THE STORY OF MY LIFE

THE STORY OF MY LIFE

BY THE LATE

COLONEL MEADOWS TAYLOR

AUTHOR OF 'CONFESSIONS OF A THUG,'
'TARA: A MAHRATTA TALE,' ETC.

EDITED BY
HIS DAUGHTER

WITH A PREFACE BY HENRY REEVE

A NEW EDITION

GYAN

Published by

GYAN

Gyan Publishing House
5, Ansari Road
Daryaganj, New Delhi-110002
Phone: 011-47034999, 9811692060
E-mail: books@gyanbooks.com

Distribution Network
gyanbooks.com
India, USA, Canada, UK, Australia, France

ISBN : 978-81-212-4549-4 (HB)
First Published, 1882

2nd Impression 2020

Printed at: Gyan Press, Delhi.

THE STORY OF MY LIFE

BY THE LATE

COLONEL PHILIP MEADOWS TAYLOR

AUTHOR OF

'CONFESSIONS OF A THUG', 'TARA: A MAHRATTA TALE', ETC.

EDITED BY HIS DAUGHTER

WITH A PREFACE BY HENRY REEVE

(1877)

NEW EDITION, WITH INTRODUCTION AND NOTES

BY

HENRY BRUCE

AUTHOR OF 'LETTERS FROM MALABAR', ETC.

HUMPHREY MILFORD

OXFORD UNIVERSITY PRESS

LONDON EDINBURGH GLASGOW NEW YORK

TORONTO MELBOURNE CAPE TOWN BOMBAY

1920

COLONEL MEADOWS TAYLOR 1873.

By permission of Messrs. Chancellor & Son, Dublin

Frontispiece.

INTRODUCTION

This *Story of my Life* has always seemed to me to be an illustration of Longfellow's catch:

> What is an autobiography?
> It is what a biography ought to be.

The interest in this case is chiefly literary and romantic. Meadows Taylor has been called, while the word still kept a noble meaning, the last of the Adventurers. Here is a surprisingly well-written record of the wanderer, so frequent in English life since Plassey, who 'runs away early to the tropics, and is at home with palms and banyans'.

I was glad to be asked, before sitting down to write about him, why Colonel Taylor should be reprinted at this date by the Oxford University Press. The least thought provides a sufficient answer: For the rare beauty of his character, and as the author of the autobiography and of his three earlier novels, *Confessions of a Thug, Tippoo Sultaun*, and *Tara*. Of his other three novels there will be a little to say in the right place. But I have not a word to say for them as literature. Instead of helping Taylor's claim to be remembered they cruelly hamper it. Inferior work can never be merely indifferent; and the three later novels must have put off many who honestly wanted to sample the writer.

As to the *History of India*, that is fully dealt with in a note. The lavish extracts made from it throughout this volume suggest the good things of which it is full—touches springing from Taylor's happy personality, accounts of places and of people he knew. Never will another History of India be attempted by any one with such a loving knowledge of its people, although the work does not meet modern standards of accuracy.

When in September 1875 Meadows Taylor, just sixty-seven, sailed from his native Liverpool on the unfortunate last trip to India, I, aged eleven, was among the few passengers. These were herded together into the old-fashioned cabin for the first meal. I remember the watery light at the end of day, the heaving of the estuary. For the only time my revolving seat was beside the old man's. In getting into his seat, being then bulky and nearly blind, he collided with me. I was surprised at the suavity, the consideration, with which he turned and apologised. I can see him standing in the dim cabin, wavering, with his face of apostolic beauty, but faded by several years from the time of that in the frontispiece. It was perhaps more like another portrait, printed in the earlier editions of the autobiography, and preserved in glass as St. Peter in one of the windows of Mitford church. Little did I then think that I should ever have the true honour of editing Meadows Taylor.

During the voyage he usually sat apart on the deck, a rug over his knees, in some suffering, not caring to be read to, or to speak much. 'Ah,' he once said, 'it is hard to have to sit like this, with folded hands, after a life of activity.' One afternoon his ribbon of the Star of India, in which he took a pride, was brought out in response to requests, and shown around. He was tended by a devoted daughter, and by his servant John. I remember John's surprise that the Red Sea was not red. 'Shure,' he said as the *Guy Mannering* steamed out of Suez, 'an' the wather's as green as Dublin.'

It is useless to go beyond Taylor's time for the beginnings of fiction in India. He has described Mohammedans much more largely, and possibly with more sympathy, than Hindus. There is an obvious reason for this in the matter of common diet, which seems, if only by illusion, to bring the Moslem world closer to European readers. This is illustrated by two early passages in Taylor, everything passing among natives of India. 'The food of us poor Hindoos would be tasteless to my lord, and therefore we have had the repast cooked by the best *bawurchees* of the town' (cookers of meat). Again: 'My mind misgives me that we . . . shall be obliged to put up in one of these wretched villages, where the *kafir* inhabitants never kill meat ; and we shall have to eat dry bread or perhaps dry rice, which is worse, after this fatigue.'

As the Moslem world is everywhere one, it is necessary just to mention the over-praised *Hajji Baba*, which was supposed to reveal it to Europe in 1824, fifteen years before Taylor's first book. The nature there portrayed is remote from human nature. Amid all the amazing things revealed by Taylor there is nothing comparable to the unaccountable way in which Hajji Baba's mother seeks his life at the end. The elemental emotions always hold true in Taylor. He owes more, and yet not very much, to the greatest book of Asia, as the discerning count it, *The Arabian Nights*.

Nor does Taylor derive in any degree from a book of Western India published in 1826, and the only possible rival to the claim of the *Thug* to be the earliest Indian novel. *Pandurang Hari : or Memoirs of a Hindoo* is not a novel but an ineptitude. Its author, William Browne Hockley, a dismissed Civil servant, does not inspire a wish for better acquaintance. Yet even in *Pandurang Hari* the few scenes from Moslem life are less ineffective, more human, than the rest.

But let those praise *Pandurang Hari* who have not read it, or who do not know the Maratha country. Taylor knew the Marathas whom he helped to administer. He speaks repeatedly of the combined turbulence and cunning of their character; but one also sees the smile which seeks to make the best of things.

The thirties of the nineteenth century, between the setting of Scott and the full rising of Dickens, were a poor time for novelists outside France. Balzac was at his height ; but that did not help things in England. It was therefore a little miracle when in 1837, in a cantonment on the borders of the jungle, a lieutenant of the Nizam, hardly twenty-nine, with no education to speak of, wrote on the arms of a long chair the *Confessions of a Thug*, published in 1839. He had been much shaken by illnesses and deaths in his little family, and was precariously recovering from an attack of the malaria which pursued him through forty years. But with the instinct of a creator he turned to the subject which had lately most stirred the world around him, making a sensation which reached to America. This was the discovery of Thuggee by his friend Major Sleeman, a discovery which Taylor had narrowly missed making himself at an earlier date. He had taken an eager part, though not in the front line, in the measures for suppressing Thuggee, which revealed still fresh atrocities. The word Thug has the meaning of deceiver. The system had flourished in India for many centuries, producing the strangest amalgam of Hindus and Mohammedans in a cryptic sect devoted to the goddess of many names, commonly called by them Bhowani. Taylor's imagination was moved by the facts which he was helping to bring to light, and in particular by a Thug informer whom he examined, a man of seven hundred murders, the original of Ameer Ali. So he wrote 'with his eye on the object'.

The *Thug* need not be read hereafter save in the delightful reprint in the World's Classics, where it rightly belongs. Even Dryasdust feels this to be a fascinating novel. It abounds in scenes and descriptions in which the lover of India must always delight. There are few of the forty-eight chapters which do not contain something distinctly good.

The theme is terrifying in its revelations of character. Ameer Ali seems to me to be a masterpiece in his suave ferocity, his sense of fate, often memorably expressed, and the conviction with which he devotes himself to evil. The entire narrative is put into his mouth, relieved by some highly artful snatches of conversation with the examining magistrate. He is a dandy, besides being all that is expressed in India by *a respectable man*. 'Have I ever broken a social tie? ever been unfaithful or unkind to a comrade? ever failed in my duty or in my trust? ever neglected a rite or ceremony of my religion? I tell you, Sahib, the man breathes not who could point his finger at me on any one of these points. And if you think on them, they are those which, if rigidly kept, gain for a man esteem and honour in the world.'

No wonder Taylor is left reflecting, till he cries aloud:

'"'Pshaw! 'tis vain to attempt to account for it, but Thuggee seems to be the offspring of fatalism and superstition, cherished and perfected by the wildest excitement that ever urged human beings to deeds at which humanity shudders."

'"Did Khodawund call?" said a bearer, who had gradually

nodded to sleep as he pulled the punkah above my head, and who was roused by my exclamation. "Did the Sahib call?"

'"No, Boodun, I did not; but since you are awake, bid some one bring me a *chilum* [hooka]. My nerves require to be composed."'

In a later passage the Thug says: 'After all, Sahib, cannot you now understand the excitement which possesses the soul of a Thug in his pursuit of men? Cannot you feel with us, as you hear my story, and follow us in my recital?'

This the reader can certainly do. The book is, of its essence, brilliant picaresque, consisting but of expeditions along the road. A little later a young man in London, some years the junior of Meadows Taylor, and more forlornly neglected in childhood, was producing perhaps the most entrancing picaresque scenes in the language, those in *The Old Curiosity Shop*. The *genre* may not be the highest, but in the *Thug* it was inevitable, and never seems inadequate. Ameer Ali's working life is spent in ruthless trips from Hindustan proper, south, west, north, and even to the east.

Delicate readers have been prevented from finishing the *Thug*, not from lack of interest, but because of its too terrible intensity. Gruesome the theme must be called, though not the handling. This is of a remarkable strength and skill. All must admit that it is well done if it had to be done at all. And his subject was imposed upon Taylor. He did not delight in horrors for their own sake, like the authors of *Timon of Athens* and too many others. He had a criminal institution to expose and to expound, as well as a story to tell.

There is no lack of variety, nor are the hues of love, both light and true, missing. Ameer Ali is outwardly an attractive youth as he issues, at eighteen, from his village after the effective episode of his slaying of the tiger. Though within the nineteenth century, those were the days when the young bloods of India, as much as the Gothic warriors in the Gaul of Sidonius some fourteen centuries earlier, delighted in putting their spare gold and silver upon their embossed shields—it is a detail that these were of rhinoceros hide. The first expedition, the most important in the development of Ameer Ali's character, naturally fills nearly half the book. He quickly excels in his grisly trade, so as to take pride in the fact that his victim is usually dead before falling to the ground. Yet his affair with Zora has something of the poignancy of 'Whom first we love, you know, we never wed.'

On his return from slippering the mother of Zora :

'"For the love of Alla, young man," cried a low and sweet voice as I passed under the gateway of a respectable-looking house ; "for the love of Alla, enter and save my mistress !"

'Fresh adventures, thought I as I looked at the speaker, a young girl, dressed like a slave. "Who are you ?"

'"It matters not," said the speaker ; "did you not pass this way yesterday afternoon, in company with two others ?"

'"I did, and what of that ?"

'"Everything ; my mistress, who is more beautiful than the moon at its full, saw you, and has gone mad about you."

'"I am sorry," said I, "but I do not see how I can help her."

'"But you must," said the girl ; "you must, or she will die ; follow me, and I will lead you to her."'

You are at once in the atmosphere of the Arabian Nights. Azima, the unhappy wife who flees from Hyderabad with Ameer Ali, never does another bold deed. 'She is tender in her love, and of an affectionate and kind disposition,' he says to the father whom he joins upon the road ; 'you must see her to-morrow ; she is now fatigued with travel.' This father, Ismail, who had murdered the parents of Ameer Ali and adopted him in early childhood, is winsomely kind. 'And you must be fatigued also, my son, and hungry too. I have a rare *pilau* ready for you.' Azima and Ameer Ali, trusting to the difficulty of Indian communications, venture to marry, and have the tenderest domestic life. His third recorded affair is with a handsome widow who shocks him by flinging herself at him upon a journey so persistently that she has to be destroyed for the safety of all.

For sheer power and pathos perhaps the climax is reached in the twenty-third and twenty-fourth chapters, relating the unavoidable doom of Nawab Subzee Khan, a warrior of rank and fame, called Subzee from his devotion to *bhang*. His is a gallant figure, suggesting that of Marmion. Unique, for the East, is the 'young good-looking girl mounted on a spirited pony' who rides openly beside Subzee Khan and prepares his favourite drink. As they near the jungles beyond Ellichpur, the place where the story was written, the Nawab says it would be a sorry fate for him to fall in an unknown spot, after a life spent in battle-fields. 'And you will do so . . . your death-blow will reach you in that jungle you dread, and no monument will mark the spot where the remains of Subzee Khan will lie.' It is amusing to hear him abusing the hardly human Gonds in a skirmish : 'Come on and try your cowardly arrows against stout hearts and ready weapons! Base-born *kafirs* are ye, and cowards ; Inshalla ! your sisters are vile, and asses have loved your mothers.'

On the destined day the Nawab sorely longs for shade. 'Here have I, Subzee Khan, gone without my usual sherbet for three days on this very account. By Alla ! I am now as thirsty as a crow in the hot weather, and my mouth opens in spite of me. Oh, that we could light on a river or a well in this parched desert ! I would have a glorious draught.'

The place is reached, and he begins to exult. 'There breathes not in the ten kingdoms of Hind a slave so skilled in the art of preparing *subzee* as Kureena yonder. . . . All the world knows that Subzee Khan drinks *bhang*, and is not the worse soldier for it. Now with a few fair girls to sing a *ghazul* or two to us, methinks a heaven might be made out of this wild spot.' That is FitzGerald before his day, and doubtless from the same source.

So the warrior fell before the cowardly assassins who always allowed three or four men to a victim. 'I had thrown the cloth about his neck, Surfuraz Khan still held his hand, and my father pulled at his legs with all his force. . . . Subzee Khan was dead—I had destroyed the slayer of hundreds !

'But no one had thought of his poor slave girl, who at some distance, and with her back turned to us, had been busily engaged in preparing another rich draught for her now unconscious master. She had not heard the noise of our scuffle, nor the deep groans which had escaped from some of the Nuwab's people, and she approached the spot where Surfuraz Khan was now employed in stripping the armour and dress from the dead body.

'Ya Alla ! Sahib, what a piercing shriek escaped her, when she saw what had been done ! I shall never forget it, nor her look of horror and misery as she rushed forward and threw herself on the body. Although master and slave, Sahib, they had loved. . . .

'"He cannot be dead! he cannot be dead!" cried the fair girl,—for she was beautiful to look on, Sahib, as she partly rose and brushed back her dishevelled hair from her eyes; "and yet he moves not—he speaks not"—and she gazed on his features for a moment. "Ah!" she screamed, "look at his eyes—look at them—they will fall out of his head! and his countenance, 'tis not my own lord's—those are not the lips which have often spoken kind words to his poor Kureena! Oh, my heart, what a pain is there!"'

The pages following would be too distressing to quote. Surfuraz Khan, who loves the girl, says: 'I have no wife, no child: thou shalt be both to me if thou wilt rise and follow me. . . . Before this assembly I promise thee life and a happy home.' But she struggles violently and he strikes her so that her beauty is spoiled. Finally he strangles her; but goes a sorrowing man to his grave.

Whether or not Meadows Taylor's name deserves to live may well be judged by these scenes. The realism here, as in other places, is relentless. But it is pity which is aroused, not needless horror. He has something of the poetical touch; and the images which he calls up are as clear-cut as the khaki landscape of India. There is art in the headings to the chapters, in the way in which these break off and go on, and in the occasional verse mottoes. He had assimilated such things in hours of study which must have been scanty. The *Thug* and *Tippoo Sultaun* are spirited imitations of a few good models. Scott, with a little of Shakespeare, and, above all, something to say, made Taylor's literary equipment. Sustained spirit in story-telling is one of the most difficult things; and it is strongest in the *Thug*.

This is shown by the way in which the story heightens. If it dips for six or eight chapters after the first expedition, it steadily increases in depth of interest, and in terror, throughout the third volume. In fact, both the early novels are wound up in interest to the end, instead of being allowed to run down.

The *Thug* is also a historical novel when Ameer Ali, with his later comrades, rides on two expeditions of mere plunder half across India with the Pindharis. The swing and momentum of these movements are well rendered: the same thing remains to be done in fiction for the more important expeditions of the Marathas. Many a student of Indian history may have wished to know a little more of the Pindhari leader Chitu, who might have left a principality like Tonk, but who 'fled to the jungles, and was killed by a tiger'. He is here in a full-length portrait, a competent man for whom the reader, like Ameer Ali, feels some respect. But even the Pindharis cannot stand the Thugs, who are soon at their old trick of strangling those who trust them.

The Thug has been eminently a criminal on horseback. But before Ameer Ali is old the institution begins to crumble, and the world becomes a bad place for Thugs. Azima, ignorant of her husband's life, is killed by the shame of the exposure, when her father-in-law is executed by being trampled to death by an elephant, in the midst of her daughter's marriage ceremonies. To the end, which is not yet, the interest never flags. 'He shall tell you the tale himself. Mashalla! he tells it with much spirit, and 'tis worth hearing.'

This is probably the least faulty of Taylor's novels, the best written, the most holding. *Tara*, of a quarter of a century later, competes with it for general excellence, but it has not the same qualities. The few points of style which afterwards became a mannerism with Taylor do not appear in the *Thug*. The English in which it is written, as the above extracts show, is pretty nearly faultless. Here are countless sentences, as lucid as a brook, with few words of Latin origin.

Tippoo Sultaun was a publisher's idea, and a good one. In 1839, behind the most picturesque figure of all history, which intervened, Tippoo still lowered from forty years before as the national foe. He was a farcical antagonist, yet terrible in his day, who had compelled us to conquer India. It must be remembered that Tippoo is one of the best-documented tyrants in history, with memoirs by himself and by others.

There is no need to apologise for *Tippoo Sultaun*, published in 1840, for having been written in haste, as it actually was, during the last winter of Taylor's exciting visit home. The haste seems to tell in the quality of impetus, which all his subsequent novels missed. The sub-title is 'A Tale of the Mysore War'. This furnished an admirable climax in the feat of arms at Seringapatam which made an abiding impression upon imaginations both in India and in Europe. But it took

Taylor out of his own country, which is the Deccan. He had passed once across Mysore and back again on the journey to Ooty when he met Macaulay and lost his earlier children. Never having seen the Himalayas, he was impressed by the sheer bulk of the Nilgiris, of which good use is made in the novel. Except for such memories, the *Mysore* of Colonel Mark Wilks was practically his sole authority. Tippoo's hunting of elephants and tigers in Malabar, the night attack upon the wall, and many a following scene are taken straight out of Wilks, supplemented by a fine youthful imagination.

In the nature of things *Tippoo Sultaun* has not the uniqueness of the *Thug*. In form it is an imitation of the historical romance of Scott, such as was attempted hundreds of times in that generation, but seldom so effectively. For it is a success, the story does come off. The writing is not identical with that of the *Thug*, nor quite so good. There is at times an approach to *ce style coulant, si cher aux bourgeois*. At other times there is rhetoric, though good of its kind; and there is a cardinal fault in the construction.

The main plot, the Indian story, begins eleven years before the fall of Seringapatam. But the interesting journey thither is twice broken by episodes of four chapters each, relating to a fresh set of characters who are never vitalised. The first has its scene in England, the second treats of the landing in Bombay and the unhappy expedition of Mathews to Bednore, all at a date four or five years before the journey; and there are two further chapters in England. Anything may be justified in fiction by the result. But this arrangement is cumbrous because it puts the reader out, setting him to look up dates in order to reconcile the order of events.

Here one comes up against an undoubted limitation in Taylor. Any arrangement could be carried off by arresting characters. Taylor probably brought in these English figures in the hope of making his story seem less strange to readers at home. But he could not then or at any time portray his own country-people well. The scenes in England, within the eighteenth century, are, like those in *Ralph Darnell*, of a curious badness. They 'have the cruel misfortune of resembling the novels of Miss Edgeworth.' Not in Scott's faintest conventional scenes do the characters have more unexceptionable pedigrees and sentiments. Yet here Taylor was only trying to depict a period some half-century or so before that in which he wrote. The half-dozen English chapters in *Tippoo Sultaun* are best omitted in re-readings.

Taylor's English officers, wooden and didactic like few whom he can have known, are less objectionable in India. It was necessary to set them forth, in the humiliating parts of prisoners and victims, before they became conquerors. The details of the Bednore expedition, as told with spirit enough in the novel, differ essentially from the same story as told in Taylor's *History* a generation later, while both accounts differ to a baffling degree from other modern compilers. I sought a disentanglement of this question, without quite attaining it, through *The Times Literary Supplement* in 1917. An extensive correspondence, both printed and private, which followed, brought me some information. The subject is a side issue to the literary study of Meadows Taylor. It awaits, without inviting, whoever cares to tackle one of the most difficult and discreditable periods of English history in India, the early eighties of the eighteenth century on the Bombay side.

For literary purposes Taylor's native heath was only Indian life and character. Except for the English interpolations, *Tippoo Sultaun* opens, continues, and ends strongly. The introductory chapters tell of the party of benighted travellers, the monsoon storm, and the rescue of Ameena from the flooded river bed by Kasim Ali the village headman. Kasim Ali Patel is one of Taylor's two or three taking young Moslem heroes. In his village he has had no chance to learn anything save marksmanship and a little Persian poetry. Some appreciation of landscape is attributed to him, admittedly against probability. But he has seen, saved, and loved the bride Ameena, hardly fifteen. In gratitude her husband carries him onward to 'the city', into the service of Tippoo.

Though this novel solicits extract less than its predecessor, the following passage is of great beauty. Abdul Rhyman Khan, nearing Seringapatam, feels obliged to confess that he has there two other wives.

'"Methinks now, to see these grey hairs and this grey beard," and he touched them as he spoke, "so near thy soft and waving tresses, I seem more like a father to thee than a husband: and yet thou art mine, Ameena. I would thou wert older, fair one!"

'"And if I were, I should not be so fair," she said artlessly.

'"I care not, so that we had grown old together; at least I should have seen thy beauty, and the remembrance of it would have been with me."

'Ameena sighed; her thoughts wandered to Kasim's noble figure and youthful yet expressive countenance; in spite of herself and almost unconsciously she drew her hand across her eyes, as if to shut something ideal from her sight.

'The Khan heard her sigh; he would rather not have heard it, though his own remark he knew had provoked it. "I have said the truth, Ameena, and thou wouldst rather I were a younger man," he said, looking at her intently. "But what matter? these idle words do but pain thee. It is our destiny, sweet one, and we must work it out together."

'"Ay, it is our destiny," she said.

'"The will of Alla!" continued the Khan, looking up devoutly, "which hath joined two beings together so unsuited in age, but not in temper I think, Ameena. Thou art not as others, wilful and perverse—heavy burdens—hard to carry—and from which there is no deliverance; but a sweet and lovely flower, which a monarch might wear in his heart and be proud of. So thou truly art to Rhyman Khan, and ever wilt be, even though enemies should come between us."'

Yet the frontispiece shows the same Khan, generous yet ignorant and sensual, for whom one feels the utmost sympathy, cutting down Ameena with his curved sword, himself to fall broken-hearted in the next day's battle. Alas for the end of sentimental love in the East!

Ameena is one of Taylor's happiest creations. Two chapters of extreme though differing excellence are those in which Kasim Ali lies wounded on the battle-field, the beasts succeeding to the birds of prey as night comes on; and then is nursed to life again in Abdul Rhyman Khan's zenana. Taylor is best at depicting humble and very human character; the meetings of travellers on the road, the humours of servants, wives who cannot read, the workings of the souls of untaught if not always poor people. The cook Zoolficar, Zoolfoo for short, is admirable. 'O coward! thou art not alone; see, thou hast the hero of the night [Kasim Ali] lying beside thee —one who has slain some men since he last ate; whereas thou hast not even slain a fowl.' One can see the flash of

Taylor's eye, hear his burst of kindly laughter at such a saying.

He has often to exaggerate the soul of goodness in such people in order to have a story to tell at all. Yet the wickedness of the East is relentlessly brought out. Peculiarly well done are the Khan's two other wives, one worse than the other, with her mother and attendants, their plottings and enchantments against Ameena. There is a quite triumphant scene of homely *diablerie*. Ameena is not killed by her husband, but awaits Kasim Ali with a persistent true love which is rewarded by happiness. Such love must be allowed even if not in the drawing; as must also Kasim Ali's candour in telling his English friends all about it at the end of the book, with the remark: 'You know, Sahib, we Moslems are not given to speaking of our wives or families.'

It is not until the original second volume of the novel that Kasim Ali beholds his master Tippoo:

'The figure of the Sultaun was of middle height, and stout; his complexion was darker than that of most of those who surrounded him, and he sat with an affected air of royalty, which, though it at first impressed the spectator with awe, yet that passed away in a great measure upon the contemplation of his face, which wanted the dignity of expression that his body assumed. His eyes were full and prominent, but the whites of them were of a dull yellowish tint, which, with their restless and suspicious expression, gave them a disagreeable look, and one which bespoke a mind of perpetual but not profound thought; his nose was small and straight, and, with his mouth, would have been good-looking, except for the habitual sneer which sat on both; his eyebrows and mustachios were trimmed most carefully into arched lines, and he wore no beard. In his hand there was a large rosary of beautiful pearls, with emeralds at the regular distances, which he kept perpetually counting mechanically with the fingers of his right hand.'

Henceforth his is the dominant figure. There is a good enough villain; but Tippoo is much more than that. Taylor's minute portraiture of him is one of much mastery, and will not be superseded while men care to read at all of such a being. Not grand enough to be daemonic, now monster, now monkey, grotesque and terrible, Tippoo is perhaps best explained by a sentence from a Moslem writer, quoted in the *History of India*: 'The most intelligent and sincere well-wishers of the house concurred in the opinion of his father, that his head and heart were both defective, however covered by a plausible and imposing flow of words.'

For this being is a chatterer, and that in a dialect of his own, a heresiarch, one who walks with spirits and relates his dreams. His gushing speeches, glowing with an uncertain eloquence, are highly amusing because conceived with genuine humour. Tippoo had his qualities, enterprise, courage enough for most occasions, a brilliant reputation during the first half of his reign. There is a tent scene before battle, when he is visited by the ghosts of those whom he has slain, including Mathews, and calls upon the spirit of his ever victorious father, which is no mean rendering of that in Richard III., with the addition of a loving girl who incites and comforts Tippoo. True pathos is in the scene where Kasim Ali, a fine fellow who cannot stand such doings, takes leave of his master. 'There sat before him the benefactor and the steady friend of years. He continued gazing on him, and often he felt the tears rush to his eyes, as though they would have had vent.' Yet Tippoo sends after him to slay him, and 'the love that was between us is broken forever'.

It is an unforgettable, ineffaceable figure, really almost as unique as that of the Thug. To this day one may commonly see a loose-limbed tiger in black and yellow, with grinning face turned around at one, ramping for ornament upon a white-washed Indian wall. That is how Tippoo, the Tiger of the Faith, survives in history and in this novel.

It is to be observed how Meadows Taylor dwells upon the likenesses, not the unlikenesses, between his readers and his characters. That is the way to command the utmost possible interest. Not too much is made of the climate, which nothing can alter, and which Indians do not mind; nor of complexions, which can never be white, though there is a tendency to seek the lightest possible, as 'a ruddy brown' or 'a light bamboo'; nor of the fact that most of the characters go about barefooted, sitting and sleeping on the ground, preferring to cook as well as to eat with their own fingers. Yet there are differences of mind which have to be shown, as Taylor shows them, because these mean character. In the comparatively recent India, as in antiquity, minds were strangely occupied by superstitious considerations, by omens, by everything that would render not absurd the words of Tippoo: 'There is much in having lucky herbs boiled under the influence of salutary planets.'

These two novels made a notable production for a young man before returning to twenty years of killing drudgery under the sun. 'Shabash! Shabash! well done, gallant fellow!' as the English officers cried to Kasim Ali.

Not all parts of the complex records of India lend themselves to fiction. In his own *History* Taylor has some discerning remarks on this subject. In Akbar's character 'romance prevails from the earliest dawn'. Under his great-grandson Aurungzeb romance lies in resistance. 'But little romance has ever attached itself to the characters of Indian history; and in this respect the difference between the Moors of Spain, and the early Mahomedans of India, is very remarkable. During the cruel and gloomy reigns, with few exceptions, of the Afghan dynasties of India, there was little scope for romantic incident, or the development of any free or chivalrous spirit among the people; and it is to the research of Colonel Tod, the Froissart of the Rajpoot clans and States, that the history of all that existed among them, exceptional as it was, is due.'

Meadows Taylor had a cultus for the enlightened Deccan dynasty of Bahmani, which four or five centuries ago ruled over many of the places of Taylor's youth. Of them he says: 'There are occasional pleasant glimpses of quiet times, and their beneficial effects, which are not to be found' in the records of Delhi. This cultus was continued for their most important successors, the Sultans of Bijapur, who had an unusual historian in Ferishta, and of whose 'superb Saracenic architecture' Taylor possibly made too much. Now it was immediately against Bijapur that Shivaji the Maratha arose to make a name in deeds of imperishable romance.

Taylor was rather obsessed by the fancied interval of just a century between the slaying of Afzul Khan and Plassey; as later by the exact century between Plassey and the critical June of the Mutiny, with the Indian prophecies on the subject. Thus there came into being his scheme for a trilogy of historical novels, *Tara*, *Ralph Darnell*, and *Seeta*. These were to set forth respectively the rise of the Maratha power, 1657 or near enough ; the rise of the English power, 1757 ; and the desperate effort to overthrow the English power, 1857.

It matters little for fiction that Shivaji's act of treachery took place in 1659, or that Aurungzeb, who overhangs the admirable narrative from a distance without entering into it, is here Emperor and Alamgir somewhat before the right dates. The plan was a good plan, had it been well executed. But *Ralph Darnell* and *Seeta* simply fail to fit into the trilogy, owing to poor workmanship. *Tara* is the only member of the set which has claims to remembrance.

Tara : a Mahratta Tale, was older and sounder than the trilogy scheme. It was suggested for *Blackwood's Magazine* by Christopher North in 1839, and soon after tentatively begun. But time and tide rushed in between. The entire twenty years of Taylor's service on end in India without furlough, resented by his friends if not by himself, intervened, followed by some years of illness. He had done his life's work as an administrator, as fascinatingly told in the autobiography. But he had lost his chance to make the utmost of the literary gift that was in him, the two things being mutually exclusive.

Seldom has a book meant so much in the writer's life. For Taylor was nursing the idea of his interrupted *Tara* through a quarter of a century of vicissitudes, perfecting his ideal, bringing the story to the rare mellowness which is its trait. All those twenty years spent near the Maratha country went, in a way, to the making of it : his early mental vigour held, for this purpose, across the gap, and was triumphantly carried over. Only thus can be explained the *tour de force* by which, in 1863, he was able to turn out *Tara* with enjoyment for a new generation of Blackwoods. To the generosity of that firm is due the possibility of this edition of the *Story of My Life* before their copyright has expired.

Perhaps I am prejudiced in favour of *Tara*, since this, read amid Maratha hills, was the second novel of my life, *Guy Mannering* being the first. The graceful figure of the soft-eyed Brahmin girl, child-widow and rescued Sati, loyal to her faith until she becomes its victim, with her upright simplicity of character, has filled a place apart in many hearts. In one of Mrs. Croker's novels there is an English general settled in India who names his daughter Tara.

Here undoubtedly Taylor has captured the shy spirit of the true romance. It is pedantic to forbid the use of the phrase Maratha Brahmin, for that is what Tara and her family were. The only familiar line of classic English verse about India relates to these same hills :

> Where in wild Mahratta battle fell my father evil-starred.

That is the romance which lives within these pages, though before the advent, for any purpose worth mentioning, of Europeans in India. Englishmen had not then founded Bombay or Calcutta, nor was the popular Indian consciousness aware of them. The stirring events of *Tara,* so intensely realised before they were recorded, pass in a world untroubled by the existence of any Europe. Taylor had for theme the conflict of the two faiths which make the woof and web of Indian life. As he says with his large humanity : 'The actors in my story are Hindus and Mahomedans ; but the same passions and affections exist among them as among ourselves, and thus the motives and deeds of my characters may, at least, be intelligible.'

Tara is the longest of his novels, reaching the generous limit of a quarter of a million words. In addition there is a certain spaciousness of treatment, a wideness of handling about it. This must be called Taylor's masterpiece, and probably the greatest Indian novel. Two subsequent novels may be mentioned in competition with it which are stronger in some respects, yet are helped out in their appeal by European characters—*On the Face of the Waters* and *Kim* : but even the inspiration of the last is largely extra-Indian.

Tara is quite as well written as its predecessors, yet differently. The sparkle is absent, nor is it missed. The brilliance of the *Thug* has here passed into a mellow general excellence, expressed in Saxon words so prevailingly short that there are constantly sixteen of them to a printed line. There is not the same temptation to quote, since neither sentences nor episodes are easily detached from the text, which is all of a piece, and all good through nearly one hundred chapters. The slight later tricks of style just begin to appear, but not to a degree as yet worth mentioning.

Though *The Times* praised *Tara* for its 'rapid action,'

there is here little impetus. Action there is in abundance, sometimes melodramatic, with yet more admirable character and description, with plain conversations which are a delight to the true Indian. But the progression is undoubtedly leisurely, 'without o'erflowing full'.

Tara has reached the age of sixteen in an anomalous position, in the steep little town of Tuljapur, a place with which Meadows Taylor had unforgettable associations, but which is unimportant except in his pages. It has famous temples of the same goddess Bhowani of Ameer Ali's strange cult, here, and nearly two centuries earlier, called Kali or Tulja, 'the goddess in the glen', Tuljamata, the mysterious mother feared by both creeds. Taylor, who was apt to overdo his architecture, has given too detailed accounts of these temples, as of the buildings of Bijapur.

Tara's father, the chief priest of the temples, was a prosperous man, still young. Yet 'Vyas Shastree had two great cares which pressed upon him heavily, and were shared by his wife. The first was that he had no son; the second, that his beautiful daughter was already a virgin widow. And these were heavy griefs.' His wife Anunda, a splendid example of the untaught Hindu wife, urges him to marry again for offspring, seeking out a bride who shall be as a sister to her. 'As she said to herself, if there is a marriage, my lord shall have a good one.'

The bride obtained is the Brahmin girl Radha, fourteen but passing for twelve, from the western mountains. She cherishes a passion for her prince, Shivaji, who as a Maratha could never marry her, and early increased his supernatural renown by turning aside from women. Radha's brother, Moro Trimmul, an agent of Shivaji, makes, with his pursuit of Tara, a satisfying villain to the end; as his accomplice Gunga, the temple girl or Murali, is a good relenting villainess. Tara, not knowing what to do, has given herself to the goddess; yet not as the other temple girls. 'I am not a Moorlee to love,' she says. This convulsive devotion on her part, which is a passing phase, and the similar worship on the part of Shivaji's mother, make the least pleasant portions of the book.

Again I can wait in the rain, beneath the withered banyan on the little hill, with the three robbers who are waylaying the amusingly cowardly and optimistic Lalla, escaping with stolen letters from the desk of Aurungzeb. They take him to the mud castle of the robber baron, Pahar Singh : these scenes, though minute, are full of spirit. The hunchback twin brothers, Rama and Lukshmun, are a pair. Rama is killed at Tuljapur ; but Lukshmun becomes singularly endearing, to Tara and to all concerned with him.

Taylor made an attempt to draw a picture of Bijapur, somewhat idealised, a generation before its extinction, in the huge episode which follows. It reaches to onc hundred and seventy broad pages, the amount of many a modern novel. Pahar Singh enters Bijapur disguised as a loathly fakir, first Hindu, then Moslem, to sell the stolen papers to the promising young king, and to save him from a conspiracy of the vizicr. One can still hear his cry, *Ulla dilaya to leonga* (If God give I will take), echoing through the unprotected palace. It is all closely knit narrative, not wordy, which improves with each reading. The trouble is that these Bijapur scenes are too much like a novel by themselves, with a separate atmosphere, and even a telling climax, the death of the handsome Persian adventurer on the spot where he had caused many another to be executed :

> ' A shiver seemed to pass through him as he closed his eyes slowly. Not of fear, for the man, a Fatalist by creed and habit, was meeting his doom stoically as a brave Moslem can do ; but a thought had crossed him which would not be put back—a vision of love and peace—of his girl wife in her rosy beauty, and of her fair boy, far away at his own village and home, in the blue mountains of Khorassan—and of a fond aged mother who lived with them. This season they were to have come to him. Who now would tell them of his fate ? '

This inset in the larger novel, as it seems, covers but the space of twenty-four remarkably well-filled hours. It is cleverly done. One becomcs intimate with a wholesome Moslem household, that of Afzul Khan the Afghan, who takes up the gage of battle against the Marathas. Afzul Khan was a complete chucklehead, else he would not hold the place which he does in history. He pretty fairly represented Bijapur. Yct he was a lovable domestic character. His daughter Zyna, fourteen, with her mother's ' bright Georgian complexion' gone somewhat browner in these latitudes, is truly engaging. She is betrothed to the vizier's son, a negro, which shows the way races deteriorate. Her brother Fazil is, together with Kasim Ali and perhaps the youthful Ameer Ali, one of Taylor's only two or three attractive Moslem lovers. Fazil Khan is weaker, yet a charming fellow. Taylor shared Scott's tolerance of a bore, to judge by the astrological chatter of Lurlee Khanum, the stepmother. Yet she is sound-hearted. There is also a capital family nurse. The entire household, especially in their treatment of Tara, who twice over falls into their hands, are an honour to human nature.

The closest companion of Afzul Khan is the Peer Sahib or priest, the holy man, inciting to the war of faith, pouring out texts of bloodshed. He is akin to the Covenanters; and it is a satisfaction to see him finally cut down upon the mountain-side along with the bluff Afzul Khan, for whom one grieves.

While Tara is being carried off at midnight from the temples by Moro Trimmul, both fall into the hands of Fazil Khan during the sacking of Tuljapur which he cannot prevent. This is how he breaks to her the news which he believes to be true: 'Sit down as thou wast, and may God keep thy heart, as I tell thee of thy misery. Yesterday there were a father, a mother, another wife, and thyself, in a happy home. Now three are gone, and thou art here.'

Tara's family has been scattered, not killed. The two mothers, Radha now settled into a good little wife, first seek and find Vyas Shastree. Sorely wounded in the defence of the temple, he has been taken into the house of the Putwari or village accountant of Sindphul. I would like to draw attention to the whole of the sixty-fifth chapter, narrating the family upsetting, with a dead negro lying in Tara's garden above, as an example of the merit to which Taylor can attain by extreme simplicity. All who have known family life must feel the following:

'For a little time, and as they silently sat beside him . . . they did not miss Tara; but Anunda's mind suddenly misgave her. Her husband, whom her arrival had aroused, had again fallen into a doze, and she went outside to ask for her. The whole court had been left to them, and the door of the outer one was closed. "Tara," she called gently, several times, but there was no reply. She might be asleep, she thought, in one of the rooms which opened into it, and she searched in each in succession. There was no one. Radha joined her. "Where is Tara?" she said. "She should have been with him." True, she should have been with her father, but she was not.

'The women turned sick at heart and sat down. A nameless terror seized them, so absorbing, that they could say nothing, but that she was not. Anunda dare not ask. Of the two, Radha was most self-possessed. Looking through the door, she saw the old Putwari's wife sitting outside it. . . .

'"The gods have given thee one precious object, sister, and taken the other," she said. "Be thankful for what is spared thee."'

Then after an interval, when definite word has been brought that Tara is a guest in Afzul Khan's household:

'Now, for once, there was no indecision or vacillation in the Shastree's mind. He could bear easy travelling in a litter; and Radha should have it by-and-by, when he grew stronger. He would not delay, and they could yet overtake the army at Wye, or soon afterwards. Very little of the household property had been lost, after all; and Anunda's store of money was at last to prove useful. That night, as with thankful hearts they spoke of their lost child, they arranged plans for setting out to reclaim her; and their friends, who crowded about them with congratulations next day, soon completed the necessary arrangements. The third day was a lucky one, according to the planets; and they moved down the pass to Sindphul, followed by many friends, and the good wishes and prayers of all who had known Tara from childhood.'

From the attack on Tuljapur, when the two streams of narrative unite, the story flows onward with a majestic current through about the last two-fifths of the novel, the interest never flagging. The country covered looks limited on the map, specially for India, being little more than a hundred miles in any direction. Yet the atmosphere is large enough to contain clashing faiths and the rise of a nationality. Two episodes in particular are of the first importance.

One is the relation, as if by an eye-witness, of the destruction of the Moslem host, treated as retribution for the sacking of Tuljapur. This was quoted to the length of five pages by the *Edinburgh Review*. As Shivaji says: 'O, the blind confidence of these Beejapoor swine! They have neither eyes nor ears, else they had guessed we are not as we seem.

But the goddess Mother has blinded and deafened them, and it is as my mother said it would be.'

The picture of Shivaji is implicit throughout the story, and the more abiding for not being on the surface. This leader vitalised Hindu history, and was so far a superman that he believed himself to be, and is believed by his countrymen to have been, more than human. Shivaji's companion, Tannaji Maloosray, with his soft black eyes, his grave deliberate manner, is impressive in Taylor's chapters, as in the Maratha ballads.

The other cardinal episode is Tara's Sati at Wye. The rescue by Fazil Khan and Lukshmun makes a gallant scene. '"I never kill Brahmuns," he said through his teeth, "but thou art a devil;" and he struck at Moro Trimmul's bare neck with all his force. As the wretched man sank to the earth under the terrible wound, the hunchback sprang to his horse, clambered upon it like a cat, and flourishing his bloody sword, though he struck no one, rode by Fazil's side onwards, unharmed.'

A historical novel after the best models, *Tara* again becomes minute yet absorbing domestic drama concerning two families; and the end is only wistfully sad. A lifetime of observation is here: 'the occasional piping of sleepless plovers', 'the huge broad leaf of the teak tree'. The conversations of humble folk are richly true to Indian life. One would like to meet that merchant of Karad, 'a pleasant-looking man, dressed in flowing Arab robes and a green turban', who so cordially receives Afzul Khan's family in gratitude for former favours.

So the book is packed with good things, though these are often latent, not salient. The reason why the frontispiece in the still current edition is distressing is that the Brahmins are seated apparently upon benches as in a dissenting chapel, not upon the ground. *Tara* must be called Taylor's best and great novel, the one most representative of India.

On the strength of these three novels, the *Thug*, *Tippoo*, and *Tara*, Taylor appeals for remembrance. It is a world that he has vividly depicted in them. In the one-volume editions they amount to some fifteen hundred pages, or about the bulk of the work which Charlotte Brontë has left.

A few minds, such as Walter Scott's, hold lights like those in cathedral windows, with banners yellow, glorious, golden. Whilc the mind of Meadows Taylor hardly holds cathedral colours, it clearly transmits the light of heaven, which is as much as can be asked in most cases. He has vigour, humour, and poetical feeling, though he could not write good verses.

It would be fatuous for any other novelist to try to portray certain figures which Taylor has given at full length. While men care at all to consider the Thug, the mad Tippoo, and the youthful Shivaji, Taylor's portraits occupy the available space. The most that could be attempted would be the different figure of the older Shivaji, defying Aurungzeb in full durbar. Taylor had the knowledge for his purposes, plus the fusing imagination. He says once that he did not understand ancient Sanskrit. If he had not studied this, which for that matter contains little of the romantic spirit outside Kalhana, he had to listen to Sanskrit deeds in his daily work.

As Taylor's younger, more successful, and loyal kinsman, Henry Reeve, wrote in reviewing *Tara*, romance may be found in the Maratha country, but seems to flee from the vast, enervating plains of Bengal. Taylor had never been within a thousand miles of these. Yet it was precisely here that he must, in pursuance of his scheme, place the climax of his next novel. He seems to flee in spirit himself from Bengal, for less than one half of *Ralph Darnell* is located there, and that without conviction. The best touch is in the mention of Clive's 'active, hardy Mahrattas, so far from their dear western mountains, looking over the sacred river which it had been their envied fate to see. How many a tale of it would be told amidst the rocky crags and deep jungles of Maharashtra, when the gallant Bombay Sepoys should return!'

There is a gulf, not in time, but in intellect, between *Tara*, 1863, and *Ralph Darnell*, 1865. The miracle of *Tara* was not repeated in fiction. The 'temporary cessation of brain power', due to overwork in India, of which Dr. Richard Garnett writes in a sympathetic article on Meadows Taylor in the *Dictionary of National Biography*, is apparent in *Ralph Darnell.*

In fleeing from Bengal Taylor rested in the England of the eighteenth century, which he had not the requisite knowledge to depict. He tried to insert loving references to his mother's family, the Mitfords ; and he knew the Northumbrian speech well. But it is impossible to remember one of his north-country young gentlemen as distinct from the other. The best figure is that of Roger Darnell, the East India merchant whose fellows were then founding an empire. For good reasons he has his nephew kidnapped, on one of his own ships, and brought to Calcutta. The figure of Clive, a stout colonel of thirty, lacks grandeur ; nor is anything made of his young companion Warren Hastings. There is a perhaps sufficient account of the Black Hole, and of Plassey, which was less than a feat of arms. Surajah Dowlah appears at some length, with the Acte attendant upon every Nero—in this case an Afghan girl devoid of charm. The hopeless thing is the marriage of General Smithson (Ralph Darnell) to the widow of Surajah Dowlah, and the way in which, after her death, he cherishes a bedizened image of her in a mysterious bedroom.

To write, as in this novel, 'Sir Horace Walpole,' Jacobin for Jacobite, and Don for Dom ; or, as in the *History of India*, 'all sexes and ages', 'the *el Chico blanco*', 'Monsieurs', and 'Edward' Pottinger for the defender of Herat—to do, or to allow printers to do, this sort of thing, is to live in a world of blurred outlines, where nothing much matters. It is idle to say that such things are unimportant : they make the works where they occur seem unimportant.

All writers sometimes have to say 'you', but a snare lurks in any possible use of the 'we'. It is easy to tell, from one conspicuous result, two of the authors whom Taylor was reading during the writing of *Ralph Darnell* and of *Seeta*. 'If I had the power and the ingenuity of Mr. Trollope', these conversations of English folk would be more workmanlike. 'If I had the genius of the late Mr. Thackeray, I' could have given a more convincing picture of the middle of the eighteenth century. Taylor caught from them the hateful habit of buttonholing the dear reader, which barely appears at the end of *Tara*. He exaggerated it well-nigh beyond belief, even to 'O patient reader'.

In 1870 appeared his *History of India* ; and in 1872 *Seeta*, the third member of the trilogy.

This novel is not as *Ralph Darnell* and *A Noble Queen*. It is a pathetic tale of woman's love; and Miss Taylor has testified to its popularity among women readers. *Seeta* is also of importance in the development of the Indian novel as the parent of a progeny. While not the earliest novel of the Mutiny, it was long the most notable. It also set the key, in many respects, for the novel of true love in India. The mixed marriage which seems so promising yet gradually becomes less so, the delivcrance from an impossible position by the heroine dying for her husband, even the placing of her among the most attractive and light-coloured of the trade castes, the goldsmiths, if one wants to avoid the incessant Brahmins—these details quickly became formulas for the imitative.

Seeta is thus pioneer work, of more historical than substantive value. The execution is fumbling. Strange to say, Taylor, who had lived memorably through the Mutiny, whose account of it in his autobiography, though not in his *History*, is so good, failed to render it impressively in fiction. The country where things happen is indeterminate. It is largely Taylor's own Berar, yet is stated to be some hundreds of miles to the north, where Hindi is spoken. Taylor's Anglo-Indians of the Mutiny are not so amateur as his English men and women of a century earlier; but they do not live. The novel begins tolerably, as is easy. It even holds for the first quarter or so, until the marriage. Nothing here is better than the figure of Seeta's grandfather. Seeta is a sweet and noble character, over whom many tears have been shed.

On his last voyage to India Colonel Taylor had with him a copy of *Seeta*, then his latest novel in book form, which went the rounds of his fellow-passengers. His skill in describing female dress, European and Indian, was much noted. This is specially evident in his later writings; though he is never so trying as George Eliot in certain chapters, where she early betrays her sex.

At this time *A Noble Queen* was appearing serially: it came out in volumes in 1878. This work leaves a mere blur in the mind, after the most conscientious readings. It is the story of a local heroine of Bijapur and Ahmednagar. The date is about 1600, some two generations earlier than *Tara*. Europeans are here represented by the Portuguese on the coast. Portuguese names and traits are confounded with Spanish;

and indeed this was the perplexing period when Portugal was exploited by Spain. Nothing is made, on the one hand, of the terrors of the Portuguese Inquisition, or on the other of the Emperor Akbar, then growing old, yet eager of heart, and campaigning, for the only time, on the dusty plains of the Deccan: even the great negro minister of Ahmednagar is left out. The day for attempting such figures had passed. It would be a mistake ever to reprint *Ralph Darnell* and *A Noble Queen*.

The six novels here discussed appeared at the dates given, first in three volumes and afterwards in one each. Together with the *History of India* and the autobiography, they make up Taylor's independent work in book form. Search by a helper has disclosed at the India Office scraps not to be found even in the British Museum catalogue, such as *The Fatal Armlet: a Legend of Ellichpur, Deccan*, reprinted at Bombay in 1872. There are reprinted lectures, articles, with contributions to architectural and other works, sometimes specimens of the actual sketching which Taylor always loved.

The Story of my Life was completed in 1874. It depended, not on an old man's uncertain recollections, but on the mass of correspondence which had passed between Taylor and his father. The style is equal to that of his best early work, strong, supple, varied, although when he wrote it he was beset by many infirmities and blindness was approaching. In the inferior books his style is often woolly, Latinistic, and confused, amounting to a confusion of thought; nor does he realise the weakening effect of such insertions as 'almost', 'perhaps', 'as it were', 'so to speak'. There is also a curious insecurity in the use of pronouns of reference, of which an isolated example occurs in the autobiography: 'I stopped the elephants, and the Resident addressed them.'

The *Life* was brought out by Blackwood in 1877, under Miss Meadows Taylor's supervision; and this is the text which, by kind permission of Messrs. Blackwood, is here followed. The one-volume edition of 1878 and the convenient abridged edition of 1882 were brought out altogether from the publisher's office.

While working at this labour of love during the last two years I have been confined to the near neighbourhood of Land's

End, and not had access to the large libraries. But Meadows Taylor, an author neither learned nor recondite, should not be heavily annotated. I could have done more with pleasure, and hope I have not done too much. In addition to the annotation I have nothing to say. Every time I go through the *Life* it seems to me more beautifully done, and of absorbing interest. No wonder that the people whom Meadows Taylor ruled in India loved him. Here was a man with heart and with brain. He is apt to be particularly good when telling a ghost story, a tiger or an elephant story. Can a better recommendation be desired?

In a world where so many things matter, spelling, certainly the spelling of Indian names, luckily does not matter. It is only a point of convenience. Yet for this reason it is well to follow thankfully, though not pedantically, and without the accents, that Hunterian system which in its beginnings vexed Taylor half a century ago. To this I have brought the Indian names in *The Story of my Life*, yet respectfully and regretfully, not with precision. I have left untouched only a few words, such as Beydur, which seemed too much bound up with Taylor's life; Ooty, one of the prettiest of names for one of the prettiest of places, of which I am able to print an original impression by Macaulay's nephew; or old poetical streams like the Nurbudda and the Krishna. But the only rule of safety, for those who do not wish to give their minds to such things, is to agree as quickly as may be with the *Imperial Gazetteer*.

To the same great compilation I am proud to be indebted for the beautifully clear map, at the end of this volume, of Hyderabad State, where Meadows Taylor's working life was spent.

Paragraphing and punctuation are unchanged. Several mistakes, probably of printers, natural in a posthumous work, have been indicated; while others have been quietly set right. Miss Taylor admirably carried out her loving labour in the editing of the original edition. To Taylor's very few footnotes I have put his initials, M. T.

If I mentioned all who have helped me the list would be, as old Colonel Wilks says, 'long and respectable'. First of all, thanks are due to Messrs. Blackwood for the permission to reprint; to Miss Meadows Taylor for similar permission, and for many contributions; and to Henry Reeve's daughter, Mrs. Ogilvic of Chesters, Ancrum, for permission to use her father's Preface. Further thanks are given to Messrs. Allen & Unwin for the illustrative extracts from *Seeta* and from *A Noble Queen*; to Messrs. Longmans for the extracts made from Taylor's *History* and from the *Life of Henry Reeve*; to Mr. Murray for similar use of the *Life of Brian Houghton Hodgson*; to Mr. C. E. Buckland, among other things, for the unrestricted use of his indispensable *Dictionary of Anglo-Indian Biography*; to Mr. F. H. Skrine for the matter in his *Life of Sir W. W. Hunter* which fits in so well as an additional chapter to Taylor's autobiography, and for other help; to Dr. William Crooke for the note which he has contributed on the modern Beydurs, and for other help; and to Sir George Trevelyan for the account of Macaulay's stay at Ooty and for his own impression of the place a generation later. The frontispiece portrait of Colonel Taylor is used with the kind permission of the photographers, Messrs. Chancellor, of Dublin, while this and the interesting sketch of Captain Taylor by Count D'Orsay eighty years ago were contributed by Miss Taylor.

There has been some trouble in getting answers to letters. One important communication turned up from India after a twelvemonth. The oldest of the serious students of Indian history, Sir George Birdwood, died while trying to assist me; while the contributions of the youngest, Miss Lilian M. Penson, are noted in the following pages.

HENRY BRUCE.

SENNEN, CORNWALL,
July 1918.

PREFACE

For several years before his death, the writer of these Memoirs had been urged by his friends to leave on record some account of his adventurous and useful life. The materials at hand were authentic and abundant ; for, not only was he possessed of an excellent memory and great powers of retaining and narrating numerous and complicated details with entire accuracy, but during the forty years he spent in India, he carried on a copious correspondence with his father and other members of his family, and a great portion of these voluminous letters has been not only preserved, but carefully transcribed in England. I venture, therefore, to say that nothing is related in these volumes upon vague recollection or traditional evidence, but every incident is told as it happened.

Although it was not the fate of Meadows Taylor to rise to a high rank in the civil or military administration of India, and he cannot lay claim to the distinction and fame which belong to the illustrious founders and servants of the British Empire in the East, there were circumstances in his career not less remarkable than in the lives of greater men. He was one of the last of those who went out to India as simple adventurers—to use the term in no disparaging sense, for Clive and Dupleix were no more—and who achieved whatever success he had in life solely by his own energy and perseverance, independent of the patronage of the great Company or the authority of the Crown. A lad of fifteen, after a few years spent at a second-rate school, and a few months in the drudgery of a Liverpool merchant's counting-house, is sent to Bombay upon a vague and fallacious promise of mercantile employment. It was long before the days of Indian examinations and

Competition Wallahs. Arrived at Bombay, the house of business he was to enter proved to be no better than a shop, and its chief an embarrassed tradesman. By the influence and assistance of a kinsman, a commission was obtained for the misfortune-stricken boy in the Nizam's military contingent. Thus only he started in life. But the stress of circumstances and the tenacity of his own character had already taught him the all-important lesson of self-reliance and independence. Already, on the voyage, he had commenced the study of Eastern languages, to which he applied himself with extreme assiduity in his new position, perceiving that until a man has mastered the language of a country, he can know little of its inhabitants, and may remain for ever a stranger to the intelligence and the hearts of those over whom he exercises authority. His perfect acquaintance with the languages of Southern India, Telugu, and Marathi, as well as Hindustani, was no doubt the foundation of his extraordinary influence over the natives of the country, and of his insight into their motives and character. It was also the first step to his advancement in his profession. At seventeen he was employed as interpreter on courts-martial, and recommended for much higher duty by the Resident; and at eighteen he found himself Assistant Police Superintendent of a district comprising a population of a million souls. Nor were the duties of that office light. They involved not only direct authority over the ordinary relations of society, but the active pursuit of bands of dacoits, Thugs, and robbers, who infested a half-civilised territory. Occasionally, military expeditions were necessary to reduce some lawless chief of higher degree to obedience. The head of the police was, in short, the representative of law and order in a wild country. These duties, at this early age, Meadows Taylor performed, and with such success as to merit the notice of the sagacious old Minister of the Nizam, Chandu Lal, and the approval of the Resident.

It would be superfluous in this preface to notice the details of his advancement in life, which are more fully related by himself in the following pages. But I may venture to point out one or two considerations on which the simplicity and modesty of his own nature forbade him to dwell. By mere perseverance and industry, he carried on the work of self-education through life, with very remarkable results; and this, chiefly, at military stations in the interior of the Deccan, with no advantages of books or European society. Having mastered the native languages, he soon found that the government of an Indian district and population means that English intelligence, integrity, and foresight are to supply all that is wanting in these respects to a less civilised people; and he applied himself to make good from such resources as he possessed all these deficiencies. Thus he taught himself the art, and even invented a new method, of land-surveying, because the revenue settlement of the country depends upon it; and without augmenting the burdens of the people, he largely increased the revenue of the State in several districts. He taught himself engineering, because the construction of roads, tanks, and buildings was an essential part of the improvement of the country. He acquired a considerable knowledge of law, both Hindu, Mohammedan, and English, because he had to administer justice to the people; and he framed for himself a simple code and rules of procedure applicable to a country where there were no courts of law and no written laws at all. He studied geology and botany, because he observed the direct bearing of these sciences on the productiveness of the soil. He brought to the knowledge of Europe the curious antiquities of Southern India, so nearly allied in form to some of the remains of Ireland, Cornwall, and France. He beguiled his leisure hours with painting and music, in which he had, I know not how, acquired considerable proficiency; and he cultivated literature with no mean success, as is proved by the series of novels, beginning with the *Confessions of a Thug*, in which the manners and superstitions of India are portrayed with wonderful fidelity, and by the *Manual of Indian History*, which is the most complete summary in existence of the annals of that country. His various literary productions, which have stood the test of time, and still exercise a fascinating power over the reader, are not so much works of imagination as living pictures of the men and women amongst whom he dwelt. There is hardly a character in these volumes that was not drawn from some real person, whom he had seen and known in his various expeditions or in the repression of crime. And he acquired, as if by nature, an extraordinary force and flexibility of style, which brings the native of India, with his peculiar forms of language, his superstitions, his virtues, and his crimes, within the range of the English reader, as no other work has done. The tales of *Tara, Ralph Darnell, Tippoo Sultaun*, and *Seeta*, were designed by their author to mark the principal epochs of Indian history at long intervals of time, and the state of society in each of them; and they form a complete work, which deserves to retain a lasting place in English literature. And when it is considered that they were for the most part written by a young officer who spent his life in active service, remote from all literary society, they are an astonishing proof of natural genius. I mention these things, not by way of panegyric, but because I hope that many a young Englishman may enter upon the duties of an Indian career with this book in his pocket, and may learn from it what may be done, in the course of a single life, to develop and improve his own character and attainments, and to promote the welfare of the people committed to his charge.

But there is a higher element and a more important lesson in this record of a life spent in the service of India. Meadows Taylor gave to the people of India not only his head, but his heart. He had the liveliest sympathy and affection for the natives of India. Thoroughly understanding their traditions and their manners, he treated men and women of all ranks with the consideration and respect due to an ancient society. The wild Beydurs whom he encountered upon his first arrival at Shorapur—men who were the terror of the country and the myrmidons of the court—said to him, after their first interview, 'We perceive that you respect us, and we will be faithful to you for ever.' And in the more polished spheres of Indian life he touched the pride of the native nobility with so light and kindly a hand, that they were as eager to court his friendship, as the peasantry were to receive his counsel and his benefits. British rule in India has, beyond all doubt, conferred the great benefits of peace and civilisation on the country; but it is sometimes wanting in gentleness and sympathy. There lies probably its greatest danger in the future. Some examples there are of men who have touched the hearts of the natives and enjoyed in return their enthusiastic and devoted regard, such as the Lawrences, Outram, and Malcolm ; but they are rare. I think the author of these recollections was one of them. Wherever he went, the natives knew and believed that they had a protector and a friend. The sphere of his power and influence was not wide, at least in comparison with the vast extent and population of the Indian Empire ; but as far as it extended they were complete. Probably there were few men in India who, at the moment of the Mutiny of 1857, could have crossed the river into Berar without troops, and held a firm grasp on the passions of an excited people : and the confidence inspired by men of this character largely contributed to save the south of India from the calamities which were devastating the North-Western Provinces of Bengal. Not only was the maintenance of peace in the Deccan a matter of the utmost importance to the suppression of the disturbances in the North-West, but Colonel Taylor was able most materially to assist the operations of Sir Hugh Rose's army by moving up cattle and supplies, which were indispensable to the sustenance of the troops.

The chief object we have in view in giving these volumes to the world, and the chief object of the author in writing them, is to impress upon those who may be called upon to take any part in the administration of India, and especially on the young men who now annually leave our schools and examination papers for that purpose, that their ability, happiness, and success in the great work before them, will depend very much on the estimate they form of the native character, and on the respect and regard they show to the natives in the several ranks of society. The highest are on a par with the oldest and proudest aristocracy in the world. The lowest are entitled to be treated as members of an old and civilised society.[1]

Meadows Taylor was never, properly speaking, in the civil service of the East India Company or the Crown, nor did he

[1] In *Tippoo Sultaun* Taylor makes one of his young Indian officers, at home on leave, insist, as he himself did (see opening of Chapter VI. below) upon the 'highly civilised and cultivated character' of the people of the country.

hold any military appointment in the British Indian Army. He was through life an officer of the Nizam. He never even visited Calcutta or Bengal. But the administration of the Nizam, both civil and military, is, to a certain extent, that of a protected government, and is largely influenced by the decisions and policy of the Governor-General of India in Council. When it became a question of appointing an officer to administer a province, though that province might be a dependency of the Nizam, it was not unnatural that the selection of an English servant of that prince, without rank in the British service, should be viewed with some hesitation and jealousy, both at the India Board and at Calcutta. It was probably owing to this cause that during the administration of Sir H. Hardinge, and when Captain Meadows Taylor had barely surmounted his first difficulties at Shorapur, he was disagreeably surprised by a note from the private secretary of the Governor-General informing him that the appointment of another agent at Shorapur, unconnected with the recent events in that State, was required, and in contemplation. Upon the receipt of this intelligence, no motive having been assigned for the intended change, Captain Taylor's friends in England took steps to ascertain whether there were grounds to justify it. I find among my own papers the following letter to myself from the late Mr John Stuart Mill, better known to the world for his philosophical writings, than for the eminent public services he rendered for so many years, in the capacity of Examiner, or Political Secretary, to the East India Company. It may be inserted here as the highest testimony to the merits of Captain Taylor as an administrator, from a most competent observer :—

INDIA HOUSE, 23*d Sept.* 1845.

MY DEAR SIR,—You can hardly feel more interested in preventing the removal of Captain Meadows Taylor from Shorapur than I do myself, because (to say nothing of personal considerations) I have a very high opinion of the merits of his administration of Shorapur. I may say, indeed, that his being at Shorapur now is owing to me, for some expressions of approval and praise in a despatch written by me was what induced the Indian Government to suspend their intention of replacing him by a civil servant of the Company, and to refer the matter home. I have endeavoured to induce the

Court of Directors to negative the proposition. I do not, however, expect to obtain anything so decided, as they do not think it right to fetter the Indian Government in its choice of instruments. But as the Court will certainly give no encouragement to the project, I think it will blow over, and Captain Taylor will remain.—Very truly yours,

J. S. MILL.

And in a second letter, written by Mr. Mill a few days later, he added:—

Whatever may be the cause that is working against Captain Taylor, I am convinced that Fraser (the Resident at Hyderabad) has nothing to do with it. Fraser, as far as I know, has always written to Government very much in his favour. Captain Taylor is quite in error if he supposes that the Nazarana[1] business has done him any harm. Fraser did not agree with him on that subject, but the home authorities and Sir H. Hardinge did, and do most strenuously.

The cloud did blow over. Captain Taylor's merits were acknowledged at home and at Calcutta, and he remained at Shorapur many years. Indeed, when the arrangement was made with the Nizam for the liquidation of the claims of the British Government by the cession of certain portions of territory, the district of Western Berar was placed under the management of Captain Taylor; and the services rendered by him were so far eventually recognised by the Government of India, that he retired, after more than thirty-eight years' service,[2] with the pension of his rank in the British service, not unaccompanied with honorary distinctions, which he valued.

The time is past when so adventurous and singular a career is possible in India or elsewhere. The world grows

[1] Occasional dues, especially upon accession. As will be seen in the text, these had been an excuse for great extortion by the Nizam's Government against Shorapur. Taylor was keen to defend the interests of the lesser State.

[2] This would run quite to the end of 1862, more than two years after Taylor had left India in 1860.

more methodical, and routine takes the place of individual effort. But the same qualities of head and heart are still the only guides to success in the government of a people different from ourselves in race, religion, and manners, but united to Great Britain by a common allegiance and common duties.

HENRY REEVE.

FOXHOLES, 25*th Sept.* 1877.

CONTENTS

CHAPTER IV

1829–37

CHAPTER V

1838

CHAPTER VI

1838–41

CHAPTER VII

1841–42

CHAPTER VIII

1843–44

CHAPTER IX

1844–45

CHAPTER X

1846

CHAPTER XI

1847–50

CHAPTER XII

1851–53

CHAPTER XIII

1853–57

CHAPTER XIV

1857–58

CHAPTER XV

1858

CHAPTER XVI

1858–59

CHAPTER XVII

1859-60

CHAPTER XVIII

1860–74

CHAPTER XIX

1874–76

NOTES

ILLUSTRATIONS

THE STORY OF MY LIFE

CHAPTER I

1808–24

I WAS born in Slater Street, Liverpool, on the 25th day of September 1808. My father, Mr. Philip Meadows Taylor, was the only surviving son of the Rev. Philip Taylor, of Old Court, Harold's Cross, in the county of Dublin.[1] My mother was the youngest daughter of Bertram Mitford, Esq., of Mitford Castle, in the county of Northumberland, one of the most ancient Saxon families of England, which still flourishes, from its origin, beyond the Conquest, to the

[1] This useful pedigree has been kindly extracted for me by the Reverend Canon Taylor, vicar of St. Just in Penwith, from the *Familiae Minorum Gentium*, page 1104, published by the Harleian Society.

John Taylor, D.D., of Norwich, d. 1761. = Eliz. Jenkins.

- Richard Taylor, of Norwich, merchant, d. 1762. = Margaret Meadows.
  - Philip Taylor, of Dublin, minister of religion, b. 1747, d. 1831. = Anna Maria, dau. of Isaac Weld, D.D.
    - Philip Meadows Taylor. = Dec. 1807, Jane Honora, dau. of Bertram Mitford, of Mitford Castle, Co. Northumberland.
      - Philip Meadows Taylor, b. 25th Sept. 1808, d. 13th May 1876.
  - John Taylor, of Norwich, merchant, d. 1826. = Susanna, dau. of John Cooke.
    - Sarah = John Austin, author of *Jurisprudence*.
    - Susan = Henry Reeve, M.D.

present time, in the enjoyment of its ancient privileges and estates.[1]

My father's ancestors were of a North Lancashire family, and have been traced to Lancaster, where they were known in the fifteenth century. They reckoned many men of sterling worth and reputation among their number; and one, Dr. John Taylor, author of the *Hebrew Concordance*, is well known to this day.[2] The Taylors intermarried with the Martineau family, after the former had removed to Norwich, which became their stronghold; and there the pleasant friendly gatherings and intercourse with Mr. and Mrs. Barbauld, Sir J. E. Smith, and other celebrities of the time, are not yet forgotten.[3]

Without making any boast of pedigree, I can at least claim descent from two ancient families of England—one Puritan, the other Royalist—and my parents faithfully preserved these hereditary distinctions to the last.

My father was educated partly in Germany, and there learnt to appreciate the advantages of rifles over ordinary muskets. He assisted in raising a volunteer rifle corps in Liverpool, which he commanded as executive captain, the Earl of Derby being the colonel; and thus had, I believe, the merit of being the first to introduce the rifle system into England. This fact was recognised by the War Office at a comparatively late period. In 1807 my father and mother were married at Walton Church, Lancashire. Five sons were

[1] In *Ralph Darnell*, chapter x., is a paragraph describing Mitford Castle. 'The site combines the utmost picturesque effect with natural strength at a period when artillery was unknown, and when bowmen, and rude engines for casting stones, could have had little effect upon defenders protected by those massive walls. . . . The beautiful Wansbeck babbles by; the rooks swing and caw in the great trees by the little church; and the Mitfords still possess those noble ancestral properties they have held round their castle for a thousand years—nay more, far back into the dim period of Saxon possession.' Again: 'If they had, like the Mitfords, indeed, all their lands about them.'

[2] This was the dissenting divine, 1694–1761, who seems to have done some good work in Hebrew scholarship.

[3] The two other families mentioned in this sentence are familiar enough. Meadows Taylor, himself a botanist, could appreciate the importance of Sir James Edward Smith, 1759–1828, who founded the Linnaean Society in 1788, and who produced an *English Botany* in thirty-six volumes. There is much about this family in the *Life of Henry Reeve*.

the issue of this marriage, three of whom survive, I being the eldest.

Soon after my birth my father removed from Slater Street to Brookfield, a pretty country-house near Liverpool; and later, for convenience in business, then very prosperous, to a house in Rodney Street, the most fashionable locality in the town at that time. I remember but little of Brookfield; and indeed my first memories of Rodney Street are dim and vague. The chief one is of my being attacked with croup, followed by a long severe illness, which changed me from a healthy, sturdy child into an ailing, delicate one, and necessitated my being sent to Ireland, to the care of my grandfather and aunts, for change of air. I grew querulous and weak, and, I fear, was a trouble in the house. I had named myself 'King Pippin', and remember lying on the rug in the room I am now sitting in, piping out miserably that 'King can't' or 'King won't' when required to do anything. I grew stronger, however, and soon became my grandfather's constant companion in his strolls about the garden, holding on by his finger, and gradually losing my awe of his deep sonorous voice and imposing manner, as was proved by a speech recorded against me, when, as he was seized by a violent fit of sneezing, I looked up in my grandfather's face, and said, gravely, 'Grandpapa, what a chap you are for sneezing.'

In due course I returned to my parents in Rodney Street, and many memories flit across me while I write. On one occasion, while on a pond with some skaters at Street Court, Herefordshire, where my mother's sister resided, I had a narrow escape of my life. The ice broke under me, and I was with difficulty rescued—my cry being, 'Help King! help King!'

I believe I could at this time read fairly, and could repeat a good deal by heart at the age of five. No great feat, truly; but I was never set up as a prodigy, nor did I begin Greek at three years old, like Mr. Stuart Mill!

My wish was to become a merchant in those days, and, watching my opportunity, I ran away to find 'papa's counting-house', and was discovered by a friend of my father's crying in the street, and restored to my dear mother, whose agony when she found I was missing was extreme. She feared

I had been decoyed away for my beauty, and that she would never see me more. I was ordered to bed, without supper, by my father; but I well remember, as I lay there sobbing, that my mother stole into the nursery with a bowl of hot bread-and-milk in her hand, and gave earnest thanks for my restoration to her beside my little bed.

Soon after this escapade, my brother Robert and myself were sent to a day-school to keep us out of mischief. Of what we learnt at the Rev. Mr. Fearon's I remember but little. I suppose the rudiments of English and the earliest lessons in Latin; but we were very happy, and it was the beginning of the little education I ever received.

Among the most distinct memories of these early days is that splendid illumination of Liverpool, the year of the peace of 1814. We elder boys were taken by our parents through the streets of the town; and although those were not the days of gas and other brilliant effects, very beautiful devices were arranged with coloured oil-lamps, and our delight was unbounded.

Nor have I forgotten the chairing of Mr. Canning and General Gascoigne,[1] on their return as Members for Liverpool, after a severely-contested election. I remember my mother presenting a nosegay of flowers (bouquet would be the word used now) to Mr. Canning, and the scarlet streamers with which it was tied, and how we children, standing on the steps, were cheering with all our might, and were shown to him. I remember his laughing face and shiny bald head as he kissed hands to my mother and drove on—the flags too, the shouting crowds, the bands of music, and the windows filled with gaily-dressed ladies; and I remember how my mother, a true Mitford, insisted that her boys should wear the Tory colours, red and blue, in opposition to my father, whose sympathies were with the pink or Whig colours of the Seftons.[2]

The same year I accompanied my parents to Norwich, where there was a gathering of the Taylor family; of this

[1] Isaac Gascoyne (thus in *Dictionory of National Biography*), 1770–1841, a general without military record in those great days, had some peculiar pull upon Liverpool, which he represented from 1802 to 1830. Canning was of the same age, and, although so bald, only forty-four.

[2] Sefton Park, Liverpool.

I have little recollection; but of our stay in London—including being taken in a wherry to Greenwich, and seeing Madame Saqui dance on a tight-rope sixty feet high[1]—I have a very distinct impression, and also that I was a hero in the eyes of my brothers on my return.

It must have been about the year 1815–16 that my father's affairs became involved. He rejected all tempting offers to reinstate his business on borrowed moneys, which were freely pressed upon him; and having honourably discharged every claim, and given up the luxurious home in Rodney Street, to which his previous position had entitled him, he took a pleasant little villa called Olive Vale Cottage, about three miles from Liverpool, to which he removed his family. My mother accepted her change of fortune with all the resignation, devotion, and nobility of her character, and was ever the truc helper and comforter of her husband.

At Olive Vale Cottage we boys lived a very happy life. There was a pretty flower-garden which was our mother's great delight, and her carnations, pinks, and auriculas were the finest of their kind; a magnolia and scarlet japonica were trained round the drawing-room windows, and showed her exquisite taste. There was a capital fruit and vegetable garden, which was my father's pride, and where he laboured diligently when he returned each day from his work in Liverpool. There was a poplar-tree too, in the highest branches of which we established a sort of nest to which we mysteriously climbed, to my mother's great dismay, and I remember my father calling to us to 'Come down, you monkeys, and don't frighten your mother', while he at the same time betrayed no small pleasure in our accomplishing so manly an exploit. Although they were very poor, my parents were very happy, and very proud of their troop of noisy boys, who throve well in the sweet country air.

The next event was my being sent to school. The one selected was kept by Mr. Barron at Holt Hall, near Prescot, and I entered as a boarder. There were, I believe, about a hundred boys, and the school had a wide reputation. It

[1] From an advertisement reprinted in *The Times of 1818* it appears that Madame Saqui was still an attraction at Vauxhall Gardens.

was a rough place, although scarcely equal to the Yorkshire school of Mr. Squeers; but I, fresh from the gentle presence and teachings of my mother, felt the change keenly, and was almost inconsolable—so much so, that I was sent home after a while, and when I returned to Mr. Barron's, it was as a parlour boarder, a distinction which caused much jealousy, and subjected me to much torment. I was the youngest boy in the school, teased and bullied by all; but after I had received an enormous cake from home, which was divided among the boys, I grew more into favour, and even became a 'pet' among them.

We rose at six in summer, partially dressed ourselves, and, with our jackets over our arms, went down to a stone bench in the yard, where stood a long row of pewter basins filled with water, and often in the winter with ice. Here, in all weathers, we washed our faces and hands, combed and brushed our hair, and went into the schoolroom a while to study; then were let out to play till the bell rang for breakfast, consisting of fresh new milk, and a good lump of bread. At ten we were all in school again, and work went on, only interrupted by the instances of severe punishment which but too often occurred. The rod was not sparingly used, as many a bleeding back could testify, and I have often been obliged to pick the splinters of the rods from my hands.

We were well fed on meat, cabbage, and potatoes, and rice or some plain pudding; on Sundays we had invariably roast beef and Yorkshire pudding. We went into school again at three. At five school broke up, and at seven we had our suppers of bread and milk; afterwards we could study or go out within bounds as we pleased. Good Mrs. Barron attended to our personal cleanliness and to our health; and at stated seasons, especially in spring, we were all gathered together in the dining-hall, where the old lady stood at the end of the room at a small table, on which was a large bowl of that most horrible compound brimstone and treacle. The scene rises vividly before me, as we all stood with our hands behind our backs, opened our mouths and received each our spoonful, swallowed it down as best we could—and had to lick the spoon clean too! Surely this was a refinement of cruelty! I presume I learnt something while at this school, for before me lies a letter from my father, praising me for the good conduct and diligence I had shown, and exhorting me to further exertions, with much sound advice on many points. A like letter was also received from my grandfather, the replies to which I had to write with great care and no blots, and which was afterwards found carefully preserved among his papers.

I could not have remained at Mr. Barron's school longer than the close of the year 1817. The ill-usage I received increased, and I ran home at last and showed my mother my bleeding hands, and also my father when he came in. The distance I had run was no great feat for me, who was always selected 'hare' in our games at 'hare and hounds'. Thus the Barron bubble burst. What was to be done with me next? Had I really learned anything, except spelling, which was well knocked into me, and has stood me in good stead all my life? I doubt whether I really had profited much.

My brother attended a small day-school in the village of Wavertree, and when I got home I was also placed there under Mr. Newby's care. I believe he was a competent teacher if he chose, but he was incorrigibly sleepy and lazy; and when her husband fell asleep and we boys became uproarious, Mrs. Newby walked in, quelled the tumult, and read her lazy helpmeet a sound lecture, which used to afford us intense amusement. She was a tall grim woman, with decided beard and moustache, and a strong Cumberland accent; but she was very kind to us boys. A short time after my attendance at this school began, I received a bite from a dog as we were going along the lane one morning. It proved a very severe one, and I was very ill; my parents were much alarmed, as I was delirious for some time, and it was three months before the wound healed. How vividly I remember my dear mother's anxious face and gentle loving care, and my little brother Selby throwing himself down on the grass and crying that he saw the sky open and the beautiful angels hovering over him and saying to him, 'Meadows won't die!' What did the child see? Long years after I questioned him about this, and he said the vision was firmly rooted in his memory!

Time passed on, but I fear my father's affairs did not

improve, and there were many anxieties and privations at the Cottage; and at length, after a visit to Dublin, on which I accompanied him, my father accepted the charge of a large brewery in James Street, of which he was to be executive manager.

Does any reader remember the Dublin and Liverpool packets of fifty years ago? Stout cutters, with one narrow cabin for passengers and berths all round it; no wonder no one went across who could avoid it. We were three days and nights at sea; and as provisions were reduced to salt junk and ship's biscuit, we amused ourselves by catching gurnards off the Kish Bank, and these split and broiled were very good. After a short stay in Ireland we returned to Olive Vale Cottage. My father wound up his affairs in Liverpool, and we embarked with all our belongings for Dublin.

The house we occupied in James Street was large and handsome, and the brewery was a source of constant and varied delight. We helped, or imagined we helped, John Reilly, the cooper, to make and mend casks; and often shared his dinner of salt herring, potatoes, and butter, with old Segrave, the porter at the gate, who had a wooden leg.

My brother and I attended Dr. Hutton's school as day-scholars. Dr. Hutton taught Latin and Greek himself, and there were masters for French and mathematics. The discipline here, too, was very severe. Was everything I learned always to be beaten into me? I made but little progress in classics, but delighted in mathematics and French, and even gained prizes in these.

There was little variety in our Dublin life. I well recollect the entry of King George IV., the procession, his portly figure, and gracious salutations to the ladies in the windows, and the deafening cheers of the crowd, on that glorious summer day. The event was a remarkable one in the history of Ireland, and its people accorded to their King a right royal welcome.

All this time my dear mother's religious teachings to us became, it seems to me now, more earnest and constant than before. From her I learnt the doctrines of the Church and the sublime sacrifice and atonement of our Lord; and how lovingly and carefully she taught us will, I am sure, never be forgotten by my brother or myself, and led to the feelings I have all my life experienced of love and humble devotion to our glorious Church.

In those days it was considered effeminate to teach boys to draw, or sing, or play on any instrument; accomplishments, therefore, were denied us. I had much desire to learn both music and drawing, but it was not allowed. I was getting on with Latin and Greek, had entered the first class, and took a goodly number of prizes in French and mathematics.

Every boy, I suppose, has one decisive fight to record; mine was with a big boy, the bully of the school. We had one encounter, in which I was severely handled. My father encouraged me, however, not to give in, and gave me private instruction, until I began to 'see my way into science'. Reckoning on another easy victory, my enemy one day called me a coward, and hit me. I returned the blow sharply. The odds were scarcely fair, as my adversary had on a jacket with a row of metal buttons down the front; however, I fought on, hitting out as my father had taught me, and at last my foe lay down, begging my forgiveness, which of course was accorded. When I got home it was very evident what had occurred.

'You have been fighting again, sir,' said my father, severely.

'Yes, sir, with J——,' I replied.

'Did you lick him?'

'I did, father, though he had buttons on his jacket.'

'Bravo, my boy, here's half-a-crown for you. Go off and treat your backers, and J—— too, if you like.'

And so I did.

I do not know how it came about, but at the close of that half-year I was told that I was to go to Liverpool and enter the office of Messrs. Yates Brothers & Co., West India merchants, and be articled to them for seven years. I did not like the prospect at all. I should leave my darling mother and my studies, in which I was beginning to take such pleasure. Why was I sent away? I am at a loss to imagine, and it is useless to speculate now, but so it was; and to the intense grief of my mother, I was taken away, young and utterly inexperienced, and placed as a boarder and lodger with

Mr. Hassal, a clerk in some office in Liverpool, who had been recommended to my father. I was duly introduced to Messrs. Yates's office, in which were several young boys—learners like myself. Mr. Ashton Yates, the senior partner, was invariably good to me, and I have a grateful memory of his kindness while I remained in the office. At first I was set to copy circulars, and such easy work; then I was promoted to being post-office clerk—not an easy task in those days, as the postage on letters sent and received was of considerable amount and variety. I afterwards became one of the clerks for attending the discharge of cargoes, sitting in all weathers in a wooden shed with the Custom-house landing-waiter, entering, under their various marks, cotton bales, sugar hogsheads, and goods of all descriptions from the East and West Indies. It was a hard life; and day after day, in snow, frost, or rain, I have sat for hours together, shivering and benumbed with cold, being allowed an hour for my dinner, in which time I had to run two miles to eat it, and run back again. Sometimes a friendly captain would ask me to partake of his meal; and I have frequently shared a landing-waiter's lunch when offered. Our nominal hour for closing office was six o'clock; but I have often been kept till ten when there was a press of work. My last office was 'assistant dunner', as it was called—*i.e.* the collection of moneys due; and late in the dark evenings have I, mere boy as I was, been walking the streets of Liverpool with thousands of pounds in bills, notes, and gold in my pocket. I was getting on; but I had enemies—why, I know not—who played me many a scurvy trick. My petty cash was often pilfered, my desk being opened by other keys. I was ordered on private errands for other clerks, and when I refused to execute them, I was 'paid off' by extra work and malicious accusations. These were, however, entirely disproved. I had a steady friend in Mr. Yates, and persevered in my work. The pleasantest part of my duty was arranging the samples of cotton according to their quality; and I have been often called into the 'parlour' to assist the partners in their decisions. I had a fine sense of touch, and became an adept in the manipulation of samples.

One incident I have never forgotten. I was returning to the office late one evening, when, passing by the door of a chapel, and hearing groans and cries, I looked in. A person stationed at the door invited me to enter and 'save my soul'. The place, a large one, was in profound darkness; a candle here and there only made the gloom more impenetrable. People of both sexes were sitting in the pews, and shrill piercing cries arose of 'Save me!' 'I'm going to hell!' 'I'm damned!' 'The devil has me!' 'I'm burning, burning!' 'Go away, Satan!' 'Jesus has got me!' and the like, with prayers so profane and shocking that I dare not write them down. Sometimes one got up, man or woman, and gave his or her experience of sins and crimes, horrible to hear, but which, nevertheless, fascinated me. I know not how long I stayed, but a girl sat down by me at last and whispered, 'Come and kiss me, you beautiful boy—come away.' I gained the door, and fled rapidly in the darkness up the street.

Early in 1824 the wretchedness I endured in the office reached its highest pitch, and malicious tales against me increased frightfully, accompanied by threats. I retorted by saying to those who were badgering me, that if I were not let alone I would tell certain things I knew of them. I was of course defied; but I felt ill—I had a fearful cough, and the doctor said I was threatened with consumption; so I wrote the whole story to my father, who had left Dublin and was settled at Apsley, near Hemel Hempstead in Hertfordshire, telling him that I must come home for change of air at once.

I went into the 'parlour' to consult Mr. Yates, who agreed I had better go for a while. I was not strong enough for work, and my enemies in the office were very malicious.

'And', he added, 'tell your father, if there is any other opening for you he likes better, or that you wish yourself, I will give up your indentures.'

I had enough money of my own to pay my journey; and on a bitterly cold morning I mounted the roof of the London coach at the Saracen's Head, Dale Street, with a thankful heart, and was in my mother's arms on the following afternoon. How happy I need not say.

My indentures were returned by Mr. Yates, after some correspondence with my father, and I had ended that phase of my life, richer in experience and general knowledge, but weak and delicate in health. With home care this soon improved.

I was not long in suspense as to my future. My father became acquainted with Mr. Baxter, a Bombay merchant, who wanted a young man to assist in the house at Bombay, and proposed to me to go out at once. It had been previously decided that I should go to Madeira for my health, so the proposal fitted admirably. We dined with Mr. Baxter, who lived in splendid style, and the terms offered seemed to me and to my father exceptionally good.

I was to receive a large and yearly increasing salary, live in Mr. Baxter's family, and to be admitted as an eighth partner when I became of age. My mother's cousin, Mr. Newnham,[1] was holding the high office of Chief Secretary to Government at Bombay, and would no doubt look after me; and I was considered a very lucky boy with excellent prospects.

My outfit was at once ordered, my passage taken in the *Upton Castle*, permission having been obtained for me to reside in India, and I returned for a few short precious days to Apsley. I will not dwell on this period; it is even yet sacred to me; but at length the 15th April came, and I parted from my dear mother in bitter grief, never to see her again. My father took me down to Greenwich in a wherry, with my boxes, and we found the *Upton Castle* there. We dined at the Falcon, and in the evening went on board. My father gave me much excellent advice and bid me good-bye, both he and I firmly believing that I should return in 'no time', rich and prosperous, a partner in Baxter's house.[2]

[1] I am indebted to Miss Lilian M. Penson for information about William Newnham. He is not mentioned in several books of reference consulted, but according to Dodswell & Miles, *Bombay Civil Servants, 1798–1838*, he was appointed in 1804, and after holding various appointments, became Chief Secretary to Government in 1823, and Member of Council 1829–1834. In 1835 he was living in England.

[2] There is a delightful Regency flavour, tempting to a novelist, about this too brief account of Taylor's childhood, with Mr. Baxter. His father, who might be a character in some early novel of Dickens, lived on for half a century, in a singularly happy intimacy with his son. But for Meadows Taylor's continuous letters to him from India, treasured up until they had served their final purpose, this autobiography would not have been what it is.

It should not be omitted that the novelist's full name was Philip

When I awoke next morning, our ship was anchored off Gravesend waiting for the captain and some of the passengers: when these arrived, we put to sea. So ended my boyhood in England. I had completed my fifteenth year the previous September.

THE MEADOWS TAYLORS

By Miss Meadows Taylor

The name Meadows has been carried on ever since two Miss Meadows married, one a Taylor, the other a Martineau. The name Meadows has been perpetuated in both families ever since. There is a valuable silver mug now in the keeping of Mrs. Mitford Taylor, widow of the Rev. Robert Taylor, only son of my father's brother, Rev. Robert Mitford Taylor, for forty years vicar of Hunmanby, Yorkshire. This mug (so goes the legend) was the property of one Sir Philip Meadows, who was in a high position in Portugal in King Charles's reign. The mug was left to his brother by my father, and descended to his son and his family.

My grandfather Taylor had great charm of manner, and was a favourite everywhere. He was not fortunate in business, and led a very chequered life. He married Miss Mitford, of Mitford, Northumberland. She was one of a large family who all married and have left descendants, so that our connections on that side are very numerous. Her brother, Admiral Mitford, was the father of the Dowager Lady Amherst of Hackney, and these cousins have always been most dear and valued.

On his father's side my father had no relatives so near, as except for his brother Rev. Robert Mitford Taylor, the remaining three were unmarried. The five brothers were Meadows; Robert; Weld, who took up lithography and latterly lived a retired life at Wimborne, Dorset; Selby and Glanville, who died within six months of each other in Ceylon, quite young men. Of these my uncle Robert and his family were the most intimate always; one of his daughters, Mrs. Robinson, lives near me now.

My grandfather's first cousins were a brilliant and talented

Meadows Taylor. The ancestor mentioned by Miss Taylor just below was Sir Philip Meadows, called 'the elder', 1626–1718, who was appointed Latin secretary to relieve Milton, and while still a young man represented Cromwell at Lisbon. He was afterwards envoy to Denmark and to Sweden, and published an account of the wars between those countries. His son, Sir Philip Meadows the younger, was long before his father's death knighted, and envoy to Holland and to the Emperor, dying in 1757, evidently at a great age.

lot, amongst them Mrs. Reeve, mother of Henry Reeve; Mrs Austin, mother of Lady Duff Gordon, whose daughter, Mrs Ross, has written an account of that branch of the Taylor family, called 'Three Generations of English Women', which is most interesting. Others of that large family were Philip Taylor of Marseilles; John Taylor, mining engineer; Edward, Gresham Professor of Music. All were notable in their way; and with many of them, especially Henry Reeve, cousinly intercourse was kept up. But the Mitford relatives always seemed the nearest to us, and we were thrown more amongst them.

My father and grandfather lived always on the most affectionate terms. My father always spoke of his mother as so lovable, and he revered her memory. His grandfather, Rev. Philip Taylor, left Norwich to take a nonconformist pulpit in Dublin. There he married a Miss Weld, who was heiress to the Harold's Cross property, then considerable. The house and what was left of the property came down to my father eventually; and we loved the old place with its delicious garden and fields adjoining. There we lived till my father's death; when, circumstances being quite altered, my sister and I sold it. It is now, I believe, covered with small houses, but the old house itself still remains. Hunmanby Vicarage is now occupied by the Rev. Edward Mitford, a distant cousin.

CHAPTER II

1824

We knocked about for a week in the Channel owing to strong adverse winds, and at last anchored off Spithead to wait for a fair breeze, and I wrote to my brother a long cheery letter detailing many a 'castle in the air', and hope of great things to come. On the 26th April we finally put to sea. We reached Funchal, Madeira, on the 26th May. I had excellent introductions from my father's relations, Mr. and Mrs. Leacock, and I was very kindly received on my arrival. I saw a great deal of the island, many new sights and much wonderful scenery, which I find described in a long letter written to my mother. We were about ten days at Madeira taking in wine for India. I was on shore all the time, and I believe some of the passengers were surprised to find 'the boy for Baxter's' at dinner-parties and the chief houses of the island. Certainly, several who had not before noticed me now began to do so. The captain and chief officer taught me the use of the sextant and to make observations, and I was soon able to be of use. Some one lent me Gilchrist's *Hindustani Grammar*, and taught me to pronounce the words, so I was able to make some progress.

The *Upton Castle* was frigate-built, and carried eighteen guns, and it was necessary to keep a good look-out against pirate cruisers about the latitude of the Azores. We were all told off to quarters, and I was constituted captain of the mizzen-top, my favourite resort for reading, and which now was garrisoned by six stout boys besides myself. One night I was keeping the first watch with Mr. Duggan the second officer, when just as the lights were being put out I raised the glass, and saw a large felucca close to us on the windward quarter. I raised an alarm, and although we hailed her several times, no answer was given. I think I hear now Mr. Duggan's order to me to 'fire', and see the long dark ship, with all its moving dusky forms, plunging past us. I fired two muskets in rapid succession; but the stranger did not turn, and we sent a parting shot after her. Our ship was in a state of wild excitement, and groups of passengers, ladies and gentlemen in every variety of costume, were gathered on deck. We had no further alarms after this. We were becalmed on the line for nearly three weeks, dull and insufferably hot. We welcomed Neptune and Mrs. Neptune on board in the approved old fashion, and I was scraped with a hoop and well ducked, but was spared the tarring.

We had one terrible gale off the Cape, but got off without much damage. I had a narrow escape of my life one day: I was upon the dolphin-striker and had struck two and hit a third, and the 'quiver' held; but instead of disengaging the line from my arm, it became twisted round my wrist, and had I not been lashed to the dolphin-striker I must have been inevitably dragged into the sea. The wounded fish turned in a last struggle, and I got the line free. My arm was very painful for some time, and I made no further attempts to strike dolphins.

As we neared Bombay one of the passengers took me aside, and asked me concerning my past life and future prospects very kindly. I told him all, and the arrangements which had been made for me in Baxter's house, and that I believed it to be a great mercantile firm. On this point I was now undeceived, as my friend said Mr. Baxter's was simply a large shop; that they had been in a fair way of business, but that Mr. Baxter's extravagance in London had been such that it was possible the firm might no longer even exist. However, he added, you have made many friends among us; we are all interested in you, and will help you if we can. I told him of my letters to Mr. Newnham and others, and he said it was impossible to have a better or more influential friend. 'I think', he said, 'you will not be long at Baxter's, and we shall soon see you take your proper place in society.' Among the ladies, especially, I had excited an interest by rescuing one of them, a lovely girl, from a watery grave. She had incautiously opened her port-hole during a storm, keeping the cabin-door shut. A great green sea poured in, flooding the whole place. I fortunately heard the rush of water, and forcing open the door of her cabin, found her lying face downwards in the water, which was pouring over the steerage deck. I carried her to the cabin of another lady and put her in, and next day was very sweetly thanked for my services.

All things considered, my voyage had been a very pleasant one. We anchored in Bombay harbour on the night of the 1st of September 1824, having been four months and a half at sea, and the whole of that glorious panorama opened on my sight as I rose early in the morning to have 'a look at India'.

I find a long letter written to my mother, dated September 3, part of which I am tempted to insert as my first impressions of Bombay :—

'Bombay, *September* 3, 1824.

'My dearest Mother,—After a long but fine passage of four months and some days, I have arrived at the house of Mr. Osborne, with whom I have every expectation of being extremely comfortable ; but having been only here a day, I can hardly judge how I shall like the business that I am about to embark in, in the town of Bombay.

'I have arrived at a very good time of the year, as the weather, with the exception of next month, which is a hot one, will get cooler and cooler every day. Even now the evenings and mornings, which is the only time you can stir out, except in a palankeen, are delightfully cool and pleasant.

'But one of the greatest annoyances here are the mosquitoes, which bite terribly ; but as yet I have escaped their torments.

'At about half-past ten on the morning of the 1st, land was descried from the mast-head, which proved to be the high land outside Bombay harbour.

'I was employed below, packing up all my goods and chattels, so that I did not come on deck till about three in the afternoon, when by that time we were close to it. It is fine high land, and is covered with green in many places—a welcome sight for us who had been so long at sea. We passed, also, two very pretty small islands, called Henery and Kenery, all covered with trees to the water's edge ; but as it was by this time six o'clock, we could not see the beautiful verdure of the trees ; [1] and as we entered the harbour by night, we

---

[1] These scraps of islands, of the size of the lesser Scillies, are about a dozen miles due south from Bombay. Henery is rightly Underi, and Kenery Khanderi. They were the scenes of fine confused pirate fighting,

missed a very fine sight, as the entrance to the harbour is reckoned one of the finest in the world. At half-past twelve we cast anchor in Bombay roads, about three miles from the town, intending to drop down early in the morning. Accordingly, when the pilot came on board about four o'clock, we weighed, and dropped down opposite the town, where we cast anchor for good about a mile from the shore. As soon as we had come to an anchor, we were surrounded by boats filled with black fellows, naked excepting a piece of cotton-stuff tied round their waist, offering fruit, eggs, milk, etc., of which you may be sure we all ate very heartily by way of a treat. About twelve o'clock I hired a boat and went ashore, taking with me all the clean clothes I had, which had dwindled to about half-a-dozen clean shirts, as many stockings, and one pair of trousers—rather a slender stock! The moment I got ashore, I hired a palankeen and went to Baxter Bros., where I was received by Mr. Osborne, the manager, who did not know of my appointment, but was very kind. He offered me his palankeen to go about in, and recommended me to deliver my letters; and I set out for Mr. Newnham's, who was very kind, offered me his advice whenever I stood in need, and told me if he could do me any service, he would with the greatest pleasure. I then went to Mr. Wodehouse, who asked me if I was entirely engaged to Baxter's; and when I told him I believed I was, I thought he looked disappointed.

'... Nothing goes down here but the "Company", and it is indeed an excellent service. There are the writers, for instance; as soon as they arrive in India, they have their three hundred rupees a-month, and nothing to do but to learn the Hindustani and Persian languages, and ride about in palankeens, with a score of black fellows at their heels. In this country there are lots of servants, and they are the laziest lot of rascals under the sun. One fellow will not do two things. If you have a fellow to brush your shoes, he will not go on an errand.[1] One of our passengers hired eighteen servants

---

yet on the smallest scale, in the days when three other Powers tried to crowd the English off the island of Bombay. Kenery passed to us with the other Maratha possessions in 1818; but it is startling to think that Henery, the island nearer the mainland, for some reason did not lapse, and was the scene of certain atrocities, until 1840, years after Taylor wrote this description.

[1] This subdivision of domestic service is one of the first points to strike a griffin. In one of the Anglo-Indian books most packed with good stories, the author, on landing at Calcutta in 1858 in circumstances very different from those of Meadows Taylor a generation earlier, is thus instructed by a family friend who did not like India: 'Caste, my dear child, is the bane of this country. Why, the fellow who cleans my boots, blowed if he will clean my shoes' (J. H. Rivett-Carnac's *Many Memories*: Blackwood).

the moment he landed! But their wages are very cheap. You get these fellows for 2, 3, 4, and 6 rupees a-month, and have not to clothe them or anything. . . . A shirt here lasts only a day—sometimes not even that. Fortunately washing is very cheap, only three rupees a-month, and you may dirty as many things as you like. I think the climate will agree with me; I do not find the heat oppressive. . . . Last night I had a walk on the esplanade, which was crowded with vehicles, carriages, gigs, and buggies, of all sorts, shapes, and sizes. Bombay is a fort; but the fortifications are not in good order. It is a pleasant walk round the top of the ramparts. I have not seen any of the passengers since I came ashore. I suppose they will all be too proud to speak to me now; but, fortunately, there was not one I cared twopence for, except young Shepheard; that's a comfort. . . . The language is not difficult to get a knowledge of; but to be a good grammatical scholar is difficult, as it is not a written language. But Gilchrist, of London, has invented a way of writing it in English letters.[1] The natives transact their business in Persian, which is a written language. This is a festival day, and the natives walk in a sort of procession, with a kind of drum, making a terrible noise. They dress up in the most ridiculous manner, carry torches in their hands, and go on with all sorts of antics.[2] . . . I have written

---

[1] The boy informs his mother with sufficient correctness. John Borthwick Gilchrist, 1759–1841, was, like several contemporary pioneers in Indian studies, a member of the medical service. His *Hindustani Grammar* appeared in 1796; and it was the discerning Marquis Wellesley who gave him a larger chance. Gilchrist was the predecessor, at Hindustani text-books, of the better-known Duncan Forbes, then a young man.

[2] In his *History*, speaking of seven years earlier, Taylor says: 'The annual festival of the Dussera was to take place on October 19, and is an occasion, in every Hindu State, not only for a military display in commemoration of the capture of Ceylon by King Rama, but for taking the annual muster of troops.' Near the opening of the *Thug* Ameer Ali says: 'As it still wanted two days to the festival of the Dussera, my inauguration was postponed to that day; for it is esteemed a particularly fortunate one by the Thugs, and indeed by all classes. On it, you are already aware, that all great undertakings are commenced by armies, and, in like manner, by us Thugs; for the breaking up of the rains gives us a hope that the adventure will not be impeded by them; and the continuance of fine weather which follows it, allows the band to travel in comfort, and with better hope of booty from the chance of falling in with travellers, who also take advantage of the break in the weather to commence long journeys. Above all, it is a day peculiarly sacred to Bhowanee, our patroness and goddess.' Yet asking his father why Hindu festivals should be acknowledged and kept by Musalmans, Ameer Ali is told: 'The Dussera is the only

you a long letter, and told you all I could think of. I shall be in daily expectation of hearing from you, and can assure you there is nothing so disappointing as a ship from England without a letter from yourself.—I am your affectionate son,

M. T.

'*P.S.*—Pray give my love to all friends at home and in London, where, I daresay, they have not forgotten me. Also to all dear friends in Dublin. When you see the boys, kiss them for me, and tell them the black fellows are such queer "jummies", with large bracelets on their arms and thighs made of silver, and rings through their noses, and strings of beads round their necks, and almost naked.

'Kiss dear Johnny for me a hundred times. I daresay he still remembers me; and give my love to Bella.

'We are going to have a new Governor, as Mr. Elphinstone is going to Madras, and a Mr. Lushington of the Treasury is coming out to succeed him.[1] The present Governor is very much liked, and the inhabitants will be sorry to part with him.

'Mr. Osborne lives in a very pleasant part of the town, fronting the esplanade, close to the fort-walls. We can see the sea—in fact it is close by—so that we have the sea-breeze all day long, without which it would be miserably hot. The houses are all built very large—large rooms, etc.; and the staircases are wide and airy.

'And now, dearest mother, I must close this letter, wishing you health and happiness; and that God may send His blessing upon you and my dear father is the constant prayer of your affectionate son.'

---

one which is observed; and the reason of this is, that it is the fittest time of the year to commence our enterprises, and has been invariably kept sacred by all Hindu Thugs.'

[1] This is quite wrong, though doubtless a rumour of the day, explained by the fact that Mountstuart Elphinstone (1779–1859) had then nearly completed the normal five years as Governor of Bombay. When Taylor landed in 1824 Elphinstone, still a youngish man, bachelor, scholar, valetudinarian, enjoyed a towering reputation as having so lately and so largely directed the annexation of that 'Maratha Continent' which had always overshadowed and confined the aspiring 'Presidency'. Elphinstone remained Governor for fully three years longer, refusing further office: his nephew it was who, in the same post, showed kindness to Taylor leaving India in poor health in 1860. Stephen Rumbold Lushington, 1776–1868, once of the Madras Civil Service, son-in-law and biographer of the first Lord Harris, the conqueror of Tippoo, was a Parliamentary politician important enough to bargain for an Indian governorship. He never went to Bombay. He was joint secretary to the Treasury from 1824 to 1827. In that year he became Privy Councillor and went to Madras as Governor for the five years following.

I had a comfortable room at Mr. Osborne's, and lived with him and his wife. He was in much perplexity about me, as he continued to receive no instructions, and the affairs of the house grew worse and worse. I could be given no salary, and as to the eighth share which I was to receive after five years, Mr. Osborne considered it purely imaginary, and his hope seemed to be that Mr. Newnham or Mr. Wodehouse would provide for me and relieve him of the responsibility. I did not write home any complaints or misgivings, but set to work to give what I could in return for the food, shelter, and indeed clothing that Mr. Osborne kindly supplied me with. I could do but little in the office, or help in accounts I did not understand at first. I could, however, make out bills for goods supplied—wine, beer, and groceries ; could draft copies of outstanding accounts, and letters for Mr. Osborne to sign. I had to sell in the shop both to ladies and gentlemen. I even one day sold some articles to the young lady I had rescued on board, and she presented me to her father, Colonel ——, with a pretty little speech, telling him the story ; and the old gentleman shook me warmly by the hand and thanked me.

I often breakfasted with Mr. Newnham, but Mr. Wodehouse seemed almost more anxious on my account, and often looked into the shop. So I plodded on, Mr. Osborne looking anxiously for letters about me that never came, and vexing himself by vain regrets.

My time of deliverance was not far distant. Mr. Newnham one morning sent his palankeen for me, with a note saying he had something to tell me, and he showed me a letter from Sir Charles Metcalfe, then Resident at Hyderabad,[1] stating

[1] Charles Theophilus Metcalfe, 1785–1846, third baronet, and Lord Metcalfe in the last year of his life, 'the liberator of the Indian Press', was from 1820 to 1825 Resident at Hyderabad, where he 'had to deal with the case of the banking firm of Palmer & Co.' He left before Taylor could have met him, returning to his former charge of Delhi: the one-volume edition of the *Dictionary of National Biography* wrongly keeps him at Hyderabad during these two years. 'The three greatest dependencies of the British Crown were successively entrusted to his care'—as Macaulay could write of India, Jamaica, and the small Canada of that day. His natural son, Colonel James Metcalfe, was an Indian officer somewhat prominent in the following generation; while the young Sir Theophilus Metcalfe, renowned in the history of Delhi, was his great-nephew.

that he had procured me a commission in his Highness the Nizam's army, and the sooner I went up to Aurungabad the better. I was of course astonished at this, but without any hesitation I accepted it at once, feeling very sure I had found a better opening than before. Only, how to get free of Baxter's ? Mr. Newnham wrote to Mr. Osborne asking that my indentures might be cancelled. Of course Mr. Osborne was surprised, but very kindly said he would not stand in my way; that I was a fortunate fellow to have such a friend and get such an appointment, and next day gave me back my indentures.

I find in a letter from Mr. Newnham to my mother that 'he is happy to tell her, her son will now quit the shop and move in his proper sphere. The Nizam's service', he continues, 'holds out the most flattering prospects; and if he qualifies himself in points of duty and in acquaintance with the native languages, the road to high and lucrative employment will be open to him. He will remove to my house, where he will remain till he is ready to proceed to Aurungabad, where his military service will commence. I shall be very happy if this change in his circumstances should prove agreeable to you and Mr. Taylor. He is a fine intelligent lad, and I saw him, with regret, articled to a house which is not in as flourishing a state as you were led to believe.—Yours very faithfully, WILLIAM NEWNHAM.'

I removed to a small bungalow within Mr. Newnham's 'compound', and a Parsi servant was appointed to attend me, who spoke good English; but I had not been idle, and could make myself understood pretty well, my ear guiding me to a good pronunciation. Arrangements for my military outfit proceeded. I needed of course uniform, tents, clothes, etc., and my generous friend, Mr. Newnham, gave me a splendid chestnut Arab, which had belonged to his late wife. How pleased he was that I was out of 'that shop'—that I was no longer 'Baxter's boy!' indeed I am sure he felt his own dignity insulted as long as I was there. 'Now', he said, 'you are Lieutenant Meadows Taylor of his Highness the Nizam's service, and we all drink your health and wish you success.'[1]

[1] 'Some men pass their lives in getting and losing chances, but Taylor was of the sort to make befriending him a pleasing office; winning,

One other temptation assailed me. Mr. Shotton, the head of the great mercantile firm of that name, pressed me to throw aside military service and join his House. The prospects were very tempting, and Mr. Newnham was greatly troubled as to what was best for me to do. Finally it was arranged that Mr. Newnham and Mr. Wodehouse should decide; and their fiat went forth that I was to be a soldier. They were right; the great House perished too, and I should have been again on the world.

So when my kit was ready I left Bombay. Mr. Newnham had generously advanced every rupee of my outfit, and I was to repay him as I could; and on the 18th November 1824 I started for Aurungabad.

HYDERABAD STATE

Our Faithful Ally, his Exalted Highness the Nizam, holds, not merely by these titles, a different position from the other princes of India. The title of a Victorian novel, *Her Majesty's Greatest Subject*, most obviously suggests the Nizam. He has been picturesquely called 'The Turk at Hyderabad'. The people of the adjoining British districts speak of *the Mogulai*, where missionaries and their agents go over the borders, among the fanatical populace, at some risk.

---

active, eager, and industrious, every one took kindly to the lad, and his high-placed relation had the discernment to see that influence and generosity exerted in his case would be repaid by the result. . . . The Nizam's army, as it was then called, now the Hyderabad Contingent, was that part of the Nizam's armed forces which had been supplied with a staff of British officers, and brought under regular military training and discipline. It comprised about a dozen regiments of infantry and cavalry with some batteries of artillery, to which were attached about one hundred European officers, most of whom belonged to the regular establishment of the Indian Army, and were detached to the Nizam's service by way of staff employ, but some of whom, like Meadows Taylor, were appointed on the nomination of the Resident, and whose commissions carried no authority beyond the Nizam's army itself.' Much is made of the unfair difference between the regular officers, who sought 'this coveted service' for 'the increased pay and promotion it conferred', and outsiders who had to enter by the back door; as also of the truly gorgeous uniforms. 'Did an officer appear at a lèvee at St. James's with an exceptional amount of gold lace and embroidery on his coat, he would usually be found to belong to the Hyderabad Contingent' (*Edinburgh Review* article, 'The Story of an Indian Life', October 1877).

For this is the surviving fragment, always the greatest in area and truly grandiose, from the Empire of the Moguls. It was once yet larger, stretching to the north and to the south, and to the eastern sea. For a century before British colonies thought of calling themselves by that name, 'the Dominions' was a familiar phrase for those of his Highness the Nizam. No Indian State can hold its head up to these Dominions. This was hardly true while the kingdom of Oudh lasted. But for more than six decades there has been no competitor.

The mere area of Hyderabad is 82,700 square miles, or as nearly as need be that of Great Britain without Wales. This area is approached by that of Jammu with Kashmir, largely mountain ranges; or even by the deserts of Kalat. But practically the whole of Hyderabad territory is good fertile country, though tending to dryness and requiring the storage of water. In the matter of population, which counts for much more, the primacy is Hyderabad's. By the census of 1911, as given in *The Oxford Survey of the British Empire*, and in the volumes of the Hyderabad Census Returns, the population was then an increasing 13,000,000. Mysore, the second State, and greatly better administered, has less than one half these figures for either population or area; while the several States following in importance have difficulty in keeping above 3,000,000.

The eighty pages of the article on Hyderabad State in the *Imperial Gazetteer* contain little that need be quoted. The statistics in the current edition have long been devoid of significance, as based upon the census of 1901. The entire State maintains a certain level above the sea, rising in places even above three thousand feet. 'It is divided into two large and nearly equal divisions, geologically and ethnologically distinct, separated from each other by the rivers Manjra and Godavari.' Of both these divisions Meadows Taylor came to have administrative experience. The portion to the north and west is trap, with black soil, a land of wheat and cotton, inhabited by the speakers of Marathi and Kanarese. This includes the Balaghat, the upper ranges which Taylor enjoyed in life, and to which he has given a poetical touch in *Tara*. The southern portion of the State, much the larger, is granitic, with bare hills and fantastic boulders, a land of rice and tanks. It is called Telingana, and the people speak Telugu.

'A greater variety of wild animals and feathered game', says the *Gazetteer*, 'is not met with in any other part of India, excepting perhaps the Mysore State.' There is a taking list, beginning with tigers and leopards, occasional bison and elephants, including wolves, tiger-cats, bears, porcupine, peafowl with blue and green pigeon, and ending with florican and flamingo on the banks of the Godavery and Krishna.

But the climate is prevailingly feverish. This is not surprising, since the mean temperature of the State is 81 degrees. There is a world of difference between that and an average temperature of a dozen, or fewer, degrees lower, that is bound to prove a burden to any European constitution; and it ruined Taylor's, within thirty-six years.

Hyderabad is, historically, the continuation of the lesser Deccan kingdom of Golconda. Taylor has told, in his *History*, how the king of Golconda, who had long felt crowded, began in 1589 to build the present city of Hyderabad, on the right bank of the Musi river, about eight miles from the fort. It was first named Bhagnagar, after a favourite Hindu mistress, Bhagmati; and when she died, after his son Hyder. 'The city was well laid out with broad streets, then sheltered by rows of trees, and the supply of water from a dam in the river above Golconda was, and continues to be, abundant.' This city has now reached half a million, and the sanitation has been much improved since Taylor's day.

About a century after the founding of the city, the Golconda kingdom was absorbed in the Mogul Empire, which was already tottering. For an uncertain generation it remained attached to Delhi. The date at which, in the first quarter of the eighteenth century, Hyderabad fell off from the empire into an independent orbit is variously stated, but is usually written as being 1724.

The founder of the State, who did with abiding success what so many Indian governors and Persian satraps tried to do, was a Turkoman nobleman or adventurer named Asaf Jah, among other names, and earlier a distinguished general under Aurungzeb. He was the first Nizam-ul-Mulk, 'regenerator of the State'. Amid the welter of the first half of the eighteenth century in India Asaf Jah strikes the imagination by his stability, and by the way he lived on, always competent though sometimes defeated. He died in 1748, 'having attained', says Taylor, 'the wonderful age of 104 years.'

His three successors, who are counted as the second, third, and fourth Nizams, assisted, during only about a dozen years, at the rise of the British power. They were all, with those after them for a century and a half, as characterless as he was full of character. The tradition of fidelity to the English took some time to get established. The Nizams of the eighteenth century were no more than just sufficiently faithful to be tolerated in the part. Their survival was largely a matter of bigness, of the attraction of gravitation, of sitting tight. Whatever provinces they lost, they held the balance in the Deccan. The real fighters, the Marathas, the Mysoreans, the English, despised but could not ignore them. Hyderabad State seems steadily to have been guiltless of any distinction, prevailing merely by mass and by inaction.

The Nizams respectively of *Tippoo Sultaun* and of the *Thug*, with two others under whom Taylor chiefly served, are as follows:

Nizam Ali, also called Nizam-ul-Mulk and Asaf Jah, counted as the fifth Nizam, was the fourth son of the founder of the line, and reigned from 1761 to 1803. As he was after all but in the second generation, exactly like Tippoo Sultan, he need not so excessively have scorned the marriage overtures from Tippoo as the son of an upstart. The Nizams had been longer on a throne, through a number of successions. Perhaps a feeling of race came in. The grandson of this Nizam Ali had still (see below, Chapter 4) 'a fair skin, ruddy complexion, and blue Tartar eyes', while Hyder was notoriously black, and his son nearly so. Perhaps also there was the feeling of the Sunni, the orthodox champion, against the fantastic zealots of the south. This ruler, who had the longest adult reign of any in Hyderabad, came to seem, by endurance and accretion, 'the great Nizam Ali' before he died.

Sikandar Jah, or Shah, the sixth Nizam, reigned from 1803 to 1829, with no more salient traits than those indicated in the *Thug*. It was his service that Meadows Taylor entered in 1824.

Nasir-ud-Daula, the seventh Nizam, reigned from 1829 to 1857, through the largest part of Taylor's service. There is no personal reference to him save the opening glimpse of a tall, ruddy, blue-eyed youth.

Afzal-ud-Daula succeeded at the crisis of the Mutiny as the eighth Nizam, and reigned for a dozen years, covering Taylor's last years in India. He was father of the late Nizam, and grandfather of the present youthful ruler. All these successions have been from father to son.

As the *Confessions of a Thug* can be so easily obtained it will be more amusing to give the references in *Tippoo Sultaun*, published 1840.

The incidents are, on an average, a generation earlier than in the *Thug*. The ruler of the Deccan, his power not yet consolidated, is here Nizam Ali, the father of Sikandar Jah; and all passes within the eighteenth century.

At the opening, 1788, a servant laments having ever 'been seduced to leave the noble city of Hyderabad', a recurrent phrase. The author speaks, among the contending powers, of 'the Nizam, whose armies, ill-paid and ill-conducted, were generally worsted in all engagements; but who still struggled on against his enemies, and in whose service titles were readily to be won, sometimes, but rarely, accompanied by more substantial benefits.' 'I like not the service of the Nizam,' says Kasim Ali, whose father had been in it. 'The Mahrattas . . . are every day making encroachments upon Nizam Ali's power, which totters upon an insecure foundation.'

The same servant boasts: 'Ay, now, at my city we have the real shooting; there, over the plains of Surroo Nuggur, thousands of antelopes are bounding with no one to molest them, except Nizam Ali, who goes out with the nobles and shoots a hundred sometimes in a day. . . . I say it is a dish for the Huzoor, and such an one as I have often cooked for his zenana.' 'Then thou wast in the kitchen of Nizam Ali?' 'Even so, Meer Sahib; there is plenty to eat, but little pay; so I left the Huzoor. . . . Ere I was a cook I was a barber; and Hyderabad is not an indifferent place to learn how to dress wounds. Mashalla! our young men are rare hands at street brawls. . . . Gradually the difficulties of the Government caused all the salaries to the officers to fall into arrears. Then came with that a train of distresses; the elephant was sold, some jewels pledged. . . . This daughter Ameena, was marriageable, and her great beauty was known; they had many offers for her, but they looked high; they thought the Huzoor himself might ask for her, and that the fortunes of the house might rise.'

As one proceeds southward 'the city' comes to mean Seringapatam. Yet that upstart place looks to Hyderabad, famous for more than its singers, with some feeling of toadyism. Tippoo knows that the Nizam is anxious to turn against the English in order to avoid fulfilling certain treaty obligations. Through intrigue Tippoo secures the sending to himself of a longed-for embassy from Hyderabad, bearing a splendid Koran, and seeming to recognise him as the head of Islam. But he spoils a promising plan.

'He had long been solicitous', says Taylor, 'of allying himself by marriage with the princely family of the Dekhan, but had never had an opportunity of proposing it; now, when the Nizam had sought him—when, humbled by the English and in dread of the Mahratta power, that prince had asked aid against both from his brother in the faith—he thought he could make that a condition of compliance. . . . But the Nizam's ambassadors were men of sound judgment; they knew that their prince had lowered himself already in sending the embassy to a self-constituted Sultaun—a low-born upstart. . . . They answered the demand in cold and haughty terms, and, requesting their dismissal, soon after left his camp.' Tippoo refuses to recall them. 'Tippoo's message was received with indignation by the Nizam,' who throws himself entirely into the cause of the English. 'Inshalla!' declares Tippoo, 'alone we will do what Nizam Ali Khan will wonder at in his zenana, as he sits smoking like an eunuch.'

There is a personal reminiscence in Taylor's account of 'that noble white-faced elephant Hyder (which was taken at the siege of Seringapatam, and still adorns, if he be not recently dead, the processions of the present Nizam)'. He is almost a character, far exceeding the other elephants in height, raising 'his white trunk high into the air' at the approach of tigers. Tippoo again speaks of 'the imbecile ruler of Hyderabad' who was drifting into that primacy of position which Tippoo might so easily have kept.

'The polite and courtly character' of the nobles of Hyderabad is elsewhere mentioned. There is a good deal about the Nizam's force in the first campaign of Cornwallis against Tippoo. 'It presented a most gorgeous Eastern display.' Half the tribes of Asia were here 'mingled with a wild confusion—men hardly belonging to any corps, and clustered round every leader's standard, apparently as fancy, or caprice, or hope of plunder dictated. The force was utterly inefficient, however, for the purposes of the war.' Its leader was bribed to inaction by Tippoo; but in the second campaign it had a more honest commander. Seven years later, at Malvilly, Tippoo exults at the sight of the green standard of Hyderabad, with 'the white crescent and ball beneath it', among his enemies. ''Tis they—the effeminate Dekhanees!—men who are no better than eunuchs . . the renegades from the Faith!'

CHAPTER III

1824–29

WHAT was I to see in the new strange world now opening before me? What was I to do and to be? My heart was full of hope, and my ambitions ran high that morning as I parted from my kind friend Mr. Newnham, whose last words rang in my ears—'As soon as you have proved that you *can* be useful, you will be *made* useful,' he said; 'be diligent and be steady, and I have no fear for you. Now go.' My things had been sent on in advance, and what little I had with me was already in the boat at the Apollo Bunder, in charge of Dorabji, my Parsi servant. We pushed off as I entered the boat, and dashed away over the clear water. The harbour was gay with shipping, and the giant Ghats in the background were wreathed with fleecy white clouds about their summits. I was in wild spirits, and could scarcely restrain myself, it was so glorious and so beautiful.

I found my horse and pony, tents and baggage, at Panvel,[1] where I landed, and in the evening went on to Chauk. There I had the first sight of a splendid Indian encampment; the Resident at Nagpur, Sir Richard Jenkins,[2] being on his way

[1] Panvel town, now of some 10,000 inhabitants, is the headquarters of the taluk of the same name in Kolaba District, Bombay. The *Imperial Gazetteer* says: 'The chief local industry is the construction of cart-wheels, of which it is said that every cart from the Deccan carries away a pair. . . . Panvel port is mentioned as carrying on trade with Europe in 1570; and it probably rose to importance along with Bombay, as it is on the direct Bombay-Deccan route.' It was at Panvel, some twenty years before Taylor's landing, that Pandurang Hari, in the novel of that name, took boat for Bombay.

Chauk, although without an article to itself, is conspicuous on the map of the environs of Bombay, the end of the first day's stage, well along the road to Poona.

[2] This is one of the figures of that triumphant epoch in India whom

to Bombay. The scene was very strange to me. The stately white tents, the camels depositing their burthens, the huge elephants, the native gentlemen arriving in palankeens, surrounded by their numberless attendants, the camp bazaar, with its booths and stalls, the variety of dresses, colours, and equipments—all formed a scene of Eastern splendour such as I could never have imagined.

As I was strolling idly along, I was accosted by an officer, and we fell into friendly chat; and when he knew where I was going, and who I was, he invited me to breakfast, assuring me that any friend of Mr. Newnham's would be welcome to Sir Richard.

I was kindly received by the Resident, and again invited to dinner in the evening, and I felt no small gratification at such kind notice being bestowed on me.

Next morning I reached the foot of the Ghats, and proceeded by the military road. How grand it was! Deep glens and ravines, bounded by tremendous precipices; trees and flowers all new to me; and fresh invigorating air, so cold and bracing, and so like, I thought, to dear old England!

On the 24th November I arrived at Poona, and was hospitably entertained by the officers of H.M. 67th Regiment at

---

one could most wish to recover in some detail. Richard Jenkins was born in 1785, the same year as Metcalfe, dying at a later age in 1853. Like Metcalfe, he came out to India in 1800, when barely fifteen; so that as far as that goes, Meadows Taylor was not exceptional in the age at which he was shipped off.

Though Nagpur was not then annexed, Jenkins, still a young man. emerged from the last Maratha war with a reputation only second to that of Elphinstone. During practically two decades he was in charge of Nagpur—for the second of these ruling in the name of the infant Raja. Of this work Taylor says: 'Material prosperity, and cultivation, had increased to an extent never before known in Berar; but the prosperity of the people only served to incite exaction, and in a comparatively short period the last memorials of Mr. Jenkins' benevolent administration had been utterly eradicated.' Incidentally, Jenkins 'suggested annihilation of Pindaris'.

After his return to England, a little past forty, he sought, with more weight than many Anglo-Indians, yet with hardly more result, to impress himself upon the public life of his countrymen. Yet he was twice M.P. for Shrewsbury, chairman of the East India Company in 1839, G.C.B., and D.C.L. of Oxford. Jenkins was probably the most eminent man whom Taylor had yet encountered.

their mess. I was shown all the sights during our evening rides, and the temple where the 'Peshwa' sat in state to see the English annihilated by his army, which, instead, was defeated at Kirki,[1] in 1817,—and many other scenes of interest; but I knew little then of Dekhan history.

We reached Ahmednagar[2] on the 29th, and were hospitably

[1] Of Kirki, Taylor in his *History* says: 'No one knew the Mahrattas better than Mr. Elphinstone: and instead of allowing Colonel Burr, the officer in command of the brigade, to await attack, he directed him to move at once on the Mahratta forces. Beyond one brilliant charge . . . the vast host of the Mahratta army did nothing; and as the British brigade still advanced, the whole took to flight.' But it is of Koregaon that the *History* relates: 'The Peshwah witnessed the fight all day from a distant eminence, and seeing the successive failures of those on whom he had relied, bitterly upbraided them for having misled him. He had now no refuge but in flight, and the British divisions allowed him no rest.'

[2] Ahmednagar District borders on the west the dominions of the Nizam, whom Meadows Taylor was to serve during some thirty-six years to follow. As it is at the core of Deccan history, the references to it in his various writings are innumerable.

Ahmednagar city lies in a plain on the left bank of the Sina, some seventy miles from Poona, and within ten miles of the nearest territory of the Nizam. In his *History* Taylor describes its founding, about 1490, by the revolting officer of the Bahmani kingdom after whom it is named. It is now a flourishing town of well over 40,000 inhabitants. About one tenth of these are Christians, the place being notable for the century-long labours of the American Marathi Mission.

Ahmednagar held her own as she could among the Deccan kingdoms for less than a century and a half. The most famous of the reigning house was Chand Bibi, 'a woman of heroic spirit, who, when the city was besieged by Murad, a son of Akbar, in 1596, defended in person the breach in the rampart, and compelled the assailants to raise the siege.' This is the protagonist of the latest of Taylor's romances, *A Noble Queen*, 1875.

In 1600 (1599 according to Taylor), Ahmednagar was captured by another son of Akbar, Daniyal Mirza, at the head of a Mogul army. 'Nominal kings continued to exercise a feeble sway' until Shah Jehan finally overthrew the dynasty. In 1707 Aurungzeb, the Philip II. of India, who ruined an empire for the sake of religion (see Stanley Lane-Poole's admirable volume in the *Rulers of India* series), died in Ahmednagar. His heart is buried in the so-called Alamgir's Darga, near the adjacent town of Bhingar.

Ahmednagar was successively under the Peshwa and under Sindia. It possesses a circular fort of stone, a mile and a half around, with a wide and deep moat, more notable in its taking than in its building—for it was captured after a severe bombardment by Sir Arthur Wellesley in 1803.

entertained by Mr. Seton, Assistant Commissioner. I spent a most interesting day there, and finally arrived at Aurungabad[1] on the 5th December.

The last marches had been through dull dreary country, endless stony plains, with scarcely a tree to break the monotony. But as I approached Aurungabad, I saw the beautiful dome and minarets of the tomb of Aurungzeb's daughter glistening in the sun, and troops at drill in the parade-ground. My tent was pitched near the mess-house; but Dr. Young came forward to meet me, and hospitably insisted that I should be his guest till I had a house of my own. I reported myself to the officer in command after breakfast, was put in orders, and directed to attend drill.

A few days later, it was arranged that I should live with Lieutenant John Stirling, who had recently joined the 6th Regiment from the Bombay army, and who had a house much too large for him. He was a noble fellow, both in person and disposition, and his untimely death ended, too soon, a friendship to which I look back as one of my greatest pleasures.

I was not long in learning my drill, and was put in charge of the two centre companies, was shown how to keep the books and pay accounts, which soon became very easy to me. The

[1] This was Meadows Taylor's first station, and always an important place in his Indian life. The name Aurungabad covers the north-western division of Hyderabad State, then the district, the taluk, and the city, which ranked until 1911 as the second in the State, now the third though without a tithe of the population of the capital. According to the Hyderabad Census, 1911, Aurungabad has 35,000 inhabitants, fewer than ten years before. During the reign of Aurungzeb the population is believed to have been 200,000, a figure which is borne out by the scale of the ruins still existing.

Aurungabad was founded as lately as 1610, under another name, by Malik Ambar, a minister of the last kings of Ahmednagar. Aurungzeb, who was appointed viceroy of the Deccan in 1635, and again in 1653, changed the name of his headquarters to Aurungabad. The first Nizam, Asaf Jah, came here some two centuries ago, before making Hyderabad his capital.

The tomb of Aurungzeb's daughter at Aurungabad, twice mentioned in this autobiography, does not appear in the *Imperial Gazetteer*. But at Khuldabad village, fourteen miles away, are certain tombs of unsurpassed interest in Indian history—those of Malik Ambar, the great negro minister of Ahmednagar; of Aurungzeb, whose heart is buried near Ahmednagar; and of Asaf Jah, the centenarian founder of Hyderabad State.

adjutant took great pains with me; and I engaged a Munshi or native teacher, and began Hindustani in earnest.

I witnessed a curious spectacle at Aurungabad, in the shape of a miracle-play, which was annually performed under the auspices of one Major Freeman, who commanded the invalid battalion at Aurungabad. During the early Musalman period, the kings of Bijapur had received and endowed many Portuguese Christian missions, and one had been located at Aurungabad, where delicious oranges and purple and white grapes still attest the fact of its former presence. A miracle-play of the life of our Lord was performed there by them, beginning with the scene of His birth, and ending with the Crucifixion. Although, no doubt, it could not bear comparison with that of Ammergau, yet it was very curious and strange. Portuguese monks chanted the story in their own tongue, interspersed with bad Hindustani, but the effect was very impressive; and the last scene, a real man hanging to the cross, was the signal for wailing and groaning from the spectators, who looked on with awe and wonder.

The ceremony may have died out with its patron and supporter, Major Freeman, but when I saw it the spectacle was complete. This Major Freeman was a strange character. When his wife was very ill, a religious friend offered to read and pray beside her, but he declined, saying, in his broken English, 'My dear friends, I do not want yous. I'se got Catholic priests, they prays for my wife; Brahmins makes *japs*[1] for my wife; Gosains sits in de water for my wife; Musalmans fakeers makes prayers for my wife; I prays myself for my wife. Little of alls is best, dear friend. Now you goes away, if you please.'

I must apologise for the above digression, and continue my story.

We were often out shooting and coursing, and one day heard of a noble boar at a village some twelve miles off. We determined to slay him without delay; and sure enough I soon saw the great grey brute emerge from behind a bush, and Stirling and I dashed after him. My horse, however, struck his chest against the opposite bank in attempting to clear a small water-course, and both he and I were a good

[1] Incantations. [M. T.]

deal bruised. But I followed Stirling as soon as I could, and met him on foot covered with blood. 'The beast has upset me and my horse,' he said; 'go and kill him.' I rode on some little way, and encountered the hog with Stirling's spear sticking through him behind the ear. My own spear had been broken in my fall, and was useless, and I sent for another. Meantime the brute took to a sugar-cane field, and could not be dislodged, charging all who ventured near him; and at last, when one poor fellow had been badly wounded, I thought it better to send for my gun, and I fired exactly between the two fierce red eyes that I saw glaring at me a few yards off, and the huge beast rolled over dead. What a reception I had! I shall never forget it. Stirling abused me soundly for spoiling the fame of the affair by shooting the hog, and it was quite in vain that I protested that no amount of 'bakshish' would induce the beaters to go near the sugar-cane. At last he was pacified, and we set off home again. My friend's wound was a bad one, and we had it properly dressed. The boar arrived soon afterwards, slung on two poles, and the whole station, ladies and all, came out to see it. I killed many a hog afterwards, but never one so large.

These were jolly days—plenty of hunting and coursing, and association with many bright, noble hearts now gone to their last long home. Erskine, Harris, Seton, James Outram,[1] and others whom I proudly called my friends, were among that goodly-spirited company. Who of them are left now?

This is no place to detail hunting exploits or tales of hard riding; but I am sure my association with these bold, true sportsmen gave a manlier, hardier tone to my mind, and was of great service to me.

[1] Of these early companions of Meadows Taylor two elude me. Of Outram there will be enough at the end of Chapter 10. The Harris mentioned was probably Sir William Cornwallis Harris, 1807–1848, a mighty hunter whose name is embedded in the *Dictionary of National Biography* as well as in Buckland. A year older than Taylor, he came out a year before him to join the Bombay Engineers. He was twice Superintending Engineer in Bombay. He made use of the despised leave to the Cape to do notable exploring and big game shooting in the interior of Africa, later negotiating a commercial treaty with Shoa in Abyssinia, for which he was knighted in 1844. Harris published several works, including *Portraits of the Game Animals of South Africa*. He died untimely of fever in India.

I suppose I acquitted myself well as a soldier, for I was chosen for detachment duty in the rainy season of 1825, and ordered to Kanhar, with 200 men, to support a detachment of the Company's 23rd Regiment, then acting against the Bhils, who were in rebellion. I do not remember that we caught any of the rebels, although we followed them into their fastnesses; but instead, I caught very severe jungle fever, which nearly put an end to me. I partially recovered, but had a relapse on my return to Aurungabad, and barely escaped with my life. I was allowed four months' leave, and my kind friend Mr. Newnham wished me to come to him. I was put into a palankeen, but was so ill at Ahmednagar that I was given over. At Poona I was again despaired of; but I reached Bombay at length, and the pure sea air and Mr. Newnham's kind nursing soon restored me, and I regained my strength rapidly. My financial affairs were by no means satisfactory. No pay had been given by the Nizam's Government for the last six months, and there was no such thing as getting it. I had been obliged to borrow very considerably; and it was a weary business perpetually borrowing at from 24 to 35 per cent when my pay would have covered all expenses had I been able to get it. I explained all this to Mr. Newnham, and also the rumours current that the East India Company were bent upon doing away with the Nizam's force altogether. He had heard the same, but bid me not despair. He thought things would improve, and there was always 'Shotton's House', then flourishing, to fall back upon.

I remained with Mr. Newnham for three months, and then returned well and strong to Aurungabad. I found letters from home awaiting me. I do not think my father liked my change of profession much. He thought we had decided hastily; and there was also a very curious letter from my grandfather, who had a remarkable dislike to a military career. 'He could only protest', he wrote, 'that it was against the laws of God that men should deliberately slay their fellow-men; and what would my feelings be if I had to kill a man (though he might be a black one) with my own hand?' and much more to the same effect. My dear mother, however, encouraged me to persevere diligently in the career I had adopted, and her counsels had most weight with me, and her words went straight to my heart.

Major Sayer had succeeded to the command of the Aurungabad Division, and proved a very valuable friend to me. He assisted me in my Persian and Hindustani studies, and told me to bring him my translations occasionally to look over. What could be kinder! I was a stranger to him, and had no introduction; but he interested himself about me, and encouraged me to work on. With his help I soon made considerable progress. There were no formal examinations in those days; but as a test of efficiency, I was directed to superintend regimental courts-martial, and record the evidence in English, and the finding of the court. In these I took my turn with Lieutenant Johnston, the adjutant, and as a reward the command of the Light Company was bestowed upon me for 'good conduct'.

With the exception of one month's leave, which I spent out tiger-shooting with a friend, I was very busy at home. I enjoyed my month's sport very much. We slew several tigers, and an occasional hog-hunt was not wanting. Small game, too, abounded—partridges and quail, peafowl and hares—and our bags were often heavy. One accomplishment I began to practise at this time. My friend was an artist, and took beautiful sketches from nature. He encouraged me to try also, and from this period dates one of the greatest pleasures of my life. He taught me as far as he could. I have the original sketches of that time—very minute, and highly finished with a fine pen—the buildings rather on the incline, and the style stiff and formal; but everything has a beginning. When my leave expired I returned to Aurungabad, and began a course of reading with Colonel Sayer, which was of great use to me. Better times came—my pay was more regular, and the debt to Mr. Newnham was almost paid off. I was very comfortable—had a good house and pleasant garden, plenty of friends, and a hopeful spirit.

About the middle of the year I was appointed interpreter to a general court-martial on a native officer of artillery—the highest linguistic test that could be applied to me in those days. I had some misgivings as to the result, but I ultimately performed my task so much to the satisfaction of the officer who had conducted the trial, that he wrote a special letter on the subject, commending my usefulness to him in 'this protracted and difficult investigation'. 'Now you are fit for any staff duty,' said the colonel, 'and I hope you won't be long without it'—a wish I devoutly echoed.

My Light Company was a fine one—mostly picked men from Oudh [1] and Bihar, handsome and athletic. I worked hard, and my men seconded me well, and the result was to me very satisfactory. We were reviewed, and I received the following flattering compliment from the officer in command: 'I beg', he said to our colonel, 'you will convey to the officer in charge of your Light Company my very best thanks, and tell him his performance this morning has been of the highest credit to him. I have noticed, with particular satisfaction, his unwearied exertions during the whole of the morning; and the appearance of the men under his command, and their steady conduct, bear testimony to his zeal as an officer.' This to me! and before every one too! Need I say how full my heart was?

About this time Mr. Martin,[2] now Resident at Hyderabad,

[1] Readers of the *Life of Sir Henry Lawrence* may recall how the magnificent region of Oudh, 'the garden, the granary, and the queen-province of India', used to impress his imagination, even more than by its wealth and its history, as being 'the native province of some three-fourths of our Bengal Sepoys—the nursery of that fine race of soldiers', etc. (Chapter xix.) Taylor, though never in Oudh, always admired the men from there as representing the finest physical type in India.

[2] Not in Buckland, or in most Histories of India. This reduction of a paragraph, page 616, in Taylor's own *History*, written nearly half a century later, indicates the course of local affairs at the beginning of his service, during the five years following 1824:

'After Sir Charles Metcalfe's departure, the office of Resident at Hyderabad was conferred upon Mr. Byam Martin, a Bengal civilian of large experience in "regulation" judicial affairs. The European agency for the administration of the dominions of his Highness the Nizam, established by Sir Charles Metcalfe, was considerably enlarged, and with very beneficial results to the people. . . . The great object to which the employment of the English officers was directed . . . was to prevent exaction. . . . The protection to the people ensured by these means resulted in an immense increase of cultivation. So long as the old Nizam, Sikunder Jah, lived, no change was made; for he had thoroughly appreciated results which had indeed become self-evident, in the check which they imposed upon the rapacity of the minister, Chundu Lall. But on his demise in 1829, and the succession of his son, Nasir-ood-Dowlah, a demand was somewhat rudely made

who also, *ex officio*, commanded the whole army, issued an order, 'that he was about to start on a tour of inspection, and with a view to rewarding merit wherever it should be found, he should advance such officers as were specially brought to his notice, and as a proof thereof, had selected Lieutenant Hampton from the whole army to the honorary post of commander of his escort', etc. Now Hampton was only a local officer like myself, and I, like many others, began to speculate on the possibilities of good things in store.

Meanwhile I was very busy. Colonel Sayer had wished me to acquire some knowledge of military surveying and fortification, and I had made a survey of the cantonment with only a compass, a chain and cross-staff, and a perambulator. I should have done my work better with a sextant; but there was not one to be had. However, as it was, I received thanks for my report when it reached the Residency at Hyderabad, and I was much gratified.

At last the Resident arrived with a brilliant staff; the station was very gay, and I was presented with all the other officers. Hampton had been promoted, and therefore the command of the escort was vacant. The Resident's camp was to move on next morning. After dinner Colonel Sayer took me up to Mr. Martin, saying, 'Allow me, sir, specially to introduce my young friend here, of whom I have had already occasion to report favourably, officially; I beg you to keep him in mind.' 'Will you take the command of my escort by way of a beginning?' said the Resident. 'I shall be happy to have you on my personal staff if you are sufficiently acquainted with the native language.' This the good colonel answered for, and I was told to prepare without further delay. I don't know how I got away: I only remember trying to keep down a big lump that rose in my throat, and the colonel saying to me, 'Now you've got a start—you will never disappoint me, I know.'

All the ladies and gentlemen of the station were present, and crowded round me with congratulations; one of my

---

by him at the instigation of Chundu Lall, who had become impatient of control, for a sudden recall of all English officers employed in civil duties; and the people soon, and very bitterly, experienced the deplorable change which the measure involved.'

friends came back with me to my house; my things were packed; we sent to the city for camels for my tents and baggage, which were despatched as quickly as possible. The night passed—I do not think I slept—and by dawn I was in my saddle, and joined the officers of the Resident's staff as they were starting on their morning stage. It was a sudden change in my life: what might be the next?

The Resident expressed himself much pleased when I presented myself at breakfast when the camp halted at a short stage from Aurungabad. We had killed two foxes by the way, my dogs having been posted beforehand. 'So you can ride,' said one of my new companions. I was then 9 stone 8 lb., and well mounted, as I had my chestnut, and a splendid bay hunter which Stirling had given to me. Yes; I could ride.

After breakfast Mr. Martin sent for me, and asked me about my family and what I could do. He then set me to converse with his Munshi, which I found very easy. I had learned to speak Hindustani like a gentleman; and here let me impress upon all beginners the great advantage it is to learn to speak in a gentlemanly fashion. It may be a little more difficult to acquire the idioms; but it is well worth while. There are modes of address suitable to all ranks and classes, and often our people unintentionally insult a native gentleman by speaking to him as they would to their servants, through ignorance of the proper form of address.

I was also examined in Persian, and Mr. Martin complimented me on my diligence. The march was delightful, and the sport plentiful; small game abounded, and we had an occasional stalk after antelope—sometimes, too, a tiger was reported. The Resident always gave me some work to do, and the days flew by very pleasantly. We halted at Mominabad,[1] a large cavalry station, where there were brilliant reviews, and *levées* of native officers, and much feasting. My dear friend Stirling had been promoted to the civil depart-

[1] Mominabad is a taluk and a town in the Bhir District of Hyderabad. According to the Hyderabad Census the town had in 1911 a population of 11,000, having come down from some 12,000 and 14,000 at previous decennial periods. It is described in the *Imperial Gazetteer* under the alternative name of Amba. Until 1903 it was a cantonment. Near by are a number of ruined cave temples, both Brahminical and Jain.

ment, and was Superintendent of a large district to the south; but the day after we reached Mominabad, the Resident received an express stating that Stirling had been killed in a fight with some Arabs who had gained possession of the town of Danduti;[1] that Major Sutherland was about to march there with his whole force, and if the Resident had any instructions to give, they were to be sent to meet him at Ausa.[2] I was inexpressibly shocked at this sad occurrence: not only had Stirling been very dear to me as a friend, but he was in all respects a *preux chevalier*, whom it had been my wish to imitate. On consulting the map I found Ausa was not more than thirty-five miles distant, and that I could ride on there and join the force. I went to Mr. Martin and entreated permission to go; and I prevailed. Before leaving him, he said very kindly, 'I find you quite qualified for civil employ, and shall therefore nominate you to succeed your friend; but the appointment must be confirmed by the Supreme Government, so you had better come to me at Hyderabad straight from Danduti.'

I was fairly astonished. The department into which I was to be transferred was the height of my ambition; the pay was 1500 rupees a-month! How I thanked Mr. Martin, or how I got away, I know not; and between my sorrow for my friend and my own unexpected stroke of fortune, my head was in a whirl. I left the camp that afternoon with two troopers as escort, but the road was unfamiliar, and we were often misled, and it was not till early morning that we reached the cavalry camp as the bugles were sounding to 'boot and saddle'. We were just in time to join the forces and ride on with them another twenty *coss*, or forty miles. Of course Major Sutherland was surprised to see me, but the letters I had with me explained everything; and after a cup of coffee we rode on. We had a good rest at the end of

[1] Danduti, probably more a fort than a town, is neither in the text of the *Imperial Gazetteer*, nor on the map of Hyderabad State, nor yet in the long list of towns in the State in the Hyderabad Census of 1911.

[2] Ausa is the headquarters town of the eastern taluk of Osmanabad District, which in Taylor's day was called Naldrug District. The population by 1911 had come down to some 5,000 from 6,000. There is a moated square fort, dating from the Bijapur kings, and once captured by Malik Ambar.

the stage, and then proceeded to Gulbarga,[1] another twenty miles, whence, after resting, we were to go on to Danduti, eighteen miles further. It had been arranged that the Arabs in possession of the fort were to be at once summoned to lay down their arms and submit unconditionally; if they refused, the place was to be stormed at daylight next morning. To me was allotted one division of the stormers with their native officers, and all preliminaries were arranged. I think few of the Arabs would have been left had the attack been made, as Stirling was very popular and all were anxious to avenge his death; but as we approached the town we heard the beat of the Arab drum and saw the enemy moving off with their colours flying, by the Hyderabad road. The Commissioner had given permission to the Arabs to depart in peace, and thus they escaped our vengeance.

I had not felt tired, and even came in first in a race proposed by one of the officers. As I slid from my horse, however, I felt very stiff, and sitting on the ground, found I had no power to rise. The surgeon declared my condition to be caused by temporary paralysis of the spine consequent on my long ride of 113 miles, and I did not recover at all till the afternoon of the next day, when a painful tingling sensation set in in my legs and back, and I soon was able to sit up. It was very clear if we had had anything to do, I should have been unable to join in it.

After-investigation proved that my poor friend Stirling had met his death by his own rashness, in proceeding alone to force the gate of the town with only twelve men against more than a hundred Arabs. As soon as the gate was opened, he fell dead, riddled by four balls which pierced his chest.

[1] This famous name applies to a division, a district, a taluk and a town in the south-west of Hyderabad State. It comes fourth among the Nizam's towns, with a population, in 1911, of 32,000—a considerable increase over former returns. Here reigned the Bahmani kings from 1347 until they removed to Bidar. Their tombs at Gulbarga are square domed buildings, heavy and gloomy, roughly but strongly built. There is a fort once remarkable, with fifteen towers and a gun twenty-five feet long. Towards the end of his life Meadows Taylor was to write much about Gulbarga, in his *History* and in *A Noble Queen*. He considers that the architecture of the dynasty improved after the removal to Bidar. 'The country was probably as well cultivated and populated as it is at present.' The modern Gulbarga is a rising commercial centre, a rival of Sholapur.

In a few days the inquiry ended, and there being nothing to detain me, I was to proceed to Hyderabad. The evening before, Major Sutherland came to me as I was sitting on the grass near poor Stirling's grave, and said,[1] 'I know you have been appointed by the Resident to succeed Stirling, and that you are only awaiting the confirmation of your appointment by the Supreme Government. Now this is very creditable to you; but I have considered the matter very deeply, and I do not think it likely that your appointment will be confirmed. Mr. Martin's patronage in the civil department will be curtailed considerably; and what I propose to you is this—do not go to Hyderabad. I want an adjutant here for one of the regiments. I will appoint you, pending your final transfer to the cavalry. You ride well, our men like you, and the pay is very good.'

It was a tempting proposal. My first wish had been to join the cavalry, and yet, when the offer was made, could I give up the chance of the coveted civil employ and the splendid opening it afforded me? Nor could I find out that my kind friend was sure of his nomination being confirmed either. How, too, could I disappoint the Resident? or how encounter the heavy expenses of a rich cavalry uniform with equipment and chargers? All this flashed through my mind in a moment, and I was not long in making my decision. I could only thank Major Sutherland, and say that 'if I did not succeed in obtaining the civil appointment, I would request Mr. Martin to put me into the cavalry'.

[1] This good friend of Taylor's youth was no mere major, but a predecessor of Sir William Lee-Warner as an authority upon the Native States. He was the author of *Sketches of the Relations subsisting between the British Government in India and the different Native States* (1833). See p. 122. In 1839 he was sent to Jodhpur to restore quiet, and held the capital for five months (J. Burgess, *Chronology of Modern India*). I am informed that further information concerning him exists in MS. in the Record Department of the India Office, to which inquirers may be referred.

P.S., March 1919.—Interesting communications from the present Resident at Gwalior supplement these facts. John Sutherland seems to have died in harness at Bharatpur in 1848; there is a statue of him in the public gardens at Ajmer. In 1843 he sailed for the Cape of Good Hope, and before returning to India three years later compiled for the Cape Government a *Memoir on the Kaffirs, Hottentots and Bosjimans of South Africa*, published in 1847.

'It will be too late then, Taylor,' he said, smiling; 'the Military Secretary will fill up the appointment at once, and I wanted you.'

'I cannot give up,' I replied, 'what may be already settled for aught I know.'

'Be it so,' he answered, 'I can say no more.' Then he, his brother, and I discussed the matter in all its bearings, and they thought I was right in adhering to my resolve.

So next morning I started; but at a place called Pargi[1] I was taken ill, and but for the kindness of the native Talukdar, Nawab Fateh Jah Khan, who sent his physician to me and nursed me tenderly, it would have gone hard with me. At last he sent his own palankeen, with orders that I was to be brought to his house for change of air. In vain I pleaded weakness and want of time. He would take no denial, and I went. This was my first introduction to the house of a native gentleman. 'You are to be one of the family,' said my host; 'you are only a boy, and the ladies will not mind you. My wife will look after you, and the children shall play with you, and I will send on your letters to Hyderabad.'

I stayed with these good people for a week, and was entertained most hospitably, and on leaving, presented my host with my old gun, to which he took a great fancy. He gave me a valuable sword and embroidered sword-belt, while his good lady begged my acceptance of a beautiful patchwork quilt and the bed I had slept in, which had very elaborately painted and gilt feet. I used these as long as they lasted.[2]

When I arrived at Hyderabad Mr. Martin sent for me.

[1] Pargi, a village of some two thousand inhabitants, is the head-quarters of the taluk of the same name in the Mahbubnagar District of Hyderabad.

[2] This experience, as it well might, made an ineffaceable impression upon Taylor's heart and imagination. It has not happened to many of the administrators of India; and it could not happen in a Hindu household. Though he is reticent in relating it, its influence may, without fancifulness, be traced in various scenes of his subsequent novels, specially in the chapters of *Tippoo Sultan* (xxxii. and xxxiii.), where the sorely wounded Kasim Ali is sought on the battlefield and then taken to be nursed into the household, almost into the harem, of the jovial old Abdul Rhyman Khan. Taylor had a natural sympathy, developed by happy experience, with the better elements of Musalman life, to which his marriage gave him affinity.

My appointment had not been confirmed, and he was very sore about it; I told him then what Major Sutherland had offered me. 'Ah,' said he, 'bad luck pursues you: thinking you were surely provided for, I gave the cavalry adjutancy away where, indeed, it was already promised. You must not leave me though; if you will join my household I will have you returned "on special duty", till something offers worth giving you.' Yes,—it was a great fall of all my castles in the air; I was not to be a civil superintendent, I was not to be an adjutant of cavalry, and I had nothing to do but to wait on, I hope patiently.

Mr. Martin was very kind to me. I did what I could to help him in return, and found his splendid library an inexhaustible treasure-field.

The State of Hyderabad in itself is by far the largest and most important Musalman dominion in India. The city is walled all round, and cannot, therefore, be enlarged, but the adjacent suburbs increase rapidly, and the population cannot now be less than 350,000 souls.[1] I enjoyed my early rides, free from parade and other morning duties, and came upon many a picturesque scene, especially along the river, with the city walls and bastions on the one hand, and the native houses of the Begum Bazaar, with their fine trees, on the other. The river-bed, too, is always a stirring sight, with its countless groups of people bathing, washing clothes, or carrying away water from holes scooped in the sand; elephants being washed or scrubbed with sand by their keepers, and evidently enjoying the operation. These, and many other objects, formed glowing pictures of colour and native costume of endless variety. The scenery, too, is very striking. From one favourite point of view of mine, the city lies stretched before you, the graceful 'Char Minar' or gate of the 'Four Minarets' in its centre;[2] the gigantic 'Mecca

[1] By the Census of 1911, Hyderabad is at last a 'half-million city'.

[2] In a rather dull section of Taylor's *History* the narrative suddenly becomes personal, as well as more detailed, when it reaches the fine adventure of Bussy at Hyderabad in 1756. 'The Char Minar, a noble edifice of the Kootub Shahy period, consisted of four open arches of great size, with a lofty minaret at each corner, and formed a conspicuous object from all points of view. The roof was a large terrace, and was nearly a hundred feet from the ground. The place commanded the

mosque'[1] standing out nobly; while the large tank of 'Mir Alam'[2] lies at your feet, and the bold rock of the Fort of Golconda rises in the distance. From hence, a rising sun gradually lighting up every object in the clear morning air, and the glowing glittering landscape terminating in the tender blue of the distance, is inexpressibly beautiful.[3] There is also a

---

whole of the city within gun-shot, and was entirely unassailable; and, manned by guns on the terrace above as well as below, was quite impregnable.'

[1] The Mecca Mosque, completed by Aurungzeb, stands to the south-west of the Char Minar. It is 225 feet long, 180 broad, and 75 high, with domes rising 100 feet higher. Nizam Ali, the ruler of long reign preceding the one whose service Meadows Taylor entered, and all his successors are buried here.

[2] After the Husain Sàgar, the chief water-supply of Hyderabad. It had been built by French engineers only a few decades earlier for the predominating Minister, Mir Alam, ancestor of the Salar Jang family. The tank was built from his share in the prize money of Seringapatam, the dam alone costing eight lakhs.

[3] Here is another impression of Hyderabad and its approaches (1900): 'Il n'y a plus de verdure, plus de grandes palmes; la terre n'est plus rouge; il fait presque froid. . . . On arrive ce matin sur le plateau central de l'Inde, au milieu des steppes de pierre, et tout est changé. . . . Des landes brûlées, des plaines grisâtres, alternent avec des champs de mil, qui sont vastes comme des petites mers. . . . Des villages, qui ont eux-mêmes changé d'aspect pour prendre un faux air arabe. L'Islam a posé son empreinte ici sur les choses,—l'Islam qui d'ailleurs se complaît toujours aux régions mornes, à l'étincellement des déserts. Changement aussi dans les costumes. . Au coucher du soleil, Hyderabad enfin apparaît, très blanche dans un poudroiement de poussière blanche, et très musulmane avec ses toits en terrasses, ses minarets légers.

'. . . Hyderabad la blanche, dominant sa rivière presque tarie, où ses troupeaux d'éléphants sont descendus dans la vase encore fraîche. . . . On ne s'attendait point, en arrivant à travers tant de tristes solitudes, on ne s'attendait point à trouver si vivante et si follement colorée cette ville perdue au milieu des terres, au milieu des steppes pierreux et gris. . . . Ce qui éblouit les yeux tout d'abord, c'est le luxe et l'infinie diversité des turbans; ils sont roses, d'un rose de saumon, ou de cerise, ou de fleur de pêcher; ils sont lilas, amarante, jonquille ou bouton d'or; ils se portent très large, démesurément larges; ils s'enroulent autour des petits bonnets pointus, et, par derrière, l'extrémité retombe, pour flotter sur la robe. . . . Les femmes, invisibles puisque nous sommes en pays de Mahomet, passent ensevelies du haut en bas sous une housse blanche. . . Vers le coucher du soleil enfin, des personnages des *Mille et une Nuits* commencent à sortir, des élégants aux yeux cerclés de peinture bleue, à la barbe teinte de vermillon, qui portent des robes

favourite place of resort of an evening for Musalman gentlemen of the city on a knoll to the right of the Masulipatam road; and I was often asked to sit down with them while their carpets were spread, and their attendants brought hookahs. Even thus early in my life, I began associating with native gentlemen, and observing their manners and customs, modes of speech and conversation. The glorious view, the air filled with golden light, the gorgeous sunsets, the mellowness which softened every object, made, I think, the evening even more beautiful than the morning. I loved to go there quietly and dream dreams. I was growing out of boyhood, and that period is always a momentous one to every man. I was sensitive and shy, and no doubt romantic. Mr. Martin was always kind, and bade me be hopeful; but I had been sorely disappointed, and felt often sad and dejected as to my prospects. At this time I was often at the house of Mr. William Palmer,[1] where I met the most intelligent members of Hyderabad society, both native and European, and the pleasant gatherings at his most hospitable house were a great relief from the state and formality of the Residency.[2]

---

de brocart ou de velours chamarré d'or, des colliers des pierreries ou des perles, et qui tiennent sur le poing gauche un oiseau apprivoisé.' —Pierre Loti, *L'Inde sans les Anglais*, pages 231-240.

[1] This man, 1780–1867, who became Taylor's father-in-law, had a lifelong fascination for him. He must have had some remarkable qualities, if only to inspire the affection which appears throughout the autobiography. He was younger brother of John Palmer of Calcutta, the 'Prince of British merchants', about whom there is a subsequent note.

Their father, General William Palmer, had been Military Secretary to Warren Hastings for several years before 1782, when he became Resident at Lucknow. He had married, evidently in youth, a Princess of the Delhi house, after a fashion not obscurely shadowed in the happy Indian marriage of General Smithson (Darnell) in *Ralph Darnell*.

Of the younger William Palmer Mr. Buckland writes: 'Founded, 1814, the great banking-house of Palmer & Co. at Hyderabad, in which the Rumbolds were partners: his heavy financial transactions with the Nizam ended in his ruin, and in the censure of the Governor-General.' It is but fair to state that the Palmers were succeeded in Berar by native farmers-general as oppressive, and as intimate with Chandu Lal, who had brought Hyderabad well-nigh to bankruptcy before he relaxed his hold.

[2] 'The magnificent mansion of the Resident' (*Thug*, chapter xviii.). 'The Residency is situated on the left bank of the Musi, opposite to the north-eastern corner of the city. The building is an imposing one, and

I was not long destined to be idle. One day Mr. Martin sent for me and told me that, under a recent arrangement in the military department, a small appointment on the general staff was at his disposal if I liked to accept it. I was delighted at the idea of having anything to do, and thanked him cordially for his kindness.

The appointment was Superintendent of Bazaars at Bolarum,[1] a cantonment of the Nizam's troops twelve miles north of the Residency, on higher ground, and consequently cooler and more bracing. My duties were simple enough. I had to regulate the markets and the prices of grain in conjunction with the principal merchants and grain-dealers. I was to decide all civil cases, try, and punish all breaches of the peace, and make daily reports to my superior officer at ten o'clock every morning in person. I was to inspect all meat killed, both for the use of the troops and private consumption; in fact, I was a sort of magistrate for the cantonment and its environs; and, as one of the Division Staff, had to attend the 'Brigadier' at all parades and on field-days.

I was, on the whole, well pleased with my office. Of course it was monotonous. What Indian staff appointment, with a daily routine of work, is not?

I was enabled to discover and check various irregularities in the prices of grain and *ghi* or boiled butter, which had escaped my predecessor, and this made the sepoys my friends. The stores of grain were kept up at their full complement, and the force could have taken the field at an hour's notice. Every one pronounced the meat and bread better than before; and as I had established a free market for vegetables, they were always plentiful and fresh.

Still, it was a troublesome post. Disputes often arose between masters and servants, debts by individuals, and the like; but I believe I firmly gained the colonel's goodwill by settling a dangerous quarrel between two infantry regiments which had arisen at one of the festivals. During the inquiry

stands in the midst of a beautiful park-like expanse, with handsomely laid-out gardens. It was commenced in 1800 . . . and was completed about 1807' (*Imperial Gazetteer*, article 'Hyderabad City').

[1] Now no longer a cantonment, but a part of Secunderabad.

that followed, over which I presided, I found an opportunity of reconciliation, of which I availed myself, and the quarrel was made up out of hand.

I did not enter much into general society at this period. High play was the chief amusement which prevailed, and I never was at that time or at any time fond of cards, or did I ever play for money, except for the veriest trifle.

I worked on as well as I could, taking care not to neglect my Persian studies, and occasionally reading with a Munshi or native teacher, and looked forward hopefully to the time when, by some possibility, I might gain an entrance into the Civil Service. The day came at length. An officer, who was Assistant Superintendent of Police in the S.W. district of the country, got tired of his solitary life, and proposed to exchange with me. Mr. Martin at once consented to the step, and wrote to me very kindly on the subject, expressing his desire to serve me to the utmost of his power, and recommending me to accept the exchange.

My arrangements were soon complete. I was to become proprietor of Captain L.'s bungalow at Sadaseopet,[1] with one or two tents; he, of my 'buggy' and horse, which I no longer needed. Furniture on both sides was valued; and when we were respectively in 'orders', I betook myself to my new duties, of which the Resident and his secretary gave me an outline; but nothing very precise could be laid down respecting them, and I was left very much to exercise my own judgment.

I left Bolarum with many expressions of kind regret from the colonel, who thanked me for my services, and declared himself well satisfied with me on all points, offering me a testimonial of good conduct and ability in case of my requiring one at any time.

Now at last I was free!—literally my own master. I had an immense tract of country to overlook, of which I knew

[1] A large emporium, with a flourishing trade in both exports and imports, in the Medak District of Hyderabad. In 1911 it had risen, unlike many towns in the State, to a population of 8,000 from 6,000 a decade before. Sadaseopet is no such distance from Hyderabad City as might be implied from the 'fourth day' below (short marches), being not necessarily more than a morning's ride to the *north*-west.

nothing, except that in going to Danduti I had crossed part of it. I took leave of the Resident and of the Nizam's Minister, Chandu Lal, who were both very kind to me; but of all the counsel and direction I received, I owe most of what was useful to me afterwards to Mr. Palmer, and he offered to assist me by letter if I were in need of help. His grand-looking old mother, the Begum Sahib, blessed me, and tied a rupee in a silk handkerchief round my arm, praying the saints to have me in their holy keeping; and I started on my journey, accompanied by my escort of police, and reached Sadaseopet on the fourth day. I had not completed my eighteenth year.

The northern boundary of my district may have been 250 miles in length, extending from Hyderabad to Parenda [1] with stations at various intervals, of which Tuljapur was one of the most important. Its general southern boundary was the Bhima river, to its junction with the Krishna, and its greatest breadth was from 50 to 60 miles, narrowing at either end. In all it may have included from 10,000 to 12,000 square miles, and its population must have exceeded one million souls.

My duties in the Revenue Department were not to begin till the Superintendent made his tour through the district after the monsoon. My police duties were very clear. There were stations as nearly as possible every 40 miles, where twelve mounted and ten foot police were posted; and these went periodical patrols from their own station to the next, returning every fortnight.

Foot police were stationed in villages averaging three miles asunder, and patrolled their beat every day. If anything occurred it was reported to the jemadar, and by him to me, if important; otherwise, it was entered in the diary, which was transmitted to me weekly.

I had altogether 50 mounted and 150 foot police under my command. The road was an important one—the highroad

[1] Prominent on the map, close to British territory, the headquarters village of Parenda taluk in the west of Osmanabad District, with some 3,000 inhabitants. It is more notable than other villages of the size as having a fort, and as having been for a short time the capital of the Nizam Shahi kings after their expulsion from Ahmednagar, early in the seventeenth century. The ruins in the neighbourhood of Parenda testify to its former populousness.

to Bombay—and the patrols had had the effect of keeping off gangs of highway robbers and *dacoits*,[1] which before the establishment of the force had become very bold and dangerous.

My predecessor had been enjoined to take active measures for the suppression of these pests, but, so far as I could ascertain, had really done nothing.

I assembled all my jemadars and native officers, and endeavoured to find out their views of what was most feasible to be done; but I found most of them were men from a distance, and possessed little, if any, local knowledge.

A district lay between the tract of land over which I had jurisdiction, and the river Manjra to the north, and it soon became plain to me that unless I had command over this as well, I could do very little to check the depredations of the dacoits, who had, as was evident from the records, become the terror of this part of the country. I therefore applied for, and obtained, the necessary permission, and was soon free to act in all directions needful to my purpose.

My position was a very pleasant one. My little bungalow was situated at the edge of a mango-grove, which lies behind the present travellers' bungalow. It consisted of one centre room, with a division all round, forming a dressing-room, bath-room, and store-room. Without, at a little distance, were the offices and kitchen, and stabling for five horses. I could not immediately start on my tour through the district, as it was the rainy season, but I had ample occupation. I gathered all the information I could with regard to thieves and robbers. I made a large collection of birds and insects for my uncle, Mr. Prideaux Selby, of Twizell House, Northumberland, who was engaged upon his great work on Ornithology.[2] Tree birds of all kinds abounded, while the tanks or reservoirs teemed with water-fowl of seemingly endless variety.

[1] *Dacoity*, robbery with violence. [M. T.]

[2] There is an article in the *Dictionary of National Biography* on Prideaux John Selby, 'naturalist', 1788–1867; high sheriff for Northumberland; published *Illustrations of British Ornithology* and *British Forest Trees*. A favourite young brother of Meadows Taylor was named Selby (see p. 7). In *Ralph Darnell* there is a reference to 'Twizell Dean, surr—that's Mister Selby's, ye ken. It's a fine place.' Again: 'They pass Twizell gates, and look up the Deàn and its hanging woods, and Mr. Selby's old-fashioned snug manor-house.'

I sent to Bombay for a Marathi grammar, and began the study of that language, without which I plainly saw I could not get on. Tẹlugu was the language of the people about Sadaseopet, and it changed to Kanarese a little distance further; but neither was a language of business. Marathi was evidently the most useful of all.

I had plenty to do. Every morning brought in reports from my officers and men, which had to be answered and investigated. Then my early bag of birds had to be skinned and prepared; English correspondence and my Marathi lesson followed; and I had always a box of books from the Secunderabad [1] or Bolarum library to occupy my evenings. I kept Mr. Newnham well informed of my doings, and his delight when I obtained this appointment was very sincere.

I rode in to Hyderabad towards the close of the monsoon to see Mr. Martin, and I told him what I was doing, and that I was collecting all the information I could about the district. He desired me to march quietly up to a spot near the western frontier, as he might have occasion to employ me actively, but said he could not be more explicit just then. So, at the beginning of October, I joyfully betook myself to my tent-life, with a sense of freedom and of joy which I still can vividly recall.

I journeyed leisurely on. The country was open and beautiful, the various crops were being sown, the air felt dry and fresh, and the march was very enjoyable. I halted near Homnabad,[2] and rode over to see the old city of Bidar,[3]

[1] A combined cantonment, covering 22 square miles, named after the Nizam then living. Secunderabad, with Bolarum, had in 1911 a population of 113,000, counted in the half-million of Hyderabad.

[2] The Nizam's State Railway has diverted the trade which Taylor describes; and Homnabad is a not very flourishing town in the Gulbarga District, with a population going down from 7,000.

[3] The later capital of the Bahmanis, some 2,500 feet above the sea. Ahmed Shah Wali, the tenth Bahmani king, founded the city of Bidar and built the fort, removing the court here from Gulbarga in 1430. It was taken from the next dynasty by Aurungzeb in 1656. The population in 1911 was 12,000. It is the headquarters of a district, as formerly of the Gulbarga Division, in Hyderabad State. In his *History* Meadows Taylor describes Bidar at much length, and with enthusiasm:

'There is no more healthy or beautiful site for a city in the Deccan

than which, I think, nothing could be more picturesque. Homnabad was a central point, where was concentrated all the trade in salt and spices from the western coast for Berar, receiving in return cotton, oil-seed, ginger, grain, etc. I found I could serve the merchants considerably, and one, Seth Atmaram, became my good friend; but first we had a quarrel. Some of my escort complained of short weight in their flour, and I had the persons who sold it fined; whereupon the other flour and retail grain dealers shut their shops, and went in a body to a grove, where they declared they would remain till I went away. I was certainly not to be intimidated; so I set up a bazaar of my own, which was well supplied by some Brinjaris, the old chief of whom had certificates from the Duke of Wellington for services in the Maratha war. Provision-sellers came from other villages, and I was independent. An effort was made to induce me to send for the fugitives, but I refused; then a complaint reached the Minister at Hyderabad, Raja Chandu Lal, that I had desolated the town by my violence, and extorted large sums of money from the chief merchants. Mr. Martin requested an explanation from me, which I, of course, gave at once. Meantime my friends began to think they had gone too far, and brought a petition to the effect that I had been misled, and that they knew the real culprits, with whom I could deal as I pleased, etc. Mr. Martin was now satisfied, and I received his commendation. The Minister sent down a special officer, who used a very lofty tone to the merchants, threatened a fine of 10,000 rupees, which I begged off; and he departed finally, with, no doubt, a very handsome private *douceur* in his pocket. When I next visited Hyderabad, old Chandu

---

than Beeder. . . . The fortifications, still perfect, are truly noble. . . . Inside the fort, the royal palaces overlooked the walls; and their present ruins attest their great extent and former magnificence. To the west extended a level plain covered with groves of mango and tamarind trees. . . In every respect, whether as regards climate, which is much cooler and healthier than that of Goolburgah, or situation, the new capital was far preferable to the old one. At the present time . . . there is no city of the Deccan which better repays a visit from the traveller than Beeder.'

There is a spirited account of Bidar, where Ameer Ali gets married, in chapter xxii. of the *Thug*.

Lal, giving me a poke in the ribs, said grimly, 'Ah, Taylor Sahib! you should have let me put the screw on those Homnabad people. You had them down so completely—and they always defied me—I might have got a lakh out of them.' 'And lost your good name, Maharaj,' I replied. 'You should bestow half a lakh on *me* for being so careful of your good name and honour!'[1]

There were no more complaints of false weights. The Dean of Guild and Town Council were made answerable for them, and the police had authority to inspect them from time to time.

My next halt was at Tuljapur, which I found a most picturesque, delightful spot. I have made it the scene of my

[1] The Maharaja Chandu Lal, 1766–1845, stands out, not only in this autobiography, as an unmistakable figure. Buckland says: 'Chandu Lal ruled Hyderabad for about 35 years: retired Sep. 1843, from the Peshkarship, on a monthly pension of Rs. 30,000.' There are some hundred pages between the first and the last mentions of him in Taylor's *History.* He was an ancestor of the Maharaja Sir Kishen Peshkar Pershad.

In that highly contentious volume, the *Life of General James Stuart Fraser*, who was later for a dozen years Taylor's chief at Hyderabad (see notes below), are more references to Chandu Lal than need be followed up. 'With an interval of less than five years . . . filled up by Charles Metcalfe's persistent attack, in spite of the displeasure of Lord Hastings, on the Palmer and Rumbold combination, the policy of the Residents at Hyderabad for more than thirty years, down to the date of Colonel Fraser's appointment, seems to have been confined to the unflinching support of the Minister, Rajah Chundoo Lall, against all his rivals, and even against his own sovereign.' He was never actually invested with the office of Diwan. He is stated to have been 'the great obstacle to reform,—the incubus that weighed heavily upon the Hyderabad State, sunk in uneasy slumbers,—and yet the removal of that obstacle seemed a more and more delicate and troublesome operation'.

General Fraser's account of his meeting Chandu Lal in 1838 is more of a picture than he often achieved, though he seems to exaggerate his age: 'Chundoo Lall, the Minister, is a remarkable man. Above seventy-seven years of age, attenuated to a mere shadow, and bent nearly double, he has yet all the active intelligence of earlier life, and the same keen and expressive eye, with that pleasing and benevolent smile that never abandons him. When he called upon me he was obliged, on alighting from his elephant, to be borne up the steps of the Residency in a tonjon [sedan chair]. He conversed with me for an hour in the most animated way possible, speaking Hindustani and Persian with equal fluency.'

historical romance, *Tara*, because of its beauty and of its history, when in 1657 its temple was plundered by Afzul Khan, whose subsequent murder by Sivaji is still considered by the people as but a fitting retribution.[1] The day I arrived, a Brahmin entered my *kacheri*, or office-tent, sat down quietly in a corner, and after remaining a while silent, rose and said—

'I hear you speak Marathi; is it so?'

'I am only a beginner,' I replied; 'but I daresay I can follow you.'

'I am struck with your face,' he continued, 'and I should like to see your hand and cast your horoscope. Do you know when you were born?'

I gave him the date, and he proceeded to examine first my forehead and then my left hand. 'It is a long and happy life on the whole,' he said; 'but there are some crosses and some deep sorrows. You are not yet married, but you soon will be, and you will have children—not many—some of whom you will lose. You will never be rich, nor ever poor; and yet much, very much, money will pass through your hands. You will not now stay long here; but after many years you will return, and rule over us. Fear nothing; your destiny is under the planet Jupiter, and you will surely prosper.'

He added further details when he brought my horoscope some hours later, one which especially struck me being that I should become a Raja, and rule over a large tract of country to the south.

[1] Tuljapur taluk, in the west of the Osmanabad District, has had the former Naldrug taluk added to it since 1905. The population of the town in 1911, 5,000, had gone down by over a thousand since the previous census.

It is in the realm of romance that Tuljapur lives. There is a description, reaching to pages, in chapter iii. of *Tara*, and onwards. 'The quaint old town, hanging literally on the mountain edge; the deep gloomy ravine of the temple opening out to the larger one; the precipices and rugged hills to the west and north, and the beautiful undulating plain to the south, over which the eye wanders as over a map for fifty miles or more, checkered with thriving villages and their rich fields and gardens,—form a striking assemblage of objects.' 'All she saw was the terraces of the houses of the town gradually descending into the great ravine; the crags and precipices of the further side; with the trees, and gilded spires and pinnacles of the temple between.'

I thought the affair curious enough, and wrote out a translation of it, which I sent home; but, to my regret, have failed to find more than allusions to it in my father's letters to me.

During that day my tent was beset by hundreds of pilgrims and travellers, crying loudly for justice against the flour-sellers, who not only gave short weight in flour, but adulterated it so distressingly with sand, that the cakes made of it were uneatable, and had to be thrown away. I sent for the civil officer of the town, who declared the flour-sellers to be incorrigible, and that the complaint was perfectly true; so I determined to take my own course.

That evening I told some reliable men of my escort to go quietly into the bazaars, and each buy flour at a separate shop, being careful to note whose shop it was. The flour was brought to me. I tested every sample, and found it full of sand as I passed it under my teeth. I then desired that all the persons named in my list should be sent to me, with their baskets of flour, their weights and scales. Shortly afterwards they arrived, evidently suspecting nothing, and were placed in a row, seated on the grass before my tent.

'Now,' said I, gravely, 'each of you are to weigh out a seer (two pounds) of your flour,' which was done.

'Is it for the pilgrims?' asked one.

'No,' said I, quietly, though I had much difficulty to keep my countenance. 'You must eat it yourselves.'

They saw that I was in earnest, and offered to pay any fine I imposed.

'Not so,' I returned; 'you have made many eat your flour, why should you object to eat it yourselves?'

They were horribly frightened; and, amid the jeers and screams of laughter of the bystanders, some of them actually began to eat, sputtering out the half-moistened flour, which could be heard crunching between their teeth. At last some of them flung themselves on their faces, abjectly beseeching pardon.

'Swear,' I cried, 'swear by the holy mother in yonder temple, that you will not fill the mouths of her worshippers with dirt! You have brought this on yourselves, and there is not a man in all the country who will not laugh at the *banias* (flour-sellers), who could not eat their own flour because it broke their teeth.'

So this episode terminated, and I heard no more complaints of bad flour.[1]

I received notice soon after that I was to proceed to Parenda and take charge of a squadron of cavalry, which was to meet me there, and that I was to co-operate with the civil authorities of the Bombay Presidency for the suppression of the rebellion of Umaji Naik—this being the special service that Mr. Martin had hinted to me. I marched at once, and found the squadron already there—two troops and their native officers. We were not idle. Umaji Naik seemed to be ubiquitous, and we had many a weary, fruitless search for this noted and most mischievous brigand, whose robberies, often attended with violence, cattle-lifting, and all manner of villany, had become the terror of the country. Umaji had a spite against all authority, hated both priestly and secular Brahmins, and enjoyed nothing more, if he could catch one, than cutting off his nose and ears. By his own people he was considered a hero. He was hunted down at last, after many years, by an English officer, who captured him as he was bathing in the river Bhima. He led us many a dance through the country, and often we were misled on false information. I scoured the hills and plains equally in vain, and became notorious by wearing a pair of red cloth trousers, made by a native artist, having worn out my own riding trousers completely. At last Umaji found the place was getting too hot for him, and withdrew, and we were released from our harassing work.

I paid a pleasant visit to the Collector of Sholapur,[2] who,

[1] This story was quoted in connection with food troubles by a Plymouth paper in 1917.

[2] The hot and prosperous district of Bombay Presidency, bordering the Nizam's Dominions to the west, south of Ahmednagar. Sholapur ('sixteen villages') has been singularly poor in history, passing alternately, during two centuries, from the Ahmednagar Sultan on the north to the Bijapur Sultan on the south. The city of Sholapur, taken by siege in 1818, is now best known by its cotton mills. It had in 1901 a population of 75,000. This had fallen to 61,000 by 1911, according to the Gazetteer of Towns in the *Oxford Survey of the British Empire*, vol. ii., 'Asia'. The name Sholapur differs by one letter from that of

I remember, was much surprised at my youthful appearance, and we discussed together the best way to repress the great crime of cattle-lifting, which had been actively carried on for years. I was amused to meet at the hospitable Collector's table some of my old shipmates of the *Upton Castle*, and to witness their surprise to see 'Baxter's shop-boy' transformed into a grave Political Agent for the whole of the Nizam's frontier. They all congratulated me, and showed me every possible attention during my stay. Mr. Newnham wrote me a very gratifying letter, saying he had heard me praised officially, and that he was quite satisfied with my progress.

I returned to my own quarters, and on consulting with my native friends, found I had not sufficient power to carry out my scheme of organising the police as I wished, at once; but I was advised to take one *pargana*, or county, work that first, and then gradually extend my system. My district was much cut up by private estates, whose owners or managers defied or evaded the orders of the Nizam's executive government, and would only obey their own masters, some of whom were powerful nobles of Hyderabad, who jealously resented any interference by the executive minister, while their agents were well-known protectors of thieves and robbers, whose booty they shared. Evidently mine was no easy task, and I must make sure my footing before I could establish or carry out any measures of reform.

I had a note from the Collector of Sholapur requesting me to meet him at a town called Barsi,[1] which I did; killing two splendid hogs on the road, single-handed, and receiving much commendation from my friend, one of the greatest sportsmen of the Bombay side. A complaint was made to us by one of the native officers about the executive department of the Revenue Survey, which was then proceeding: it was averred that bribes were taken and other corrupt practices

---

Shorapur, the wild little State in the south-west of the Nizam's Dominions, with which Taylor was later to be so uniquely associated: the names are once confused in the original edition.

[1] An important town of Sholapur District, population in 1901, 24,000, conspicuous on the map as an inset into Hyderabad territory, between Parenda and Osmanabad. Barsi has a temple of Bhagwan and a big reservoir.

carried on, and numerous documents were sent in as proof. We looked into the matter, and found not only much ground for complaint, but also that a great deal of the work was good for nothing. I had the pleasure afterwards of learning, through Mr. Newnham, that I had been the means of bringing heavy frauds to light, and had done essential service.

In regard to my plan of frontier police, the Collector saw many difficulties, unless, indeed, a regular force were organised; and I had yet much to learn.

I determined, therefore, to begin at my own end of the district first, quietly feeling my way. In some places my orders had met with a hearty response, in others they were totally disregarded.

My camp was pitched at Ekeli,[1] when one afternoon I saw some persons carrying a native bedstead, which was put down opposite my tent: there was something lying upon it concealed by a bloody sheet; when this was withdrawn, I saw a young Brahmin literally covered with sabre-cuts. He was very faint, but after the barber had dressed his wounds, he told his story, saying that the night before, the Raja, as he was called, of Karamkot had attacked his house, had murdered his father, uncle, and grandmother, and had then proceeded to plunder the dwelling; that the Raja was still abroad, and purposed committing another dacoity that night at a village he named.

There was no time to lose; this at any rate might be prevented. I had ten mounted men and five available foot police, and I prepared in all haste.

The perpetrator of the outrage was a noted character, Narayan Rao, and I had heard of him as being a very dangerous man. His village was very strong, and he had recently repaired the *garhi* or castle, with its gates and bastions, and it held a strong garrison of desperadoes. I was determined to have him if I could. My friend, Balram Singh, knew the country well, and was our guide. We had thirty miles to march, but eventually the night's work proved far more.

It was dark as we neared the village of Kulur, where the proposed dacoity was to take place, and leaving four men

[1] A town approaching 6,000 inhabitants in 1911, Bidar District.

for its protection I took on the other nine, including Balram Singh and another jemadar of police ; I had also two grooms who rode my baggage-ponies ; and these constituted my little party.

We rode first to a town called Sulupet, where Narayan Rao was reported to have been seen in the bazaar ; but we were at fault, as he had left it and gone, the people said, to Kulur ; but as there was no other road than the one by which we had just come, we knew this could not be the case. Balram Singh fancied the Raja must have heard of the wounded Brahmin having been brought to me, and therefore had retired to his fort ; and he was right. We all partook of some refreshment, as we were tired, and then started for Karamkot —the Raja's village.

It looked very strong as we approached in the early morning ; the fort stood out in the centre with its large bastions and loopholed walls, all in excellent repair. We halted under a little grove of mango-trees, and when the gate was opened to allow the cattle to come out, we rode in boldly, and though the guard seized their matchlocks, no one attempted to fire. In reply to their questions I answered, 'I have been travelling all night and am tired, and intend to rest here a while.'

'We will send word to the Raja,' said several.

'No,' I answered, 'I will speak to him myself'; and we rode up the main street. I thought for a moment that it was rather a rash proceeding, for on the bastions of the fort many men appeared, showing themselves on the parapet and calling to us to go back. The Raja lived in the fort, and some men came out and stood on the steps leading up to it, and asked me what I wanted.

'The Sahib Bahadur wishes to see your Raja Sahib,' said my jemadar, 'and he is tired,—he has ridden all night.'

'My master is asleep,' rejoined the man, 'and I dare not disturb him.'

'I must see him, and at once,' I said ; 'if he does not come, I shall go in myself,' and the spokesman went in, returning directly with a young fair man, who was tying a handkerchief round his head.

He saluted me, and inquired haughtily, 'why I had come

into his town, into which no Feringhi had ever before entered without his leave ? '

I stooped down and said in his ear, ' You are my prisoner, and must come quietly with me ; if you or your people resist, I will drive my spear through your body. Now we will go, if you please.'

The street was narrow, and as my horsemen spread themselves behind us, no one could get near us. I do not remember ever feeling so excited as I did when the Raja and I went down to the gate by which we had entered. He said nothing ; but his men were crowding on the walls and house-tops, all armed and calling to each other. Perhaps they noticed that my long hog spear was within six inches of their Raja's back !

When we reached the gate he merely said to the guard, ' Don't follow, I shall return soon ' ; and we all passed out safely.

' Now,' said I to one of my men, ' let the Sahib ride, Bhadrinath ' ;[1] and as he dismounted from his mare, I bade Narayan Rao get up

' If you don't, you're a dead man,' I said ; and Balram Singh advised him to obey ; ' for ', said he, ' if you do not do as my master orders you, he will put his spear through you.'

So the Raja mounted, and as this was seen from the gate towers not a hundred and fifty yards from us, one of my men happening to look round, called out, ' They are going to fire ' ; and we had scarcely time to put our weary horses into a canter, when a regular volley was discharged, knocking up the dust behind us.

Bhadrinath had scrambled up behind the Raja with a merry laugh, and kept consoling his companion by telling him the shot would hit him first. Narayan Rao, however, maintained perfect silence, and told me afterwards he expected to have been hung upon the first tree, and supposed this to be my reason for ordering him to mount.

Now I had my prisoner, where was I to put him ? My camp was forty miles distant, and I resolved at last to take him to Chincholi,[2] where there was a fortified court-house,

[1] This name was transferred to one of the best drawn characters in the *Thug*, the fat Brahmin inveigler, Bhudrinath, so suave and callous.

[2] Headquarters of the north-eastern taluk of Gulbarga District. Chincholi is in hilly country ; in 1901 it had a population of 4,000.

which could be easily defended in case of a rescue being attempted; and when we reached it the Raja was safely located there, having been first put in irons.

The surviving relations of the murdered Brahmins came that evening, and were confronted with the Raja, who did not attempt to deny the murders. The family were his own near relations, but they had a good deal of silver plate, which had excited his cupidity.

All that night we were kept in constant alarm. Shots were fired at our gates and bastions, and dismal and unearthly shriekings and howlings were kept up by our enemies. I was glad when morning came, and brought my servants with clean clothes and a guard of five soldiers. It was a busy day; people crowded in with complaints and accusations against the prisoner for exactions and dacoity. Strange to say, he admitted them all, and directed us where to find the plunder. I sent for it, and it was brought; massive silver, copper, and brass vessels, and a quantity of valuable cloths and silk. The villagers sent me eight men who had assisted at the dacoity, and their confessions enabled me to apprehend ten more.

I determined to take the wretch himself to Hyderabad. This he heard of, and sent me a private note, which ran thus:—

'You are all-powerful and merciful. Send the enclosed to Homnabad, and you can get cash or bills for 24,000 rupees. When you get this, allow me to depart.'

'So that is your game, my friend,' I thought; 'perhaps you may be corrupting my people.' So I ordered my bed to be taken down and placed across his door, and talked to him most of the night.

'I was a fool', he said, 'not to shut the gate when you were inside. My people would have killed you.'

'It wouldn't have helped you much,' I replied; 'your village would soon have been knocked about your ears, and you would have been hanged. Now you are safe. Chandu Lal will not hang a Brahmin.'

'Not unless your gentlemen make him,' he said, 'as you do your own people when murder is done. I hated them. I only killed my uncle. He was the worst.'

'And your grandmother?'

'Ah!' he said, and was silent. He then asked if I had sent for the 24,000 rupees in money or bills?

'No,' I said, 'English gentlemen do not take bribes. The Minister will get the money at Hyderabad.'

'God forbid!' he exclaimed; 'take 50,000, take a lakh. Ah, sir! for your mother's sake let me go. I cannot go to Hyderabad alive!'

It struck me he might have poison concealed about him, so I had him stripped and searched. I told him frankly, he must go to Hyderabad, for that I had no power to deal with him.

But it did not seem an easy matter to get him there. My scouts brought in word that the Raja's people were out in great numbers on the road, and intended to dispute my passage. My escort was very weak; I had nineteen prisoners. But a happy solution occurred to my difficulties. My men on the look-out reported that some English troops had arrived, and going up myself, I saw the flags of an English regiment being set out for an encampment. I dressed quickly and went to the officer in command, who at once ordered a native officer and twenty men to accompany the prisoners. I started early next morning, and made a long march, clearing the jungly tract in which the rescue had been planned, and which would very possibly have succeeded had my escort remained as it was. I reached Hyderabad on the third day, and was immediately summoned to the Residency, red trousers and all; told Mr. Martin my story, which amused him very much, and showed him the order for the 24,000 rupees. He desired me to go at once to the Minister, and we did, hot and travel-stained as we were. Chandu Lal was very cordial and gracious, and his keen grey eyes twinkled when I handed him the order for the 24,000 rupees, and he laughed heartily at my account of the whole scene.

'Why did you not get the lakh, Taylor?' he said; 'now it will be hidden.'

Narayan Rao sat trembling in the corner, making frantic appeals for justice, and I took my leave as I heard the order given for 'close imprisonment'.

'The Minister might have given you a present out of the money you brought,' said Mr. Martin; and indeed I thought so too, especially as three of my best horses died soon after.

I received a very handsome official acknowledgment from Mr. Martin for the service I had rendered, praising my 'zeal and promptitude in an arduous and trying business', and much more that was very flattering and pleasant. I left Hyderabad within a week; but, alas! my horses had been in an infected stable, and I lost all except my white pony. It was in vain that I asked for some help to replace them, although they had done valuable service, and were a loss of 3,000 rupees.

I mentioned my loss when writing to Mr. Newnham, and he sent me most kindly and generously a magnificent bay—a timely gift, and one I highly prized.

When I returned to my district, in company with my chief, Mr. Colvin,[1] we determined to look into the revenue settlement of the country. We stayed a few delicious days at Bidar, roaming through the grand old city, revelling in its beauty, and recalling its past histories. We could have stayed there dreaming on, but work was before us, and we pushed on to Homnabad.

I am not going to inflict details of revenue settlement on my readers. We found the Bengal system, with which Mr. Colvin was familiar, would not suit the country at all, and that the best plan was to continue the former settlements, with here and there some slight alterations; and as I could do this alone, he left me. I worked at this and my registration of village police in every county and along the road, getting on as well as I could, and my old hope of having a district to myself was renewed, as Mr. Colvin was dissatisfied and would not stay, and thought it likely that I might be appointed in his place.

[1] John Russell Colvin, 1807–1857. In 1827 Colvin was appointed second assistant to the Resident at Hyderabad. Here he regretted 'the old common village responsibility for payment of land revenue', with collection through the village headmen.

Colvin is believed, as secretary, to have had too much influence in Lord Auckland's Afghan policy. Mr. Buckland writes: 'He worked with extraordinary industry, and greatly increased the business of the Government.' Colvin succeeded Thomason as Lieutenant-Governor of the North-West Provinces in 1853, dying in the midst of the Mutiny, and leaving behind him a heated controversy. No reader of *Forty-one Years in India*, where so few unkind things are said, can forget the scathing picture of the state of things at Agra in 1857.

Some very curious and difficult cases of disputed inheritance came before me. One [1] I very well remember, in which two families claimed the same land under a grant from King Yusaf Adil Shah, who began to reign A.D. 1480. The papers were exactly similar. No forgery could be detected either in the registries or seals; both seemed genuine, and we were fairly puzzled, till, after dinner, holding up the paper to the light, I saw an unmistakable water-mark—a figure of an angel, with 'Goa' underneath. Now, Goa had only been taken by the Portuguese in A.D. 1510; therefore, there could have been no Goa paper in existence in 1488, and Indian paper has never any water-mark. The falsification, therefore, of the deed written on Portuguese paper was conclusive.[2]

Mr. Colvin was obliged to go back to Hyderabad, as his health was suffering, and I had an immense increase of work; but I determined to make myself acquainted with every detail, in order to fit myself to succeed him if he should leave.

Returning after an absence of a month through my district, I was met by some very startling revelations. The police, and chiefly my faithful Balram Singh, had reported some very unusual occurrences. Dead bodies, evidently strangled, and in no instance recognised, were found by the roadside, and no clue could be discovered as to the perpetrators of their death. In two places, jackals or hyenas had rooted up newly-made graves, in one of which were found four bodies and in another two, much eaten and disfigured.

The whole country was in alarm, and the villagers had constantly patrolled their roads, but as yet in vain. All we could learn was, that some time before, two bodies of men

[1] 'Readers of Miss Edgeworth's novels will remember a similar case described in *Patronage*' (*Edinburgh Review* article, 'The Story of an Indian Life', October 1877).

[2] In *Tara* the forgery of a horoscope is thus described: 'The paper on which it was written was new, but it was not paper of that part of the country; it was from his own district. An ornamental border was quickly drawn round it, in red, black, and yellow lines; the signatures of the witnesses were carefully copied; finally, the whole document was held over wood-smoke till it was of a proper brown colour, then rubbed and frayed at the edges, and creased here and there as if it had been often examined; and, lastly, it was perfumed with camphor to remove the smell of wood-smoke, and with the odour of benzoin and sweet pastille.'

had passed through the district, purporting to be merchants from the north going southwards, but that they appeared quiet and respectable, above suspicion. During these inquiries it transpired that numbers of persons of that part of my district were absent every year from their homes at stated periods. These were for the most part Musalmans, who carried on a trade with Belgaum, Dharwar, and Mysore, bringing back wearing apparel, copper and brass vessels, and the like. Who could these be? Day after day I tried to sift the mystery, but could not. I registered their names, and enjoined Balram Singh to have the parties watched on their return home. But as the monsoon opened that year with much violence, I was obliged, most reluctantly, to go back to my bungalow at Sadaseopet.[1]

I was very anxious about this time also on another point. Lord William Bentinck, then Governor-General, had adopted as one of his political measures the alteration of the treaties between several native States with the Honourable East India Company, which provided for the support of Contingent forces established during Lord Hastings' government. When it was known that the Nagpur force had been abolished, and all the officers of the Company's army remanded to their regiments, and the local officers discharged

[1] One of the earliest references in English to the mere name of the Thugs, before anything characteristic was known about them, occurs in *Pandurang Hari*, chapter xi. The date of the incident is within the first decade of the nineteenth century; the novel was published in 1826. Pandurang relates to the village headman how he and his party had been robbed with violence, having sallied out in the morning while it was still unaccountably dark.

'He replied, "If you will be so rash as to set out on such a journey in the dead of night, you must expect to be robbed." "Dead of night!" I exclaimed; "what do you mean? I heard the birds chirping in the trees, and felt assured morning was about to dawn." "*Arry*!" exclaimed the potail; "you have fallen in with the *Thugs*!" Upon inquiring who they were, he told me a class of persons in that part of the country who lived by plundering travellers; and, to avail themselves of the darkness of the night, the better to conceal themselves and carry on their predatory schemes with surer success, they mounted into the trees and shook the branches. The birds at roost on them, being thus disturbed, begin immediately to chirp, as if it were near daybreak; and thus travellers, who are resting for the night in villages or farm-dwellings, are too often deceived and fall an easy prey.'

with gratuities of a few months' pay each, it was impossible not to feel the direst anxiety as to the fate of the Nizam's Contingent, which occupied a perfectly similar position.

It was expected that we should receive four months' pay each, and then I should be thrown again upon the world.

Had the old Nizam lived, or had he been in a condition to transact business, he might have yielded to the offers made him; for the force was a very expensive one, costing forty lakhs or more, and it was expected the Nizam would gladly pay twenty or thirty as an escape from further liability. But his end was now approaching, and for a time we had a respite.

Mr. Newnham wrote to me bidding me 'come to him again and he would do his best to further my interests'; and in the event of our force being abolished I should have done so. Mr. Palmer advised my remaining at Hyderabad and becoming a merchant, and promised me a rapid fortune. So waiting and speculating I kept on, often very weary and anxious.

The old Nizam, Sikandar Jah, died at the end of June 1829, and was succeeded by his eldest son, not of the highest degree of marriage; but he was favoured by the Minister, Chandu Lal, and was confirmed as his father's successor at Calcutta.

The first use he made of his power was, at the 'durbar' which the Resident attended to congratulate him on his accession, to demand roughly, 'that the Feringhis, who were interfering in his country, should be recalled'. Of course no immediate reply could be given, as the establishment of the civil control had been at the request of his father, who was sufficiently wise to see that the best chance of prosperity for his country was its being placed under English gentlemen.

It was the general opinion that the withdrawal of the civil officers would be the prelude to the total abolition of the Contingent. Reference was made to Calcutta, and it was decided to accede to the wishes of the Nizam. After living some months in a state of feverish anxiety as to my fate, I received orders in October to rejoin my regiment at Hyderabad as the civil control was to be discontinued. I earnestly entreated to be allowed to remain even a short time to prosecute my inquiries respecting the mysterious murders which had been perpetrated in my district. At first the Resident listened to me incredulously as I unfolded my tale; but he soon saw I was in earnest, and he wrote to the Minister to request permission for me to stay: but Chandu Lal replied that the Nizam had become so impatient and imperious that he dare not sanction my continuance; and with a very heavy heart I rejoined my regiment, the 6th, stationed at Bolarum. Had I been allowed to remain, I should have been the first to disclose the horrible crime of Thuggee to the world; [1] but it fell to the good fortune of Major Sleeman to do so afterwards. My inquiries were very active, and I found that parties of apparently most respectable Musalmans

[1] Taylor missed this, and without complaining; but missed it so completely that his name is not in the list of more than a score of officers to whom Sleeman makes final acknowledgment, in a note at the end of chapter 13 of his *Rambles and Recollections,* as having 'aided in the good cause'. All these, however, were either of the Civil Service or of the regular army. So far as can be told in the absence of initials from this list, it includes four men who were Residents in Hyderabad while lor served there in a subordinate capacity—Mr. Martin, Colonels Stewart and Low, and General Fraser, besides Taylor's friend Sutherland.

One might think it would have been a pleasure to Sleeman to mention Taylor, who was his acquaintance, and who always praised him. The English officer before whom Ameer Ali is taken at Saugor may or may not be meant for Sleeman: 'A tall, noble-looking person he was, and from the severe glance he cast on me I thought my hour was come, and that ere night I should cease to exist.' In the Introduction to the *Thug,* dated July 1839, Taylor quotes a passage 'from Colonel Sleeman's introduction to his own most curious and able work'. He also acknowledges 'the obligations I am under to Colonel Sleeman for much valuable information, and also for a copy of his work'. In Taylor's *History of India,* written long after Sleeman's death, are two capital paragraphs, setting forth Sleeman's achievement, and never mentioning himself.

William Henry Sleeman, 1788–1856, had published at Calcutta in 1836 a Vocabulary of the peculiar language used by the Thugs, called *Ramaseeana,* a book of sufficient interest to be pirated in America. This should be the book referred to by Taylor, who wrote almost entirely from first-hand material. In 1840, the year after the *Thug* was out in London, Sleeman published at Calcutta his famous *Report on the Depredations committed by the Thug Gangs of Upper and Central India, from the Cold Season of 1836–7, etc.* The year before he had also issued from the Serampore Press a minor *Report on the System of Megapunnaism.* This is one of the varieties of Thuggee which Taylor mentions in his

occasionally passed through the district, having charms, amulets, and medicines to sell. 'Our trade', said one to me, 'is to take with us from Aland,[1] old and new *saris* and waistbands and trade with them, getting in exchange brass and copper pots, and gold or silver ornaments; these we exchange again when the rains begin. We don't take our wives; they and the children remain at home as hostages for the rent we owe.' What could seem more plausible; and who could conceive the horrible crimes that were concealed under so fair a semblance?

The subject haunted me; why should so many men follow the same calling? Where did they go? Were they speaking the truth? My people were at fault, and Balram Singh shared my suspicions. He and Bhadrinath volunteered to follow and watch these men, and they were both absent disguised as fakirs when I was recalled to my regiment, and thus the mystery remained unsolved!

All chance of civil employ was now over, but still the service was safe, as the Nizam had promptly refused to do away with the Contingent and substitute a payment of twenty lakhs, as had been suggested. He took pride in the force, and the English Government now declared that it should not be disturbed, but that its cost should be lessened by sundry reforms. The pay was made to assimilate with that

---

Introduction as having been brought to light since the *Thug* was written: 'The most refined in guilt are those who murder parents for the sake of their children, to sell them as household slaves, or to dancing women to be brought up to prostitution.'

The two Indian classics bearing upon Thuggee have been issued from the Oxford University Press. Sleeman is represented not by any of his Reports, but by the book of his whole life, the racy *Rambles and Recollections of an Indian Official* (1844). Thuggee here occupies only a chapter of a dozen pages, called 'Thugs and Poisoners', with a note at the end of the volume by Sleeman's grandson. The *Times* in reviewing this edition, in the Indian Series, 1915, said essentially that Sleeman's revelations would not have gone far had not Meadows Taylor, in his novel, given them wings to fly with. This *tour de force*, the *Confessions of a Thug*, appeared in the World's Classics in 1916, with a map, a better glossary than before, and an excellent short Introduction by Mr. C. W. Stewart.

[1] A town of some 10,000 inhabitants in the west of the Nizam's State, Gulbarga District. 'Aland is a commercial centre of some importance.' The name recurs continually in *Tara*.

of the Company's army, without any consideration of the pensions, passage-money, and other advantages of the Company's service: we 'locals' were to have our bare pay only—in my case as a lieutenant it was 290 rupees a-month instead of 400. New regulations were drawn up providing promotion to the rank of captain after twelve years' service: but no pension was allowed; and the whole was summed up by a sentence which carried despair to many a heart—

'The Nizam's Government can grant no furlough to Europe.'

No more sight of home! no future meeting with my mother! never again to visit England, unless I left the service and returned to be a burden to my people. I can never forget the numbness which crept over me as I thought of it, now that all pleasant anticipations were gone, and my congenial employment exchanged for the dull routine of regimental duty. My old company received me with affectionate greeting, and I made up my mind, for the present at least, to remain. I was now twenty-one.[1]

[1] In his *History*, p. 630, Taylor tells how Lord William Bentinck's principle of non-intervention, carried too far, 'served to weaken the paramount authority and prestige of British power in India. In Hyderabad, a wasteful minister was allowed to weary the people by exactions and want of faith, which seriously impaired the revenue, and created a horde of usurers, Arab chiefs, Patans, and native bankers, whose extortions from the people of the districts assigned to them, in payment of loans and advances, are remembered with terror. As a relief to the State, an offer was made by the governor-general to disband the contingent, for a partial equivalent in money payment; but the services of this force were invaluable to the Nizam's Government, as a counterpoise to its own turbulent feudatories and military chiefs, and the offer . . . was declined. The pay and allowances of the contingent were, however, reduced to the standard of the company's forces.'

In 1835 a remonstrance came from the Court of Directors. 'These remonstrances had, however, little practical effect, and the minister, taking courage from the prevailing non-interferent policy, made no change in his system.'

CHAPTER IV

1829–37

I HAVE, perhaps, no right to intrude upon my readers the doubts and fears, crude hopes and impossible aspirations that filled my mind, as was only natural in one so young. I had met with some disappointments, bitter ones, already; but I had courage and good health remaining, and I always look upon this period as a turning-point in my life. I was exposed to much temptation. In those days in India men drank hard and deep, and high play was the rule, not the exception. However, I cared for none of these things, and kept much aloof; I was esteemed exclusive and unsociable, but I did not mind. I had my own recreations after my own taste; among these my boat on the large Husain Sagar Tank [1] was my chief one, and scarcely an evening passed that I did not drive over from Bolarum to have a sail. I had rigged her myself with three sprit-sails, after the fashion of the Liverpool ferry-boats, and I fully enjoyed sailing her in company with the other tiny yachts which were always out. I studied Persian and Marathi, and if I had been drawing all day long I could not have complied with the requests that were made to me to fill the albums of my fair friends.

[1] This, 'the far-famed Hoosain Sagor, or, as it is more often called, Secunderabad', described with evident personal delight in the *Thug*, was built by a Sultan of Golconda, in the sixteenth century, before Hyderabad was fairly founded.

'The Husain Sagar, a large sheet of water, which when full extends over an area of 8 square miles, lies between Secunderabad on the north and Saifabad, a portion of Hyderabad, on the south, and is the source of water-supply for the Residency and suburbs north of the Musi river. The dam is 2,500 yards long, and forms the road connecting the northern suburbs with Secunderabad' (*Imperial Gazetteer*, article 'Hyderabad City').

Mr. Martin was removed from the Residency at Hyderabad and transferred to an appointment at Delhi. He had never been popular, and his manner was cold and formal except to those he really liked. To me he had been invariably kind, and the tears stood in his eyes when I took leave of him. 'I would have done more for you if I could,' he said; 'I feel as if you were among the few really true to me.' He soon afterwards took furlough to England, and did not resume his public life.

In November 1830, Colonel Stewart, formerly Resident at Gwalior, was promoted to Hyderabad. From him and his charming family I experienced kindness and hospitality unbounded. He was generous and open-hearted, and belonged to the school of 'non-interference' politicians. The Nizam expressed himself anxious to effect reform in many departments, but ended by doing very little.

At the end of the Maratha war of 1818, the finances of the Nizam's State were in the utmost disorder, and the Government of the Nizam had no credit whatever in the money market. Had it not been for the continuous loans made to it by Messrs. Wm. Palmer & Co., it must have become bankrupt in all its State obligations. The Nizam had large private hoards, but these he refused to allow his Minister to touch for any public purpose. The loan of £600,000, authorised by the Indian Government, from the house of Wm. Palmer & Co., did for a while satisfy some pressing needs; but no attempt was made to introduce economical reform, or to raise depressed revenue to the ordinary standard. Therefore, financial distress continued. Villages were deserted; large tracts left uncultivated; rebellions ensued which the Government was too weak to check; and it was when things were in this condition that Sir Charles Metcalfe proposed the introduction of the superintendence of English officers into the civil departments—a measure sanctioned by the Court of Directors, and approved by the old Nizam.

The measures enforced by these officers were the settlement for five years of every village which duly received its lease. Waste lands were let at small increasing rents, till a fair average should be attained in five or seven years; cultivation increased rapidly; emigrants returned; much good was done, and much exaction prevented. The officers of the Nizam's Government made the collections, and generally managed their own districts, but no demand for extra cesses or oppression of any kind was left unnoticed. These native officers considered the check and superintendence of the English a great grievance, and appeals were entered against them; but on the whole, the system worked harmoniously and beneficially to the people.

Now, however, that the civil control of the English was abolished, the country was thrown open to the Minister and his creatures, and the old scenes were enacted anew. The fine rich cotton-growing country of Berar suffered terribly, and many more likewise. Districts were farmed out to speculators, or money-lenders—whoever chose to make the highest advance; and it was a grim joke at Hyderabad that every man who took a district rode the first stage with his face to his horse's tail, to see who was following him.

To Chandu Lal's policy Colonel Stewart appeared indifferent. The Nizam had been offered power to dismiss his Minister, and had refused to do so, professing himself perfectly satisfied; so things grew worse and worse.

I have not yet mentioned the prosecution of Obid Husein, the late Resident's Munshi, on the part of the trustees of the house of Wm. Palmer & Co. This person had been an immense favourite of Mr. Martin, I think. But for his influence the Resident would have given Mr. Palmer every assistance in the recovery and liquidation of the large sums lent by the House to the Nizam's Government: but from the moment of his arrival there was a perceptible difference; and not only was no help given in recovering sums which had already been decided in favour of the House by the Musalman Civil Court of Hyderabad, but every difficulty that ingenuity could suggest was thrown in the way, and Chandu Lal and others amused themselves by telling Mr. Palmer how much money they were giving to the Munshi to get the claims altogether quashed. Sir Charles Metcalfe's opinions were adverse to the House, and debates ran high. There were Palmerites and Metcalfites; and I, young as I was, took part in the discussions, maintaining only that 'if the whole of the claims were dishonest, why did Government pay any of them? Why had the English Government applied to the Court of King's Bench for a mandamus to adopt a despatch in Messrs. Wm. Palmer & Co.'s favour? And why had the Hyderabad Courts given awards in their favour amounting to £100,000, the payment of which was hindered by the intrigues of Mr. Martin's Munshi?' No doubt I spoke as a lad, and with all the zeal of youth; but now, forty-four years after,[1] I find my opinion unchanged.

Mr. Palmer's house continued my chief resort. There was a fascination about him quite irresistible to me, his knowledge was so varied—classical, historical, and political. His father, who had been secretary to Warren Hastings, had taken part in all the most eventful scenes of early Anglo-Indian history, and had married, as was very usual then among English gentlemen, a lady of high rank, one of the Princesses of the royal house of Delhi; and his fund of knowledge and great store of anecdote made him a delightful and improving companion.

In 1830 (I forget the exact date), my prospects brightened. The adjutant of my regiment, having completed twelve years' service, was promoted to the rank of captain. I was the next in seniority, and my claims were recognised by the Resident, Colonel Stewart. I passed my examination in Hindustani 'with credit', and my name appearing in orders, I assumed my new duties. My pay was increased considerably; and I was much amused, when I asked a young lady to dance at a ball one night, to overhear her ask her mother's permission, 'as I was now an adjutant'.

'Are you quite sure, dear?' said mamma; 'if you are, you may do so. He is quite eligible *now*.'

I could not repress a smile as I led the young lady out to our dance. Are mammas still so watchful?

During the rainy season of 1830, I met with a very severe accident in riding after a panther, which led us a long chase. He got away through some high grass at last, and mounting my horse, with my gun in my hand, I made after him. My horse put his fore legs into a deep hole, as we were going at speed, and I was shot out of my saddle, and thrown on my shoulder with great violence. I got up directly. ran on to the garden where the panther had taken refuge, and pushing

[1] 1874.

through the hedge I saw a fine young sepoy keeping him down with his bayonet, and another poor fellow sitting at a little distance holding his arm, which was nearly severed above the elbow. I tied his arm up with my handkerchief, and soon after the doctor arrived. He asked me if I were likewise hurt, remarking I looked very pale, and I owned to much pain in my right shoulder. On examination it turned out that I had not only broken my collar-bone, but also the scapula and the socket of my right arm. I did not recover the use of it for many months.

At the close of the year, H.H. the Nizam expressed a desire to review the whole of the troops at Secunderabad and Bolarum. I had then charge of my regiment; and the unusual size of our men, and their steadiness, excited the envy of officers of the Madras corps. As the Prince passed slowly on his elephant we dropped our colours, which no other regiment had done; and he then learned, perhaps for the first time, that such troops belonged to him. After parade we were all to breakfast with his Highness. I was late, and could not easily find a seat, which the Resident observing, offered me one close to himself. The Nizam, a fine-looking man over six feet in height, with a fair skin, ruddy complexion, and blue Tartar eyes, at once recognised me and inquired my name. 'He has already done me a delicate but important service,' he said to Colonel Stewart, 'and I am glad to have this opportunity of thanking him. He will tell you what it was.'

So I related how, one evening, my camp being pitched at the town of Kalyani,[1] I was told that a lady of rank, attended by her secretary and a few followers, was without,

[1] A jagir town in Bidar District, with a population of 13,000 in 1891, but 11,000 at the two following decennial periods. Kalyani has a notable history. It was the seat of the Chalukyan kingdom about the period of the Norman kings in England. It was the birthplace (*Imperial Gazetteer*) 'of Basava who founded the Lingayat sect'. In his *History* Taylor has a long paragraph on the story of this 'Brahmin named Busappa', whose faith 'became the means of accomplishing a great dynastic and religious revolution'. His tenets 'remain to the present time, professed by perhaps the majority of the middle classes in Southern and South-Western India'. When Kalyani was no longer a great capital it belonged to various kingdoms, was sacked by the Moguls, and the fortress taken by Aurungzeb in 1656. Its fine temples have been demolished or changed into mosques.

in a palankeen, asking to see me. I went out at once, and my fair visitor told me that she was the youngest sister of the Nizam, married to the Lord of Kalyani, who had ill-used and even struck her; that she had left his fort, daring his people to molest her; and had come to my camp, where she was sure the English flag would protect her. Now she wanted an escort of police-horse to conduct her to Hyderabad. This I gave her, and provided escorts from stage to stage until she reached Hyderabad.

'Did you report this?' asked the Resident.

'No,' I replied; 'the Begum especially desired the matter should be kept private. I have recorded it in my Mahratta diary, but it is not a circumstance I could report officially.'

'You are right,' he said; 'and you see your service has not been forgotten.'

The Nizam was quite at his ease, conversing with Colonel Stewart, and occasionally asking me various questions about the country and what I had done.

Shortly after this, the Nizam's brother, Mubariz-u-Dowla, collected a number of Arabs and Afghans, strengthened his house in the city, and proceeded to press claims against his brother which could not be for one moment entertained. The case becoming serious, and disturbances being imminent, Colonel Stewart was called upon to repress the disorder by sending in a force from Bolarum. I was still in charge of my regiment, and, preceded by two guns, we marched into the city. Had there been any fighting we should have fared badly in those narrow streets, lined with terraced houses, all covered with armed men; but happily not a shot was fired, though the guns at the palace gates were unlimbered. The officer commanding the brigade had preceded us and induced the rebel to proceed according to orders to Golconda, and to trust to his brother's generosity to settle all disputed claims; and so, for a time, there was a hollow peace patched up.

Mubariz-u-Dowla, however, could not rest content, and the Minister had overlooked the fact that in his personal retainers he possessed the means of doing much mischief. The treasury at the Fort of Golconda[1] is one of the most ancient in the

[1] The fame of Golconda is not wholly due to its association with diamonds, which were never found in the near neighbourhood. It is

State, and at this time contained 100 lakhs, or a million sterling; and the Nizam, wishing to remove some of the money, sent his treasurer, with a small guard, for the purpose. Mubariz-u-Dowla refused admittance, and the others, being too weak to fight, placed a guard at the entrance. There was great consternation at Hyderabad. Five thousand Arabs, Rohillas, Sikhs, and other foreign levies, including some of the old French 'Ligne', were marched out to Golconda, and took up a position in the outer *enceinte*; but they made no impression on the Prince, and indeed were supposed to be well affected towards him. After days of useless negotiation, the Minister, on the part of the Nizam, requested the assistance of the Bolarum Contingent; so we all marched out on the 6th January 1831, and encamped opposite the north or Delhi gate, on the plain on which stand the noble mausoleums of the Kutb Shahi Kings. It was an absurd state of affairs. The interior was held by the rebel Prince, the outer *enceinte* by the Nizam's levies, who also treated us as enemies, not only refusing to allow us to enter, but threatening to fire on

---

a fortress and ruined city five miles to the west of its daughter city, Hyderabad. The fort was built by a Raja of Warangal, who ceded it to the ruler of Gulbarga. 'In 1512 the place passed from the Bahmanis to the Kutb Shahis, who had their capital here till the foundation of Hyderabad. In 1687 the city was taken by Aurungzeb after a siege of eight months, and the last of the Kutb Shahis was deported to Daulatabad' (*Imperial Gazetteer*).

The fort is over three miles round. The granite tombs are crumbling, while the enamelled tiles have been stolen from them. The fort is garrisoned now, much as in Taylor's day, by a few Arabs and by the special Golconda Brigade.

It is at Golconda, as a convenient point outside Hyderabad, that, in chapter xxi. of the *Thug*, Ameer Ali has tryst with Azima, whom he marries. 'As we passed over the brow of an eminence, the tombs of the kings of Golconda broke on our sight, occupying the whole of a rising ground in front. . . . I was astonished at their size and magnificence, even from that distance; how much more so when we approached them nearer! . . Their immense size, and the beautiful groups which they assumed as our point of view shifted, struck forcibly on the mind, while the desolation around them added to their solemn appearance. . . . From the other side of the terrace the whole of the large tombs were seen at a glance—each by itself a noble and striking object; but rendered still more so when grouped with others of smaller size, whose contrast increased their massiveness.'

Loti has a graceful, sentimental chapter on Golconda (*L'Inde*, 1903).

us, and training the fort guns on the wall so as to command our camp. I rode to the edge of the counterscarp one morning, but was warned off. However, I managed to have a look at the ditch, and saw that it was wide and deep; and by dint of exchanging good-humoured 'chaff' with the men, escaped unharmed.

We remained inactive until the 15th February, when we were suddenly ordered into the fort, and the Nizam's troops at the same time ordered to leave it. We took up a position not far from the Prince's palace, between it and the treasury, and pickets were immediately posted. I held the advanced picket with two guns and four companies. I had my guns loaded with a double charge of grape each, and as the Prince's men were watching us very closely, they must have seen that we were in earnest.

The Nizam's people began removing the treasure, but it was slow work, and for four days and nights I had not even time to change my clothes; the weather, too, was very hot. I believe mine was the post of honour, as it would have been of danger had any fighting occurred. But it was annoying to be kept there perpetually on the stretch, with constant alarms that the Arabs were coming to attack us, and with the sound of their peculiar drum and their war-songs constantly in our ears.[1]

I was not sorry when, on the fifth morning, one of the staff rode up and told me I might withdraw my men, for the Prince

[1] What were so many Arabs still doing in Deccan history? They were survivors from the anarchy which had been ended only a dozen years before. Taylor resented their continued intrusion in Hyderabad affairs, their fanatic influence, and their manners. Chapter 5 gives a picture of the Arabs at Aden, just before its annexation, swaggering about 'stroking their moustaches in very Hyderabad fashion'. There is also a significant passage in the *History of India*, telling how 'all the fugitive Arab mercenaries had collected', in 1818, at the fort of Malegaon in Khandesh. After a notable defence they were allowed, writes Taylor, 'to march out under promise of payment of their arrears of pay, and a free passage to Arabia. This generous treatment was, however, misunderstood. The Arabs considered they had had the best of the contest; and the result ever since then has been held up as an instance of successful resistance by Arabs to English troops which could not be overcome, and at Hyderabad and elsewhere has produced many bad consequences.' Loti notes the Arabs in Hyderabad.

had agreed to send away his levies and keep only his immediate retainers.

A scene followed which affected me very deeply. I had drawn up my four companies, and released the guns from their position, when the men burst into loud shouts of—

'Bolo, Mahadeo Baba Ke Jey!' ('Victory to the son of Mahadeo!')

I hardly understood it at first; but my friend S., who came to look after his guns, clapped me on the back and said, 'I do congratulate you, Taylor, with all my heart; no truer proof could have been given you of the men's affection; you will never lose your title—it will follow you all your life.' 'Bolo, Mahadeo Baba Ke Jey!' he shouted to the men, and heartily did they respond; while, as I proceeded to dismiss them from parade, the cry was taken up by hundreds of both the regiments present.

Even our chief came out to say a few kind words. Captain S. was right, my *sobriquet* never left me, not even in the Mutiny, and it may still linger among the descendants of those who conferred it.

The force was to return to cantonments, but the request of the Nizam was complied with that six companies should remain in charge of the fort, and I was appointed to take command. I was to see that no levies joined the Prince, and I was to be the medium of communication between the Prince and the Resident. 'You can read Persian,' the Resident said to me, as he gave me my orders, 'and you are to open and read all letters the Prince sends you, whether to the Nizam, the Minister, or me: what he has hitherto written are so insolent in tone, that if the others are like them, you need not forward them. If you can make up this quarrel between the brothers, do so, and I shall be obliged to you; but on no account make it worse.'

So I remained at my post, and for a few days no notice was taken. I sent for my boat, and used to sail about on the fine tank which washed the walls of the fort, and see the Prince spying at me through a telescope. At length his Munshi came out, and I offered him a sail one evening. In return, dishes arrived for breakfast and dinner, delightfully cooked, and I reported this friendly intercourse to the Resident.

At last letters were sent—one to the Resident, another to the Nizam, very violent in tone, which I returned; others followed daily for more than a fortnight, gradually improving in tone, but not right yet. 'You've hooked your fish, Taylor,' said the Resident, laughing, 'but he is too strong to land yet; I'll not help you or interfere at all;' and I was very glad he did not.

By-and-by my friend grew sulky, but this did not last long; and one evening the Munshi arrived with some extra good dishes for me, and food for the whole detachment. 'Would I be pleased to draft a letter that would satisfy all parties—his honour was in my hands,' this was the message delivered by the Munshi. I did draft a letter, and the Prince flew into a violent rage over it, and abused me for having so small an idea of his dignity. We wrangled over it for a week, and he ended by placing his case unreservedly in my hands, and writing what I dictated. I made the draft in English so as to be sure of my meaning, and it was afterwards translated by me into Urdu with my own hand, to assure the Prince that it was really mine. The letters were brought to me the next afternoon; and as the Munshi and I sailed about, the Prince waved a white flag by way of salute, which we answered from the 'Zora', with twelve shots from her little pieces.

I took the letters next morning to the Residency. That to the Nizam was forwarded at once, and was pronounced very satisfactory. He would send his mother directly to Golconda with his assurances, and would make proper arrangements for his brother's return. When I returned to Golconda, I found the old Begum Sahiba had already arrived, and two female servants were sent to my tent to report that she and her son had fallen on each other's necks and wept much; and in a day or two Mubariz-u-Dowla was escorted to the city with all possible respect.

I received the thanks of the Nizam for having 'for the second time rendered a service to his family'.

Mubariz-u-Dowla sent his secretary to me afterwards, when my intended marriage was announced, with a 'Fard' or memorandum in Persian, which was presented on a silver salver covered with a napkin of cloth-of-gold. He hoped I would accept for my future wife the articles mentioned in the list, as a mark of the gratitude he felt for the services I had rendered him. The presents he wished to give were very valuable, including shawls, necklaces, ornaments for the head, bracelets of diamonds and other gems, a zone of gold set with precious stones, and a necklace of seven rows of pearls with diamond pendant, the aggregate value about 20,000 rupees; but alas! I could only thank him for his kindness, and tell him I was not permitted to accept his gifts. He afterwards got into trouble by his connection with the Wahabi conspiracy of 1839, and eventually died a State prisoner at Golconda. During my stay I was only once permitted to ascend the hill whereon the fort stands, and I wrote my name in the mosque, now disused; but I never could even enter the gates afterwards, nor, since the temporary occupation of the place in 1831, has any Englishman ever been allowed to enter its precincts.

On the 25th August the following year, I was married to Mary Palmer, daughter of Wm. Palmer, Esq., Hyderabad, by the Rev. W. J. Aislabie, chaplain of the station, at Secunderabad Church; and in December of that year my regiment was ordered to Hingoli, where we took up our abode.

Hingoli was a dreary place enough [1]—scarcely a tree near it, no gardens, and altogether desolate. There was no amusement to be had at the station, and we passed our evenings in reading French and Italian, and my wife tried to teach me to play the harp; but suddenly one day the sounding-board and back split up under the heat, and my progress was rudely interrupted.

On the 4th of June 1833 we were ordered to march to a place called Goligaon, the chief of which, Jaluji Naik, had rebelled against the Government, garrisoned his fort, and was plundering the country. The town was reported to be forty miles distant, and we started under a blazing sun.

[1] The account of Hingoli town and taluk, Parbhani District, in the *Imperial Gazetteer* bears out Taylor's description. The town is the eighth in the State, with 17,000 inhabitants. 'It was a cantonment of the Hyderabad Contingent up to 1903. Since the removal of the Contingent, some of the Nizam's troops have been stationed here. Hingoli is a great cotton mart, and is famous as one of the first places in the Deccan where operations for the suppression of *thagi* were commenced about 1833.'

We were obliged to halt several times, but by dint of resting during the heat of the day and going on at night, we at last sighted the place, lying in a hollow beneath us, and keeping up a sharp fire from its walls. We had, in reality, come upwards of a hundred miles, and the thermometer had been 114° under the shade of a thick banian-tree at our last halting-place. How our men, laden with forty rounds of ammunition and two days' provisions each, did it I don't know. I helped them as much as I could by dispensing with pantaloons, which were tied up in bundles and placed on the spare carriage-bullocks. Many a Hindu song was sung in chorus as we marched, relieved by the old cry, 'Bolo, Mahadeo Baba Ke Jey!' and on calling the roll, when we reached the camping-ground, I found that, with the exception of five men who had been left to burn a man that had died of cholera on the road, every one was present, and apparently fresh.

Jaluji Naik, the rebel, was still in the fort, and maintained a continuous fire, some of the balls cutting the branches of the tree we were under; and it was arranged that we should attack the fort the following day. It was a very strong place—a square mass, with a large bastion at each corner, loopholed for musketry and wall-pieces. The height of the wall was fifty-two feet from the parapet to the ground; the whole was in excellent repair.

We held a council of war, and arranged matters as follows:

First, the fort was to be shelled by the howitzer. I was to occupy the crest of a rising ground opposite the village, and advance through the village in case the shells did not take effect, and attack the outworks. Captain T—— was to set fire to the village, so that the sparks and burning thatch might be carried over the fort by the wind, which was very strong.

I reconnoitred my post that evening, and had a narrow escape, a ball passing through my cap; but I saw enough to show me the place was 'ugly', and might prove tough work for us. I think we all felt it so, though little was said as we parted for the night. We were to take up our position at earliest dawn. The stars were very bright, and the ceaseless firing kept up from the parapets of the fort had, I remember, a very beautiful effect. The place seemed full of men.

Suddenly a sentry challenged, and we all sprang to our feet. I called out not to fire, and ran forward with some of my men. A moment later, a short figure advanced and threw himself at my feet, and I found it was Jaluji Naik himself, with five or six attendants, who all gave up their arms. I sent him in at once to Captain T——'s tent, and received orders from him to take two companies and occupy the fort at daylight. I felt very thankful for this termination to the affair, especially when I saw the place we were to have attacked. As soon as it was light we marched to the entrance-gate, and desired the garrison to come out singly, first depositing their arms inside. There were eighty-five men only, as the remainder of the three hundred were absent at the Mohurrum festival, not expecting our visit. What a place it was! The courts and their entrance-gates grew narrower and narrower, till the last one would not admit two men abreast. There were store-houses filled with grain, rice, and *ghi*, stables and cattle-sheds, stores of forage and provisions. It seemed deserted now, except for a few women; and my men began to remove as much as possible of the grain and other property, which was sold at the drum-head, and the proceeds divided among them. I secured the rebel's household gods for my share, and a matchlock inlaid with gold.

Some camp-followers had set fire to a house in the village, and the wind blowing strong towards the fort, brought with it pieces of burning thatch and volumes of smoke. The stacks of forage took fire, and the wood-work of the buildings followed. I was about to depart when I fancied I heard the wail of an infant, and searching hurriedly about, I found a young woman lying insensible upon a bed, with a very young baby beside her. I took both in my arms, and staggered out through the fire and smoke, and meeting two of my men, who were anxious about me, they relieved me of my burden, and we left the place to the flames. The rebel Raja was told of the rescue of his wife and child, but he only replied, 'They had better have died,' and relapsed into sullen silence. His atrocities had been fearful. Persons had been suspended by the heels over the battlements of the fort; others had had their ears stuffed with gunpowder, which was ignited; but I may spare the reader these. He was made over to the Civil Superintendent of the district, and I do not know what his fate was eventually. His surrender alone prevented his being hanged on a bastion of the fort.

We returned to Hingoli on the 21st June by twelve easy stages, instead of the three we had marched the distance in before. Some rain had fallen, and it was cooler.

Now I became very busy. Those famous discoveries in regard to the practice of Thuggee had recently been made at Jubbulpore and Saugor by (then) Captain Sleeman, which made a sensation in India never to be forgotten.[1] By the confessions of one gang who were apprehended, many Thugs in Central India were brought to justice; and at last the Thugs of the Deccan were denounced by these approvers, and as many lived near Hingoli, they were at once arrested.[2] I volunteered my services in the labour of collecting evidence, and they were accepted. Day after day I recorded tales of murder, which, though horribly monotonous, possessed an intense interest; and as fast as new approvers came in, new

[1] 'The town of Saugor was, and is now, a large and busy place, built on the edge of an immense lake, nearly as large as that of the Hoosein Sagor; the cooling breezes which travel over it make it a delightful spot. . . . The country between Jubbulpoor and Nagpoor is a wild waste. Villages are not met with for miles and miles, the road is stony and uneven, and the jungle thick and dangerous for nearly the whole way. On this account the tract has always been a favourite resort of Thugs, and more affairs have come off in those few marches than perhaps in any other part of the country frequented by us' (*Confessions of a Thug*).

[2] 'At the cantonment of Hingolee, the leader of the Thugs of that district, Hurree Singh, was a respectable merchant of the place, one with whom I myself, in common with many others, have had dealings. On one occasion he applied to the officer in civil charge of the district, Captain Reynolds, for a pass to bring some *cloths* from Bombay, which he knew were on their way accompanied by their owner, a merchant of a town not far from Hingolee; he murdered this person, his attendants, and cattle-drivers, brought the merchandise up to Hingolee under the pass he had obtained, and sold it openly in the cantonment; nor would this have ever been discovered had he not confessed it after his apprehension, and gloried in it as a good joke. By this man too and his gang many persons were murdered *in the very bazar of the cantonment*, within one hundred yards of the main guard, and were buried hardly five hundred yards from the line of sentries! I was myself present at the opening of several of these unblessed graves (each containing several bodies),' etc. (Author's Introduction to the *Thug*, London, July 1839).

mysteries were unravelled and new crimes confessed. Names of Thugs all over the Deccan were registered, and I found one list containing the names of nearly all those whom I had suspected in my old district. The reader will remember my intense anxiety on this subject in 1829, and my conviction that deadly crime existed and was only awaiting discovery; now it was all cleared, but I felt sore that it had not fallen to my lot to win the fame of the affair.

Some men of the artillery and some camp-followers deserted at this time. They were also Thugs; and it was a horrible thought that these miscreants had been in our midst, and it made many in the station, and especially the ladies, very nervous. We had searched for bodies of murdered people wherever we were told to look by the approvers, and invariably found them, sometimes singly, sometimes whole parties, and the details were so sickening we resolved to open no more graves. I wrote and sent home to my father an article on Thuggee, which was shown to Sir Edward Bulwer, who sent me word that had he possessed any local knowledge of India or its people, he would write a romance on the subject; why did I not do so? I pondered over this advice, and hence my novel, *Confessions of a Thug*.[1]

The year did not end pleasantly. A horrible plot, said to be of Wahabi contrivance, to murder all Europeans at Bangalore, and sell their women as slaves, was discovered. There were disturbances in Oudh and other northern provinces, and famine was rapidly spreading from Kathiawar and Guzerat over the Deccan. We did what we could at Hingoli, first individually, then by general subscription. A Brahmin cook was engaged, whose bread and boiled pulse all would eat, and a good meal was given to each person once a-day. The system worked well, and our relief-books showed that three thousand persons received food daily and were all in good health. But in the rural districts thousands of people and cattle must have perished; the gaunt attenuated forms

[1] This was an interesting genesis for a first novel in so remote a part of the world. I have always wondered if Taylor saw anything of the first Lord Lytton when at home a few years later, at Gore House or elsewhere; but no record of such a meeting could be found by the Earl of Lytton, who kindly examined his grandfather's papers.

of some who arrived to ask for aid were pitiful to behold, and the roads were strewn with the bodies of those who died on their way from weakness and starvation.

During the next three years I had much domestic trouble. The birth and subsequent death of two dear children,[1] the severe and continued illness of my wife, and my own very narrow escape with my life from terrible jungle fever, contracted at Gudalur,[2] at the foot of the Nilgiri Hills, whither we had been ordered by the doctors for change of air for my wife,—all these events saddened our lives and caused us much distress.[3]

Of the beauty of the scenery on the Hills I need not speak here. It has often been described and enlarged upon since, but at that time it was less familiar to those at home; and I find my letters teeming with descriptions of our journey—of wooded hills and towering mountains, of trees and waterfalls, of precipitous crags and deep wooded glens, of ferns and blackberries and violets to remind us of dear old England, of sunsets and sunrises, rolling mists and cool fresh breezes—and, above all, of gratitude for my wife's returning health. My enemy, the fever, however, came back when I was at Ootacamund with renewed violence, and the medical men looked grave, and spoke of a voyage to England as my only hope of life. How could this be accomplished? Furlough was prohibited, and the only chance was a voyage to the Cape—

[1] Two boys. No record exists of the births of Colonel Taylor's children. Indeed, as has now been brought to light, there was no system of registration of births in India until more than a generation later.

[2] There is nothing vital in the *Imperial Gazetteer* about Gudalur, the headquarters of the western taluk of the Nilgiri District. It lies much lower than the rest of the district, on the road from Ootacamund to Calicut, with a dwindling population largely speaking Malayalam. The region is reverting to jungle since the decline of the coffee industry and the mining for gold and mica. In the *Oxford Survey of the British Empire*, vol. ii., 'Asia', is a striking photograph of Gudulur (*sic*), Madras, showing the development of, apparently, feathery bamboos.

[3] The journey by road of the harassed young man, through half-a-dozen degrees of latitude southward from Hyderabad, yet towards the saving altitudes, right across the tableland of Mysore, made an ineffaceable impression. There are traces of it in his second novel, *Tippoo Sultaun*, written some five years later.

dreary enough, but still it must be tried ;[1] and meantime we stayed on, mostly at Coonoor, where I amused myself trying to sketch some of the most striking views, and was always enchanted with its beauty, so varied and so picturesque on every side. It was at this time, when I was in sore trouble at the loss of my second child, that I had the good fortune to be introduced to the then Governor-General, Lord William Bentinck, He was staying at the Hills and had often noticed my boy, not knowing whose child he was. When he died, he wrote me a kind letter of sympathy, asking me to come and see him. I did so as soon as I was able, and so faint and weak was I that I could not stand when I entered his room. He took me in his arms, laid me down on a sofa, and sent for some wine. I told him, when I was stronger, that I had two letters for him which I had been unable to deliver before—one from Mr. Newnham,[2] and the other from my uncle, Captain Robert Mitford.

'You don't mean it,' he said, as his face beamed with pleasure ; 'he is one of my dearest friends ; why did you not come to me at once ?'

'I have only just received this letter,' I replied, 'and I did not like to intrude before having received an introduction.'

'Now what can I do for you ?' he asked.

I mentioned that the Paymastership at Hingoli would soon be vacant—could he appoint me ? and he promised to assist me if he could. 'Only', I added, 'I fear I shall be obliged to go to the Cape on leave, this fever has so shattered my health.'

'Why not to England ?' he asked.

[1] The time when Taylor contemplated the Cape was not far from the days when the isolation and crudeness of life there were such that no worse threat could be made to Napoleon's followers when troublesome at St. Helena than that of being taken to the Cape and dropped. Yet it was glorious shikar country—a fact of which Taylor's friend Cornwallis Harris was even then making good account.

[2] This is the last mention in the autobiography of the kind friend (retired, 1835). *Tippoo Sultaun*, 1840, (and it must have been a satisfaction to Taylor) bears the inscription : 'To William Newnham, Esq., my best and earliest friend in India, this volume is with grateful esteem dedicated.' Miss Taylor believes that he died soon after ; but has no further knowledge of him or of his descendants.

Then I poured forth the tale of the furlough grievance, and he could scarcely credit that such an order had been passed. He sent his secretary for a copy of the orders, and saw it was all true.

'I shall put in a minute at the next Council,' he said; 'we can get over this, and I shall record that my friend Mr. Taylor is to be allowed leave to England when necessary. That will be enough for you.'

'But, my lord,' I said, 'though I am more grateful than I can express for your kind consideration towards me, my case alone will not help my brother-officers. May I plead for them as well?'

'Certainly,' said Lord William, 'you are quite right; and though my minute as regards yourself will stand in case of urgent necessity, yet all of you shall be released soon from this restriction. Write to-day to the senior officer of your "locals", bid him send in a memorial without delay, and I will have it passed.' [1]

The friend I wrote to despatched the memorial as soon as he could obtain the signatures, and the question passed through Council without difficulty.

After this interview I dined frequently with the Governor-General, meeting there many charming and interesting characters, amongst others the then Mr. Macaulay, whose conversation I found intensely fascinating; his seemingly boundless

[1] This reception of the ailing subaltern was altogether worthy of the way in which Bentinck had received Victor Jacquemont (1801–1832) in Calcutta in 1829. In 1834 he was sixty, and himself ill, which was the reason for his being at Ooty: he died five years later. Only this once, through all the century, could a Governor-General have been found residing in South India.

Bentinck seems to have been the only Governor-General whom Meadows Taylor met, though he had correspondence with others. His administration of nearly seven years occupies some twenty pages in the *History*. The brilliant triumphs of earlier English rulers 'are wanting in the peculiar and hitherto non-existent charm which is attached to the memory of Lord William Bentinck. During his incumbency, there were no glorious victories to be recorded, for no enemies remained to be overcome; but the successful development of moral force, and the conversion of long-existing prejudices into a steady policy of improvement and advancement, is a triumph even more transcendent in the aggregate than that of successful war.'

knowledge of life, his acquaintance with history and philosophy, his fiery zeal in argument, and his calm eloquence in oratory, opened to me new subjects of thought for future study.[1] Oh, if I had been among such men always, I thought, I should have been very different!

I grew stronger in health, and my regiment being ordered to Ellichpur[2] at the end of December, we left the Hills about October 10. We did not return by the way we had come, for we had only too much cause to dread it, but went by Coonoor and Coimbatore,[3] where there was a most extraordinary

[1] It is this meeting with Macaulay which stands out in the early record of Taylor's life, as it did in reality. In the summer of 1834 he was a young man not quite thirty-four, spending June to September with the Governor-General before both proceeded to Calcutta where they belonged. It is still the chief literary memory of Ootacamund. I have put at the end of this chapter a note on Macaulay at Ooty, compiled by permission from the *Life and Letters*, with an original impression of the place contributed by Sir George Trevelyan.

Macaulay was seeing so much, or rather seeing with such effect the surface, of Indian things. He was also missing so much; as in Calcutta he missed the documents, lying under his hand, which would have justified Warren Hastings. He saw enough for his literary purposes; and for the two essays, written years later. These have been called Indian history masquerading on the field of the Cloth of Gold. This may apply to the *Clive*; but the *Hastings* is not history at all. To test the *Hastings* by facts is to begin to feel a queer shakiness about the *History of England*, which, however, is constructed on different principles.

A letter to Hunter, in Skrine's admirable *Life*, throws light upon 'the true causes of the feeling which arose' against Macaulay in Calcutta. 'The subsequent change in feeling was partly due to what you say—the limited conversational powers of Calcutta society and its inability to appreciate Macaulay, and he was not slow in expressing his disgust. Then the lawyers began to grow irritated with a bird which was fouling his own nest, as they said, and who was said to have called them a tribe of horse-leeches.'

[2] Ellichpur town, with a population of some 26,000, was until 1905 the headquarters of a district of the same name. It is hard to tell which was ever the capital of Berar, where no one place predominates. Taylor later on distinctly calls Buldana (quite a small place) the head station. The *Imperial Gazetteer* says: 'Until the Assignment in 1853, when Amraoti became the administrative headquarters of the province, Ellichpur was always regarded as the capital of Berar,' although in Akbar's time Balapur became 'the headquarters of the Imperial army of the Deccan'.

It was here that the *Thug* was written some years later.

[3] 'Coimbatore, picturesquely situated on the left bank of the Noyil

collection of large figures of horses in terra-cotta. I have never heard of these in any other part of India, and could obtain no tradition of their construction or their origin. They were reverenced by the people as offerings to a divinity they locally worship, but possess no particular value.

At Bangalore I was pressed to stay and act as interpreter to a court-martial about to sit, as, strange to say, no competent linguist was available; but I could not do it without much loss of time, so we pushed on, and finally reached Ellichpur on the 3rd February. We found two infantry regiments, one cavalry, and some artillery, at the station, so that there was no lack of society. I practised my drawing, and began to paint in oils, victimising many friends to sit for their portraits, and finding endless occupation and delight. Thus with military duties, and shooting, and excursions to various places of interest within reach, our time passed pleasantly.

It is not fitting for me here to undertake political discussions, or to comment on the career of the illustrious man who at this time quitted India; but I feel I must add my tribute to his integrity of purpose, liberality of action, and the commencement of that system of progress which is now bearing ample fruit. No more eloquent tribute to a statesman was ever written than that by Mr. Macaulay, engraved on the pedestal of Lord William Bentinck's statue at Calcutta. It contains no flattery, but a simple record of the real motives of the man 'whose constant study it was to elevate the moral and intellectual character of the Government intrusted to his care'. To me individually, and to our service, he had rendered inestimable benefit. I was told a testimonial was to be presented to me for what I had done, but I checked the scheme as soon as I heard of it. There was only one man to whom gratitude could be expressed, and that was the Governor-General. He was succeeded by Sir Charles Metcalfe.

Mr. Palmer's affairs seemed mending. An award was made by Mr. Macleod [1] for a portion of the debt, and twenty-

---

river, . . . is a healthy and pleasant town with a light annual rainfall and moderate mean temperature' (*Oxford Survey*). Yet the population has been going down from about 50,000.

[1] 'As soon as the dispatch reached India, the Governor-General appointed an umpire, Mr., now Sir John, Macleod, an able member of

four lakhs were paid in, the Nizam advancing most of the money, and the creditors were repaid in full. But the other awards of the civil courts against other debtors, for whom the Nizam's Government was security, were not adjusted; and these, together with the first balanee of twenty lakhs upon the great loan, remained to be settled.

The balance was not disputed, and they were left for payment, and still remain unadjusted and due, in spite of many memorials to successive governments, which have been hitherto without effect.

In December[1] I was promoted to the rank of captain, having completed twelve years' service; but I was allowed for a time to fulfil the duties of adjutant.

The following year I began my tale *Confessions of a Thug*. I had never attempted any work of the kind before, and I found it intensely fascinating—the work seemed to grow so rapidly in my thoughts and under my hands, and I enjoyed the sensation ardently. I remember giving the first few chapters to one of my brother-officers to read, and his constant demands for 'more', and his perpetual scoldings for my 'laziness' in writing so slowly, were accepted by me as a high compliment.

Mr. Palmer, too, encouraged me to proceed. He criticised, and commended, and his marginal notes were of great use to me, and often very amusing.[2]

---

the Civil Service, who proceeded to Hyderabad,' etc. (Taylor's *History*, p. 626). Sir John Macpherson Macleod, 1792–1881, was a fellow Law Commissioner with Macaulay.

[1] 1836.

[2] Here may be best inserted a passage from Taylor's preface to the 1873 edition of the *Thug* (Kegan Paul), testifying both to the extraordinary demand for the book when first published, and to the more extraordinary spirit of the fever-stricken, untaught youth (he was not twenty-nine until towards the end of 1837) who wrote it.

'Few authors can perhaps look back so long to their first essay in literary occupation with more satisfaction and gratitude than myself. In 1837, when serving with my regiment at Ellichpur, in Berar—weakened and distressed by repeated attacks of jungle fever—I wrote the Confessions to amuse myself, reclining in an easy-chair, with a board on my knees, for I was too weak to sit up much—little thinking, or perhaps even hoping, that they would ever be printed. I was sent to England to recover; and in 1839 the first edition appeared, published

In 1837 we made a charming excursion to Burhanpur. My old friend Major Sutherland had been appointed Resident at Gwalior, and invited a party to meet him and shoot tigers. It was a very beautiful journey, and I could fill pages with descriptions of all the places of interest through which we passed. I took several sketches at Burhanpur, every street and turning abounding in subjects for the pencil, so that the difficulty was in knowing where to begin.

Burhanpur had been always famous for its brocade weaving.[1] We visited some of the looms, and watched how the gold and silver threads were deftly woven in. But the most interesting part of the work was the making of the gold thread itself, which we followed through all its stages.

A piece of silver about the length and thickness of the middle finger is first gilt several times, according to the value of the thread to be produced. It is then hammered out into a long bar, as it were, and drawn through plates of fine steel, perforated with holes, which are changed each time to one smaller, till the wire becomes as fine as a hair. This is then drawn, two wires at a time, through a still finer plate, over a bright steel anvil by a man who hits each a sharp blow with a steel hammer. Thus the whole becomes a flattened wire of exquisite fineness and ductility, which is then wound on a reel. A long and very thin silk thread, with a spindle at the end, is now passed over a hook in the ceiling, and a man, giving the spindle a dexterous twirl, applies the gold wire to it,

---

by the late Mr. Richard Bentley. The subject was new, strange, and exciting, and at once gained a place in the public mind. No attempt, except in "Pandurang Hari", had ever been made to depict, in a familiar or dramatic aspect, the manners, customs, and thoughts of Indian people, or the scenes in which they live; and more perhaps for this reason, than the recital of the Thug's Confessions, terrible as they are, was the work received with favour, which indeed was little short of fascination. The old editions are now entirely out of print, and have so completely disappeared that it was found impossible to procure one for the re-printing of the present, and I was obliged to devote the only copy I possessed to the purpose.'

[1] Two thousand persons are still supported by this industry at Burhanpur (on the Tapti, Nimar District, Central Provinces). Taylor's *History* speaks of the architecture here as showing 'an appreciation of comfort in fresh air and ventilation foreign to the habits of the present people of India'.

which he runs up as far as practicable. The gold thread thus made is wound upon a reel, and the next length begun. The manual dexterity shown, and rapidity with which the process is accomplished, is very curious. I have never read any description of it, and hence am tempted to make this digression.

We had capital sport and a series of tiger-hunts while enjoying the splendid hospitality of the Resident. One incident occurred which amused us all. I had given up my seat on Major Sutherland's elephant, and my guns also, to another gentleman, as I was disinclined to go out that day, when one of the sirdars came up and asked me why I was not going.

'Oh,' said he, 'take my elephant and see the fun, even if you do not shoot. He is very small, but very easy, and will not jolt you.'

I accepted his offer, and mounted the little beast, on which I sat comfortably astride on a well-stuffed pad. As I passed my tent I called for my sun-hat, and my old tent-pitcher ran out, crying—

'You are not surely going without a gun, sahib? Take mine; I have just cleaned it, and I will load it for you with ball to shoot the tiger.'

This ancient weapon was a French musket of the last century, only known to explode on rare occasions. I had myself seen its owner sitting behind a bush snapping it at a hare which was calmly sitting at a short distance quite unmoved, but he was unable to get it to go off, and when it did, the hare had taken its departure after all. This venerable piece, which had taken part in the wars of Bussy, was brought to me.

'It will kick a bit,' said the old man, as he placed it in my hands; 'but you won't mind that when you kill the tiger.' He then made a salaam to it, patted it, and said to it: 'Do well, my son; you will be with the master'; and we started, I flourishing my weapon, and being not a little 'chaffed' on my accoutrements.

'Never mind,' said I, 'I'll kill the tiger'; but at the same time I had not the smallest intention of discharging the gun at all.

The place was reached—the tiger found. Every one fired—no one hit him. I retired to a piece of waste ground some distance off to be out of the way, when, with a great roar, the tiger dashed forward, ready to spring, within a few yards of my little elephant, which stood like a rock. I fired instinctively, I think, though the recoil nearly knocked me backwards, but the tiger did not move. I told my driver to get off, as he was going to spring, when the man exclaimed—

'He's dead, sahib—quite dead!' and as he spoke, the fierce grim head fell to one side. The old 'Frenchman' had for once done his duty, and the triumph was adjudged to me.

I had had a very narrow escape, for my little elephant was not higher than the door of a room, and the result must have been terrible had the tiger made his spring.

The hot-weather season was especially trying, and brought back my fever, with severe neuralgia, and I was racked by pain.

'This won't do,' said the doctor. 'You must go away; we can do no more here.'

My wife answered quietly, 'Yes, doctor, we will go'; and so it was settled: and on the 1st November I received my certificate and three years' leave of absence.

Had the old furlough rule still existed, I must, humanly speaking, have died.

We travelled on by easy stages, visiting Ajanta and its marvellous caves, now so well known by photographs, and Major Gill's splendid fresco-paintings, which met so untimely a fate in the great fire at the Crystal Palace.

We also visited the Ellora caves,[1] and the cool air invigor-

[1] The articles on Ajanta and Ellora in the *Imperial Gazetteer* are full of information. But Loti is preferable when attainable. He has a long chapter on 'Les Épouvantables Grottes' (*L'Inde*, 1903) at Ellora, which he had to reach by night in a bullock cart.

'Elles sont consacrées à toutes les divinités des Pouranas; mais les plus immenses sont à Siva, Dieu de la mort. Des hommes, dont le rêve fut terrible et colossal, s'acharnèrent jadis, durant des siècles, à les tailler dans des montagnes de granit. Il en est de bouddhiques, de brahmaniques, d'autres qui remontent au temps des rois Jaïnas. . . Siva, toujours Siva. . . . Ces éléphants cariatides, alignés pour soutenir les édifices du centre, étonnaient dans ce lieu par leur tranquillité.

ated me, and brought back a feeling of health to which I had been long a stranger. At length we reached Bombay, pitching our tents on the esplanade.

I had been ordered not to proceed direct to England, but to linger in Egypt or Arabia on account of their dry climate, and I set to work to see how this could be effected.

The only steamer about to start was already full, cabin accommodation being very limited. Various schemes were thought of and failed. At last my agents told me one day that an Armenian gentleman had taken his passage on board a large Arab 'buggalow', bound for Mocha, which had capital accommodation, and we could manage well if we took our servants.

We went to see the ship, a large one of her class, about 400 tons burthen. She had come from Batavia, and was going to Mocha, with a light cargo. She had a poop and stern cabin, which occupied the whole breadth of the ship, with a bathroom attached. In front, the cuddy and two cabins—one for the captain, the other for our Armenian fellow-passenger, who, fortunately, spoke Arabic like a native.

We found our servants very willing to go with us, and we laid in our stock of provisions, live stock and liquors, not forgetting abundance of bottled water, several goats, two small tents, carpets and rugs.

Some of our friends thought us very rash, but I argued if a vessel could come safely from Java, she could go to Mocha with a dead fair wind, and we felt no alarm. So early in January [1] we sailed out of the harbour, all things promising us a fair voyage.

. Les temples monolithes du milieu étaient polychromes, eux aussi, en leur temps; des nuances comme on en voit à Thèbes ou à Memphis, des blancs, des rouges, des ocres jaunes y persistent encore aux places abritées.'

Mr. Bernhard Berenson has written to me of the frescoes at Ajanta as constituting 'India's greatest pictorial achievement'. He adds: 'I have a weakness for Indian art before say 1200. Since then it has gone from bad to worse, and fallen at last into the lowest degradations of pornography.'

[1] 1838.

MACAULAY AT OOTY

By Sir George Otto Trevelyan, Bart., O.M.

. . By the evening of the 24th June [1834] he was once more on the road; and, about noon on the following day, he began to ascend the Neilgherries, through scenery which, for the benefit of readers who had never seen the Pyrenees or the Italian slopes of an Alpine pass, he likened to 'the vegetation of Windsor Forest, or Blenheim, spread over the mountains of Cumberland'. After reaching the summit of the tableland, he passed through a wilderness where for eighteen miles together he met nothing more human than a monkey, until a turn of the road disclosed the pleasant surprise of an amphitheatre of green hills encircling a small lake, whose banks were dotted with red-tiled cottages surrounding a pretty Gothic church. The whole station presented 'very much the look of a rising English watering-place. The largest house is occupied by the Governor-General. It is a spacious and handsome building of stone. To this I was carried, and immediately ushered into his Lordship's presence. I found him sitting by a fire in a carpeted library. He received me with the greatest kindness, frankness, and hospitality. He is, as far as I can yet judge, all that I have heard; that is, rectitude, openness, and good-nature personified.' Many months of close friendship and common labours did but confirm Macaulay in this first view of Lord William Bentinck.

'You need not get your map to see where Ootacamund is: for it has not found its way into the maps. It is a new discovery; a place to which Europeans resort for their health, or, as it is called by the Company's servants,—blessings on their learning—a sanaterion. It lies at the height of 7,000 feet above the sea. My bed is heaped with blankets, and my black servants are coughing. I travelled the whole four hundred miles between this and Madras on men's shoulders. I had an agreeable journey on the whole. . . .

'I am very comfortable here. The Governor-General is the frankest and best-natured of men. The chief functionaries, who have attended him hither, are clever people, but not exactly on a par as to general attainments with the society to which I belonged in London. I thought, however, even at Madras, that I could have formed a very agreeable circle of acquaintances; and I am assured that at Calcutta I shall find things far better. After all, the best rule in all parts of the world, as in London itself, is to be independent of other people's minds.'

'If I live, I shall get rich fast. . . . At Christmas I shall send home a thousand, or twelve hundred, pounds for my father, and you all. I cannot tell you what a comfort it is to me to find that I shall be able to do this. It reconciles me to all the pains—acute enough, sometimes, God knows—of banishment.'

The months of July and August Macaulay spent on the Neilgherries, in a climate equable as Madeira and invigorating as Braemar; where thickets of rhododendron fill the glades and clothe the ridges; and where the air is heavy with the scent of rose-trees of a size more fitted for an orchard than a flower-bed, and bushes of heliotrope thirty paces round. The glories of the forests and of the gardens touched him in spite of his profound botanical ignorance, and he dilates more than once upon his 'cottage buried in laburnums, or something very like them, and geraniums which grow in the open air'. He had the more leisure for the natural beauties of the place, as there was not much else to interest even a traveller fresh from England. . . .

Unfortunately Macaulay's stay on the Neilgherries coincided with the monsoon. 'The rain streamed down in floods. It was very seldom that I could see a hundred yards in front of me. During a month together I did not get two hours' walking.' He began to be bored, for the first and last time in his life; while his companions, who had not his resources, were ready to hang themselves for very dulness. The ordinary amusements with which, in the more settled parts of India, our countrymen beguile the rainy season, were wanting in a settlement that had only lately been reclaimed from the desert; in the immediate vicinity of which you still ran the chance of being 'trod into the shape of half a crown by a wild elephant, or eaten by the tigers, which prefer this situation to the plains below for the same reason that takes so many Europeans to India; they encounter an uncongenial climate for the sake of what they can get'. There were no books in the place except those that Macaulay had brought with him, among which, most luckily, was *Clarissa Harlowe*. Aided by the rain outside, he soon talked his favourite romance into general favour. . . .

'When I was in India I passed one hot season in the Hills; and there were the Governor-General, and the Secretary of Government, and the Commander-in-Chief, and their wives. I had *Clarissa* with me; and, as soon as they began to read, the whole station was in a passion of excitement about Miss Harlowe, and her misfortunes, and her scoundrelly Lovelace. The Governor's wife seized the book; the Secretary waited for it; the Chief Justice could not read it for tears.'

An old Scotch doctor, a Jacobin and a free-thinker, who could only be got to attend church by the positive orders of the Governor-General, cried over the last volume until he was too ill to appear at dinner. The Chief Secretary—afterwards, as Sir William Macnaughten, the hero and the victim of the darkest episode in our Indian history,—declared that reading this copy of *Clarissa*, under the inspiration of its owner's enthusiasm, was nothing less than an epoch in his life. After the lapse of thirty years . . . the tradition of Macaulay and his novel still lingered on with a tenacity most unusual in the ever-shifting society of an Indian station.—*Life and Letters of Lord Macaulay*, chapter vi.

I never shall forget the three months I passed at Ooty in 1863. I used to think that looking down on the plains, stewing below, must have been like looking down from the floating island in the account of Laputa by Gulliver (*Letter to Editor*).

CHAPTER V

1838

I AWOKE the next morning and went early on deck. How delicious it was, the cool pleasant breeze and the ship rolling lazily along under her enormous sail! The captain, mate, and some others were on the poop, and I was greeted with a general 'salaam aliekoom', which I returned, Arab fashion, and we all sat down. Presently the captain's breakfast was brought, rice and fried fish. 'Bismilla, sit down with us,' cried he; 'here we are all one, Arabs and Christians. Thank God! we have got away from those Kafirs of Bombay, who were no better than Hindus! Come, sir, and eat with us.'[1] I did eat heartily, and found the viands very good indeed.

[1] A fascinating monograph might be written, by one with sufficient knowledge of the subject, upon the interactions of Hinduism and Islam. Some of these have taken forms surpassingly strange—none stranger than the devotion to Bhavani on the part of Mohammedan Thugs during at least several centuries. This has been already touched upon in a note on the Dasara festival. In the *Thug* Ameer Ali's sympathetic adoptive father delightfully expounds the muddle which had been made of two faiths. 'I am a Thug, a member of that glorious profession which has been transmitted from the remotest periods, to the few selected by Alla for his unerring purposes. In it, the Hindoo and the Moslim both unite as brothers: among them bad faith is never known: a sure proof, that our calling is blessed and sanctioned by the divine authority. . . . Besides, it is Fate,—the decree of the blessed Alla! and who can withstand it?'

On another occasion Ismail instructs his son as to the origin of 'our profession, which is intimately connected with the faith of the Hindoos, and by whom we Moosulmans have been instructed in the art of Thuggee'. 'This is wonderful; how do you reconcile any connexion between the faith of unbelievers and that of the blessed Prophet?' 'I cannot pretend to solve the difficulty; but as their religion is far more ancient than ours, and no doubt had a divine origin, there are many points in

At noon the mate, to my surprise, brought out a sextant, took the sun's altitude, and worked it out in English figures. He had three chronometers for longitude, and said he would take a lunar for correction in a day or two. All seemed so perfectly regular—for I had checked the calculations—that I was quite satisfied we could come to no harm through bad navigation. We had plenty of air and room, our own servants, and in our Armenian fellow-passenger an intelligent, agreeable companion. He had brought with him large stores of

---

it which one of the true faith may follow without offence, so that he does not join them in all their forms and professions. Indeed this is impossible, as no one can become a Hindoo [only partly true]; but, as I told you before, Thuggee is one of the means by which Alla works out his own ends,' etc.

In the exchange between the creeds the elder, the more intellectual and literate faith has given stronger impressions than it has received. To be sure the veiling of women, nowhere indigenous in India, was adopted in some parts. On the other hand, the Indian reverence for animal life has influenced both Parsis and Mohammedans, so far as to preserve the curs of Constantinople. Vishnu has been confounded to some degree with the Imams. And many Indian Musalmans claim to observe some sort of caste, which would prevent their sitting down, at least under observation, to eat with Europeans.

This point of commensality, of being able to eat together, counts for almost everything in the way of good fellowship and of social intimacy. It makes it possible to chum up with fellow-travellers in a way that Englishmen have always enjoyed doing with Turks and Arabs, and to a lesser degree in India.

Even to the spellings of names, I have not meddled with the descriptions which follow of Arabia and of Egypt—lands outside Meadows Taylor's beat, and singularly inferior to India in originality, in variety, in true charm, to say nothing of size. Egypt, nearer to Europe, enjoyed better material conditions than India eighty years ago: Taylor notes that the temples were better built, the dancing girls more accomplished, and remarks on the apparently lavish scale of living among the people. Here again commensality came in to assist intercourse. Save for the ophthalmia, things seemed to conspire to give an enchanted time of rest and change to Captain Taylor, not yet thirty, jaded with the thirteen years of his first stay in India, carrying home with him his first and most brilliant novel. There even seem signs of that unique thing, a cultus of the Red Sea. But by his return voyage the happy balance of circumstances had vanished, and he writes: 'To Suez, down the Red Sea, always hot and uncomfortable'.

In the September of 1838, at the opening of which year Taylor sailed upon his three years' furlough, his future master for a dozen years, General James Stuart Fraser, entered upon his unprecedented period of fourteen years as Resident at Hyderabad.

Armenian beef, which was delicious, and is prepared in this wise.

'Take pieces of lean, but good juicy beef, two or three cubic inches in size, boil them partially, then rub in salt, pepper, and a *soupçon* of onion. Fry in melted butter, or lard, or oil. Put loosely into jars, and pour boiling water over all till the jar is full. The beef will keep for years if closely covered.'

Altogether it was like travelling in one's own yacht, and was most enjoyable. I had told the captain that I belonged to H.H. the Nizam's service, and knew all the Arab sirdars of his court—Abdula ben Ali, Umr ben Uz, and others—and he said I should find their names very useful to me on my journey.

We sailed past Cape Partak, with its grand bold precipices descending into the sea, and its perpetually varying colours and tints. Then headland after headland, all of the same bold type, succeeded, until we cast anchor not far from shore opposite the town of Shahar.

Presently the sheikh left the fort, and his procession looked very gay as it wound down to the beach, where several boats were waiting; they then put off with slow, measured stroke, the rowers singing in chorus as they approached our vessel. The sheikh, a fine old man, courteously invited us on shore and made us welcome. My wife was carried off to the women's apartments, and I conversed with our host, gravely smoking *nargailés* (water pipes) and sipping coffee the while. In the evening he took us to his garden without the town, and after that more pipes and more coffee, till the sun went down, when one of the men cried the invocation to prayer: carpets were spread, and all present performed their devotions. We then took our leave and returned to the ship, the starlight being more brilliant than I ever remember seeing it before. We continued our voyage next day, having landed our cargo and halted at Macullah. This proved a very picturesque and curious place, lying at the foot of huge mountains dipping into the sea. We went ashore, but the sheikh here was surly and indifferent, and after pipes and coffee we took our leave. The captain told us the sheikh was in a bad humour about the 'Aden affair', and we should soon find out all about it at

Aden, which we reached in due time, casting anchor in the back harbour as the sun was setting.[1]

'I do not see any English ships,' said the captain; 'I wonder there are not some here.'

Next morning he and I landed, and took donkeys to ride into the town. When we came to the barrier fortifications, the guard at the gates refused to let us pass, but eventually allowed us to sit in the guard-room till permission should be obtained from the sheikh for our entrance.

The sheikh himself soon appeared, followed by a numerous company, and sitting down ordered pipes and coffee. I did not like his look or that of his people, who swaggered about stroking their moustaches in a very Hyderabad fashion. I was not noticed; and in a conversation which ensued between the sheikh and our captain, I saw the face of the latter become very grave, and my Arab servant, as he handed me some coffee, stooped down and whispered, 'You must get back quickly or they will seize you.' This was not a pleasant prospect, as the gate was closed and resistance would have been hopeless. I could not understand a word of what was going on. At last I heard 'Nizam' and 'Abdula ben Ali', occurring in the wrangle; and after a while the captain told me I might go, and with a smile the sheikh offered me his hand and bade me 'depart in peace'.

[1] There is need to say little about this 'peninsula, isthmus, and fortified town' on the southern coast of Yemen, well known as a part of the Bombay Presidency. According to the *Imperial Gazetteer* the total area is 80 square miles, the population 44,000. 'It is a well-ascertained fact that long residence impairs the faculties and undermines the constitution of Europeans, and even natives of India suffer from the effects.' But a few further extracts will show into what a pretty kettle of fish Captain Taylor fell, sailing from Bombay just when he did.

'In 1829 the Court of Directors thought of making it [Aden] a coaling station, but abandoned the idea owing to the difficulty of procuring labour. . The chief soon afterwards committed an outrage on the passengers and crew of a British buggalow wrecked in the neighbourhood; and in *January, 1838*, Captain Haines, on behalf of the Government of Bombay, demanded restitution. It was arranged that the peninsula should be ceded for a consideration to the British. But various acts of treachery supervened; and it was captured in January, 1839 . . . the first accession of territory in the reign of Queen Victoria.'

'Go at once,' said the captain. 'I will tell you all afterwards.'

You may be sure I was only too thankful to make my way back to the ship, and I learned afterwards that my being in the Nizam's service and knowing two of his Arab chieftains intimately, had alone saved me from a very unpleasant detention. The English, said the sheikh, had been intriguing with a member of his family to get possession of the place, and he disapproved of the whole transaction. The English had fired from their ships and killed many people, and he had determined to keep me in irons till an indemnity had been paid.

What an escape I had had! The people were much excited, and but for my Hyderabad friends, I had a poor chance of getting away. I was indeed very very thankful for the great mercy shown to me, and we were heartily glad when the captain weighed anchor and we left the dreary rock behind us.

We continued our voyage to Mocha, where we parted company with our good captain, who transferred us to another Arab vessel commanded by a friend of his, Salim ben Ahmed, son of a rich merchant at Jeddah. At Mocha I found an English agency house, and some officers of the Indian Navy, who scarcely believed that I had visited Aden and had got out of it again. I had been in the greatest danger, for, as soon as a force could be sent, Aden was to be attacked, and my life would surely have been forfeited.

Our new captain was anxious to proceed. We were to sail inside the reefs in smooth water, by day only. It was strange work threading our way in and out of the reefs. The weather was delicious, and every evening we made for some rocky island and were moored to it for the night. We often, in the evenings, took the boat and went out among the islands, occasionally landing to collect the lovely shells which abounded, or we took out our lines to fish, and were generally very successful. Such strange creatures we fished up! Such varied forms and brilliant colours! I began to make a collection of drawings of them, which I afterwards exhibited at the meeting of the British Association at Newcastle-on-Tyne, and eventually presented to the Linnæan Society, for which I received the distinction of being elected an honorary member.

The beauty of the beds of coral on these still evenings was indescribable: they were like huge beds of flowers—pink, red, emerald, yellow, and purple, mingled with grey and brown; and the extraordinary clearness of the water gave us a feeling of hanging in the air which was very strange. We were really sorry when we neared Jeddah, and cast anchor in the harbour. Salim and I had concocted a scheme that I was to leave my wife at his house at Jeddah under the care of his mother, while he and I went to Mecca to see the *haj* (pilgrimage). 'No one will recognise you,' he said; 'you are browner than I am, and I will lend you clothes: we shall do the journey in the night.' So we landed, and next day we were to start. We had, we thought, kept the secret safe; but it had leaked out somehow, and our consul at Jeddah came to me and told me the Pacha had sent for him, and asked him whether I was going to Mecca.

'He will be in danger without a firman from the Sultan, tell him,' said the Pacha, 'and I cannot give one.'

'You had better come and tell the Pacha you will give it up,' said the consul, 'for the gates will now be carefully watched, and you are not safe.'

I saw there was no use resisting, and very reluctantly I went to the Pacha. He laughed heartily when I assured him I would not go, and answered in French—

'I do not care, but others do, and your life would be in peril.'

An English ship lay at anchor in the harbour, and proved to belong to Messrs. Palmer of Calcutta, my wife's relations.[1]

[1] Mrs. Meadows Taylor's uncle, John Palmer, 1767–1836, was only two years dead. He it was who was styled in his day the 'Prince of British merchants', and on his tomb 'the friend of the poor', his bust also standing in the Calcutta town hall. His name was brought up at the opening of 1917 by the death, at a great age, of his grandson, Sir Charles Parry Hobhouse, third baronet, born in Calcutta, January 2, 1825. John Palmer was a much older brother of Taylor's invariably stimulating and beloved father-in-law at Hyderabad. Mr. Buckland, who gives no authorities, but who is priceless upon many an occasion such as this, says that John Palmer left the Navy in 1783 and joined the firm of Burgh, Barber & Co., becoming sole manager as Palmer & Co. 'He had great public spirit, and gave his support to J. S. Buckingham' in a notable contest for the liberty of the press the year before Taylor reached India, but with which he expresses sympathy in his *History.* Palmer died, 'universally respected and regretted', January 21, 1836.

The captain insisted on our coming at once on board, and we lived there most luxuriously for nearly a month. I had little hope of getting on to Suez during the *haj*, and our good friend, Captain Hill, offered to send us on to Tor, at the entrance of the Gulf of Akaba, in the beautiful long-boat, in which a cabin could easily be rigged up by awnings, and which would be under the command of the boatswain; but this plan was frustrated by Captain Hill receiving orders to return sooner than he expected, and the long-boat would not have time to rejoin the ship.

I heard of a good *buggalow* about to sail for Suez. We took our passages in her, and left our kind friends with regret. We intended to land at Tor, go to Mount Sinai, and thence to Jerusalem for Easter.

The morning we sailed I awoke hearing an unusual shuffling of feet and a buzz of many voices. On going on deck, to my horror I found it and the poop both crowded with pilgrims from Mecca, who, the captain said, had been sent on board by order of the Pacha.

In vain I remonstrated, representing that I had taken the whole poop. The captain would or could do nothing, and I told him I should appeal to the authorities at Yembo for redress. On arriving there, I sent my servant to the Pacha, requesting him to come and see the plight we were in. Men and women constantly intruding into our cabin, a frightful crowd, the effluvia and vermin from which were sickening, and quite impossible to describe; added to this, we suffered terrible abuse for being 'infidels', and my wife was afraid to leave her cabin.

The pilgrims lived mostly on dry biscuit, and very pungent bitter cheese. Few only had the privilege of cooking any food; and I very much feared that some frightful epidemic would break out among them soon.

At length a Kavas, one of the Pacha's messengers, arrived, with the servant that I had sent before; he brought a kind message from his master, entreating us to come ashore at once. This was impossible, as we durst not leave our baggage; but the Kavas carried off our captain, who was in a terrible fright, and then returned with a handsome boat belonging to the Pacha, and orders to take us and all our belongings to a

Government vessel, where, he said, the Pacha would meet us in the morning. We were not long in complying with this civility; we once more breathed the fresh air, and the last I saw of the vessel was a scramble among the crowd to get near our cabin and flock into it.

Next morning the Pacha visited us, accompanied by his secretary and staff. He was dressed beautifully, in a costume made of fine brown cloth, with a profusion of braiding of a darker shade of the same colour, and had several decorations on his breast. He spoke French with fluency, and a little English, and nothing could exceed his courtesy and kindness. 'I am afraid to treat this rascal as he deserves,' he said. 'If I had the power, I would have bastinadoed him severely; but he belongs to the English agent at Suez, and I dare not; but I can at least release you from your present uncomfortable position. I will put a crew and Reis on whom you may depend on board this vessel, and you can dismiss them whenever you please. All you have to do is to give them their wages and food, which amount to very little. Take the ship to Tor, and if the wind is against you, you can take her on to Kosseir.' I accepted his kindness most gratefully. That afternoon our new Reis arrived, and early next morning we left Yembo with a handsome present of dates, Turkish sweetmeats, and new live-stock, fodder for our goats, and all we needed, from our kind friend.

I was now my own commander, with a crew of twenty-four men and a pilot. I could go where I pleased, and the Reis proved a good navigator. Yembo, from the sea, was the handsomest Arab town I had yet seen. It is built on the margin of the shore, up a rising ground, and the lines of whitewashed houses had a pretty effect. This town is the port of Medina, and the residence of the provincial governor, and there seemed to be a good number of Turkish troops stationed there. We gave passages, at their earnest solicitation, to a Turk and his wife, who had been with us on our former ship. He was old, and in bad health, and their state was really pitiable. His wife promised to be useful, and proved eminently so during our voyage.

We had a delicious sail up to Tor, between the reefs and the mainland, and at night we made fast to one of the islands, or cast anchor in shallow water, and then went off in the boat seeking endless treasures in shells, fish, and coral. The colours of the shallows seemed to grow more intense and vivid—of all shades, from the deepest violet and purple blue, to the most brilliant turquoise, emerald green, and red; and as we threaded the often narrow channels the effects were charming. The coast up to Yembo had been comparatively flat and uninteresting, but from thence it grew much bolder in character. Fine headlands were seen in front of us dipping into the sea, and the voyage increased each day in interest, till at length the rocky peaks and precipices of the Jebel Antar range stood out before us, and behind them lay the Gulf of Akaba. In this portion of our little voyage the scenery was very striking, and the atmospheric effects wonderful, as the sun ran its course, and the shadows of the peaks and ravines changed till all was merged in a soft violet tint as evening closed in. We were alone; we saw no fishing-boats or other craft, no sign of dwelling or life upon the shore, which looked utterly desolate and barren in its grandeur. Very grand, too, is the mouth of the Gulf of Akaba, with the range of Jebel Antar to the south, and the far more lofty and imposing mountains of the Peninsula of Sinai to the north. The gulf itself was like a large lake shimmering in the mid-day sun as we entered it, the ranges of mountains on either side being veiled in lovely violet mist.

Very soon the little town of Tor lay before us, and as we anchored, and hoisted our English flag, a boat put off with one likewise flying at her stern; and we found our visitor was the secretary to the English agent, who brought his chief's compliments, and asked what he could do for us.

We ordered pipes and coffee, and sat down to talk.

'If this wind holds', said our friend, 'you can go on to Suez; but if a *shimal* or north wind blows, you may be kept here for a fortnight; the sea is dangerous then for your small vessel.'

'And Akaba?' I asked.

'Impossible,' he answered; 'even the Sultan's firman is at present useless. The Arabs are fighting, and the passes quite closed. You must give up that idea.'

'Well, then, can we get to Mount Sinai, and to Jerusalem?'

'I fear not,' he replied; 'but I will go on shore and ask the sheikh. Perhaps you will come with me?' and I went.

The old English agent was very civil, ordered pipes and coffee, and we proceeded to discuss the business, the Arab chiefs having come in.

'You could only do it by yourself,' they said; 'we could not carry you there with the lady: you would not fear a few shots if you were alone. Have you a firman from the Sultan?'

'No,' I said; 'only a passport from the Bombay Government.'

'Ah!' said they all, 'that is of no use; we could not be responsible for any Englishman without one from Constantinople.'

So Sinai was given up, and a *shimal* coming on, the Reis said we could not stay where we were; there was no use in staying—the wind would soon moderate, and we could cross over to Kosseir very quickly and safely. So next morning we started with a fresh cool breeze, and we had, at least, the whole of Egypt before us, and the sights that we had to see would be ample compensation for our disappointment.

Our voyage was most propitious; we reached Kosseir very quickly, without touching a rope. On our arrival we found no difficulty in procuring camels; and my servant Abdula, who had been there before, and knew several of the principal people, was a great help to me. We remained on board our ship till all our preparations were complete, and our tents pitched under some date-trees near the town. Then we landed, and walked through the place, once the ancient Berenice, with no trace left now of its former greatness, except the ruins which lay on either hand.

No accommodation for my wife's journey could be devised, except large *kajawas* or panniers, slung upon a huge camel, with an awning above to keep off the sun; and with soft bedding these were made endurable enough. For myself, I had a camel, and two donkeys in reserve. The Turk rode a donkey, and his wife a camel, on which were all their worldly goods.

So we set out on our first march into the desert which lies between Kosseir and Kench, the old beaten track of Egyptian, Greek, and Roman traders, each in their turn through ages of the past. My previous idea of a desert was that it would be flat and sandy, but instead our road lay through a hollow, with considerable hills on either side, affording striking and pretty views at every turn. Here and there the valleys were very narrow, and high precipices towered on either hand. Again they widened into lateral ravines, which seemed interminable. In many places the rocks had Egyptian, Greek, or Roman characters carved upon them. Does any one know of these, and of their purport ? [1]

It was not very hot, for the north wind blew cool and fresh, and we could travel all day. I had never left my camel, and towards evening became very tired. I lay down on some warm sand near our tents, and gradually stiffened, to the great alarm of my wife ; but my servant and the camel-men said they would soon cure me. I was turned on my face, and my back rubbed with castor-oil well heated. By this time some large cakes of *dhoura* meal had been prepared and partly baked, and these smeared with oil were bound on my back, the whole length of the spine, and partially covering my ribs. They were almost too hot to bear, but I obeyed orders, and allowed myself to be swathed up like a mummy. Next morning, to my great delight, I had neither pain nor ache ; the remedy, rough though it was, had been effectual.

On the fourth morning we met some men driving camels, and carrying water-melons on their heads—how refreshing they were ! I think I see now our old Turk, whose lips were much chapped by the dry wind, sitting on a stone, intensely appreciative of the large slice I handed to him. A few miles

[1] Though not attempting to annotate the Egyptian journey, it struck me how well it would be if this one question, and another about the good physician who saved Taylor's eyesight at Cairo a few weeks later, could be answered by the first living authority. And here is what Dr. W. M. Flinders Petrie has kindly contributed. I have not consulted the work mentioned, which is out of my reach.

'The Qeneh-Qosseyr road is always known in archaeology as the Wady Hammamat. The inscriptions are of various ages, and have been often published, the most complete record being by J. Couyat and P. Montet, 1914, in *Memoirs of the French Institute of Oriental Archaeology*. This deals with the Egyptian writings, and the later ones have not been completely collected.

'I have not many details about Dr. Abbott. He was American, I believe, but died long before I went out in 1880, I believe before 1864.'

further, from the crest of the pass, we had our first look at Egypt.

It was very beautiful; the cultivation reached nearly to the foot of the descent, of a vivid green, and most luxuriant; wheat, barley, pulse, cotton, and sugar-cane, with fields of yellow and blue lupins in flower, patches of crimson clover, with date-trees, and sycamore, and our Indian *babul,* or mimosa, everywhere.

My Hindu servant cried out, excitedly, 'India! again India! are we come back to it?' No, it was not India certainly, but it was inexpressibly lovely; and our hearts were full of gratitude to God for His goodness in bringing us so far in health and safety. No more rough travelling, no more privation; but instead, a sojourn among glorious scenes of antiquity and beauty which we had longed to see.

A few miles more and we had reached Keneh, which seemed exactly like an Indian (Deccan) town, with its clay-roofed terraced houses; and we were taken at once to the house of the English agent, who placed very comfortable rooms at our disposal, and took all the trouble of dismissing my camel-men off my hands.

The house was scrupulously clean, and our friend's wife was a first-rate cook. I remember two dishes in particular—one of quails, fried somehow in vine-leaves, and another of long cucumbers, stuffed with delicately-flavoured mince-meat—that would have satisfied much daintier palates than ours. We often wished to be able to converse with our host, who was a Copt, apparently a merchant, in good circumstances; but the only mode of communication was Italian, of which he knew a very little, so we did not make much progress.

I had some pleasant shooting—quail were plentiful, and I found snipe, too, in the little swamps, so that my bag was generally a good one. One day we sent out our tents a little distance from the town, and had a picnic, spending a quiet, dreamy day under the shade, enjoying the delicious cool wind, the great river flowing past us, and the peaceful scenery beyond. 'You must see Dendera to-morrow,' said our host; and we went, crossing by a ferry-boat, and finding donkeys waiting for us on the other side. We breakfasted at the vestibule of the temple, and then set to work to examine it, and the old Roman town beyond it. My servant declared we must be in India, because there was a real Hindu temple; but the temple of Dendera was more imposing than any I had ever seen, and its grand proportions, at first not easily understood, grew upon one hour by hour. The roof is covered with names, modern and ancient; Greek, Roman, Egyptian, and Arab, as well as every European nation, has its record of the 'John Smith' of the inscriber, and I added mine to the number.

The Roman town interested me very much; for not only were the narrow streets clearly defined, but some of the houses and walls, which were nearly perfect, and the round arches, though built only of sun-dried bricks cemented with mud, remained as they had been first erected, perhaps two thousand years before. We left the place with regret, grim and desolate though it was. The temple looked very grand in the evening light. No rain falls here, which accounts for the preservation of mud walls and arches. No rain for 2000 years—can one realise it?

We had seen all the sights, our clothes had been washed, our boat was ready—a small *dahabieh*, very clean and comfortable—our luggage was stowed away on board; but what were we to do with our Turk and his wife? He was very feeble, and she was of great use to us, so they were allowed a corner on board; and we bade farewell to our kind friends, who gently declined any recompense, until at length I bethought myself of my small tents, which I offered them, and which were gratefully accepted. On our arrival at the river, we came upon an Arab woman frying pancakes and omelets for the boatmen. The woman had good fresh butter, and the smell was very appetising; so we sat down and had our meal of the pancakes and omelet, with salad and hard-boiled eggs, and ate till we could eat no more. How good it was!

Our intention was to go up to Assouan and Philæ, then return and stay a while at Thebes, and so go down to Cairo. If the *shimal* lasted, we should run up to Thebes very fast. If we lost it, we might have varying winds; but not a *khamsin* for a good while. It seemed a very pleasant programme: we should see all the wonders of Egypt, we should sit in the gate of Ethiopia; and as our boat was very light, there was no fear of the Cataract.

The Nile is far better known now than it was in those days—drawings, engravings, paintings, and photographs have been made of the scenes along its banks, and are familiar in England to all, so that any description of mine from memory now, would, I fear, be incomplete and tiresome. Yet there are some scenes which can never fade or change as long as memory lasts. Who that has seen them could forget the granite quarries above Thebes, with the blocks of granite split from the native rock ready for transmission down the river? or cease to wonder at the means of transport and erection? Who can forget the grandeur of the giant figures of Abu Simbel, or the perfect temple at Edfu? Above all, who can forget the wild scenery of the Cataract and Assouan—the shouts during the ascent amid the seething waters; or the welcome change to the placid pool above, with exquisite Philæ beyond, sitting a queen indeed upon the waters, glowing in the bright sunlight?

We stayed at Philæ for five days, living in the temple during the day, and sleeping on board our boat at night; and our enjoyment was intense. English visitors were rare then, and many boat-loads of natives came alongside to have a look at us, and bring us presents. I think, among all the many scenes which rise in my memory as I write, that those evenings spent at Philæ were the most beautiful, when the still, long pool reflected the brilliant tints of the sky, among the dark basalt rocks, till all faded into dim grey; and the moon, near the full, cast over all a flood of silver light, and the temple, the ruins, and the feathery palms were bathed in it, till they seemed hardly of this world, and we sat on and watched the stars appearing, one by one, and drinking in the strange 'eerie' beauty around us. If there is a place on earth where one's heart swells, and one's throat seems to tighten, it is Philæ.

Back again to Thebes, very pleasantly. Our crew were hard-working, good-humoured fellows, full of fun of one kind or another, singing merrily to their oars when the sails could not be used, and their voices sounded mellow and sweet in the choruses. No doubt there is monotony in Nile boat-life, and yet it is very pleasant, and very restful. If I pleased, I could go ashore and have a day's shooting. My crew delighted in acting as beaters, and game was plentiful enough. Frequently we received presents from the chief man of the village—sour milk, the same as in India, live pigeons, vegetables, melons, or anything he thought might be of use to us; and he would beg in return a little English powder for firing, or a pencil, or a little tea. Sometimes I accepted an invitation for the evening, and smoked my pipe and drank coffee with the village elders, longing always to be able to talk to them without an interpreter.

They were much interested in India, and I had to answer many questions about its people and religion. I enjoyed these homely, but to me very interesting, meetings exceedingly; and I read in after-days, with deep interest, the story of her life in Egypt, so touchingly described by my cousin, Lady Duff-Gordon, in her delightful letters, and was able to feel how real and true are her descriptions.

We remained at Thebes, I think, a fortnight, visiting all the places of interest, and especially the ruins of Karnak, where I made many elaborate sketches, now, alas! lost. We crossed the river to the Memnonian Palace, part of which we had swept out for our abode. We were close to the great sitting statues, and could watch them at all times of the day, and in all the changing lights. In the morning and evening nothing can exceed their grim, uncouth grandeur. How they were brought from the quarries, how erected, who can say? One can but look and wonder!

Of course, too, we visited the tombs of the kings. I need not enlarge upon them, or on the interesting fresco-paintings which illustrate not only the costume and customs of ancient Egypt completely, but also its wars and processions, the employment of the Jews during their captivity in making bricks, helping to drag large building-stones, and the like—the Jewish features being always discernible. The passages were hot and stifling, full of bats, and the smell of the castor-oil lamps almost unendurable; but we persevered, and saw all there was to see, enjoying our return into the cool fresh air afterwards.

'Should we like to have one of the tombs on the hillside above us opened,' asked Abdula; 'the Arabs were willing, if we wished, to open one for a certain amount of *bakshish*.'

I agreed at once, and next evening they returned with many curious objects: a chair, perfect except for its rush bottom, which had decayed; a necklace of beads the colour of turquoise; several scarabei, and small blue enamel figures; the best of all, two most elegant terra-cotta boats, one of which had good, well-modelled figures at stem and stern, and an altar in the centre of the boat, at which a priest was offering. There were also some mummies of ibis, one of a small crocodile, and another which seemed to be a cat. They had likewise picked up a woman's mummied hand and part of an arm; the hand was plump and beautiful in shape. The boats, and two of the scarabei, when examined at the British Museum, were found valuable, as they proved the establishment of different kings, filling up gaps in one of the dynasties; and I received, I think, £47 for them. All the minor articles I gave to Dr. Abbott, the famous collector at Cairo, for his museum.

The north wind had moderated very much, and we were anxious now to get on. We stayed a day or two at Keneh with our old host and hostess, who would take no denial. A fantasia of dancing-girls was to come off in my honour: I had never seen one, and was curious to see what the Alimeh of Egypt were like. Certainly their dancing, or rather posturing, was very strange, some of it both elegant and spirited, as they twisted scarfs about each other, and waved their arms and bodies in time to the music. It had an almost mesmeric effect upon me. Again, nothing could be wilder than some of their rapid movements, appearing to lose all consciousness of self in their ever-varying gestures. Their singing was wild and plaintive by turns, but it did not interest me, as Egyptian music is very monotonous, the chief aim apparently being to produce long, high, quavering notes, which received due applause from the bystanders. Their costume was rich and good; far more elegant, as were also their performances, than those of Indian nautch girls. They wore necklaces and bracelets in profusion of what appeared to be gold. I saw nothing indelicate or indecent in what they did during the whole performance.

Laden with gifts from our kind friends, of flour, eggs, semolina, vegetables, sour milk, and fresh bread, we re-entered our boat, and started again down the river. There was not much variety in the scenery, but it was very pleasant, and the tall sails of the Nile boats, both traders and *dahabiehs*, and the towns and villages which we passed, always formed pretty objects in the landscape.

We were still seven days from Cairo when I was attacked with ophthalmia in its worst form. The pain was horrible, and we were very thankful when we reached Cairo, where I was at once taken to the hotel, and put under the care of Dr. Abbott, through whose skill, under God's blessing, my eyes were saved; but he said another day's delay would have been fatal. I was quite blind for some time, and I can never forget the joy and thankfulness I felt when I saw again, though very dimly, my wife's dear face. With very great care I eventually recovered, but for a long time I appeared to be looking through milk-and-water with opal tints upon it. At Cairo, I was told by the English vice-consul that a long complaint had been laid against me by the owner of the *buggalow* from which I had been delivered at Yembo. I was accused of breach of faith, violence to the Reis of the vessel, and other misdemeanours; and the official was stiff in manner, and far from agreeable. I showed the decision of the Pacha at Yembo, which he forthwith entirely ignored. My copy of the agreement made at Jeddah, and signed by Mr. Ogilvie, was, however, very different to the one filed on the plaint and unauthenticated, and my friend began to doubt. 'Had I any witnesses?' he asked. I had only my servant and the old Turk, who were desired to proceed next day to the vice-consulate. Their account of the affair simplified the matter very much, and the vice-consul told me they gave evidence in no measured terms, and descriptions of our state which I dare not record; so the question was referred to the consul-general at Alexandria, and I promised to appear when called for. I was not allowed to go out, except with my eyes closely bandaged; but after some time we were given leave to prepare for our journey. A boat was engaged, and we left Cairo, the scene of so much suffering and so much mercy. As we rode on in the early evening after leaving Boulak, Cairo, with its groves, minarets, and domes, and its lofty citadel, with the rugged hills beyond it, was before us on one side. On the other, date-groves, villages, green fields, and the mysterious Pyramids in the distance, behind which the sun was setting, and a glory of crimson light-tinted clouds hung above them, and spread over the southern and eastern sky, reflected in the broad still river; and as the sun sank lower, the distance changed to the deepest violet, and at length a still misty grey veiled it from our eyes. What a picture it would have made!

On my arrival at Alexandria I was summoned to the consulate at once, and most courteously received. My affairs were under investigation, and the result was that all my passage-money was returned, and the owner of the *buggalow* fined into the bargain, and threatened as well with the loss of his agency if he ever attempted imposition again.

My cousin, Mr. Philip Taylor of Marseilles, was then inspector-in-chief of the 'Messageries Royales' steamers, and knowing I was on my way home, had desired the captain of the steamer then at Alexandria to inquire for me. Finding we had arrived, he very kindly sent off for our baggage, and when we went on board we found the best cabins reserved for us. We had to take leave of our faithful Turk and his wife; the latter clung to my wife, crying, 'Take me to England with you!' and refusing all payment. 'Why should you ask me to take money?' she said; 'I have plenty—my husband has plenty; why should you think of it?'

All I could persuade her to take was one of the Deccan goats. The other I gave to the mistress of the hotel at Alexandria; and when I returned on my way back to India it knew me again, and rubbed its head against me!

Off again,—to Smyrna first, in such luxury as we had long been strangers to—such delicious beds and sofas! such a cook! such excellent wine! and a captain who could never do enough to make us comfortable, and help to pass the time agreeably. We had English and French books on board, chess, piquet, and other games; but my great delight was to lie lazily watching the sea, to feel the delicious climate, and, as they express it in Indian idiom, to *eat* the air.

We ran across from Smyrna to Crete, coasting along its eastern shore to Syra, where we were to stop; threading our way among the islands before a balmy wind, through the Ægean Sea, now passing barren uninhabited rocks, again fertile islands, all combining to form sea-pictures of surpassing beauty. Leaving Syra, where I did not land, being satisfied with our captain's account of its dirty streets, and strange pyramid of terraced houses, which looked sufficiently picturesque from the sea, we bounded on past more islands, more headlands, those of the south of Italy being very grand; and so to Malta, where we were boarded by the officer of health, and carried away to the gloomy-looking quarantine lazaretto.

Here we had airy rooms, and a *guardiano* appointed to us as our sole attendant. As we had a clean bill of health we thought it very hard, but we had to submit to twenty-one days' detention nevertheless. Our *guardiano,* Michele, was a merry fellow, and did his best to cheer us.

'Did he know Mrs. Austin?' I asked; 'and was she still at Malta?'

'Who does not know that kind lady, who is as a mother to us all?' was the reply. 'Was I her brother?'

'No, her cousin,'[1] I said; 'and she will come and see

[1] A relative and friend worth having, 1793–1867. If Sarah Austin did not, as was believed, help Disraeli to write *Vivian Grey*, she secured the Clerkship of Appeals for her nephew Henry Reeve at twenty-four. And for the *Thug* she made better terms than Taylor could have done, saving him from having to publish in India, like Sleeman and Outram.

Mrs. Austin was a daughter of that Mrs. John Taylor (see pedigree) who has been described, in *Three Generations of English Women*, as 'darning her boys' grey worsted stockings while holding her own with Southey, Brougham or Mackintosh'. This Sarah Taylor married John Austin, 1790–1859, whose *Jurisprudence* is still used as a text-book. Her daughter Lucy, 1821–1869, wife of Sir A. C. Duff-Gordon, baronet, was author of the *Letters from Egypt* mentioned above. Like her mother, Lady Duff-Gordon translated much. The *Life of Henry Reeve* is full of the Austins, and the marriage of his cousin.

How did Mrs. Austin happen to be living in such a place as Malta? 'In 1836 Mr. Austin and Mr. Lewis were associated in a commission of inquiry into the affairs of Malta, where they resided for some time.' Memorial article on Sir George Cornewall Lewis in the *Edinburgh Review* for July 1863. One must see in this the hand of Henry Reeve, who succeeded Lewis as editor in 1855, and who was consulted by Lewis's family as to the publication of his writings. The best thing in the article is a selection from his letters, giving a picture of the Malta of that day. 'I have seen Hookham Frere, who found himself in Malta

us when she hears we have arrived'; and so she did, coming to the Parlatorio, which had a double iron grating, too distant one from the other for us even to shake hands. I told her how we had travelled, and what we had done, and she seemed wonderstruck that we had performed such a journey so well. I also confided to her about my book, *The Confessions of a Thug*. She was about to start for England, and asked me to give her my MS. to look over on her journey. I did so; but the three volumes were first scored through with knives, then smoked with sulphur till the ink turned pale, and finally delivered to her, by means of a pair of long tongs, through a narrow slit in the grating!

A few books had fortunately been left in our quarters by charitable predecessors; and with these and bathing, swimming about within the prescribed limits, our time passed somehow.

At length we were released, and took up our quarters in the town; but the glare was trying to my eyes, and the heat very great, as it was June, so we were not sorry to leave Malta, and embarked again, passing Etna, then Messina, where we stayed a few hours; and Stromboli, casting up its red-hot stones into the dark heavens answering Etna, whose illumined pillar of smoke towered grandly to the sky miles astern. On to Naples, where we were refused permission to land, owing to a dispute about port-dues between the French and Neapolitan Governments. So to Leghorn, and the lovely gulf of Spezia, and all the glorious beauty of the Riviera, till, finally, we arrived at Marseilles on the 3rd July, and were met by a hearty welcome from our relations.

One amusing incident occurred. I had two large jars of Indian preserved tobacco, and our captain assured me these would inevitably be confiscated. I had no wish to lose my tobacco, and was determined to pass it if I could. My panther and tiger skins were ruthlessly seized, to my great dismay,

---

fourteen years ago at his wife's death, and has forgotten to return to England. . . . The misery which prevails among the mass of the people is caused by the excess of their numbers,' then 120,000, since doubled. Lewis had attended Austin's lectures at London University. 'The vigour and clearness of Mr. Austin's mind acted powerfully on that of his pupil, and had, we have no doubt, great influence in forming his habits of thought.'

and I trembled for the precious jars. I wish I could give the conversation in the original French as it occurred.

'What is this ?' asked one of the *douaniers*, politely.

'Oh, taste it,' said another. 'I daresay it is a preserve.'

That gave me my cue.

'Yes, gentlemen,' I said, 'it is an Indian preserve that I have brought with me. Will you do me the favour to taste it ?'

'Is it sweet ?' asked one ; 'it has a strange smell,' and he sniffed at the open jar.

'Ah, yes,' said I—'peculiar, no doubt ; there are many strange things in India.'

'No doubt, sir—no doubt ; but is it sweet ?'

'Surely,' said I ; 'it is prepared with sugar and spices ; do try it.'

'Well,' he returned, 'here goes,' as he put in his forefinger, and swept out a good lump, which he put into his mouth.

Now if there can be anything more inconceivably nasty to the taste than another, it must be prepared Indian tobacco ; and the man, after sucking well at the lump, spat it out upon the floor with a volley of oaths, while the others stood round in fits of laughter.

'You do not seem to like it, sir,' I said, as gravely as I could ; 'but it was surely sweet ?'

'Sweet ! yes,' he cried ; 'the devil's sweetness ! Horrible ! horrible ! *sacre !* . . . horrible !'

'Perhaps', said I, looking round, 'some other gentleman would like to try it.'

'Is it hot ?' said one ; 'Indian things always burn one's mouth.'

'There is no pepper whatever in it,' I replied.

'And how do they eat it ?' asked another ; 'is it with bread-and-butter ?'

'Well,' I returned, 'there are many ways of using it—every one to his taste, you know.'

'Certainly, sir, certainly ; every country has its peculiar tastes ; may we try it ?'

'By all means,' I said.

Then there was a rush at the jar, and all put in their fingers and hooked up bits to taste. It was impossible not to laugh, and my cousins fairly roared at the scene that ensued, the *douaniers* spitting, spluttering, swearing, declaring the preserve only fit for the devil to eat, and getting rid of their quids as fast as they could; but one turned his head on one side, and said—

'Do you know, my friends, I rather like it? one would soon grow fond of it. May I take some home to my children?'

'Shut up the jars!' cried the chief, gruffly; 'let us have no more of such nonsense! Let them go to the devil! I beg your pardon, monsieur, but the taste will not leave my mouth—like rotten cabbage with sugar on it! Bah! we cannot charge duty on poison like that. Take it away!'

So I carried off my two jars in triumph.

We pushed on after a few days' stay at Marseilles, where for the first time in my life I saw and examined machinery of the highest interest. Mr. Philip Taylor had lately embarked in marine engineering work, as well as in the manufacture of powerful machines for oil-mills and the silk trade, and his comparatively small establishment grew rapidly into a large concern.[1]

[1] Meadows Taylor was never intimate with this branch of the family. But his cousin Philip Taylor, uncle to Henry Reeve, should have had an interesting life as a captain of industry in France. These are the only references to him, not merely scrappy, in Sir John Knox Laughton's *Memoirs of Henry Reeve.* In the early autumn of 1840 Reeve, with his mother, went by sea from Havre to Bordeaux. 'Thence through the south of France to Marseilles, where Mrs. Reeve remained, on a visit to her brother Philip, who, in 1836, had established some engineering works, which subsequently developed into the Société des Forges et Chantiers de la Méditerranée.'

In 1853 Reeve had an interesting talk with young Philip Meadows Taylor of Marseilles 'on the French steam navy, which it is the fashion here greatly to overrate. He says that they have no steamships really fit for war' save two; . . . 'that besides his own house, which Louis Napoleon has christened *Forges et Chantiers de la Méditerranée,* there are but two private establishments in France capable of turning out powerful engines, and neither of these is fully employed'. He introduced his cousin to Sir James Graham, then First Lord of the Admiralty under 'good old Aberdeen'. 'But he was more anxious to defend his own opinions and proceedings than to listen to P. Taylor's facts. . . . One takes a different impression from P. Taylor's account of his own workshops, in which he has, at Marseilles and at Toulon, some 1,500

We found the journey by diligence to Paris very fatiguing, and probably we suffered more than others from having led such a free open-air life, and the close cramped-up vehicle seemed stifling. However, Paris was reached at length, and after a few days' delay, spent mostly at the glorious Louvre, and also in refreshing our, by this time, very dilapidated wardrobes, we set off again, reaching London at last, after a weary night journey from Dover in the coach.

---

men, all bitterly hostile to the Emperor, and for the most part socialists.' Finally, in 1867 Reeve and his wife went from Geneva to Marseilles, where his uncle, a hale old man of eighty, was still living, with his wife, 'some seven years younger, and not at all old in figure, look, and voice'.

Miss Taylor believes that after the death of Philip Taylor and his sons the connection of the family with Marseilles and Toulon ceased. Descendants are living.

CHAPTER VI

1838–41

I RECEIVED an affectionate welcome from all the members of my family who were in London. I had left them a boy, and had entered on a life which was quite new and strange to them; and I think some were surprised to find I 'had the manners of a gentleman', as one remarked to me, 'and did not show traces of contact with the savage tribes of India!' nor could he be persuaded that the people among whom I had been living were highly civilised, and in many ways resembled ourselves. I determined not to speak of India unless I were asked direct questions, or to tell Indian stories, which might not be believed.

Mrs. Austin, to whom I had confided my precious MS. at Malta, had been much interested in its perusal, and kindly introduced me to Mr. Bentley,[1] in whose hands I left it; and to my infinite delight he eventually accepted it, and the agreement was duly executed. Thus one great wish of my life was to be fulfilled. I had hopes, too, of obtaining further literary employment, and as my long journey had been terribly expensive, and my means were slender enough, I looked forward to both pleasure and profit in my work.

I attended the meeting of the British Association held that year[2] at Newcastle-on-Tyne. I exhibited my drawings of Red Sea fish, but as I had no knowledge of ichthyology,

[1] Richard Bentley, 1794–1871, the brother and the father of publishers who are also in the *Dictionary of National Biography*.

[2] 1838. I have had to alter the dates at the top of the pages, which are most confusing in this chapter as printed in the original edition.

I could only explain the localities and circumstances in which I found them. As I have said, I gave them to the Linnæan Society, and was not a little proud when I was elected an honorary member. I paid a visit, too, to my uncle, Mr. Prideaux Selby, at Twizell, and was pleased to find the collection of birds and insects I had sent him from India in excellent preservation, and much appreciated by him.

We spent a happy time visiting among my dear mother's relations at Mitford, Twizell, and North Sunderland; and my book was going slowly through the press. My MS. proved too voluminous: much had to be curtailed and condensed; a great deal was pronounced really too horrible to publish; and at last I found it advisable to return to London to see about it. Mr. Bentley wrote to me that I must come and hurry it, as 'Her Most Gracious Majesty the Queen' (to whom Mr. Bentley was Publisher in Ordinary) 'had directed sheets, as they were revised, to be sent to her—and, having become interested in the work, wished for further supplies as soon as possible'.

I worked hard at my proof-sheets, and was very busy. I was asked to write an article for the *British and Foreign Quarterly*, on 'The Disposition of the Native Princes of India towards England' in the event of a protracted struggle in regard to the Afghan war, and I freely confess I was afraid to undertake it. However, I set to work, and did my best, and it was approved of, and, I was told, excited much interest in England, and particular attention on the Continent, and that it was translated into several languages. I founded my article on Major Sutherland's little book upon Native States, which he had written while secretary to Sir Charles Metcalfe, and which I unearthed in the department of the President of the Board of Control, uncut. I referred to my article lately, and among the native states there recorded, some, as Oudh, Nagpur, Satara, and Jhansi, have been annexed to the British dominions, and are now integral portions of its empire of India; but the remainder exist as they were, the treaties being strengthened by her Majesty's proclamation on the assumption of the government of India by the Crown; and though some modifications of older treaties have occurred, they in nowise alter those which are recorded in Major Sutherland's work. I received ninety-five guineas as my honorarium for this article,[1] the first money I earned by writing, and I do not think I ever felt prouder or more pleased. In this, and all my undertakings, I have ever had the soundest advice and most steady help from my dear cousin, Henry Reeve,[2] whose faithful love and friendship have never failed me all my life.

I went to see Lord William Bentinck, who was then in London. He received me very kindly; and I felt more and more, as the intellectual aspect of London society was opening upon me, that, but for his generous interest in me when I was in sore strait, I should never have returned to my native country. He was much interested in the introduction of vernacular education into India, and also of translations of English works; and he charged me, as I agreed with him, to do my utmost to support the cause in England, and to assist it in India. I never saw him again. His health

---

[1] Such payment could only have been for an article of disproportionate length, as this was. Miss Lillian M. Penson has looked it up in the *British and Foreign Review*, or *European Quarterly Journal*, No. xv., January 1839. 'The author of the article is not given, but it takes the form of a review of Captain Sutherland's *Sketches of the Relations subsisting between the British Government of India and the different Native States*. It comprises ninety-one pages—rather surprising, as Captain Sutherland's book is quite short, and Taylor's article appears to be rather a summary than a criticism of this subject.'

[2] This second cousin, 1813–1895, nephew to Mrs. Austin, was a singularly mature young man. Five years younger than Taylor, he was already in the centre of the swim, where he was to remain for more than half a century following. The references to Meadows Taylor are surprisingly few and colourless in the *Memoirs of Henry Reeve* by Sir John Knox Laughton (2 vols., Longmans, 1898), a book full of interesting things about other people. In 1840 Reeve joined the *Times*, the foreign policy of which he controlled for the next fifteen years. He may well have had something to do with Taylor's dozen years' connection with the leading journal; but nothing is said. The only mention of the cousin from India during the two and more momentous years at home occurs in November 1839: 'Meadows Taylor writes to me of one of his Indian friends, who swallows his tongue from time to time, suspends respiration, and is buried for three months or so; in order, as he says, to meditate.' Reeve proposes doing the same thing in order to be able to work.

was terribly broken, but his interest in these subjects never flagged.[1]

I got back to the north for Christmas. Such cold, as I had long been a stranger to, set in ; and as I could not get further than Manchester by railway, I had to mount the coach, there being no inside seat. Well do I remember that drive, the biting north-east wind, and the keen frost—I sitting by the coachman ; and at last, when he could hold out no longer, I took the reins ; and I believe the excitement of driving the 'wild teams', as the coachman called them, kept me up, for I had never felt such cold before. At every stage we found hot tea ready ; and if possible every team was wilder than the one before ; but we drove in turn : and when, on reaching Leeds, I tendered my half-crown, the man would not take it. 'No, no, sir ; not a penny from a genl'man as helped a fellow like me to get through such a night ! If it hadn't 'a bin for you w'd ha' been on top of Blackstone Edge a-lyin' in the snow, for I couldn't 'a drivin ye !' And I assure you I felt proud of the good fellow's hearty commendation.

The year that was expiring[2] had been very memorable to me. When I reflected on the great distance we had safely traversed, the variety and interest of the scenes we had witnessed, the merciful protection we had enjoyed, my recovery from long and severe illness, and the restoration of my sight—my heart was lifted up in thankfulness to the Almighty Giver of all these mercies. Besides, there was the reunion with my family : all had received me with open arms. A few dear faces were missing, certainly—one I never ceased to mourn, who would have shared my pleasures and my troubles, and whose loving sympathy was always ready for her boy ; but my life was a very happy one, and the dawning hope of literary employment, however humble, was very precious to me.

[1] Died June 17, 1839. So the *Thug* was later dedicated by permission to one to whom Taylor was introduced by Lady Blessington, George, Lord Auckland, 'who is vigorously prosecuting those admirable measures for the suppression of Thuggee which were begun by the late Lord William Cavendish Bentinck'.

[2] 1838.

Returning to London in spring,[1] I found my book, *The Confessions*, had been received with much greater interest and success than I had ever ventured to hope for; and not only did the London papers and periodicals take it up, but the provincial press teemed with flattering reviews and long extracts from it. It was curious to hear people wondering over the book and discussing it; and evidently the subject was a new sensation to the public. It passed rapidly through the first edition, and a second was in preparation. I was asked also to write another book, which should take the place of an historical novel, and become the forerunner of a series of such Indian works, and Tippoo Sultan was chosen as the subject. I remonstrated, as I considered the theme too recent; and what could I make out of it? To be sure, I had travelled through Mysore, and could describe local scenery and objects, but I fairly despaired of making a readable story out of Tippoo. But my publishers were not to be convinced, and I promised to do my best.

I required some information in regard to points in the Duke of Wellington's transactions with the family of Tippoo Sultan, and I wrote to him asking him to be so good as to help me.[2] To this request I received a short and very

[1] July 1839 is the date of the important Introduction.

Taylor, having once consummately depicted Thuggee, did not touch it again save with the left hand. Thugs are shown, but only incidentally, in *Tara* and in *Seeta*, the historical dates of which are separated by two centuries.

As to the attempts of others to make literary capital out of this gruesome theme, two such are recorded by Mr. Edward Farley Oaten in his *Sketch of Anglo-Indian Literature*. George Powell Thomas produced in 1847 a volume of *Poems*, mainly narrative. 'Chief among them was *The Bridal Party*, a tragic Indian tale, in Spenserian metre, of a happy marriage wrecked by the "roomal" of the murderous Thug.' In 1851 Colonel C. J. C. Davidson went one better by combining two horrors of Indian life in *Tara the Suttee*, a play. Tara leaps on the burning funeral pile in order to escape the Thugs. 'In *Tara the Suttee* Lieut.-Colonel Davidson showed that the drama of native life possesses great possibilities for English writers.'

[2] These points were, after all, not mentioned in the novel. But Taylor's memory of the interview appears in some glowing sentences. They are in the account of the battle at Malvilly (called Malavelly in his *History of India*, Malavalli in the *Imperial Gazetteer*), some forty miles from Tippoo's capital, fought on the 27th of March 1799.

characteristic reply, written on a scrap of foolscap paper, dated from the House of Lords.

'The Duke of Wellington is too busy at present to answer Captain Taylor's note; but if he will attend at Apsley House to-morrow at eleven, the Duke will endeavour to remember what Captain Taylor requires.'

The note was the merest scrawl, but was precious to me in remembrance of the very courteous interview that followed. His memory was perfectly clear, and he had forgotten nothing in regard to his own part in the first Maratha war. He told me *The Confessions* had fairly taken him back to India.

I spent the summer in Ireland, principally at the dear old house at Harold's Cross, in which I now reside. We travelled, too, to Killarney and Limerick, and visited my father, who was then living in the Co. Clare.

On our way, I had the strangest speech made to me by an old beggar-woman that I think I ever heard, even in Ireland. As we drew up at Naas, the usual clamour for charity began. I was on the box-seat, wrapped up in a coat bordered with fur, and doubtless looked very cosy.

Wellesley, a colonel not thirty, commanded the 33rd regiment of foot.

'The Sultan was in an ecstasy of delight. Little imagined he then to whom he was opposed; that one led the troops, which he expected would fly like dust before the whirlwind, to whom fear was unknown—who bore within him the germ of that renown which has raised him to the proudest, the most glorious pinnacle of heroic fame—Wellesley! Wellington! What heart so callous that does not bound at those illustrious names, recalling with them victories upon victories to his remembrance—not the result of fortuitous circumstances, but of devoted bravery, of admirable foresight, of consummate skill, of patience and fortitude under every privation through a long series of years—the most splendid array of triumph that ever the world beheld, which, already so glorious, will yet increase in after times to a renown more brilliant than we can at present estimate.' At Malvilly, though the Sultan at first exulted with some reason: 'It was a sight which curdled his blood: his favourite corps turned—they dared not abide the charge of the British and Nizam's division, led by the gallant Wellesley; and the cavalry, headed by his old enemy Floyd, dashed out upon them.' (Sir John Floyd, baronet and full general, 1748–1818.)

One of the old women called out—

'Ah, thin, comfortable gintleman, throw us a copper!'

I was dubbed 'comfortable gintleman' by the crowd till I could no longer resist, so I threw down a shilling to be divided. On this my old friend dropped on her knees in the mud, and raising her clasped hands, cried—

'Ah, thin, that yer honour might be in heaven this night, sittin' wid the blessed Virgin Mary upon a binch!'

At Killarney we fairly bothered the beggars by speaking to them in Hindustani, and thereby escaped importunity.

'Hasn't he moustaches?' said one. 'He is a furriner. What's the good o' axing the likes of him? Bad cess to him.'

In spring I went to London again, having devoted the winter to the writing of my new book,[1] and to enjoying Dublin hospitalities.

[1] *Tippoo Sultaun; a Tale of the Mysore War*, 1840. The publisher's suggestion had been fruitful. Tippoo had been the national enemy four and five decades before; and though Napoleon had intervened, the fascination of this weird figure still held, and holds. Not only is Tippoo made vivid in a form which must be final for most readers, pathetic and terrible and ludicrous, but he does not overshadow an independent love story of much charm. The only weakness lies in the half-dozen chapters, out of fifty, where Taylor tries to show English people in their eighteenth-century homes. The masterly Indian novelist never learned adequately to portray his countrymen even in India.

Taylor could not have written *Tippoo Sultaun*, or would have written it quite differently, even to the spelling of the word Sultan, but for Colonel Mark Wilks. He writes of Tippoo: 'It has been said of him by an eminent historian, whose account of the period is a vivid romance from first to last, that "his were the pranks of a monkey, with the abominations of a monster."'

There are said to be no materials for a biography of Mark Wilks. The usual books of reference give the chief dates of his official life, with his birth probably in 1760, and his death in 1831. He was closely connected with Madras and with Mysore, where he was Resident for the five years before he left India in 1808. From 1813 to 1816 he was Governor of St. Helena, and he was the first and the genial gaoler of Napoleon.

Wilks's *Mysore* is a true classic of Anglo-India, though at present out of commission. The original edition in three volumes is hard to get even at a great price. There was a reprint at Madras in 1869 in two volumes, aggregating a thousand close pages. Few books more loudly call for an edition with modern apparatus, edited if possible by some

I had the *entrée* into much delightful society in London, and became acquainted with many distinguished characters.

Lady Morgan [1] was insatiable about Indian stories, and I had to invent or improvise when my memory failed me. At her house we had rich treats in music, Moscheles, Liszt, and others frequenting her rooms constantly, besides many gifted amateurs.

I was free of Gore House too, and look upon the evenings spent there as among the pleasantest reminiscences of that period.

It was most interesting and fascinating to me to meet so many men of note under such charming auspices as those of Lady Blessington.[2] Most of these now, perhaps, are gone to their rest, and there is no need to mention names. Does any one remember the strange, almost 'eerie' speech that Prince Louis Napoleon made one evening there, when, leaning his elbow on the mantelpiece, he began an oration declaring the policy he should adopt when he became Emperor of the French? And I remember too, when this really happened, how his actions actually accorded with that strange speech. When Lady Blessington rallied him good-naturedly on what he had said, he put his hand on his heart, bowed gravely, and told her that he was never more in earnest in his life, and that she would understand it all by-and-by. Maclise [3] and I walked home together, and could speak of nothing else.

As I came to know Prince Louis Napoleon better, he proposed to me to join him in a tour through India which he contemplated, taking with him Count D'Orsay.[4] He was

scholar conversant with South India. The notes are particularly good, affording glimpses of a group of men who, about a generation later than Colonel Guy Mannering in India, made the same difficult effort to keep in touch with Europe regarding things of the mind. 'A man of much erudition considering his imperfect opportunities.'

[1] Sydney, Lady Morgan; *The Wild Irish Girl*, 1806; died 1859. Like Mrs. Austin and some other entertaining women writers, she was married to a husband writing upon particularly dull subjects.

[2] Marguerite, Countess of Blessington, 1789–1849.

[3] Daniel Maclise, 1806–1870. 'His frescoes—the greatest historical paintings of the English school' (*Dictionary of National Biography*).

[4] The only mention here of Alfred Guillaume Gabriel, Count D'Orsay, 1801–1852. Fortunately Miss Taylor wrote to me in time: 'I have a sketch by Count D'Orsay of my father in 1840. This was lithographed,

CAPTAIN MEADOWS TAYLOR 1840.

To face p. 129.

to apply for my services as long as he required them, and the plan appeared delightful.

I heard from him direct, after I had returned to India, asking for information on various points of equipment, etc.; but the Boulogne affair and what followed put an end to the whole scheme, to my infinite regret.

I remember, too, another very interesting evening at Gore House, when I was presented to the son of the great Russian Minister, Count Nesselrode.[1] He had been specially sent over to glean intelligence of the English designs in Asia, and he set himself steadily to pick my brains on all sorts of Indian subjects. He was, or affected to be, surprised at my account of the number, discipline, and equipment of the native army in India, of the condition of the cavalry and artillery, and especially when I told him that I should not hesitate to put my own regiment of native infantry in brigade with H.M. Guards, and that they would work with them as well and as effectively as any regiment of the line.

I was complimented afterwards by several present on having spoken out some very home truths fearlessly, and I hope they were of use. That night La Blache and Tamburini sang by turns, and imitated the singing of Grisi and Persiani, in the most surprising way, in falsetto, quarrelling over it very amusingly. But I may not linger over these memories, which few who shared them could have forgotten. It was to be my last season of such society for many a long year, and I prized it accordingly.

---

and I have also a framed copy. I am having the original sketch photographed for you.' This is the profile opposite. It is of revealing interest, showing, as nothing else could have done, the young man, hardly thirty-two, who had produced two downright good as well as lengthy novels, and who was returning to the twenty years' unrelieved grind in the wilderness which was to ruin his health.

[1] Charles Robert, Comte de Nesselrode, 'a Russian diplomat. He was plenipotentiary of the Tsar at the Congress of Vienna and directed the foreign policy of the empire under Alexander I. and Nicholas, from 1816 to 1856' (*Petit Larousse*). The curious *Cassell's Biographical Dictionary*, to which Meadows Taylor contributed Indian articles at the end of his life, says that Nesselrode was born at Lisbon, where his father was Russian ambassador, in 1780, and died in 1862. After the Congress of Vienna he 'became minister of Foreign Affairs, a post which he filled with extraordinary ability under Alexander I., Nicholas, and Alexander II., till the treaty of Paris in 1856'.

I pass over the intervening time which we spent in farewell visits among our friends and relatives, and we left London in November,[1] on our return to India.

I had attended the last *levée* of the season, 'on departure for India', and as I knelt to kiss her Majesty's hand, she said to me very graciously, 'I wish you a safe voyage, and trust I may see you again.' And so she did, exactly twenty years later.

Back again, through Paris and Marseilles, from Malta to Alexandria and Cairo, and so to Suez, down the Red Sea, always hot and uncomfortable, and we were glad at last to reach Bombay early in January,[2] after our long absence.

We sent on our luggage on carts to Poona, and ourselves started, just as I had done seventeen years before, on my first journey to Aurungabad to begin life.

How was I to go on? Was I to rejoin my regiment, and continue its dull routine of duties, or was a fresh career before me? My mind was filled with speculations on these and many other points.

I need not go over again my old route to Poona, where we did not stay long, but went on to Sholapur. All along the route I found luxuriant and continuous cultivation, instead of the waste land and deserted villages of 1824. The original survey operations had been improved, the assessments had been reduced and arranged on a proper valuation of the land, and the change in the aspect of the country was as remarkable as it was beneficial. The early millet and pulse of the first crop of the season had been reaped on the uplands, but in the lower ground the later millet and wheat were fast ripening, and the sheets of golden grain were truly beautiful. All over the upland stubbles were large flocks of ortolans, of which I shot numbers, affording us delicious eating; and every afternoon I rambled out with my gun, and seldom failed to bring in a bag of hares, quails, and partridges.

It was a most enjoyable journey throughout. We had a very pleasant party of fellow-travellers: a lady and her family, who came with us from Bombay on her way to join her husband; and the children were charming companions,

[1] 1840. [2] 1841.

boys and girls both accompanying me in my rides, mounted on stout ponies, and scrambling all over the country. The only uncomfortable member of the party, I believe, was their tutor, a Frenchman, who found the people barbarians, the country barbarous, and the language worse. Above all, there were no hotels, no wayside inn, even, where one could procure a cup of coffee. His chief delight was to come out with me, and see partridges and quails shot *flying*.

We reached Sholapur in due course, and found tents sent for us by Mr. Palmer. We halted there for two or three days, and then pursued our march by the Naldrug and Homnabad road, through my old district of 1827–29. From Sholapur to Hyderabad in those days there was, strictly speaking, no road, only a track; but I knew every mile thoroughly, and that I could obtain assistance everywhere if it were required.

The tents were very comfortable; the children, and even Monsieur, were enchanted: they were lined with pretty chintz and carpeted, and had double walls and roofs to keep off the sun, and were a luxury we had not expected.

I received a perfect ovation through my old district, and it was very gratifying to find I had not been forgotten. At Naldrug, where we halted a day or two, the townspeople visited me in great numbers; and both from the Nawab's agent in the fort, and from the zemindars, came presents of provisions, trays of sweetmeats, barley-sugar, and almonds, not only for ourselves, but for all my servants and followers. At every village, as we entered it, the authorities came out to meet us with jars of milk, baskets of eggs, and humble offerings of flowers, while the piper played us past the village.

At one resting-place, parties of women came to visit my wife, and tell her stories of me, and how 'at first they used to be afraid of the gentleman with the "red trousers"; but he had done them no harm, and the country was not so quiet now as when he had been with them', and more that was pleasant to me to hear.

At Homnabad, in particular, the welcome given to me was on a great scale; all the merchants and others assembled about half a mile from the town headed by my old friend Atmaram, the dean of guild; and there were baskets of flowers, sweetmeats, and fruits, which I had to accept. The town pipers and drummers played us to our tents; provisions were provided for all the party; and in the afternoon crowds came to visit me, and have a talk over old times in their simple, homely fashion.

They were very curious about England, and I had to recount all my doings since I had left them. My wife, also, had her assembly of women; and told me afterwards, with tears in her eyes, how precious it was to her to hear how these people really loved me, and wanted me to come back to them.

Next day we proceeded to Ekali, where it may be remembered I had marched after the insurgent rebel before-mentioned. He was still confined at Hyderabad, and had been fined heavily; but was said to have become a reformed character, and to have grown very humble and religious.

At Sadaseopet, my old residence, I had another similar ovation; but my little bungalow had been removed, and a larger one built for the accommodation of travellers, and I was rather sorry not to see it again.

On the 26th February we arrived at Hyderabad, having been just a month on the road; and Mr. Palmer was over-joyed to see us again. I put a copy of my new book, *Tippoo Sultaun*, into his hands, and in some respects he liked it better almost than *The Confessions*. He told me that nearly every one doubted my really being the author of *The Confessions*; and said it was fortunate that I had sent him the work in manuscript as I did, so that he could assure all sceptics that he had read it in my handwriting before I had left India, thus ending the discussion.

General J. S. Fraser had succeeded Colonel Stewart as Resident at Hyderabad, and received me most cordially, recommending me very earnestly to pursue my literary work, and prophesying that I should find ample occupation for my pen.[1]

[1] During two decades there was to be no time for literary work, except articles, which gradually became crowded out.

James Stuart Fraser, 1783–1869, appears rather well in *The Story of my Life*, less well in Sir William Lee-Warner's *Life of the Marquis of Dalhousie*, which will be cited in due course. General Fraser was about the oldest man who has ever controlled an Indian State as Resident. He was the contemporary of Elphinstone, of Jenkins, and of Metcalfe, whose labours in India were long since over; of his namesakes William

My regiment, the 6th, was at Bolarum, and the men and officers came to see me in numbers, and to welcome me back again; but General Fraser was making other arrangements for me. I was to go to Hingoli to take command of the 8th, whose commandant had gone on furlough to Europe. It was a long march in the hot weather; but orders had to be obeyed, and we started on the 13th March, making as long stages as we could.

During our stay at Hyderabad, the festival of the Moharram had occurred; and I was gratified to find that my description in the *Thug*,[1] although written from memory, was correct in every particular, yet hardly giving an idea of the grandeur of the scene.

One sore disappointment awaited me. I had hoped that my little savings, upon which I had not drawn during my absence in England, would have increased materially; instead of this, all had been swept away, with a very small hope of

---

Fraser, shot dead while Resident at Delhi in 1835, and William Fraser's brother, James Baillie Fraser, author of the *Life of Colonel James Skinner* and of some faint beginnings in Indian fiction.

General Fraser, who was a French scholar, held, in the last twenty years of his service, the residencies in Mysore, in Travancore, and at Hyderabad. He is fortunate in having to his credit a distinct little campaign, that against Coorg, to annex it 'in consideration of the unanimous wish of the people'. In his *History* Taylor says: 'To take possession of the province, a force invaded it under the political direction of Major-General J. S. Fraser, which, though gallantly resisted in some attempts to penetrate the stupendous passes and defiles, was eventually successful, and the capital, Mercara, was occupied on April 6, 1834. The rajah, who surrendered to General Fraser, was removed,' etc. Thornton describes the same events at great length. Fraser became full general in 1862.

[1] This is the clear-cut account covering the opening pages of chapter xv., 'Setting forth how Ameer Ali spends the ninth night of the Mohorum, and how he loses his mistress.' He watches the successive processions from Zora's house. A painfully vivid incident is the rage of a mishandled elephant who tears a man from the crowd 'by the waist with his trunk, and whirling him high in the air dashed him against the ground, and then kneeling down crushed him to a mummy with his tusks'. The most striking sight of all was the Char Minar itself, sometimes in the light of torches, sometimes in the blaze of a thousand blue lights. 'The pale sulphureous glare caused the white surface to glitter like silver; high in the air the white minarets gleamed with intense brightness; and, as it stood out against the deep blue of the sky, it seemed to be a sudden creation of the genii,' etc.

recovery, and I had to begin afresh. Had I died then, my dear wife and child would have been left penniless; but God was merciful to me in all things. Before I left Hyderabad, General Fraser warned me to make no arrangements to reside at Hingoli, as I might be sent on to Ellichpur to act as staff-officer and paymaster. And so it proved. We again marched on the 19th April, and reached our destination safely. Since our departure from Bombay we had travelled very nearly seven hundred miles, and we were truly thankful to be at rest, and with a delicious climate to live in. The brigadier had the privilege of residing at Chikalda, upwards of 4,000 feet above the sea,[1] where there was no heat, and the nights and mornings were almost cold. My eyes, which had suffered much from our march in the heat and glare, now improved rapidly; and I would fain have remained at Chikalda during the monsoon; but as soon as the rains set in, the brigadier and the doctor moved into cantonments, and we were forced to follow.

I then began a new book, but my eyes proved too weak for writing, and I was obliged to give it up.[2] I could paint better, and amused myself by taking portraits of my friends.

[1] 3,664 feet, says the *Imperial Gazetteer*. Chikalda is on a plateau in the Satpura Hills, less than twenty miles from Ellichpur, thirty by a good road. The first bungalows had been built by officers of the Ellichpur brigade only two years before this date. The heads of departments in Berar spend a portion of the hot season at Chikalda. 'The scenery is beautiful, and the vegetation luxuriant and varied in character—roses, clematis, orchids, ferns, and lilies succeeding each other with the changing seasons.'

[2] This was probably the first draft of *Tara: a Mahratta Tale*, begun afresh more than twenty years later, published 1863. The story is told in chapter xviii. of the autobiography. In the Prologue Taylor supplements the very scanty account of his literary friends in England:

'In the year 1839, I became acquainted with the late Professor Wilson; and in course of conversation on the possibility of illustrating events in Indian history by works of fiction, the details of the present story, among other subjects, were slightly sketched out by me. He was interested in them, and suggested my writing the tale for *Blackwood's Magazine*. I could not, however, then commence it, and deferred doing so till my return to India; but, falling into political and civil employment there, was never able to continue what I had begun, till my return home.' The Wilson of this paragraph was obviously not the Professor Wilson of the next note, but John Wilson, 1785–1854,

I managed, however, to send an article to England on 'Educational Measures for the People of India', which was called forth by a controversy then raging between the Arabic, Persian, and Sanscrit party, and the English and vernacular, whose cause I espoused, not only in the Indian press, but in my letters for the *Times*, which were then regularly sent by every mail. My advocacy of their measures did not slacken until they were finally adjusted; for the practical benefit to the people by their adoption far exceeded what might be looked for from the ancient system and languages so ardently insisted upon by Wilson and others.

I need not now enter into the particulars—they are matters of history, and out of date; but I have never regretted the part I took in this discussion when I see the noble results which have been already attained, and are rapidly advancing year by year, all over India, in all its regions, and in all its vernacular languages.[1]

At the latter end of October my tenure of staff employment came to an end, and I was ordered to rejoin the 8th Regiment at Hingoli. A pretender to the person and claims of Appa Sahib, the ex-Raja of Nagpur, who had escaped from custody after the Maratha war of 1818, had arisen in rebellion in the Nagpur district, and, joined by bodies of Rohillas and others,

---

Christopher North, 'elected', says the *Dictionary of National Biography*, 'on strength of his tory principles professor of moral philosophy at Edinburgh University, 1820'.

[1] This was the cause of vernacular education which Lord William Bentinck had charged Taylor, at their meeting in London at the end of 1838, to maintain. It was opposed by Horace Hayman Wilson, 1786–1860, a name that must be venerable in Oxford, Boden Professor of Sanskrit from 1833. Like Leyden, H. H. Wilson was an outstanding example of the Indian doctors who have been scholars. Mr. Buckland calls him 'the greatest Sanskrit scholar of his time, combining a variety of attainments as general linguist, historian, chemist, accountant, numismatist, actor and musician'

In his *History* Taylor has a good paragraph on this Battle of the Books in Calcutta during the thirties. 'Able men argued on their respective sides with great pertinacity. Dr. H. H. Wilson led the van of the Orientalists, and was opposed by Sir Charles Trevelyan, Mr. Brian Hodgson, and Dr. Duff of the Scotch Church, with a host of others; and the question was finally debated in Council, where Mr. Macaulay gave pure Orientalism its death-blow. Then the English language, with its flood of light and truth, was opened to the people of India,' etc.

was plundering where he could. The 8th Regiment was already in the field, and I was directed to join it without delay. So I started through a wild and almost depopulated, but very beautiful, tract of country, and in a few days came up with the regiment. The campaign, however, was concluded by Captain Johnston's capture of Appa Sahib, after a truly surprising march of 78 miles in 32 hours. Another brilliant attack was made on a party of Rohillas by Brigadier Twemlow, at the head of a detachment of cavalry: 150 of the enemy were left dead upon the field, and the rest captured; the cavalry lost eight killed and wounded only. This was a truly gallant affair, for the Rohillas (Afghans) are well known for their bravery, and for good use of their weapons.

My contributions to the *Times* were apparently liked, for I heard at this time that I had been appointed 'Special Correspondent', on a yearly stipend; and this honour I continued to enjoy for many years.

Events in India were deeply interesting at this period; the miserable retreat from Kabul, the failure of Lord Auckland's Afghanistan policy, and the safety and relief of Sale's brigade, were universal subjects of interest and speculation. Before I left Ireland I had become acquainted with Lord Fitzgerald and Vesci,[1] and was honoured by his friendship, while I supplied him with all the information he needed, as far as my experience carried me. I had now become his regular correspondent, and so continued as long as he held office as President of the Board of Control, and by him I was strongly recommended to Lord Ellenborough, the successor of Lord Auckland. Although Lord Auckland had not been able to give me permanent employment, or transfer me to the cavalry in the absence of vacancies, yet he had, since my introduction to him by Lady Blessington, shown a very kind solicitude respecting me and my advancement, which, had he remained in office, would probably have been attended with good results.

[1] William Vesey Fitzgerald, 1783–1843, a statesman little known: envoy to Sweden and paymaster-general; succeeded to his mother's peerage, 1832; created an English peer, Fitzgerald and Vesey, 1835; President of the Board of Control during the last two years of his life. The Sir William Vesey Fitzgerald who was Governor of Bombay from 1867 to 1872 was his second son. Taylor gives the alternative spelling of one of the oldest of baronies.

Now I had to look to Lord Ellenborough, to whom I sent Lord Fitzgerald's letter of introduction, and I was much gratified by receiving an autograph letter from him in reply, which showed more knowledge of my doings hitherto than I anticipated, and contained kind expressions of goodwill.[1]

Shortly after I joined the 8th Regiment I had occasion to return to Hyderabad, and there was appointed to do duty with the 4th Regiment stationed at Bolarum, where I took a house, and for some months we led quiet and happy lives. The weather was delicious, and we had some pleasant parties to Golconda, where we entertained our friends. Although the country is bare of trees, the locality of the Kings' Tombs presents many picturesque features. The noble mausoleums themselves, the grim old fort and its massive walls, the city of Hyderabad in the distance, and several large lakes or tanks

[1] It is pleasantest to say as little as possible of these two Governors-General. It is enough that Taylor returned, at the opening of 1841, to an India singularly fallen in prestige and in power from the India which he had left three years before.

Another year, and Sir W. W. Hunter can write of the situation: 'A month after the news of the annihilation of our Kabul force reached Calcutta, Lord Auckland was succeeded by Lord Ellenborough on February 28th, 1842. Lord Auckland's long Governor-Generalship of six years ended amid a gloom such as had never overshadowed British rule in India since the Black Hole of Calcutta in 1756.'

Taylor had no delusions about these two men, though he had dedicated the *Thug* to Auckland, and though he thought an appreciation from Ellenborough worth recording. His account of their administrations covers seven chapters, and some third of a hundred close pages, in his *History of India.* For the beginner there is no better grounding in the vanity of interference in Afghanistan than Taylor's exposition of Auckland's meddling, which was actually based upon legitimist theories. With no exception worth mentioning, expert opinion condemned this war in advance. As a plain personal account of much of its course, commendation must be given to chapters v. to xi. of Sir Thomas Seaton's *From Cadet to Colonel.*

Of Ellenborough Taylor writes that 'a new and more vigorous man had arrived in India', and 'found his predecessor prostrated in mind and body by the events which had occurred'. Ellenborough is described as 'a man of much brilliant talent, and apparent determination, possessing ample theoretical experience in Indian affairs, and filled with ambition'. Of his one abiding measure, the annexation of Sind, Taylor's disapproval was so vehement that it will require special notice at the end of chapter x.; while he has recorded his shame at having to read aloud the Somnath proclamation.

sparkling in the sun, contribute to form one of the most striking views in the Deccan. After Golconda we all assembled near the tomb of Burhani Sahib, on the east of the city, the Nizam's deer-preserve, where, as I had permission, several fine bucks were shot.

Here, on the 23d November, just as I had ridden in from Secunderabad, I received a note from General Fraser desiring me to come to him at once, as he had something important to communicate; so I rode in to breakfast, after which we entered on the business for which he had sent for me.

THE EXTINCT STATE OF SHORAPUR

There is something tragical in the thought of a State which for any reason has forfeited its separate existence, which has run its course like a mere human being—*vixit.* This, a thing which has happened comparatively seldom in lands of European civilisation, was more frequent than is easy to grasp during long centuries of Indian history. It was not far from the normal condition of things, and somewhat peculiarly so in the Deccan. The flux and incessant change of kingdoms, perhaps by that fact shown to be organisms of a low grade, were only arrested by the English predominance about a century ago. After that, until and during the Mutiny, each successive death of a State caused so distinct a shock to public feeling that it seemed best to guarantee its impossibility for the future.

The next six chapters in this autobiography, with their sad supplement in two later chapters, amounting to about one half the work, make its most characteristic portion. Equally, in Taylor's career, the dozen years following 1841, with his last years in India, 1858 to 1860, are the unique thing. Shorapur was the core of his life, the place of which he must have kept the most poignant memories, the interesting entity which he struggled to preserve from deserved dissolution, while doing a vast amount of good among the populace which loved him. His life at Shorapur was too close to him to be used by him in fiction. But as here told from contemporary letters it has so many of the colours of romance, such drama, such completeness, as to tempt other novelists, perhaps delusively. No made-up record could equal his own simple tale, truthful yet artistic. At least a hundred Residents in India, of better official standing than Meadows Taylor, have had his chances to make vital the life of a native State—notably his chief at Hyderabad during most of this period, the dreary James Stuart Fraser. Only Taylor, so far as I know, has preserved, as in some magic crystal, the fluctuating life of a race apart, the Beydurs, of a little State which is no more, of a reigning house as doomed as the Atridæ.

The Beydurs and Shorapur have been nowhere else so described as in the following chapters. Taylor was less happy when writing about them elsewhere. In his *History*, and in *Tara*, are references, hardly worth gathering up, to the robber Beydurs threatening Bijapur, and half a century later Aurungzeb, from their strongholds at Sagar or at Wakingera. When the place last named, which is not to be found in the *Imperial Gazetteer*, was taken, the chief, Pam Naik, about 1707, 'retreated to a stronger position in the hills, which, under the name of Soorpoor, or Shorapur, is still the capital of the district'. In *A Noble Queen*, where all the outlines are faint, the Beydurs are portrayed about a century earlier: in another note I have quoted quite enough from this description of them. At the end of Chapter XII. is an ethnological note upon the modern Beydurs by Dr. Crooke.

Shorapur while independent was six or eight times as large as one might think if judging from the present district of Shorapur. In fact it was about one half the size of Wales, or of Palestine. According to an account sent me in 1918 by the Director-General of Revenue, Hyderabad, Shorapur State some seventy years ago included Deodrug, Dehgaon, Andola, Shahpur, and miscellaneous regions in addition to the capital town and district. With one exception all these places stand out plain upon the map of Hyderabad State affixed to this volume. It will thus be seen that Shorapur filled the good wide country between the Bhima to the north and the Krishna to the south, including the Dhon flowing into the Krishna from Bijapur. The Director-General of Revenue counts up to an area of about 3,500 square miles for the kingdom of Shorapur, which approaches the 4,000 square miles of Taylor's estimate; and to a population then of a third of a million, as compared with Taylor's half a million.

Shorapur made an inset into the flank of the Nizam's territories on the west which must have seemed an ugly gap during the two years it was held by the British. It is in sixteen degrees of latitude, almost reaching seventeen. While lying in the south-west of Hyderabad State it does not form the south-west corner, which is occupied by the classic country close around the former Vijayanagar.

To Taylor's surviving sister-in-law, Mrs. W. Fallon, of Saifabad, Hyderabad, I owe the recommendation of a little book called *Shorapur, an Ancient Beydur Raj*, by Nawab Framurz Jung Bahadur. 'It is', she wrote, 'very interesting, and gives you an insight into many little things connected with Col. Taylor. The Nawab is a friend of ours, and a great admirer of the old Col.'s. I wish we had more like him nowadays.'

This is a volume of 117 pages, in boards, published by

Higginbotham, Madras, in 1907, at, I believe, a rupee and a half. The Nawab is described as 'First Talukdar (Collector), Raichur District'. He served at Shorapur from 1904 to 1906, and was 'seized with a very strong desire to find out all I could of the place, so as to make this interesting part of the country more generally known'. Of course the name of Meadows Taylor, unjustly forgotten elsewhere, predominated just there. The Nawab also met 'a descendant of one of the ancient families of Shorapur, a man named Hakim Papia Shastri', who had some records of local history written on palmyra leaves, it is not stated in what language. He speaks of writing English 'as a foreign language'.

The second half of Nawab Framurz Khan's monograph consists of a shortened paraphrase of those eight chapters of Meadows Taylor which I have praised above. But from the earlier chapters a few extracts may be made.

The word Beydur is said to mean fearless, as Surpur is the City of the Gods (City of Valour, says Taylor). Apparently from his own knowledge of them the Nawab writes of the Beydurs: 'They are highly honourable and never break an oath. . . . Their moral character is high, but they are very illiterate.' Chapter ii. gives twenty pages to an abstract of Papia Shastri's palmyra chronicle of the Shorapur kings. This is the sort of thing, unverified and unverifiable, which has always gone down in Asia as history. No matter what volumes of it may be printed, it does not help one to any knowledge of the past. The dates here, not even agreeing among themselves within a few lines, might as well have been sprinkled from a pepper pot. The pity is that the same may be said of the dates upon too many pages of Taylor's own *History of India.*

Nawab Framurz Khan counts the Shorapur Raj as beginning from 1515, which would give it a run of nearly three and a half centuries to 1858. It is said to have originated in a grant from the Maharaja of Satara. I would particularly like to know more of the Maharajas of Satara in the sixteenth century.

There is a rather good story of a Raja Gaddad Pid Naik, seventeenth century, who with his staff overcame a mad elephant of the King of Bijapur. 'No sooner was the beast set free than it commenced breaking houses, shops and trees. Pid Naik came in front and the elephant wished to get hold of him, but Pid Naik soon managed to get on the elephant, and struck a severe blow, with his staff, on its forehead. The elephant, being wounded, commenced to run away, and Pid Naik continued thrashing the beast, so much so that it became helpless. The mad elephant being led in the presence of the King, Pid Naik caught the tail of the elephant and got on its back,' etc.

There is another of Raja Pam Naik in the eighteenth

century, by which time the allegiance of Shorapur had shifted to Hyderabad. He had captured a robber Raja as ordered. 'Pam Naik reached Hyderabad with the Rajah, who was ordered to be blown off with a cannon ball. Pam Naik refused to do it himself, urging that the Rajah was his nephew, thereupon the Artillery men were ordered to fire, they attempted thrice, but without success, then the Rajah told them to take away the charm he was wearing, no sooner the charm was removed, the Rajah was successfully blown off.' By such stages one comes to Kistapa Naik, who, though the date of his death is wrongly given, was the reputed father of the little Raja whom Meadows Taylor reared. 'It was in his time that the decline of the Shorapur State commenced—although he was a wise and educated man and said to be religious too, yet the expenses exceeded the income and the State was getting into hopeless debt.'

Chapter iii. is of the Manners and Customs of the Beydurs or Berads. Their progenitor Kannaya could have said, with Homer in Plutarch :

> Work was not dear, nor household cares to me,
> Whose increase rears the thriving family.

For when the god appeared to him in the forest, offering him a choice of boons, 'Kannaya prayed Shiv to make him and his descendants sure shots, and to make his and their lands grow corn without much labour or water. The god granted his prayer, and all Beydurs are good marksmen and live by hunting and fowling, growing only the *rabi* crops which want neither much water nor much care.' That is why Shorapur still lacks irrigation, though seated between two noble streams.

The Beydurs, according to this little account, which is useful as supplementing, not repeating, Meadows Taylor, are not a cleanly folk. They must be so dark as to approach blackness. The touch, 'of middle height, with round faces, flat cheeks, thin lips and lank or frizzled hair', is not attractive. Further on one reads that though they rank themselves with 'Mahratta Kunbis and other field-working classes', high-caste Hindus rank them below Musalmans. 'Their home tongue is corrupt Kanarese, and some out-of-doors speak incorrect Marathi. The well-to-do live in one-storeyed houses, with either stone or mud walls and terraced roofs, costing from Rs. 60 to 200 ; the poorer families live in huts which are built at a nominal cost.' Even in 1906 the Nawab could write that 'his food costs a man about one anna a day', or a penny. 'They are great eaters, but poor cooks.' So among Hindus it is not surprising that 'Beydur' is a common term for sloven. Yet as a class they are now 'orderly, hard-working, thrifty, hospitable, and free from crime'. They 'may be considered a rising class'.

CHAPTER VII

1841–42

I HAD been aware that an officer of cavalry, a very accomplished and able man, had been employed as Political Agent at Shorapur for more than a year in adjusting affairs at issue between that State and the Government of H.H. the Nizam, in pursuance of Act 17 of the Treaty of 1800 between the British Government and the Nizam, which stipulated for interference between the Nizam and Shorapur in case of the latter withholding payment of tribute and just claims due to the former.

The original tribute had been comparatively low ; but the Nizam's Government had increased it on various pretences, and on the succession of the late Raja, who had very recently died, a Nazarana, or succession fee, of fifteen lakhs (£150,000) had been exacted by the Nizam's Minister, which was to be liquidated by instalments.

These demands led to many complications, in which the British Government had always been obliged, under pressure of the treaty, to take a part. Money had been borrowed from local bankers under the signature of British officers to pay instalments of tribute and succession fees, which the impoverished State could not meet ; and there were disputes between the Shorapur State and the bankers, the bankers and the Nizam's Government, which altogether presented a very complicated and eminently disagreeable state of affairs.

The officer in charge had just concluded a proposed settlement of all these matters, and had submitted an exhaustive report on the country and its revenues and resources, when the Raja, Krishnappa Naik, died suddenly, and his elder

Rani, Ishwarama, assumed the administration as regent to her son, a boy of seven years old or thereabouts.

The Rani was a woman of much energy and cleverness, but she was dissolute to a degree—in fact a very Messalina, and hardly second to the famous Maharani of the Punjab.[1] Her infidelities were known to her husband and his family, but could not be checked. On the death of her husband she defied all parties, resisted the settlements made by Captain Gresley,[2] and called out the military forces of the country, about ten thousand men, whom she rallied round her, inducing the leaders to promise to support her on oath.

The late Raja's family, who headed a strong party in the State, had declared themselves opposed to the Rani because of her infamous character; and acting according to their declaration, the late Raja's brother, by name Pid Naik, had been proposed as regent during his nephew's minority, an arrangement which was ratified by the Governor-General in Council. This measure, however, had been violently resisted by the Rani, and she defied her brother-in-law and the British Government alike.

Affairs having reached this point, and Captain Gresley having no disposition to temporise, he applied for a force to disperse the adherents of the Rani, to establish Pid Naik in office, and to assist him generally to carry out the measures he had proposed, and which had received sanction.

General Fraser, however, did not consider an exhibition of force necessary, nor had he, he thought, a sufficient number of troops at his disposal to render it sufficiently imposing. Our army was then evacuating Afghanistan, and there was no security in the Punjab after the death of Maharaja Ranjit

[1] This widow of Ranjit Singh, 'a woman of most licentious habits', was notorious in India throughout the forties. Of her conduct in 1848 Taylor writes in his *History*: 'The Ranee's intrigues spread rapidly to native courts in India, urging an effort to drive the British into the sea. . . . The seeds of revolt, so deeply sown, were already springing up vigorously in various directions.'

[2] Francis Gresley, Nizam's Contingent, several letters from whom (but none from Taylor!) are in the *Life of General Fraser*. In 1842 he took a small fort garrisoned by rebel Arabs and negroes. Of this Lord Ellenborough writes: 'Captain Gresley must be a good soldier, and seems to have his heart in the business.'

Singh.[1] Troops from the southward had been marched northwards, a measure which had caused outbreaks of mutiny in some corps of the Madras army; and while the movement across the Punjab was in progress, it was felt that any outbreak of war elsewhere might be only as a spark to a magazine of general treason, which might explode with fearful consequences.

When the assistance of a force was denied him, the political officer reported that he could do no more than he had done; that the position of the Rani was growing stronger; and that if she were supported by Arabs, Rohillas,. and other mercenaries whom she had funds to maintain, the result would be a costly and bloody little war, always to be deprecated.

He had already been able, by seizing the ferry-boats on the Bhima and Krishna rivers, to prevent the crossing of those mercenaries; but the rivers would now soon be fordable, and no security would then exist. He therefore begged to tender his resignation, and to be relieved without delay.

'Will you take up this matter, Taylor?' asked General Fraser of me. 'If you succeed, it will be a good thing for you, and you are at any rate independent. I cannot spare any other officer just now on whom I could rely.'

I saw it was a very, very difficult matter—one in which a very able man had failed; but it was a chance of political employment, for which I longed; and I was confident in myself, and knew that if I should be so fortunate as to succeed, Government would be obliged to me. So I accepted the offer at once, and said I would do my best to bring the refractory lady to terms. No doubt I was rash, but I could but do my best, and did not anticipate a long absence.

I went at onee to Secunderabad, packed up what things I required, took my tents, and marched the following morning to Hydcrabad. I employed the next day in reading up the very voluminous papers eonnected with the case, and afterwards again visited the Resident to have a final consultation. He explained his intended line of policy, which was to abstain from using force as long as negotiation could be carried on, and the interest of the Government seeured; that, in fact,

[1] June 27, 1839.

he had no available troops till the regiments now on their march should reach Hyderabad ; and then, if necessary, he would support me with four regiments.

I started alone the following morning, and on the fourth day reached Maktal, a distance of 120 miles.

On my way to Shorapur I went to Captain Gresley's camp, and heard from him an entire exposition of his transactions with Shorapur from first to last. He told me that the Rani's paramour, a man named Chan Basappa, was now paramount ; that Pid Naik was in dread of his life ; that the Rani was insolent and confident to the last degree ; that she knew of the British reverses in Afghanistan ; and that her astrologers were filling her mind with the most absurd stories of the evacuation of India by the English.

'I have twice failed in my negotiations with this woman,' said my old friend, 'and I could not humiliate either myself or the British Government by trying a third fall with her. You are a new hand, and may be more successful ; but I advise you to be very cautious, for no one is to be trusted in Shorapur, where the people, though outwardly civil enough, are at heart treacherous savages, and you would not be safe among them.'

This was not encouraging. I remained two days with my friend ; but the more I heard and the more I considered, the more the business seemed hopelessly involved. His views were convincing enough. He maintained that had he been at first supported by a regiment, with other forces at hand in case of need, all would have been arranged quietly without firing a shot ; but he was quite hopeless of my success now, as more mercenaries had already joined the Rani, and the Beydur militia were at her entire command.

He showed me, too, a letter from Colonel Tomkyns, part of which ran thus :

'If Taylor settles this matter without troops, he will be a cleverer fellow than I take him for !'

Not flattering, certainly, but quite enough to put me on my mettle, and I had formed a little plan of my own which I longed to test.

Next day I was at Shorapur.

It was a grim place to look at, certainly : a mass of granite mountains rising abruptly out of the plain, and though apparently several miles long, had no connection with any other range.

To the north, a second line of lower rocky hills ran parallel to Shorapur, and a flat valley about a mile or mile and a half wide lay between. The Shorapur hills were masses of granite, whose denuded tops appeared in strange *tors*, and piles of rocks exceeding in magnitude any I had before seen. There was no appearance of a city.

My tents were pitched in a pleasant tamarind-grove close to a suburb, and I was told that the town was over the brow of the hill before us, and lay in a hollow between the highest part of the range to the east, and a somewhat lower portion to the west. I found two companies of my old regiment, the 6th, and a few cavalry, as my escort.

About mid-day I was visited by Raja Pid Naik, who brought his nephew, the little prince, with him, several members of his own and the Rani's family, and a banker named Lakshmangir, a Gosain ;[1] and I read out the letter from General Fraser, which announced my mission, and in which he hoped that the measures of Government would be adopted without further delay, and recommended all parties to sink their differences in the common good of the State. I then warned them of the fate of many other States which had from time to time rejected and opposed the Government, and had perished under their own eyes, and entreated them not to be over confident, but to be very careful.

The Rani's brother formed one of the audience, and seemed very attentive. I told him that, as Pid Naik had been selected by Government, no other could be admitted as regent ; and after the warnings Captain Gresley and I had both given, any opposition to these orders would be considered rebellion, and without doubt would be dealt with as such.

[1] In the glossary to *Tara* Taylor writes : '*Gosai* or *Gosavee*, a sect of Hindu devotees, who are sometimes bankers.' In *Pandurang Hari* there is a deal about the Gosains. Frere recalls how, a century ago, they oppressed the inhabitants of Poona, living in a quarter by themselves, in houses which were like forts and which looked 'palatial amid the meaner houses of the surrounding town'.

I could see, however, that Pid Naik had no party, and that to set him up and pull the others down was almost a desperate matter, and I nearly inclined to Captain Gresley's opinion that force would be necessary. I requested that all the officers of the State troops, and the heads of the Beydur clans, might be sent to me next day, that I might explain to them the views of Government; and to my surprise they came to a man—about a hundred of as wild-looking fellows as I ever saw—and were introduced to me one by one, by one of the State officers. Pid Naik stayed away, and I was glad he did not come.

I spoke to them for some time. A few grew violent, and swore they would acknowledge no authority but the Rani's, and would fight for her and Chan Basappa to the death. Others were quiet, and, I thought, determined; and some appeared irresolute. I had done enough for that day, and dismissed the whole assembly with the ceremonious gifts of *atr*, and betel-leaf, and a garland of flowers.

'You treat us with respect,' said one of the jemadars or officers, 'and we thank you for it.'

'I always treat my friends with the respect I hope to receive myself,' I replied; and I believe this simple act of courtesy at least softened many.

Next day I went to return the visit of the little Raja, and to submit my demands to his mother.

If I had listened to all the warnings I received, I should never have ventured at all. Many, I was told, had vowed to make an end of me: the town was full of the Beydur militia, who had sworn to turn me out of Shorapur, and the like.

I had to ascend by a roughly-paved road, about 400 feet, into the city, which appeared well built and well populated, lying between portions of the rocky range which varied from 400 to 500 feet in height. Being completely screened from without, it seemed, as it had been described to me, a very stronghold of freebooters.

I was politely received in the outer court of the palace by the little Raja, where a great crowd of armed men were assembled, and then led into another court, and through a passage into a third, well built of red brick, and of two storeys. It contained two open halls, neatly covered with white cotton cloths, with large pillars at intervals. The little Raja, who was a delicate-looking though cheerful boy, was by no means disconcerted, and asked me many questions pleasantly, and at last invited me to come and see his mother.

She was in the next room, and sat at the door behind a bamboo screen—through which, however, she could see me, though I could not see her. She spoke neither Hindustani nor Marathi; but I had a good interpreter in one of the members of the family, who had been at Hyderabad, and was quite a gentleman. For a time she spoke very pleasantly, and the little Raja had, of his own accord, come to me, and was sitting in my lap. 'See,' said the Rani, 'my son has gone to you, as he never did to his father, and now you must be father to us all.'

This speech led the way to business; and when I told her it would be far from wise to pull her own house about her ears as she seemed to be doing, she replied, in the most innocent manner possible, 'That she was quite unaware of having offended any one, and could only look to the British Government to protect her and her son, as it had already done for several generations'.

We talked for four hours without ceasing, and at last I handed her a paper, in which I had embodied my demands.

1*st*, To give an account of the revenue for the last three years.

2*d*, To give over the Raja's seal of office.

3*d*, To make over all the armed men to Pid Naik.

This sadly bothered her, and she was as slippery as an eel; but it would not do. I said I would not leave her till I had her determination from her own mouth; for I had no faith in letters or messages, and I doggedly kept my seat.

This did good: for, though arguing bravely, the Rani was driven from her positions, one by one, and at last agreed to all my demands. Would she keep to her word? That remained to be seen. The only objection which I thought was a reasonable one was about the seal, which, being the Raja's, could not be used by his Minister; but, as she suggested, a seal of regency might be engraved and used. After this interview was over, I walked to Pid Naik's house through the crowd outside, and saw his three fine boys and two girls, while his wife sent me a kind message. He appeared more hopeful, and thought we were getting on.

Next day the leaders of all the armed men came to me again by appointment, and I requested they would at once give me agreements to serve Pid Naik and not the Rani. How I had to argue and coax by turns, I can hardly describe; but at last one came over to me, then another and another; but some remained unconvinced and went away.

I then wrote to the Rani; and, after a day's intermediate delay, she sent me about 400 men—those on whom she could least rely—and I made them over at once to Pid Naik. The Rani now began to see that she must either come down quietly or be pulled down, and in two days more I had secured 600 men. But still I was not satisfied.

The Beydurs had not come to me, and I was very anxious about them, as they were the representatives of the 12,000 militia, and the Raja's body-guard, on whom the Rani had lavished much money. I also had much anxiety respecting the garrison of Wondrug—a very strong fort, about ten miles off, in which there were 300 picked men. On the seventh day after my arrival I had secured 1400 men in all. The last 700 were Beydurs, as fine and bold a set of fellows as ever were seen, well armed with sword, shield, and matchlock.

'Tell us,' cried their leader, 'are you going to make Pid Naik Raja?'

'By no means,' I replied. 'He will only be Minister. Your little Raja is my son, and I will put him on his throne with my own hands before I go.'

'And you give us your word about this?' they asked.

'Certainly I do,' I cried, 'and the word of the British Government.'

'Enough!' was the general shout. 'And now put your hands on our heads, and we will be your obedient children henceforth.'

Then they crowded round me, and I placed my hands on a number of heads, many prostrating themselves before me, some weeping, and all much excited.

I had sent for baskets full of wreaths of flowers and betel-leaves, and I gave each of the leaders a garland, hanging it about their necks myself, while my attendants distributed the same to the others. As they filed down before me, each division gave me a hearty cheer: 'Jey Mahadeo Baba!'—the old cry of Golconda! How had they learned it? I confess it moved me deeply.

No fear now, thought I; and I was right, though there were some trials yet to undergo. All these men were sadly in arrears, and I took up money sufficient to give to each two months' pay. I did this solely on my own responsibility; but I saw the necessity, and felt sure I would be supported by General Fraser.

That evening they went of their own accord and made salaam to Pid Naik, who could hardly believe his senses when he saw them. The day after, all the horsemen of the State came to me. They had Chan Basappa in their charge to protect him from me, but promised obedience like the rest. I saw it was the time to demand him at their hands. To this most of them demurred, as they were on oath to the Rani; but they said, 'Though as a point of honour they could not give him up, yet they would have nothing more to do with him.'

Next day the Rani's agent came to try to get a promise of probation for Chan Basappa; but he found me utterly obdurate, and I suppose he went and told him it was no use resisting, for in the afternoon Chan Basappa himself came to me alone, and threw himself at my feet, making no conditions. 'He had now no protector from his enemies,' he said, 'and submitted himself to me to be dealt with as I pleased.'

I quote here the following passage taken from one of my letters to my father:—

'I hear the Lady is very sore, and I hope she is. There is a long account to settle with both—that is, with the Rani and Chan Basappa. They owe the Nizam's Government two lakhs, arrears of tribute which I must get; and they have paid none of the bankers whose instalments are in arrear. It will be no easy matter to get this money; but patience will do a great deal, and as yet no force has been used. Collectors have been sent into the districts to collect the revenue now due, and to establish Pid Naik's government; and I have only to hope all may go on quietly. Besides the papers to Pid Naik, I have taken others from all the mercenaries and the Beydurs, in the name of the British and Nizam's Governments, pledging themselves to obedience and allegiance, on pain of punishment if they go in opposition to the future management of the State.

'I have already found out that four days after the Rani had reported to the Resident that she had made over the Government to Pid Naik, she bound down all the Beydurs by oath, and many others, not to obey him, but to stand by her; and if she could have been joined by the Arabs and Rohillas, which Captain Gresley's vigilance alone prevented, she would have caused the Government of India much anxiety.'

I had now been at work ten days, and hard, anxious work it was.

So far, I had carried all my measures. My proceedings were entirely approved of, and I received the following official letter from the Resident on the 22d December, after my report had reached him :—

'These despatches demand from me nothing further than the expression of my entire approbation of the temper, judgment, and firmness which you are now exhibiting in the discharge of the duty intrusted to you; and it will be very gratifying to me to state to the Supreme Government, that under your judicious management the affairs of the Shorapur State may be arranged in a satisfactory manner, and without the necessity of having recourse to arms. . . . Nothing remains to me but to transmit to you my entire and unqualified approbation of all your proceedings.'

(Signed) 'J. S. FRASER, *Res*[t].'

Captain Gresley also wrote from Maktal :—

'You have managed admirably, and deserve very great credit. I could never have done the thing so well. General Fraser ought to be much obliged to you.'

These letters were very gratifying and encouraging; but the following, which the general was so good as to write to my wife, was even more so :—

'MY DEAR MRS. TAYLOR,—I cannot resist the pleasure of telling you, because I am sure it will give you pleasure, that I have received three despatches from my *chargé d'affaires*, your good husband, at Shorapur, and that he is succeeding admirably in the duty intrusted to him—even getting the better of a lady!—the Rani Ishwarama—which of all diplomatic transactions is probably the most difficult.

'He has exhibited the most perfect temper, tact, and judgment, and I have been delighted to express my entire and unqualified approbation of the whole of his proceedings.

'The requisite communication has also, of course, been made to the Governor-General, and it gratifies me to think the despatches must equally meet the approval of this higher authority.—Very faithfully yours,

'J. S. FRASER.'

And the following extract from a letter from the Secretary of Government followed very shortly afterwards :—

'The Governor-General directs me to express the great satisfaction with which he has perused these reports, and his entire concurrence in the just approbation you have bestowed upon the temper, judgment, and firmness evinced by Captain Taylor in the several transactions he has detailed.'

(Signed) 'T. EDWARDS, *Assist. Secy.*'

In addition to the above, I had almost daily private letters from the general, which were very encouraging; but I have kept no copies of them, nor, indeed, are they needed here.

I had not, however, by any means, done with the Rani yet. After my first flush of success, her party again assumed formidable dimensions, and I feared might incite her to fresh opposition. I had only myself to rely upon, for Pid Naik was utterly useless and helpless. I did not relax in any of the demands which I had made, for which the Rani alone was responsible, having collected the revenue for many years; and finding I would not give in, she sent to me to say she was preparing bills for a lakh of rupees.

These were, however, so long in making their appearance, and there were so many evasions and excuses for which I could not account, that I grew more suspicious, and discovered at length that Chan Basappa, who was in my camp under surveillance, was sending the Rani private messages to delay; that I 'should soon be turned out, as Captain Gresley had been, and that I had no force at hand to use in case of resistance'.

At last the Lady sent the banker to me with an impudent message, to the effect that if Chan Basappa were released unconditionally by me, and if she were allowed to have her own way in the direction of affairs, she would then pay the lakh of rupees.

This was displaying the cloven foot with a vengeance, and it was evident that so long as Chan Basappa remained, these secret intrigues would go on. I heard, too, that she was endeavouring to incite some of the 12,000 Beydur militia to attack my camp and rescue her paramour, and my men had noticed a great number of them prowling about, and posted on the hillsides at night. I therefore determined to send Chan Basappa at once to Lingsugur,[1] the cantonment of the south, where he would be quite safe and kept out of mischief. One of my *chaprassis* or messengers knew the road perfectly, and the Krishna river was fordable.

Twenty-five of my cavalry were therefore ordered to prepare for a night march; and about nine o'clock, when all was quiet, I went to Chan Basappa, and told him he had forfeited his word, and was leading his mistress into fresh trouble. He did not deny the charge, but confessed the Rani had sent him word that she would rescue him. I told him I had likewise heard the same, and that he must gird up his loins at once and mount the horse that awaited him.

In five minutes more he was on his road, guarded by the cavalry escort, and reached Lingsugur the following morning in safety.

Long afterwards this man thanked me, with tears in his eyes, for having saved him, and the Rani too, from much evil—perhaps even from death; and told me, also, how narrowly I had escaped myself. If I had not been very vigilant, I would have been attacked by clans of the 12,000 whom I had not seen. I wrote to my father thus :—

'Great was the indignation and consternation of the

---

[1] There was a former district of Lingsugur, as there is still a taluk of the same name in Raichur District. But the headquarters of Lingsugur taluk are the larger town of Mudgal (see note below, on the Christian colony there). Lingsugur town has a population of some 5,000. 'The Mahbub bazar, 2 miles north of the town', says the *Imperial Gazetteer*, 'was the site of a cantonment while the District was held by the British from 1853 to 1860'—and evidently earlier. Lingsugur cantonment appears in the following narrative as Taylor's nearest point of contact with civilisation from Shorapur, and the place where he took his wife for aid when dying.

Lady in the morning. She beat her head, and, as it was reported to me, knocked it against the wall, roared and cried, and then, in a violent passion, rushed into the outer court of her palace, and called upon all good men and true to help her to get Chan Basappa back again. This was the crisis that I expected, and upon it would turn everything, hostile or peaceable. But nobody stirred. Only six negro slaves loaded their guns, and threatened everybody; but, being threatened by others, quietly fired them off, and were placed under surveillance.

'Well, my lady then was down on her marrow-bones for a few days, and my humble servant. She had her palankeen prepared to come and see me, which, I declared, without my wife's presence, would be indecent. Then began a series of sorrowful letters, with presents of partridges and quail, fruit and vegetables; but it would not do: I must have my lakh of rupees; and it came in two days in bills, which I very gladly despatched to Hyderabad.'

I now determined to discharge certain of the mercenaries; and in consequence of the Rani's obstinacy about the money transactions, the Resident thought it would be too hazardous to attempt the measure without some backing up. The 26th Regiment, Madras Infantry, which was on its march to Secunderabad, was therefore ordered to make a diversion to Shorapur, and to await my orders. In reality I did not want the regiment; but the Resident was more cautious than I, and thought prevention better than cure. I had no trouble with the mercenaries. Those who were needed for ordinary duty were retained; superfluous men discharged, their arrears for four years being paid to them according to their amounts. I thought the garrison of Wondrug were inclined to be restive, but the men all came into camp, a very fine set of fellows; and when I had inspected them, looked at their arms, and complimented them on their steadiness, I called for volunteers for a hog-hunt, and I think more than half the men responded at once: so we started, the officers of the 26th Regiment joining heartily, and showed them good sport before we returned.

Another very anxious crisis thus passed over; but the Rani said she had no more money, though her own accounts showed she had more in hand than the 75,000 rupees I had asked for, and I told her that I had no alternative but to attach her private estates if she remained obstinate; and at last I did so by sending small parties of cavalry into her villages, and this so completely humbled her, that, in consideration of her having complied with the former demands made, I begged that the balance still remaining might be remitted. She was literally at my feet for one day: though I told her not to come, she arrived in her palankeen at my tent, to lay all her sorrows before me. I could not turn her away; and as she entered she fell prostrate on the ground, and placed her son in my arms. Both were weeping bitterly. She begged hard for her estates; but as the attachment had been made at the instance of the Nizam's Government, I could not take upon myself to withdraw it, and could but assure her that I did not wish to punish her more, and that I trusted Government would be lenient in the end. The Rani had arrived just after breakfast, and sat with me till sunset, surrounded by her women and secretaries, unveiled, nor did she ever seclude herself afterwards.

I had sent for my wife, who, with her brother, soon afterwards arrived from Hyderabad, and I selected an open spot within the walls, about 500 feet above the plain, to which we removed. The Rani now asked permission to come and visit us, and I was glad that she should do so. She offered many valuable presents—shawls and ornaments—and tried to put a large string of pearls round my wife's neck; so that I was obliged to tell her firmly that if she attempted again to force presents on my wife, or to talk to her about her affairs. I should be forced to forbid all communication between them,

The next day we returned the visit, and were introduced to all the family.

The late Raja had had three wives, and in all there were fifteen children. Among these, one lively child, of about ten years old, became our prime favourite, and she engaged me in a game of romps, pelting me with roses, and laughing merrily. There was not the slightest attempt on the part of any of them to hide their faces, nor was there any of the stiffness usual among native families.

The more I became acquainted with the State affairs, the more anxious I grew to have the remainder of the Rani's debt to the Nizam's Government remitted. Under cloak of British authority, it had, on the late Raja's accession, not only imposed a fine of fifteen lakhs (£150,000), but an additional yearly tribute of 56,000 rupees. It was no wonder, therefore, that under an improvident and neglectful Government the State affairs had fallen lower and lower, and it required very careful treatment to enable them to recover.

Eventually, at my suggestion, a new arrangement was entered into between the Nizam's Government and the State of Shorapur. Another division of the *parganas* or counties was authorised, ceding that of Deodrug[1] to the Nizam, and retaining that of Andola[2] on the frontier line, whose people were most unwilling to be transferred.

The Nizam's Government was to give up all claim for arrears of tribute and succession fine, and the annual tribute was now fixed at 60,000 rupees a-year. These were the best terms I could get; and it was only by showing how entirely the successive Residents at Hyderabad had been misled by reports from temporarily deputed officers to Shorapur, and how the original sum demanded under the treaty of 1800 had been increased, that I gained my point. If, as in justice ought to have been the case, past exactions had been repudiated, the Nizam's Government would have been obliged to refund; but all these exactions had been recognised by us, English officers had been deputed to levy them, and their transactions were immutable. The retention of Andola, and remission of all arrears of tribute—the interest on which, at the ordinary market rate of 12 per cent, would be 60,000 rupees—were certainly some service done to the State, and were the most favourable terms I could procure. But the Nizam's Government grumbled terribly at being obliged to give up its dominant position and revert to its original status. It could no longer make extra demands through us, and get us

[1] Headquarters of the taluk of the same name in Raichur District, with a population of some 7,000. 'Deodrug', says the *Imperial Gazetteer*, 'contains an old fort enclosed on all sides except the west by hills, and was the stronghold of the *poligars* of the Bedar tribe, who were so powerful that the first of the Nizams sought their alliance.' It is a place unforgettable in Beydur history, as Taylor's text will show.

[2] Not to be confounded with Andol, in Medak District, at the centre of the Nizam's territories. The *Imperial Gazetteer* has articles only on the taluks of Andola and Andol, so the towns must be unimportant, though given with beautiful clearness in the map of Hyderabad State.

by treaty to enforce them. It could not impose a succession fine on the young Raja. It could only get what I had proposed, and which was ratified by the Supreme Government.

Of course, owing to these arrangements, my friend the Rani got back her estates and the revenues collected, which had been kept in deposit; but her appanage was reduced from 30,000 to 18,000 rupees a-year, the Raja's expenses being borne by the State. I think at the time she was very grateful, and the reduction of the Nizam's Government demands seemed to strike every one—most of all Pid Naik. Indeed, with careful management the State would be easily able to pay them.

I soon perceived that it would be necessary to lose no time in placing the young Raja on his *gadi*, or throne, that he might be publicly acknowledged. My reason was this. For some years after her marriage, the Rani had had no male child, nor had any of the other wives. In fact the late Raja had formed two other marriages, in hopes of having an heir.

If there were no male heir born to him, his brother Pid Naik naturally succeeded; but Pid Naik declined succession for himself, and put forward his eldest son for adoption, who had been generally acknowledged, although no ceremony of actual adoption took place.

However, when hope was nearly at an end, the Rani had a son, and Pid Naik's son was thrown out. It came to my ears that Pid Naik, encouraged by his boon companions at his drinking-bouts, had said that 'Now he could do as he pleased, and had the ball at his feet, and he would show them all so after I had been withdrawn.' In any case, whether this were true or not, he was very cool about the ceremony of placing the young Raja on his *gadi*. He made many excuses. It would cost a great deal of money; the Beydur clans must be brought together, and he was by no means sure of them; an auspicious day must be selected, and was far distant, and the like; and if anything went wrong, he would get the blame. However, I simply told him I had received orders from the Supreme Government to proceed with the ceremony on the earliest possible date, and according to the rules and customs of the family on such occasions, and that it must be done forthwith.

And so it was. Arrangements were made of all kinds. There proved to be enough money in the treasury to pay the expenses of the ceremony. Invitations were sent to the neighbouring families and people of rank, and the State observed its usual profuse hospitality to all, and its charitable doles to beggars, dancers, jugglers, acrobats, etc.; and for three days previous to the ceremony the feasting was perpetual. Finally, when all the Hindu rites had been concluded, I took the little Raja, who had been sitting close to me, as his mother had implored me not to allow him out of my sight, and leading him to his *gadi*, or cushion of embroidered velvet, placed him upon it in the name of the Government of India and the Nizam.

'Whoever', I said to the crowds about us, 'is the friend of your Raja Enketappa Naik' (and I added his titles), 'is the friend of both Governments; and whoever is his enemy is our enemy, and will be dealt with as he deserves. The British Government will protect your Raja and his interests till he reaches his majority, after which his possessions will be made over to him. It is, you see, a long journey to travel: some will faint and fall by the way—some will fail; but in the end, if ye are all of my mind, ye will joyfully repeat this ceremony.'

Then followed great clapping of hands, and again the old cry, 'Jey Mahadeo Baba!' and afterwards the distribution of *pan* and *atr*, with handsome shawls and dresses of honour, according to degree. The ceremony being ended, the little prince rose, and thanked all present in, for his age, a very dignified manner; and I took him back to his mother, who embraced him passionately. Whatever the Rani may have been, there was no question that her love for him then was devoted, and that she was very grateful to me.

'This would never have taken place but for you,' she said to me, as she embraced my wife, who had been with her all the afternoon. 'What can I give you?—how can I thank you both? My child is in truth yours, and you must guard him henceforth as a son.'

We submitted, as a matter of form, to be enveloped in rich shawls, and soon afterwards took our leave. Pid Naik had accompanied us to the entrance of the inner court, but it was not etiquette for him to proceed further, and he waited for us and went with us to our tents, amidst firing of guns and noisy music.

So far, I hoped I had done my duty, but I felt uncertain as to the future, for no definite position had been assigned to me as yet.

CHAPTER VIII[1]

1843–44

My position, however, had meanwhile been considered by the Governor-General, and shortly afterwards I received the following despatch from General Fraser, dated 18th May 1843 :—

'I transmit for your information and guidance the accompanying letter from the Secretary of the Government of India.

'The sentiments of the Governor-General regarding the administration of the Shorapur State during the minority of the Raja Enketappa Naik are so fully and clearly expressed in this despatch, that it is only left for me to request that you will be strictly guided by them.

---

[1] There is a passage in the *Life of James Stuart Fraser* which belongs to the opening of 1843. Colonel Hastings Fraser cannot have been a very accurate person, considering the two words which I have underlined in the only sentence which he has about Taylor: 'Captain Meadows Taylor, mentioned in the following letter to Lord Ellenborough —well known *subsequently* as author of *Confessions of a Thug*, and several other works—was one of the local officers of the Nizam's Army, and had been, at General Fraser's instance and with the Minister's consent, placed in charge of the small State of Shorapore, tributary to the Nizam, which had fallen into confusion during the minority of its Rajah, and under the disputed guardianship of his *step*-mother.'

General Fraser writes to the Governor-General, Hyderabad, January 7, 1843: 'I beg to send your Lordship four private letters from Captain Taylor, which may perhaps aid his official ones in giving a correct idea of the state of affairs at Shorapore. I am quite satisfied with the manner in which Captain Taylor is conducting his proceedings there, and I shall not now hesitate in the execution of measures for reducing the Ranee of Shorapore to obedience, and to oblige her to render an account of her past administration. The Shorapore business is sufficiently illustrative of the general state of confusion and disorganisation of the whole of the Nizam's country. It is upon a small scale what the latter is upon a large one; and the same remedy would be found equally efficacious in the latter case as in the former.'

'I shall be glad, however, to be informed that the caution enjoined in the fourth para. has been observed, and that the system upon which it has now been determined that the administration of Shorapur shall be for some time conducted, is in conformity with the wishes, not only of Raja Pid Naik, but also of the most influential persons in the State.

'You will be so good as furnish me with such occasional reports of your proceedings as may be necessary for my information, and for eventual submission to the Government of India; and I shall be glad to be informed of the measures you may deem it advisable to adopt, with a view to give a good practical education to the Raja; and I beg that you will from time to time make me acquainted with the character and disposition he manifests, and the extent or degree in which he profits by the instructions you may have the opportunity of giving, or causing to be given to him.

'It will be highly gratifying to you to have received the Governor-General's entire approbation of your conduct; and I am happy to be able to add, as the expression of my own personal sentiments towards you, that I place the utmost reliance on the judgment and discretion which you have hitherto manifested, and which are so essentially necessary in the official connection of every British officer with the natives of India.'

(Signed) 'J. S. FRASER.'

Copy of despatch from the Secretary to the Government of India with the Governor-General, to Major-General Fraser, Resident at Hyderabad:

'POLITICAL DEPARTMENT, AGRA,
3*d May* 1843.

'SIR,—

'1. The Governor-General has read with regret Captain Taylor's letter and its enclosures transmitted to me in your letter of the 20th ultimo.

'2. The Governor-General was in hopes that the administration of the Shorapur State might have been carried on during the minority of the Raja, ostensibly by Raja Pid Naik, with the general advice and support of Captain Taylor, but without his assuming a prominent part in the government.

'3. The facts stated by Captain Taylor, and the decided opinion expressed by him, in which you coincide, with the admission of Raja Pid Naik of his inability to carry on the government, and his request that you will appoint a gentleman who, in conjunction with himself, will arrange the affairs of the Shorapur State—all these circumstances compel the Governor-General to adopt, most reluctantly, the conclusion that a British officer will be necessary, in order to secure

M

to the inhabitants of the Shorapur State, during the minority of the Raja, a just and beneficial government, and to enable the State to perform its pecuniary obligations towards the Nizam and its creditors.

'4. The Governor-General considers it desirable that, notwithstanding the transference of the administrative authority in Shorapur to a British officer, Raja Pid Naik should, as far as possible, be put forward as the head of the State during the minority of the Raja; and it will be obviously expedient that the British officer should act in concert with Raja Pid Naik, and place the young Raja upon the Hindu throne (*gadi*) with the usual ceremonies.

'5. The Governor-General therefore authorises your directing the adoption of such measures as will be necessary for the adoption of these objects; it being understood that the proceedings be in conformity with the wishes, not of Raja Pid Naik alone, but of the most influential persons of Shorapur.

'6. The Governor-General intimated, on the death of the late Raja, the interest he took in the welfare of the minor Raja succeeding under such painful circumstances; and his Lordship particularly directs that every consideration be upon all occasions shown to the young Raja; and that every measure be adopted which the judgment of yourself and the British officer at Shorapur suggests, for the purpose of imparting to him a good practical education, such as may render him capable of administering the government of his State with benefit to his subjects.

'7. It is not sufficient to place in the hands of the Raja, on his attaining his majority, a prosperous and well-ordered State. It is due to his people—it is necessary to our character—that the State should be confided to hands by which prosperity and good order may be preserved.

'8. The Governor-General has much satisfaction in seeing the difficult task of restoring the State of Shorapur to the condition it seems to have once enjoyed, confided to Captain Taylor, whose good disposition, ability, and discretion, have been manifested in all the transactions in which he had been engaged.

'9. The Governor-General requests that you will communicate to Captain Taylor his entire approbation of his conduct.'

(Signed) 'J. THOMASON,[1]
Secy. to the Govt. of India.'

---

[1] This was the James Thomason, 1804–1853, of whom his admirers think so very highly. After being Foreign Secretary he was Lieutenant-Governor of the North-West Provinces for ten years from 1843, having been appointed Governor of Madras on the day of his death. Taylor came to disapprove greatly of his land revenue system.

It was in consequence of these instructions that the young Raja had been placed upon his throne, and I was very grateful for this proof of Lord Ellenborough's entire approval of my conduct. I had received neither from General Fraser nor the Governor-General any specific instructions as to the details of the future government of the State, and I felt, as these appeared to be left entirely in my hands, that no greater proof of confidence could have been manifested. I had given Pid Naik a fair chance from the time I had put him in charge as regent. I had assisted him to the very utmost of my power; but he was utterly helpless and incompetent. I had suggested many systematic improvements for his treasury; for collection of the revenue; for provision for the tribute he would have to pay, and the like,—not one of which plans was there the slightest intention, apparently, to carry out. On the contrary, he seemed to be surrounded by a new set of harpies and obstructors of order. He gave himself up occasionally to fits of intoxication, from which no one could arouse him.

His excellent wife made piteous complaints to me and to my wife on the subject, and so did his sons, giving me sad accounts of his bad habits, and how sometimes for days together no one saw him, when he and his special favourites continued their drunken orgies night and day. If I remonstrated privately he cried like a child, promised most humbly to amend, and was as bad as ever directly afterwards. His brother, his uncle, and all the Government officers reasoned with him, but in vain; he was indeed hopeless.

I had explained the purport of the Government despatches, and had quoted to Pid Naik and all concerned, including the chief bankers and merchants, the points to be observed, and they expressed themselves perfectly satisfied. The population, too, of the villages and districts seconded the others with every expression of confidence; but still, I thought more was necessary; and as I was summoned to Hyderabad as a witness on a court-martial then about to sit, I wished to take the opportunity of laying the whole subject before General Fraser, with a view to obtaining his specific instructions with regard to Raja Pid Naik.

There were many important matters to arrange. The

local bankers had claims, they alleged, upon the State for nearly twenty lakhs (£200,000). There had been no revenue settlement of the land for more than half a century; but I need not describe the condition of an effete State which had been going rapidly to ruin under heavy pressure from without and absolute neglect within. No hand had been stretched out to save it; and, I think, more pity and consideration ought to have been shown to the oldest princely family in the Deccan, which, through all wars and revolutions, had preserved its possessions without committing itself with any one since the earliest period of the Adil Shahi dynasty of Bijapur.

Fortunately, I was not obliged to leave Shorapur till August, when the first violence of the monsoon was over, and the weather was delightfully cool and pleasant. Although we had lived all through the hot season in tents on the open ground, none of the party had suffered in the least, and our time had passed very pleasantly. My wife was a great favourite with the ladies of the palace, and with the children, who came sometimes to spend the day, playing very much like other little ones, and bringing their dolls with them, for whom feasts were made.[1] Sometimes the Rani herself, or one of the other matrons, accompanied them, and the young Raja came too; sometimes Pid Naik's sons and their mother,

[1] A dolls' feast among grown girls is described in *Seeta*.

There is a pleasant page upon the subject in Taylor's *History*: 'Toys and playthings for young children are common in all parts of India; they are made both of wood and earthenware, and being mentioned in the earliest dramas and poems, appear to have existed from very remote times. . . . What the girls of India, whether Hindoo or Mahomedan, would do without dolls, it is hard to say, and they are at least as numerous as they are among English or French children. . . They are of wood, painted, and are frequently frightful enough. . . . In India the Hindoo or Mahomedan girl of good family and ample means has her doll's-room specially set spart. . . . Dolls' ornaments and clothes are frequently very expensive, and I have known instances, in a princely family, of a doll's trousseau and jewels costing some thousands of rupees. Dolls sometimes need change of air, and there is a children's party at a garden-house, or in the fields under the trees, and a feast, with a happy gathering of young people and a merry return home by moonlight. Were it not for dolls, therefore, Hindoo and Mahomedan girls might have a dull time; but . . . the interest and affection is the same, and may not have varied for thousands of years.'

who was very delicate: in short, there was no constraint among them, and they went and came as they pleased.

I had heard these Beydurs called 'savages'; but in truth they are no more savages than other nations of India. They are perhaps somewhat more blunt and less obsequious, far more natural in manner, and we liked them all the better for that. My own tent was open to all comers from breakfast-time to sunset—no one was refused; and although I did not personally inquire into cases of complaints, I referred all such petitions to Raja Pid Naik by endorsement. If I could have spoken Kanarese, I should have felt more at my ease; but many who came spoke Marathi and Hindustani, so that I managed to get on very comfortably on the whole. I had selected a site for a house during one of our evening rambles—a small level plain on the top of the plateau to the west of the city, and directly overlooking it, the mountain beyond it, and the plain beyond that again. The view was certainly very fine; and as the site was 400 feet above the town, it would not only be cooler, but more healthy than below.

The ground was being cleared, and the places marked out for house, stables, and servants' offices. I hoped, on our return from Hyderabad, to find the building had commenced; and there were plenty of first-rate masons and other work-people in the city. It was impossible to say how long we might be detained at Hyderabad, so I could only leave all the directions in my power to Pid Naik; and having done this, we started, and marching as rapidly as we could, we reached Hyderabad on the tenth day.

Before leaving Shorapur, however, I had the great pleasure of receiving the following extract from a private letter from Lord Ellenborough to General Fraser, who wrote—

'It gives me great pleasure to send you the subjoined extract from a *private* letter from Lord Ellenborough, on the subject of your management of recent affairs at Shorapur.'

(*Extract.*)

'The account Captain Taylor gives of the proceedings of the Beydurs, and of the arrangement with them, is very satisfactory. He has managed the affairs in which he has been engaged extremely well.'

And I considered that a private letter from the Governor-General was much more complimentary and comforting than a public and formal despatch.

After all, I was not long detained at Hyderabad, and arrived once more at Shorapur on the 1st September. My presence was very necessary, but as everything was going on well and quietly, there was no need for any anxiety about me. During my short stay at Hyderabad, General Fraser and I had fully discussed the Governor-General's despatch, which I had already communicated to Pid Naik, and all the principal persons of Shorapur, including the Rani ; but it was necessary, I was of opinion, for the Resident to write himself to Pid Naik on the subject. The commencement of an English direction of local affairs was a momentous event for Shorapur ; and no room for doubt ought to remain, or any question of the purpose of the British Government. My own position, and that of Pid Naik, should be clearly defined. General Fraser desired me to prepare the draft of a letter in English and in Persian, to be sent to Pid Naik, embodying the wishes and directions of the Governor-General. This I did ; but the Resident did not approve of it, and said he would make one himself. When the two were compared and checked by the best Persian scholars, who were called in, mine at last was adopted.

I had availed myself of Mr. Palmer's directions in correcting my own draft. He was a first-rate Persian scholar, and could at once suggest the most expressive, as well as the most courteous, and plain, and decided phrases that a paper of the kind required, as applicable to persons of Pid Naik's position and understanding. Mr. Palmer's assistance to me had proved very valuable. I wish I possessed a copy of this document, but I do not find it amongst my father's collection of my letters and papers.

My position at Shorapur was declared to be supreme, and that of Pid Naik executive ; and sound advice was given him to practise rigid and systematic economy, until the financial difficulties of the State were overcome.

Pid Naik was styled 'Raja Pid Naik Diwan',[1] and was to be allowed a seal as such. He had claimed the same title as the Raja, 'Balwant Bhiri Bahadur' ; but this was a

[1] Regent. [M. T.]

ridiculous assumption, and would have been resented by the Raja, the Rani, and others of the family. Doubtless he would feel chagrined by the title proposed, and by the whole matter; but I had no resource but to do my duty, and let him down as easily as I could.

As soon as I arrived at Shorápur, Pid Naik paid me a visit. Everything had gone on smoothly during my absence, and I complimented him upon all he had done. I then delivered to him the Resident's letter, and he sent away his crowd of attendants and followers in order that we might discuss the subject unrestrainedly between us. It had been left optional to him to accept the orders of the Governor-General or not, as he chose; and I was ready to transmit his wishes, whatever they might be, whether of entire and *bona fide* acquiescence in the orders issued, or his objections to them, as he pleased. If he acquiesced, it would be my duty and care to make the execution of these orders as light and pleasant to him as possible; but if he objected, I could only transmit any letter or paper that he might give me.

He said his honour and reputation were in my hands, and he would think over the letter from the Resident, and give me an answer as soon as possible. This he did; and the reply, when it came, was quite satisfactory, and expressed his desire to work faithfully with me for the good of the State. Between us we made out a budget of the State revenues for the year, and I found that we might have 240,000 rupees, out of which the local charges would be 100,000, leaving 140,000 for payment of tribute and interest, with a balance to go on with.

A few days after this interview there happened a disagreeable affair in Shorapur. One of my *chaprassis*, or messengers, was buying some grass in the market-place from a Beydur woman, and was badly wounded by an armed Beydur standing near. Whether my *chaprassi* had insulted the woman or the man, or whether they quarrelled over the price, I never knew; but he was never accused of having done so. I had just set out from my house to ride up to my new works on the hill, and had turned into the market-place, when I saw the Beydur run off, brandishing his bloody sword; and after procuring what assistance I could for my wounded *chaprassi*,

I went after the Beydur who had cut him down. I met him in the main street, and ordered him to give me up his sword, which strangely enough he did at once (I had only a slight riding-whip in my hand), and telling my prisoner to go before me, I took him to the palace guard, and gave him in custody to the men on duty there, to be kept safely until Pid Naik, who was out shooting, should return. I then rode on towards my new buildings, and returned shortly before sunset.

It was still quite light as I rode back into the town, and I found a crowd of armed men before the palace gate, shouting and much excited. The first idea that occurred to me was that there might have been some collision between my escort of twenty infantry and the Beydurs; but I had sent my people word to remain quiet, and they had done so.

As soon as I appeared I was surrounded in an instant on every side, so that it was impossible for my horse to move one step, and the shouting and peculiar shrieking of the Beydurs were indescribable. Many matchlocks were pointed at once close to my body; and I saw one fellow's match pressed into the priming-pan by the trigger twice, and grains of powder igniting on the end of it each time it was withdrawn. For a moment I gave myself up; but, by the mercy of God, the piece did not go off. Drawn swords were also brandished close to my face, but no blow was made at me; and the whole passed in less time than it takes me to write.

At that moment several men ran out of the palace gate, one of whom I knew to be the Raja's own body-servant. He pushed through the crowd, struck up the matchlock then touching me, and calling out to the crowd, pushed them aside right and left, telling me not to be afraid. He then accompanied me to my house, where I found my escort under arms and much excited.

The Rani sent me word that both she and the Raja would come to me at once, if I would allow them, and stay with me, or would I come to them? But there was no need now, though I felt in my heart I had nearly tasted death. The men of my escort were very savage; and it was as much as I could do to prevent their marching to the palace court and taking the offending Beydur into their own custody. Pid Naik shortly after arrived in a terrible fright, and offered to stay with me all night, but I felt no further alarm. The Beydurs, however, went to the palace guard at night and carried off the prisoner to the hills. He was a champion among them, a wrestler and athlete, and had the appellation of 'Bich Kati', or 'Thrower away of the Scabbard'.

In the morning all the clans of the 'Twelve Thousand' were found to have gone out upon the hills, where they were shrieking, blowing horns, and beating their drums all day, vowing they would not surrender the man unless they had a guarantee from me that his life would be spared.

A row with the Beydurs would have been very serious, and I was determined not to have one if I could help it; at the same time I was equally determined not to give way an inch. Pid Naik was in a desperate fright; but I would not allow him to give in, and he obeyed my orders, insisting that the prisoner should be sent back to him.

By evening the Beydurs grew tired, and made over the prisoner to Pid Naik, who forthwith put him in irons, at my suggestion, though he was more than half afraid of his own people. I daresay they did not like it; but it was no time to show the white feather. Having waited for a day to see that all was quiet, I urged Pid Naik to make the Beydurs bind themselves down by strong bonds to behave quietly for the future. At this they took fresh alarm; but they did not go back to the hills, and I knew my game was safe; and so it proved in the end. I made known to them that I would take no further steps in the affair until the issue of the wounded *chaprassi's* case was known; and I was very glad for all parties concerned that he seemed going on well. I sent them all away, with a present for the wife and family of the imprisoned Beydur, as it appeared they subsisted entirely on the fruit of his labour, and all seemed satisfied and happy.

I daresay my *chaprassi* was a good deal in fault—for he was a bit of a coxcomb, and no doubt had given himself airs—and I only put the Beydur in irons in order to make an example.

A few weeks after, on the occasion of the Dasara—a great anniversary festival of the Hindus—the head men of all the clans of the Twelve Thousand came to me with a very humble petition on behalf of the Beydur still in confinement, and said they would esteem it a direct favour if the man were released to them. They were ready to make any agreement or bond with me, and to obey me implicitly in all things. My *chaprassi* had nearly recovered from his severe wound; at all events, his life was no longer in danger from it: and as he too joined in the request that his assailant should be forgiven, and the young Raja, Pid Naik, and his brothers, and other influential persons, backed up the petition, I saw no reason to refuse. By consenting, I had a fair hope that this hitherto utterly lawless and uncontrollable body of men might be brought under some kind of subjection for the future. I therefore complied with their request, and the Beydur prisoner was released before them. He came blubbering to me, falling at my feet and begging pardon. He then prostrated himself before my *chaprassi*, who also forgave him. But I had impressed upon Pid Naik the necessity of requiring from all the heads of the clans much more stringent and more formal engagements than they had given before, which, it now leaked out, they repudiated as irregular and not binding. At the first hint of what was intended, the Beydurs took fright, but they did not go back into the hills; and after a consultation among themselves, under their great tree of assembly in the centre of the town, they gave in, and professed themselves ready to do as I wished. The agreements, which contained several clauses, were drawn up by me. They secured to the clans all hereditary lands and privileges, but made me, as the chief authority in the State, supreme judge in criminal cases, and in any other trials which could not be settled by their own *panchayat* (court). My drafts were copied by their own chief registrar, and signed by him, and by all the chiefs, and many others. When the agreements were ratified in all respects, I held a court, and the papers were presented to me formally, and I crossed hands over them with the chiefs of every clan. It was a very anxious period, and the complete success of the affair was a very great relief to me. General Fraser, too, had been very anxious; for any disturbance among the 'clans of the Twelve Thousand' would have been most embarrassing after what had at first occurred. However, in the end he was satisfied that I was in reality now stronger than ever.

Several years afterwards, I heard the truth of the whole

affair, and I was thankful I had not known it at the time. The plot had been originated by Krishnaya, Pid Naik's especial favourite and boon companion, whether with his master's knowledge and connivance or not I cannot say; but Pid Naik was, whether accidentally or on purpose, absent that day on a hog-hunting expedition.

The plan was this: One of my men—any one—was to be quarrelled with and cut down by the Beydur champion, on which it was presumed that I would immediately attack the Beydurs to recover possession of him, and thus a general *mêlée* would ensue, in which I would be made away with. The scheme, I daresay, seemed perfectly feasible, for no blame would have attached to any one, except, perhaps, myself. But, through God's great mercy, I escaped.

As soon as I could leave Shorapur after the Dasara festival, I determined on making a short tour to see the country and become acquainted with the rural population, and also to give directions concerning the first settlement of revenue. I had, too, some cases of border raids and robberies of cattle by Beydurs on the northern frontier, to inquire into and adjust. I found that for generations past no notice had ever been taken of such depredations by the Rajas, and the issues had been left to the strongest. This, however, would not do now. I found that, wherever the land was under cultivation, the crops were, for the most part, very fine, but that there was comparatively little under tillage, when the large areas of village lands were considered. For these the people were clamorous for leases. I was obliged to tell them at present I could do nothing, but that I hoped to return as soon as I could. Meanwhile I was picking up all the information in my power, in my rides over village lands. There was plenty of game everywhere, and my bag was generally well filled; the people were exceedingly well-disposed and civil, and my time was passed very pleasantly. In November I received official notification of my promotion:—

'Captain Meadows Taylor, 6th Nizam's Infantry, is promoted to the rank of "Captain Commandant", with effect from 7th July last, *vice* Doveton resigned the service. Captain Commandant Meadows Taylor is posted to the 7th Regiment, but will continue in charge of the affairs of Shorapur.'

I was therefore secure of a regimental command in case of any alteration in the arrangements at Shorapur. I returned there about the middle of November, and was distressed and vexed to find that Pid Naik had been at his old work, drinking very hard.

'I find', I wrote to my father on the 22d November, 'Pid Naik is seemingly on his last legs, morally and physically. He looks very shaky, and has been seriously ill, after some days of beastly drunkenness; and I am sure more will follow when I leave again.

'I had to counteract endless petty schemes and dirty tricks. "Who is the man who prevents these?" said his Brahmins; and he replied—

'"Ah, it's all very well for you; your knuckles are not rapped: it is only mine."

'I would not be put off with excuses that so-and-so had peculated or intrigued, but would only exclaim—

'"You are the executive, and you have full power to check all irregularities. If I did the work myself, you would grumble, and I look to you. Why cannot you go on comfortably, and in a broad, straight road with me? You know you always suffer in the end. Why are you so foolish? If you want money, say so—come and ask for it. The treasury (for I had established one with some difficulty) is not yours or mine; it belongs to the State. You can have what you require for State purposes; but do not steal from it, or allow cheating."

'Personally we are very good friends, and now and then he really does some trifling business; but where the State moneys are concerned, he has no idea of honour or principle. He has not been seen for the last two months in public, except when he has come to visit me; and the people whom he employs have largely increased their power. Here is an instance of what goes on:—

'A learned man and very holy Brahmin who returned from the annual pilgrimage to Tripatti,[1] and had charge of

[1] A shrine of superlative sanctity in North Arcot District, some hundreds of miles away. Tripatti or Tirupati is a town of about 15,000 inhabitants, 'crowded at all times with pilgrims to the famous shrine on Tirumala'. This, or Upper Tirupati, six miles distant and 2,500 feet high, is the holy hill. The temple is dedicated to an incarnation

the State funds and expenses there, was asked to send in his accounts; and when examined, a debt of 2,500 rupees (£250) was proved against him, which I directed he was to pay—and he promised to do so in fifteen days. This caused a very great sensation.

'"So great a Brahmin! so holy a Shastri! That he should be made to pay!"

'"Why not?" said I. "Has he not cheated the State, and Tripatti also? and, moreover, acknowledged to having done so?"

'"Oh yes," was the reply, "but he is a Shastri, and has spent it at the shrine of Shri Ballaji."

'"So much the better," say I. "But Shri Ballaji is just. He did not like the stolen money, and he sent the Shastri back to pay his debts!"

'"Ah, truly, that may be the case," said a knowing old clerk; and after a very long discussion, the assembly finally gave it as their opinion that I had hit the right nail on the head.

'Pid Naik had, I knew, been offered 500 rupees as his share of the spoil, if, indeed, he had not already bagged the money; and he not only proposed that *no* demand should be made against the Shastri, but that he should be given another 500 rupees, as a mark of approbation!'

My house was getting on very well. Building was very cheap, and I hoped to finish it for 2,000 rupees. It was all of granite, which the stone-cutters sold in large blocks 1½ foot long and 4 to 6 inches thick, 6 to 10 inches broad, for 3 rupees a thousand. I got the wood for the roof for nothing, for there was a lot lying at an old fort in the Nizam's country, which the land revenue officer seemed delighted to get rid of, as no one had claimed it for years.

There were about forty-six beams of various sizes, which answered my purposes capitally, and were well seasoned, saving me a very great expense, both in procuring wood and

---

of Vishnu, familiarly called Shri Ballaji below. According to the *Imperial Gazetteer*, for long no Christian or Moslem was allowed to ascend the hill, as none has yet entered the temple. 'Up to 1843 the temple was under the management of Government, which derived a considerable revenue' from the offerings to the idol.

conveying it perhaps a hundred miles. Lime, too, was very cheap ; but the building was principally done with mud and stone, and only pointed on the outside so as to keep out damp.

I employed about forty people. They did not work so fast as English workmen, but on the whole I was very well satisfied. A mason's wages at this time were about 6d. a-day, and the women, who assisted largely, had from 1½d. to 4d. On this they lived well, and many possessed gold and silver ornaments purchased out of their own earnings! I was obliged to write to Bellary, seventy miles off, for an estimate of carpenter's work, as the making of doors properly was an art quite unknown in Shorapur. The fitting stones to the corners of the doors and windows involved employing a different class of masons, those who worked with chisel and hammer, and were quite distinct from the wall-builders. Their wages were higher, and they had to find their own tools, which were all of the best steel.

The arch between the two centre rooms was turned in one day by two men in good stone and mortar work : it was 12 feet span, and 2 feet thick. I suggested to them to make a rough wooden frame to build over, but they shook their heads, and so I let them alone ; and they proceeded to build up the form of the arch between the piers with rough stones and mud, then struck the circle at the top, and smoothed it over with mud ; this soon dried in the sun, and the next day the arch was built over it, and was as firm as a rock. I often wondered what English workmen would have said to it all.

I laid out a flower-garden too, and the soil turned out very good. I had to clear away some rocks, and make the ground tolerably smooth. The Rani kindly gave me a piece of ground in one of her gardens, at the foot of my hill, in which was a good well, so I did not despair of having plenty of plants, and wished to try and induce a taste among the people for English flowers and vegetables. I sowed beans, peas, cabbages, broccoli, and cauliflowers, which eventually throve and flourished. I was often amused on a holiday to watch the crowds of people who came up from neighbouring villages, and from the town, to see what was going on. Sometimes one, wiser than the rest, endeavoured to explain to the others 'all about it'; but they only put their forefingers to their teeth, shook their heads, and marvelled silently.

My friends the Beydurs were now very peaceable, and conducted themselves very quietly, cultivating their fields, and sometimes coming down from their hills with presents to me of partridges or other game. They generally had their dogs in leashes, and carried falcons on their wrists.

As soon as I could leave we went out again into the districts, and I began my work in earnest through the country.

I found the people very distrustful at first, and I was not surprised at it, as their own Government had never kept faith with them at any time; and it was but natural that they should be suspicious of me.

'How do we know', they said, 'that your agreements with us are binding?' and I replied—

'I shall inquire into your condition before I sign your leases, and I shall visit your villages and look into your accounts; and, moreover, I give you my word, the word of an English gentleman, which cannot be broken.'

'But you may go away?'

'If I do, another will succeed me.'

'Well, we shall see. If you keep faith with us for one year, we will take heart, and cultivate all the waste lands in the country.'

These scenes and conversations were of constant recurrence, and soon the people began to talk to me, and to consult me on their business affairs, and I felt pretty sure that when the revenue settlement was begun, the people would trust me, and get over their shyness and suspicion. I had determined to admit no strangers as clerks; clumsy as they were, the hereditary officers of the State had the first claim for employment, and must be educated into regular system if they were to be of use afterwards. I therefore made my selection, leaving the others with Pid Naik. An extract from a letter, written in December 1843, will give some idea of the condition in which I found the head village of the *pargana* or county which I first visited :—

'These districts are in the worst conceivable condition. No accounts whatever have been kept; no record of the revenues, or of the land in and out of cultivation for sixty-seven years, and you may well imagine the work of cleaning out and reorganising the Augean stable of abuse and corruption. Whole villages in this county are deserted, and are little more than heaps of ruined houses. This village, Hunsigi, had formerly a weekly market and many dealers in grain, a hundred families of weavers, and a host of other tradesmen. Now, there are left only one grain-dealer and two weavers. Half the cultivators' houses are in ruins, and the land is more than two-thirds waste. The revenue used to be 4,900 rupees a-year, or £490. Now, it has declined to 875 rupees, or £87, 10s., and is collected with difficulty ; what could be done ? I will tell you what I have done. I invited back the weavers on a low tax of three rupees a-year—they ought to pay twelve ; but then they have to rebuild their houses. With them come other tradespeople, cultivators, grain and flour sellers. While we have been here fifteen families have returned from the British territory, and more are coming in. I can get no better terms than three rupees per *kuru*, and I have accepted that for three years, with an addition of three for the next three years, when the land is to be reassessed ; the present assessment being 30 rupees per *kuru* per year—that is, 40 acres for £3 per year. Matters may differ a little in each county, but I can get land taken on no other terms. People cannot trust the Shorapur authorities, and mistrust me too for the present. They are very shy—however, that is wearing off very fast, and during the last three days they have come forward pretty freely. It is hard work, however, but I don't despair, and hope to lay a foundation for future revenue arrangements. Oh that I were rid of Pid and his crew, who grow more and more obnoxious, idle, and altogether mischievous!'

The year 1844 opened very brightly upon us. I had arranged three small counties ; the rent had been only 2,000 rupees a-year—it would now be upwards of 3,000 rupees, and hereafter would produce 8,000 on the new leases. I was beginning to see my way ; and as we approached the Bombay frontier, farmers came in numbers, asking to be allowed to settle and take up new land, as much as I would give them. Of course I made no objection, and they became registered landholders.

We were in excellent health, and found our tent-life very agreeable.

The people came in crowds wherever we encamped. I have had a couple of hundreds about my tent, and they seemed much interested and amused by our ways, which of course were quite new to them. It pleased us to see the confidence they had in us; and they constantly brought some little gift as token of their friendly feeling. I felt very thankful for all this.

I never worked harder, or felt stronger in my life—sleeping soundly, and eating heartily, and the climate was delicious.

My wife and I used to take our morning rides together over the fields. I had to inspect the lands, and sometimes very amusing scenes took place when gross peculation and roguery were discovered. One was in reference to the *patel*, or head of the village, at which we were encamped, Kembavi. This personage had a fine estate and farm of 2,410 *bighas* under excellent cultivation. Some of it was a free grant for services performed by his forefathers; but by the original deed of grant he was to pay 1,600 rupees, or £160 a-year for the whole. The land was all under rich crops of *jowari* or large millet, wheat, cotton, linseed, and pulse. The *patel* had been paying only 600 rupees a-year for the last sixty-eight years! and had the assurance to ask me for a remission of 200 rupees out of the 600, as some of his crops had failed! This led me to examine into the case carefully, and to go over the whole property, and we rode over literally miles of fields, which were far more like 10,000 *bighas* than 2,410. Of course I gave no remission, and the *patel* voluntarily agreed to pay his full rent of 1,600 rupees next year if I would not charge him for arrears!

Here is also another instance.

The *patel* of a village near asked me to come and look at his land, as the crops had dried up. I told the people to meet me on their boundary at sunrise, and I went. The crops were certainly poor; but I said, 'In the Company's territories no man has more land than he pays rent for, therefore remissions are allowed. You seem to have a great deal more than you write down, suppose we try one field'; there were in it about 15 *bighas* of wheat, the same of linseed, the same of pulse and cotton—all very fine; and a patch of *jowari*, poor and dried up. Altogether, by pacing it, it appeared to me 90 *bighas*, of the best quality, and all well tilled.

'How much do you pay for this piece?' I asked; but there was no answer.

One fellow nudged another, but no one spoke. I asked a

second, and a third, with the same result. At last a fine old soldier of the village, a Musalman, spoke out.

'Please your lordship,' said he, 'the *patel* pays two rupees (four shillings) for it per year.'

'Two rupees!' cry I. 'O *patel* of bad destiny, two rupees for all this land! Say, how much am I to remit out of that? Are you not ashamed of yourself to enjoy all this land for two rupees? Now let me see more of your fields.'

'They are all the same,' cried the sturdy soldier. 'Please your highness, that *patel* takes all the fine land and puts off the poor land upon us poor people, paying what he chooses to the Government; and they are all the same.'

'Well spoken, O Khan!' cried a chorus of people; 'it is the truth!'

Looking at the honest soldier, I asked him, 'Now, where are your fields? if they are bad, you shall have a remission.'

He drew himself up, proudly enough, and replied—

'My fields were sown in the rains, and God has been good to me. I have reaped and stored the crop, and my children are eating it. I have paid my rent too, and want nothing but your favour.'

So I patted him on the head, and bade all the rest go and do as he had done, and I heard no more of remissions.

So it was in every village; the powerful paid no rent in comparison with the poor, and thus the revenue had been diminishing year by year. No accounts of land had been taken for fifty years or upwards; no one had paid the least attention to the subject, and it would necessarily take some years to get to the bottom of all the defalcations, and to establish a new and honest system.

Nor had even the rent which had been collected been forwarded to the treasury; in some places half the sum, or even less, was expended on the village itself, and the balance handed over to the collector. What wonder that the revenue declined?

It was very hard work, beginning at seven every morning, and lasting till after midnight, except one hour for each meal; yet I was very well, and the work had to be done somehow. At Shorapur everything was quiet and prosperous; but Pid Naik's good wife was very ill, and he wrote despairingly about her. I was very sorry for this, for I knew well if she died he would be enticed by his other wife, who was as great a drunkard as himself, and both would go rapidly to the dogs; but remonstrances, and even entreaties, were of no use. He made promises which he never fulfilled.

As, after much inquiry, there was no specific charge proved against Chan Basappa, except that of wasteful extravagance, and even this seemed to be more the Rani's fault than his, I had him released from Lingsugūr, and he came direct to my camp. Whether he had been the Rani's paramour or not was no business of mine. His account of the whole matter was of course a different affair altogether. He said he had been trying to do what I was doing, but the corrupt practices prevailing were too strong for him. He said that Lakshmangir, the Gosain banker, had desired the management of affairs; but that the Rani had preferred him, and therefore he had become a mark for slander and misrepresentation to Captain Gresley. He would not permit almost unlimited peculation by the *daftardars* and other ministerial officers, and they resented his interference with them, and as he was a Lingayat, all the Brahmins hated him; and no doubt there was a good deal of truth in these justifications.

As to Raja Pid Naik, I knew now very well what he was, and it was scarcely likely that the Rani, a shrewd, clever woman, who had known him since she was a child, would give in to him, or allow him and the Gosain banker to domineer over her; and she had never forgotten the proposed adoption of Pid Naik's son by her husband. That feeling rankled at her heart, and until her own son had been formally recognised by the Government of India she had never been free from anxiety. With me, and to me, I must say that Chan Basappa behaved extremely well. His office was an hereditary one as keeper of the treasury and wardrobe; but he did not wish to resume the actual performance of these duties, and he never interfered with the current business in any respect, while, if I required information on any point, he gave it readily and clearly if he could.

In one respect, indeed, he was highly commendable; he had taken under his charge certain detached villages, and all the Rani's private estates had been managed by him. In these the people were content and prosperous, the lands were well tilled, and the accounts had been well kept for several years; while he was evidently much liked and respected by the people.

Early in February Raja Pid Naik's good wife died. She had been the mother of seven children, and was much respected for her charity and piety. I went into Shorapur to pay him a visit of condolence, but I found him very low and despairing about himself.

His chief anxiety, however, appeared to be that the State should allow him 3,000 rupees for his wife's funeral expenses, gifts to Brahmins, etc., and that a market should be founded in her name. I could do nothing without instructions, at which he did not seem pleased; and I felt no doubt that, had I not come in from the districts, he would have taken advantage of the occasion to have appropriated at least 10,000 rupees—so dishonest was he. I told him I could not lay out the Raja's money on his private expenses, but if I received permission from the Resident, the expenditure should be authorised. I saw more clearly every day that had it not been for my presence, the whole of the money would have been made away with, as Pid Naik's people put it into his head that he was in truth Raja of Shorapur, and none else; and the poor little Raja would have scarcely been able to hold his ground unaided.

I also visited the Rani and the Raja, who were overjoyed to see me. I had appointed Mr. Murray, the medical attendant attached to me, as instructor in English to the Raja, and I found he had made very fair progress, being able to read easy stories, and write very fair copies. I was much pleased, and told him when I came to reside in my own house I would look after him myself. He was very intelligent, and never tired of asking me questions about my country, its customs, and its people. He was also learning Persian, Marathi, and Telugu, the language of business, and got on very well with all. I found three rooms of my new house were roofed in, and the walls plastered inside; the rest was in active progress, and I hoped all would be ready for us by the time we wished to return.

Meanwhile my work continued, and the condition of some of the towns and villages was truly distressing to witness. One, the town of Narribol, used to pay, according to the accounts given me, 26,000 rupees a-year, comparatively a very few years ago. Now 5,000 rupees were collected with difficulty per annum, while no regular accounts had been given in or taken for eighty years!

By this time, however, it was well understood that I should require accounts and returns properly made out by next season; and there was less trouble, when they saw I was in earnest.

Personally, Lord Ellenborough had been very kind to me; but as special correspondent of the most influential paper in the world, it was impossible to pass over his policy in regard to events in Afghanistan or elsewhere. His proclamation in regard to Sind, and other transactions, are now matters of past history, but live fresh in the memories of those who were contemporaries of that time, and still survive. He had been appointed Governor-General, and had arrived in India at a very critical period. Not only had Lord Auckland's policy, as regarded Afghanistan, broken down utterly, but the force at Kabul had perished miserably in their retreat; an attempt under Pollock to force the Khyber Pass and relieve the brave garrison of Jellalabad had failed. The Sikhs were to the last degree unquiet, and had been so since the death of Ranjit Singh in 1839. The Maratha State of Gwalior was in a very shaky condition; there were strong indications of disturbance in Sind; and instances of mutiny in the Madras army had occurred, under the impression that the native portion of it would be required to proceed to Afghanistan. It might have been supposed that Lord Ellenborough, considering his undoubted character and reputation, would have struck out some definite policy, so as to meet the crisis in a spirit suitable to the emergency.

It is true that, thanks to the indomitable spirit of Pollock and Nott, Kabul was again occupied, and all the captives were rescued, and that the forces under these generals were successfully marched out of Afghanistan. But there were no indications of support from the Governor-General; on the contrary, for a time timid vacillation, and in the end pretensions of having achieved the success which was due to others. This was very painful to witness then; and when the force actually returned, safely guided through the tumultuous upheavings of the Punjab, the famous proclamation issued by the Governor-General, which was to be read at every native court, was treated as it deserved by the press of India and of England.

I, in my humble capacity, never had so humiliating a task put upon me as the reading of that proclamation to Raja Pid Naik, and all the authorities of Shorapur. Not only did they not comprehend it, but they considered it, as it really was, a piece of bombast, only intended to conceal the disaster of Afghanistan, of which every one knew perfectly, and many no doubt rejoiced over in private, and of which the most exaggerated details were given. If the policy in regard to Gwalior shows finer and more generous features in the non-annexation of the State after the victories over its mutinous armies—long the nucleus of every discontented and ambitious chief of Central India—what shall be said in regard to the policy in Sind, which, placed in the hands of an unscrupulous man, ended in the destruction of that ancient State, with whom the British Government had made treaties of eternal friendship ?

These are now, however, subjects of history, and I need not revert to them ; but I cannot accord with the opinion, in regard to the actors and the acquiescers in this tragedy, 'De mortuis nil nisi bonum' ; and posterity will deal with them as they deserve.

CHAPTER IX

1844–45

I RECEIVED during this time an official despatch from the Military Secretary's pay department fixing all my future allowances, which relieved me from further anxiety on that score. The Resident had behaved very handsomely to me, and I had every reason to be grateful.

We spent three days on the banks of the Krishna—a glorious river, with grand rocks and streams, and dark pools below. I tried fishing; but although fish were plentiful, I could not succeed at first owing to the want of proper tackle. The beauty of the scenery was very great—wild and striking—and the river was much broken by islands: the water reached above a man's waist, and in one place the river divided into five large streams, each more than two hundred yards in width. Higher up I heard there was a fine waterfall, which I should have liked to visit, but I did not care to delay just then, so we deferred it to another time. We remained out in the district until the end of March, when the heat became suddenly very oppressive and unbearable, and we began to long to inhabit our new house, which, from its lofty position on the hill, would insure our having plenty of air, and cool refreshing wind at any rate at night. I found the house entirely roofed in, and several rooms, quite enough for our accommodation, ready; and we were very soon greatly the better for the change.

But I was not happy about Pid Naik's goings on. He was engaged in an intrigue at Hyderabad, through Lakshmangir, the Gosain banker, the object of which was, absurd as it may appear, to get himself recognised by Raja Chandu Lal, the

Minister of the Nizam, as Raja of Shorapür. This scheme was to be backed up by the Nizam himself, in order that, as in the case of the district officers in 1829, the interference of the English might be withdrawn. I personally did not care about this; but I saw it would unsettle the little mind Pid Naik possessed, and that he was conducting himself now far more like the Raja than the Diwan. He spent and threw about money just as he pleased, in defiance of his own promises and my directions, and this could not be permitted. I therefore desired him—

1*st*, To give no orders upon the treasury without my counter-signature.

2*dly*, To allow no persons except the regular Government officers to interfere with State affairs; and,

3*dly*, To appoint any day in the week most convenient to himself for a General Durbar or Court, at which I, with the Raja, would attend to receive reports, hear petitions, and transact general business.

I never received any reply to these proposals in writing; and though Pid Naik came over and over again to see me, and promised most faithfully that he would do all that was required of him, I was told by some of his own people that he had not the slightest intention of fulfilling his promises.

In May the reports of the Shorapur intrigues became so notorious at Hyderabad, that my friend Captain Malcolm, assistant to the Resident,[1] wrote several times to warn me of them, and desired me to keep well on my guard against them, etc. As affairs stood at present, according to Captain Malcolm's account, Lakshmangir had got the support of the Minister and of the Nizam himself. The Minister had been promised 30,000 rupees, with 20,000 to some subordinates; the Nizam himself was to have 100,000 rupees, or £10,000.

[1] Several letters from D. Malcolm, Assistant Resident, dated the year before, and having nothing to do with Shorapur, are given in that fearful volume, the *Life of James Stuart Fraser*. The Resident at Hyderabad writes (1918) that 'one Captain D. A. Malcolm, 3rd Regiment, Bombay Native Infantry, an Assistant in the Thaggi Department, Hyderabad, was appointed Assistant to the Resident at Hyderabad on the 30th June, 1838'. He is mentioned in Taylor's Introduction to the *Thug*, 1839, as having charge of the operations against Thugs for 'the *whole* of the territories of H.H. the Nizam'.

And all had been led to believe that the Shorapur treasury was full, and that the amount could be paid over to them at once.

'If you will refer to my previous letters', I wrote to my father, 'you will find, I daresay, that a balance of five lakhs of rupees was said to be due to the Nizam's Government when Captain Gresley made his settlement. When I became perfectly acquainted with these affairs I thought otherwise, and was convinced the balance was due to the other side, and to a large amount. I therefore wrote a letter on the subject, and a very earnest one, to get the Shorapur estate excused the balance on account of its poverty. To this the Resident would not listen; but as I had no reply from the Governor-General, I thought my letter would have struck him, and that he might have referred the subject to England. Whether he did so or not I know not; but orders have since come out from the Court of Directors that the balance is *not* to be taken, and whatever may have been paid by the Shorapur State since the late settlement (£16,500) is to be refunded.

'Now the Nizam's Government does not like this at all, and has not answered the Resident's note on the subject. Malcolm thinks the Nizam will make a reference to the Governor-General, which will not be successful; for this balance of five lakhs is sheer robbery. What the end of all will be I know not; but if the Governor-General abandons the policy he deliberately undertook, it will be most strange and unaccountable. I do not think he will; and I believe when he hears of their intrigues he will take the bull by the horns, and place the country entirely under my direction, or that of some other English officer, which would be the only means of retrieving the State from ruin and destruction. As to the intrigue, I am not uneasy since I heard it was known at Hyderabad; and if the Governor-General comes down on the Nizam to refund the £16,000 I shall be all right.'

Shortly afterwards General Fraser wrote again to Pid Naik, enclosing copies of extracts from his former letter, to which no reply had been vouchsafed. The General's letter now required replies, even in the ordinary course of politeness and etiquette. Pid Naik evaded an answer for several days, offering to send his agents; but I would take no verbal answers, and he said he was too ill to write; and so we continued to skirmish, and still Pid Naik would give no reply either to the Resident's letter or to mine. His chief counsellors now were a boon companion of his who was once a religious mendicant, and went out accompanied by a boy begging for rice—another, the holy man who was dismissed for cheating in his district last year. The third was the chief spiritual adviser of Lakshmangir, the Gosain banker (whom I had sent to Hyderabad), a man who had again and again complained to me of Pid Naik's indifference to him, at the same time extolling his own holiness. The holy man came to me when he saw that his friend Pid Naik must soon go to the wall, and abused him and the rest, betraying all their confidence. What a pack of scoundrels they all were, to be sure! Contemptible and most villainous! Pid Naik was gullible to a degree, and believed all these rascals told him. He asked for money on the most foolish pretexts. He wanted musical boxes, and an English carriage, although there was not a road within miles of Shorapur where one could possibly be driven,—indeed I had long been endeavouring to persuade him to mend the roads into the city; but he objected, urging that his so doing would impair the impregnability of the place!

Every day he promised to do exactly as I asked him, and every day he did the contrary, or evaded, or shuffled in some way, till I was obliged to be very imperious in my demands. Then he came cringing and begging me not to tell of him, and agreed to some trifle, by way of a *sop*, and the whole scene was re-enacted. However, I did not keep silence, and I regularly sent copies of our correspondence and details of our communications up to Government, accompanied by some very severe remarks, and I could only hope that Lord Ellenborough would give them his attention in time; and as Pid Naik was perfectly deaf to all remonstrance from me, I could but look to Government to support me.

At last, after much weary waiting, a note came which ran as follows:

'I have understood the letter of the Resident to *you*, also the Persian extracts which accompany it, in every respect. I consider you to be in the place of the Resident. According to his orders to you, do you act truly.'

Pid Naik was evidently determined not to reply to the

Resident himself, and I sent a copy of the foregoing to Hyderabad, to which the Resident answered privately :—

'I need not say how much I regret the difficulties you have experienced from the incapacity and unaccountable obstinacy of Raja Pid Naik. It is now a question before the Government of India whether he can at all be retained in the office of Diwan or altogether removed, and yourself installed as the sole and exclusive manager of the district. Recent despatches from the Court of Directors have, however, intervened regarding Shorapur, upon which I have been obliged to write largely, and these circumstances may perhaps occasion some delay in the coming to a specific decision in the case of Raja Pid Naik.'

After much vexatious delay, I received an account of receipt and expenditure, of which no details were given whatever.

Revenue	235,000	rupees.
Expenditure by Raja Pid Naik	110,000	,,
Government debts, including tribute	110,000	,,
Reserve fund	10,000	,,
Losses and extras	5,000	,,

Now the Nizam's Government had only received 50,000 rupees on account, and thus 60,000 were due from Pid Naik on that head ! Every one ought to have been paid out of the sum set down, but there were 40,000 rupees of arrears due ; and thus a deficiency of one lakh, or 100,000 rupees, had occurred in the financial year. There were about 4,000 rupees in the treasury, and about 10,000 rupees of outstanding balances difficult of realisation. Now there was a new debt of quite a lakh, and how much more had been concealed from me I could not say. If affairs had been honestly conducted, we should have had a surplus to carry on to the next few years. How Pid Naik had got rid of the lakh of rupees which he had thrown away I could never discover ; but I imagine much of it had gone to support the intrigue at Hyderabad. Now the accounts would have to be forwarded to Hyderabad, and would tell their own disgraceful story, needing no comment from me. Nothing had come of the intrigue at Hyderabad ; and nothing was likely to come of it. The Nizam and his Government had taken warning by the movement of the Supreme Government of India and the Court of Directors, and had thrown off Lakshmangir and his false promises with contempt.

* * * * * *

In August I took my wife to Lingsugur for medical advice—she was ill and suffering. I had arranged to send her home to England for a time to recruit her strength, which had suddenly and unaccountably declined. I trusted that the means used would enable her to undertake the journey, and that the complete change would set her up. God saw fit to take her from me very suddenly at the last.

Of that time I cannot write. It is many years ago, and all the scene with its sad details rises fresh before me. I tried humbly to bow to the will of God; but I had lost in her not only my loving and beloved wife, but my steady, true friend, my comfort and my happiness; so tender in her love, so gentle; so firm to do right, and so keen to detect wrong. Henceforth I must be alone at Shorapur, and work on as best I could without her loving presence and her wise, calm counsels, without human aid or sympathy of any kind. Well—it was a bitter grief, and it had to be borne; so, after a very severe illness which detained me for some time, I returned to take up my work again at Shorapur alone.

I found my house quite finished now, and looking really beautiful inside and out. What a mockery it seemed to me! The dear presence that would have made it home to me; the deft, skilful hands that would have delighted in making it habitable and homelike—these were at rest now, free, at all events, from future pain and suffering; and in this thought was my only comfort. . . . Fresh anxieties were in store for me at Shorapur.

* * * * * *

I had been hearing for some weeks past very disagreeable reports in relation to a conspiracy at Shorapur to destroy the young Raja at the Dasara festival, when great crowds usually assembled. Pid Naik's favourite, Krishnaya, was at the head of this most villainous scheme.

The young Raja of Gadwal,[1] a neighbouring principality,

[1] This lesser tributary State, with all its violence, survived while Shorapur went down. Gadwal Samasthan (or Keshavnagar) is given in the *Imperial Gazetteer* as a tributary 'estate' in the east of Raichur

had been shot in his Durbar with his father and brother, and their bodies had been cast out of the town.

My watchful friend, Captain Malcolm, wrote to me to be on my guard, and look well to the river ferries, because reports were rife that Arabs and Rohillas had moved in my direction, so as to arrive at Shorapur at or during the Dasara festival.

The Rani was in the wildest state of alarm about her son, and about me; but I had brought another company of the 6th Regiment with me from Lingsugur, and I had now 170 men—quite enough, I considered, to prevent any disturbance. I had also requested Pid Naik to send Krishnaya to me, as I suspected he was implicated in the plot; but instead he had despatched him to the fort of Wondrug, nine miles off. To my surprise, however, General Fraser ordered a regiment of infantry and 200 cavalry to march on Shorapur, and they all arrived the day before the festival. Evidently the Resident was anxious and determined to use every precaution in his power. Very soon after the arrival of the troops, Pid Naik

---

District, Hyderabad. The town, Gadwal, had 12,000 inhabitants in 1911, having varied greatly in population at recent periods. Out of a revenue of three lakhs the tribute paid to the Nizam is some 86,000 rupees. 'Gadwal existed long before the foundation of the Hyderabad State. It formerly issued its own coin, which is still current in Raichur District.' Nothing is known of its earlier history. The fort, the residence of the ruling family, was completed more than two centuries ago by Raja Somtadari. The land in Gadwal, upon the Krishna and the Tungabhadra, is alluvial, and thus extremely fertile. Silk saris, turbans, and superior dhotis with gold borders are busily produced in the town.

For evident reasons I could not accept the figure, approaching a million, given in the current edition of the *Imperial Gazetteer* as the population, in 1901, of Gadwal, the feudatory of a feudatory. Referring the question to Hyderabad, I have received, after a year, through the Residency, an answer from the Director-General of Revenue. After giving figures from a vernacular book on Hyderabad State he says that in the *Imperial Gazetteer* there has been a misprint, and the integer 8 has crept in between 6 and 4. 'It is thus clear that the population of this Samsthan which was 82,608 prior to 1901 rose to 96,491 in 1901, which later on increased to 113,000 by 1911 A.D.' The area of this prosperous little State has curiously varied, from a recorded 707 to 864 square miles, and again to 813 according to the Census of 1911. Shorapur had, more or less, four times this area, revenue, and population. Gadwal is now the outstanding feudatory of Hyderabad.

came off to see me in the direst alarm. 'What was the meaning of these troops?' he asked. I verily believe that he imagined they had come for him! And as I did not care to erase this impression altogether, I only told him that there were reports of a dangerous and bad character afloat at Hyderabad, relative to some intrigues going on at Shorapur, and that the troops had been sent by the Resident's orders to be ready in case of emergency and to prevent trouble; but that no one would interfere with him, or molest him in any way, if things went well and quietly.

Two days afterwards, two of Pid Naik's confidential servants came to me privately, saying they had something to disclose; I therefore took down their depositions. A sad revelation, indeed, of contemplated treachery! They professed to have warned their master, but in vain, and therefore came to tell me in the hope that mischief might be prevented. Evidently I had arrived just in time—the scheme was all ready to be carried out. My informants were fearless men, and gave their information clearly and unhesitatingly. In all respects it accorded precisely with Captain Malcolm's private information received at Hyderabad.

The heads of the depositions were these :—

That for a long time past Pid Naik had tacitly allowed Krishnaya to intrigue; and that he, finding all his efforts at Hyderabad unsuccessful and thwarted by me, had at last grown desperate, and had laid this diabolical scheme to make away with the poor little Raja and with me also during the procession by means of some villains whom Pid Naik had sheltered (although he had denied having done so to me), and who were rebels from the Nizam's country and notorious desperadoes.

The man who gave the best evidence was manager in Pid Naik's late wife's household. He deplored what had occurred, and how Pid Naik had gradually been brought to listen to Krishnaya's vile plot. He said he did not think his master had any bad intentions of himself, but had been talked over by the others whose names he gave me, and they agreed with those against whom I had received warning from Hyderabad. He said he thought Pid Naik had despatched Krishnaya to Wondrug because he felt certain that I had discovered the plot, and he would wish to appear well disposed towards me by punishing the chief offender. For as the man said, 'If there had been no plot, he would have written to you evasively; as it was, why should he put his favourite directly into prison as soon as you asked for him?'

The *karkun* or clerk who sat at Pid Naik's gate also gave similar evidence. I requested Captain Stoddart, who was in command of the troops, to move his force nearer, so as to command the entrance to the gate below my hill; but owing to a deep ravine coming in the way, he could not post them nearer than a mile from the gate; however, the road was a good one up to it, and the force could easily move along it in case of necessity.

This movement created some fear, but I sent word to the townspeople not to be afraid—that no harm was intended, and that the procession was to go on as usual.

I was also much surprised by a visit from Krishnaya's most confidential Brahmin, who came to me openly—a man I had never before seen; but he said he could keep quiet no longer, and was most willing to give evidence before Krishnaya himself on oath anywhere. I was indeed delighted, and encouraged him to make a clean breast of it, and a very pretty revelation it proved. He told me he it was who had sent me anonymous warnings and hints on several occasions, and appealed to me whether they had not turned out to be true. And in the present case he said it was he who 'had told it to a friend, who had told it to my agents, who had told it to me'! Now all he desired was to be openly confronted with Krishnaya. I took down this deposition also and forwarded it to the Resident; it accorded with the previous ones in every respect.

I then sent for Pid Naik, and without informing him how far he was implicated, told him of the horrible plot that had been discovered, and informed him, before Captain Stoddart as a witness, that I should hold him responsible in life and person for any riot or disturbance, and also for the safe custody of Krishnaya. He did not like this at all, and pretended to be greatly shocked at the contemplated villainy; but when I told him further particulars, and what conclusions had been arrived at from his recent acts, he seemed to comprehend the danger to himself if he did not at once exert himself to prevent mischief. He agreed to give the necessary orders, and to see that peace was preserved during the procession, and in fact I think the shock quite sobered him, for I never saw him so collected or so earnest and clear-headed.

The procession takes place at night, and the Raja had to proceed from his palace to an open space about a mile off. All the Beydur clans were present, all the State soldiers, and crowds of people. I had a party of a hundred picked men, giving them orders to keep close to the Raja. We went down to the palace about five o'clock, a rather formidable-looking party. I was on my elephant, with Captain P——. who had come in from Lingsugur; and then my little force of picked men followed. When we arrived at the palace we dismounted, and each taking the little Raja by the hand, we led him between us to his elephant, which was waiting, placed him upon it, and then remounted our own. We proceeded very, very slowly, any one might have taken a shot at us that pleased; but God protected all—the fatherless boy and those with him—and we were unhurt. Not a word was spoken, every one was most respectful to us, and we passed on to the place where the ceremonies were performed, under the hill whereon my house was situated. The crowd baffles description; after the ceremonies were ended the fireworks began, and were very fine; one bouquet of two hundred rockets was superb. About eleven o'clock we returned to the palace with the Raja, whom I restored to the arms of his anxious mother. She had been in a state of the wildest alarm and anxiety; and of her grateful feelings when her child was brought back safely to her I need not speak here.

Thus was I again, through God's great and infinite mercy, preserved through imminent danger.

The next day I demanded Krishnaya from Pid Naik. I hoped that when he was delivered up, the Government would be convinced of the rascality prevailing at Shorapur, and would be disposed to assume a firmer aspect, and make a final settlement of affairs.

Pid Naik, finding he could make no impression on the Nizam's Government, now began writing letters to Hyderabad complaining of me—and very much calculated to set the Nizam and the British Government by the ears—and sent an agent with them to Hyderabad to deliver them to the Resident and to Colonel Tomkyns. I warned the Resident of what was coming, and then sent for Pid Naik, told him I had heard of his proceedings, and asked him what he had been doing, and what he had written. Then he swore solemnly 'on his children's heads' that all was false. However, in due time Pid Naik's agent arrived at Hyderabad, and delivered the letters to Colonel Tomkyns and to the Resident. Colonel Tomkyns took the letter, but turned out the man who brought it, and the Resident did exactly the same. Both of them forwarded the letters to me without having opened them, and I sent for Pid Naik as soon as I received them, and showed them to him with the seals unbroken. He could say nothing, he could make no excuse or frame no lie, he was so utterly dumbfoundered; but he went home, and was dead drunk for the next three days!

Meanwhile Pid Naik's agent at Hyderabad had again, through Lakshmangir, the Gosain banker, got the ear of the Nizam's confidant, and he reported to his master that the Nizam was going to interfere on his behalf; and Captain Malcolm wrote to me privately confirming this report. The Resident, however, had already written a spirited note to the Nizam's Minister requesting that these disreputable intrigues might be put an end to once for all, and the reply was all I could wish for. Orders were issued to seize Pid Naik's agent; but he had been evidently informed of his danger, and had made his escape. I showed all these letters and documents to Pid Naik, who begged me to transmit a letter of apology to the Resident, denying that he had ever sent an agent, and requesting that if any person came hereafter, purporting to have been sent by him, or by his orders, he should be at once forwarded either to me or to himself.

That evening the young Raja and Raja Pid Naik came up to my house to hear the band of the 2d Regiment play on my terrace. It was a glorious moonlight night, and I had never seen Pid Naik so pleasant. In the morning, of his own accord, he sent all the treasury orders to be countersigned by me, and the accountants with all the accounts, imploring me to try and *save his credit.* It would have been poor spite in me to notice the past any longer. I did my best to set him upon his legs again, and I told him I intended to hold him up as long as he deserved it.

I believe the reason of this very sudden change for the better was that I took the fate of the rascal Krishnaya into my own hands, and placed him in confinement, heavily ironed, reporting proceedings *afterwards* to the Resident. I felt it was a case where decision was needed, and I exercised it at the risk of being found fault with. I considered it due to the welfare of the State, and the safety of the Raja and myself, to keep this mischievous character safe, as he was always inciting Pid Naik to some villainy or other. Another evil influence was also at an end by the sudden death of Krishnaya's friend, Bhim Rao. He, it was said, took poison on hearing of Krishnaya's arrest, fearing awkward disclosures.

With the removal of these two, all opposition to me ceased, and, as I have said above, all my demands were complied with without further hesitation. Would it last? I often wondered; but I hoped Pid Naik had had a severe lesson, and that he had found both the Government and me too wary to look for success in any future plot.

The effect of all this was very successful; the first proof of the confidence it had inspired was given me in a very gratifying visit from the heads of the Beydur clans, who came to me with offerings of flowers, begging me to forget the past, and from henceforth to consider them as my children. I took the opportunity of making them a little speech, and with good effect. I told them it had pleased God to afflict me in the loss of my dear wife, and that I had no tie now to bind me to Shorapur, except my wish to serve their young Raja, and to do my duty to those who had sent me there, and that it was very hard to have to bear all this anxiety and my own sorrow too. 'Relieve me of that', I cried, 'and you take a heavy load from me.'

This touched them deeply; they crowded around me, placing their hands on my feet and neck, and earnestly exclaiming, 'They would never *vex her spirit* by causing me pain or anxiety.'

I saw my opportunity, and spoke at length. I warned them against crime—cattle-lifting and dacoity, both of which had before been considered honourable achievements—and I offered them advances for trade or for land cultivation to the utmost of my power. They listened very attentively, and I believe I won them entirely ; having done so, I determined to keep them. When I had ended, I offered them *pan* and flowers, and sent them away.

Another proof of confidence in me was the increase of revenue in the contracts, the contractors having previously held back to see how matters would go. They would not give Pid Naik last year's amount ; but they agreed with me for 13,000 rupees above it, which was no unwelcome addition to our finances. The crops promised well, both grain and cotton, and the price of grain rose from 12 to 20 rupees a *candy*,[1] owing to the increased demand.

I endeavoured to show Pid Naik the folly of his previous course, which would have been to levy additional heavy taxes, that he proposed as soon as the people were at all more prosperous. For this year I was content to have a moderate increase of revenue, to bring peculation to light, and to see the people more contented and more happy.

Pid Naik and I worked away at the accounts, and he could do his work very well when he was not drunk !

The treasury arrangements were concluded, and the pay of the establishment settled, which amounted to 90,000 rupees a year. The contingencies, which last year amounted to 73,000 rupees, would be only 25,000, and there were 100,000 set aside for Government demands and arrears. I had the control of the whole, and not one anna could be disbursed without my counter-signature.

I also, at *Pid Naik's request*, began several roads, which were much needed. I had to study road engineering as well as I could, and lay them out, and superintend the whole ; those leading from the several gates of the town were specially essential.

Shorapur was a regular mountain fortress, a robber stronghold. To make it stronger than it was by nature, it had been fortified, and all the gates were rendered nearly impassable to any one except footmen by large loose stones being thrown

1 'Candy. A weight used in southern and western India, varying greatly in different parts, but averaging 500 pounds av.' (*New English Dictionary*).

down upon the passages to the plain. These had gradually become a horribly rough kind of pavement, so slippery and so loose that any horse unaccustomed to it tripped and stumbled at every step. No cart could have attempted to enter the town! Pid Naik's people had been laying out a road to the river Krishna, and part of it led over a gap in the hills, rough and bad. They told him they could not clear it, and advised him to apply to me—hence his making this request, which had surprised me not a little. I instantly set thirty men to work, looking after them myself morning and evening. The road was now complete, twenty feet wide, and made of rotten granite, which became almost as hard as stone in a very short time.

When I had completed about 1,200 yards all were delighted, and crowds came to see the wonder.

'Why not carry it through the gateways?' said some one.

'Why not?' I rejoined, 'and then no more necks will be broken on those polished stones.'

Pid Naik assented, and I instantly put on additional workmen, thirty-five to each gate. From the gates the roads were carried through the town, and up to the Raja's palace, and I could scarcely get them done quickly enough to satisfy the people. This was indeed a great step in the right direction. I had high hopes now, and even dreams of a good school, public dispensary, and suchlike institutions; but I was obliged to be very cautious.

One day we very nearly had a row. One of my English household shot a dog which was carrying off a fine fat duck in its mouth. The dog, it appeared, belonged to a Beydur. A body of these went off to Pid Naik to complain, and I told him to settle the matter as he pleased; but he would do nothing, and one of the scoundrels thought it a good opportunity to make a disturbance. So next morning, as Mr. A—— was going into the town to see the Rani's brother, he found about a hundred armed men on the road, who refused to let him pass, and threatened him. He came to me to make his complaint, and during that time about fifty men went to his tent and bullied his wife, terrifying her by yelling, screaming, and pointing their guns at her.

I wrote to Pid Naik at once that if these people were not

punished immediately I would leave Shorapur; but I did not expect he would have the courage to do as I asked: however, to my surprise, the ringleaders were seized, and the row was put an end to. The whole had been a got-up affair to try and pick a quarrel with me, and had been instigated by one of Pid Naik's bosom friends and boon companions.

I wished to reach Lingsugur in time for Christmas-day, and as I had a good deal to do before the year closed, I went out for a while into the districts, and worked very hard. From eight in the morning till eight in the evening people crowded in, and I only allowed myself half an hour for breakfast and dinner. It was weary work, neither gratifying nor amusing—a constant unveiling of acts of tyranny and oppression, lying and cheating; but it had to be done, and the more I worked, the more intricate it seemed to grow.

'Why', said a fellow to me one day, quaintly enough, 'do you take all this trouble in combing people's hair? You only break your combs, and don't get out the tanglements; the best way would be to shave it off and let it grow again, and then you could make it as smooth and straight as you please.' But this was rather too severe a measure, and I preferred plying the comb with patience.

I had my reward in seeing the people more prosperous, and the trade of my little State increasing, and apparently in a fair way to become the highroad of commerce from the Company's districts into those of the Nizam and others. I lowered the duties, and the carriers were now protected at every halting-place by the very Beydurs who used to plunder them, steal their cattle, and annoy them in every way!

During this year there was not one single complaint of border outrage or cattle-lifting, and the country at large seemed to know that such doings must cease under the new *régime*. The people came forward boldly with their complaints, instead of going about in armed parties against those who had wronged them, burning their stacks of corn, and perhaps wounding or vexing inoffensive people in revenge for their injuries.

Pid Naik now was quiet and obedient, and having placed the expenditure on a proper footing, I trusted all would go on regularly in that department. I had as yet made no proper report on the state of affairs generally, but intended to do so after Christmas, on my return from Lingsugur. I did make one special report on the state of the accounts, showing the waste that had occurred, and the Resident agreed with me that it had been very deplorable ; but ended by saying, that as long as everything showed so fairly for the present, and as Pid Naik had no means of making up the deficiencies, and had listened to reason, he should be excused from any demand on account of it, and this was what I had myself proposed. I am sure this decision was a very great relief to Pid Naik himself, while to me the General wrote :

'Your despatches contain ample proof of a most unwearied and unremitting attention to business, and a zeal in the discharge of the duties of your office that can scarcely fail to be attended by the happiest results. It may be expected that time and patience should be necessary for the purpose among a people so entirely unaccustomed to any kind of regular and just government.'

I left Shorapur on the morning of the 24th December, at 1 A.M. Such glorious moonlight, as I well remember, and very cold. I was glad to stretch my legs with a walk of five miles, and arrived at Lingsugur a little after sunrise.

And so the year 1844 ended—one very eventful to me—one full of sad, sad memories, and bitter, grievous trial. Yet through all I had been strengthened and upheld by my heavenly Father to bear the burden He put upon me ; and He too, in answer to my earnest prayer, gave me courage and hope to cheer me on. I had, in some measure, succeeded beyond my hopes—I had won the hearty approbation of the highest in the land. I had gained, and was hourly gaining further, the confidence of the people ; they were more peaceful and content, improvements were progressing, trade and crops were promising. I had good health and constitution, and though often weary and sadly sick at heart, the thought that my efforts had so far succeeded gave me strength to fight on ; and somehow I had a liking for my work, and a certain pride in it, which carried me through many a difficult task. If I had not felt at times so unutterably lonely, I should have been quite happy; but the thought of what I had lost in her who would have cheered and supported me, was at times almost too much to bear.

India, too, had made a great stride that year. Mercantile and other projects were advanced. A new Steam Navigation Company was started, the shares in which were bought up directly; so with the banks, of which there were three, if not more, in North-western India, and others in Bengal, Bombay, and Madras, all doing well, and paying interest at 10 or 12 per cent on their original capital. Also there was the plan for the Bombay Railway, of which all the shares were snapped up by English and Indian capitalists. Yes, India was stirring in these respects, and was likely to advance in all peaceful undertakings under our veteran General,[1] who apparently thought of anything but fighting, and busied himself with roads, bridges, education, and trade—one and all of which his predecessor seemed to think out of his line altogether, and perhaps beneath his notice.

The new year opened brightly enough. On my return to Shorapur I found the Raja well and happy; and as I had persuaded some of my friends to accompany me from Lingsugur to see my house and my little State, I had quite a gay time of

[1] The first Viscount Hardinge of Lahore, afterwards Field Marshal, who had come out overland half a year earlier after being Secretary at War to succeed his brother-in-law Ellenborough.

Of him Indian history, and Meadows Taylor, who in such judgments represents the voice of history, must speak well. Taylor writes in his *History*: 'It was not only for the vigorous prosecution and successful termination of the Sikh war that Lord Hardinge's administration of three years remains a memorable record in the history of India. . . . In a true spirit of humanity, Lord William Bentinck's edict against Suttee was extended to the territories of native princes and chiefs, accompanied by earnest requests that the suppression of infanticide and slavery should follow. A strange portion of old customs had remained in Sunday labour in all departments of the State, which was finally abolished. Amidst so benevolent and so wise a career, the unexpected return of Lord Hardinge to England was a subject of universal regret; and he finally sailed on March 15, 1848, having won the reputation of a great soldier and statesman, which the lapse of time has materially enhanced.'

The perplexing *March* here should be January—an example of the unmanageable errors of date in the same *History*.

it. My party consisted of three ladies and four gentlemen, and their advent created quite a commotion in the town. We pitched our tents at Bohnal, a small village seven miles west from Shorapur, where there was a very pretty tank or artificial lake, of considerable size.

I had drawn out a plan for a sailing-boat of tolerably large dimensions, and had had her built at Lingsugur ; and finding her quite finished, I put her on a heavy artillery-waggon, and conveyed her to Bohnal with many a misgiving, as she had been built altogether by the drawings I had given. She was now quite ready to make a start, and was put into the water on her trial trip, and I was very glad to have so large a gathering on the occasion. We awaited the great event with much anxiety, and it was looked for by all the natives with intense curiosity and eagerness. First, out came the Rani and all the *élite* of Shorapur, to have a look at the boat, and their admiration was unbounded, and most amusing. As to the little Raja, he was wild with delight, and hugged me with all his might for having made the boat for him. The Rani was for being out half the day ; and once, when there was 'a bit of sea', and the little vessel was dashing through the water, throwing up the spray about her bows, she was in absolute glee. She, the English ladies, and the children, went out thus with me two days running, and great was the fun and merriment among us all.

It was certainly an unprecedented thing for the Rani and me to be together in the 'same boat' ; and it was wonderful to see how the native ladies, wild and secluded as had been their life hitherto, opened out under the influence and companionship of their English sisters. Indeed my friends told me they had imagined the Rani a perfect tigress, and that they were most agreeably surprised to find her so pleasant and so polite. My boat had turned out a pretty thing—20 feet keel, and 24 feet over all, a good beam, and three masts—old Liverpool ferry-boat fashion—a bowsprit and jib, topmast and sails. She was very stiff in the water, and very safe ; in fact, she worked well, and was beautifully finished in every respect, built of teak, copper-fastened throughout ; yet she had been entirely the work of two common carpenters of the country. I felt rather proud of my first experiment in shipbuilding ; and my boat was a constant source of amusement and recreation, as, although the lake was not very large, it was sufficiently so for an hour or two's sail in the evenings when work was done. It was about a mile across, and one and a-half long. Its depth, when full, was 20 feet ; but as the *Raja* only drew 2½ or 3 feet, there was always plenty of water for her. The exclamations of the natives were very amusing sometimes. 'Dear me,' said one, after we had been sailing along briskly for some time, 'see how that grass is running ! was ever such a thing seen before ! '

'But', said another, 'that hill is moving away, and there goes a tree ! Well, to be sure, it is miraculous ! '

And so they would go on till I convinced them of the truth.

My party soon broke up. They expressed themselves charmed with the novelty and beauty of all they had seen, and it certainly must have been a change from the dull routine and gossip of station life.

I determined to build a cottage at Bohnal for a refuge from toil at Shorapur, and before I left I marked out the foundation. It was to consist only of two rooms and a small bath-room, with a veranda round them. The view was very pretty, looking over to the old fort of Wagingera, and across a wide plain with the Deodrug Hills in the distance. Stone was to be had for the picking up, lime was plentiful, as also was long grass for thatching, so that the cost was very moderate.

I made a contract for a road between Bohnal and Shorapur, which promised to be very pretty, as there was a good deal of wood and firm red soil, and I hoped that all these plans and projects of mine would in time produce a civilising effect upon the natives and induce them to follow my example.

I now returned to my district work, and the conflicts over false returns were as troublesome as before. Still I observed a good deal of progress, and the demand for taking up waste lands was very great. Numbers of old Shorapur families had returned to their villages, and there seemed to be abundance and prosperity everywhere. An insurrection had broken out in the month of February in the southern Maratha country,[1]

[1] In Kolhapur and Savantwadi States.

and the British authorities were most anxious about the Beydurs of Shorapur, as the movement was within sixty miles of them, and had they joined in it, things might have taken a very serious turn. I lost no time in sending an urgent appeal to them all, not to be enticed into the rebellion; and they responded most warmly and joyfully, and proved their loyalty to me in the most practical manner, as not one Beydur of my district joined the rebellion. At last I felt I had them well in hand, and I know that the Bombay Government were very thankful to me for my control over so formidable a body.

In March another great ceremony took place—the first removal of the young Raja's hair! It is usual in Musalman, and most Hindu, families, not to cut the hair of a male child until he has attained a certain age. In the Raja's case, his father and mother had fixed the period at nine, eleven, or fourteen years of age. It had not been done in the ninth year, and the present was the eleventh, which could not be passed over, and I was glad of it, for the boy suffered greatly from the weight and heat of the tangled and matted hair falling about his shoulders.

As this was a state ceremony, I requested the Resident to allow me to bestow what was needful in the way of funds, and I was permitted to give the Rani five thousand rupees from the State treasury, to which sum she added as much of her own, and the following is the description of the affair which I sent home:—

'There was a great gathering of all classes of people to partake of the Rani's hospitality. I don't know how many Brahmins and others were invited; all were fed and received gifts of clothes and alms. The crowds were enormous. All the members of the family were feasted for two days, and received turbans, scarves, and other presents, and every one seemed pleased and happy. The ceremony itself took place in a tamarind-grove near a suburb in the plain on the south side of Shorapur; the Rani had had comfortable tents arranged for me, and I arrived from camp in time for the beginning of it. I did not see what was taking place, as no one entered the enclosure but the Brahmins; but the beating of kettle-drums, blowing of horns, and firing of guns, announced the ceremony completed. I was sitting with the Rani the whole time, and she was very thankful to me for my presence there, and the assistance I had been allowed to give.

'As the camp could not move into the city that night, I remained, and there was a grand *natch* under the trees, and fireworks, which had a very pretty effect, the whole grove being lighted by torches, with occasional Bengal and blue lights. Next evening all went up to the city in grand procession. The Raja on his superb elephant, with his little wife beside him, who had arrived from the Mysore country just in time. She is rather dark, but a pretty child about eight, with glorious eyes. I rode and *drove* another elephant, and we were surrounded by all the horsemen and foot-soldiers, and the Beydur clans. Such a scramble! When we got into the city we were joined by others, and there were literally thousands, and all the house-tops were covered with well-dressed women and children. By this time it was dark, but there were hundreds of torches and blue lights; and the effect of the crowds in the streets, the horsemen, and the women on the flat roofs, was very fine. It was the best procession I have seen. We proceeded to the great temple, where the Raja and his people went to return thanks and make offerings. I remained as I was. I joined them afterwards, when we all went on to the palace; and after sitting a short time in Durbar, the little Raja told me he was very tired, as well he might be—so I broke up the assembly, and took him to his mother, thanked her for her hospitality and came away. I stayed the next day at Shorapur, because Pid Naik was beginning his old tricks of spending money without authorisation. He complained that his people did it—they would not listen to his advice or orders; and the latter was the truth. What could I do but preach and caution? I found the little Raja getting on very fairly, and I send you a note of his in English as a specimen. He reads easy stories nicely; but is best in Telugu and Marathi, which, after all, he needs most. Would that I could send him to England! but that is impossible.'

Inquiry had been in progress at Hyderabad regarding the alleged debt to the Gosain bankers; and a suspicion arose in the minds of the Resident and Captain Malcolm that the interpolation of *one line* in the Marathi document was a forgery.[1] This provided a bonus of 15,000 rupees on one transaction, and interest at two per cent per month on the whole; and the bonds were sent down to me. There could be no possible doubt of the forgery. The writing, and the colour of the ink, were quite different from those of the

[1] 'A Mutsuddee may be a rogue, but he should have discretion,' as the Lalla, 'a poor Khayet, a Mutsuddee only' (clerk), quotes the Persian proverb in *Tara*.

remainder of the document. I took the deposition of the clerk who had written the paper, and he declared at once that the line in question had been interpolated, and that the writing was not his. The original draft of the bond was then produced. I took depositions from a number of experts, and also from all the secretaries and clerks who were present when the bonds were written and sealed—all unanimously declared the line to be an addition, and false. If the forgery could be proved, the State would be relieved of debt with interest to the amount of two lakhs, or £20,000.

These inquiries led me into an investigation of the sums paid by the Shorapur State for fifty-two years to the Nizam's Government, and I found it to have been no less than one crore and seventy-nine lakhs (£1,790,000), on various pretences; whereas all it was entitled to was 50,000 × 52 = 26,000,000—twenty-six lakhs only (£260,000); so that the excess paid to the Nizam's Government was £1,530,000, and yet more was required! My father very naturally asked me what law there was in Shorapur, and I find I wrote as follows :—

'As to administration of justice, it lies entirely in my hands. Pid Naik will do nothing. He does not see the necessity of any law or justice; therefore I have to decide all minor cases myself. No court of justice has *ever* existed in Shorapur; but the people are used to *panchayats* or arbitrations, which seem very fair. They are properly courts of five members—two plaintiffs, two defendants, and one person named by them; but here as many as will, sit—and their judgments are really excellent.'

In June I was rendered very anxious by a report from Hyderabad, apparently to be relied on, that a Bengal civilian was to be sent to Shorapur, which was to be entirely severed from Hyderabad. This, it was said, had been resolved on by the Court of Directors, on the examination of correspondence for many years past, and the discovery that the security Government had entered into for the Shorapur State amounted now to £90,000.

It was strange that no answer had been given either to the Resident's despatches or my own, on the subject of Shorapur management, for upwards of a year now; neither he nor I knew whether we were doing right or doing wrong—we had only acted to the best of our judgment and capacity ; but for some time past I had begun to find the Resident very reticent, and apparently unwilling to take further responsibility on himself.

For my own part, I was satisfied I had done my duty to the utmost of my power. I had reported all irregularities and their consequences ; I had requested special and detailed instructions as to the wishes of Government, and I had received none beyond what I have already given here. Lord Hardinge was now Governor-General. I wrote to his private secretary, and pleaded what I had already done ; showed what further measures I had in view, and their results, for the good of the State, if they were carried out ; and left my case in the hands of the Governor-General, awaiting an answer with considerable anxiety.

It came at length, and was unfavourable. It ran as follows :—

'DEAR SIR,—In reply to your letter of the 12th instant, I am directed to state that the arrangements contemplated by the Governor-General for the arrangement of the Shorapur affairs will require the appointment of another agent unconnected with the recent events which have passed in that State, and I very much regret that I cannot hold out any expectations that the retention of your services will come within the scope of the measures now under consideration.'

(Signed) 'C. S. HARDINGE,[1]
Private Secy.

'CALCUTTA, *28th May* 1845.'

However, I was determined not to let the matter rest here. What I had at first written was in general terms ; what I wrote the second time were more particulars referring to the many despatches I had forwarded, in which I had made urgent application for the instructions of Government as to the arrangements of the Shorapur State. This letter, like the first one, was transmitted through the Resident, General Fraser, and he wrote a long despatch on the subject, which, Captain Malcolm informed me, was the clearest and most

1 Charles Stewart, second Viscount Hardinge, 1822–1894. He was his father's only private secretary in India ; and wrote the volume on Hardinge in the *Rulers of India* series.

complete State paper he had ever seen from the Resident's pen.

As many small matters constantly arose which required references to the Nizam's Government, and also in regard to other local business, I had maintained an agent at Hyderabad, by permission of the Resident, and the Nizam's Minister, Suraj-ul-Mulk; and my agent now reported that he had been directed by the Minister to acquaint me with what had occurred at the Nizam's court in reference to Shorapur; and this was the substance of his communication.

The Governor-General had applied to the Nizam to have the State of Shorapur made over to the British Government during the minority of the Raja, and to have all its affairs managed quite independently of the Nizam's Government and of the Resident.

To this the Minister, Suraj-ul-Mulk, had replied, by direction of the Nizam, that Shorapur was a State tributary to him, and not to the Hon. E.I. Company, and had been so recognised in the treaties.

That when the late Raja died, his Government had made no opposition to the appointment of a Diwan; and if the Company were dissatisfied with him, he should receive no support from Hyderabad, and might be removed from office at the pleasure of the Company.

That no opposition had been offered by the Nizam's Government to my appointment; and as I had hitherto acted in the interests of both Governments, being a servant of both, so I ought to be allowed to continue to act, the Nizam's Government, on its part, having perfect confidence in me.

That the Nizam's Government could not see on what principles the British Government could take its tributary out of its hands, especially as there was now profound peace at Shorapur.

'If' (I quote from one of my letters to England) 'the Nizam's Government has really written this, as I am informed, I cannot but think it will have its effect upon the Government of India; and it tallies with what Captain Malcolm wrote to me some time ago, that the Nizam had sent a crusty note about Shorapur, and my agent was told the purport of it as above, with orders from the Minister to tell it or write it to me on the first opportunity.

'Meanwhile a new subject of anxiety to Government has sprung up. I wrote last month that Pid Naik was very ill of combined drunkenness and disease, and that I did not expect him to live. He has lived, however, but at the expense of his intellect. He is now quite foolish, sometimes insane. His people have sent for two Musalmans, who are famed for making charms and amulets, and the belief is that he is bewitched. With one charm he rubs his eyes, another is burnt by his bed,[1] a third is washed off the paper, and he drinks it. My apothecary reported some time ago that he had an attack of *delirium tremens*, which, as no one here knew how to treat it, has resulted in insanity. When I went to see him, a few days ago, he knew me; but I could not make him understand, except that, when I asked him about his seal of office, he said, "Do you use it while I am ill." I have reported all to Government; but until the larger questions are settled, the lesser ones lie by. It is useless to enter upon speculations: God only knows what turn things will take; and to Him I have committed all, most sure that, whatever His will is, it is good.

'Since I last wrote, my new road has been completed, and it is the best and prettiest I have ever made, the ground being so nicely wooded. My greatest achievement has been the driving of my new phaeton to the end of the road every morning to exercise the horses and look after the workmen, and it ran beautifully, and indeed is, I flatter myself, a very stylish thing. The horses did not like the hills at first, but now are quite accustomed to them, and I shall soon take the little Raja out with me for a drive.

'This new road has opened out Shorapur completely: all the artillery and troops in the kingdom could march straight through it without difficulty. I have been finishing a picture of Shorapur for you in oils, and I hope it will give you some idea of the town. In the foreground is the Raja on horseback, attended by his usual retinue, nearly a hundred figures. I have attended closely to detail and costume in those nearest the eye. It is perhaps too ambitious a subject for me; but I have done my best, and it has afforded me much amusement and pleasure. I have also been attempting my own portrait for the Raja, who wished very much to have it.'

The cholera broke out with great severity during the months of June and July. When I returned from a short holiday I had taken to Lingsugur, it was still very prevalent, attacking children very fatally, and in fact sparing neither

[1] Such paper charms are employed to cure Ameena, when ill, in *Tippoo Sultaun*—*i.e.* among Mohammedans.

age nor sex. Fully five hundred souls were swept off in Shorapur alone. On one day I remember fifty-one persons died, and for several days the average was twenty to thirty per day. Thank God! the disorder did not come up my hill, but was confined to the town below. A good fall of rain checked it, and it ceased as suddenly as it came.

The people were greatly rejoiced at its departure, and there was much sacrificing of sheep and buffaloes, and, rather to my dismay, the clans of the Twelve Thousand asked my permission to hold a grand sacrifice to their ancient divinities in Shorapur, which do not belong to Hinduism, but are remnants of original beliefs. The authorities came to me in a great fright and said this *puja* [1] had not taken place for eighteen years, and that on the last occasion the Beydurs had fought among themselves, and that some of the State soldiers had likewise been killed and wounded; and that if the ceremony were allowed, guards must be posted around the place of sacrifice.

'But', I said, 'why do you not trust the Beydurs?'

'They are not to be trusted,' was the reply.

I, however, sent for the head Beydurs and told them if they would promise *by my feet* not to make a disturbance, I would let them have their *puja*, and feed them well: and as their little Raja was a child, and the Diwan, Raja Pid Naik, ill and imbecile, they had only me to look to, and I hoped that as I was about to place great confidence in them, they would not disappoint me. They declared they would not.

'Send one of your *chaprassis* to us,' they said, 'and he will be as much as an army.'

So I sent the one *chaprassi*, and one or two steady old Brahmins who knew the people. About 6,000 Beydurs assembled. There was plenty to eat and drink. About 400 sheep and 50 buffaloes were killed during the ceremonies; and there was not one drunken man in the streets, nor a quarrelsome word spoken, yet all were armed to the teeth! I wondered whether at a gathering of Irish, or English even, such order would have prevailed.

[1] *Puja*—worship, a religious function. [M. T.]

I had never before been so perfectly satisfied with the Beydurs, and was very glad to be able to forward good accounts of their steady behaviour to Hyderabad. I had felt great anxiety, owing to the evident reluctance of the authorities of the place to have this *puja*; but I knew if I flinched at all, or had put them off with promises, there might have arisen ill-feeling against me. Now all was right—and fortunately a good deal of rain fell, which was attributed to the goddess being pleased.

The great suspense I had now for some time been enduring, was happily relieved on the 19th July by a private letter from General Fraser, which ran as follows:—

'My dear Taylor,—I have several times informed you that the whole circumstances of your removal from Shorapur were to me a perfect and most unintelligible mystery, and I am happy to tell you that I have just received the extract of a despatch from the Court of Directors to the Supreme Government, of 19th March 1845, in which the whole of your conduct is spoken of in the highest terms. This, with some other matters, will form the subject of an official communication from me to you in the course of to-morrow or next day.

'It gives me great and sincere pleasure to add that the Government have intimated to me that, pending the receipt of the honourable Court's reply to a letter from Government, dated 12th April last, the Governor-General in Council has determined to suspend the resolution which related to your removal from Shorapur and the appointment of another officer. On this latter part of the subject, however, it is not probable that I shall have occasion to address you officially, as I do not think I have ever informed you officially of the resolution of Government to remove you.—Believe me, my dear Taylor, ever sincerely yours,

'J. S. Fraser, *Resident*.'[1]

'*P.S.*—I have just received your letter of the 12th. I think you ought to report to me officially the good conduct of the Beydurs on occasion of the late grand *puja*. This is very creditable to yourself personally, and I shall be glad to report it for the information of the Supreme Government.'

---

[1] Thus ended the obscure intrigue discussed by John Stuart Mill in the two letters of the September following, given by Henry Reeve in his Preface to this autobiography. It seems to have been chiefly due to the fact that Taylor's post at Shorapur had become good enough to be acceptable to members of the ruling service.

The loyal article on Meadows Taylor in the *Edinburgh Review* for

The official despatch which came from the Court of Directors is too long for insertion *in extenso*, but I subjoin a few extracts.

Extract from a despatch from the Honourable the Court of Directors, No. 9, *dated March* 19, 1845.

Para. 64. 'Captain Taylor's reports, dated 30th December 1843 and 18th January 1844, afford very favourable indications of his capacity for the task intrusted to him, that of reforming the administration of a State always one of the most backward of the petty States of India, and now much debilitated in condition by over-exaction and other mismanagement.

'In this difficult enterprise Captain Taylor seems to be in no respect aided, and in some degree thwarted, by the Diwan, Pid Naik, who, from indolence and weakness, rather than from evil intention, is, though profuse in promises, sparing in performance. If Captain Taylor's ability and perseverance should fail in sufficiently overcoming this obstacle, Pid Naik must be reminded that he occupies his position solely by your appointment, and that not he but your Government is the guardian of the young Raja and real regent of the State. At the same time, Captain Taylor should by no means lose sight of the importance of maintaining a good understanding with Pid Naik. Great allowance must be made for the natural mortification of that personage at his supersession in the supreme authority which, on being nominated Diwan, he expected to exercise. His rank in the State must render the tone of feeling displayed by him greatly influential in the country, and the measures of Captain Taylor cannot fail to be more acceptable to the population, if taken with his concurrence and approval. Captain Taylor therefore should endeavour to conciliate his co-operation by every token of conciliation and respect.'

Then follows approval of my plans and arrangements for the collection of revenue, leasing lands on five years' leases, and inducing the ryots and weavers to return, and proceeds :—

October 1877, looking back over more than thirty years, speaks of 'secret influences at work on this occasion' which were never fully understood even at the India House. 'Apparently the Governor-General, Sir Henry Hardinge, was acting under the influence of the secretariat at Calcutta, jealous of the claims of the covenanted civil service to all preferment of the kind, and wishing to secure the appointment for a member of that body.' There is an earlier protest against the rules, 'degrading as well as ludicrous in their application to educated English officials', which distinguished against the 'uncovenanted' service.

'We are of opinion that it is both right, and the duty of our Government as the Raja's guardian, to do what, according to the ideas and practice of the country, he will have a full right to do when he assumes the Government—namely, to resume all alienations of revenue which were either excessive in amount or improperly bestowed. The time and mode of effecting such resumptions, and the extent to which they should be carried, are subjects for the consideration of the local authorities under your general guidance.

67. 'Captain Taylor's attention is vigilantly directed to the reduction of expenses, and he has proposed a schedule of expenditure amounting only to one lakh instead of 179,303 rupees as formerly,—independent, however, of all payments to the Nizam's Government and creditors.

68. 'We are glad to observe that Raja Pid Naik's opposition will not be allowed to defeat the needful arrangements for the young Raja's education and gradual initiation into public business.

70. 'Captain Taylor has hitherto abstained very properly from introducing any judicial changes, the revenue system and the regulation of the public expenditure being matters of more immediate urgency. When these subjects, however, shall no longer engross his attention, we shall hope that he has been able to introduce some tolerably constituted court of criminal justice. Heretofore, he says, there does not appear to have been any administration of justice whatever. There is no kind of court, civil or criminal. The place, however, of civil courts, is in some degree supplied by the ordinary native expedient of *panchayat*.

'True extract. F. CURRIE,[1]
Secretary to Government of India.'

Raja Pid Naik's earthly career was fast closing now. He was not only very dangerously and incurably ill, but the following correspondence will show that the Government of India had at last come to the determination of dispensing with his services :—

From F. Currie, Esq., Secretary to the Government of India, to Major-General Fraser, Resident at Hyderabad.

'FORT WILLIAM, 18*th July* 1845.

'SIR,—I have received, and laid before the Governor-General in Council, your two letters of 10th and 27th ult., Nos. 64 and 69, with enclosures from Captain Taylor, and in reply I am directed to state that the Governor-General in

---

[1] Sir Frederick Currie, 1799–1875—one of the sturdy figures who used to win baronetcies in India and found families. He was Foreign

Council authorises your instructing that officer to set aside Raja Pid Naik entirely should he be living when you receive these orders. And his Excellency directs that Captain Taylor assume the entire charge of the administration of the Samasthan pending further orders, which, as instructed to you in my letter of the 4th inst., No. 1913, will be communicated to you on receipt of the sentiments of the Honble. the Court of Directors on the affairs of Shorapur.—I have, etc.

'F. CURRIE, *Secy. to Govt.*'

General Fraser wrote as follows on July 30th :—

'I have the honour to transmit for your information and guidance the accompanying letter from the Secretary to the Government of India to my address, No. 2024, under date the 18th inst.

2. 'It may be almost superfluous that I should suggest to you the propriety of carrying into effect the measures therein directed, with every consistent regard for the feelings of Pid Naik, and in such a delicate and cautious manner as shall avoid giving any offence or jealous suspicion to the Beydur population or other inhabitants of the Shorapur Samasthan.—I have, etc. J. S. FRASER, *Resident.*'

I found it, however, quite a hopeless task to communicate the contents of this letter to Raja Pid Naik, who lingered on, suffering from the effects of his paralytic seizure, and was now both speechless and insensible. He lived till the 8th of August, and then died without apparently further suffering. I went to visit him a few days before he breathed his last, and as he revived a little, his sons believed him to be sensible. I think, perhaps, he was conscious for a few moments, for he took my hand in one of his, while he passed the other all over my face and person, trying the while to speak, but no articulate sound came from his lips. I promised his sons, who were in bitter grief, that I would return if he revived at all ; but he did not, and passed away quite quietly.

I made every arrangement for his obsequies, and for the expenses necessary for their performance ; and the morning after his death attended the funeral in full dress as a mark of respect. When I went to the house, I found the late Raja

---

Secretary, accompanying Sir Henry Hardinge in the first Sikh War ; and was Resident in Lahore at the final outbreak. Taylor did not care for Currie's conduct in 1848, as appears from the *History*.

dressed in rich garments, with all his jewels on, set out on a terrace in the courtyard, the body placed leaning against a wall, and seated on his velvet cushion of state, and his sword and shield lying beside him. The face was disfigured by paralysis, bloated, and under the pale hue of death was most distressing to see ; but all his retainers, many of the chiefs of clans, and friends were bidding him a last farewell, and were saluting him. When the ceremony was concluded, the body was taken up, and placed sitting in an open chair, and then, taking his two eldest sons by the hand, I led them after him, amidst the firing of guns and the wailing of the crowds all around us, to the place of cremation, where, divested of its jewels, the body was placed on the pyre, to which the eldest son applied the first torch ; and as the wood had been thoroughly saturated with oil and *ghi*, or boiled butter, together with camphor and incense, it burst into a fierce blaze, and the cremation was soon complete. I remained with the boys till all the ceremonies were ended, and then conducted them home,—paid a visit of condolence to the sorrowing widow, and then took my leave.

It would have been indelicate, it appeared to me, to open the subject of my succession at once ; but when the first few days of mourning had expired, I held a court, in order to explain publicly what I had previously made known privately to all.

There was at first some little difficulty with the heads of departments. I laid down my plan of proceeding very decidedly, and adhered to it. At first they greatly wished that the Rani should have a voice in all that went on, and that nothing should be done without her concurrence. A few trifling orders even had been given in her name ; but I cut all this very short, and distinctly stated that I would stand no sort of interference whatever ; and to put an end to all controversy on the subject, I went to visit the Rani after my Durbar was over, and she protested vehemently, not only that she would never attempt to hinder me in any way, but, on the contrary, that she would assist me to the utmost of her power.

I arranged that the State seal with my signature was to be the only authorised authority for documents in the State.

The seal was a mere matter of form, as all orders, receipts, and the like, were examined during the week, and on Monday mornings were produced, and explained to the little Raja, and sealed up in his presence, so as to show the people that he was in reality considered their Raja, and the head of the State. The people were glad to see him put forward, and all discontent soon subsided. Even the keys of the treasury were brought up every night and put under my pillow; and those of the stores and groceries were kept by the Rani, as she wished to have them.

Another great blessing was vouchsafed to us; a plenteous rain fell at last, which had been sorely needed. Grain had risen in price, and I was growing anxious, for a famine seemed inevitable. The young leaves of the early grain were withering; but still all knew if rain fell it would sprout again. The wells were dry; but they filled rapidly, and in a few days the grain looked green again, and everything seemed cheerful. My lake at Bohnal was now really a noble sheet of water—good two miles from corner to corner, and six feet more in depth than the previous year. As if, too, all I had endeavoured to effect had taken place at once, I heard privately from Captain Malcolm that the Nizam was about to remit the payment of four lakhs and a half, which was still due on the old accounts. He had seen the Minister's draft of an official note on the subject, and assured me I should soon have it officially. I need not say how great a relief it would be to me when it came.

I continued to pay frequent visits to the Rani, and took her and the Raja drives in my new carriage. Her ecstasies were very great, and her remarks most amusing when she was driven to places where she had never been before. I visited Raja Pid Naik's family also very often. He had left no will, nor any directions as to the disposal of his property or estates; and as, several times when he was sensible, he had put the hands of his wife and children into mine before all his people, so now they all requested that I would take sole charge of their estates and affairs, and manage them for the benefit of all—and I consented. The head steward and accountant, with all their papers, were then made over to me, and so long as I had charge of their affairs I never had trouble with any of the family.

Poor Pid Naik! with many faults he had many kindly qualities; but he was utterly unstable, quite unable to resist temptation, and too obstinate and puffed up by the people about him to attend to orders issued by Government. He fancied himself Raja of Shorapur, and at heart desired to gain the succession for his eldest son. Brahmins, mostly of bad character, had obtained complete ascendancy over him, and he was too weak, and too credulous and superstitious, to resist their suggestions. I do not think he ever went into extreme wrong but once, when, if he did not actually embrace crime, he certainly shook hands with it. The temptation was great, for if the Raja had been killed, his son would have become Raja in his stead. Pid Naik left eight children,—six by his excellent wife Madama, one by the other wife, and another illegitimate.

CHAPTER X

1846

I WAS obliged to be absent for a short time on private business, and there had been many attempts made to induce the Rani to defy my authority, but as yet she appeared firm. She had, however, set up a new paramour, one of the menials, and under such circumstances was not to be depended upon, and I was obliged to watch very narrowly. Not long after my return to Shorapur a letter was intercepted by one of my Beydurs, who had obtained it for a few rupees from the messenger that was to have taken it to Hyderabad. The writing and the seal were those of an old Brahmin of rank, who I knew aspired to be head manager under the Rani, and the letter was addressed to one of the Nizam's confidential servants, urging him to send 1,200 Arabs and Rohillas without delay.

Before the copy of the letter and my report could reach General Fraser by express, Captain Malcolm wrote to me privately that 400 Arabs had actually left Hyderabad, and begged me to stop them.

I showed this letter to the Rani in confidence, and warned her ; but she protested entire innocence, and the old Brahmin suddenly and mysteriously disappeared. I found out that my absence had been interpreted as a recall, and that the Rani had been making profuse promises to her adherents ; but I took no notice of these stupid intrigues, which could only be stopped when they came to a crisis. The authorities at Hyderabad were very busy sifting this plot, and its intrigues seemed interminable.

The year 1845 closed pleasantly for me. In the first place, General Fraser sent me a copy of a despatch which he had received from the Secretary to Government on the subject of Shorapur affairs, which was very gratifying, as the first from Sir Henry Hardinge.

'Foreign Department.

'Dated CAMP ZEIT, *7th November* 1845.

'SIR,—I have received and laid before the Governor-General your despatch, dated 17th October last, No. 129, submitting copies of correspondence with Captain Taylor in regard to the Shorapur Samasthan.

'In reply, I am desired to state that his Excellency does not consider, after perusal of the papers submitted, that they call for any orders from him beyond the expression of his opinion that Captain Taylor would appear to have shown zeal, ability, and judgment in the conduct of the affairs of the Samasthan during the past season.—I have, etc.

'F. CURRIE, *Secy.*'

Lastly, it had pleased God to grant to the people one of the finest harvests ever remembered, though in the beginning of the season the anxiety, owing to the want of rain, had been so great; and what could be a happier opening for 1846 than a cheery letter from my father, bringing good news of all my dear ones at home? I had recovered from a sharp fit of fever and ague, which left me as weak as a child for a time; and the people were orderly and quiet through the country—no cattle-lifting, no robberies or outrages—and some of the most notorious thieves and robbers had taken to farming quietly and contentedly, and I endeavoured to encourage more to follow their good example.

The Rani and her intrigues were the only cause of anxiety, and she certainly was in a queer humour, exalting her new favourite with all her might and main in the most shameless manner; but the townspeople seemed quite weary of her profligacy, and were very gentle and perfectly easy to manage; but I never saw in any place, or among any natives, morality at so low an ebb among the higher classes, or such entire absence of the commonest truth and honesty. I often felt there was no chance for the poor young Raja among them all. I went out into the districts as usual, and got through all my routine of work just the same as the year before, and a few extracts will suffice.

'*February* 1846.—I got to my camp all right, and yesterday moved on to Andola, six miles. Such fields of *jowari*! such glorious crops I never saw before, and the people say have not existed for ten years. One ear of *jowari* I pulled, which contained a countless number of grains, all nearly ripe, and like so many pearls. The cotton, too, is very fair, but not quite so fine as the *jowari* perhaps; and there is a good local demand for manufacture on the spot, so my farmers will make a handsome profit.

'All hands are very grateful to God. Their worship is not ours, but their gratitude is the same, and we may well hope will find acceptance in His sight. . . .

'I don't know how *jowari* would mix with wheaten flour. I don't think it would rise, as the flour wants the gluten of wheat; but it is highly nutritious, as the robust frames of our peasantry testify—no fat, all sinews and muscle,—enduring vagabonds as ever helped at a border fray or drove their neighbours' cattle. Now, all are as quiet as mice. . . .

'I am informed that the Rani is now in great admiration of me, and swears she will have nothing to do with any nonsense such as was going on. I wonder what she means, and what is in the wind now!

'The Governor-General's hands just now are too full of the Sikh war to attend to anything else, and the post has brought the news of the victory over them, about which I was not a little anxious.[1] . . .

'*February 24th.*—Bitter cold wind till noon; worked hard all day. In the evening I went into the village, carpets were spread on the terrace, and we had a *natch*. I sat in state for an hour, and then went and saw the children who had been married: one about eleven, very pretty and fair for a native; she came and sat in my lap very confidingly, but would not open her eyes till I put my watch to her ear, showed her the works, and the "tic tic" within. Such eyes they were! well worthy to be painted. The other was a sly puss, but came at last to me. Then fireworks, and I took my leave. . . .

'The General has authorised a new line of post, which has saved me at least three days, and is a great comfort. Are not these wonderful victories over the Sikhs? The Peninsula can hardly boast a more brilliant series. We have fought no such battles in India before.[2] . . .

---

[1] Sobraon, February 10, 1846.

[2] Taylor's accounts of the Punjab battles, in his *History*, while not free from errors, are among his better writing. Through them one can feel the contemporary thrill; and also the *Times* correspondent, whose business it was to be well informed, although not upon the spot. Of Ferozeshah: 'Never before had so hardly-contested a battle been fought in India, nor, with eventual victory, had ever such great peril of defeat been encountered.' At Sobraon: 'Nearly 10,000 Sikhs perished in two hours. . . . The battle had begun in earnest at nine

'I have quite secured the additional revenue I hoped for; altogether my accounts will show 30,000 rupees extra over last year, and I hope the big folks will be satisfied.' . . .

On the 24th April, as the heat was very great, with scarcely any shade, and the thermometer averaging from 125° to 127°, I returned to Shorapur. There was also another very severe visitation of cholera, and the poor little Raja was very ill, with terrible inflammation and suppuration of the glands of his neck. Native remedies had proved useless, so I insisted upon being allowed to see what I could do, and I sent to Lingsugur for some leeches, which I applied, and afterwards lanced the place, putting on soothing poultices. He slept all that night, and he recovered his health and strength, which had been greatly reduced; and I believe my renown as a physician was widespread.

There were great rejoicings on the recovery of the Raja, and among other entertainments a Hindu play, which I had never seen before, taken from the Bhagwat, or recitation of the poem relating to Krishna.[1]

The chief performer was a handsome young girl, who was a capital actress and singer, very richly dressed. She personated one of Krishna's wives, lamenting his absence from her. The text was all given in recitation, with here and there an air and chorus, the language, Kanarese,[2] which I could not

---

o'clock, and by eleven there was not a single Sikh soldier, except the dead and wounded, on the left bank of the river.'

[1] 'The amorous blue-throated Krishna playing to the damsels of Muttra' (*Tara*).

[2] Of the chief language of these parts (see the beautiful language maps in the map volume of the *Imperial Gazetteer*) Taylor had already written in *Tippoo Sultaun*: 'As quiet as . . . the natural discordance of their own language (the Canarese) would allow.' He seems never to have cared for the sound of this Dravidian tongue, which he did not know. In *Tara,* written much later, a traveller is kept awake by the noises 'from the women, who ground at the mill so early in the house, singing a discordant Canarese song'. A guide rolls forth 'a volley of hard Canarese village names'. After Taylor's cross-country journeyings were over he made a character say: 'Ah, by-and-by, you will know what a Canarese coss is.' Fazil Khan, going out in disguise, is told by Bulwunt Rao: 'Only keep that courtly tongue of yours quiet, or if you speak at all, let it be in Canara, which somehow suits you better than our soft Mahratta, and let it be as broad as you can make it.'

follow. One plaintive air with a chorus was excellently given, and I wish I had been able to take it down. Her acting was admirable : grief, sadness, hope, jealousy, despair, all depicted in turn, and her joy at the last when she found she had been tormenting herself for nothing after all ! Yet the whole was performed by stone-cutters, who could neither read nor write ; and the plays had been learned by rote, and were traditional in their families.[1]

Some of the Hindu dramas acted in this way must be very beautiful. Sir William Jones [2] has translated *Sakuntala, The Toy Cart*, and others admirably. Rude as it may appear, one can trace the ancient system of chorus—the actor appealing to the chorus—and the chorus answering the actor or actress, advising, pitying, etc. That which I saw was not strictly a play, but one of the sacred books dramatised. There were comic interludes, to enable the female performers to rest, and these, too, were very clever. Altogether, the children, for whose entertainment it was given, were highly delighted, and so was I ; and we all sat on the ground together.

It seems absurd to mention more intrigues, but I was forced to check one which was growing troublesome. The head of the *daftar*, or account department, one of the chief peculators in Pid Naik's time, set himself up as the Rani's champion, and she gave him valuable presents, and abetted him very shamelessly. At last he took it on himself to declare to her that he had been appointed by the Nizam her Minister, and gave her a sum of money out of the treasury.

This could not be allowed. I therefore suspended him, put the *daftar* papers into the hands of the real hereditary head of the office, a clever young fellow, and sent the defaulter to his house, under a guard of twenty of my Beydurs, who

Yet the same speaker again says of the southernmost, as perhaps the purest, Sanskrit language in India : ' I dread thy courtly speech breaking out even of our rough Mahratta tongue.'

[1] There is a full account of the rendering of a Katha, or sacred play, running through three nights, before Shivaji, in *Tara*; chapters lxxii. and lxxiii.

[2] 1746–1794. On literary grounds, as a piece of English, no rendering of *Sakuntala* can compare to *Sakuntala : a Play in Five Acts*, Indian Press, Allahabad, 1902, by J. G. Jennings, then of the Educational Service. ' The original story has been treated with great freedom.'

kept him safely. No one grieved at his degradation, for he had been insolent to all classes.

In a few days the Rani came to me, and was very penitent, wept very much, and promised to be so good in future ; but I cannot say I trusted the lady !

From the first I had determined to allow no outsiders in hereditary offices. I had to teach those who held these posts what their duty was and how to keep systematic accounts. I had a day-book and a ledger in the treasury, and they were kept very neatly and correctly. On examination at the end of the financial year, I found that, after paying the Nizam's tribute and other debts and arrears, I had still 70,000 rupees of surplus balance, notwithstanding all the extra expenses of the family in ceremonials which could neither be delayed nor avoided. The account stood thus in the final reckoning of the year :—

Total revenue . .	Rs. 321,716	10	6
Total expenditure . .	246,818	4	3
Balance in favour of the State	74,898	6	3

Of this General Fraser sent me ample approval, which I need not copy in detail ; the concluding paragraph shows the spirit in which he wrote.

'The mode of accounts which you have adopted is clear and explicit, and appears well calculated to afford that information to the Supreme Government which it will no doubt desire to possess. With regard to your management of Shorapur, I highly approve of the zeal, ability, and unremitting exertion with which you discharge the duties of your present important office, and your gradual establishment of order and well-regulated administration in a district hitherto proverbial for maladministration, corruption, and every species of disorder. (Sd.) 'J. S. F.'

I find that but little of interest took place during the remainder of that year. All was flourishing and peaceful. Now and then petty intrigues occurred on the part of one or another. Lakshmangir and the lady herself were generally at the bottom of the mischief, or her paramour Kasima. He indeed disseminated ill-will between two sections of the Beydurs, with a view to set them all by the ears, and thereby to bring disrepute on me. There was a small riot in the town, and some grain-dealers' shops were injured; but the offenders came to me and 'begged pardon' like naughty boys. Happily in November Lakshmangir was summoned to Hyderabad, and I obliged him to go and we had some peace.

Among themselves the Beydurs were rather at strife, one accusing another of having more land than he ought to possess, and suchlike disputes. However, with these I never interfered. I was too weak, and they knew it, to break up a clannish faction of 12,000 men and more, who held the finest lands in all the villages, and so long as they were orderly, it was all I required. Had any serious quarrel arisen I must have interfered, and I often told them it was to their interest in the end to keep together and remain peaceable.

Rather a curious incident occurred during this year. A Brahmin, who had been absent from Shorapur for two years, came to me, and said that he had cast up the table of my nativity, and had brought me the result. As I had never seen or heard of him before, and as he himself wished to know whether it tallied with my own experience hitherto, I was anxious to see the paper, which ran after this manner. I had not, nor could I have, given him any sort of information as to the date of my birth or other particulars, as I did not know of his existence.

From birth under the *Sun's* influence. Neither favourable nor unfavourable. I was weak and delicate, sometimes ill. Six years.

Next under the *Moon's* influence. Generally good; few crosses, and those which occurred resulting in good. Ten years.

Next under *Venus.* Neither good nor bad. The ordinary run of life. Seven years.

Next under *Saturn.* Bad. Losses; grief. No worldly advancement; no wealth. Never long in the same place; unsettled; frequent disappointments. Eighteen years.

Deduct on account of astrological months, five years, two months.

End of troubled period, thirty-five years, ten months.

Since when I have been under the influence of 'Brihaspat' or *Jupiter*, of whose sway one year is already nearly past, and it will continue from its commencement, sixteen years.

Add to the previous calculation the one year of Jupiter, and the result is—thirty-six years; which was my exact age.[1] The Brahmin inquired whether that was about right, as he had been rather bothered in the calculations regarding the moon's influence, which could not be rendered with as great certainty as the others. No one here knew my age, that I was aware of; but the result seemed to me very curious. I wished to know how the calculations had been made; but my friend could only explain them in Sanskrit, and this I did not understand. I sent the paper home to my father, and it afforded a good deal of interest and amusement to friends at home.

The details of my daily life were too monotonous to be of general interest—one day passed like another, only varied by my daily rides and drives to look after my roads and other public works; and I propose to introduce here a short sketch of the history of the Shorapur State, which may not be uninteresting, and may serve to relieve the sameness of my story.

The Beydurs are a race of aboriginal descent, numerous in Mysore and in the Southern Maratha country. They profess to be Hindus, some following Sivite Brahmins, some Vishnavite, and many, perhaps most, the tenets of the Lingayats; but at heart they are believers in the original demons, sprites, and local spiritual beings in whom their ancestors had faith in the earliest period of their race, and their worship is still actively maintained, all the opposition of the Brahmins and Lingayats notwithstanding. These spiritual creatures have various names and various attitudes, merciful, protective, and destructive, and one or other is worshipped according to

[1] Born in 1808, as stated in the opening sentence of the autobiography, Meadows Taylor can have been of no other age than thirty-eight in September 1846. These additions and subtractions are too suggestive of the divine by whom, a dozen years earlier, Macaulay was assaulted upon alighting at the Residency in Mysore. 'I can assure you that, if you write Napoleon Buonaparte in Arabic, leaving out only two letters, it will give 666.' 'The man looked at me as if he thought me a very wicked fellow; and, I dare say, has by this time discovered that, if you write my name in Tamul, leaving out T in Thomas, B in Babington, and M in Macaulay, it will give the number of this unfortunate Beast.' Taylor, like Scott, had a weakness for astrology, and could make too apt use of it in fiction. But his own life was to contain two remarkable examples of prediction in the horoscopes of himself (Chapter iii.) and of the little Raja (Chapter xi.).

necessity—for children, for good crops, for any vow made in any need or emergency, for destruction of enemies, for staying of disease among men or cattle. Sacrifices are made to rude stones in their honour; but they are not represented by images, nor do they dwell in temples. Large pipal, nim, or banian trees, and most frequently deserted spots on village boundaries, are the places which the deities are supposed to like best. Although the Beydurs arrogate to themselves pure descent from the Kshattriyas or warriors of ancient times, they have no pretension to caste, as understood in a Hindu sense—no Hindu, even of the lowest caste, would take water from their hands, or eat food dressed by them. In short, they are *mlechas* or outcasts, and form part of that great mass of aboriginal population which—as the Gonds, Bhils, Mangs,[1] Santhals, and many other tribes—underlie Hinduism all over India.

In character they are violent, fickle, and often treacherous —adepts in lawless pursuits, and often engaging in serious organised crimes, as dacoity, cattle-lifting, etc., in which they take a pride. They are brave, and Tippoo's famous infantry was mostly composed of them; but they are impatient of control and difficult to manage. In the service of the Vijayanagar State, in the fifteenth and sixteenth centuries, they were very numerous, and were at times more than a match for the Musalmans of Gulbarga and Bidar. Among themselves they are merry and quarrelsome by turns, fond and jealous of their women, industrious in some respects, and idle in others; devoted to field-sports of all kinds—hawking, coursing, hog-hunting, and deer-shooting. None of them are mechanics or artisans in any form or degree; and but for their association with civilising Hindu, Musalman, and British influence, they would most likely relapse into their original savagery.

The family of Shorapur came originally from Ratnagiri, in the Mysore territory, where they were lords of a hill-fort and a considerable district. They were one among many

[1] In the *Thug* the Mangs sent for as executioners are called 'these wretches, everywhere the vilest of mankind'. Towards the end Ameer Ali says: 'Who cares about Mangs and Dhers? they are always villains and robbers.' But in *Tara* there is a Mang watchman of singular faithfulness even in his cups.

such 'lairds' who were feudal vassals of the Hindu State of Vijayanagar, and who served their masters with all the clans of their own tribe after the first Musalman invasion and subsequent settlement of the invaders at Gulbarga, and declaration of independence of Delhi by Alla-ud-din Hassan Gangu Bahmani, in 1347. The Hindu State of Vijayanagar was obliged to defend its own frontier against Musalman inroads; and some of the Beydur clans were settled in the tract between the Krishna and the Tungabhadra rivers, among whom were the Beydurs of Ratnagiri.

In the wars between the Bahmani kings and the Hindus, these Beydur clans always took a distinguished part, and afterwards in those with the Musalman dynasty of Bijapur; but as the Hindu power declined, the Shorapur family joined the Musalman, and became his feudal vassals. The river Krishna had been hitherto the boundary between the Hindus and Musalmans; but the latter now occupied the Doab, a tract lying between that river and the Tungabhadra. Gradually, partly by military service and partly by encroachment, the Shorapur clans took possession of countries north of the Krishna. They built a fort at Wagingera, on the west side of the Shorapur hills, where they became more settled and powerful, and their chiefs were raised to noble rank at the Bijapur Court, with extensive privileges for the collection of dues from the country round, and which was, in reality, black-mail; and so matters continued till the Emperor Aurungzeb captured Bijàpur and annexed its dominions, in 1686. The Beydur chief of Wagingera, however, resisted the Emperor for some time, and refused to come to his Court, though very earnestly and cordially entreated to do so. At length he consented; but being jeered and insulted by the courtiers, he returned to his fastness, more determined than ever to rebel. It was quite in vain that the Emperor wrote him letters of pardon and assurance, impressed with his own right hand dipped in ground sandal-wood—in vain that he wrote, 'Would that you were a Musalman! you would be to me as a brother.' No impression could he make upon the rebel chief, who was assisted and encouraged by Shivaji, and his famous commander, Dhannaji Jadow. At last the Emperor attacked Wagingera, was a second time repulsed, and it was not until after a siege lasting seven months that the fort and town of Wagingera were eventually stormed, with the aid of the army from the south, under General Zulficar Khan. Driven from his fastness, the rebel chief, Pam Naik, selected the secluded spot where Shorapur now stands. Its proper name is 'Sur-pur', the 'City of Valour'. Here he was allowed to live in peace, and eventually became good friends with the Emperor, who bestowed high titles upon him, created him a 'Commander of Five Thousand', conferred on him a large addition to his territory, confirming all previous grants by the Bijápur monarchy, and also extended his collections from villages over a great portion of the Deccan and Carnatic.

As the Musalman power declined, the Beydur chiefs maintained their position, and though nominally tributary to the Peshwas, never performed actual service. If their district collections were interfered with, they plundered the Peshwa's country till the interference was withdrawn. They were in a somewhat similar position with Nizam-ul-Mulk, who was Viceroy in the Deccan; and when the Nizam and the Peshwa concluded their treaty at Yatgir, on the frontier of Shorapur, in 1785, the two Powers consulted as to whether the Beydur chief should not be at once attacked, and his dynasty suppressed as a public nuisance. The reigning Beydur chief, however, partly by showing a very bold front, and partly by the high reputation of his clan for valour, and also by agreeing to pay 50,000 rupees a-year to the Nizam, escaped the threatened danger.

The Shorapur State was then very flourishing, the revenue being between twenty and thirty lakhs a-year. There were two battalions of disciplined sepoys under European commanders, and a park of artillery, and these, with the Beydur militia, 12,000 in number, and a considerable body of cavalry, made the reigning Raja, Enkappa Naik, truly formidable. Hyder and Tippoo, each in turn, tried to induce him to join them, but he was content to remain as he was; and Tippoo, though he overran part of the neighbouring District, made no attempt to attack Shorapur.

Enkappa Naik was a great patron of Hindu learning, and established a Sanskrit College, which I found still existing in a reduced form. He was a good soldier, and skilful administrator, according to the customs of his tribe, and the manner in which he brought his principality out of the troubles and difficulties of those times was truly admirable ; but the fortune of the State passed away with him.

The Marathas grew stronger, and sweeping away the Shorapur dues from their district, imposed instead heavy demands on Shorapur. The Nizam repudiated Aurungzeb's grants, and annexed all the territory north of the Bhima river. In the State was not only bad administration, but waste and extravagance. On the death of the late Raja's father, the Nizam's Government demanded a succession fee, or *nazarana*, of fifteen lakhs, which the then Resident at the Court of Hyderabad, Mr. Martin, declared to be an 'equitable addition to the Nizam's Government'. The amount was partly paid in cash, and, except the final balance of four and a half lakhs, by loans taken upon British security from the Gosain bankers of Shorapur, year by year, until Raja Krishnappa Naik died, the State being then virtually insolvent.

It was soon afterwards committed to my care, in the hope that, in some degree, the past might be redeemed, and the family placed in more comfortable circumstances for the future.

This short sketch will, at any rate, show the reader that the Shorapur family was one of the oldest, and the most distinguished of the Deccan ; that they had attained high rank under the Bahmani and Adil Shahi as well as the Mogul dynasties ; had been respected by the Peshwas and Tippoo : and if, through misfortune and bad government, they had fallen into a lower grade of power and wealth, they deserved better treatment than they had received at the hands of the British Government in its intervention.

After my first tour through my districts the agricultural classes became anxious for a settled revenue, and spontaneously offered me a gradual increase for a term of five years. I could not at once grant it, nor during the uncertainty of political affairs could I even propose any such settlement to the people as an advantage.

Now, however, all hindrances had been removed, and I considered that such an arrangement would conduce to the welfare of the people. I had no actual data, by survey or measurement, for assessing the land ; but the old accounts in the possession of village registrars were freely brought forward, and the assessment made by a former Raja, fifty years ago, 'Enkappa Naik the Great', was accepted by all as just, and was a good foundation on which to begin.

Between this assessment and the present one existing, a mean was struck, and the difference in prices of grain, etc., and the amount alienated in grants, were all allowed for. The maximum of settlement was then decided, and fairly distributed over lands under cultivation and waste, for which the rates at first settled by me were the standard.

The people seemed quite content, and in some instances offered an increase on the rates of their own accord; but of course the settlement was very roughly done, and not with the accuracy with which one founded on an actual survey could have been executed. At all events, it opened up the road to the employment of local capital, and, above all, it satisfied the people.

My own work was, of necessity, very heavy, but proceeded very successfully, as one by one the different districts were arranged on five years' leases, and the result in the immediate application of capital to the reclamation of waste lands was most satisfactory. The rents were regularly paid, and the crops and harvest exceptionally good, and I anticipated a very favourable balance-sheet.

One instance I record, among many, which I gave in letters to my father.

'The *patel* or head man of a large village where I was encamped, had been very poor, and was thoroughly disheartened by repeated exactions. His wife, a homely, excellent woman, had complained to my dear wife that her husband was idle, and begged I would speak to him. "If he wants money," she said, "I will pledge every ornament I have to buy bullocks." I, however, assisted him from the State with sufficient money to set him up. This year the man and his wife came to me together, and she was the speaker.

'"God has prospered us," she cried; "we have now 32 bullocks, beside cows and buffaloes: we used to pay 32 rupees, but all our land is cultivated now, and we pay 322 rupees"; and there were hundreds and hundreds like him, prosperous, secure, and thankful.'

I was then on the right bank of the Bhima, and one day received a deputation from a large village called Sinnur, on the left bank, the estate of an officer of the Nizam's household who had charge of the royal tent establishment, and I went to them next day. The village women and children, all neatly dressed, met me, poured libations of water before my horse, and offered me flowers and garlands. A carpet was spread in the *patel's* house, and I sat with the assembly for a long time, hearing accounts of how the Beydurs used to come in bodies, cut down their crops, drive off their cattle, and keep them in perpetual fear. Now all was secure, not a head of corn was touched, and all their distant lands were under cultivation, as well as those near to their dwellings. The same Beydurs who used to plunder them came unarmed to their weekly market, and all was peace.

Many men showed me scars of sword and bullet wounds received in those affrays, and indeed the whole frontier must have been in a sad state. I need hardly tell you how very gratifying this visit was to me, and it was followed by many others to my frontier neighbours with the same result.

If I have as yet left the affairs of Sind unnoticed, in regard to the great political transactions of Lord Ellenborough's government of India, it is because they have long since become subjects of general history; commented upon by all writers, and therefore beyond the province of this record of my life. During the process of annexation, however, I watched the progress of Sir Charles Napier with the keenest interest. Outram was one of my earliest and closest Indian friends, and we corresponded as frequently as his and my own heavy duties allowed of. I do not believe that Lord Ellenborough ever desired the conquest or the annexation of Sind; but he was in the hands of a man who, led on by personal unscrupulous ambition and daring, which no one can question, formed, as it appears to me, from the beginning, the resolution of displacing the Amirs, and, regarding its strategical importance, of converting Sind into a British provinee. History and Sir William Napier's *Conquest of Scinde* tell how this was achieved: how, by one traitor among their brotherhood, Ali Murad, Sir Charles was misled and deceived; how the Amirs were literally goaded on to war, and defeated in the bloody battles of Miani and Dabba. and lost their State and their treasure.

In my letters to the *Times*, I was able, with my friend's assistance, to detail the progress of political events as they occurred ; and I believe I told the truth, without sparing any. No one could question the high military capacity and valour by which the victories were won by a handful, comparatively, of British soldiers, against perhaps the bravest Indian troops that ever took the field, and whose numbers far exceeded those of the British forces.

By the splendour of these victorics, the people of England were perhaps dazzled, and the political events of the time were thrown into the shade ; but they are ineffaceable, and will remain for ever a blot upon the record of Indian history ; not as the effect of any national or Governmental policy, but as the consequence of the acts of one man who, uncontrolled, had entered Sind under a foregone conclusion, and brought about the result. Lord Ellenborough could be just and merciful in the case of Gwalior, the troops of which were more treacherous and more dangerous to the peace of India than the Beluchis of Sind; and it is difficult to estimate why he confirmed Napier's aggressive policy in the one instance, while he contradicted it in the affair of Gwalior, which he conducted in person. In both these instances the troops of the State were the aggressors, not the principals themselves, and except for one man's ambition the results would have been the same.

In a short time, comparatively, Sir William Napier's glorification of his brother appeared in the *Conquest of Scinde.*

It was impossible for Outram to remain silent under the attacks made upon him and his reputed share in these political transactions, and I, and many other friends, urged him to write and publish a vindication of his acts, and a revelation of facts, which in Sir William's book were either omitted or glozed over to justify Sir Charles's execution of his mission. Sir Charles had taken £70,000 as his share of the Amir's wealth. Outram, a poor man, had declined to receive a penny of the proceeds, though his share was a large one,[1] and therefore he was entirely independent. He roused himself to the task, and wrote, sending the manuscript to me for approval and correction, and I cheered him on. At first his expressions

[1] £63,000. Taylor's *History.*

were laboured ; but his style soon became clear and vigorous. It was the fashion, when his commentary appeared, to say that Outram never wrote a word of it, and that he was unable to do so ; but if such an opinion still lingers in any mind, I can at least declare that I saw and read the whole from beginning to end in his own handwriting, bold and large. I advised him to have the document roughly set up and printed in Bombay, and then sent home for final reprinting, after being duly corrected for the press, and I myself revised all the proofs, suggesting here and there rearrangement of the matter, so as to form a more continuous narrative and commentary ; and, so revised, the whole was forwarded to Edinburgh, where it was finally published. I altered none of the writing, and the book is as I saw it when in manuscript, with the excision only of any repetitions, and here and there a slight variation in the arrangement of detail. I kept the original letters and much of the manuscript by me for many years.

Whether Sind was a profitable annexation or not was a question deeply considered by Lord Hardinge's Government, and by the Court of Directors, who at one time appeared very much disposed to repudiate the conquest altogether ; and in my opinion it would have been well to have done so on the discovery of Ali Murad's treachery.

Sir Charles was very sensitive on this point, and issued one of his famous proclamations 'To his Soldiers' to prove that Sind was profitable, and that he had actually remitted revenue from it. This assertion was taken up by the press of India very earnestly ; but as no details were given on the other side, Sir Charles had pretty much his own way. I, however, was supplied from my own sources of information in Sind and Bombay with authentic copies of unpublished public accounts ; and was permitted to use them. I saw I could prove by the details that if Sir Charles remitted ten lakhs (£100,000) of surplus revenue from the province, after paying all its civil charges, that in reality on the military side the cost was a million and a half sterling, for which there was no provision at all ! And with the consent of the editor of one of the leading papers I opened a series of letters on the subject of this costly annexation and its political character. Occasionally these were answered by an article in Sir Charles's defence, very ably and speciously worded; but they could not bear down the weight of actual results, and after a while the editor gave judgment in my favour so warmly and heartily for the public service I had rendered, that I was amply rewarded for my trouble.

Whether the conquest of Sind now pays its expenses I know not—in any case it is well governed and prosperous. No question could be raised as to its importance in a strategical point of view; but the mode of its acquisition is a dark blot on the record of Indian history.

TAYLOR, OUTRAM, AND NAPIER

These strong sentiments seem to be sound, however they may startle some modern readers. Taylor is very apt to be safe and orthodox in his views.

In his *History of India*, written some years before this autobiography, and a generation after the events which he denounced as they happened, his voice is the same, expressing vehement feeling with dignity, in words telling because restrained. The story is well told in only two and a half pages from page 660. 'It is impossible to deny high military skill, ability, and bravery to Sir Charles; but in regard to knowledge of the country and its people, temper, or ordinary courtesy to native princes, a worse selection could not have been made. . . . The conquest of Sinde was indeed achieved; but it had been based upon violence, injustice, and deliberate perfidy, which, questionable as many transactions in the English conquest of India may be, has happily no parallel. No one ventured to vindicate it.' In a sense it laid the seeds of the Mutiny of fourteen years later, since various Indian regiments refused to go to Sind. 'There is no doubt of its value in a strategical point of view; but the mode of its acquisition forms one of the darkest records of British Indian history.'

Taylor condemns, as any one must do, the Napier of a later date who, as Commander-in-Chief, sought to exalt the military power above the civil. As has been said, Napier was then old, and not himself; or perhaps too much himself. Yet both in the *History* and in *Seeta* Taylor admits that Napier showed more prescience than most in regard to the coming storm.

CHAPTER XI

1847–50

In January 1847 I lost my faithful friend and manager of one of the largest of my districts, Balram Singh, who had been an officer of my police in 1827–29. He was one of the best natives I ever knew, most faithful and intelligent. The district under his charge was the worst in the country; but he had managed it well—had encouraged the people to increase cultivation—and had laid a good foundation of eventual prosperity. With his last breath he committed his wife and children to my care.

On my return to camp I had to wait till daylight at a village about half-way, which I reached in the evening. The good old mother of the *patel* being sure, as she said, that I was very tired, had prepared a delicious warm bath for me, and a most abundant and well-cooked supper, consisting of various capital dishes of vegetables and light *jowari* cakes. The family were strict Hindus, and did not eat meat. They had also got ready a comfortable bed, with fresh clean sheets and pillows. This spontaneous hospitality touched me very much; and it was just the same wherever I travelled.

As the Resident had applied to me to report what kind of a revenue survey would be necessary for the country, I selected a village of average size, and began a regular survey of it, field by field, partly by cross-staff and chain, and partly by prismatic compass, for I had no theodolite, and finished all, including the map, myself; and then forwarded the whole of the papers, field-books, and registries of proprietors to the Resident, with a report.

I was, however, in no hurry to begin a survey. I considered it would be time enough when the present settlement was at an end, as many of the occupants had measured out their own lands, and were becoming more and more correct. This season was the coolest I had ever felt in the Deccan. I find on the 25th February the thermometer varied from 68° to 76° in my tents, and at Poona there had been a frost. It did not, however, last long, and was succeeded by extreme heat.

In March the Raja's youngest sister, a very pretty little girl of six years old, was married to the Raja of Sonda,[1] near Madras, aged twenty. He was a courteous, well-bred young man, and the little child was a great pet among us all, so pretty, and very fair, even rosy in cold weather, and quick and clever too. She was being educated in Telugu, and her favourite book was extracts from the *Pilgrim's Progress*, which, indeed, was liked by all classes at Shorapur, and there were occasional readings of portions of it by the Brahmins.

As head of the State, and *in loco parentis*, I had to perform all ceremonies, except going to the temples, and others of a purely religious character. I wanted the parties to wait till the child was thirteen or fourteen, but her affianced could not delay, as he wrote to me to say he could not be installed as Raja of Sonda while he was single; and as royal families of Beydurs were very scarce, he was forced to take this child. There was no use preaching in such matters, so I remained neutral, and allowed them to do as they thought proper themselves. The Rani came to me for 20,000 rupees for the expenses of the ceremony; I could but refer the request to the Resident, who would sanction only 3,000 rupees expenditure by the State, and the Rani was very much disgusted.

In May the Raja had another terrible fever, and narrowly escaped death. He was brought up to my house for change of air, when a turn for the better came, and he recovered. If I could have kept him with me longer I would have done so,

[1] Sonda is a little extinct Raj in the hilly country of Mysore, now in N. Kanara (Brit.) District. The words 'near Madras' are loosely used, Sonda town being 390 miles N.W. of Madras. The chiefs were apparently Beydurs, and the representative of the family still holds a position of honour in Goa, where it was compelled to take refuge after the destruction of the city in 1764 by Hyder Ali (*Imp. Gaz.*, art. 'Sonda'. See also Wilks' *Historical Sketches* (1810), i. 456 etc., and *Wellington's Despatches*).

as the clear cool air on my hill would have renewed his strength, and he much preferred being with me, as his mother's horrible profligacy and want of chastity shocked him terribly: but this he could only tell me secretly, and weep bitterly, poor boy, at the shame it cast upon him.

If Government had removed the Rani Ishwarama from Shorapur, as it had done the Rani of Kolhapur, and also at Lahore, all trouble would have been avoided; but it was not to be so.

However, I reported, as it was my duty to do, her now openly shameless conduct; and in June I received a despatch in relation to her, from which the following are extracts:—

'2. It appears to us a preferable mode of disposing of the case would be that of requiring the Rani to retire entirely from Shorapur, and to take up her abode in her father's house at Ratnagiri. . . .

'5. I do not apprehend that the mere banishment of Kasima (chief favourite), and other paramours, would be productive of much benefit with a woman of her immoral character. These personages would probably follow each other in succession, notwithstanding any engagements you may receive from her to the contrary, and you would have the same inconveniences, and the same evil influences to surmount which you have at present.'

But neither the Resident nor I had power or authority to remove the Rani, or suggest to her 'change of air'. It was a question which the Governor-General alone could decide.

My report for the revenue year past, 1256 *Fasli*,[1] was considered by the Resident to be 'eminently satisfactory'; but it is too long for insertion here, and too full of local questions to be interesting to the general reader. The Resident was gratified at the low rate of assessment, which was on the general average eleven annas, or 1s. 4½d. per *bigha*,[2] that for the Nizam's country being upwards of four rupees, or eight shillings; and he was satisfied that the increase did not proceed from extra rates of taxation. The result of the accounts was as follows:—

[1] See p. 258.

[2] The standard of the *bigha* varies in various provinces, but it is generally about one-third of an English acre. [M. T.]

	Rupees.		
Revenue under all heads	351,556	2	9
General expenditure—loans, advances, village expenses	245,276	11	6
Cash balance	106,279	7	3
Balances of loans and advances recoverable .	15,124	7	0
Total in favour of the State . .	121,403	14	3

At last I had a lakh in the treasury ! safe after all payments, including tribute to the Nizam. The Gosain bankers' claim, after being checked in England on their own accounts, transmitted by me, dwindled to 121,000 rupees, on the decision of the Court of Directors, after scrutiny by actuaries. I discovered that the bankers had not credited a payment of 52,000 rupees, received by them from assignment on villages, which was proved by their own receipts to the villages ; and if I had not had the control of the whole State accounts after the death of Pid Naik, and of those of the villages also, I should never have discovered it. The original claim was admitted to be 380,000 rupees. Now 52,000 with interest thereon amounted to 72,000, which had been deducted, and the balance due was therefore considerably reduced, but Lakshmangir and his brethren were in no case to receive it. They were all quarrelling among themselves, and the Resident declared that, until he knew to whom the balance was to be paid, he would give no order on the Shorapur treasury. He thought it very possible that I might discover other fraudulent transactions, and I was not without hope that I should.

On my report of the previous year, I had the pleasure to receive a copy of an extract from the Court of Directors' political despatch to the Governor-General, which was as follows : —

'Para. 29. From Captain Taylor's report of 12th September 1845, it appears that the *Fasli* year 1254 had produced an increase in cultivation the preceding year of 17,656 rupees, and of net revenue 18,852 rupees, and that the whole revenue had been collected, except some trifling balances in course of collection.

'30. We agree with the Governor-General that Captain Taylor appears to have shown zeal and judgment in the conduct of the duties of the Samasthan during the present season. His report contains much valuable information respecting the landed tenures and revenue system of Shorapur, and he seems to have adopted means well suited for gradually improving the revenues of the country, without introducing such changes of system as might hereafter be embarrassing to a native Government.'

In reference to my official report on the current year, the Governor-General was pleased to write as follows.

The letter is dated Simla, 23d August 1847, to General Fraser, from the Secretary to Government with the Governor-General.

'Sir,—I have the honour to acknowledge the receipt of your letter, dated May 22d last, No. 62, submitting Captain Taylor's report on Shorapur for 1846, and in reply, to state that the Right Hon. the Governor-General considers the report satisfactory, and very creditable to the zeal and ability of that officer, to whom you are requested to convey the favourable sentiments of his lordship.

'2. If the removal of the Rani Ishwarama, the mother of the young Raja, will tend to benefit the State, the Governor-General will not object to the adoption of the measure. It must, however, his lordship observes, be done with all the forms of courtesy, care being taken that the allowance she is to have in her own country be not too much contracted; but she must be given to understand that its continuance must be contingent on her discreet behaviour.

'The Governor-General approves of Captain Taylor's proposal to register the military class, and other Jaghirdars of Shorapur; and also sanctions that officer's proposition to make a survey of the whole country, with a view to its final settlement.—I have, etc.,

(Sd.) 'H. M. Elliot, *Secy.*'[1]

Need I say that I was more than satisfied with this cordial letter from Lord Hardinge? and I felt certain that the issue of the current year's work would assure him that improvement was progressing, slowly perhaps, but I hoped surely.

About this time I had a very strange interview with the

[1] Henry Miers Elliot, born in the same year as Taylor, but more favoured. He was Foreign Secretary to the Government of India; accompanied Lord Hardinge and Lord Dalhousie to the Punjab; and received the K.C.B. for negotiating the Sikh treaty in 1849. This is the Elliot familiar in the eight formidable and rare volumes of *The History of India, as told by its own Historians*, published long after his death. He died at the Cape of Good Hope on his way home, at the end of 1853, aged only forty-five. Like Augustus Cleveland in the century before, who also died trying to reach the Cape, he has been called the *dulce decus* of the early Bengal Civil Service.

Rani. She had been ailing for some days, and reports were rife as to the cause of her illness, which were disgraceful enough. However, she sent for me early one morning, having, as her servant said, passed a sleepless night, and being very much excited and troubled in her mind. As soon as I had taken my breakfast I went to her. I found her lying on her bed in her private room, seemingly very restless and in pain, moaning incessantly, but apparently dozing. I sat down in the outer room, as I did not wish to disturb her, and the little Raja came to me crying bitterly.

'"She is going to die," she says,' he whispered. 'She has abused me shamefully. She says I am not my father's child, and bade me go away. Where am I to go? What am I to do? Indeed I am so frightened, and you are the only one I can look to. I have hidden all her shame and my own, and this is too much! I fear for my life!'

I comforted him as well as I was able, and told him I would bring his mother to reason if I could, and that if he really continued frightened, he should come to my house or go to the cottage at Bohnal. As we were speaking, I heard the Rani call loudly,

'Is he come? Is Taylor Sahib here?'

I went in at once. She was still excited, and her breathing seemed oppressed. I really thought she was dying, and she complained of being 'all on fire inside'. I had brought a small bottle of sal-volatile with me, and asking for one of her silver drinking-cups, dropped into it what was requisite; and when one of her attendants had added water, she drank it up, and fell back upon her pillows. After a time she roused herself, and desired one of her servants to go for the *purohit* or family priest.

'I am dying,' she said, 'and must tell you all. You are the head of the family and the State, and should know everything.'

When the priest arrived—a man I knew very well, as he was always in attendance, and one of the professors, as it were, in the Brahmin Sanskrit College—the Rani told him to bring a certain box which contained the secret papers of the house; and when he had brought it she unloosed the key from a necklace she had on, and bade him open it. The man demurred.

'These papers have never been seen by any one but my lord the Raja, who is gone to heaven, yourself, and me. No one else knows of them,' he cried; 'why should you show them to Taylor Sahib?'

The Rani sat up straight in her bed, and glared at him. I had never seen such a look on any human face before.

'Do as you are told,' she cried, savagely; 'what is it to you what I do?'

The *Shastri* trembled all over, and without speaking, he unlocked the padlock and opened the lid. The first thing I saw was a roll tied with red silk.

'Tell him first about that,' said the Rani, and fell back again.

'It is not fit you should hear it,' said the *Shastri*, who spoke both Marathi and Hindustani fluently.

'It is the Raja's horoscope which I wrote. The moment he was born I noted the time, and the conjunction of planets, and the result was bad.'

'Yes, it is bad!' cried the Rani, seizing my arm, as I was sitting on the ground by her bedside—'it is bad! All that concerns that base-born boy is bad! Why did his father die? Why did I not strangle him with my own hands rather than let a wretch like that live to be the ruin of the State? Yes! he is fated to die *in his twenty-fourth year*, and I shall not see it! I am dying myself, and you English have made him secure to glory in my death! Ah, yes! he will die before he is twenty-four complete; we, my husband and I, sent that paper to Nassik, to Benares, and everywhere that there are wise Brahmins; but they all returned the same answer. He must die in the twenty-fourth year after birth. Is it not so, *Shastri*? Did we not spend a lakh of rupees over this, and it availed nothing?' and she stopped for want of breath, her eyes flashing with excitement. 'Is it not so? Tell the truth!'

'You speak truth, lady,' said the *Shastri*, who was sobbing. 'It is only the truth, Taylor Sahib; I have tested all the calculations and find them exactly conforming to the truth according to the planets. The Raja is safe till then; but when that time comes, how, I know not, but he will surely die. He will never complete his twenty-fourth year! never! never!'

'No!' cried the Rani, interrupting him—'he will not live; he is the last of his race. He will lose his country, and all the lands, and all the honour that the Samasthan has gained for five hundred years. Would that he were dead now, the base-born dog and slave!' and then she uttered language that I dare not write.

I was obliged to rebuke her sternly, and threatened to go away if she spoke so again; but she cried the more.

'Slave! slave! I wish he were dead, and the State safe! It might go to you—to the English. I would give it freely, now—now—but not to that boy! Listen! never go from him until he is dead—then take the whole yourself. Behold, I give it to you, and the *Shastri* is witness I give it to you and your children—they shall have it. O Taylor Sahib! you have been as a father and mother to me, and I have often used you very ill. I am a wicked woman, and deserve punishment; but listen to me—forgive me! Never leave that boy, Enketappa Naik, till he is dead, and burned like Pid Naik—will you promise me this? I am dying—dying!' she paused for breath, and went on.

'Now I have told you all the secret I had in my heart, do not tell it to any one till he is dead; do you put your hands upon my neck and swear this.'

'I promise you I will not,' I said, 'on the faith of an English gentleman,' as I put my hand, with the *Shastri's*, on her neck.

'Enough!' she cried, 'I am content. Do not suppose I am mad or excited, I am quite myself, only for the pain I suffer. I do not think you will care about the other papers; they are some of the emperor's grants to our ancestry, and there are some foolish letters from chiefs in the Maratha country, asking my husband to rise with them against the English; but he was too wise to do that.'

'I will seal up the box in your presence and that of the *Shastri* with the State seal,' I said; 'and I will add my own seal when I reach home'; and to this she agreed.

I sent for the seal, and the priest and I sealed up the box. There was no one else present. I had desired the Raja to go to his lessons when I went to his mother, so he was in his private apartments. The women in attendance had been dismissed by the Rani, so that no one could have heard what passed. I showed the Rani the box sealed up.

'That will do,' she said; 'keep it now yourself; it is safer with you, whatever happens, than with me. Now I am very weary, and would sleep. Do not think ill of me; but I have only told you the truth before God! I have given you much trouble in coming here to-day—now leave me.'

I went. The Raja sent word I was to come to him; he was learning his Persian lesson with the *munshi*; as I entered he bade the man depart and leave us alone.

'What did she say to you, *appa*?' (father), he said, anxiously; 'what is in that box?'

'Only papers,' I answered; 'the papers of your house, those from Bijapur, and the emperor, and others. Your mother is ill, and thought herself dying. I will take care of them in future, and I have sealed them up.'

'And what did she say? I heard her so angry.'

'It was not with me this time,' I said, 'though you know we do fight sometimes. She only told me what to do in case of her death!'

'And will she die, *appa*?'

'Not this time,' I replied; 'but she is in pain, and how it may end, who can tell? Do not go near her at present, she has gone to sleep, and may feel better to-morrow.' I could not tell the poor boy what she had said of him.

'I will send you word by-and-by how my mother is,' he said, presently; 'and now leave me.'

In the afternoon they sent to me to say she was better, though still weak and in pain, and that she and the Raja were playing *chausar*, a kind of draughts, together.

As I had much to discuss and consult on with the Resident, and a meeting would save endless correspondence, I proposed that I should go up to Hyderabad, and he told me to start without delay.

My journey was somewhat deferred by a heavy case which I had to dispose of relative to a large gang of robbers, whom I was lucky enough to catch, and who during the year past had perpetrated several most daring gang-robberies, attended with murder in the Company's districts to the southward. I obtained, as I expected, great commendation for this capture, as the Bombay Government had been very hot on the matter, and very angry with their magistrates in Dharwar about their apparent neglect. It was not their fault in the least, as the robberies were planned by men about 60 miles northward of me, and the men who committed them had travelled at least 140 miles to the scene of their pillage. They were *brinjaris*, or carriers of grain, and were quietly encamped at a village about 24 miles off, trading most unsuspiciously in grain and salt. Captain Hervey [1]—an able assistant in the department for 'Suppression of Thuggee and Gang-robbery'—was lucky enough to get hold of fourteen of the gang at another encampment about 40 miles south-west of me; and having obtained both information and confessions from them, sent me the particulars so as to enable me to follow up the trail. It was not easy at first to discover their whereabouts; when I did, I sent out a strong party, and to my joy they returned with one leader and sixteen men. The other chief was absent with thirteen more men on some expedition. I secured, however, their wives and families, also their cattle (295 bullocks, 438 goats), and other property, amongst which were many stolen articles recognised by the approvers. Hervey and I broke the power of this gang very materially. I was anxious about the thirteen men that had escaped us, and I issued notices to all on the frontier to be on the alert in the hope of catching them on their return.

I left Shorapur at last on the 3d October, reaching Hyderabad on the 9th. The Resident and I discussed all our business very amicably, and the Resident agreed with me on several material points. First, that it would be wise to delay the commencement of the survey for a time; next, to delay also the proposed inquiry into the Beydur lands, of which they were very jealous, and it would be like thrusting one's hand into a hornets' nest; and again, that it would be well to make a second reference about the removal of the Rani Ishwarama.

I did not, of course, tell the Resident of the strange scene which had taken place so recently. Since then she had been amicable and quiet; but who could trust her?

I remained a short time at Hyderabad, and greatly enjoyed

[1] As General Hervey, published *Some Records of Crime* in 1867.

a little intercourse once more with my own countrymen and women. What a treat it was to hear some music, and to exchange ideas with men of one's own kind after the life of solitude I had led so long! There was a grand fancy ball too, to which I went as a 'nobleman' of the Nizam's Court—a quaint simple dress of white muslin, a small green turban, a shawl and dagger, etc. I wore no beard then, and an artist from the city came and fastened a splendid one on to my chin, so as to join with my whiskers. As I spoke Hindustani fluently, and could assume all the native manners, nobody found me out; Captain Malcolm and I went together, he as a Mohammedan Doctor of Laws—a capital dress; and as we went with Suraj-ul-Mulk's nephew, and entered the room with him, we passed off well. It was very amusing to be spoken to by the native gentlemen as one of themselves, and to parry their questions as to where I had come from, etc.

Captain Malcolm soon after left Hyderabad, and was a very great loss to me individually, and to the people. They assembled in crowds to see him off, and accompanied him for twelve miles out, and presented him with an address. Such a tribute had never before been given to any Resident or Assistant.

My return to Shorapur was most unpleasantly delayed by an accident which turned out very serious. The horse I was riding fell under me, and I was injured internally, and confined to my bed for several weeks. The Resident was most kind—coming constantly to sit with me, and I was tenderly nursed at Mr. Palmer's house. My only anxiety was about Shorapur; but the Resident comforted me, saying, 'If there is any row, Taylor, I shall go down myself and act for you, so don't be anxious about your affairs.'

Nor was I, at first; but the lady, finding my absence prolonged, began to be again very mischievous. Her paramour, Kasima, told her that my being reported ill was only a blind, and that the State affairs were now to be made over to her; that I had been removed from Shorapur, and was under the heavy displeasure of the authorities, and the like. One act of hers annoyed me excessively. I had desired the Raja occasionally to write to me as an exercise in English. Some time elapsed, and I received no letter. I wrote to inquire the cause, and an answer came, a good specimen of handwriting to show the Resident. The Rani had been absent when the note was written and despatched. On her return she sent for her son, and beat him very severely with her own hands for daring to write to me and to ask when I was coming back. The poor lad was terribly frightened, and sent me word privately to come *quickly*, for that much evil was going on ; and he afterwards managed to write to me in Telugu urging me to make haste, 'for his life was not safe '. The Rani was gathering all the heads of the Beydur clans together about her, under Kasima, feasting them, and giving them silver ornaments and other presents. One day the runner who carried the post-bag was going as usual along the road when four Beydurs jumped out upon him from behind a hedge and demanded the bag. The man would not give it up, and fought well with a stick ; but this was of no avail against the swords of the Beydurs, and the poor fellow's left hand was struck clean off, and he fell senseless under repeated blows. The bags were then seized, and were afterwards found in a lonely place, but they were empty. A large reward was offered, but no clue could be obtained as to the perpetrators of the outrage. I strongly suspected female curiosity was at the bottom of it, and that the Rani wanted to find out what was said of her by me. She gained nothing, however, as I took care not to write anything about her or her doings by the post. The town was reported to be full of parties of Beydurs, going about with drawn swords ; and at an assembly a resolution was passed that no orders of mine were in future to be obeyed. This resolve emanated solely from the Rani's party ; the remainder, who were likewise the majority, were yet, or appeared to be, stanch.

I had recovered pretty well from my severe illness, and was growing very anxious to return to Shorapur. My detention had happened at a very awkward time ; but still, under God's blessing, I believe my life was saved, as had I been at Shorapur, with no skilful surgeon near, my life must have been in all probability forfeited. So as soon as I could get leave I started, having first had a long consultation with the Resident, who was of very decided opinion that the Rani must go—and that at once ; and that Lord Hardinge's order should be carried out.

A letter from the Resident to the Rani was soon drafted, and troops were desired to be in readiness to march on the shortest notice upon my requisition.

I reached Shorapur on the 3d February, having been absent three months. The Raja came out several miles to meet me, and embraced me, imploring me 'not to let him go back to his mother any more'. We went up together to my house. The city seemed full of armed men, but I took no notice of them; my main object was to prevent collision between the two parties of the Beydur clans and the Raja's personal adherents, which, if it occurred, must have led to disastrous consequences.

The next morning I had a translation of the General's letter ready for the Rani; and during the night, she, anticipating being taken to task for her proceedings, had assembled all her men in Shorapur, and sent out orders for all those in the districts to come in; and these were fast arriving across the hills in detached parties. When my letter reached the palace, there were about five hundred of her adherents outside, who rushed about the streets with drawn swords; but happily there was no collision. I sent warnings to them in vain, and so did the Raja; but his messengers were insulted, and all declared they would obey no orders but the Rani's. I had posted all the trusty Beydurs inside the palace, and had sent for the garrison of Wondrug, which was stanch to the Raja, and thus had nearly four hundred men about him. My great object was to prevent collision between the parties; and the palace guards behaved admirably. When the rebellious party thundered at the gates, demanding the Rani and Kasima, who were inside, no one stirred, and the Raja controlled his people with admirable temper. As darkness fell the insurgents retired to a high conical hill, the headquarters of some of the clan, and consulted how to make a night attack on my house; but I, as well as my position, were too strong for them; and finding that but few of the country Beydurs joined them during the night, they sent to me for terms. I would take none but unconditional surrender of the leaders and their arms; and in an hour or two sixteen of the leaders were brought to me, and the insurrection was at an end.

General Fraser, the Resident, had written to me to say that he wished to come down to Shorapur himself; and I thought he expected some disturbance on the Rani's removal. I therefore awaited his arrival, according to the instructions I received from him, before finally sending off the Rani. During the night painful scenes had passed between her and Kasima, each reviling the other in no measured terms. He had threatened to murder the Rani, and had drawn his sword on her. The Raja had interposed; but Kasima said he would not give up his sword to any one but me. Accordingly the Raja sent him to me, when he and five of his brothers placed their arms before me on the ground, and all were put into confinement. Several other leaders gave themselves up during the day; but three of the very worst remained at large, trying to rouse the district Beydurs. However, nothing came of their efforts. In the afternoon the Rani sent for me, and I went. She was quiet enough then, but was crying bitterly. She told me she had been behaving very ill, and that she knew I must carry out the orders of Government. She also confessed to having concealed valuable State jewels, etc.; and when they were brought I sent them to the treasury. Her only hope was that she would be treated with courtesy; and this, I assured her, would be the case. Her son's delight that this interview passed over so quietly was indescribable: he and his little sister and brother clung to me, and I could hardly get away.

On the 11th the General arrived, and I went out to meet him and bring him in. As he entered the town and ascended the hill, a salute of seventeen guns was fired from the ramparts, and a second from the guns near my house. All the officers were assembled at my house to receive him, and a guard of honour of the 1st Regiment presented arms as he alighted from his palankeen. A few minutes after the young Raja came up, with a great concourse of people, and was duly presented to the General by me. He was remarkably well dressed, and behaved very properly, answering all the General's questions with the ease and precision of a well-bred gentleman. All the male members of his family accompanied him, and also the most respectable inhabitants of the city, who were introduced by me, one by one; and after sitting for a while they took their leave, and the General was left to refresh himself after his journey.

The Resident was very complimentary to me on my arrangements, and was especially struck with the success of my plan at the palace for cutting off the Rani and Kasima inside from their adherents outside. I told him the Rani was ready, and had agreed to go; and he thought with me the sooner she was off the better. I therefore went down to the palace, having previously sent on her tents and some of her baggage and attendants. I was busy for four hours, making all final arrangements and settlements, and at last she was ready. Up to this time she had been quiet; but of course at the last there was a scene. Her women set up a howl which was heard at my house, and she cried a great deal. She refused to see the Raja, which I was glad of; and he did not desire to see her. She asked me for a note to the Collector of Bellary, which I gave her. She then rose, requested me to take care of her children; and I led her to the door of the outer court, where her palankeen was waiting. As she entered it she said, 'I know this is all my own fault. Forgive me. You could not help it.' And kissing my hand, she closed the doors, the bearers took up their burden, and in ten minutes she was beyond the gates, the escort closing round her.

I then went to the little Raja, who threw his arms round me, saying, 'He had only me now, and he hoped I would take care of him, there were so few he could trust.' I told him not to be afraid. I had had a very painful task to perform; but now it was over, and I hoped we should have no more disturbance or anxiety. I then took my leave, and returned to my house and to the Resident, who had been very anxious, and shook me warmly by the hand, congratulating me that this much-dreaded event had been so quietly got over. Indeed I had again deep cause of thankfulness for the happy issue of what might have been a fearful scene of tumult and strife.

The Resident paid a return visit next day to the Raja, and was taken to the Rani's late apartments, where several members of the family were awaiting us. After some conversation the men retired, and I went for old Kesama, great-aunt to the Raja, and all the children, who came nicely dressed;

and the General took two on his knees, and was much amused by their chat. He promised the old lady to be kind to the children and the State; and then she took the Raja, and begged the Resident to put him into my arms, which was done, to her infinite satisfaction. This over, wreaths of flowers were hung about our necks, *atr* was given us, and we departed. We went round the city on elephants, and I showed the Resident all through it. We passed the Beydurs' large 'tree of assembly', where about 1,500 of them had congregated all armed, and lining the road. I stopped the elephants, and the Resident addressed them, assuring them that their Raja would be cared for and their State also. It was now dusk, and a host of torches were lighted, and blue-lights stuck on poles preceded us. The effect was wonderful, revealing wild rocks and wilder faces, most picturesque and startling in the fitful glare.

Next day I showed the Resident the lake at Bohnal, explaining to him my project for enlarging it, which he approved. He left next morning, having expressed himself most heartily pleased with all he had seen, and saying he would write to me from Hyderabad officially, and in due time the despatch arrived. I subjoin a few extracts.

From General Fraser to Captain Taylor, on special duty at Shorapur. No. 179 *of* 1848.

'SIR,—I have the honour to acknowledge the receipt of your several letters noted in the margin. . . .

'2. Having had an opportunity of fully communicating with you in person at Shorapur regarding the affairs of that district, I have now the gratifying duty to perform of placing on record my entire and unqualified approval of the whole of your recent proceedings. . . .

'4. Your very judicious measures, taken previously to their arrival (the troops), had already restored tranquillity, and reduced the insurgent Beydurs to obedience, besides obtaining the assent of the Rani Ishwarama to remove from Shorapur to Ratnagiri. . . .

'6. You will be pleased to order an immediate investigation to be made into the conduct of the Beydur prisoners transmitted to Lingsugur under charge of the 1st Regiment (Nizam's Infantry). I think it desirable that this inquiry should be made by a Commission, presided over by yourself, with Captain Commandant Johnston, and any other officers whose services may be conveniently available, as members. . . .

'9. The proceedings of this Commission will be forwarded

by me to the Government of India ; and pending the decision of that authority as to the ultimate disposition of the prisoners, you will be pleased to request Captain Commandant Johnston to detain them under custody sufficiently strict to prevent any risk of their escape, but without unnecessary severity.

'10. I shall submit the whole of your correspondence, now acknowledged, for the information of the Government of India, and I shall be happy to bring to the special notice of the Right Honourable the Governor in Council the ability, judgment, and firmness by which you succeeded in averting the serious danger which threatened the district of Shorapur, and perhaps the necessity of having recourse to actual military operations, which might have proved a source of much present inconvenience, besides involving a consequence still more to be deprecated, that of injuriously affecting the relations subsisting between the Beydurs and yourself, and substituting fear and distrust in lieu of that confidence and attachment which I feel assured the majority of the people now bear towards you.—I have the honour to be, etc.,

'J. S. FRASER, *Resident*.

'HYDERABAD, *17th February* 1848.'

To this I, of course, returned a suitable reply ; but I was obliged to go out at once into the districts, as my long detention at Hyderabad had materially interfered with my work and I could delay no longer. The Commission of Inquiry was therefore postponed for a time. As the settlements now only required supervision, my labour was comparatively easy ; but the crops were bad, the cotton and wheat were blighted, and other products injured by excess of unseasonable rain. And I had to make some material remissions which in the end satisfied everybody. Lord Dalhousie had now succeeded to the office of Governor-General and took his seat in January,[1] and the whole of the Shorapur correspondence would be laid before him. I was anxious for the result, and it arrived at length. It was most satisfactory. His Excellency in Council expressed his entire satisfaction with the manner in which the affair of the Rani had been conducted, and 'directed' that his 'approbation of the ability, firmness, and judgment' I had displayed should be conveyed to me. It was all very gratifying ; but I could not but miss more than ever the dear face that would have lighted

[1] January 12, 1848. There is an amusing account of the landing and inauguration, in the gathering darkness, in Lee-Warner's *Dalhousie*.

up with loving joy and pride at my success, and I never liked to return to my beautiful house. Old wounds would reopen, and I longed for a kind word or a loving smile to greet me there. I determined then, however, to live out my life alone, and that I would never seek marriage with another; and I have kept faith to her who is gone and to myself, and shall do so till I die. This determination was the result of a very curious and strange incident that befell me during one of my marches to Hyderabad. I have never forgotten it, and it returns to this day to my memory with a strangely vivid effect, that I can neither repel nor explain. I purposely withhold the date and the year. In my very early life I had been deeply and devotedly attached to one in England, and only relinquished the hope of some day winning her when the terrible order came out that no furlough to Europe would be granted. One evening I was at the village of Dewar Kadea, after a long afternoon and evening march from Maktal, and I lay down very weary; but the barking of village dogs, the baying of jackals, and over-fatigue and heat prevented sleep, and I was wide awake and restless. Suddenly, for my tent-door was wide open, I saw the face and figure so familiar to me, but looking older and with a sad and troubled expression. The dress was white, and seemed covered with a profusion of lace, and glistened in the bright moonlight. The arms were stretched out, and a low plaintive cry of 'Do not let me go! do not let me go!' reached me. I sprang forward, but the figure receded, growing fainter and fainter, till I could see it no longer, but the low sad tones still sounded. I had run barefooted across the open space where my tents were pitched, very much to the astonishment of the sentry on guard; but I returned to my tent without speaking to him.

I wrote to my father. I wished to know whether there was any hope for me. He wrote back to me these words:—

'Too late, my dear son. On the very day of the vision you describe to me, —— was married. . . .'[1]

Shortly after my return to Shorapur, I succeeded in catching two of the Beydurs who had escaped. One of them tried to stab himself when apprehended; but, being prevented in

[1] Οὐκ ὄναρ, ἀλλ' ὕπαρ ἐσθλόν, ὅ τοι τετελεσμένον ἔσται. τ 547.

time, only scratched his stomach. They both made a confession which cleared up everything in regard to the late insurrection. It was they who, with two others, attacked the post-runner and took his bag from him by order of the Rani and Kasima, in order to find out what I had written. In all, they had hoped to raise 10,000 men, and relied on the treasury for payment, which was to be seized by them. I was to be prevented from entering Shorapur unless I promised to accede to all the Rani wished; but the Raja coming out to meet me, which they had never contemplated, put an end to that part of the scheme. So far all was clear enough, but subsequent declarations and confessions by other parties proved contradictory, and others were accused by them as well as the Rani. So I took the witnesses to Lingsugur to be examined before the Court then sitting, and left it to the Resident to unravel what he could. I never had had experience of anything at all like the lies and counter-lies recorded on that memorable occasion; they beat all that had come to my knowledge.

I had a letter from my friend the Rani, who preferred remaining at Bellary, and I was glad she did so, as she was more under surveillance at a large station; she expressed herself content and satisfied, and I answered her note telling her of her children and their welfare.

The accounts of the State would possess no interest for the reader; but the table given below will show how I was progressing.[1]

[1] Here, as nearly as possible, belongs the only passage about Taylor, besides the one quoted at the opening of Chapter VIII., in that waste of personal and financial controversy, the *Life of James Stuart Fraser*. Other references are bare mentions, sometimes in connection with the forwarding of Taylor's letters to the Governor-General of the day. The interesting visit of the Resident to Shorapur in February 1848 is never mentioned. A little later General Fraser seems to have gone on leave to Singapore, while his place at Hyderabad was filled by his subsequent successor, that fine officer, Colonel John Low. By August 30 of the same year Fraser, writing to the new Governor-General, Dalhousie, shows that Taylor had not been without his anxieties during 1848.

'I beg to transmit for your perusal a private letter, with the enclosure to which it gave cover, from Captain Meadows Taylor, the officer in charge of Shorapore, as they refer to a matter which I do not propose to make the subject of an official communication to the Government of

Balanee in favour of the State for 1253, '54, '55, '56, and '57 *Fasli* :

1844 (1253 *Fasli*), balanee	Rs. 45,456	7 6
1845 (1254 „ „ .	41,805	11 9
1846 (1255 „ „	74,898	6 3
1847 (1256 „ „ .	181,391	0 6
1848 (1257 „ „	308,547	0 0

while the whole cash account of the treasury, whieh ineluded reeeipts from other sources, shows the balance in hand to be Rs. 348,977 : 14 : 9.

How quiet was everything at Shorapur for the next two years. No intrigue ! no suspicion ! no combinations ! The Raja, as he grew up, advanced in intelligenee, and daily attended to all the eurrent business, working with me eheerfully and well, and I had no apprehensions on his account. The Nizam's Government had withdrawn their demands for balance claimed, and the Court of Direetors had repudiated any elaim for interest on the bankers' bonds on the discovery of their forged interpolation. It beeame now a question whether they were not debtors to the State ; and so 1849 opened pleasantly. 1848 had been a turbulent year in many parts of India, but though the seeond Sikh war was not concluded, there was no doubt now as to its issue, and in March 1849 the Panjab was annexed to the British Empire.

I was summoned to Hyderabad to report on the proceedings of the Court on the Beydurs, and I was obliged to state that not only had I never been summoned as a witness, or as a

India, unless Captain Taylor insists upon it, or that your Lordship thinks I ought to do so. Captain Taylor wishes to have a military force stationed in Shorapore for the purpose of overawing his Bedur population ; but I think I have already sufficiently guarded against any danger from these men, . . while, in the case of any outbreak in Shorapore, every necessary reinforcement might be rapidly sent from Bolarum or Secunderabad. I do not feel at all disposed to have a military force permanently placed within the district of Shorapore. Independently of the immense inconvenience of our sparing troops for that purpose, I wish Captain Taylor to accustom his Bedurs to be kept quiet by moral influence rather than by military coercion. He is, by his disposition and qualifications, better suited than any other man I know to effect this object, and think that his present suggestion arises in a great measure from a needless distrust of his own powers of control.'

prosecutor, but that the Court had wandered into extraneous matter, and had been at the mercy of false witnesses both for and against the prisoners. That the chief points of the insurrection had never been inquired into at all—that is, the assembly in arms, etc. My paper was sent in to the Court, and at length I was summoned; after which the final finding of the Court was that the prisoners had been guilty of overt acts of rebellion; but in consequence of their long imprisonment, they were recommended to mercy—and the Rani, who had never been on her trial at all, was acquitted! The whole proceedings were forwarded to Lord Dalhousie, who eventually confirmed the finding of the Court; and some of the prisoners were released. He blamed me too, for having been misled—why, I could not understand. The measure of removing the Rani was one of Lord Hardinge's which I had to see carried out, and it was done without bloodshed. Perhaps the Court was bewildered by the great mass of contradictory evidenee before it; and possibly even his lordship's astute mind was too, for he made ample amends to me hereafter.

The Rani was to be allowed to return, but when or how was not specified.

In July we had another visitation of cholera, and the Raja's half-brother died of it, to the great grief of the family. He was a very interesting and promising child; but no care availed to save him. I sat up myself with him for four successive nights, and he died, poor little fellow, in my arms.

I was greatly interested in the extension of the lake at Bohnal; it was my first essay at irrigation works, and proved a complete success. I had taken careful levels of the whole of the ancient embankment, which was much higher than was necessary. I added 12 feet to the escape-weir, and took advantage of some natural hillocks beyond the weir to extend the embankment in accordance with the old portion. The lake filled in September, and was a truly noble sheet of water, 2½ square miles (rather more than 1600 acres) in area, with an average depth of 12 feet. I had built a small schooner for the Raja, and we sailed matches against each other, to his infinite delight; he never cared how hard it blew.

The despatch of the Court of Directors upon my reports for 1847 and 1848 was very cheering and acceptable to me.

Its length alone prevents my giving it here ; but it was evident that all I had already done and proposed to do had been well and carefully considered and approved.

The Raja had removed from the palace in which he had lived with his mother to the older and original residence of the family. It was badly built, and during the heavy rains of the present year, one night a corner of the building fell, and so shook the whole that repair was impossible. I therefore asked and obtained permission to build a new palace ; and I set to work to make designs for it. The building was handsome and commodious when finished, but I could have wished a larger space for it to stand in.

Several other tanks were in progress, and I determined to try, in these ways, to lay out the surplus in the treasury to the best future advantage of the State. Bohnal works cost 6,000 rupees, and this was entirely paid back during the very first year by the increased return of rice and sugar-cane produce.

On the 20th May 1850 my friend the Rani returned! having been away from us for more than two years. She had got terribly into debt, and had nearly been sent away from Bangalore to Vellore in consequence of her intrigues. She had been ill too ; but in spite of all, here she was again!

She stayed some days at Lingsugur, where a house had been taken for her, and I had a very amusing account of her most absurd demands and unreasonable requests.

She wanted three good houses belonging to private individuals, who were to be deprived of them ; and if she did not get them, she vowed she would come up to my house and live there! This was indeed an alarming prospect for me! However, I, with the Raja and all the principal people, went to meet her at the Krishna, the frontier, where the Raja's new suite of tents had been pitched for the first time for her especial accommodation ; and as she crossed the river, we went forward to welcome her, and conduct her to her tent. She refused to enter the large one ; but chose a dirty little one belonging to her servants ; and a very stormy and disgraceful scene occurred, which, as my last illustration of the lady's temper and disposition, I copy from a letter written to my father.

'We were all there, and after a short interval, glaring at us one by one, she burst out—

'"Well! and what have you sent for me for?"

'"We did not send for you," said I, and several others.

'"Yes, you did. Do you think I would have come of my own accord? You had better kill me, and throw me into the river, or put me in the guard-house. How very proper and pleasant it will be to be in the guard-house! Why shouldn't I live in the guard? Have you got those houses I ordered?"

'"No, Rani Sahib!" I answered. "The houses you ordered are private property, and you cannot have them."

'"Can't have them?" she cried; "who are they to deny me? Am I not Rani of Shorapur? Can I not do as I choose?"

'"No, not quite," I returned; "not with what belongs to other people."

'"No? I can't? we shall see," she cried. "Did not General Cubbon[1] and Mr. Pelly,[2] and —— and —— and ——" (hurling at me a host of names), "and a lot of other people, tell me I could do whatever I liked? and yet it seems I am not to have my very first wish gratified. Am I less than those people? Are they not my slaves? Well," (after a torrent of abuse) "and where am I to go?"

'"To the palace, Rani Sahib," I replied.

---

[1] Sir Mark Cubbon, 1785–1861, who had a career in a native State longer than that of James Stuart Fraser, though not as Resident. Few English names are so bound up with a single place as his with Bangalore. From 1834 (when he entertained Macaulay) for twenty-seven years he was sole Commissioner of Mysore, ruling it 'despotically but successfully, through native agency, and exercising a profuse hospitality'. Taylor wrote in his *History* that Cubbon's benevolent measures 'are remembered with gratitude and affection'. His stay without a break in India far surpasses anything related of Lord Metcalfe. He never married, nor left India until he retired in 1861, at an age which may hold the record for active service, upwards of sixty years after he had landed. Like so many Anglo-Indians, including Sleeman and Meadows Taylor, he died on the journey home—in this case, at Suez. Mr. Buckland says: 'His equestrian statue is in the Cubbon Park at Bangalore; when unveiled, it had been daubed with the three Brahmanical marks on the forehead.'

I am unable to learn under what circumstances General John Carnac died in 1800 at such a place as Mangalore, 'on a sea voyage', at the age of eighty-four. If he was still in the subordinate employment which he had solicited from Warren Hastings, this would surpass anything known of an Anglo-Indian. His brother-in-law, James Rivett, to whom his name and fortune went, also died at an advanced age as member of the Bombay Council.

[2] Sir George Birdwood feels sure that this could not have been the subsequent Sir Lewis Pelly.

'"The palace! I won't go there! no, not to my old place! I won't be taken there except by force. Why don't you tie me hand and foot? You are powerful, and I am only an old woman." (Here the Rani began to whimper.) "Put me into the river at once. I'll *not* go to Hyderabad, or to Bangalore, or to Bellary. I'll go on pilgrimages. I will not stay here. I won't! I won't! No, I won't!"

'"But," I said, "Rani Sahib, you seem to forget that your son, the Raja, is sitting near you; you should go with him and me, and we will both try and make you as happy and comfortable as we can."

'"My son!" she screamed. "My son! He is no son of mine, the base-born! He my son!" and a volley of invectives followed. "I wish he were dead! Why did he live, and not my sister's child? Yes! you killed him among you, just to vex me!" (and more abuse succeeded, which I could not translate). "He my son indeed!"

'Poor little Raja; how he bore it I know not: but every now and then he pulled at my coat, or squeezed my hand, and whispered—

'"How can you bear it? Come away."

'I told him we would bear it as long as we could, for I was in hopes the storm would spend itself, and that she would be more amenable afterwards; but there was yet a very ticklish subject to introduce—viz., her former estates, or *jaghirs*; she being now only dowager, and the young Rani having the estates; an allowance having been substituted for her lands.

'How she raged and foamed when I told her! What a fierce war of rage and passion waged when I explained matters to her! Her allowance had been fixed at 1,000 rupees a-month. She became quite beside herself when she heard this, and made use of language that made one's blood creep. The idea of pay was worse than anything.

'"Am I a servant?" she yelled, "that I should take pay? Have not other Ranis their estates? Why do you take mine?" Then a fit of crying, then more abuse; till at length my patience and temper could stand it no longer, and I fairly told her that if she did not come to Shorapur, as she was directed and permitted to do, I should dismiss her escort, and leave her where she was. That the decision of Government could not change; sooner would the current of the river turn and flow upward. I strongly advised her to return to Bangalore until she was in a more reasonable frame of mind; and I ended by telling her, that if she continued so violent I should report everything that she said to Government, and that she would probably get deeper into trouble. At length, at sunset, after having endured her society for nearly four hours, we left her.

'At eleven at night she sent for me again. What a life

this woman led me! I took a relative of hers with me, a respectable man. She was restless and uneasy, said she was sorry for what she had uttered, that she had lost her temper, that she could not sleep because I had left her in anger, and had sent for me to tell me so, etc.; and that she had determined to go to Shorapur next day, and would do exactly as I bid her. Also she proclaimed that she intended to live privately, and to have no men about her; that they had all cheated her, and brought her into trouble. As I found her cool, and reasonable, I gave her a lecture, appealing to what feelings she had, and showing her how her own evil doings had led her into disgrace and banishment, and would inevitably do so again if not controlled. She seemed to feel my words, and kept repeating, "I have no true friend except you. Forgive me! forgive me!"

'After a long talk I left her and came home to bed, tired and worried enough. Next day we all started, the Raja riding a fine horse; and about 3 P.M. the Rani came to his tent, and seemed more pleased to see him. In the evening we started for Shorapur, about seven miles, she and I in palankeens, the rest all on foot or on horseback—a motley crowd, but very numerous. The Rani appeared in very good humour, and thanked me for having received her with so much honour. When she arrived at the palace, all the children, with dear old Kesama, met her; but she took no notice of any one except Kesama, at whose feet she fell, praying her to forgive her, and to place her hands upon her head—which the good old lady did at once.'

Thus the Rani subsided into her old palace and old associations. She had brought a poor half-caste with her, and amused herself by writing English letters to officials she had known during her absence; but as these were invariably returned to her, she addressed the Resident with the like result. Her allowance was higher than she expected—12,000 rupees a-year—and she professed herself content.

She sent for her old friend Kasima, who came to me in much alarm.

'What am I to do?' he said. 'I have had quite enough of her and of her schemes—she is a devil.'

'She was kind to you,' I replied; 'she had you married in state, and made her son, your prince, walk before your palankeen; you should not abuse her. All you have to do is to keep quiet'; and he took my advice.

When I came in from the country in August the lady was very quiet, and returned my visit, bringing some of the children with her, and staying nearly all day amusing herself in my garden; but I found her chief object was to present me with a schedule of her debts! These amounted to 62,000 rupees, and there were more behind. I had no authority to pay any such sum, which had been borrowed by her chiefly in Mysore; and whether permission would be granted for the payment of these debts or not I could not tell. Eventually 500 rupees a-month was deducted from the Rani's allowance to give to her creditors, a decision which set her frantic; and she announced her intention of appealing to Parliament, though utterly ignorant of what that tribunal was, or where!

NOTE

The following explanation of the word *Fasli* (see p. 235, etc.) has been kindly contributed, too late for insertion as a footnote:

'"FASLI—the revenue or agricultural year. In the Deccan it was established in A.D. 1636–37 (A.H. 1046) by Shahjahan. The Madras Government reckons the beginning of the year as from July 12" (Cunningham, *Book of Indian Eras*, 1883, p. 82).'

CHAPTER XII

1851–53

A COPY of a despatch from the Court of Directors reached me in December. It was most satisfactory, and reviewed the transactions of 1847–48. It was full of honourable commendation, which I need not here repeat ; but the State had made great advance since then in material prosperity, and I was glad to have an opportunity of showing it to Major Johnston, then military secretary at Hyderabad, and he promised to write to Sir Henry Elliot, at that time secretary with the Governor-General, and to tell him all he had seen, and about the improvements in progress. I found the Rani very ill and miserable—she had had a stroke of paralysis that had affected all her left side, and more particularly her face, which was now hideous ; and there was little doubt that dropsy had set in, in addition. The apothecary who had charge of the public dispensary and hospital did what he could for her, but had a very bad opinion of her case.

In March my public report for the year past went in, and was reviewed by the Resident, General Fraser. He was perfectly satisfied ; and on the report of Major Buckle, engineer-in-chief at Hyderabad, sanctioned my estimate for the new tank at Kachaknur, near Bohnal. Major Buckle had great experience in irrigation works in the Madras Presidency, and was kind enough, during one of my visits to Hyderabad, to instruct me in the principles of the construction of dams, sluices, and the like. I had put these instructions into practice, and sent up all the estimates, with survey, plans, and sections, for this new work. I was very anxious to complete it, if possible, during my stay at Shorapur. It would be of considerable magnitude—the dam 1,872 yards in length ; the greatest depth of water-storage 50 ft.; the average of the whole basin about 20 ft.; and the area of water 6¼ square miles. It would be a noble sheet of water, and very profitable, as it would irrigate upwards of 10,000 *bighas* of rice. As soon as my estimates were sanctioned I began the work, and the Raja opened it with all due ceremony, turning the first sod, and carrying the first basket of earth.

The concluding paragraph of General Fraser's despatch was as follows:

'I consider it, however, due to you to place upon record the renewed expression of my entire approval of your public conduct, and my highest commendation of the unremitting and devoted attention which you give to the discharge of your important duties.'

Could I desire more? Still my life was lonely and dreary: I had no society whatever; and only at rare intervals a short visit from some friend or passing traveller. If it had not been for my daily work, which lasted from seven in the morning till eight at night, and sometimes longer, I could not, I think, have endured the entire isolation of my life, all official praises notwithstanding.[1]

During my wanderings over the Shorapur district in this and former years I had discovered, in many places, cairns and dolmens, some of them of very large size, corresponding in all respects to similar monuments in England, Brittany, and other places. I mistrusted my judgment in regard to

[1] In that curious example of biography by essay-writing, Sir W. W. Hunter's *Life of Brian Houghton Hodgson* (1800–1894), in the most human chapter, 'A Solitary Heart', are similar complaints. Hodgson's official duties were few. Differently treated from Taylor, from the age of thirty-three he had been full Resident in Nepal, where it was thought that the introduction of a white-faced woman would be 'the downfall of their empire', upon £4,000 a year. He too had wayward and wanton queens to deal with. But he had not 'seen the fringe of a petticoat for eight years'. 'The sense of isolation becomes more intense as the years roll on.' In 1833 he writes to his sister: 'I am, and long have been, secluded from society, without wife, child, or any other object of affection.' He is afraid of 'petrifying within'. 'I am thirty-three—the last thirteen years passed in the wilderness without wife, children, or the presence of a female. No change, no society! What think you I am likely then to be?' 'I read and read and read, and love nothing so well as my books. Yet have I a fund of constitutional gaiety and feeling; only there is no one to draw upon it!'

them for a long time: but at length I drew up a paper on the subject, accompanied by sketches; and followed it up by another in regard to the contents of cairns which I had opened. In one spot, near Shorapur, I found most curious remains—a large barrow, with a parallelogram of rocks, 440 ft. by 280 ft. The rocks were in regular line, some of them 12 ft. long and 9 ft. thick, and from 5 to 6 ft. high. They had been rolled from the granitic range, a distance of 1½ mile. Another place contained an immense number of large rocks, placed in regular rows, direct and diagonally, leaving squares of from 5 to 6 yards between. In this area were some cairns. I sent my article on the subject to the Royal Asiatic Society in Bombay, who did me the honour to elect me a member. These stone monuments of Shorapur tallied exactly with European examples; but it seemed to me so strange a discovery that I almost doubted whether European archæologists would admit it. They did so most fully afterwards, and my discoveries at Shorapur were followed by others even more interesting in other portions of lower India.

For a long period the affairs of the Nizam's Government had been in a critical state. It owed nearly one million sterling to the British Government, which it could not pay. The Contingent was constantly in heavy arrear, and Lord Dalhousie, urged by the Court of Directors, pressed for a settlement. The subject had been under reference to England for several years; but it appeared now nearer a conclusion.

The Nizam had tried several Ministers in succession, who had failed. He then attempted to govern himself, and failed more signally than his Ministers. The State had no public credit, and the administration in the provinces was oppressive to the people, and utterly corrupt. Now affairs seemed to have reached a climax. Provinces, detailed in a minute I wrote by desire of the Resident in January 1851, were to be made over to the British Government, and I was to be put in charge of one of them.

'The experience and past services of Captain Meadows Taylor', wrote Lord Dalhousie to General Fraser, 'at once point him out as the proper person for undertaking the direction of those districts which lie near Shorapur, if his present occupation will admit of his entering on this additional charge.'

It would have admitted of it, for no new measures were required at Shorapur, and the Raja was gaining enough experience to manage fairly for himself, with a little assistance now and then. He transacted most of the current business, and did it very well. His new palace was finished outside, and nearly inside also, and the upper apartments were very airy, cool, and spacious.

My only dread was on account of his mother, who, I feared, was endeavouring to drag him into her toils by the worst possible means. However, the new arrangement with the Nizam was not to come into force at once. I was summoned to Hyderabad, to be given charge of a province, but returned as I went—the appointment being delayed. When there, I ascertained many more particulars of the condition of the Nizam's Government than I previously had knowledge of, and in some respects it was worse than I thought.

The first instalment of the Nizam's debt, 40 lakhs, £400,000, had been remitted to Calcutta, and the second was due; but there were no funds to meet it. The Nizam sent to his Minister, Suraj-ul-Mulk, jewels, which his Highness valued at 30 lakhs, to be pledged for that amount; but the bankers only valued them at 10 lakhs, and they even declined to give four for them. The principal bankers were so shaken, in fact, by their previous loans, that not only were they unable to make money, but some were even threatened with insolvency. At the instance of capitalists at Madras an advance had been made on the Nizam's jewels of five lakhs; but this was a mere drop in the ocean.

The first 40 lakhs had been raised by officers newly appointed to several large districts, assisted by the bankers. It was now proposed to raise a similar sum by putting in new men and turning out the others. Nobody dared to mention 'cession of territory' to the Nizam, and thus the vessel of the State drifted on without sail or helm to the rocks, on which it might go to pieces at any time. I was sorry for the Resident, who, if he trusted to Suraj-ul-Mulk's word, was sure to be deceived; yet I believe Suraj-ul-Mulk had every wish to fulfil his promises if he could; but there were literally no assets to work on, and no credit to be had, and all waited for Lord Dalhousie's next move.

In November I received a private and confidential note from the Rani of Gadwal, a State smaller than Shorapur, but occupying the same political position.

She knew of the prosperity at Shorapur, and wished me to take charge of Gadwal in the same manner. The offer, spontaneous as it was, gratified me much, but unless I were placed in charge of the Raichur Doab, in which her State lay, I could do nothing for her, and in any case I could not myself propose the measure. The Rani was a woman of irreproachable character, and would, I felt sure, be easy to deal with.

In December I received orders to go to Bijapur to meet the Commissioner of Satara and the Collector of Sholapur, who, with myself, were to form a commission for the investigation of lines of traffic and roads from all sides, with reference to the opening of a new port on the western coast at Viziadrug.[1] I had been suffering much from fever and other ailments, and the change of air and scene was delightful to think of. I had never yet seen Bijapur, and had longed to visit it for years, on account of its noble remains of Musalman architecture.[2] We met, and made out a report, which I had

[1] Given as Vijayadurg in the *Imperial Gazetteer*; and best of all known as the pirates' nest, Gheria. It is a natural port of some beauty, with about 2,000 inhabitants, in Ratnagiri District, 170 miles south of Bombay. But, as with other ports along this enchanted coast, nothing can force greatness upon it; and Vijayadurg still languishes.

[2] During these memorable weeks Taylor had the long-nursed tale of *Tara* in his mind. His enthusiasm for Bijapur must be treated with respect: only specialists can say if it is overdone. Superlative it is, as shown by the statement (Prologue to *Tara*) that Bijapur 'rose to be the greatest, as it was the most magnificent, city of the Dekhan'; and that (*History*, p. 195) it was 'destined to become one of the largest and most magnificent cities of India, or indeed of Asia'.

Bijapur (Town of Victory) is now the headquarters of Bijapur District, which lies southward from Sholapur and westward from the Nizam's Dominions. The town, most uninteresting in its modern aspects, has a population of some 24,000, not a third of whom are Moslems. Taylor has described, in his *History*, the advantages of Bijapur as a capital. 'There is nothing picturesque in its situation, for around it are undulating downs, and the country for the most part, though fertile, is stony and uninviting.' It is backed, however, to the east, by the unequalled fertility of the Dhon valley.

to write, and we were a very pleasant little party; but my chief delight was in sketching, in which I was unwearied, and found ever fresh objects for my brush. Had I had three months, instead of three weeks, to spend, I could not have half exhausted the subjects that presented themselves everywhere—palaces, mosques, interiors, exteriors, combinations of ruins and landscape, extended views, and choice 'bits', all most picturesque and beautiful. I brought away as many drawings as I could; but I would willingly have lingered had I had leisure.

As the majority of the Raja was fast approaching, I drew up, at the Resident's request, a report upon the results of my management of Shorapur from the commencement; and this he transmitted to the Governor-General, with a letter requesting instructions as to the date on which the Raja's minority should expire, and proposing, on his own part, that I should remain at Shorapur after that event, in the capacity of political agent on the part of the Government of India, on a salary of 1,500 Co. rupees per month, to be paid by the State of Shorapur. I did not think it likely that the Raja would desire the presence of any political agent, if he were allowed the option, much less that he would agree to maintaining one at the cost of 20,000 rupees of the local currency; but the Resident's letter had gone on to the Government, and

---

In more than one place Taylor has told the rise of the Adil Shahi dynasty, founded by an offshoot of the Grand Turk in 1489, through its never quite glorious fortunes, to its fall with the taking of Bijapur by Aurungzeb in 1686. It 'had reigned, for the most part in great splendour and prosperity, for 197 years'. The date of the fall of Bijapur is wrongly given, doubtless by the printers, at the end of *Tara*. In a former siege a large part of the city walls had fallen down after unusually heavy rains.

It is impossible to accept all Taylor's statements in what follows: 'Few in England know that the contemporary of our Queen Elizabeth in the Dekhan kingdoms was a woman of equal ability, of equal political talent, of equal, though in a different sense, education and accomplishments, who ruled over a realm as large, a population as large, and as intelligent, and as rich as England.' The Bijapur dominions may conceivably have covered 50,000 square miles, since they included, with uncertainty, the home lands of the Marathas. But Taylor is elsewhere more moderate in feeling that the material resources of Bijapur can never have been great.

I could only await the reply. When it came it was very satisfactory.

Extract from despatch from the Secretary in the Foreign Department to the Resident at Hyderabad.

'*15th January* 1852.

'SIR,—I am directed by the Most Noble the Governor-General to acknowledge the receipt of your letter, dated the 22d ult., No. 218, with its enclosures, and, in reply, to observe that the report upon the management of the affairs of Shorapur exhibits results in the secured prosperity of the Prince, in the tranquillity of the State and contentment of the people, highly honourable to the industry, the perseverance, and the ability of Captain Meadows Taylor.'

The period fixed for the majority of the Raja was the completion of his eighteenth year; but in relation to the political agency, his lordship stated that 'though it would be in the highest degree advisable, yet if, on attaining his full age, which the Raja would then have reached, and finding the State orderly, and his means adequate to his expenditure, he should decline to comply with the suggestion, his lordship does not know on what grounds the Government of India could insist upon it.' The question, therefore, was to be referred to the Court of Directors.

A few days after the receipt of the foregoing, I had the pleasure to receive from F. Courtenay,[1] Esq., private secretary to the Governor-General, a letter, written privately, by desire of Lord Dalhousie, which assured me his lordship wished me to know that he had himself drafted the despatch before-quoted to General Fraser, and that he was glad of having had the opportunity of expressing his opinion of what I had done, and that, in regard to the blame he had attached to me on the proceedings of the Lingsugur inquiry, he now completely exonerated me from it, being convinced, from the Rani's dangerous and obnoxious intrigues and general ill-conduct in Mysore, that I had done no more than my duty in removing

[1] Sir William Lee-Warner tells how, as a young man in charge of the Board of Trade, Lord Dalhousie had found ready help in his secretary there, F. F. Courtenay, 'who afterwards accompanied him to India' He it was who received the midnight note: 'If you are up and have your breeches on come here. If not, without them.—D.'

her from Shorapur. Mr. Courtenay added, in a postscript, 'His lordship has read this, and desires me to say that you may consider it as having been written by himself.'

Could I have wished or hoped for more ? My friend, Major Johnston, was with me when the despatches arrived, and I sent for the Raja to read them to him, and make over the executive authority in Shorapur itself to him, as I had proposed to do that of several departments, informing him also at what period his minority would cease.

He took these communications in a very proper spirit—not greedily, but gratefully, and even sadly. 'Till now', he said, 'he had not felt his position or its reality ; but he would try and be worthy of the confidence of Government.' He seemed most anxious about his mother, whose conduct was now horribly profligate ; and soon after his return to Shorapur he tried to capture her chief favourite ; but the man escaped at night, and the Rani, in a furious rage, shut herself up in a far wing of the palace.

'What will they do', he said, 'when you leave them ?' Though he did not love his mother, yet she had power over him to tempt him into vicious courses, and this she did not neglect to exercise.

In June I received the Resident's reply to my general report for the financial year, 1851–52, which was probably the last I should make, as the Raja would soon have the management of his own treasury. The cash balance in the preceding year had been 377,334 rupees, the highest figure it had yet reached : this year it was 309,442 ; but the extra expenditure on public works—such as the new palace and the irrigation works, three large embankments being in progress—fully accounted for the diminution of the balance. Indeed I applied money as rapidly as I could to these useful undertakings, with a view to their future profit to the State. The great embankment and sluices at Kachaknur were now getting on fast ; and I had the satisfaction of hearing from Major Buckle that 'my plans, surveys, and estimates were most creditable to me as an engineer'.

The Resident's despatch ran thus :—

'Par. 37. As the time approaches when the Raja will have attained his majority, and be intrusted, under the sanction of the Government of India, with the administration of his country, it becomes a matter of much interest to us to be assured that nothing has been wanting on our part to ameliorate the condition of the country and of its inhabitants during the time that it has been under our direction.

'Par. 38. On this subject, therefore, it is particularly gratifying to me to reflect that you have done honour to the office you have held, and that you have discharged its several important duties with the most marked ability, and a devotedness of time and labour that has had no intermission.'

The Nizam's affairs continued in the same deplorable condition. In June 1852 I had not received my pay for December 1851. I had long ago warned the Resident that he was being deceived, and he now began to acknowledge that I was right. What would be done ? Would the Government of India demand a cession of territory for the pay of the Contingent only ? or would the whole State be placed for a time under British surveillance ? all the foreign mercenaries discharged, who were a perpetual source of uneasiness and disquiet, if not of actual alarm, and the establishment reduced so as to pay debts and leave the State prosperous ? This was the Resident's advice ; but at present no move was made in any direction.

I have not as yet alluded to my friend, the Rev. Mr. Kies, whose occasional visits were a very great pleasure to me. He was a member of a German mission[1] emanating from Basel, and supported by Germany.

He was so simple in his ways, and so learned at the same time, that he won the respect and esteem of the people wherever he went. He made no display, travelling on his stout pony from village to village, trusting to hospitality, which was never denied him, and meeting the learned Shastris on their own ground, being fully versed in all their sacred books, and speaking Kanarese perfectly. He and I had many a talk on the subject of missions and mission work, and his experience led him to believe that there were great numbers in many parts who were really dissatisfied with their own Hinduism, yet lacked courage to break through the trammels of caste, and separate themselves from Brahminical influences. That

[1] A German-speaking Swiss mission well known in India.

eventually the Christian faith would prevail, he did not doubt; but at present there was but little to show for the patient, humble teaching of many years of labour. In one note I had from Mr. Kies, he told me that the priest of a village where he had previously preached the Gospel was dead, and with his last breath had laid injunctions on his people to receive him as their future Guru (spiritual teacher); and this they did, listening 'simply and reverently'.

Another letter I find, which is, I think, worthy of a place here.

'I am afraid, sadly afraid, that missionaries who go or who write home to Europe, make it appear as though they were securing more conversions, or hoped to do more, than they can effect. I think they have begun at the wrong end, by abusing Hinduism and idolatry, instead of meeting the natives on their own ground—the Shastras, their scriptures—and showing them how unreasonable, illogical, and void of all comfort they are compared with the belief of a Christian. The finest work they have, religious and philosophical, is the *Bhagwat Gita*, an episode of the Mahabharat; but though there are fine thoughts in it, and fine doctrine, it rests upon no basis that the mind feels, and is intermixed with physical absurdities. You should, if you can, read Schlegel's Latin translation; it is the best, as being nearest to the original Sanskrit. There is an English version; but I do not know how to get hold of it. The missionaries are now, I believe, at last aware of the necessity of meeting natives on their own ground; but for thirty years it was not so, and the mass of vituperation of Hindus that has been printed is enormous—at least what they consider vituperation. Put it to yourself, as for instance, in Italy, where there is much image-worship very like idolatry, would it answer any good purpose to call Saint this, a rogue? or Saint that, a thief? or Saint t'other, an impostor? Krishna deserves all these names; but it answers no good purpose to bestow them. I am often surprised at the supineness of the English chaplains of the Established Church. Missionaries take the trouble generally to learn at least one native language; but among English clergymen I do not know of one who really makes native languages his study, and many of them can hardly speak intelligibly to their servants. Why is this? Is there no field of work for them as well as for missionaries? no good to be done to natives around them? no translations to make? Of course there are. The work is plentiful; but it is not done. Good classical scholars generally find little difficulty in learning native languages; and why should not a chaplain preach in a plain, simple fashion, and be able to read the service to the natives at his station? Much good, it strikes me, might be done were this subject rightly considered.'

Mr. Kies was beloved and respected by all; and his visits were eagerly looked for. He laboured on as long as I continued in India; and I believe, at last, owing to ill health, returned to Basel, where he died—an honest, upright, humble follower of his Lord, and one who, by his simple faith and kindly feelings, won many converts.

In September, all being perfectly quiet and prosperous at Shorapur, I went up to Hyderabad for medical advice. The Raja had married his third wife, according to the custom of the family, and his first wife's half-sister had also been married at the same time to the Raja of Sonda. She was one of my Shorapur children, for whom I had always felt a great affection; she was so clever, and yet so gentle, and very handsome, and the Raja of Sonda had fallen in love with her at first sight, and would not be refused. The expenses of these marriages, the ladies' *trousseaux* and their jewels, were very heavy—hardly less in all than a lakh of rupees; but the money was their own, and devoted to their own purposes.

At Hyderabad I was very ill; the fever I had previously suffered from returned with great violence, and my life was almost despaired of. Under God's great mercy I again recovered, and felt far better than I had done for several months before I left. The Resident wished me to remain, pending the final instructions of the Governor-General regarding Hyderabad and the debts of the Nizam's Government, which were increasing every month. The Governor-General and the Resident were at issue in regard to the policy to be adopted with respect to the Nizam. The Resident proposed that the whole of his Highness's dominions should be placed under the management of the British Government, and all useless expenses reduced in order to pay the State debts, which were estimated at four millions and a half. Lord Dalhousie, on the other hand, protested very strongly against any interference with his Highness's affairs, which had been guaranteed by the British Government in the Treaty of 1800; and he required only a partial cession of territory to provide for the payment of the Contingent and liquidation of the debt to the Company. These views, so essentially different, were irreconcilable; but

I was not prepared for the result. The Resident came to me one evening and said, abruptly, 'Taylor, I have sent in my resignation; I have just posted it myself, and I have told nobody—not even my wife; but I confide it to you. In a day or two it will be made public.'[1]

I was much grieved. I had worked under him and with him for more than nine years without a difference, and his kindness, both officially and privately, had been uniform and continued, nor can I ever forget his unwearied care of me and attention in my illness.

While I was still at Hyderabad his resignation was accepted, and he began his preparations for departure. I left Hyderabad on the 26th December, bidding him good-bye with extreme regret. Colonel Low,[2] who on a former occasion had acted

[1] Yet some time before this General Fraser, hurt at an expression from the Government of India, had said to his wife, 'Be prepared to leave in a month' (*Memoir and Correspondence*, p. 410).

Taylor's grateful attachment is characteristic. It is easy to believe that the general was pleasanter as a superior than as a subordinate. The references to him in Lee-Warner's *Life of Dalhousie* are such as his fame would be better without. After his absence, due to his daughter's illness, Fraser 'on his return to duty had to be checked in his eagerness to force matters to a determination'. In March 1850 Dalhousie writes that India is tranquil, save for some plundering in the Nizam's Berar. 'General Fraser makes mountains of these mole-hills, sends me more official papers on the march of a Subadar's party of the Contingent than were produced by the battle of Waterloo, and dins into the Government day after day with provoking pertinacity his one remedy, the assumption of the Government by us—that is, by himself. They are going from bad to worse, and to that it must in all probability come at last.' This is the only other reference, save for bare mentions. 'Elsewhere', writes Sir William Lee-Warner of Dalhousie at the end of 1852, 'the prospects before him were brighter. General Frazer [*sic*] had relieved him from difficulties by resigning his post as Resident at Hyderabad, where he was "personally obnoxious to the Nizam", and therefore an inconvenience to the Governor-General.'

[2] Afterwards General Sir John Low, 1788–1880. He was but for half a year in Hyderabad. Low, together with his friend Sleeman, was among those who served in India to an age approaching seventy, thus rivalling James Stuart Fraser and Sir Mark Cubbon. Low's longest service was in what Hunter calls 'the supremely important post' of Resident, from 1831 to 1842, at Lucknow, which the natives call Nacklao, but which Outram's biographer, in his wilful way, spells Lakhnau. When Outram went there in 1854 Low wrote reminding him that the King of Oudh must meet an arriving Resident outside the city, take him upon the royal elephant, and in this way conduct him to

for General Fraser, was appointed his successor, and would, it was presumed, bring with him the final orders of the Governor-General in Council. He was expected early in March, so I should not be long in suspense.

I returned to my districts, and began my last revenue settlement. There was but little to do; the period of five years had expired, and all that remained was a general revision and adjustment, with the remissions or other provision for outstanding balances. On the whole we had been unlucky as regarded seasons, and had had three bad, through excess of unseasonable rain, against two good. I could therefore make no demand for an increase of rent, and the leases for waste lands taken up had been necessarily irregular. A regular system of returns of cultivation and revenue, in all villages in correspondence with the treasury, worked well, and the most ordinary supervision on the part of the Raja would keep everything straight. I had not been long in camp when the Raja came out to me, and remained for a few days' shooting. He appeared, for the first time, restless, and somewhat petulant, wondering how soon the orders would arrive regarding him. I could only assure him he could not be more anxious than I was on the subject; but I could do nothing till they came. The Rani had again been ill, and when her son visited her, had told him that unless he exerted himself he would never get the country out of my hands, and that he was now no child, 'Why did he not act as a man?' No wonder, I thought, that he was petulant, and perhaps suspicious too. I had informed him of the probable political agency; and a draft of a letter was prepared from himself and others of the elder members of his family, declaring that no political agency was needed, and that the Raja was fully able to manage his own concerns. Some signed these papers; but others, especially the Beydurs, refused to do so, except a few, who sent me word they had done it under compulsion. The

---

breakfast at the palace—a ceremonial in singular contrast to the sullen first reception of General Fraser by the Nizam.

In his *History* Taylor commends Low's 'spirited conduct' both at Lucknow in 1837, when he determined the succession at some risk to his life, crowning the new King with his own hand, and at Hyderabad.

Rani, to her credit, declared to her son that he would ruin himself if these papers were forwarded. I never heard of them till afterwards, so I suppose the Raja was guided by her counsel.

On March 10th the Resident wrote to the Raja that the Court of Directors and the Governor-General approved of his taking up the affairs of his State; but they desired that I should remain as political agent to advise him in State matters, and thus preclude the recurrence of former disorder and irregularity: to this the Resident requested a distinct reply, which would be forwarded for the orders of the Governor-General. On receipt of this letter, the Raja wrote to me asking the meaning of 'political agent', which I explained, and he sent his reply to the Resident, which was at once forwarded; but the question of political agency was evaded under his assurance to Government that 'his reliance in all matters was restricted to the favour of the Supreme Government'.

Perhaps if the Raja had been from the first assured that he would not have had to pay for the agency and its establishment, he would have consented to the step as a mark of distinction to his State, but the prospect of having to pay 20,000 rupees a-year was formidable. Lord Dalhousie had very distinctly given his opinion that the measure could not be forced upon the Raja; and even if he consented, he ought not to be considered responsible for the heavy charges it would involve. I had always looked on the subject as extremely uncertain; for unless the Court of Directors sanctioned the expenditure, I did not see how the Governor-General could authorise it. Everything, however, must soon be finally settled.

The Raja had come of age the previous October, and the delay in his public recognition by Government was only making him restless and suspicious. If the Raja had agreed to the appointment of a political agent, I should of course have remained with him; but I had no wish to do so for many reasons, and I wrote privately to Colonel Low on the subject. The rumours of a transfer of territory by the Nizam became again rife in April, and as I felt sure my services would not be passed over, I waited patiently for the issue. I could not have remained at Shorapur ; but if I were given charge of the Raichur Doab, I could still look after it. The Raja's vices were becoming notorious, and I cannot write of them ; and his temper, to his own people, was growing like his mother's.

The Raja's answer to the Resident not being considered satisfactory by the Governor-General, the Resident again wrote, detailing the exact sum to be paid to the agent, 1,815 Shorapur rupees per month—equivalent to 1,500 Government rupees—and there would be additional sums for sepoys, etc. I was at Shorapur, and the Raja brought the letter to me, and asked me what he was to say.

'I cannot pay this large sum to any one,' he said ; 'you know I cannot.'

Indeed I was of the same opinion, and thought the expenses might well have been shared by the Company and by the Nizam's Government.

'But', continued the Raja, 'I suppose they will be angry with me if I refuse, and, indeed, I don't want you to go away. I know I shall do no good when you are gone ; you don't know the people I have about me.'

'Yes,' I said, 'I do, as well as you ; and if you only act rightly, you will be able to control them far more easily than I did.'

'O *appa*!' he cried, leaving his chair, and throwing himself at my feet—'O *appa*! if I were only a little boy again to lie in your arms, and for you to love me as you used! All that is gone for ever.'

'No, no,' I answered ; 'if I go—and I must go soon—I shall not be far away from you, and if you are in any trouble or difficulty send for me and I will come. You can always write in English "Come", and I shall understand.'

'I will,' he said. 'I know, whatever you may hear, you will not forsake your boy.'

And I gave him my promise. That, except once more, as I shall have to relate, was the last time I was ever alone with him. He wrote his answer to the Resident on the 1st May : it was clumsily worded, and Colonel Low did not like the style ; but the Raja did not intend it to be disrespectful or arrogant. He declined the political agency on the terms on which it was offered, owing to the great expense; and I thought him right.

Meanwhile events at Hyderabad were in full progress towards a settlement. The Resident had received his final orders, which were to demand that territory in payment of the Contingent might be ceded in perpetuity to British management, and the districts I had named in my minute of January 1851 were the basis of the transaction. The old Contingent was to be remodelled; all the local officers pensioned, and the force no longer called the 'Nizam's Army', but, as the 'Hyderabad Contingent', to be an auxiliary one to the Government of India. Should any reader desire to refer to these transactions, they are to be found in their entirety in the Blue-book of 1854, April 4th, and are in truth very interesting, as explaining measures on which Lord Dalhousie has often been arraigned. The Nizam objected to the 'assignment in perpetuity', and the treaty was duly executed and signed without that condition, leaving him at liberty to redeem the provinces if possible, at some future time.[1]

[1] In Taylor's *History* are three pages (pp. 695-7), which bring the affairs of Hyderabad to the critical year 1853. The concluding passage is given in the note just below. Other portions concern the persistent Palmer claim, the financial wrangle ending in the cession, and the successors of the wicked but picturesque old Chandu Lal, who had had to clear out in 1843. The following sentences are of value as illustrating under what conditions Meadows Taylor had to serve the Nizam.

'It was a common saying at Hyderabad, that those who accepted new district offices in payment of advances, rode out of the city with their faces to their horses' tails to see who followed them. In the districts, rival Talookdars went to war with each other; the people were ground by exactions; and crops of villages might be seen standing under attachment, eaten by the birds and destroyed by the rains, long after the season of harvest was past. Of administration in the departments of public justice and police, and of the regulation of the irregular army, which amounted to 50,000 men, of whom 16,000 were Arabs and half-caste Arabs—there was not even a pretence; and local disorders, robberies of mail-posts, and the oppression of [by] foreign mercenaries—Arabs, Rohillas, Sikhs, and Patans—was grievous and notorious. Remonstrance had had no effect, and any remedy short of assuming the administration appeared impossible.' The pay of the contingent force, to which Taylor belonged, was normally four months, but often more deeply, in arrears.

I was still at Shorapur. The Rani intended to go on a pilgrimage to one of the great temples in the south of India, and took leave of me in apparently real grief.

'Do you remember, Taylor Sahib,' she asked, 'what I once told you about that boy? You have not forgotten it?'

'No, Rani Sahib,' I replied, 'nor ever shall.'

'Ah,' she continued, 'he is the last—the last of his race! He will lose all his ancestors ever gained; and all the pains you have taken with him, and all the money you have saved for him, will be poured like water into the sea; and you will be grieved—sorely, sorely grieved! But I shall not see it, for I am dying, my friend, dying fast now. Will you forgive me all that I have done to you? I am a mean old woman: you are going one way, and I am going another; we shall never meet again.'

I bent over her as she lay upon her bed, and touched her hand with my lips. She could not speak; but smiled, waved her hand gently, and I left her.

Next day she went to Lingsugur, and being again seized with paralysis, died there on the 27th May. She was but forty years old; but when I last saw her she seemed seventy, haggard and wasted almost to a skeleton. The Raja rode over to see her the day before her death, but she was insensible, and he disgusted all those present by his levity and the unruly crowd he had with him.

He returned to Shorapur while she was yet living, and made no attempt to attend her funeral rites. I called upon him the day after her death, according to Shorapur etiquette, but he hardly mentioned his mother at all, except as having 'been very foolish'.

So ended the Rani Ishwarama.

If there were some good points in her character, generosity and charity to the poor, her profligacy and baneful influence over her son were terrible to think on, and continued to have effect on him to the last.

Suraj-ul-Mulk, the Nizam's Minister, was dead; and his nephew, Salar Jang, a most gentlemanly, well-educated young nobleman, had been appointed in his stead by the Nizam, with every prospect of success. He has since risen to the very highest eminence in India as a statesman, and by him the

Nizam's State has been rescued from the decadence with which it was threatened.[1]

I was now summoned to Hyderabad to receive instructions respecting the district that was to be given into my charge—which of the five that had been ceded was not made known to me. I arrived on the 11th June, and having reported myself, received a polite note from the Resident, asking me to come to dinner, as he had much to say. He received me most kindly, and I was charmed with him, he was so frank, and clear-headed, and decided in all his expressions; and I saw, at once, that I should work happily under him. Next

[1] In Taylor's *History*, p. 697, one may read: 'It is impossible to pity, or sympathise with, the wilful extravagance and mismanagement of the Nizam's government, during a period of twenty-five years, and under repeated warnings of their consequences. It is equally impossible to overlook the fact, that under General Fraser's arrangements of 1851, the settlement remained in the hands of the Nizam's government alone. . . . Suraj-ul-Mulk, after a long illness, died very shortly after the treaty had been executed, and his nephew, Salar Jung, young in years but of great ability and promise, was appointed minister, and whose admirable administration still continues. At the period of the assignment of territory by the Nizam, the Raja of Shorapur attained his majority, and his country was made over to him. The revenues had been doubled during nearly twelve years of careful management, and every inducement existed to hope that he might continue what had been established.'

There is a good deal about Salar Jang and his uncle in the *Memoir and Correspondence of General James Stuart Fraser*. Hastings Fraser believes 'it may fairly be said that the measures of reform carried out by Sir Salar Jung, in quieter times, and with a larger and more cordial support from our authorities, were constructed on the lines laid down by his uncle and my father, and placed by them on record'.

Nawab Sir Salar Jang, 1829–1883, had a remarkable career as Prime Minister of Hyderabad during thirty years. Mr. Buckland writes: 'He disbanded large bands of Arab troops, subdued robber chieftains, and put down lawlessness: refilled the Treasury, which was almost empty.' He was finely loyal to us during the Mutiny, if not twenty years later. The vain ambition of his life was to obtain the restitution of the Berars. He was a great gentleman, ever loyal to the Nizam, though 'always an object of suspicion to his jealous master'.

It was as the guest of Sir Salar Jang that Colonel Taylor went to Hyderabad in 1875. To him, as 'Leader of all the advancing civilization of the Dekhan', *A Noble Queen*, 'illustrative of a portion of its history', is dedicated. There is a *Life of Sir Salar Jang, G.C.S.I.*, 1883, by a friend who had accompanied him to England some years before, Syed Hossein Bilgrami, which I have not been able to obtain.

day the districts were assigned. At first I was given Berar, the largest; but an express arrived from the Bombay Government particularly requesting that I might be given that portion of the ceded territory which lay contiguous to the Bombay Presidency, and I was nominated to that instead.

The following extract from an official letter from the Resident to me, was at once both explanatory and gratifying:—

'Para. 14. As I understand that you have felt surprised, and perhaps somewhat disappointed, at finding that districts of comparatively small extent are to be made over to your management, while larger districts are allotted to other Deputy-Commissioners of less experience in civil duties than yourself, I think it is due to you to assure you that the circumstance in question has not occurred from any want of confidence on my part in your qualifications or zeal for the public interests—indeed quite the reverse; for my original reason in determining to send you to the western districts was my belief that many of the duties in that quarter will be of a peculiarly difficult and delicate nature, arising from the numerous Surf-i-Khas [1] districts in that quarter, the revenue management of which remains, according to agreement with the individuals who enjoy them, with the Nizam's Government, while the police and judicial duties of those villages are to be conducted entirely under your orders.

'15. I may also mention that long-pending and intricate disputes respecting boundaries and frontier taxes, etc., etc., must be inquired into and settled in communication with the collectors of Ahmednagar and Sholapur of the Honble. Company's territories; and I knew that I could rely on your tact and judgment, and general experience in civil duties, for the purpose of bringing these disputes to a satisfactory conclusion. Moreover, I may as well mention the fact that it is within the last three days, and after the allotment of districts to the several Deputy-Commissioners had been arranged, that the western districts have been curtailed to their present extent at the particular request of the Nizam, who originally promised eight lakhs in that direction, making up the difference by adding lands to the southern portion of Berar. That fact, however, does not in any material degree alter the difficult duties above alluded to connected with the western districts, which I consider you so well qualified to overcome.'

I had sent on all my tents and heavy baggage towards Berar by way of Bidar; but I now recalled it, as I was required

[1] *Crown*, as an adjective.

to go first to Shorapur, and then to my new district: it was, in fact, part of my old district of 1828–29, and a fine healthy climate, which to me Berar was not; and as one end bordered on Shorapur, I should have no difficulty in getting there. The Raichur Doab, to which I had looked as my probable destination, was divided into two portions, and Berar into two, and mine appeared to be the largest in area, though not in revenue. '"You won't mind that,"' said the Resident, as I wrote to my father; '"your district requires a person of tact and experience of more than ordinary character, and therefore I send you"'—a flattering and gracious speech, for which I made due acknowledgment. It was curious that my destination should be so very suddenly changed.

The treaty, ratified by the Governor-General, had not as yet arrived from Calcutta; and as there was a great deal of detail to be arranged about the establishments and general management of the new districts, the Resident requested me to draw up a minute on the subject, which I did as rapidly as I could; and by the time the treaty had arrived, and the Nizam fixed the 18th July for a public *durbar* to receive and sign it, my minute was ready. On the appointed day, the Resident, accompanied by a numerous staff, of which I was one, went to the *durbar*. His Highness was in excellent humour, chatted freely and gaily with Colonel Low, and seemed highly pleased that the differences between the two Governments had been so speedily and so amicably arranged. Next day, I and the other new civil officers who were at Hyderabad received our credentials, and there being no need for further delay, I returned to Shorapur to make my final arrangements, and to give over my charge to the Raja according to the instructions I had received. Lord Dalhousie had not been particularly pleased with the tone of the Raja's reply to his despatch, which he characterised as 'presumptuous'; yet, as there was no pretext for compelling him to retain the services of a political agent, he directed that the State should be made over to him, at the same time warning him—

'That if he allowed his country to fall into disorder, the Supreme Government would interfere and establish order,' or perhaps set him aside altogether.

I had appointed the 30th June for the final ceremony, and had written to tell the Raja to be ready. On my way to Shorapur I fell in with Captain Balmain, who had been appointed to Western Raichur, and took him on with me. My future assistant, Lieutenant Cadell, awaited me also at Shorapur. I will give the detail of the last few days from my letter to my father, written at the time.

'I had prepared proclamations and other documents directing all persons to obey the Raja, and Cadell and I went to the palace in the evening. There were many people present, and the letter from the Governor-General was first read: then my proclamation; and I made a short speech, saying I hoped that all present would be faithful to the Raja, and serve him as they had served me—that I trusted they would do so, and take care of the State, and not relapse into evil ways.

'Then, as I hung a garland of flowers about the Raja's neck, and gave the State seals into his hand, a royal salute was fired, and the ceremony ended.

'The Raja seemed to take it all very coolly and as a matter of course, and said nothing; but he whispered to me that he could not say all he would in such a crowd; but would send for me, or come up to me in a day or two.

'We remarked that there was no manifestation of satisfaction among the assembly, or among the crowds outside the palace; on the contrary, many were weeping.

'The Raja's first act was to seize his illegitimate half-sister, or rather take her away from her mother, and marry her by a left-handed ceremony, obliging the members of his family to be present, to their great disgust. For two days he was busy with this ceremony, offerings at temples, and the like, and on the 3d July he wrote to me, begging I would come to him in the evening.

'He asked me what he should write to the Governor-General, and I gave him verbally the outline of a plain grateful letter. He then asked to be allowed to purchase my house, which was a great satisfaction to me, and he offered 20,000 rupees, an offer I gladly accepted, provided Government made no objection. He afterwards sent every one away, and spoke about his affairs more sensibly than I had ever heard him do before; and as he gave me this opening I improved upon it, and showed him how, during the short time he had managed his affairs, he had already contrived to spend every rupee of ready money—how his servants and soldiers were even now in arrears of pay; as was the case in his father's time, and he himself obliged to borrow here and there in advance of the collections. I told him I did not see what it would all come to if he did not take pains to make things better, and much to the same purpose, when he began to sob, and cling about me, saying he had now no friends, and how he was to get on he did not know, but he would do his best. He said he saw there was no use in soldiery, which his people told him were necessary (this was in relation to the proposed enlistment of Arabs and Rohillas, which I had heard was intended), and that he would discharge many of them, and reduce his extra expenses. He then told me there was one thing which he wished me to know, and which had long been on his mind—namely, that if he died without legitimate issue he wished the British Government to annex his State, and provide for his family and dependants. I begged he would write this in a letter to the Resident, which I undertook to forward; but I represented that he was very young, and that I hoped to hear of his having a family and an heir.

'In such conversation our time passed, and I mentioned everything I could think of in regard to the future management of the affairs. He said he did not know how to thank me, or show his gratitude; but that if he were permitted to settle on me an allowance for life, and a village or two for my maintenance, as a proof of his regard, he would be thankful.

'The next day he asked Cadell and me to dine with him. The letters, including that about my estate, were all ready, and were duly forwarded on the 7th July. The village selected for me was an outlying one within the British territory, and yielded 2,500 Company's rupees, or £250 a-year, and I shall be very lucky if I get it.

'The following day—Cadell having started in the morning—I went to the palace to bid the Raja good-bye; and not only he, but all the members of the family, and the chief people, male and female, in Shorapur.

'It was a painful process; there were crowds of people all about me, clinging to my palankeen, as I went from house to house. The Raja had gone out to one of his hunting retreats, leaving word that he could not bear to see me go. As I proceeded, the people and the Beydurs, men and women, gathered in the streets, and accompanied me, and it was as much as I could do to get away at all. The Raja's wives, whom I had known as children, clung about me. Poor old Kesama, now nearly ninety years old, blessed me: "I cannot weep," she said, "my old eyes are dry; but I bless you, you and all belonging to you."

'It was a most exciting scene, and very painful. Mine has been a long sojourn among a strange people, and whatever may have been their faults, there was no doubt of their warm attachment to myself.'

The crowds followed me to the gates; but as my bearers quickened their pace the numbers soon fell off. At every village I was met by the people, and at the last one on the frontier a great concourse had assembled of all the head-men, *patels*, and *patwaris*, and principal farmers. I do not think there was even one man who had a hope of the Raja's maintaining his position, and as to themselves, they said—'We must escape oppression as best we can. It will be a hard struggle.'

So ended my connection with Shorapur for the present. It was hereafter renewed for a time under far different circumstances. I had tried humbly and earnestly to do my duty to its people of all degrees; and could I give *in extenso* my long letters to my father, they would show more of what my inner life and occupations were, and of my schemes and plans for the welfare of the State. They are far too monotonous, however, and all I have been able to do is to note such events, and quote such extracts, as would give some notion of my endeavours and their results.

In one of his despatches General Fraser characterised the State of Shorapur as 'a wild and barbarous district, replete with disorder and irregularity of every conceivable kind'. And no doubt it was so when I took over charge. The Beydurs were the same, and their power was the same as in the time of Aurungzeb, or indeed from the fifteenth century, and their feudal condition of service to their chief was the same. Sometimes, owing to their numbers and position, they had been able to dominate over all classes of the people; sometimes their power had exceeded that of their own chiefs, and had forced these to act as they pleased. Sometimes the Rajas had in their turn brought them to submission; but they had never bent to any Musalman or other foreign yoke, and none of the civilisation that such a process insured had ever reached them. As long as times were disturbed, they plundered at their will throughout the Deccan and Mysore, and it was only when stronger and more peaceful Governments had the rule that they were restrained. But if the old raids and forays could not be indulged in, there were at any rate cattle-lifting and *dacoity*, and other crimes, to fall back upon; and they looked upon these as most honourable achievements until the late interference with Shorapur by the British Government.

This violence I had at least suppressed, and for years before I left there had not been one single complaint of any such doings beyond the frontier.

One of their systems, however, was not easy to eradicate. A man who had a quarrel with his village for any cause could always obtain the aid of Beydurs willing to take his part as a point of honour, and these proceeded to issue threatening notices, such as—

'To the authorities of ——. In the name of Mahadeo!

'The fire is on the hills! We are out on murder and violence because you have injured ——, and you had better settle with him.'

If this notice were obeyed, all was well; if not, the people of the village were kept in perpetual alarm, their crops injured, and persons wounded, indeed often killed. This state of things was bad enough in the country itself, but when it extended to parties across the frontier it was far worse.

On one occasion a man of a small village near the river Bhima quarrelled with his family, and went to the Beydurs of Adur, which was fifteen miles distant, in the Nizam's country, where about a thousand of them were to be found. He returned with a party, who harried the Shorapur village, burnt corn-stacks, and wounded the head-man desperately, besides seven others, also sending me an impudent message that the Shorapur Beydurs were cowards and old women. My Beydurs were furious, and asked me to lead them on to avenge this insult; and I daresay they thought meanly of me because I did not. As the Nizam's local authorities would or could give no redress, I appealed to the Resident, who desired me not to stir, and sent down a detachment of infantry to march on the rebel village. It resisted, was stormed, and afterwards burnt; and some of my Beydurs were present, which was a satisfaction to them, though they would rather have gone under me. Not long after the offenders sent a deputation to me, praying for forgiveness, and they never transgressed again. They invited me to come and visit them, which I did, finding them on a fine level plateau—a much cooler climate than the plain.

As a body the Shorapur Beydurs had been free from crime. They were not dishonest, and there was no petty thieving or roguery among them ; they used to say they were too proud for that sort of thing. Though scarcely belonging to any caste, they were not given to intoxication, and rarely drank spirits ; few even touched *sendhi*, which is the sap of the palm, fermented in a peculiar manner, and very exciting. In the years that I had been at Shorapur there were, I think, only two murders among them. They never dreamt of resisting authority in such cases, but gave up the offenders to justice at once. In civil cases I never interfered with their usages, and they never complained of injustice. Their *bhats*, or bards, and their elders, had a traditional knowledge of their laws and customs, and always attended the *panchayats* ; but I do not think there was much difference between their law and that of the Hindus.

The elders of the clans sat every day on their platform, under the great *nim* tree in the town, and attended to all complaints. They were grateful to me for respecting their former privileges, and elected me *gurekar*, or head executive over all the clans. They certainly never abused their claims, and by working well as rural police saved me both labour and anxiety. I was very thankful that during my stay no blood had been shed, nor a single shot fired in anger among them.

All the members of the clans had had lands allotted for their original support, which had descended hereditarily. The minimum amount was one *kuru*, or thirty *bighas*, but some held as much as three hundred *bighas* nominal. Ordinarily they farmed these lands themselves, and divided the produce, but never the land, among the family. When general security began to prevail, many took leases for waste lands, and were assisted by me with capital ; but it often surprised me to see how much was cleared and planted by them without help. I opened out to them also a new occupation, that of carriers of cotton, and other Shorapur products, *to* the coast ; and of salt, spices, and English piece-goods *from* the coast,—and this business was proving very profitable. I introduced the best seed of cotton and other produce that I could get, and established a small manufacture of indigo, and tried by every means in my power to promote peaceful and civilised undertakings. I think, and hope, that I left these wild people better than I found them ; they certainly were more prosperous. They were highly honourable, and once they had really solemnly sworn faith to me they never swerved. Not even their Raja could tempt them when he tried ; and they told him very sternly that they had pledged their faith to me, and till I made them over to him they would not break it—nor did they.

As a class these men were fine athletic fellows, constantly exercised in gymnastics and in the use of arms. They lived well, eating no meat except game, and they were comfortably housed, their habitations having solid mud, or mud and stone walls, and clay terraced roofs. There was no savagery among them, such as prevails among the Bhils and Gonds, and other tribes.

Their ordinary dress was a pair of loose trousers, of cotton cloth, descending to the calf of the leg ; a turban, and waistband, with a chintz tunic for festal occasions. Their hunting or war costume was a brown leather cap, gathered in round the head ; brown leather drawers over the cotton ones ; and a leather jerkin or jacket without sleeves : they only carried swords. Their women were well made, strong and hardy, and very cleanly in their persons and in their homes, and were excellent housewives, making their husbands' clothes, spinning yarn for the weavers, and working in the fields, watering crops, and suchlike. It was rare to hear of a Beydur having more than one wife, and they were kind to their women as a rule.

The moral character of these people was very high, and such infidelities as did rarely occur were tried among themselves at their own *panchayats*. They were very illiterate, and considered it ' low ' to be able to read or write, or cast accounts. That was the work of Brahmins ! They joined in some of the Brahminical observances of the State, and the *Dasara*, and the *Uaydi* or *Bassant*, were always attended by them. The *Dasara* I have before mentioned as a State pageant ; the *Bassant*, or Springtide, was very different. In the morning all the clans in Shorapur assembled on the hills around, dressed in clothes dyed yellow, and accompanied by their horn-blowers, drummers, flag-bearers, and pipers, marched to the open space before the great temple on the terrace where the Raja and I used to sit. Games were then begun—

wrestling, leaping, etc.; but that most appreciated was climbing the poles. Six of these, from twenty to thirty feet high, were put up, each with a small pavilion at the top, in which sat a man provided with jars of some slippery mixture. Large slices of pumpkin hung from the bottom of this cage, and the feat was to tear away one or more of these slices, and it was no easy task. Four, six, or eight stout fellows placed themselves round the base of the pole, others climbed on their shoulders, others again upon them, and so on, until one essayed to swarm from the last to the top, amidst clapping of hands and shouting. Meanwhile the man in the cage diligently emptied his jars of slippery stuff and water over them all, and often the whole structure would collapse, and the men fall in a heap. When any fellow, stronger and more fortunate than the rest, did succeed in snatching away the prize, the excitement was unbounded, and he was brought in triumph to the Raja to receive his reward. These people also had a very popular game, which closely resembled prison-bars; and I taught them leap-frog, taking a back myself at first; and I have seen hundreds flying merrily over each other. I also introduced racing in sacks, which caused great amusement. Besides these sports, they had marbles, peg-tops, hop-scotch, and trap, as well as kite-flying, each in its season, as with us; and it was curious to find these games amongst a people who had never known the English; they were played, too, exactly in the same manner as with us, and are universal throughout India. Beydurs are keen sportsmen; with their sharp spears they attack panthers, wild hog, and often even tigers, fearlessly. They are skilled at hawking, both with large falcons and sparrow-hawks, training the latter to kill quail, larks, and snipe; and the former, partridges, wild duck, floriken, and hares. The last mentioned, however, were generally drawn into nets, and then knocked on the head with sticks. A sporting Beydur, 'specially got up', was a very grand fellow indeed. He wore a large handkerchief tied round his head, of some showy pattern in brilliant colours. In the centre of his forehead was a large patch of crimson, which was brought down to the end of his nose, and across his eyes he had drawn his hand covered with dry ashes. Dabs of crimson ornamented his back, round which a delicate muslin scarf of some bright colour was brought and tied in a bow, the ends being finished with some gold tinsel ribbon, which hung down in front. Round his loins was wound a strong piece of cloth, with a knife stuck in the waist. His trousers, tight round the body, looser to the knee, and after that very wide to the ankle, are generally white, or of pale salmon colour. His sandals are nicely oiled ; and altogether, with his falcon or sparrow-hawk on his wrist, his two dogs at his heels, and a stout quarterstaff in his hand, he was an imposing, handsome - looking fellow, and was quite aware of the fact ! Some wear gold ear-rings, silver rings above the elbow round the arm, and silver waist-chain. Sometimes a father took his little son out with him ; and these juvenile 'swells', dressed exactly to resemble their fathers, sparrow-hawk and all, were very amusing.[1]

[1] This account of the people among whom Taylor laboured may be supplemented by extracts from the paragraphs about them, written at the very end of his life, in *A Noble Queen*, pp. 253-256 :

'The Beydurs, under the name of Veddur, still used by the wilder part of the tribes who inhabit the mountains and forests of south-western India, are what is termed ordinarily one of the aboriginal races, as seen in their native condition in the forests of Travancore and Mysore. Other portions of the tribe which remained in the plains of southern India and of Mysore became, in some respects, civilised, and at one time attained a considerable degree of power, which, however, was shattered by the great Hindoo dynasties that gradually arose long before [?] the Christian era, and the Veddurs, now adopting the appellation of Beydur, became soldiers and tillers of the soil, but never artisans, or reaching any degree of education. . .

'The Beydurs as a people are essentially different from ordinary Hindoos. Some of them attend Hindoo services and conform to the ministrations of Brahmins, but for the most part they are followers of the Lingayet doctrine, or hold to their ancient aboriginal worship of natural objects, glens, water-falls, rocks, trees, and the like. They do not accept or desire education in any form, and are of a freer, bolder type—both in manner and customs—than ordinary Hindoos. They are great sportsmen in all respects ; bold in following tigers, panthers, and bears on foot ; and ordinarily they live upon whatever game they can shoot or snare. In person both men and women are remarkably neat and clean, and their homes and villages well kept. They are also industrious cultivators and farmers, and own a great quantity of land in their province. They are also public carriers of cotton and salt to and from the coast ; and, in short, are rarely idle, and by no means dissipated. Formerly they were dreaded for raids on their neighbours, and in cattle-lifting especially were most daring and expert ; but these

I need not attempt to describe the ordinary classes. They resembled most others of the Deccan, mixed Musalman and Hindu, but were ruder in manners than the corresponding classes in the British and Musalman territories of the Nizam. They were industrious farmers, and the way in which they reared and cultivated American cotton-seed, and applied their capital to increase the produce of their country, was admirable. They were litigious and quarrelsome. In heavy criminal cases I employed courts, or *panchayats*, of the chief persons in Shorapur, Lingayats, Hindus, and Musalmans, without exclusiveness as to their class, and including members of the Raja's family; a President was then selected, and specific charges or indictments made against the prisoners. The evidence for prosecution and defence was recorded, and the court gave written judgment, which contained summing up and sentence. I found this plan very simple and efficacious, and the proceedings were always carried on with the greatest regularity. Where sentence of death was recorded, as in murders, the judgment was translated by me, with the evidence and defence, and forwarded, through the Resident, to the Governor-General for confirmation; and I had not one instance of disapproval to record. Cases involving fine and imprisonment, with hard labour or without it, I used to try myself. No law had ever existed in Shorapur, nor even the semblance of a court of justice, civil or criminal. Ordinary civil suits were tried by civil *panchayats* not limited to five members, and there were but few appeals to me from their decisions.

The population of the principality by census was about 500,000, or 130 to the square mile. The town itself and its suburbs 30,000.[1]

---

times and deeds have passed away, though their memory lives in many a song and legend.

'Beydurs hold themselves to have no caste, and they eat everything except carrion, and such birds or beasts as feed upon it. They also object to beef, because the slaughter of kine is offensive to Hindoos, and especially to Brahmins. They marry exclusively into their own tribe, and rarely have more than one wife, though their chiefs take as many as they can support.'

[1] I had supposed these numbers to be impossibly large, but it is difficult to compare figures owing to the great changes in area which have occurred. The Director-General of Revenue, His Highness the Nizam's Government, has kindly sent me, through the Hyderabad

The public dispensary and hospital at Shorapur were very useful, and medicines were dispensed under the orders of the apothecary attached to the staff. In visitations of cholera, medicines were sent out into the districts, and competent persons despatched in charge of them. Vaccination made great progress at Shorapur; and in the country, I myself was the chief operator, my tents being surrounded every morning by crowds of women and children so long as my supplies of lymph lasted or could be obtained.

My school at Shorapur was well attended, and both Marathi and Telugu, with Persian to Musalman boys, were well taught. I had even a few English scholars, some of whom turned out well. In the districts there were plenty of schools where Kanarese and Marathi were taught; and to these I gave small grants in aid, and books which were used in the schools of the British provinces.

I have already spoken of what I had begun and done in public works. The lake at Bohnal was a complete success, and had repaid the money spent upon it several times over. The other irrigation works were incomplete, and there was but small hope that the Raja would carry them on, although he promised very faithfully to do so. One grand scheme I formed—that of diverting the waters of the river Krishna from their bed, and bringing them through most part of the principality for irrigation purposes—had to be abandoned for want of funds, though perfectly practicable, as I had ascertained by levels.

I had made and cleared many roads, one of which extended to Lingsugur, through a wild and rocky track, for 36 miles, and opened up traffic between Shorapur and the south.

I had planted many thousand mango and tamarind trees about the town and elsewhere, intended both for ornament and produce. When I left, the road to the Krishna, six

---

Residency, detailed calculations and information which show that, close to Taylor's day, the Shorapur District had an area of 2,901 square miles, with 637 villages; and that 'the figures given by Colonel Meadows Taylor are for all practical purposes quite correct. The decrease in the population of Shorapur must no doubt be due to the decline which inevitably followed the downfall of the principality in 1858 A.D., since when it has ceased to be the capital of an independent Raj.'

miles in length, was bordered on each side by a double row of fine young trees, which gave ample promise of fruit. All these undertakings were gradually accomplished without distressing the revenue in any way; indeed there were ample funds for all such contingencies.

I have not the final returns of the revenue at hand to refer to; but I know that it was nearly, if not quite doubled; and with the average liberal expenditure, there was a surplus of a lakh and a half. There were no debts whatever now, and I think, when I made over charge to the Raja, that the State possessed every element of comfort and independence that could insure prosperity; but there was small hope of its continuance.

Even in the brief period that had already elapsed the Raja had spent every anna he found in the treasury, had not paid the stipendiaries, and had only the usual year's revenue to look to. My warnings on this point had been quite fruitless.

I need say little of myself. Since my great sorrow I had led a cheerless, lonely life; no society, no one to speak to from first to last, except the very rare visit of a friend or traveller. The palace children often came to see me, and loved to hold their dolls' feasts among my flowers with their playmates. Native friends would come up in the evenings, and a game of chess with one or other often followed. In the country, the village authorities would gather round to hear of England and the world beyond India, of which they had no conception whatever. Sometimes travelling minstrels or singers, accredited from other courts, such as Mysore, Baroda, Gwalior, or elsewhere, arrived, and the State hospitality was exercised, and performances given and attended, and on these occasions I gave my parties.

Neighbouring 'lairds' had to be received and entertained, for Shorapur had to maintain its character for hospitality and kindly feeling to those adjoining it.

My books were my constant delight, and with these and my telescope, a fine Dollond, I had always plenty of occupation. I read up Herschel, and other works on astronomy, to enable me to understand something of what I saw. Night after night I have thus wandered about those glorious fields of the heavens, ever new, ever resplendent, leading thought irresistibly into the Infinite. I could not go on with literary work, as, at the day's close, my brain was generally wearied out. My work was seldom less than twelve hours a-day, with little variation, so to write was impossible; but I felt I was gaining more and more real knowledge of native life and character, under circumstances that fall to the lot of very few Englishmen, and that hereafter, if life were spared, I might turn my experience to good account. I kept up voluminous private correspondence, particularly with my father; and this, with my usual letters to *The Times*, official reports and translations, and occasional articles for the Indian press, were all I could manage to get through in my busy life. I was very thankful for the many blessings given me, and tried to discourage the feeling of utter loneliness that would at times oppress me.

Ten years [1] of my life were given to Shorapur—a blank to me in many respects as regarded intellectual intercourse and literary progress; but yet, with all its drawbacks, more interesting than the dull routine of a small cantonment.

Now they had passed over, and a new phase of my life was opening before me in an enlarged and more important sphere of action. Through all danger, through all illnesses and weariness and trials, I had been mercifully preserved and tenderly protected, and was grateful to God for His great mercies—praying that in the future they might be continued unto me.[2]

THE MODERN BEYDURS

By William Crooke, C.I.E.

The *Census Report*, India, 1911, gives as follows:

Beda, Bedaru, 318,444—distributed:

Coorg .	97
Madras .	49,893
Mysore . .	268,454

[1] It was more like twelve years, as he says elsewhere, since Taylor first went to Shorapur in November 1841.

[2] I have fortunately been able to supplement Taylor's account of the Beydurs whom he knew by this contribution from the foremost authority upon Indian tribes and castes.

With them are often confounded the Vedan, numbering 46,799 in Madras.

Census Report, Madras, 1902 (i. 145) gives 'Bedaru (62,273), a caste of Canarese Shikaris akin to the Tamil Vedans and Telugu Boyas', with references to *Mysore Census Report*, 1891, 256-7. Buchanan, *Mysore*, i. 123, 248. The Vedan are described (*Madras Census Report*, 1902, i. 183) as numbering 25,519, 'a Tamil-speaking labouring and hunting caste, the members of which were formerly soldiers and subsequently dacoits. The name means "a hunter", and is loosely applied to the Irulas in some places. There is some connection between the Vedans and the Tamil Vettuvans, but its precise nature is not clear. Marriage is either infant or adult. Widows may marry their late husband's brother or his agnates. Some employ Brahmans as priests. They either burn or bury their dead. They claim descent from Kannappa Nayanar, one of the 63 Saivite saints. Their title is Nayakkan' (*Census Report*, 1891, para. 538; *Madura Manual*, Part ii. 63; *North Arcot Manual*, i. 234; Mateer, *Native Life in Travancore*, 60).

Thurston (*Castes and Tribes of Southern India*, i. 180 ff.) gives an account of the Bedar, occupying 29 pages. He gives Boya as the equivalent of Bedar, and says that Wilks mentions them as soldiers of repute in the eighteenth century. There are two divisions of Boyas—Pedda, 'big', and Chinna, 'small',—and by another account there are four endogamous sections. They have long myths of origin. They are the chief beaters at the annual pig hunt on Telugu New Year's Day. In Mysore their chief deity is Tirupati Venkatamanaswami. They have a number of exogamous septs, obviously totemistic. Marriage is done by a Brahman who makes the pair stand on the lower half of a grinding-mill—a form of fertility magic. Divorce is allowed. The Uru Bedas bury their dead: but in Mysore they are said to cremate the corpse. Spirits of men who die unmarried become dangerous spirits, known as Virika or 'heros', which give trouble if neglected.

The Vedan of Coimbatore (*ibid.* vii. 331-5) are described as 'a very degraded, poor tribe, living by basket-making, snaring small game, and so on. The delight of a party at the gift of a rupee is something curious.' The hill Vedans of Travancore 'live in wretched huts amid the rice-flats at the foot of the hills, and are employed by farmers to guard the crops from the ravages of wild beasts. The upper incisor teeth of both men and women are filed to a sharp point, like crocodiles' fangs.' The Mala Vedans apparently possess no temples or shrines, but Hindus permit them to offer money at the Hindu shrines from a distance, in times of sudden sickness or during other seasons of panic. Their god Chattan, or Sattan, has no fixed abode, but, where the Mala Vedans are, there he is in the midst of them. They kindle fire by the friction of wood, and eat the black monkey. Their implements are bill-hooks, bows and arrows. They weave grass baskets, which are slung to their girdles, and contain betel, etc. When their wives menstruate, they are secluded, and their husbands have a feast on the ninth day. Until the evening the husband dares to eat nothing but roots, for fear of being killed by the devil.

According to the *Mysore Census Report*, 1901, i. 514, the Beda are identical with the Tamil Boya. They are also called Nayaka or Nayakamakkalu. They provided most of Hyder Ali's celebrated peons. They now cultivate and serve as Government peons. The eldest daughter of a family in which there are no sons is made a Basavi or prostitute. They eat fowls, sheep, goats, hogs, deer, fish, and drink spirituous liquors. They can have as many wives as they please, but can divorce them only for adultery. Widows are allowed to remarry, though they are permitted to live as concubines of another Beda. They bury their dead. They claim descent from Valmiki Muni, the author of the *Ramayana*.

The Machi or Myasa Bedas have a curious mixture of customs. They do not eat pork, but use beef, and they are the only Hindu tribe which circumcise their boys at the age of 10 or 12. They practice also Brahmanical rites, such as the *pancha gavyam* (the use of the five products of the cow), the burning of the tongue with a *nim* or margosa stick. Women in childbed and menstruation are isolated. They are said to avoid liquor of every kind, and eat the flesh of only two kinds of birds—the *gauja* (grey partridge) and *lavga* (rock-bush quail). They cremate their dead, and next day scatter the ashes on five tangadi trees (*Cassia auriculata*). Their aversion to any kind of drink is so great that they never use date branches for building purposes, and do not even touch them.

CHAPTER XIII

1853–57

ALTHOUGH suffering from a severe attack of acute rheumatism, I, with my assistant, Lieut. Cadell, pressed on to Sholapur, where it was necessary that I should meet the Collector, who congratulated me very heartily on my appointment to the district, which joined his own, and we could work together with good accord, and looked forward to much pleasant intercourse from time to time.

My assistant had no knowledge whatever, or experience, in civil affairs ; but I thought it best to place him at once in a prominent position, and to give him general directions which, as he was very clever and willing, I thought would suffice. I therefore made over to him part of the small establishment I had collected, and directed him to take possession of all the ceded districts which lay along the left bank of the Sina river, between it and the range of hills that formed the Balaghat[1] or upper portion of the whole province ; and with an escort of cavalry he set out to do what he could.

Fortunately the cession had been made at the close of the financial year, so there was no confusion of demand and account between the outgoing administration and the incoming one. I did not anticipate any opposition ; but the British forces at Sholapur and Ahmednagar had been warned to hold themselves ready to assist me in case any resistance might be made.

[1] The *Imperial Gazetteer* defines this as a range of hills in the western half of Hyderabad State, with a length of some two hundred miles east and west and a width of from three to six miles. The name is *Bala*, above, and *ghat*, a mountain pass. 'The country formed by the range and its two spurs forms a plateau, known locally as the Balaghat.' See map. This was Tara's native land—'a ballad of the Balaghat'.

Naldrug[1] had been fixed upon as my headquarters, and I proceeded there without delay. I found a squadron of the Contingent cavalry encamped without the fort, which was in the possession of a large body of Arabs, who refused to allow the cavalry to enter, and whose temper appeared very doubtful.

At first, too, I was refused admittance. Their chief declared that he held a large mortgage on the fort and its dependencies, and that his men were in arrears of pay, and that until all his demands were settled, or I gave him a guarantee from the British Government that they would be settled, he would not give me up the fort. I, however, took no notice of his demands whatever. I told him the Nizam's Government was the only one with which he could have dealings, and that if he and his men did not at once march out, I had no resource but to summon the military force at Sholapur, when I could not answer for the consequences. All the Arabs blustered a great deal, but finally retired inside to consider matters ; and a message was brought to me in the evening, to the effect that in the morning the fort would be given up. And so it was ; and as soon as they had bivouacked outside on the esplanade, I marched in at the head of my splendid cavalry escort, hoisted the English flag I had with me, and took possession forthwith. I should have regretted exceedingly if the obstinacy of these Arabs had brought

[1] Any glory which it once had has passed from Naldrug. The name of the district has gone to Osmanabad (Dharaseo); while the former Naldrug taluk has been amalgamated with Tuljapur taluk. Naldrug is now but a village of 4,000 inhabitants. One can watch the leadership passing in the account of Meadows Taylor, who, though personally well and happy there, records it as so unhealthy as to be unfitted for a headquarters station. Soon after his day the headquarters were removed to Dharaseo, as mentioned in the note on that place.

There is a long account of Naldrug, with its river and lake, in *Tara*, chapter lii. Also in *A Noble Queen*: 'It was, indeed, very beautiful: the lake shimmering in the sun, with the black precipices, hung with many-hued creepers, reflected into it; while, after it had shot through the arch on the dam, the river brawled down the valley till it was hid from view by the projection of the hills below. The air was cool and refreshing, for they had risen to a considerable height above Sholapoor.'

The *Imperial Gazetteer* says: 'The fort of Naldrug is situated above the ravine of the Bori river, and is one of the best-fortified and most picturesque places in the Deccan.'

about any collision, for their example was looked to by all the various parties of Arabs in the province ; and had they resisted my authority, all the rest would have done so too, and the Arab chiefs of Hyderabad were almost in possession of the whole tract.

They held it in assignment for their pay and debts ; and it was a convenient district for them, as fresh men could constantly reach them from Bombay and the coast without attracting observation, and be forwarded to Hyderabad to reinforce the main body. Also many private individuals living at Hyderabad possessed estates and villages in the province, and had mortgaged them to the Arabs—so that, in point of fact, the whole area was under their control, with very little exception ; and the tenacity with which they stuck to their possessions, whether for arrears of pay or any other monetary consideration, had been too often experienced to be doubted now. The Arabs in my fort of Naldrug could not have held it against any force, as the guns were useless ; but had they continued their opposition, our occupation of the country would have assumed a very different aspect, and might have caused a disturbance and collision with the Arabs at Hyderabad—a consequence which would have had, in all likelihood, serious results.

Although I had often before been at Naldrug, I had never seen the interior of the fort, nor the English house belonging to it, which had been built by the late Nawab, who in old times had been a great friend of mine. The ladies of his family had used it, and now it was to become my residence. I found it a handsome building, although not very commodious. In the centre was a large hall, with two semicircular rooms on each side ; above the hall, a bedroom of corresponding size, with bath-room attached, from which there was a beautiful view all over the fort, the town, and the adjacent country. In front there was a broad veranda, supported upon pillars, and near at hand the portion set apart for the zenana, and which was still occupied by the ladies, who were to leave shortly. In the fort itself were several massive buildings, terraced and bomb-proof, which had been used in former days as barracks, hospital, powder-magazine, and guard-houses. There were also some other good native houses—all empty now, but useful for my English clerks and escort, and for conversion into treasury, jail, and public *kacheri,* or court, until more commodious buildings could be erected, or possibly another head station fixed upon.

The fort of Naldrug was one of the most interesting places I had ever seen. It enclosed the surface of a knoll or plateau of basalt rock, which jutted out into the valley or ravine of the small river Bori from the main plateau of the country, and was almost level. The sides of this knoll were sheer precipices of basalt, here and there showing distinct columnar and prismatic formation, and varied from 50 to 200 feet in height ; the edge of the plateau being more or less 200 feet above the river, which flowed at the base of the precipice on two sides of the fort. Along the crest of the cliff, on three sides, ran the fortifications, bastions, and curtains alternately, some of the former being very firmly built of cut and dressed basalt, and large enough to carry heavy guns, and the parapets of the machicolated curtains were everywhere loopholed for musketry. On the west side the promontory joined the main plateau by a somewhat contracted neck, also strongly fortified by a high rampart, with very roomy and massive bastions; below it a *faussebraye,* with the same ; then a broad, deep, dry ditch, cut for the most part out of the basalt itself ; a counterscarp, about 20 or 25 feet high, with a covered-way ; and beyond it, a glacis and esplanade up to the limits of the town.

The entire circumference of the *enceinte* might have been about a mile and a half, and the garrison in former times must have been very large, for nearly the whole of the interior was covered by ruined walls, and had been laid out as a town with a wide street running up the centre. All the walls and bastions were in perfect repair, and the effect of the fort outside was not only grim and massive, but essentially picturesque.

Naldrug held a memorable place in local history. Before the Musalman invasion in the fourteenth century, it belonged to a local Raja, who may have been a feudal vassal of the great Rajas of the Chalukya dynasty, A.D. 250 to 1200, whose capital was Kalyani, about 40 miles distant ; but I never could trace its history with any certainty, and during the Hindu period it was only traditional. The Bahmani dynasty,

A.D. 1351 to 1480,[1] protected their dominions to the west by a line of massive forts, of which Naldrug was one; and it was believed that the former defences, which were little more than mud walls, were replaced by them with fortifications of stone. Afterwards, on the division of the Bahmani kingdom, in A.D. 1480, Naldrug fell to the lot of the Adil Shahi kings of Bijapur; and they, in their turn, greatly increased and strengthened its defences. It was often a point of dissension between the Adil Shahi and the Nizam Shahi potentates—lying, as it did, upon the nominal frontier between Bijapur and Ahmednagar—and was besieged by both in turn, as the condition of the walls on the southern face bore ample testimony, as well from the marks of cannon-balls as from breaches which had afterwards been filled up. In 1558 Ali Adil Shah[2] visited Naldrug, and again added to its fortifications, rebuilt the western face, and constructed an enormous cavalier near the eastern end, which was upwards of 90 feet high, with several bastions on the edges of the cliff; but his greatest work was the erection of a stone dam across the river Bori, which by retaining the water above it afforded the garrison an unlimited supply. I quote from a letter to my father, written a few days after my arrival:—

'I was greatly delighted and surprised by the view from the back of the house, where there is a balcony. You look up and down a valley, in which there is a fine brawling stream; and about a quarter of a mile below the house a huge dam of solid masonry has been built across the ravine, which holds the water back, and forms a pretty little lake. Above this, on the south side, the walls of the fort are built on the side of a precipice of about 50 feet to the water's edge, and the tall grim bastions have a fine effect. The dam connects the main fort with one opposite to it on a knoll on the north of the lake, whose bastions and curtains extend down the north

---

[1] In his *History*, p. 183, Taylor says correctly of the Bahmani dynasty: 'It had reigned, for the most part, in great glory and power, from 1347 to 1526, or 179 years.' But as a power the dynasty ended in 1482.

[2] This monarch reigned in Bijapur from 1557 to 1579. Taylor's *History* mentions the visit to Naldrug. The account of the reign covers some pages, since it included the momentous battle of Talikot, 1565. Chand Bibi, the widow of Ali Adil Shah, is the heroine of *A Noble Queen.*

side of the ravine; so on looking down you see the two forts, one on each side of the valley, the lake between, and the precipices beyond. The dam is truly wonderful—it is 90 feet high, 300 yards long, and 100 feet broad at the top. The river at its ordinary height runs over the crest of the dam in channels arched over, and the water falls into the pool; but when there is a flood, the whole of the water runs over the crest of the dam, forming a huge cataract, and is indeed a magnificent spectacle. About the centre of the dam there is a flight of steps by which you descend into a small, beautifully-ornamented room, in the Saracenic-Gothic style; and there is a very ingenious contrivance by which, even when the river is in full flood and the cataract falling in front of the balcony of the room, the water which comes down the staircase is turned off down a tunnel in another direction, and cannot enter the room. The look-out from this apartment is extremely picturesque—the great pool below, the sides of the ravine clothed with shrubs and creepers, and the brawling waters as they run down the valley, forming altogether a striking and very beautiful picture, of a character I had never before seen.'

It may easily be imagined that I was quite content with my new quarters; and in a few days' time, when all the rooms had been well washed out, and the broken panes in the excellent English glass doors and windows repaired, my pictures hung up, my precious books unpacked, and some furniture and carpets I had brought with me placed in the large room, the result was a very comfortable apartment. There was, too, a good garden about the house, which was very soon cleaned up, and eventually became one of my greatest pleasures—for nowhere that I had been in India did English flowers and vegetables grow so well; and there were several fine orange-trees and vines too, which, when properly looked after, gave abundant produce, as did the other fruit-trees, with which the garden was well stocked.

My first task was to take stock of my new province. Its boundaries had been ill defined at Hyderabad, and had to be rectified before the whole could be brought well together. To the west, the river Sina, from a point nine miles from Ahmednagar to its junction with the Bhima, formed an excellent general line. Inside this lay portions of British territory belonging to the Collectorate of Sholapur; but that did not signify. To the north a range of mountains, which bordered the valley of the Godavery, formed another distinct frontier. The river Manjra, which flowed eastwards, rising among these mountains, gave another distinctly-defined boundary to a certain point, where it diverged; and from this point to Afzulpur on the Bhima, an arbitrary line had been drawn, which, as it included several large counties that were private estates belonging to one of the chief nobles of Hyderabad, could not be attached. Within the general boundary too, many portions had either been wilfully concealed or improperly and dishonestly retained. However, the whole province, as defined in the treaty, would have been more than was really required; and in the end, after I had gone over the whole carefully, my boundaries became more definite, and it was satisfactory to think that all the country lying within them was under my own control.

As fast as I could get them, I despatched managers to the different head-centres of counties with my orders, and to convey my assurances of goodwill to the people. The Arabs were fast betaking themselves to Hyderabad, and neither my assistant nor I had experienced any except very temporary difficulties from them. In almost less than one month I was able to report that we had established the authority of the British Government of India in every part of the province. My assistant's father, Mr. Cadell, was an eminent Writer to the Signet in Edinburgh; and I was much amused when he wrote to his son that the proceedings of two men, with a small escort of cavalry, taking possession coolly of a province half as large as Scotland, with a strange population, were, to his perception, the 'most consummate piece of assurance' he had ever heard of; and 'pray, how were we going to govern it?' Our district was rather more than 15,000 square miles in area; but though the shrewd old Scotch lawyer saw, I daresay, a thousand difficulties, I saw none which could not be overcome by patience, hard work, and steady perseverance.

It was a fine climate, fortunately, and very healthy. The tract lying between the Sina river and the hills was lower than the rest; but it was open, free from jungle, and for the most part well cultivated. From it the basalt plateau named the Balaghat rose to a height varying from 400 to 1,000 feet, some of the highest summits showing 2,400 feet above the level of the sea. This plateau, culturable from its very edge, sloped gradually eastwards to the Manjra river, and joined the northern mountain boundary, which extended to Ahmednagar.

Naldrug itself lay 2,200 feet above the level of the sea; and, compared with Shorapur, the climate, even during the hottest part of the year, was much less trying, while in the cold season it was very cold indeed, and not unfrequently frosty.

The Balaghat was renowned all through the Deccan for its luxuriant crops of wheat and barley, pulse and oil-seed. Cotton did not thrive, and what was produced was of very short fibre, harsh and unfit for export. Sugar-cane grew well, and there was a good supply of hemp and linseed; but the beautiful white millet of Shorapur was wanting, and that grown was coarse and hard in comparison.

I had known the people before, when I was a boy, and many still remembered me and my red trousers, and came to see me. The population was almost entirely agricultural—thrifty, industrious, practical farmers and gentry, who tilled their somewhat hard soil with singular perseverance and success; they were better farmers than those at Shorapur, and kept improving their fields till they would have done credit to an English landowner.

I had liked the people in my early days because of their sturdy, independent character. Marathi was the only language spoken,[1] and this I had at my command—a circumstance which, I felt sure, would inspire confidence, for everybody soon knew that they could come to me and speak out their minds freely whenever they had occasion, without any go-between, or interpretation, being necessary. I knew, too, that the normal crime of the district, *dacoity*, not only still existed, but was largely and desperately practised—and this, which had defied me in former years, must now be eradicated with a strong hand.

[1] 'Changed to the sweet Mahratta vernacular, that all could understand' (*Tara*, chapter xlviii.).

I believe that the people at large, with the exception of the small portion forming the hereditary criminal class, welcomed the new rule with sincere delight. They knew it meant security of their land and possessions, as well as justice and protection, and extension and protection of trade. Those who were unacquainted with the working and ways of English rule in other districts were, perhaps, somewhat disturbed at first at the idea, but they were few, and the feeling soon wore off.

When I took possession of the province, there was no court of law or justice whatever, civil or criminal, any more than there had been at Shorapur, and none such had ever existed within the memory of any person. The agents of the Nizam's Government, and the Arabs, used to punish gross criminal offences, and, in some cases, petty thefts; but in the great crime of *dacoity* all seemed to have had a share, inasmuch as the agent always received part, according to his share, of the property stolen! As for murder, no one ever noticed it, or thought of bringing the perpetrators to account.

After a great deal of very hard work—during almost night and day while it lasted—I had gained, partly from old accounts and partly from the details sent in from my new managers, a tolerably correct estimate of the resources of the province, which I submitted in a report to the Resident.

If I had taken the province according to the estimates and orders of transfer of the late Minister and the *daftardars* of Hyderabad, I should have had a revenue of about *two and a half lakhs*, and a few scattered portions of territory, and there would have remained within my boundary-line large tracts of country not under my jurisdiction. This would have caused much confusion and vexatious embarrassment, and probably constant disputes would have arisen. Now, when I had got all together in a kind of ring-fence, as it were, I found, according to my rough estimate, that I should have about *eleven and a half lakhs* of Hyderabad rupees.

Colonel Low was just going away to Calcutta to be sworn in as a member of the Supreme Council; and before he went, he wrote me his very hearty approval of what I had been able to effect in so short a time, and particularly his great satisfaction at the complete and bloodless expulsion of the Arabs.

I must here, likewise, record my grateful thanks and remembrance of the very essential services rendered to me in respect to the latter by the native officers and men of the cavalry detachments sent for my assistance. The native officers were all gentlemen by birth, most intelligent, and highly respected by the people wherever they went. They proved excellent negotiators, and were fully trusted by all, even by the Arabs themselves.

At Ausa, a far stronger fort than Naldrug, my manager presented my letter to the Arab chief commanding the garrison, requesting him to evacuate the place. The request was indignantly refused; but on the appearance of a squadron of cavalry which I sent to my officer's assistance, the Arabs received the native officers with 'honours', marched out at once, and gave up all the large dependencies they had held in mortgage from the Nizam's Government without any demur. Ausa was the last, indeed the only place, that caused me any anxiety; and I knew that the Resident had also been very anxious about it, owing to its reputed great strength and the large number of its garrison. In Ausa, Parenda, and Naldrug, I now held the three strongest forts of the Deccan;[1] yet all had submitted without using any violence, and no further display of force than I have mentioned.

So ended my preliminary operations in my new province; and I was about to leave Naldrug, in order to start on a tour through the district, when I received a note from the Collector at Sholapur asking me to come to him and arrange many matters pending between us. The prospect of a little holiday and society was very pleasant, and I went. His wife was an excellent musician—both sang delightfully; and it was a great treat to me to hear once more the music of great composers skilfully executed, and to try my own voice in concerted pieces—a pleasure to which I had for so long been a stranger.

[1] This is a doubtful statement. Yet Taylor had a reasoned admiration for these forts. In his *History* he writes that the fortresses of the Bahmani kings 'far exceed any of the same period in Europe. They are of all kinds, both on the plains and on the crests of mountains, from baronial castles to forts of the grandest dimensions'. Out of not less than fourteen of these enumerated by him as remarkable and beautiful, Parenda and Ausa, he says, 'are the most perfect, according to military science'.

They were very kind and very patient with me; but I fear I gave the ladies some trouble, I had grown so rusty.

Owing to my very unsettled life latterly, my letters to *The Times* had become irregular, and I could not keep up the necessary communications for news which were required for fortnightly letters.

There were no posts through my district; and letters and newspapers would, of necessity, reach me very irregularly, while the same objection applied to my despatch of letters. I reflected, also, that whereas hitherto my position at Shorapur had left me comparatively independent, I was not so in my new appointment, and that I was not justified in writing so unrestrainedly on political subjects as I had been used to do. I therefore resigned my office of 'special correspondent' to the great paper, which, from first to last, had uniformly treated my opinions and contributions with the greatest courtesy.

I could not, either, agree with the now confirmed annexation policy of Lord Dalhousie, which began in 1853, and seemed likely to be continued; and I knew that among the people generally the annexations of Jhansi and Nagpur, and the transactions in regard to the latter especially, were spoken of with unmeasured mistrust and suspicion. The proceedings [1]

[1] The continued proceedings of this Inam commission were among the causes of popular discontent alleged in the Marathi warning sent to Lord Elphinstone early in 1857. At the end of his special Mutiny letters, included in the present chapter, Taylor guards himself against being thought to be 'against the annexation policy of Lord Dalhousie'. Yet his intellectual allegiance to the great Governor-General was sorely shaken by some of the doings of the year when he gave up his connection with *The Times* rather than defend or attack them. In his *History* is a short chapter on Nagpur and Jhansi, beginning: 'Of all the period of Lord Dalhousie's administration, the year 1853–1854 most abounds with remarkable occurrences.' As he says, Jhansi was small. But the extinction of so noble a kingdom as Nagpur, or Berar, could not take place in silence. Taylor gives its area as 76,500 square miles—which approaches the present size of the Nizam's Dominions. But its population was then less than five millions, and it is still scanty.

This, Gondwana or the land of the Gonds, though a good country, was one of the empty spaces of India, without archaeology or antiquity, with no history that can go back three centuries. Until 1853 the Nagpur Raj had run on pretty well through more than two decades upon the impulse given it by Sir Richard Jenkins (see earlier note). At the end

in the Bombay Presidency in regard to the inquiry into free lands, charitable grants, and the like, had been, or were being, badly conducted, and had excited much discontent. My very outspoken Marathas took no pains to conceal their censure of the conduct of Government as evincing a spirit of greed and bad faith which was strange and painful to many of them, and in these views people and gentry alike coincided.

During my period of connection with *The Times*, however, I had enjoyed the privilege of discussing and explaining, as far as possible, all the great subjects which pertained to the period : education and its results on the people—for vernacular education had long since become a declared policy—trade, railways and communications of all kinds, cotton cultivation, irrigation in all its forms, along with the general political events of the previous ten years, momentous as they had been. I do not know whether these humble efforts of mine had any effect in bringing India and its people, its interests, and its increase of civilisation, more directly under the notice of thinking people in England. I hope so ; and I was vain enough to think they might have some such effect, as they were generally backed up by leading articles in the paper itself, and thus attained some importance.

Now, there were other correspondents in the field,[1] newspaper articles were better written, and their number had increased largely, so that the exponents of India's condition and wants were manifold, and there was no use in my continuing to send communications which must necessarily be unconnected and desultory. My correspondence all these years with my faithful friend Reeve never slackened, and his

---

of November the Maratha Raja died heirless; and in December Nagpur was annexed. 'The State of Nagpur,' Dalhousie proclaimed, 'conferred on the rajah and his heirs in 1818 by the British Government, has reverted to it on the death of the rajah without any heir.'

Taylor's discussion of the question shows how his conscience was hurt. If the annexation was unpopular and alarming, the mode in which it was carried out, he says, was worse. W. W. Hunter and Talboys Wheeler tell the story in their *Histories*. The latter says that the people spoke of 'Dunkin Sahib' (Jenkins) with affection, while 'all the middle and lower classes were heartily desirous of British rule'.

[1] One of these was to be Sir Joseph Archer Crowe, the later diplomat and historian of art, 1825–1896, who was in Bombay for two years from 1857, and *Times* correspondent during the Mutiny.

letters were a great source of pleasure and encouragement to me in my work, and kept me informed of what was going on in the political and literary circles in London, so that I did not feel quite so much my exclusion from them.

On my return from my pleasant little stay at Sholapur, I went out to my tents, which were pitched at Tuljapur, my old favourite resort in 1825. How beautiful it was! The hills were all clothed with verdure, and the view from my tent was lovely. On the north side of the promontory where I was, lay the town, built on both sides of a deep ravine, and at its head the celebrated shrine of Bhowani or Kali, which lay in the hollow beneath—not indeed, in itself, a remarkable edifice at all, but surrounded by picturesque cloisters and courts, always thronged by pilgrims, and which formed a curious combination of all kinds of Hindu architecture.

Above the temple towered rugged cliffs on either side, and the ravine opened out into a large amphitheatre, bounded by precipitous hills, that seemed like buttresses to the plateau above. To the south was a great undulating plain, stretching to the dim blue horizon, dotted by thriving villages, surrounded by luxuriant cultivation, and checkered by ever-varying masses of light and shade. The line of the hills and plateau extending towards the east or Naldrug direction, was broken by headlands and ravines descending to the lower country. There was no wood, it is true; but the diversified outlines, now rugged, and again more regular, redeemed the landscape from any monotony.

The climate was delightful, like that of an English summer day, in turn cloudy and sunshiny, with occasional light showers. On the day of my arrival, I had just breakfasted, and sat down to begin work in my *kacheri*, or office tent, when an old Brahmin came in, and for a time sat down quietly in a corner without speaking. Seeing that I was alone, he came up to my table, and peering closely into my face as he leant upon his staff, he said, 'Are you the Taylor Sahib who came here many years ago?'

When I answered that I was the same, he produced a bundle of old papers, and asked me whether I recollected them. As I looked over them, I saw that I had put my initials to each of them, but forgot at the moment why I had done so; for in any case of inquiry or settlement it was my habit to initial all the papers, and I thought these documents must relate to some old claim or suit to be revised. I was soon undeceived.

'Have you forgotten, sahib,' said the old man, 'that I once cast your horoscope, and told you that you would return here to govern us after many years ? And see ! it was true !—you have come ; and, indeed, there is little difference in the time I recorded—twenty-five years ! I had not the exact data, if you remember, that I wanted—you could not give it to me.'

It was all true enough ; there I was, the 'ruler' over them, and I then recollected how strange it had appeared to me at the Residency when my destination was so suddenly altered from Berar to these western districts, on the requisition of the Government of Bombay. The prediction had certainly been a strange one, and was as strangely fulfilled, even to the very letter of time.

'And you have been a "raja", too,' continued my old friend, 'and have governed a country to the south for ten years ; that I recorded—see, sahib !' and he pointed excitedly to the document. 'See, there is no mistake there either !'

'Not quite a "raja",' I said, laughing, 'only manager of the country while the raja was a child.'

'It was all the same,' returned the old Brahmin ; 'you were all-powerful, and just like a raja, and you governed the people. And you have seen sorrow too, sahib ; you were not married when you were here, and now you have lost wife and dear children, I hear ? I wrote that. I saw it all plainly—it is here. And you are not rich, they tell me ? Yet lakhs of rupees have passed through your hands. Did I not tell you that too ?'

'No, indeed,' I replied, 'I am not rich ; indeed much the reverse, and I have had heavy sorrows.'

'It could not be avoided,' he said ; 'no one could have mistaken what I discovered just twenty-five years ago. You were born for work, not for the indulgence of wealthy idleness, and so you will continue. If you want these papers I will give them to you ; if not, let them remain with me,' and so saying, he took his leave. He soon afterwards went on a pilgrimage to Nassik, and there died.

I did not want the papers, and he kept them. I cannot account for his prediction. I only relate what happened. I told my old Serishtadar, Baba Sahib, about my horoscope and its results ; but he was not in the least surprised.

'We Brahmins', he said, 'believe in astrology, and you English laugh at it ; but when one who understands the art casts a horoscope and calculates it scientifically, the result is seldom wrong. You were to have gone to Berar, and yet your fate has brought you here to Tuljapur again, at the very time appointed, twenty-five years after, in spite of yourself and also of the Resident. Can you doubt, after this ? Is there not more in astrology than you believed ?'

I made no comment. How could I, in the face of the simple facts that had occurred ?

It was the rainy season, but there was so much to see after that could only be done on the spot in each division of my district, that my personal convenience must not be studied in any way ; and I marched along the edge of the plateau from one division to another, halting at the head station of each for the purpose of investigating old accounts, records of cultivation and the like, and, above all, gaining, as I went, knowledge of the people.

A settlement of the country for five years had been directed, and inquiries were necessary before any attempt could be made to carry out the measure. I did not even know what the revenue of the whole district might amount to ; and the accounts received from Hyderabad, if not actually designed to mislead, were at all events most incorrect and incomprehensible, proving to be of no use whatever. I therefore began at the foundation—the village accounts—and was glad to see that they had been far better kept than those of Shorapur, when I began a like inquiry there. The village accountant had proper lists of proprietors and occupants of land, according to the ancient Deccan system, which had never been altered, however much it might have been abused ; and among the records of some of the chief towns and villages, were ancient settlements of the officers of the Bahmani kings of Gulbarga and Bidar, and the Adil Shahis of Bijapur. The most regular and valuable records were the settlements by Malik Ambar, the great regent of the Ahmednagar State, which were more minute than those of the Emperor Akbar, and were founded upon an actual survey of the lands and their assessment, according to their productive quality. But these had only been preserved here and there, and it would be impossible to found any new settlement upon those that existed as a basis for all. The Nizam's Government had taken no record of cultivation; but the sums received from villages were entered in an account for every *taluk*, or division, which was signed by the hereditary ministerial officers of each county, and which, up to the last financial year, had been regularly sent up to the head accountant's office at Hyderabad. From these documents, compared with the village accounts and registries, I could see my way to a new form of account which would embrace all particulars ; and copies of these forms were made by the village accountants, to be filled up when the yearly period of settlement arrived.

It was very tedious work; but unless it were done, it would be impossible to submit to Government any clear or complete statement of the general revenue, or whence it was derived. My progress was necessarily very slow.

In the original instructions given to the Deputy-Commissioners, they had been directed to make use of the existing local courts of the Nizam's Government for the trial of all cases, civil and criminal; but as no local tribunal or judicial office of any kind was found by me, and none had existed for years, I determined to introduce a code of laws of my own, civil as well as criminal ; and I took the regulations of Bombay as my guide, drawing up a short definition of crimes and their punishments—and in civil cases, of general procedure,—simple and intelligible to all classes. I assigned various powers to *patels*, or heads of villages, to *taluk* officers, to my assistant, and to myself—mine being the highest court of appeal in the province from the decisions of subordinate courts, and the Resident being the final one to whom all appeals against me were to be referred.

This code and general plan of mine were approved of as a temporary measure at Calcutta, and I put it in force as soon as it was sanctioned. It lasted till Macaulay's penal code was sent for a practical trial in the assigned districts, but the civil procedure I had drawn up was, I think, retained. These, with instructions for the guidance of police, revenue proceedings and collections, and for the conduct of every department, occupied a great deal of my time ; but all were as brief and concise as possible, though necessarily embracing every point for general direction.

After Colonel Low's departure from the post of Resident at Hyderabad, several distinguished officers were named as his probable successors. Sir Henry Lawrence, to whom I believe Lord Dalhousie offered the appointment, and my old friend James Outram, whom I would have gladly welcomed, were among those talked of ; but as the office of Resident now involved the head administration of the assigned districts, and as everything in regard to them was still in an incomplete state, a civilian of administrative experience was held to be the fittest person ; and Mr. Bushby, once an assistant to the Resident at Hyderabad, was appointed to the office, which, until his arrival, was conducted with much ability by (then) Captain Davidson.[1]

It was his wish, as it had been that of Colonel Low, that my district should have a well-defined frontier; and all the boundaries, except those to the north, had been gradually adjusted. I had even been exempted from the vexatious task of administering justice and police affairs in the reserved portions which lay along the Bhima to the south-west, and they remained under the charge of their native proprietors. But to the north, on the borders of the Ahmednagar and Nizam's territory, there remained a small tract, hitherto undefined, and often much disturbed, the British and Nizam's villages lying confusedly together.

This was by far the prettiest and most picturesque portion of my province. The plateau of the Balaghat continued to the hills forming the Ahmednagar range ; but at one point it lowered considerably, breaking into ravines, which ran south

[1] Cuthbert Davidson, 1810–1862, who runs through the *Life of James Stuart Fraser*, and whose niece Hastings Fraser married. He was first assistant at Hyderabad under Generals Fraser and Low, Resident at Baroda for three years, and finally Resident at Hyderabad from 1857 to his untimely death in August 1862. 'Distinguished for his courage, composure and resolution,' says Buckland. What Taylor has to tell of Colonel Davidson shows him as one of those who held steadiest in the evil days.

towards the Sina, and north-east to the Godavery, a very rough tract, with a corresponding rough class of inhabitants, who required to be kept well under control.

While encamped at Patoda,[1] the station of my native collector, I explored the whole of the crest of the plateau towards the north-west, and found the scenery very beautiful. There was no jungle, but the grassy hills afforded fine pasturage for cattle, and the views from the summits of the highest knolls were, in some instances, very grand.

In one place a small river, the Incherna, which received the drainage of a great portion of these hills, fell into the lower level of the western portion of my district with one leap of 398 feet, sheer perpendicular fall, and now, being well filled with water, formed one of the most graceful waterfalls I have ever seen. I did not expect to come upon anything so grand or picturesque as this fall and the basalt chasm into which it precipitated itself, and I was lost in admiration, remaining at the place for several days, in order to sketch the ravine and waterfall from every point of view. I have described it fully in my novel of *Seeta*, to which I refer any curious reader who may wish to know more.[2]

[1] A village of 3,000 inhabitants, headquarters of a 'crown' taluk in the south-west of Bhir District. The Manjra river rises in the hills to the west. 'The taluk is situated on a fertile plateau, and is hilly toward the north and west.' The *Imperial Gazetteer* article on Bhir District says: 'The climate is generally healthy and temperate. Patoda, on the Balaghat, is the highest part and is cool even in the hot season.'

[2] The opening paragraph of *Seeta* describes a waterfall somewhat like this. But the reference must be to chapter xxvii., 'The Gao Mookh,' or Cow's Mouth. It is placed seven or eight miles from Nurpur, which in some respects is Nagpur.

'Before them lay a deep valley, the sides of which were sheer precipices of basalt, some four hundred feet in height, which showed the richest colours, from black to brown, yellow and red. . . . At the upper end of this amphitheatre, which was of no very great width, a portion of it narrowed sharply, and out of it spouted a jet of water of considerable volume, which fell clear of the precipice in a cloud of fine spray, wafted here and there by the wind, and showing portions of brilliant rainbows as the bright sun caught its changes. At the foot of the fall was a deep, dark pool, fringed with graceful bamboos and reeds, which continued down the glen and up the sides where there was no rock. A dull roar from the fall came up to them now and then, mingling with the murmur of the river above and below as it chafed in its rocky bed.'

'It's a strange place', says Brandon, 'and I think most lovely.

I deseended by a well-known pass to the low eountry north of my distriet, and found, as I had anticipated from a copy of the trigonometrieal survey map, exactly the frontier I desired. A considcrable stream flowed from the west, almost in a direct line eastwards. Its name was the Suitana; while a smaller one, the Domeri, rising on the plateau, flowed due north, aud fell into it. Within this line were sixteen scattered villages of the Nizam's mingled with British villages and my own; and after representing the diffieulty of maintaining all three jurisdietions in a state of amity, they were transferred entirely to me, under the orders of the Nizam's Government. The whole tract had been in a state of chronie feud for years, and the correspondence and other references, regarding all manner of disputes, had been vexatious and endless. I found no less than *seventy* boundary disputes had to be adjusted, of which I settled the worst, leaving the traet for the final supervision of my assistant, who now joined me. I determined to proceed to Ahmednagar, in order to confer with Mr. Bcll, the Collector there, as I had already done with Mr. Loughman, the Collector of Sholapur, upon all matters which required settlement.

Cadell had had a littlc adventure at Parenda, by far the strongest fort in the distriet, situated in his division. He had not been able to visit it personally before, and when he arrived the garrison shut-to the gates, mounted the bastions, and deelared they would not give it up. He might do what he liked with the dependencies, but thcy were thc garrison, and they declared that until they reeeived orders from Hyderabad, they would not open the gates. Finding remonstranee useless, Cadell wrote to me for help, in the shape of a troop of cavalry, with whieh he eould watch the place to see that no

The rivcr is the Incherna . . . which rises in the hills about thirty miles off. You see there is comparatively very little water in it now, but it must be a magnificent fall in the monsoon. You can make out the white mark, high up, on both sides of the head of the water.' As another says, 'a great body of water would fall straight down, whereas, look at those beautiful swayings to and fro which it has now'. A further account, from a different point of view, speaks of 'the huge spout of water, blue as a sapphire. . . . All the rocks were vivid with colour, while flocks of wild blue pigeons and green parroquets wheeled hither and thither in the air.'

malcontents got in to help the garrison. I wrote to the *kiladar*, or castellan, desiring him to evacuate the fort, to which he demurred ; and I then wrote again, saying he *must* do so, or fight, for that no orders could come now from Hyderabad, the country having been entirely ceded to the British Government. The troop of cavalry arriving almost immediately after my letter reached him, the *kiladar* saw that I was in earnest, and thought 'discretion the better part of valour'; so he opened the gates, and as Cadell marched in and took possession, the garrison laid down their arms, which he at once returned to them. He described the place as the strongest he had seen, and quite perfect in every way, and there was a very respectable garrison of Rajputs. I was glad on every account that the affair had been tided over so peaceably. I visited Parenda myself afterwards, and shall describe it later.

Having made all the arrangements I could in the newly-acquired territory of Manur, I went on to Ahmednagar. One of my villages lay within nine miles of the station, and, owing to its beauty, was a favourite resort for country parties and picnics. I met Mr. Bell there, and he hospitably invited both Cadell and myself to his house, where we spent some days very pleasantly at the great station. I had not been there since the year 1826, and found it greatly improved and enlarged.

In my journey both to and from Ahmednagar, I had been much struck with the capabilities of the country for large irrigation works, and in particular for tanks. Streams, descending from the table-lands to the north, and tributaries to the Sina, afforded ample supplies of water ; and the ground, from its peculiar character, provided most convenient basins, which only required dams at certain places across their mouths to be converted into tanks.

In one instance a stream which had a catchment area of upwards of 200 square miles, after leaving the hills, ran through a nearly level plain of about four square miles in area, which ended in two bluffs about a quarter of a mile asunder. A dam of fifty feet high was perfectly practicable at a comparatively small outlay, and the water held back would form a lake twice the size of Bohnal. I determined, with as little delay as possible, to get up a report on the subject, and try to have some works of the kind begun for a country which was absolutely thirsting for water, and where every drop that could be procured from wells or from streams was used for the production of sugar-cane, ginger, turmeric, and other rich and valuable crops.

Mr. Bell met us at a village which we had agreed upon, where there was good camping-ground, and which, though under his charge, was within our frontier, and there we passed some days in November very agreeably. As he had brought his establishment with him, we compared our work, and he was not a little surprised, I think, to find mine quite as regular in all respects as his own, except in the revenue department, the particulars of which we had still to unravel, whereas his had been decided by survey. I was now settling three divisions in order to enable my assistant to work for himself; and when these were completed, I left him, to look after my eastern districts on the table-land, which I had not yet visited.

By the end of the year 1853 the whole was in fair working order, and giving me no anxiety, except as to the scarcity which seemed to threaten us owing to failure of crops. There had been no rain since September, and comparatively little before that. Portions of the Bombay Presidency were already suffering, and Shorapur was also in distress. The accounts from thence were very sad. Neglect, riot, and crime prevailed; and I was indeed grateful that, although I was worse paid as a Deputy-Commissioner than I should have been as Political Agent there, yet I was spared the pain of seeing all the fair structure I had striven so long and so hard to raise rapidly falling into ruin and decay.

All we Deputy-Commissioners had been placed on a salary of 1,200 rupees a-month, as a temporary rate of payment, and, as yet, we received no 'deputation' allowance, but were promised it, to provide for the expenses of tents and moving about our districts.

When the local officers were pensioned, we hoped that we, who had now become servants of the Company, might be granted our Nizam's pensions apart from our pay, as was at first arranged; but ultimately this was not allowed—both were included in the pay of a Deputy-Commissioner, a proceeding which I have always considered unjust, for we were not serving the Nizam but the Company ; and if the Government of India had set us aside and sent its own officers, it would have had to pay both charges out of the revenue of the cession. When we were transferred to the new service, our rank was recognised in all respects as those of 'Company's officers' of corresponding length of service ; but in this respect also were we painfully deceived—we were placed in the category of 'Uncovenanted servants', by which we lost all our former rank and privileges, and were reduced in status. One of our number laid down his rank, and would never resume it. However, hard as it was, we were grateful for employment at all, though I have never ceased to consider it an ungenerous act of the great Government of India, to take advantage, as it seemed, of our necessities, and to give us lower pay than it gave to its own servants in like employment, and in charge of far smaller districts and with less responsibilities than ours.

I will state the question clearly in figures. My pension from the Nizam's Government was 300 rupees a-month, or £360 a-year ; my pay 1,200 rupees a-month.

Had I received 1,200 rupees a-month and my pension as well, my receipts would have been 1,500 rupees a-month. Now I was to receive in all 1,200 rupees—that is, 900 rupees pay and 300 rupees pension ; so the 300 rupees were saved, which we considered taking rather a mean advantage of us. We were no more Nizam's servants, but had been taken over into the Company's service, and, as such, should have received salaries on the same scale as those already in their employ.

By the close of the year I had already made considerable progress in the suppression of the terrible normal crime of dacoity. Several old dacoits had turned approvers, and had given details of robberies and murders, which had been shockingly numerous. Through them stolen property was traced, and recovered too, to a very large amount ; and out of one dacoit's house at Ausa, articles of various kinds, to the value of 1,200 rupees, were taken, which had been his share of the plunder secured on that occasion. I was blamed at first by the Resident for raking up old cases ; but I held my ground, for those I had tried were all comparatively recent, though the crimes had been committed before the cession. I was determined to eradicate the pest if I could, and I thought the only chance lay in attacking the old gangs and in bringing their crimes home to them. This had been done in Thuggee, why not in Dacoity? The question was referred to Calcutta, and soon decided as regarded the assigned districts. All criminal offences, such as dacoity and murder, were deemed open to trial within a period of ten years from the date of their perpetration; and according to this rule I was at liberty to work, and I did so vigorously. Already I had achieved something, and more would follow.

By Lord Dalhousie's request I kept up my correspondence with Mr. Courtenay; I think his lordship liked to know unofficially what I was about, and I wrote free and unreservedly. A report I had sent in upon my system of administration had interested him a good deal, and I heard he took it away to study in private, and that he desired I might be told this. He had also entirely acquiesced in my plan of revenue settlement to precede a survey; and to hear that what I had done was approved of, was very cheering.

I found the eastern portion of my district in a far worse condition than the western, and I find myself writing thus to my father in March 1854:

'While at Nilanga[1] I was more oppressed with work than I had been anywhere. I found the district in shocking order: no proper accounts, and no confidence among the people; a ruined, impoverished set of pauper cultivators, who have been so long oppressed and neglected under the Arab management, that they are, I imagine, blunted to all good perceptions. Murder, robbery, attacks on villages, plunder of cattle, and destruction of crops, had got to such a height last year, that civil war could not have had a worse effect upon the people or on the revenue; and all agreed that if British rule had not come in this year, the whole district would have been utterly ruined and wasted. I never saw anything like it. I thought Shorapur bad, but this is infinitely worse, and the labour it is to get anything put right has been excessive. I can only say that I have been obliged to work frequently from 4 A.M. to 8 P.M., with only respite for dressing and

[1] A village of some 3,000 inhabitants, and headquarters of a taluk, in Bidar District.

breakfast; but there is no help for it. I have been giving five years' settlements to such villages as are ready to take them, but there are many which are so disorganised that they require to be specially nursed.'

I had likewise introduced a regular system of village accounts with the rent-payers and the treasurers, which I will briefly detail.

Each village accountant kept a day-book and ledger, in which the sum he was to pay was entered to his debit, and his payments successively at stated times to his credit. His account was entered in the village ledger in the same manner. If he paid an instalment, it was entered to his credit in his book as a receipt; and this payment was entered into the day-book, and afterwards posted to his account in the ledger. Peculation was therefore almost impossible, or any undue exactions, and the people now began to understand the protection that the system implied. The district treasury had a similar account with villages, and the particulars of each village instalment were forwarded to the head treasury with the general remittances. Any error or any exaction by any individual could thus be traced up to its author at once, and the check and counter-check were quite efficient in practice. The village accountants were at first rather clumsy about their books, but they soon grew accustomed to the system; and before the season of collections was over, I had the satisfaction of finding that the plan was working easily and well in every portion of my province.

Before I returned to my headquarters, Naldrug, I had the satisfaction of beginning two new irrigation reservoirs near Tuljapur, on plans and surveys which I had previously submitted. I intended that these should form the commencement of a system of tank-irrigation from Tuljapur to Ahmednagar, a question in which the Governor-General seemed much interested, and in which he encouraged me heartily to persevere.

The Resident also, Mr. Bushby, began to see the necessity of it; and I was the more rejoiced at obtaining sanction for this, because great distress was prevalent, though it scarcely amounted to famine yet, and three new works would enable me to employ a great number of persons. I was glad, too, to find that both my neighbours, the collectors of Ahmednagar and Sholapur, had become strong advocates for irrigation-works, and had sent in urgent representations to Government on the subject. In these undertakings I had to make the surveys, plans, and calculations entirely myself; but I always managed to find time to do these before my daily work began, so that other business was never interfered with or postponed. It seemed strange to me that though irrigation-works were progressing in the North-West Provinces with great energy, in the Bombay Presidency no one seemed to take the least interest in them, and, had it not been for these gentlemen, would probably ever have given a thought to the subject; and indeed, to this day, I believe but little progress has been made in these most useful works.

I had great difficulties to encounter in the treasury department for the first year or two. Rents had been paid in all sorts of local currencies, and I was required to account for them in Company's rupees. Now I had as many as fourteen different kinds of rupees current in my province, each with its separate value, and the market value was often fluctuating; the assay rates did not correspond at all with the market value, and, in short, the whole was a system of inextricable confusion; and I was obliged in the end to notify that none except Company's rupees would be taken in payments to the State, and this relieved us of all difficulty.

For a long time the proposed revenue survey caused much trouble and vexation. A small manual had been sent us from the Punjab of the system in use there, which was by plane-tables,—and plane-tables were sent afterwards. Every Deputy-Commissioner was to have a school of instruction, and to teach the *patwaris*, or village accountants, to survey their own lands; and the work was to begin at once. This was all easy enough to write about; but the carrying such orders into effect was a very different matter. I believe I happened to be the only Deputy-Commissioner who knew how to survey, and the rest looked to me to begin operations.

Extensive correspondence on the subject took place, and cost me much additional time and trouble; but I could not use the Punjab instruments and the compasses with which the work was to be done—it was impossible; and after much writing and loss of time in useless endeavours at explanation, I introduced a plan of my own. I had some better plane-tables made, and worked them by backsight, like a theodolite, and my plan succeeded very well. I also established a school of young men, instead of the *patwaris,* who proved apt scholars, and did good work, and I sent in my report with some specimens of surveyed lands. My plan was approved, and I was simply desired 'to go on'.

I found distress very great at Naldrug—not so much among the people of my own district, as among starving wretches who came there from all quarters so emaciated, and so shrivelled and weak, that all, men, women, and children, were fearful to look upon. Often, during my morning rides, I came upon dead bodies lying by the roadside, creatures who had sunk down to die before they could reach the town; and many crawled in who were too far gone to be recovered. Except at Hingoli I had never seen famine in its worst form before, and this was horrible to witness. I did what I could myself, and every one at Naldrug did the same: my own share amounted to several thousand rupees, which I could very ill afford; and it was not for a comparatively long time that I could get any answer to my earnest request to be allowed to use what money I needed, to give employment to those able to work. At length, however, I got a favourable reply, and about four thousand miserable wretches were set to work to cut down the scrubby jungle in the fort, and to clear out the old ruined works. Gradually, as rain fell and prospects brightened, the people began to return to their various homes. What would have become of us at Naldrug if the famine had been universal, I can hardly conceive; for its results from which we suffered were fearful enough.

The monsoon was heavy, and all the month of September proved very unhealthy at Naldrug. My establishment, and nearly all the clerks, both English and native, suffered from fever, dysentery, and other complaints; so that to get through the needful work was very trying. We had no other convenient shelter, and so were obliged to remain; but I thought it doubtful whether the place could be retained as a head-station.

However, a further trial of it was directed before it was given up.

The year 1854 had been a truly laborious one to me, and except during the very short period of the late rains, I had been under canvas since July 1853. The work accomplished had been enormous. In English, Persian, and Marathi, the references and letters had been 34,474, upwards of 9,000 of which had passed between my assistant and myself, many being on very intricate and tedious subjects. We corresponded officially always in Marathi.

For my own share I had had 272 criminal cases to dispose of, thirteen of which were indictments for murder: of civil cases and appeals I find no record among my letters, but no doubt they may have been mislaid or lost.

My revenue for the financial year was all collected—except about 3,000 rupees, which still had to be remitted—and amounted to 10 lakhs and 66,000 rupees of all sorts; which, allowing for large deductions, exchanges, etc., became Rs. 886,565 13 3.

The revenue for the previous year had been, according to the local accounts, Rs. 699,305 11 8, so that there had been an increase of Rs. 187,260 1 7. The amount of land previously under cultivation had been 1,192,395 *bighas*; that for the present year 1,221,947 *bighas*, or an increase of 29,552.

Further particulars are unnecessary, and would scarcely interest the general reader.

In spite of a little fever, from which I suffered at Naldrug, I was in rude health. I enjoyed the climate of the district, and along the edge of the table-land it was generally cool in the hottest weather.

I was always able to work at least twelve hours every day, and often more, except on Sundays, when I always read the service in my tents to my English clerks.

Every department of the district was now in fair working order, and I was quite prepared to show the Resident, if he came to see it, as it was hinted he would, all my interior economy, and wished it to be compared with other districts of the same class.

I was directed by the Resident to meet the Collector of Sholapur on the frontier, in order to settle a boundary dispute which had arisen between the Raja of Akalkot's[1] territory and the Nizam's, and in regard to which there had been some serious fighting and bloodshed; so I made for the spot early in November, expecting that everything would be satisfactorily arranged in a few days.

It proved, however, that I had to survey 26 miles of disputed boundary, and to make a map of it, before the question could even be understood at all; documents on both sides had to be examined, and evidence taken. Finally, after recording our opinion in separate minutes, part of the boundary was laid down; but the Akalkot men came in the night, pulled up the stones which had been placed as landmarks and threw them away.

As I could wait no longer, and the Collector had no authority to enforce our decision, I left the place on the 18th December, heartily regretting that my detention had been so long and so unprofitable; and I moved to a village on the eastern frontier to begin the revenue settlement for the year. I should then be close to the Resident's line of march from Hyderabad to Naldrug, and could easily join him at the nearest point.

I was glad to find the people on the eastern and western frontiers taking heart; and I had the pleasure of letting nearly all the uncultivated lands, which had become covered with low mimosa jungle. There was a better spirit abroad in the country, and the local bankers were ready to make advances for the cultivation of these waste lands on low rates of interest to any extent. The fact was, that agents from some of the great mercantile houses in Bombay had acted upon a circular which I had sent them some months before, pointing out to them the capabilities of my province for the production of oil-seeds and other staple commodities of trade; and they had sent agents with bills of exchange to a very large amount to invest in these purchases. One of these agents had bills to the extent of three lakhs (£30,000); and in all I traced more than £60,000, which was a very welcome addition to

[1] A pleasant little country if not a good neighbour. Akalkot State has some 500 square miles, a growing population which was 82,000 in 1901, a tolerable climate, an army of fifty men. It is watered by the Bori, the Bhima, and the Sina.

former capital. No such influx of money had ever been known before, and I recommended the agents to deal directly with the farmers, without the intervention of any third party; and they took my advice, and ultimately all were quite satisfied.

The Resident and his staff left Hyderabad on the 20th December, and I met him at Kaliani, in the Nizam's territory, on the 1st January 1855. He received me very kindly. As I rode into camp, he was just starting on his elephant, and he asked me to come with him, which I did, and we were soon deep in friendly talk about all sorts of things. We travelled together to Naldrug, where I had plenty to show him—all the treasury books and accounts, the jail, etc., etc.; and I had collected the *patwaris* of a number of villages and their books, and explained my system to him. He was pleased to say 'he could hardly believe that so perfect a system could have been organised'; and he was more and more satisfied as we proceeded further, and the books of other groups of villages were shown to him. He did not like Naldrug at all, and said there must be another head-station—and in this view I quite coincided; but there could be no change made for the present.

I was very anxious to lay my projects for irrigation-works before him, and he marched with me to Tuljapur, where the largest tank had been marked out, and this seemed to decide him in regard to the more extended system which I had advocated. He said he was very anxious to show that the 'assigned districts could do as much for their size as the Punjab', and promised to send on to Government all the plans and estimates that could be prepared.

He could propose no change in judicial matters, as my small code was working very satisfactorily; and he confided to me that I was the only Deputy-Commissioner who had attempted to introduce anything of the kind.

The Resident had not very much time to spare; we therefore went on from Tuljapur to Ausa, but I regretted his being unable to see the prettiest part of the district, which lay along the edge of the table-land.

He was immensely struck, however, with the regularity and beauty of the fine old fort of Ausa; and indeed, if the

Arabs who formed the garrison when I first took possession of it had chosen to resist, the place could only have been taken by a regular siege. I left the Resident at Bhalki,[1] a point on the Hyderabad road ; and we had, when we parted, settled everything as far as we could. I showed him the survey work, which pleased him. No other Deputy-Commissioner had as yet even attempted a commencement, and it gratified him that I had done so, in spite of my refusal to make use of the Punjab system. We parted very good friends ; and as I fancied, on his first coming, that he had acquired rather a prejudice against me, I was the more pleased at the result of our meeting. I knew my district was in a much more orderly and regular condition than any other ceded at the same time, and I was anxious it should be inspected.

At the request of the people, I chose the site of a new market-town near Nilanga. There were more than a hundred applications for sites, so I designed a market-place and a hall of assembly ; and the Resident having given his sanction we began to build at once. Nilanga was now a place of trade and a resort of merchants, yet how it was reduced ! The old accounts showed its revenue to have been 12,000 rupees a-year ; now it did not reach above 3,000.

After much tedious and lengthy correspondence respecting the difference in value of currencies collected during the first year, which I had cut short by accepting only Company's rupees in payments during the present year, I was able to submit my accounts of revenue and collections at an early period ; and the following copy of a memorandum I sent to my father in July will show what progress had been made :

'*Cultivation.*—Contrasting the returns of 1852–53 with those of 1854–55, and after adjustment of all transfers of villages attached to proprietors, lands released, etc., there is a clear increase of new cultivation of *bighas* 139,190. A *bigha*, by the average of local measurement, is here upwards of an acre—about 1·30.

---

[1] Plainly shown upon the map, with a rising population of 6,000. Bhalki is the headquarters of a taluk of the same name in Bidar District.

'*Revenue*.—The gross and net revenue of 1851–52, including all estates rcsumed by us, customs duties, etc., was :—

Gross revenue, Hyderabad rupees . .	856,263	7	5
Villagc expenses	164,882	13	5
Balance, net revenue, Hyderabad rupecs .	691,380	10	0
Gross revenue for 1854–55 in Company's rupees	922,666	8	0
Deduct village expenses . . .	97,993	8	9
Balance, net revenue, in Company's rupees	824,672	15	3

Result.

Net revenue, 1854–55, Company's rupees .	824,672	15	3
Net revenue, 1851–52, Hyderabad rupees .	691,380	10	0
Increase in tale . .	Rs. 133,292	5	3

'The value of the different rupees is not here given ; and either the Hyderabad rupees may be turned into Company's at 21 per cent, or the Company's into Hyderabad, and here is the result :

Company's rupees, 824,672, at 121 for 100 Hyderabad rupees . . .	997,853	1	11
Net revenue of 1851–52, as above . .	691,380	10	0
Net increase, value, Hyderabad rupees	306,472	7	11

Or, if the Nizam's Government's share only of 1851–52 for the whole province is reckoned, the amount will stand as follows :

Net revenue of 1854–55, as above, Company's rupees, 824,672, at 121 per 100 .	=997,853	1	11
Realised by the Nizam's Government in 1851–52, according to account .	562,457	14	9
Given to the Nizam's Government by cession on the result of 1854–55, in Hyderabad rupees	435,395	3	2

'Even this is not all, for the Rs. 562,457 14 9 contained the customs duties abolished in 1854–55. These amounted to

Rs. 35,000 ; and there is a further profit in decrease of village charges, which were 19·41 per cent on the gross revenue in 1851–52, and in 1854–55 10·84 per cent.

'The average rate of assessment per *bigha* or acre, is nine annas and two pies (about one shilling and three halfpence); and there is no other tax or cess whatever.

'In reference to the gross revenue of 1854–55, the total remission from unrealised balances is Rs. 620 5 6 ; or 922,666 8 Company's rupees have been realised, all but Rs. 620 5 6 ; or £92,266, all except £62.'

There remained, therefore, no doubt whatever that the cession of this province had been highly profitable to the Nizam's Government. The actual receipts had very nearly doubled, and the revenue was secured in Company's rupees instead of in fluctuating currencies. The local profits of the Nizam's *talukdars,* or collectors, had been enormous. They had collected all the revenue, for the most part, in a local currency, which was little short in value in the market of the Company's rupee ; but instead of giving their Government the benefit of the exchange into Hyderabad rupees, they had paid Hyderabad rupees only by bills on Hyderabad, which were cashed in the local debased currency of the city itself.

If this were a specimen of one province, what must have been the result from them all ? Berar, like Naldrug, showed a similar difference of value and increase in favour of the cession.

In August of this year the distress seemed almost greater than the year before. There had been no rain since June, and the poorer classes, who were accustomed to gain their living by weeding fields and other agricultural work, were now starving, and flocking in crowds to Naldrug. We all did what we could, as we had done the year before, and it was a heavy drain on private individuals. I urged the Resident to allow me to begin the roads to Sholapur and Hyderabad, which he had promised, and which would have greatly relieved the local strain upon me and others, but I had to wait a weary time for an answer.

During this month, too, I lost the valuable services of my assistant Cadell. He had gone to Hyderabad on leave for a month, and when there, Bullock, who was Commissioner in Berar, applied for furlough to England on medical certificate ;

the Raichur Commissioner was ordered to act in Berar, and Cadell was sent to Raichur. I was very sorry to lose my friend. He had managed four out of my ten divisions admirably from the first; he was always kind, courteous, and considerate to natives of every degree, and had won golden opinions from all. We had worked well together, and he was thoroughly acquainted with his duties in every respect. Personally, I was very much attached to him, and shall never forget, while I live, our pleasant days together.

No assistant was appointed in his stead, and the whole work of the province fell upon me, without any additional pay; but I was grateful for excellent health, though I hardly hoped it would long hold out under the terrible strain now put upon me.

We had no rain till September; but the new roads, to the commencement of which a tardy sanction had at length been given, provided labour for upwards of 4,000 men, women, and children, and saved them from starvation. I also cleared out the fort altogether, and thus employed 1,500 more persons: every old wall was levelled, and the stones were thrown into hollows and covered with earth. In October heavy rain fell all over the district, and we thanked God that all dread of famine was at an end. The very early crops had withered, but now every acre of land was being re-ploughed and sown, and the prospects were very cheering. Another road to Tuljapur was sanctioned, and put in hand; and I had completed thirty miles of one and fifteen of another, having been obliged to do all the surveying and laying out myself. They were only cleared and levelled to begin with, and would be metalled afterwards.

My brother-in-law, William Palmer, was at last appointed as my assistant. He had served in a similar capacity in North and South Berar. In the latter province no system whatever had been introduced, neither revenue, account, nor judicial, and the Resident had gone there on a tour of inspection. Cadell, too, wrote from Raichur to say that he had everything to originate there, and he did not like it at all; but I hoped he was in a fair way for promotion. The work at the large tank at Tuljapur had been stopped, pending formal sanction by Government—but this had been granted; and after testing all my old levelling by a new instrument which my father sent to me from England, the embankment was begun in earnest. In December all looked well—crops were luxuriant, work progressing, and people happy and contented; and for this peaceful close to a very trying year, I felt most grateful. I again received orders to meet the Resident on his return from South Berar to Hyderabad, at any point nearest to my boundary. I therefore, while waiting for him, carried on the survey of the road from Tuljapur to Kaliani, and contrived to get through from seven to nine miles per day, laying down marks for the contractors and workmen. I finally met the Resident at his camp at Bandapur on the 14th January 1856. He was exceedingly kind and friendly towards me. He expressed himself dissatisfied with the condition of South Berar, and was pleased to say many flattering things about the order and regularity in all departments which he had found at Naldrug. As still further improvement had continued since his visit, I would have liked to have taken him through part of my district; but time did not permit of it, and he could not delay longer his return to Hyderabad. There was no difference of opinion between us except in regard to the survey, as to which I consistently maintained my first position, that unless it had a scientific basis and the surveyors had a practical education and knowledge of their work, they could not deal with village lands like those of Naldrug, some of the areas of which were from 20,000 to 30,000 acres in extent; and that to persevere in the Punjab scheme would not only entail loss of time, but of money also.

We had several hot arguments about this; but at last the Resident confided to me that the Punjab work had been an utter failure when scientifically tested, and he showed me some of the correspondence, which was convincing.

I was therefore allowed now to work out my own tables in my own way. I had a number of clever pupils, who were ready to set to work at once, and I promised to show results in a very short time, which I hoped would be considered satisfactory. All official clouds and differences were dispersed, and we were of one accord in all matters. In private Mr. Bushby was one of the pleasantest of companions; and we sat up each night into the small hours of the morning, engaged in pleasant talk, and schemes for the further improvement of my district. He had sent on all my plans for roads and irrigation-works; and estimates, exceeding a lakh of rupees, had been passed by Government. All this made me very hopeful.

I thought very earnestly at this time of taking furlough to England, and seeing my father once more, and of bringing out my children to India, if it were practicable. My heart yearned to see them and all the dear ones at home, yet there were many difficulties. I had no society, and no means of continuing their education; and Naldrug, or life in tents, was quite unfit for them. I could not, either, go home on medical certificate, for, thank God! my health was first-rate; and no doctor in Bombay, seeing my ruddy cheeks and strong frame, would have ventured to give me one. So I had no alternative but to wait patiently the tide of events.

I was not without a hope, that as a head-commissioner was to be appointed to superintend the whole of the districts, I might be nominated to the post. This would have involved residence at Hyderabad, where I could have had home and friends for my children; but in this I was disappointed. Alas! I was not a regular Company's servant, only an outsider, 'uncovenanted', and the Company's rules could not be infringed! Already, I heard from Mr. Courtenay, there existed much jealousy in regard to the offices held by 'local officers'; and much as Lord Dalhousie wished personally to serve me, he dared not provoke further dissatisfaction.

On the 6th March, Lord Dalhousie departed from Calcutta for England, leaving behind him a minute, which has its place in history, in which he detailed what he had done during his vice-royalty. His last annexation had been Oudh; but that had not been his own work. It had been for some time imminent, and was finally decided upon by the Court of Directors and the Government of England. It is only in future histories of India, and from his own papers, should they ever be published,[1] that the character and acts of Lord

[1] These add little to the facts which Taylor knew. A sentence in the chapter in the *History* on the annexation of Oudh, 1854 to 1856, in which the local agent was his early friend Outram, shows how obstinate were his questionings of the measure: 'All these are patent facts, which no one, even among the most bitter censurers of the annexation,

Dalhousie as Governor-General can be properly estimated; as yet, he has had his eulogists, and his bitter opponents, almost, indeed, amounting to defamers.

To my humble perception he was the most practically useful and single-minded ruler that India had ever possessed. His great mind took in every question with a singular clearness, whether it were large or small, momentous or unimportant, and he improved everything he touched. To him India owes electric telegraphs, railways, extension of practical education, large irrigation projects, roads, and the removal of many disabilities under which natives suffered. No one who ever worked under Lord Dalhousie could for a moment question his unerring detection of any weak point, and the great power of mind and application which distinguished him, and at no period of Indian history had the administration of India been so admirably conducted.

To receive a word of praise from him was the desire which lay nearest every heart; and when given, it was never in a cold or niggardly spirit, but warmly and most encouragingly. To myself personally, though I knew him not, he had been, both privately and officially, kind and considerate from first to last; and I only regret that I cannot find among my papers the last expression of his lordship's sentiments towards me, in transmitting a copy of the last despatch of the Court of Directors in reference to the affairs of Shorapur.

I have spoken of my own work, and have called it hard, lasting from twelve to sixteen hours daily; but this was made up of the petty details of one province. Lord Dalhousie did as much each day, with the direction of all India on his mind. 'No one can record,' wrote *The Times*, 'for few knew, of his daily toil, or how, with a delicate frame, he overcame it, but which overworked and destroyed his physical powers, and in 1860 sent him to his grave.'

---

has ever disproved, or sought to disprove; and yet the question remains open as to whether the course pursued was justified by the emergency, and whether the abrogation of treaties, and cancelling of all claims by a dynasty on which, in its sorest times of need, the British Government in India had relied without ever experiencing disappointment, and to which its obligations had been placed on record for nearly a hundred years, was not a breach of national faith.' The chapter closes with a paragraph from the *Times* article of which a sentence is quoted below.

When he left her, India seemed secure and peaceful, and he retired with a very sincere conviction that so she would long remain!

I was desired in February to meet a native commissioner from Hyderabad, to settle the boundary of jurisdiction, which had been under dispute, and we were to act in concert. I waited wearily for a month, losing the best period of my season; and when at length the commissioner arrived, he had received no instructions, and further delay ensued. At length, after he had made references to his Government on various points, we arranged affairs amicably.

I was principally engaged in trying criminal cases, which were both numerous and heavy; but there were no dacoities now, and these cases belonged chiefly to the period before the cession. As a proof of what I had to do in judicial affairs, I may here mention that Mr. Compton, who was judge of Sholapur, sent me a memorandum of the result of his work within a certain period. He had tried 72 cases, whereas my file showed 172 for the same!

My police system was working well. Every *patel*, or head of a village, was made a local magistrate, with certain powers, and a small allowance; and as a mark of distinction, the post was much esteemed. It gratified me also to find that my rules for the police were ordered for adoption in every province of the cession.

My accounts were made out, and sent up to Hyderabad with the administration report in July. The increase of cultivation in three years had been 184,000 acres. In 1855–56, 72,000 acres of new land had been taken up, but 34,000 were abandoned in the famine, which would not have been the case had rain fallen, and we should have had, with that, 218,000 acres of increase. As the revenue augmented, petty taxes would be remitted, as I had arranged from the first. This year 40,000 rupees would be struck off, yet the whole revenue would not be seriously affected. I need not give again all the details, as those of the previous year will suffice.

In August Mr. T. N. Maltby, of the Madras Civil Service, was appointed head-commissioner, and Mr. Bushby was relieved from the extra duties which had been imposed upon him, and which were very onerous. We looked out now for changes and amendments, which would form part of a more regular system than we had yet experienced. It was very evident to our commissioner, in the first place, that without increased establishments, the demands for regular reports, constantly increasing, could not be complied with, nor could the strain on any one who could and would do the work be borne much longer. As some relief to me, my head ministerial officer, 'Baba Sahib', a very shrewd and excellent revenue officer, whom I had brought with me from Shorapur, was promoted to the rank of extra-assistant;[1] and he, with my assistant Mr. Palmer, relieved me of much of the petty detail which had distressed me before. Cadell had been appointed Deputy-Commissioner in South Berar, and Eastern Raichur had been added to the western portion as part of the new arrangements. He was now, I was glad to see, on the high-road to promotion, and he had truly well earned his advance. My work never slackened in amount; and in reply to my father's query as to how my day was spent, I wrote as follows:

'Up at 5 A.M., and go out about the survey of the roads. In by eight o'clock and answer letters, English and Marathi, till ten; bathe, and breakfast over at eleven. Then to *kacheri* work, trials, etc., till 6 P.M., without stirring—often, indeed, till seven. Dine, and sit an hour or so with Palmer, if he is there, or with some native friend, by way of a rest, which brings up the time to half-past eight or nine. Then to my room, and work at translations or other business till eleven or twelve. Count up all this and you will see there is no time for anything except hard work; yet, I am very thankful to say, I have neither pain nor ache.'

The public works did not slacken either. Every road I had surveyed and marked out was in active progress, and there were now six long distances under the labourers' hands.

Our new Commissioner had written to me to say that he proposed taking my district the first in his projected tour of inspection. He was to leave Hyderabad on the 20th

[1] Cyril Brandon's Serishtidar, Baba Sahib, runs similarly through *Seeta*, even to this appointment. There is a further detail: 'It was gratifying to him to receive the order of the Star of India, and a high pleasure to know that in the same grade had been included the name of his old faithful friend and constant companion, Baba Sahib.'

November; and as I had a little leisure time and needed rest, I went into Sholapur[1] on a visit to my kind friends, Mr. and Mrs. Compton. What a treat this was to me! She was a highly-accomplished and exquisite musician, and it was delightful to listen to her. I had heard so little music since I had been in England, and had nearly forgotten all I knew; but it came back to me, and I had the great delight of singing all my favourite duets, Italian and English; and they were so kind and sympathetic, these dear friends, that my heart warmed to them both, nor did our friendship ever lessen. My pleasant stay ended abruptly, as I had to return to Naldrug sooner than I expected. Another assistant was added to my staff, Lieutenant Temple of the Madras Army, who, having passed an examination as civil engineer, and having been employed in the survey, and as superintendent of roads and tanks, would be of the greatest use to me.[2] He arrived at Naldrug on the 30th November, and was followed by a second native assistant, Jewanji Rustomji, a Parsi, so that now I had two English and two native assistants. Mr. Maltby had seen at a glance that it was no use overworking

[1] This would be the period when Taylor was getting to be fifty, and stout, covered by the recollections kindly contributed by Sir George Birdwood. The father alluded to in them was Christopher Birdwood, 1807–1882, 'Birdwood Maharaja', who had forty-five years actually in India, becoming full General in 1877.

'Meadows Taylor was a great friend of my father, and used to stay with him whenever he came into the Presidency of Bombay. When, after fifteen years' absence, I returned to India as a full-blown Assistant Surgeon in the service of the Honourable East India Company, in 1854–5, I saw a great deal of him at my father's house at Sholapur, where my father was commanding the 3rd Native Infantry. I saw Meadows Taylor again sometime in 1856–8 in Bombay, where my father was Commissary General for some years during and after the Mutiny. Taylor was for me and for everyone else at Sholapur simply a thorough English gentleman and loyal friend, and the most cheering of companions, with none of the airs of an author about him, or the slightest trace of literary pretension and pride. We all had read his books; but he never talked about them. . . . Taylor was highly respected by both Hindus and Muslims.'

Sir George Birdwood has also written: 'I knew Abingdon Compton, Judge at Sholapur, well. . . . He was a typical Civilian of the fine type created by the Honourable East India Company.'

[2] In *Seeta* is a 'young Temple', similarly appointed from the Army to be a civil assistant.

his Deputy-Commissioners. He unfortunately met with a severe accident, which prevented his leaving Hyderabad; and I was much concerned at this, for I had looked forward to his coming with sincere pleasure, and I knew that he was one to appreciate all I had done and was striving further to accomplish.

During my little visit to Sholapur I made the acquaintance of the surveyor-in-chief for the railway, and I asked him to come with me to see my embankment works, roads, etc., and, above all, to test my survey with the theodolite. He came to Naldrug, tested the surveys of three considerable village lands, and gave me a certificate that he could find 'no appreciable error whatever'. Here was a grand triumph for me! Government had refused me a theodolite, and I had been working in my own fashion, and somewhat in the dark.

My system with the planc-tables was quite new to my friend, and he did me the honour to ask me for one of my instruments, which I considered a high compliment. The certificate he had given me was too valuable to retain, as it entered into full details of his tests, and I forwarded it to the Commissioner.

Although he had not seen them in actual working, Mr. Maltby ordered at once the adoption of my system of accounts in all departments, and directed it to be put in force in all districts of the Commission. My police regulations had already been adopted, and, at length, what I had been working for so hard seemed to be appreciated; and I received, by a minute of the Supreme Council, the 'special thanks of the Governor-General in Council for my valuable services'. And so ended the year 1856, with many thanks to God for all His merciful protection. Everything around me was peaceful and prosperous; there was good hope of a fine season; my roads were opening out lines of traffic all through the country; and trade was brisk and profitable.

I had held many criminal trials during the year; but the last one in 1856 was more than usually extraordinary. A farmer and shepherd, the possessor of some wealth, had two wives—one old, the other young. The elder wife had no family, and he had married a younger one in the hope of having an heir born to him. Much jealousy existed between the women, though they did not live in the same house, or even in the same village. One morning, early, the shepherd was found dead in his sugar-cane field, which he had gone to watch alone during the night. His head was literally knocked to pieces with large stones, but the body could be perfectly identified. There had been a feast in his house the evening before, and a kid had been killed by his nephew, and many of the neighbours had partaken of the dinner, at which the shepherd and his elder wife had appeared to be on the best terms. At the inquest and local investigation, many suspicious circumstances were brought forward against the elder wife and the nephew, and both were committed by me for trial. One of these was, that the wife of the nephew declared her husband had been absent most part of that night; and when he returned home he threw a thick sheet over her, which he had with him, saying she must be cold, and that he was going to her village, and she must follow. On this sheet were large patches of blood, which she had not observed at night; but she had given it to the police when they came in the morning. I had sent the sheet to Hyderabad in order that the blood-stains might be analysed; but it could not be proved that the blood was human, and the male prisoner swore that it was that of the kid which he himself had killed for the feast.

There was a great deal of circumstantial evidence in the case; but it was impossible to convict the prisoners upon this only, and they were very ably defended by a native advocate. When the defence was closed, I was on the point of recording an acquittal, although I was inwardly sure the prisoners had done the murder; and I had taken my pen in hand to write, when the woman, a tall masculine figure, began to beat her breast, and cried out with a loud voice—

'Stop, Sahib! do not write! You do not know the truth; you would write what is wrong. All that my advocate and the witnesses have said to you is false. Lies! lies! lies! *I* did the murder, and' (pointing to the nephew) '*he* helped me! He knocked him down with a big stone, and then we killed him between us.'

It was quite in vain that I cautioned her that this confession must be made use of against her if she persisted in it. She only said the more—

'Lies! lies!—we did it, he and I, and he will tell you so himself. Is it not all true?' she said, turning to the other prisoner. 'Don't be ashamed of it. Speak the truth before God and the Sahib.'

'It is all true', said the young man, quite calmly—'quite true; and I will tell how we did it. Was I not his heir? and he had always denied me my share because he said he would have children by his new wife. Could I bear that, Sahib?'

'Could I bear his leaving me for a wooden-faced girl?' cried the woman, beating her breast violently. 'No, no! I did it! I did it! I and he; and if he were alive now, and we two were free, we could not let him live. Take down all I say!' she shrieked—'take it all down, and hang me afterwards, for my heart is burning! burning! burning!'

I recorded their confessions, which were long and very circumstantial, not only corroborating the evidence in every material point, but explaining how the murder had been long planned,—how the woman had engaged five men of a village in the British territory to do it, and had given them two rupees each as earnest-money; but their courage failed them, and they had given the money back to her: then, as she said, there remained no one to do it but her husband's nephew and herself. After all was recorded, I passed sentence of death upon both. The proceedings were sent on to the Sadar Adalat or Supreme Court of Calcutta, the sentence confirmed, and the horrible pair hanged together. I shall never forget the look and action of that woman as she cried out to me 'not to write', and poured forth a torrent of confession which she could not repress.

In another case of dacoity which followed, the clear evidence of the widow of the owner of the house attacked, who was a young and very beautiful Brahmin girl, affected me very deeply; and the subject of that trial forms the opening of my romance of *Seeta*. The deposition of Seeta given at the first inquiry is that of the Brahmin widow, with very slight alteration.[1]

[1] This scene, and the events leading up to it, occupy the eight opening chapters of *Seeta*. It is all very workmanlike, readable narrative, yet without the brilliant touch which tempts to quotation. It is one of the

Indeed my operations against the dacoits of my district were beginning to tell heavily upon them. One large gang, very notorious in 1827–29, were at length brought to justice, and stolen property to a very large amount was recovered from them and recognised. A zemindar of the adjacent British province, a great man in his way, was also tried and convicted on many charges of dacoity, and was sentenced to fourteen years' penal servitude; and these instances of conviction, and many more, purged my province of dacoits.

New-Year's Day of 1857 found me at Nilanga, where I had been for two days. All was now very prosperous, and the crops were splendid. Every one was in good heart, and applications for waste lands were very numerous; in a comparatively short time none would remain to be taken up. My new assistant, Temple, had gone to work steadily, and was studying Marathi with every prospect of becoming a proficient. He liked the people, and they liked him; and, as I had before done with Cadell, I made several yearly settlements to show him how the work was done, and he was a very patient and good-tempered scholar. He had been with me on the Hyderabad road so far as it extended, and he completed the survey of two branch lines from Nilanga and Sowara to Latur [1]—all of these I left to him to look after, as he could afford the time; but the works were making rapid progress everywhere. From Nilanga I went to Kharosa, half-way to Ausa, as I was very anxious to see some Hindu cave-temples of which I had heard a good deal, and none of the archæologists of Bombay seemed to know anything about them. I found them well worthy a visit—excavated in a cliff of laterite or coarse stone; but some

few contributions to fiction from the magistrate's bench. Seeta, the goldsmith girl, has brown eyes like the Brahmin Tara, but without the alleged flecks of violet. 'For a native woman, Cyril Brandon had never seen any one so fair or of so tender a tone of colour. Such, he remembered, were many of the lovely women of Titian's pictures—a rich golden olive, with a bright carnation tint rising under the skin—and Seeta's was like them.' As Brandon says later: 'It only proves how little we know of native women, and how impossible it is to know anything more except in a case like this, which breaks the ice.'

[1] This is a town in the Ausa taluk of Osmanabad District. Its population had gone down from 10,000 in 1901 to some 7,000 in 1911. 'Latur is a great centre of the cotton and grain trade in communication with Barsi railway station, 64 miles distant.'

of the pillars left were richly decorated with carving, and several of the halls of the temples were large and airy. The whole were a miniature, apparently, of the caves of Ellora, but very humble copies of these noble temples; and though there did not exist even a tradition of their origin, I concluded they must have been the work of the Rajas of Kaliani—either the Chalukyas, or their successors the Yadavas of Deogarh or Daulatabad. I could discover no inscription to copy and send to the Asiatic Society of Bombay, but I measured the temples and sent plans of them, as I did also those of the fine Buddhist excavations near Dharaseo,[1] which in many respects were very remarkable, and had been previously unknown.

The day I arrived at Kharosa I received the melancholy intelligence of the death of the Resident, Mr. Bushby.[2] He had over-fatigued himself when out on a country excursion, and brought on an illness from which he never rallied. I regretted him very much; for although we had had some differences of opinion on various local questions, yet to me individually he had been kind and encouraging. We corresponded constantly, and he was ever urging me on to attempt and begin further public works, and expressing satisfaction at the result of those already completed. It was impossible to conjecture who might be his successor.

After staying a few days at Ausa, for the trial of the prisoners confined in the jail there, I went by the new line of

[1] This name may be found in parentheses, under the prominent word Osmanabad, in the map at the end of the volume. The town is of some 10,000 inhabitants, the headquarters of a taluk and a district. The *Imperial Gazetteer* says of Osmanabad: 'It lies in the Balaghat, and was formerly known as Dharaseo. . . . When the District was temporarily ceded to the British, from 1853 to 1860, the headquarters were removed here from Naldrug, owing to the healthy climate of the place.' This fact does not appear from Taylor's account of the period up to 1857. The *Gazetteer* calls Osmanabad a great centre of trade; and adds an evident reference to the caves explored by Taylor. 'Two miles north-east of the town is a group of seven caves, four of which are Jain, while the others are probably Vaishnava.'

[2] 'A cemetery close by contains, among other tombs, those of two Residents, Mr. G. A. Bushby and Mr. Roberts, who died respectively in 1856 and 1868; and of Sir W. Rumbold, Bart., a partner in the house of Palmer & Co., who died in 1833' (*Imperial Gazetteer*, article 'Hyderabad City').

road to Sowara and Naldrug. This latter portion was quite finished, and measured 24 feet in width, looking like a good gravel-walk the whole way. This had beforc only been a rough track for carts, indeed sometimes merely a path winding among the great basalt boulders. At Naldrug, the first building I had used as a jail was now too small, and I began enclosing the large magazine with a wall 21 feet high and plastering it inside. There were now 400 prisoners in the jail, and I had established a school of industry, which was going on well. Some of the prisoners were making rope and tape, others weaving, and more manufacturing carpets of strong cotton—some of these were very pretty, and showed much skill. Nor did I allow the women to be idle; they made various articles in a kind of knitting which was taught them, and other kinds of work. The prisoners were likewise set to build the new jail wall, and were useful in a multitude of ways.

After a good look round Naldrug, just to see that all was right, and testing all the surveys of villages within reach, I went on to Sholapur for a few days' rest, and to indulge myself in a little music; and I promised to go there for a long visit during the rains, when I could not move about my district. My friend the surveyor-in-chief was not at Sholapur, but Lieut. T. of the Artillery, who had belonged to the Trigonometrical Survey of Sind, accompanied me to Tuljapur, bringing his theodolite with him. He was curious to see what I was doing, and he remained long enough to test my surveys of several large villages—all of which, I am glad to say, he found correct.

I asked him to make a report to me on the subject, which he did, explaining in detail the tests he had made, and their results, which I sent on to Mr. Maltby—and if the Commissioner had any doubt about our work, I knew this report would remove it; but he wrote word that he was sure we were fully able to carry it on correctly; and I was rejoiced to find that my plan of using the plane-tables was turning out so thoroughly successful.

I had now leisure to make measurements for the completion of the noble embankment at Bhatodi,[1] which was one of my

[1] This name, though not in the *Imperial Gazetteer* maps or index, is mentioned in the article on Ahmednagar District. 'The Bhatodi lake was constructed by Salabat Khan . . . and was restored by Government

principal projects. The high-water level showed an area of upwards of two square miles; the water would have an average depth of 25 feet, and the irrigation channels on the right bank of the stream would carry water to Ahmednagar itself, which needed it sorely. This great work had been begun, according to tradition, by Salabat Khan, the great Minister of Ahmednagar, who died in 1588, and whose mausoleum overlooks the admirable site for the lake which he had selected. As each would benefit alike by the work, the Nizam's and the British Governments were to share its expenses; and I was so anxious to see it put in hand, that I worked very hard at all the plans, sections, and surveys. Bhatodi was one of the most delightful of all my villages, and I had constant visitors from the cantonment. Lieut. Cotgrave of the Engineers, with an assistant, was sent to help me.

Between us all, we finished what we had to do; and the cross-levels of this basin gave a result of upwards of sixty millions of cubic yards of water-storage, while the expenses of the work would be comparatively moderate. Mr. Cotgrave had not had experience of tank-engineering, but he very soon took in the project, and entered into its details with great spirit and zeal; and on looking into the particulars of the former portion which had been completed, we were both exceedingly struck by the profound science which had been evinced by the ancient Musalman engineers.

A survey of the high watershed lying between my district and the great valley of the Godavery river was necessary in order to calculate the amount of rainfall for storage in the large tanks I had proposed; and I began this from Bhatodi, and finished about 100 square miles of it, which all fell into the basin I had tested when I came first to the district.

I had now gained the amplest data for irrigation projects both here and at Bhatodi; and when I should find leisure to

---

in 1871. It is 10 miles from Ahmadnagar. . . . When full it has an area of 315 acres.'

Taylor's *History* says that in 1588 Salabat Khan, then an aged man, was allowed to return to Ahmednagar, and died the same year. 'His noble mausoleum, erected on a lofty hill south of the city, is still in perfect repair, and is used by pleasure parties from Ahmednugger. It commands a grand view over the mountains to the south and east, and over the broad valley of the Godavery river.'

do so, would submit them with my administrative report. How anxious the people were for water!—not only for cultivation, but for their cattle; and what noble memorials would these works be of our rule in the province! I had discovered among the hills a refuge in hot weather—a village 2,470 feet above the sea-level by barometer and boiling-point of water. I did not leave it till the end of March, and then it was quite cold at night and very agreeable during the day. The scenery was beautiful all along the mountains to Ahmednagar westwards, and over my own district eastwards; while to the north lay the wide plain of the Godavery, and Aurungabad and its hills beyond. Even with the naked eye I could see the glitter of the marble dome of the great tomb of Aurungzeb's daughter in the far distance, and of other domes and minarets in the city; but my time was up—I had to meet my assistant Palmer, and to lay out a new piece of road south to Dharaseo and north towards the city of Bhir. After all was done, the rainy season would begin, and we should assemble at Naldrug.

My plans were changed by a note received from Colonel Davidson, from Baroda, where, after leaving Hyderabad, he had been appointed Resident. Now, it appeared, he was promoted to the vacancy at Hyderabad, and sent me word that he should be at Naldrug on the 12th April. I received his note while at Manur on the 6th, and I had 120 miles to travel over as best I could in order to meet our new chief, who was an old friend of mine. By relays of horses, and a palankeen from Tuljapur, I managed to reach Naldrug on the morning of the 10th, as the sun was rising, and I found everything looking very nice. Next day at 4 A.M. the Resident arrived, and I was very glad to welcome him, and to congratulate him on his new appointment. He had been overworked at Baroda, and looked ill; but the offer of the Hyderabad Residentship was too tempting, and he had abandoned his previous idea of going on furlough to England for a few months' leave, until he should have established himself in his new position.

As soon as it was light, he asked to be shown all over the fort, expressed his approval of the new jail, and heard all about my schemes for roads, and all the irrigation projects, to which he promised his help and countenance, declaring that one of his first undertakings at Hyderabad would be to complete the road to a junction with my frontier. I explained the progress of the survey, and, in short, everything connected with my work in all departments, and he had not one single objection to offer to any of my plans. He stayed with us till the evening, Temple having ridden in from Ausa during the day; and we then sent him on, with our hearty good wishes for a safe journey, and after this relapsed into our usual monotonous routine of daily work.

I returned to my camp, and made surveys and plans for the last large tank I had to prepare for execution in the ensuing year. It would collect the drainage of 57½ square miles; would have an average depth of 24 feet, and an area of 13¼ square miles; and would, when completed, be a truly noble work.

I had much anxiety at this time about many things, and one especially was the very severe illness of my father-in-law Mr. Palmer, who throughout my life had been so steady, loving, and truly helpful a friend to me in all my doings. He recovered, however, very slowly; but his son, my assistant, was obliged to leave me and go to Hyderabad for advice about his eyes, which began to fail him terribly. He could now scarcely see to write his name, and was unfit for duty. I took charge of his subdivision myself; and the travelling season being over, returned to Naldrug by the close of May.

On my way to Naldrug, my assistant Baba Sahib had met me at Dharaseo, and in course of a conversation which we held privately, he told me that very disagreeable rumours had been flying about that disaffection prevailed in the British territory, and that it was reported an attempt would soon be made to turn the British out of India altogether.

I had heard this myself, but it had made no impression upon me. Who could or would think it could be true, while the whole of India lay apparently in profound peace? Who could dream of any rising?

'Do you remember', said Baba Sahib, 'the anonymous letter sent to you by the Bombay Government some time ago? I think it was in February; that was a warning, and kindly meant, though it sounded rude and insolent. Now the almanac for this year 1914 [1] is most alarming ; it goes back to the " hundred years " of the battle of Plassey, and declares that the rule of the Company must come to an end in bloodshed and tumult. This is what is disturbing men's minds, and we must be very careful. When I saw the almanac for the year, I had almost determined to write to you to have it stopped, and prevent the public reading of it if possible ; but I knew that you would say such a step would give it too much importance. Do you not hear ugly rumours yourself ? '

I scarcely liked to confess that I had ; but since February I had been receiving several anonymous letters sent through the ordinary post, with various post-marks, all warning me, as a friend to natives, to take furlough to England and join my family, and leave the district to its fate. They were worded mostly in this way—

' Although you have many friends, and the people worship you, you have still enemies who will approach you when the time comes, and you will never know who strikes you down.'

All these letters were marked ' private ', or ' to be read by himself ', and, like other anonymous productions, which were common enough, I had read them and then torn them up. I had not the smallest fear of the people in my district ; but these letters, taken in connection with those which had been sent confidentially to Lord Elphinstone,[2] had more effect upon me than I cared to acknowledge.

The advent of 1914 had been preceded by frightful cholera

[1] These were favourite ideas of Meadows Taylor, developed in *Seeta*, in his *History*, and elsewhere. It was, of course, by the Samvat era of King Vikramaditya, beginning in 57 B.C., that 1914 corresponded to 1857–58. Taylor calls it ' Sumbut 1914 ' in the *History*, where are various passages illustrating unsuspected causes of discontent, with warnings which very few Englishmen were in a position to hear, and still fewer to regard.

[2] John, thirteenth Baron Elphinstone, 1807–60. He was nephew to Mountstuart Elphinstone, who died only half a year before him. Lord Elphinstone was Governor of Madras during an uneventful period, 1837 to 1842 ; and the efficient Mutiny Governor of Bombay between 1853 and 1860. In his *History* Taylor tells of ' a very remarkable letter or petition ', anonymous, but evidently well meant and well founded, received by the Governor. It ' contained a solemn announcement of treason, accompanied by the enumeration of causes of general discontent.'

and floods in Bengal, discontent about the greased cartridges, and the mutiny of the 19th Bengal Native Infantry ; but such events seemed to have no possible connection with the general uprising of the people ; and even if, in Bengal, they were suspicious of infringements of caste, what could that possibly have to do with the peaceful and apparently loyal farmers of the Deccan ?

In Bengal, however, there now appeared to be real alarm. Lord Canning's proclamation of May 16th proved that there was, as there seemed to me to be, direct sympathy between what the people of Bengal were warned of by Lord Canning and what I knew was being felt all round me. I could only infer that the evil prophecy of the curious almanac, the same in purport everywhere, had in reality disturbed the minds of the unthinking and superstitious. What could be done ? I heard the same apprehensive reports from Hyderabad. The Resident and others wrote to me about them ; and from Ahmednagar, Sholapur, Berar, and other localities, came the same tidings: and out of all the letters which reached me and Temple, there was scarcely one which did not make some reference to the subject.

I confess I was considerably relieved when I received an order to remit all the money I had in the treasury to Bombay for the Persian war. I felt, in any case, it was better to be without it.

I well remember the receipt of the 'Extra' from Meerut of the 11th May. Who that was in India at that time can forget it ? One could not but shudder at the awful news ; but there arose a hope that it might only be a local mutiny which could be checked without spreading further, and that peace would soon follow ; and yet, if common precaution had been taken at every station as early as February or March, before the evil wind of 1914 [1] began to blow, many and many a valuable life would have been spared. Now it was too late, for throughout the Bengal army disaffection was widely prevalent, and was beginning to bear fruit almost day by day everywhere. Warnings had not been wanting. Friendly natives had endeavoured by many means to put Englishmen on their

[1] A remarkable anticipation of another 1914.

guard; but no hints were taken, no precautions used, and the blow fell at last.

The following letters were written home to my friends, though with no view to publication at the time; but for the convenience of my family and others interested in the subject, they were printed and circulated privately without my knowledge:—

'NALDRUG (WESTERN CEDED DISTRICTS, DECCAN),
June 21, 1857.

'No Government despatch that ever left India will be looked for with such anxiety as the mail which takes this. The close of the Afghan war was a period of intense excitement; but then it was for an army retiring, and one which could, united as it was, have borne down everything before it. Now the fear arises from the army itself. To say that a Bengal army exists, is, I fear, hopeless. The list of regiments that have broken into open mutiny, or have been disbanded because of disaffection, has extended to more than half the regular regiments already, and who shall say how far it may not extend? How will it be possible to trust any after this? Happily, as yet, no disaffection has been manifested in the Bombay or Madras armies, and the native States are one and all faithful. There has been excitement at Hyderabad, of course, and one night a standard was planted, around which some rabble assembled; but the Minister sent a party of Arabs to keep order, and those assembled fled, nor has any attempt at sedition been renewed. Davidson has a small detachment and a few guns at the Residency, more to assure the people at the Residency Bazaar than aught else; and all is quiet. There had been suspicion of communication between disaffected parties in the native regiments and the city rabble, but no trace could be found; and such reports have been common at all times, for the last twenty years, in any periods of general excitement. The Minister and Nizam are steadily with us; and it seems they have the Arabs *in hand*, which perhaps some doubted. Of course the general interest is now centred in Delhi; and I think and hope that you will hear of its fall by this mail. News, by electric telegraph, to Davidson, of the 2d, from Delhi, said that a breach had been made; but the most material was, that the king had thrown himself on our protection, and that the mutineers were divided among themselves. They had been defeated with great slaughter outside the walls, by our troops, under General Barnard; and the results of their two attacks on the outpost of the Meerut post on the Hindun,[1] were also slaughter and defeat. That

[1] The battles on the Hindun river, on the way from Meerut, on the last two days of May, have a couple of paragraphs in Rice Holmes's

the whole will be quelled, and speedily too, I have not the least doubt; but, meantime, it is a period of intense anxiety and excitement, as you may believe. It is most satisfactory to see the *people* of our newest provinces—the Punjab and Oudh—as yet unmoved by what is going on. Those of the North-West have not been loyal, and more plundering has been carried on by the rural population about the large stations than by the mutineers. Here we are all perfectly quiet, and I trust in God may remain so. With a purely agricultural population there are no elements of excitement; and unless it be among any of the chiefs in the Southern Maratha country, no chance of disaffection exists on this side India.

'One naturally asks what has been the cause of all this—of a whole army becoming at once disaffected, and officers and men, Hindu and Mohammedan, abandoning allegiance, pay, and pensions,—risking all in this wild attempt to subvert the Government, for no one can doubt that that is the end aimed at. It is not only that present advantages have been risked, or considerations of them thrown away; future considerations are involved as well. All sepoys, or most of the Bengal army, are connected with land,—there was hardly a farmer or proprietor of any kind who had not a son or relative in the army; many were themselves landed proprietors: all are known, and, as traitors, have forfeited their estates. It would seem also, by the wanton butchery of officers, and by the measures at once pursued, that it was desired to leave no chance of accommodation or retreat. I suppose all this will come out some day. It is impossible but that a commission must be appointed to sift the whole to the bottom, and devise a remedy. The authorities, blindly confident, or timid, or conceited as they may have been, must open their eyes now, and not only look danger in the face, but provide against its recurrence. Some people talk of Russia; but I cannot think what she can have to do with it, or how secret means could have been devised for the corruption of the army. That a general conspiracy was made, who can doubt?—the fact of the circulation of those mysterious cakes of bread last year showed this, though no one suspected the sepoys, or at least declared that they did.

'But observant men have done so for many years. I have never met an officer who had seen Bengal troops, who was not amazed at their lax discipline. Colonel Jacob,[1] long ago,

---

History of the Indian Mutiny. 'Wilson had done something to retrieve his tarnished reputation'; though it was the opinion of John Nicholson, who was not present, that 'he was driven into fighting at the Hindun, and could not help himself'.

[1] John Jacob of Jacobabad, 1812–58. His cousin on the Bombay side, afterwards Sir George Le Grand Jacob, 1805–81, was the General

said that the "normal condition of the Bengal army was *mutiny*", for which he was nearly losing his commission; but it was fact. At Multan,[1] and through the whole of the Punjab war, the men were hardly to be trusted; and after it, Sir Charles Napier had to quell one mutiny, which had not the appearance of being an isolated ebullition of feeling, though it did not spread. Caste has been the bane of that army, and it has been most strange to me always to hear caste spoken of as an advantage. Brahmin sepoys are, no doubt, a fine race; physically, no finer men exist; temperate and well-behaved always, and they are liked by officers; but they have viewed with dread the gradually extending territory of the British beyond seas, which to them are dreadful, and yet where they might sooner or later have to go—nay, *would* have to go. Enlistment is only made for general service now; and while it has been made by young hands, to get the only service possible, the old hands had not taken the oath, and it must have been an object of the lower and younger grades to free themselves from theirs. There are many reasons why mutiny has broken out, which I see are prominently given in the newspapers—foreign service, suspicion about the Enfield cartridges, general lax discipline, absence of European troops, and the like; but there are others which I do not see noticed

---

Jacob whose vigorous action at Kolhapur, and as Commissioner in the Southern Maratha country, is repeatedly commended by Taylor. Neither Jacob is mentioned in his *History of India.* Sir George Jacob published in 1871 *Western India before and during the Mutiny*, a book much used by Mr. Rice Holmes in his *History of the Indian Mutiny.* See note, opening of Chapter XV., concerning General Jacob's strictures upon Taylor's account of this subject.

[1] Siege of Multan, first and last, from September 1848 to January 1849. In *Seeta* the Brigadier traces much of sepoy disaffection to the siege of Multan, when Bengal troops had to work with Bombay troops. 'And we all saw the difference to our shame. . . . Those little Mahratta fellows would work in the trenches like Englishmen, and never took off their accoutrements on guard, as our petted men who jeered them, did. Do you think we dared to ask our high caste people to do the same? Not we; there would have been a mutiny on the spot. Yes, Jacob's clever letter went to the root of that matter and many another! but who would or *dare* attend to its wise and practical considerations?'

The situation before Multan is further illustrated in Taylor's *History*, p. 691. 'The Bombay army . . . had a more exact internal discipline than the Bengal. On these points, the contrast between the men of the two armies at the siege of Mooltan was very evident; the Bombay Sepoys were taunted with performing ordinary duties which had never been imposed upon the high-caste Brahmins of the Bengal army, and opinions and discussions had run high in camp and throughout India on the subject.'

at all, but which strike me as having had some effect. These are: 1st, The way in which the Commission in Oudh has been working, and its result as regards the landholders. This class—petty Rajas, Thakurs, and landholders of all degrees—are powerful under the native governors, and lawless to a degree. They had as much land as they liked, and paid only what they chose. The Government was at perpetual feud with them; and they had the best of it, I suspect. Now that is all changed, and there can be no distinction of persons. 2dly, It is said that the appointments in the Commission, as regards the heads of it, were not good—too many regulation men—and that the revenue screw was not spared at all. I do not know how this is, but suspect that all combined has had more to do with the Mutiny than any other cause—or if not more, that it has had the effect of arousing to action all other subjects of real or fancied discontent. 3dly, I doubt also whether the revenue system of the North-West Provinces is sound—Thomason's system, so belauded by its supporters. It has *not* secured property to the middle classes; and the yeomen, who are our sepoys, have lost lands, which are swallowed up by moneyed men. The Santal rebellion [1] was of this kind; but there, interest and exorbitant charges on money transactions had driven *savages* to despair. The middle classes of tenants in the North-West are not savages, and watch and have watched with jealousy the operation of laws and courts which have sold up old properties and encumbered new ones. I cannot dilate on these subjects; but keep them in mind, and I think you will see hereafter that they have had effect banefully to weaken attachment which might have been secured by other means.

'I am confident in your English resources. It will be seen that a very large force of European troops is needed for India, and that henceforth they must be *en masse*, as Sir Charles Napier most truly observed and urged. Isolated parties are of no use, and, as in case of the assembly at Delhi, can only be got together after long delays, and then inefficiently. I have no doubt the Government will send from 10,000 to 20,000 men directly, and meantime what there are will hold their own *at least*; but I hope the Delhi matter will have been settled by this time, and, after that, the rest is rather of detail only. Without money, without leaders, without guns, resources, or ammunition, what can a rabble of sepoys do? Social mischief only; and that, horrible as it has been

---

[1] During the second half of 1855. In the *History* there is a paragraph about the Santal rebellion, referring to and praising the young W. W. Hunter's *Annals of Rural Bengal*. This, when Taylor wrote, had only recently appeared, and had been made by him the subject of an article in the *Edinburgh Review*.

and may be, is the price at which we are purchasing experience. Perhaps, in the end, all will be better than before. Illusions will be dispelled, and there will be no trifling with danger. There must be a native army, but that of Bengal will not be what it has been. There will be more European cavalry and infantry, and more artillery; more irregular levies or armed police: in short, we shall be wiser and sadder, and shall not trust, as we seem to have been doing for many years, to our good fortune or *prestige*. This, too, may have been one of those solemn warnings, given in God's providence, resulting from struggles in men's minds between forms of belief—the *fact* between heathenism and Christianity. What the Saxons were to Charlemagne, the Hindus, *mutatis mutandis*, may be to us. A great struggle between light and darkness, civilisation and savages, is no doubt progressing, and, like others before it, will have its phases of excitement and misery. Lord Canning is doing well *now*, but was not decisive enough perhaps at first. Yet who shall say it? [1]

'MEADOWS TAYLOR.'

---

[1] The military will say it as represented by Sir Thomas Seaton, who was doing more conspicuous work than Meadows Taylor in this and the following year. He fought before Delhi as a volunteer, having lost his regiment. Very indignant he was that Lord Canning, 'who seemed to rush from blunder to blunder', decided against the prize money, giving six months' batta instead. A soldier chalked up on the walls of the palace: 'Delhi taken and India saved for thirty-six rupees, ten annas; or one rupee, one anna, per battle'. Seaton says that this was reported to Calcutta, and that 'My Lord', or 'his stupid adviser, stung to the quick, directed every exertion to be made to find out the author of the pasquinade'. Of course no one would 'peach'. Some soldiers dashed their money on the ground. Two years later: 'I thought that I could never again look upon a sepoy or the natives of India with the same kindly feeling I had previously entertained for them, and that I should thus be prevented from serving the Government with satisfaction.' *From Cadet to Colonel*, chapters xvii. and xx.

The first Viceroy runs through Taylor's account of the Mutiny. He sums up, when Lord Canning was leaving in March 1862, to die in three months, having given his life for India: 'It was evident that the first fierce clamour against his clemency had been softened by a late, but full, recognition of its justice and necessity. . . . Future historians, while they may notice his natural slowness of conception and of action, will not fail to recognise the inherent firmness and unostentatious greatness of his character. . . . At the worst period, and when surrounded by panic-stricken men, he never lost confidence in himself or his means, and his calm courage and perseverance, while they cheered and encouraged every subordinate authority, gained him an eventual success, the value of which will be enhanced by time.'

Earl Canning, like his father, is remembered among the few best makers of Latin verse at Eton.

'NALDRUG, *July* 6, 1857.

'You will read with horror in England the accounts from the Bengal stations, where regiments have mutinied. I will not dwell upon them. Mutiny, and a declaration for the sepoy's cause, whatever it is, might have been expected in an organised rising of this kind; but it is clear now that the extermination of officers, with their wives and families, was one main object—and, alas! it has been accomplished with fiendish barbarity in many instances. I cannot think otherwise than that England will be stirred as she has rarely been stirred before; and that it has needed but the perusal of the accounts of the last month, and even of the last fortnight, to arouse a spirit of vengeance against these miscreant sepoys, such as has been rarely, if ever, displayed among you, and that troops will be sent out instantly in large numbers. We have not yet heard of the fall of Delhi—that is the point on which all interest centres at present; and the operations there are not known, except that General Barnard had repulsed three sorties from the place, with great loss to the mutineers. By the last accounts—that is, up to the 16th—the General was waiting for some reinforcements from the Punjab, which had reached Umballa on their way down to him. I daresay the place is strong; and as all in it are fighting with halters in prospect if taken, they are doubtless desperate; and it is clear nothing can be risked. Reports have come down country to Bombay that the place has been taken, but they are not officially confirmed as yet; so we must wait in patience. They are strong in Calcutta, and I daresay by this time have some of the Chinese troops there; if so, they will be pushed up the country with all speed. The Punjab is quiet—no rising or disturbance—which speaks well for the local administration. All through the Deccan and south of India there is entire tranquillity. Hyderabad is well in hand by Davidson, who will get credit for what he has done. The Nizam and the Minister are stanch, and the Arabs well in hand also; they have no sympathy with the Bengal movement, or with a king of Delhi, and will be faithful to us. Here we are all quiet and peaceable as any one could wish, and also in all the adjoining districts, British and Nizam's. We were rather apprehensive, a week ago, that a regiment of Nizam's Contingent cavalry, which had mutinied at Aurungabad, and was at first stated to be in full march on its station, Mominabad, about sixty miles from this, might make a dash at us for the sake of the treasury; but that report was false. No men moved from Aurungabad till General Woodburn's force arrived there by a forced march of seventy miles from Ahmednagar. The General went straight to the cavalry lines, surrounded the regiment, when the greatest number of the men submitted at once—in fact, joined him; but some remained till a charge or two of grape was sent among them, when they fled for the most part, sixty-four being taken prisoners. Of these, several have been hanged, and some transported; and the example will have a good effect—no doubt, indeed, has had, for no one has stirred elsewhere. I have about eighty of the men of this corps on duty in the district, but all have behaved well, and seem right glad to be out of the mess. There was an ugly sort of conspiracy at Satara, when the matter first broke out; but Rose, the Collector there, who is a good officer, has nipped it in the bud, and all is square again.

'You will see that the ex-king of Oudh has been confined, and that Government have a clue to his participation in the matter. I have from the first thought that Oudh was the cause of this. Our Bengal army are Oudh men for the most part; and, as I may have said before, the check on habitual lawlessness in Oudh, and no less lawlessness in the ranks of the army, was hardly to be endured. No doubt the conspiracy has been long matured. It has been no cartridge question, or any other question, but a struggle to break bonds, which were getting tighter every day. If this outbreak had not occurred, the crisis would have come in some other form, and might possibly have been worse. As it is, it is only a question of time. The Ganges is rising fast, and steamers can get up with troops easily and quickly. 5,000 men from China will hold everything till you can send us more; but for some years to come India will require many more European troops than she has had. In this Lord Dalhousie failed, that he trusted the native army when it was clear they were not in hand as soldiers should be. With a new annexation at one end in the Punjab, and one in the middle—and considering the character of Oudh, which was far more lawless than the Punjab ever was—there should have been a heavy European force there and at Delhi. All this is too late now: we have only to retrieve the losses, and our power will be stronger than ever, and the attachment of all well-disposed classes greater; for it is clear to all, when any disorganisation ensues, what will be the result to property. Government will be sadder but wiser; and the administration of India for the next hundred years more civilised than it has been since Plassey. The savagery of the worst State in India has had its burst—a fearful one it has been—but the retribution will be as fearful. All these men are landed proprietors in Oudh. Dare they return there to be hunted down? Every man's name is known, and his place of residence; and when our turn begins again, woe to them! Small mercy will be shown to the violators and murderers of English women and helpless children. As it is, there appears a lull. About half the Bengal army has not stirred. Many of the corps are doing good service, and will perhaps wait to see the issue of Delhi. By-and-by, as corps move up from Calcutta, the rebels will be between two fires. We know they have no ammunition or material in shot and shell but what may have been got at Delhi, and no ammunition but what was found there. Where are they to get caps for their muskets, which are all percussion? We see at Benares that they threw away 1,400 stand of arms. Now, if they kept their arms and discipline, they might be formidable; but without either, they are no more than the rabble, which has never yet stood—and never can—regular armies. So I see good hope in prospect; and as we must have had it *out* one day, the worst is over, I think. Every one will blame Lord Dalhousie, I daresay. I only see that he was wrong in not covering his annexations with sufficient European troops, and this the Russian war prevented his doing. We ought to hear by the mail coming in what you say at home to the beginning of the Mutiny. But we cannot hear what you know of the worst for another fortnight, or month perhaps. This mutiny will give us an electric telegraph to you, no doubt, when you can hear daily news from India. But we should be thankful that we have at least steam to carry over distress to you in a month, and perhaps gain help. You will see that men are equal to the emergency. Lawrence at Lucknow has done wonders. Colonel Neill and his Madras Fusiliers are renowned already—a gallant-spirited man as any we have. In the Punjab, too, they have determined men and troops enough, as they have got rid of all the Bengal men. We only want troops for the North-Western Provinces and Central India, and we shall be all right in a few months. Meanwhile, the more anxious England is the better.

'You will see what Lord Canning has done about the press. I think it was needed now; but it may be relaxed, except to native prints, hereafter. And I hope these murders and massacres will ease Exeter Hall and its party of some of its cant in regard to "sympathy with natives".

'I am quite well—and here, but that we read newspapers, should have no anxiety whatever. Tell this to all who ask after me. God bless you! and believe me ever yours faithfully, MEADOWS TAYLOR.'

[In the month of August Captain Taylor was promoted to the Deputy-Commissionership in North Berar, and proceeded to his new station at Buldana.]

'JALNA, *September* 7, 1857.

'I have got so far on my journey to my new country,—that is, about three-fourths of the distance. We cannot travel luxuriously as you do, but I have come about 180 miles in nine days, with my tents and servants well up, which is not bad work. I give all a rest here, and hope that Bullock will come in from Buldana to-day, till when I shall occupy myself with writing, and first to you. I had intended to have done so on the road ; but the double marches, evening and morning, though they are not over ten or twelve miles at the most, interrupt every attempt to settle to anything. My journey has been a very pleasant one ; there was no rain to speak of : and through the Nizam's country, in which I could not possibly have been treated with greater civility and distinction had I been the Resident himself, deputations met me from all the large towns and stations, and I was helped on in every way I could desire. The country is perfectly peaceful and loyal to us. But it is sad to see so much of it waste, and to hear the people complaining, not so much of active oppression, as of no one taking the least interest in them, except to screw what can be got out of them. I see, however, changes for the better in the system of district management, and there seems to be a system at last ; but it must be, even with Salar Jung, that he has little assistance, much opposition, and in all cases very lukewarm co-operation. I trust, however, that a man so thoroughly in earnest and single in purpose will succeed as he deserves to do. His conduct through the trying crisis of June and July has been very admirable ; and as it has passed the ordeal of the Moharram safely, Hyderabad may be considered thoroughly safe, I think, as its people throughout the country are entirely well affected.

'You ask me in your last what the effect of this mutiny upon the princes of India seems to be. It is not an easy question to answer, but I will give you my opinions ; and, unless we sustain very unlooked-for and serious reverses, I do not think they will alter. At present, then, I think all is in a satisfactory state. Certainly there is no sympathy with the mutineer sepoys, neither politically nor as far as creed is concerned. The papers will give you details, but not one of the large States has moved or openly displayed sympathy with the sepoy movement. Wherever these Purbia[1] sepoys, whether Hindus or Musalmans, have had service, they have mutinied and gone towards Delhi, as they did from our service. Contingents of native princes which at first appeared loyal to us, but which consisted of the *same classes* of soldiers as our men, broke away as well from us as from their nominal masters and joined the general confederacy. You see this exemplified in the events at Indore and Gwalior, and the cases of the Kotah contingent, Bhopal people, etc. ; but as soon as Holkar was rid of his mutinous soldiery, who marched to Delhi, and his own Marathas rallied round him, he welcomed the Resident back, and matters now are much safer and quieter than before. The princes of Rajputana have been loyal and stanch, I believe, to a man, helping with their men

---

[1] This is defined on following page as Hindustani, and particularly as having to do with Oudh. The word Purbia means 'eastern'.

as far as was needed. I can, however, readily understand their not sending large bodies into the field, with an infectious spirit abroad, and without any apparent head, knowing that there is amongst them as strong a love for plunder and anarchy as existed in the time of the Pindharis, nay worse. Native States have therefore kept quiet, sending only what they themselves could entirely depend on; and in this they have been right.

'That there is any combination among native States against us, I have no suspicion; and a combination to set up a head, as an Emperor of Delhi, would, I should think, be the last thing that any one of them wanted. If it were possible that such a result followed, even for a while, the impossibility of cohesion is most transparent to all; while the certainty of exaction, extortion, plunder, and insecurity of property, is alike clear to every one. Better, therefore, as it is, to them; and they are accordingly quiet, if not active and sympathising friends. At a first glance you might think that the Nizam State would sympathise with a "Delhi Raj". But the Nizams were faithless to Delhi, utterly so, and would have to pay a heavy reckoning, nay, be utterly extinguished, if possible. The Maratha princes, what remain of them, hold territories wrested from Delhi. Would they be spared? The Rajput princes, the oldest feudatories of Delhi, have, as I have said, displayed active sympathy with us, retaining and protecting the political agents with them, and helping with supplies, and in other ways of which the papers give details. I have from the first looked anxiously to see whether any grand political movement or confederation could be detected, but as yet there appears none, and I think the Government will have the same intelligence from the Governor-General. No; as yet the movement appears confined to the Bengal army, and to that portion of it which is called Purbia or Hindustani. The Sikhs will have none of it: Gurkhas are stanch; but wherever these Purbias are, there are disaffection and open savagery of the worst description. The reason of this is as yet a profound mystery. That the whole of the Bengal army was prepared to rise about the 15th May, there can be no doubt now; and that its rising was not simultaneous, has been providential. Even now, regiments that have been disarmed break away occasionally. Corps of irregular cavalry that have been considered stanch, mutiny and make off to plunder, and join, if they can, the Delhi or Rohilkund parties, even without arms, or pay, or plunder. To doubt, therefore, a preconcerted plan in this mutiny would be absurd. It has existed, and exists; and out of the whole Bengal army I do not think there are at present more than half-a-dozen Purbia regiments who are stanch, or who have proved loyalty by action. It will be long before the origin of the movement is known. Whether, as has been supposed, it is in reality a plot of the Delhi princes to attempt to regain sovereignty,—whether it is owing to intrigues in Oudh,—whether an attempt among a powerful body, bound together as the Hindu Purbias are by one bond of religious belief, to establish a dominion of military priests as existed in the ancient days of Hinduism,—or whether it is one of these outbreaks of savagery against civilisation, of which we have instances innumerable in the history of civilisation, remains to be seen. My own impressions lead me much to the latter belief. Civilisation is pressing hard on Hinduism, perhaps also on Mohammedanism : I do not say Christianity, for that as yet is far off ; but that amount of civilisation which has proved progression of knowledge to be incompatible with Hinduism, and to be sapping its very existence. This may have led to conspiracy among Brahmins, and by them the Rajputs or Kshattriya classes have been aroused to action. These classes compose the Bengal army. There are no others. Hindustani Musalmans are much Hinduised, and were originally part of the Hindu people. Hence, when it became necessary, there has been for the time a complete identification of the interests of all. Again, for the last fifty years we have been breeding up a race of stalwart priests for our army. In the most deplorable manner we have strengthened every prejudice by enlisting none but them. The magnificent *men* of that army were the admiration of all, they were accordingly pampered and indulged by all ; they *would not allow* intermixture of other classes ; they recruited themselves ; and each corps, from the officers down to the lowest private, were not only classmen, but fellow-priests as Brahmins, or holy warriors as Kshattriyas. Can anything more pregnant with mischief be imagined ? Yet so vain were Bengal officers of their men, and of their men's *caste*, which was the strangest thing, that mention or thought of anything low-caste was ridiculed,—and the Madras and Bombay armies held as things of nought. So it went from bad to worse, as regards discipline ; and while the sepoys strengthened themselves in their regiments, civilisation was treading hard on their heels outside. Sepoys were not educated men, except in ceremonials as Brahmins. Education was spreading over Bengal and the North-West Provinces very fast. It would have followed into Oudh, and as yet Oudh was a stronghold of dark Hindu fanaticism. The Oudh Brahmins are known by other Brahmins for their attachment to, and study of, the mystic rites of Bhowani or Kali. These rites are held in abhorrence by Deccan Brahmins ; they call them fearful and unholy, and those among them who have knowledge of them are held in dread by the rest. Of such are the Bengal sepoys, the Brahmins and Rajputs of Oudh and as far south as Benares. And since they have broken forth and shown themselves in their true colours, it has not surprised me to see that the mask completely thrown off has displayed in savagery that spirit which in those districts produced Thuggee, which had its most noted leaders from among these very classes. I have given you these reasons to explain why I think this more a movement of savagery against civilisation than aught else, and I still adhere to my opinion that the annexation of Oudh was the incentive to this outbreak. Perhaps the way in which Oudh was managed at first, and till Lawrence got it, made it more immediate than it otherwise would have been. Outram took Oudh, but has always eschewed details of management. The first managing man under him was a thorough-bred Bengal civilian, as the phrase goes,—haughty, quarrelsome, imperious, and a red-tapist of the worst school.[1] So I have heard him described. He did much mischief, no doubt; and *then* must have begun the organisation, or the idea of it. Strange to say, Lord Dalhousie could not see danger in trusting a new country to the military

---

[1] This culprit, though not in books of reference, is easily run to earth. In his *History* Taylor writes: 'In Oudh, the new administration, which had promised fairly at first, became in the last degree unpopular, from the mistaken and over-zealous proceedings of the commissioner, Mr. Coverley Jackson, and his subordinates; and though Mr. Jackson was removed and Sir Henry Lawrence appointed in his room, the evil already done could not be remedied.'

Mr. Rice Holmes, in his *History of the Indian Mutiny*, calls Coverley Jackson 'a smart revenue officer from the North-Western Provinces. . . . No more unfortunate selection could have been made. Jackson was best known for the violence of his temper. . . . Only a man of the greatest tact and firmness could have reconciled the classes who had thriven under the corrupt native government to the rigorous purity of British rule: but Jackson had no tact.' Lord Canning only superseded Jackson 'when his pertinacity had outraged all patience, and when it seemed too late even for Lawrence to repair the mischief which he had done. For the deposed King of Oude was complaining bitterly of the unmanly cruelty with which the English were treating his family, even the delicate ladies of the zenana.' It was shown that 'C. Jackson . . had taken possession of one of the palaces set apart for the royal family'.

The same point is mentioned (though not indexed) in the cumbrous *Life of Outram* by Sir Julian Goldsmid. There were many other complaints, with a lamentable atmosphere of contention. Finally, there are pages about this in the great *Life of Sir Henry Lawrence*, from which a few sentences must suffice. Lawrence reached Lucknow in March 1857, and soon afterwards wrote to relatives: 'Mr. Jackson has received me amiably, though he feels bitterly his supersession. He is an able and energetic man, but, like us Lawrences, has strong passions not under much control.' 'Mr. Jackson was not altogether to blame. He is a violent but able and kindly man. When thwarted he could not restrain himself, and lost his judgment. He stayed eight days with me, and was very amiable, though I told him he was very wrong in some of his acts, and in more of his expressions.'

occupation of a people whose freedom (lawlessness is a better word) his measures were curtailing every day. He too believed in the Bengal sepoy as others did. Yet he was bringing that sepoy's father and brothers into subjection, looking after and taxing their lands, preventing them from indulging in outrages and dacoity. For years and years we have recruited from Oudh; and for years and years we have known the Oudh population to be the most lawless in India. Was it expected that it would like civilisation, or a strong Government, or restraint of any kind? And were not the very men we enlisted as lawless in their way as their brethren at home,—refusing foreign service, refusing discipline, refusing intermixture of other castes? All this was: some saw it, and some wrote about it. Those who did write about it, either to the public or to Government, were marked and ruined men; they were never advanced. Many people are getting courage to speak out *now*, but it is too late. It was a pleasant delusion, that Bengal army, while it lasted; and so were all other Bengal delusions pleasant—nothing was like them. The men who held them were inflated; they were, in fact, Bengal civilians, and who should gainsay them? —— wrote to me only the other day that he knew every one, for years past, who had striven publicly or privately to expose these delusions, had been a marked man. So it went on. One would have thought that when last year the cakes of bread flew through the North-West Provinces, it would have aroused suspicion of some intrigue, or would have been traced. What notice was taken of it? None, that I know of; or if any suspicion was entertained it was shut up. If Government knew of suspected disaffection—or if at any time what Napier wrote, what others hinted, what even broke out in occasional mutiny, was known,—and I am impressed with a conviction that it was known, and feared too,—why was India left so defenceless in regard to European troops? But this is another part of the subject now, alas! causing waste of life and treasure, which will keep India back for years.

'There is another matter, or cause of disaffection, which I will briefly mention, because it affects the *people* of the country. I have doubted the revenue system of the North-West Provinces very much ever since I knew it. It has made village communities throw off attachment to Government, I think, by weakening the bond between them; and it has reduced the bond of the landholders, whether great or small, to a simple question of money-payment, the most easily broken. It has also given headmen too much influence, and reduced village communities to a state of vassalage to them, rather than retaining them in a direct communication with Government authorities. This system is the far-famed "Thomason" system; one which, no doubt, got in most money with least cost—but otherwise, *I* think, and have always thought, was regardless of the people, and regardless of the bond which should have been maintained, rather than broken. You see the result now in some shape. Leaders of villages have abused authority, petty chiefs have leagued with them, both parties have taken to plundering property not belonging to their own classes. Here and there, there are symptoms of revulsion, and the *people*, tired of being plundered, have risen on their headmen, and invited back the European magistrates; and this will progress, I think and trust, as if to show, without doubt, the utter inability of these people to rule themselves without plunder and massacre, and the utter insecurity of property in whatever shape it may exist. This may have its effect in time in restoring order; but the operation of reducing to order a country which has become disorganised is necessarily slow at any time, and one can hardly see or think whom to trust when Government has crushed, as it will crush, the originators of the Mutiny. It is sad to think, too, that all the promotion of natives to offices of trust and confidence has in most instances proved futile to check disorder or maintain authority. There have been, it is true, some faithful men, some bright instances of personal exertion to aid our authority, but they are lamentably few; and it must be almost more bitter to those who have selected these authorities to see them supine or faithless, than to encounter the mad savagery of the native army. It is too soon now to speculate upon final results as to the civil government of the country. It may, it is true, be comparatively easy when order is once more established; but the shock to all has been a rude and violent one. The civilisation of mind, which most of us thought had made progress, proves to be only skin-deep, and not to have affected the masses of the people at all, and will have to be commenced again, I hope in a more earnest and practical spirit than before. I adhere to my opinion that a government on the part of the Crown will be the best policy to pursue, and there can be no doubt that a double Government will not answer. Whether it is understood by the people, that the Company has been, as it were, abandoned by the Crown—that it only occupies the place of "farmers" of the country, or is in the position of a weak interloper, and can be thrown off—I do not know; but there is much in the discussions on the renewal of the charter, and the comparative absence of European troops, to favour the supposition in minds which cannot understand European politics or the constitution of our own country. I see that Sir Erskine Perry [1] has already made a motion on the subject;

---

[1] Rt. Hon. Sir Thomas Erskine Perry, 1806–1882, who had been Chief Justice in Bombay. Later, when for a few years M.P., he attacked Lord Dalhousie's administration and spoke constantly on Indian affairs.

Perry was member of the Council of India for the lengthy period

but the extent of the calamity must be fully known before a remedy can be applied, and I think the result will be a Government into which no division of authority can enter. No one will be hardy enough now to support the doctrine that India can be governed by opinion. It must be by European troops well distributed that government can be maintained. I shall be anxious to see what turn your counsels take on this subject, one on which all in India are well assured that England is doing her best, and that the past will be retrieved in time.

'I have nothing particular to say of myself. I was very sorry to leave the Naldrug district; the people were quiet and attached, the country was fast improving, and improvements as to roads and other matters were in active progress. I do not know on what principles Berar has been managed, and have to get acquainted with the people,—a long matter, with a district of its size. I will write you more from Buldana by-and-by, and when I see my way into what is before me. God bless you.—With my dear love to all kindred, believe me ever yours faithfully, MEADOWS TAYLOR.'

'BULDANA, NORTH-BERAR, *September* 26, 1857.

'I arrived here on the 14th, and took charge of the district, and your letter of the 6th of August reached me a few days after. I wrote to you from Jalna, when staying there to wait for Bullock, and I hope that letter has come safe to hand. I do not think I have missed any mail since this war began; for such as my opinions are, and means of observation, I am anxious you should have the result of them for yourself, apart from all public discussions which reach you from India and are made in England. You have done my first letter much honour,—more than it deserved, I fear, for it was written in a hurry, and in some alarm perhaps, and more than there need have been; and yet I cannot say I have ever felt alarm for anything south of the Nurbudda since the Mutiny broke out, and as yet, you see, we are safe. So long as Hyderabad remains quiet and attached, there is no apprehension, I think, for Southern India; and I sincerely believe that it is both. The Moharram passed off quietly, and there is no excitement at present. On one point they appear obliged to temporise, which is, the trial of Torra Borg Khan, the Rohilla zemindar who led the attack on the Residency. He has not been hanged, as he ought to have been, nor given up, nor will the head of the Adalat in Hyderabad condemn him for taking part in a *holy war*; it would be against Mohammedan laws,

---

from 1859 to 1882. It was to him that the remarkable letter from W. W. Hunter in 1878, urging the merits of Meadows Taylor and the claims of his daughters to pensions, was addressed, which is printed in full at the end of this volume.

and the Minister appears helpless in respect of bringing him to punishment for the present. He is, however, still in confinement, and it is safe policy not to press anything at the present. I have no apprehension of any Maratha league. In the Deccan the old Maratha families are weak, and I do not think there is any one who would have sympathy with Sindia after the long break there has been in the connection. The Brahmin influence was never liked by the true Maratha families, and *he* would not join Nana Sahib, the representative of the Peshwa, nor would the Satara family. There have been reports that Sindia was deposed by his troops, and Delhi proclaimed. But this wants confirmation, and is not believed. Holkar, the Gaikwar, and the Kolhapur chief, the Jaghirdars in the South Maratha country, are all stanch and quiet, and, whether singly or collectively, are too weak to attempt coalition; such at least is my impression, and I imagine Lord Elphinstone says the same. The Maratha people of the Deccan, too, are well off as to employment and landed settlements; they appear to me to have ceased to be warlike in every way, and, under a good system of government and easy taxation, have fairly abandoned old ways and settled down into active farmers. No doubt there were some intrigues at Satara which were put down with a strong hand by Rose, the Collector, who behaved admirably.[1] There were some plots also at Poona and Belgaum, got up by low adventurers, without leaders or means, but having a bad *animus*. These also were promptly discovered and the conspirators executed. The reported mutiny of one Bombay regiment at Kolhapur caused some alarm for the time lest it should spread; but it was an attempt by the Hindustanis of the regiment, which was, beyond anything we have seen yet, insane and futile; and these men were disposed of very gallantly by the Maratha Horse and the true men of their own corps. In this matter the Kolhapur Raja was well affected, and gave what help he could; and you know he is one of the representatives of Sivaji, and many of the old Maratha families hold by him and

---

[1] These small intrigues are not mentioned in Taylor's *History*. The *Imperial Gazetteer* merely says: 'During the Mutiny a widespread conspiracy was discovered at Satara to restore the Maratha power with assistance from the North; but the movement was suppressed with only trifling disturbances.' Mr. Rice Holmes gives half a page to it, mentioning Mr. Rose, and stating that seventeen conspirators were executed, while the family of the late Raja were transported.

As to the rising at Kolhapur, below, Taylor, in his *History*, writes: 'Captain Kerr, commanding the Mahratta Horse, with fifty troopers, marched from Sattara to Kolapoor—seventy-six miles—in twenty-four hours, and pursuing the mutineers, came up with them in a temple where they were resting, and slew most of them.' Mr. Rice Holmes relates these and kindred events in great detail. Kerr lived until 1919.

his little court. The Brahmins of the Deccan are not military people in any way, and they are well represented and provided for in Government employ. I do not think there is discontent among them, and if there were, they have no sympathy among the Maratha people, who do not like them. Under all these points of view, I do not think there is ground for apprehension of any Maratha rising or combination, and I hope my views may be ultimately correct.

'Now the more I look back to what I wrote to you first, the more I am inclined to adhere to the opinions I then expressed, and have since repeated. The Mohammedan sympathy in the movement has been secondary as far as the people are concerned, even in the North-West Provinces, but the share of the King of Delhi and his large family of *soi-disant* Shahzadas in the original plot, while it remains to be investigated, is meantime borne out by facts. I have long considered the Bengal army utterly unsafe. It had become impossible to control the priestly faction of which it was composed, and to which all others were subordinate; for the Mohammedan portion of it was just as arrogant in respect to caste prejudices as the Hindu, and followed the Hindu lead. It was impossible to convince Bengal officers of the mischief attending any caste as an element of military service under us. No attempt was made, or could have been made (except by taking the bull by the horns, which no one dared to do), to break down the caste influence, except by the very partial effort of the enlistment of sepoys on oath for general service—which of course, and as might have been foreseen, was useless in contact with the old and very powerful element of the former system. I daresay this was admitted by those who chose to think—and I will venture to say there were few who did not; still, the old prejudice in favour of high-caste Brahmins, arising no doubt out of the comparative ease by which they were managed as soldiers in garrison, the fine appearance of the men, and the bravery *occasionally* displayed in recent times, with the *prestige* of old victories, all combined to perpetuate the illusion; and while the soldiery were led to look up to the service as an hereditary right, they became the less disposed to brook any interference with it. You see how these men were spreading fast into the Bombay army. As Hindustani men rose to rank as *subadars* and native officers in general, and returned to their native villages, they were employed to bring down batches of recruits, fine stalwart young fellows, who enlisted readily, and no doubt served well. Marathas, as their country has been settled, and become, as it is, one expanse of cultivation, needed no employment for their young men, and, except the very lowest classes, did not enlist in the army. Those regiments into which a Hindustani element has been once infused, became more and more Hindustani from year to year; and the 16,000 men said now to be in the

Bombay army would have been doubled in a few years more, with the same kind of contrivance, the same views, and no doubt eventually the same conduct as the Bengal army itself. Happily, most happily, this has been broken up. The design of enlisting any more of these people, and the danger of even allowing what there are to remain, is too imminent to be overlooked, and it will be averted. In the Madras army I believe there are a few Hindustanis here and there, but very few, and they will, I trust, be got rid of. But in the Madras army there is another influence not unlike what prevailed in Bengal, which needs to be checked in time; this is the Mohammedan, and you will do good service by bringing it to notice in those quarters where it can be remedied. The military portion of the Mohammedans of the Madras Presidency lie about Arcot, Seringapatam, Vellore, and other places, and are exclusively military, looking, as the Bengal and Oudh Brahmins did, to hereditary services. They are known to be bigoted, and even natives mistrust the Thal Ghat Musalman as turbulent and unfaithful. They have their old ideas of rule under the Mysore dominion of Hyder and Tippoo, brief but brilliant; possibly have no sympathy with Delhi, but true sympathy with the cause of Islam. They are not cultivators, like the Sikhs and Marathas, but look to service as sepoys—in short, to a military life, rather than to any other, and have found it in the Madras army to a great extent. It is only necessary that this combination, which provides all the cavalry and many of the infantry regiments, should not be allowed to proceed as it has done in Bengal; and there is plenty of time to avert it. I have known many men who thought that the more a regiment was connected by family ties the better; but we now see the danger of it as regards the Bengal army, and, under the constitution of the native mind, everywhere the same; and the danger attending combination induced by a sense of power, I think should be prevented. I am not writing or thinking any wrong of the Madras army, which as yet has proved wonderfully stanch and obedient in many trying times and foreign wars: I only wish to prevent the possibility of its becoming other than it is and has been—the possibility of its gaining that conviction of power, which has destroyed the Bengal army, as it will assuredly any other army which is infected by it. By what means this can be best effected is not in my power to state. It must be done silently, gradually, and without exciting suspicion. I have often thought a partial admission of half-castes, as also enlistment of negroes, or some of the martial Cape tribes, would be good, and negroes best of all;[1]

[1] Negroes in India would afford subject for a monograph. Their military value, under superior direction, has been illustrated in West, East and North Africa. In India they could not always be controlled.

and often and often, in old letters, have I dwelt on this subject, and alluded to the increasing predominance of *caste power* in the native armies, particularly in that of Bengal; but who attended then? Another idea is, that part of every native regiment should be European,—say one flank company or both flank companies, with more English non-commissioned

---

There were several short-lived negro kings even in Bengal. To use the word Abyssinian, as is conventionally done, is of course an absurd equivalent for East Coast negroes of whom the one thing certain is that they were Moslems. On the Bombay coast they are represented by the Habshi, the Grand Negro as one may say, of Janjira: his petty State is called Habsan, 'the African's land'. The other word for negro, Sidi, perhaps a corruption of Saiyid, is also located here. To be a Sidi in Janjira is to be a person of distinction, probably related to the Nawab and in possession of State grants. Many good sailors come from Janjira island.

Even a European feels the sense of intrusion in reading of so many Arabs, and more particularly of negroes, in the history of Hyderabad. Indians might well have felt the presence of negroes, certainly when dominant, an unequalled profanation to the sacred soil of Bharata. They probably did, but could not help themselves.

Without quoting references to Abyssinians in Taylor's *History*, here are two passages from the full picture of the Bijapur polity in 1657 in *Tara*: 'At this period the Dekhanies and Abyssinians were rival factions in the state. The latter were more amenable to discipline than the former, who were descendants of . . . Toorks, Tartars, and Affghans. . . . Was it wonderful that they at length became arrogant, and that, to maintain an equipoise against them, another element, the Abyssinian, was admitted into this state?' It is a Hindu who later says: 'Take some of your . . . Abyssinians; they know no fear, and are more certain than the braggart, plundering Dekhanies, who are afraid of the Mother who sits in the glen, though they are Mussulmans.'

In the attack upon the temple at Tuljapur it is a huge negro who strikes down Tara's father. It must have been humiliating to live upon a plane whereon the big bodies and the docile vigour of the negroes gave them an advantage. At the opening of *Tara* the Wazir of Bijapur is a treacherous Abyssinian, a former slave, dreaming of kingship, who gets slain. His son, Kowas Khan, betrothed to the delicate Zyna, must have been a negro, perhaps with some dilution of Indian blood. Taylor has not dared to make speaking characters out of either of these historic figures. 'We feel that we do not know much of this young man,' he weakly says at the end. The Slave Kings of Delhi were of very different race.

It is but just to say that the most recent testimony of missionaries in Western India who have had the training of negro boys taken from slave ships is that they far surpass the lower-caste natives of that countryside in energy, strength, and industry. The standing example of the enlightened negro is Malik Ambar, minister of Ahmednagar at the opening of the seventeenth century, died 1626. In his *History*

officers. The French mixed natives and Europeans together in this manner with good effect, both as to work in the field and discipline in garrison, and it prevented combination. It has long been the opinion of able men that artillery should be exclusively European, and natives used only as assistants, as I may say, under them; and in this I entirely coincide. It is the artillery only of the mutinous Bengal army which does any execution, and costs us men to recover; and yet the guns have not in general been well fought, and are taken by comparative handfuls of our troops. But I am wearying you, I daresay, with these disquisitions.

'The siege-train has reached Delhi, and the final result there cannot be delayed. Every one knows by this time of the munificent aid you are giving us, and the rest is but a work of time. The cold weather is before us, the British army will have the best of the year for field operations, and it is little to say, I think, will perhaps, in the end, be disappointed that there is so little left to do. I myself think there will be comparatively few left in Delhi when it is assaulted, and that our final operations will be in Oudh, where most of the mutineers will fight *pro aris et focis*, and not for the King of Oudh, or any potentate whatever. It will be satisfactory to you to see how few persons of rank are concerned in this movement, and how few of the people in general, when the millions of which the population of Hindustan is composed are reckoned. Idle savagery exists everywhere, and the country has never been disarmed. Plunder and violence might be expected from such classes, and it has no doubt abounded, to the misery and disgust of those better classes who were secure under us. I cannot but think that this has had a great effect in our favour throughout the country, and most, too, in the worst districts about Delhi and in Oudh. I trust the complete disarming of the Bengal Presidency will be the first work of the *new* Government. It has worked well in the Punjab; and indeed for all India a "licence to carry arms bill" would be very advisable. Oudh must be disarmed, of course. They did not hesitate to disarm the Punjab almost as the first measure, and we see the benefit of it now; but they dared not attempt to disarm Oudh, because it would have affected the Bengal army, and so it remained as before, strong in itself as having perpetually resisted the Oudh Government, and stronger as being part of ourselves, with which we dare not interfere. It will be broken now and reduced, and with it will be broken all military *prestige*, and I hope combination, not only of the

Taylor calls him 'one of those Abyssinians who, little better than savages in their own country, displayed in the Deccan abilities as statesmen and generals which were hardly exceeded by the more civilised Persians'. But he neglects to make him a speaking character in *A Noble Queen.*

Brahmins and Rajputs, but of the petty rajas and zemindars who abound. In our next revenue settlements, too, we might break up combinations in regard to land, and by seeing that every one gets what he requires for cultivation, make him dependent more upon Government than on his feudal chief. I mistrust those North-West settlements, I assure you, very deeply, and think that had the Government made grants to the people instead of to the middlemen, they would have had more content, more real attachment than in the other course. That course, however, got most money at least cost of collection, and so was persevered in.

'I do not go into details of events; those the newspapers chronicle steadily. A few Bengal regiments remain stanch, and do good work, as the 31st at Saugor, etc.; but the rest are gone, and happily, I think, sparing our Government any chance of sympathising with them afterwards. You will know the sad, sad particulars of Cawnpore in time; and I beg you to read the deposition of a subadar of the Bombay army, who for his faithful conduct has been promoted, with 1000 rupees, and the military order of merit. I dare say, and hope, that there will be many such examples come to light by-and-by. You may hear by this mail that Delhi has been stormed, and Lucknow relieved by Havelock and Outram. If they do not kill the King of Delhi, I hope he will be transported to England with all his family. The King of Oudh should go too, and be kept there, as Dhulip Singh is, in honour and respect. There should be no flinching in this, I think.

'I would not have you think, from anything I have said, that I am against the annexation policy of Lord Dalhousie. The fault was, not guarding it sufficiently; and if, as I believe, it has been the direct means of showing the true temper and worth of the Bengal army, it has been the more welcome now that we are free to remedy it. We should have been hard pressed if this outbreak had occurred when we had the Russian war on our hands. I am delighted to see the question of the Queen's Government openly canvassed; and it should be carried steadily through till Queen Victoria's proclamations are in every village of India belonging to her.[1]

---

[1] No more moderate and illuminating comment upon the Mutiny can well be found than in these contemporary letters. But *Seeta*, Taylor's only novel dealing with the Mutiny, does not offer as much illustrative matter as might have been expected: the intellectual quality does not predominate there.

In his Introduction to *Seeta* Taylor brings out a favourite point. 'The Sumbut year 1914 commenced on March 25, 1857, and closed on March 19, 1858, before the war had come to an end. It had been preceded by deadly epidemics and disastrous floods, and in addition to these, tumult and massacre, as predicted, had marked its course.' Many natives clung to the belief that 'the English are just in the end'.

'This is a nice little station. Myself, Captain Grant, and his wife, are the only tenants of it. Bullock's house, which he lets me live in, is very comfortable. The situation is on the table-land just above the Ghat, on the south side of the Berar

---

Yet this belief was sorely tried by the annexations above discussed. 'They are all-powerful, and in the main they are just; but why so greedy? Is no one to be left?' These disquieting facts were supplemented by rumours which would not have gone down in all lands. 'The childish credulity of the ordinary Hindoo native of India', says Taylor, 'has no equal in the world. Trained in his youth to believe the astonishing, and to him beneficent, miracles of his gods, his mind is prepared, as it were, to receive any human exaggeration and invention without question, and for any cause.'

The speech of Azrael Pandé to the Oudh sepoys at Barrackpur in chapter xx. has some good points. Which of them used not formerly, when stepping into any of the holy rivers, to cry out first 'Jey Gunga Mata!' and next 'Jey Kumpani Bahadur!'? 'With such cries our fathers went to battle, and won a thousand victories. But that is past. The "Kumpani" is not as it used to be; it is no longer an incarnation of our gods. It has changed into a mean, cheating robber, who farms this great Hind of ours from the Government of England, and robs it of all it can carry away. Where do those great ships yonder take the cotton, and the indigo, and the silk which the poor ryots have produced, but to England? Do they bring us anything in return? No! nothing but what we have to buy, and very dearly; and even the old Moghuls did not tax our salt and our opium. . . . In the west they took Sattara, and the family of Sivajee are beggars.'

Then comes the obscurantist argument that the former muskets were good enough to fight with—reminding them of a grievance. 'Did not the old win all Hind for the English? win it with your fathers' blood, freely poured out? Did not thousands of our people perish in the Khyber amidst the snow and ice—whose blood cries for vengeance? Did not these same men die with the old guns in their frozen hands?'

The judge, returning from Calcutta, speaks of the grumbling of the sepoys; 'and between you and me, they don't ever grumble for nothing. . . I hate these new-fangled laws; can't they let the people alone?' Next year it has become: 'And so around them the trouble thickened, for the evil storm of 1914 was raging fearfully everywhere.'

In contrast to so much discrimination as to the causes of the Mutiny, an interesting passage in *From Cadet to Colonel* illustrates the merely military point of view. Seaton returned to command his regiment in 1855 after an absence of ten years. At once he noticed 'a marked deterioration in the bearing and conduct of the sepoys towards their European officers. . . . The men were quite careless of showing respect to any officer but those of their own regiment. Riding in uniform past the guard of other regiments, I constantly observed that the sepoys would stand with their arms folded, their legs straddled, their noses raised in the air, and that they would salute with mock respect, or purposely with the left hand. . . . Every governor-general and

valley, six miles east of a place called Dewal Ghat, which I daresay you will find in any good map. The climate is very good—just now most delightful; and I am quite hearty, and well as ever I was in my life, I am thankful to say. Now good-bye, and God bless you all!—My most affectionate regards and remembrance to all, and believe me ever yours most faithfully, MEADOWS TAYLOR.'

I cannot find my usual statement of revenue and cultivation for this official year, 1856–57, which would have given the details of each department. I only find in a letter to my father, dated June 4, that the net amount of revenue was 919,000 rupees in round numbers, and that the 40,000 rupees lost by abolition of customs duties had been nearly made up.

The increase in cultivation had been very nearly 35,000 acres in the year, which, together with the previous increase, made a total of 219,000 since the cession. 237 miles of road had been completed, and much more had been surveyed, marked out, and was in progress.

The survey showed a result of 260,000 acres completed; and the surveyors, who could not do field-work in the rains, were now occupied in making fair copies of village maps and registries. These maps were most creditably executed, and some of my pupils evinced decided talent as draughtsmen.

---

commander-in-chief, including that most mischievous double functionary, Lord William Bentinck, had done something tending to the ruin of the native army. Lord William Bentinck gave it the first and most serious push down the incline.'

Not only did he abolish some allowances of the officers, but he abolished corporal punishment in the native army. 'There are two things the natives of India revere as much as they do their deities: money and power. Lord William Bentinck mulcted their officers in both.' Sir Thomas Seaton testifies: 'There is naturally a great deal of the gentleman about the sepoy.' But: 'Take away the lash, and in a campaign your army will soon become a disorderly rabble. I have commanded both English and native troops, and know it well. . . . Lord Dalhousie, governor-general, and Lord Gough, commander-in-chief, men of natures as noble and merciful as could be found, recognised the absolute necessity of re-establishing corporal punishment in the native army, and carried it into effect.'

Yet they reduced the officer to the condition of King Log. 'In time commanding officers found themselves like Gulliver, so tied down by innumerable little strings, that they could move neither hand nor foot. The weapon that kept the wild beast in awe was taken out of their hands; the beast rose up against them, and they were weaponless, prostrate, and helpless' (*From Cadet to Colonel*, chapter xiii., 1866).

I was in daily expectation of a reply in regard to the principles and working of the survey which I had drawn up, and submitted in November 1856 ; but eight months' work had shown decided and continuous improvement in every respect ; and as the tenures of land had not entered into the first propositions, and I had to make many explanations in regard to future contingencies, my final report was delayed. My readers would scarcely understand the minutiæ of village and landed tenures, and I will not inflict them upon them here ; but I may mention that I found a great proportion of the occupants of land to be *mirasdars*—that is, persons who hold their portions of land in hereditary occupancy, and had so held it for generations, on a fixed rent. Most of these had suffered from local exactions, and but too many had thrown up their ancestral lands, and had emigrated to the British provinces. Of these great numbers had now returned, and had taken up their former estates where they were in possession of yearly tenants. Others, in cases where the land had been improved, had paid the occupant a sum of money for reoccupancy ; but all *miras* rights were reclaimable within a period of forty years of absence. To preserve the local rights of these *miras* proprietors, the tenants of *miras* lands had only been recognised as yearly tenants ; but they were not disturbed so long as they paid their rent regularly.

The third was a fluctuating class, who took up lands which generally belonged to the village area, on yearly tenure only. These were constantly changing, and passing from village to village, for the most part unthrifty people, with neither capital nor credit, and but few cattle.

I could see plainly the advantage of settled classes, and of giving them security of tenure, in order to induce the employment of capital and the improvement of their estates ; and I proposed that all holders of land should be made proprietors, and that the land should be not only actual property to all, but that it should be allowed to be bought and sold or mortgaged like any other marketable commodity. Also, as the lands in all surveyed villages had now been defined, that the owners and occupants should have the option of taking out title-deeds for them, on stamped paper, which at the head should have a map of the land or estate, whatever it might be, great or small; and that in the body of the deed the boundaries and general description of every field or division should be detailed, the estate to become the hereditary property of the holder, subject only to a lien on the part of Government.

I fixed the term of thirty years for the first settlement of revenue, at the expiration of which period a revision should be made, and the rent fixed as a permanent settlement in perpetuity.

The Bombay survey was admirable, as far as it went, and the occupants of land were secured by registry; but I thought that possession required more security than registry, and that actual title-deeds would provide this, enable the land to be bought and sold, and satisfy the proprietors. I saw, too, that by the plan I proposed the real marketable capital of the country would be enormously increased, and the intrinsic value of the land would become a source of wealth to every individual holder. I also, at the same time as the land survey, carried on a survey of village sites. Every house was numbered, and its boundaries defined and measured, and title-deeds for this description of property were to be given separately.

When all my rules were drawn up and completed, I made a translation of them into Marathi; and having assembled the chief men of villages, the officers and *mirasdars*, as well as other landholders and occupants, as many as would attend, I laid before them the paper I had drawn up, telling them what I proposed to do if permitted by Government.

At first anything so definite and so valuable was doubted, and I believe the people, who had all through their lives been under a system of exaction and oppression, thought there was some dark sinister plan lying below the surface; but when they came fully to comprehend the projects laid down, and received my assurance that title-deeds would be given for all lands, even the smallest holdings, the delight (for I can call it nothing else), the enthusiasm, and the gratitude of the people knew no bounds. It seemed to all as if a new life were opening before them—peace for themselves, and their descendants after them.

Two years previous to this, I had saved the people from a measure proposed on the system of the North-West Provinces, by the Supreme Government. This was, to make a settlement of my district, and all the others were placed in the same category, with zemindars. Now there were no zemindars, in the Bengal sense of the term, in the ceded districts, with whom any settlement could be made. The officials who went by that name were the ancient hereditary officers of counties, not necessarily landed proprietors, except in payment of their local services. It was impossible to elevate such persons into land-holders, or to give them the rank and position of such, or to transfer to them properties which belonged to other people. Such a course would have interfered seriously with those landed proprietors in villages who were very sturdy in maintaining their hereditary rights; and the settlement in this manner seemed to my perception utterly impossible, and any attempt to force it on the people would have produced not only universal discontent and anger, but in all likelihood a serious insurrection. I wrote, as I was obliged, a great deal on the subject, and I believe I was considered 'most impracticable and obstinate', and incurred, I have little doubt, much ill-will; but for that I cared absolutely nothing. I could not uphold what I believed would be an injury and a wrong to my people, or become a party to any course which I considered was not only unjust and unpopular to the last degree, but which would abolish all those ancient hereditary tenures to which the people had clung with devoted pertinacity through all revolutions and vicissitudes for many centuries, and which the old Musalman kings and rulers of the Deccan had continuously respected.

My view of this question was very strenuously supported by my friend Bullock, Commissioner in Berar; and, in the end, I rejoice to say that we so far prevailed as to enlist the sympathies of our Chief Commissioner on our side, who earnestly protested against the system proposed from Bengal, and was successful in his opposition, inasmuch as the question was deferred for 'future consideration'. In his Administrative Report of 1870, Mr. Saunders, Resident at Hyderabad, and *ex-officio* Chief Commissioner, states, p. 14:—

'Orders were actually issued by the Government of India for a settlement of rights on the basis of the village community system, and were suspended only in deference to the earnest protest of Mr. Maltby, the then Commissioner of the Hyderabad Assigned Districts, some of whose assistants, such as Mr. Bullock and Captain Meadows Taylor, had passed their working lives in the Deccan, and perfectly understood the nature and meaning of the facts they had to deal with in their newly-acquired provinces.'

Again, after the final territorial arrangements with his Highness the Nizam in 1860 were completed, the question was revived by the Government of India, and orders were again issued in the most stringent terms. All honour is due to Mr. Saunders, who, although himself a Bengal civilian, possessed ample means of studying the question from previous reports and local observation, and had the firmness to resist and maintain the existing system; and, as he states, 'when the report was drawn up, the final orders of Government were passed, and the system of field assessment and recognised recognition of cultivating occupancy was formally sanctioned.'

The people of Berar had also obtained a zealous advocate in Mr. Lyall,[1] Commissioner of the province, also a Bengal civilian, whose report, after study of all previous correspondence, formed, perhaps, the basis of those by Mr. Saunders, and rescued the rights of the hereditary and all other classes of occupants from transfer to a class of persons who had never possessed them, and who, indeed, made no pretence whatever to them in any way. I had the subject much at heart, and must apologise for this long story about it; yet I cannot refrain from quoting Mr. Lyall's own words, which explain the system on which the new settlement was made in 1869:—

---

[1] In J. H. Rivett-Carnac's *Many Memories* is a charming picture of life during the following decade in the larger Berar, the annexed kingdom of Nagpur which became the Central Provinces in 1861, and the next year received Richard Temple to 'initiate good government'. He obtained, to help him, Alfred Comyn Lyall, who became Commissioner in 1867. But when Temple applied to the Punjab for James Broadwood Lyall, the answer came: 'Oh, you want J. B. Lyall, do you? Well, he is the very best of our young men; and don't you wish you may get him!' The work in 'an out-of-the-way jungly Province like ours', carefully to be distinguished from Taylor's restricted Berar, must have had a morning freshness comparable to that of the earlier administrators in India.

'The English Government has now placed the tenure of land in Berar on a stable foundation. After some hesitation, for a settlement on the North-West Provinces model was first actually ordered, the Bombay system of survey and settlement according to fields has been adopted. The whole country is being marked off into plots, and assessed at rates which hold good for thirty years. Subject to certain restrictions, the occupant is absolute proprietor of his holding; may sell, let, or mortgage any part of it, cultivate it, or leave it waste, so long as he pays its assessment, which is fixed for the term of thirty years, and may then be raised only on general principles; that is, the assessment of an entire district or village may be raised or lowered as may be expedient; but the impost may not be altered to the detriment of any one occupant on account of his improvements. . . . When the registered holder alienates his estate, he does it by surrender and admittance, like in English copyholding. Indeed the Berar occupancy has many features resembling the copyhold estate in the reservation of manorial rights. Thus, in fifteen years, the Berar cultivator has passed from all evils of rack-renting, personal insecurity, and uncertain ownership of land, to a safe property and a fixed assessment.'

All this is in exact accordance with the plans laid down by me in 1856 as the principle of my own survey of the province of Naldrug; but in my humble opinion it does not go far enough. It neither gives title-deeds for the land, nor does it assure the landholder that after the expiration of the thirty years' assessment any further adjustment of rates shall be final and unchangeable in perpetuity. Possibly the grant of title-deeds may be deferred only till the present term of thirty years has expired; but I rejoice to see that a perpetual settlement with all *bona fide* proprictors of land throughout India is now publicly advocated, if not publicly notified; and I trust the bill to be passed on the subject will include the issue of title-deeds. I cannot imagine a more beneficial or more popular measure, or one more calculated to secure the gratitude of the agricultural classes of India. These dceds would be issued by millions, and the property in land would be an enormous addition to the national wealth of India.

I feel that this digression may have been wearisome to some of my readers, but in writing the *Story of my Life* I cannot pass this over without notice, as it was a point on which, firmly believing myself to be in the right, I deliberately risked not only the goodwill of the Government of India at that time, but my own employment as Deputy-Commissioner. I would never have agreed to carry out the unjust measure proposed in ignorance of local tenures by the Government of India, and my friend Bullock and myself were prepared to have resigned our appointments in case stringent orders were issued on the subject; and there is no act of my public life which, to this day, gives me more sincere pleasure and satisfaction than my successful resistance to the orders of Government to the settlement being made according to the North-West system.

It was hoped the Mutiny would be confined to Bengal; but very early in June the regiment of cavalry stationed at Aurungabad, or a portion of it, was decidedly in a mutinous condition, and was, perhaps, only checked by the attitude of the infantry and artillery who were loyal. Application had been made to Ahmednagar for assistance, and the General marched at once upon Aurungabad with part of a dragoon regiment and some horse-artillery. Hearing of their approach, some of the native cavalry broke away at once, and proceeded to Hyderabad and Homnabad, exciting much alarm throughout the country. The dread was great lest the whole Contingent might be infected with the spirit of the army of Bengal, for most of the Contingent infantry were from Oudh, and thus their example might have spread to the Madras army; happily, however,—most happily and providentially—the Contingent remained otherwise firm.

The re-establishment of a new empire at Delhi would not at all have suited the Nizam; for his ancestors had declared themselves independent when the empire had fallen into decadence. And this consideration alone, had others been wanting, would have preserved his loyalty.[1]

[1] During the early weeks of the Mutiny South India depended upon the Nizam's loyalty—which held. As the Governor of Bombay telegraphed to the Resident: 'If the Nizam goes, all is lost.'

It shows the faintness of personality to which any Nizam, after the first, has been allowed to attain, that there was just now a change in the Nizamat which did not cause a ripple. Nasir-ud-daula died in the critical May of 1857, after a reign of twenty-eight years. At his accession, in June 1829, he had asserted himself in a way which meant much in Taylor's early life. He was the fine-looking prince, ruddy, fair, and with blue Tartar eyes, to whom Taylor was able to render the delicate

It was impossible not to feel great anxiety at Naldrug. After the mutiny among the cavalry was known abroad, and I think, when the mutineers arrived at Homnabad, they must have had some communication with those who were with me. They seemed uneasy for several days, and the native officer who was in command seemed uneasy too; but the men professed entire loyalty when I went among them; and as they were quartered in the town, they could not do much harm to any one. They were watched carefully by the police. Eventually three of the troopers broke away at night and went towards Homnabad—the rest remained at their post. I had no means of pursuing the fugitives, indeed my doing so would not have answered any good purpose; and even supposing the cavalry had come to Naldrug, on account of its treasury, and attacked it, as it was reported they intended to do, I had ample garrison inside the fort, in police and infantry, to have repelled them. The great gate was the only mode of communication with the interior, and the approaches on all other sides were defended by inaccessible precipices. Sholapur, too, where the troops were quite loyal, lay within twenty-six miles of us, and a reinforcement could be obtained in twenty-four hours at any time if needed; but the stout old fort no doubt induced a feeling of security which might not have been felt in less well-defended quarters.

On the 23d July, I was very agreeably surprised by a letter from the Chief Commissioner, Mr. Maltby, informing me

---

service recorded in Chapter IV. Nasir-ud-daula was practically the Nizam of Meadows Taylor's lifetime in India. Yet his disappearance is not mentioned either in the autobiography or the *History of India.* He was succeeded by his son Afzul, unmentioned personally in those two works.

In his *History* Taylor writes of 1857: 'Brigadier Stuart, at Dhar, was doing good service with the Malwah field force, part of which was composed of the cavalry and infantry of the Hyderabad contingent. During July and August, Colonel Davidson, the Resident at Hyderabad, had, with excellent judgment, assembled a strong brigade of the contingent at Mulkapur in Berar; and throughout the subsequent campaigns no force rendered more able and gallant service than the Nizam's contingent, which, composed as it was of the same elements in men as the Bengal army, and excited by the prevalent rumours and events, might, under inaction, have proved mutinous.'

that I had been nominated 'settlement officer' and 'surveyor-in-chief' to all four districts of the cession, on a salary of 1,500 rupees a-month for the present, and 300 rupees travelling allowance. All my maps and proposed plans of settlement had been approved and confirmed, and I was to set about collecting an establishment as soon as possible, so as to begin my work directly the monsoon admitted of my so doing. This was indeed good news; and I looked anxiously to the time when I could surrender all revenue affairs to a successor, who I hoped would be Cadell, as he knew the district and the people so well, and all were attached to him. My new duties would be infinitely more congenial and agreeable ones to me I felt; and to get rid of the interminable details of revenue business would be a very great relief. I was in high spirits at the prospect opening before me, and at the thought that all my labour at the commencement of the survey would now bear good fruit for the people and save me much trouble. Mine was, however, 'the only district in which any attempt had been made to carry out the orders of Government, and my proceedings, from first to last, had been eminently successful, and reflected the highest credit upon me'. So wrote Mr. Maltby; and I was very much gratified at his kind expressions.

I was quite easy about my district in every respect. The revenue would increase up to two lakhs, which would be its maximum, till the conclusion of the survey; and in all other respects everything was progressing steadily and well. There had not been a single case of dacoity for upwards of a year now!

But I was doomed to disappointment, and all my pleasant dreams rudely dispelled, at least for the present, by the receipt of an express from the Chief Commissioner, on the 24th August, informing me that I had been appointed Deputy-Commissioner of Berar, *vice* Bullock, who was transferred to my district; and I was to proceed there with all possible speed.

With this public notification came private letters from the Resident and Mr. Maltby, both to say that my immediate transfer was a necessity—but why, they did not tell me. Their letters urged me to make no delay whatever, and the Resident's note was characteristic :—

'Go to Berar directly, and *hold on by your eyelids.* I have no troops to give you, and you must do the best you can. I know I can depend upon you, and I am sure you will not fail me.'

I would have started that very day, but my camels were out grazing in the country, and Temple was absent, to whom I must make over the treasury and all current business. What would come of the survey now I knew not, nor of my appointment as 'settlement officer'. I saw the call was very urgent. It was not a time to waste words or thought in idle speculations. My duty was clear before me, and the times were too exciting to venture to ask any questions. I was, however, assured that I should be promoted to be a Deputy-Commissioner of the first class on a salary of 1,500 rupees a-month.

It became known later that the survey operations had been suspended till more peaceful times, and all public works as well—till the present threatening aspect of affairs was at an end.

On the day appointed for me to leave—the 27th August—I was presented with a public address from all the official and principal persons of the province. This ultimately received 1,622 signatures, and I append a translation of it here. I had not the least conception that such a proceeding had ever been intended. The address was beautifully written in Marathi, and presented to me on a very handsome silver salver, which I now use constantly.

True Translation of a Marathi Address to Captain Meadows Taylor, Deputy-Commissioner, Dharaseo District, August 27, 1857.

(After the usual preliminary compliments.)

'Since your arrival in this country we have all been happy and prosperous. Now an order has come from Government that you are to go to Berar, and Government has no doubt directed this because of your qualifications, and fitness, and ability for that duty. As it is a higher office than this, it will be a source of pleasure to you; and we all pray to God that He will be pleased to protect so kind and merciful an officer, and we shall be very grateful, so God will hear our prayers.

'But now we are to be separated from you, and are thereby

fallen into a sea of grief. We shall never be able to give sufficient praise to you for the manner in which you have protected the people hitherto—how you have created means of prosperity—and for your various good qualities. Still we have it in our hearts to address you in some sort, and you are to be pleased to accept it in order to gratify all.

'In the year 1853 you came to this district as Deputy-Commissioner; and, considering its circumstances then and now, there is a very great difference in its condition, of which you are the sole cause. When you came, there were no good roads in Naldrug; all the village streets and paths were filthy and useless, and even men travelled with difficulty. But you, with much personal exertion, have made proper arrangements for the good comfort of all. We all know this, and it has all come of your kindness.

'There was an immense quantity of waste land in the district. This has been cultivated since you came, and is now inhabited; and by provision of water and other circumstances in the country, hamlets, villages, and market-towns have been founded and built, and trade has very greatly increased, by which all obtain a livelihood, and there is no distress of any kind.

'Before, in this district, dacoits and gang-robbers and plunderers who openly committed murder, used to go about in force, and the inhabitants were much afflicted by them. But you established police, and settled everything, and so entirely extirpated these people, that not even a trace of them remains. From this protection of life and property, one of the principal benefits which result from the British Government was secured to this district.

'In the year 1855 there was a very heavy famine in this land, and it was difficult even for rich people to support themselves. In that hard time many poor people were at the point of death; many could get no food, and in their straits even abandoned their children. We all saw this. Then you made great exertions to save these poor people, and began with large establishments to clear the fort, and to make roads —as well to the advantage of Government as to the people; and thus you maintained the poor, who had no other means of subsistence. Of those who were not able to labour, you, from your own private funds, supported thousands. So if we seek for benevolent and useful people like you, we find few of them.

'From the tanks which you strove to get constructed, this district will be greatly benefited, and from this your name will be sung with praise when our women grind at their mills. But if we now say all we have to say it would only fatigue you, and take up much time; therefore we will be concise, and close this with what is due to your good qualities.

'But what shall we say? You were as father and mother to the ryots. You heard the complaints of the poor and protected them. In your *durbar*, as flies to honey, all classes and degrees of persons gathered and mingled together without apprehension; but we never saw yet that you ever used harsh expressions to any one. Your perfect knowledge of our language assured complainants, for they knew they were understood, and were contented; and never, on any occasion, have we seen that any one was treated with indignity or affronted in your *durbar*.

'We, who are the servants of Government in this district, as also all the ryots, well know what your conduct has been, and know also that your kindness to us has never decreased. You have taken care of us as of our children. Were we to relate how you have exerted yourself for us, we should never make an end of it. It will be difficult for us to obtain another superior like you, and we considered it good fortune when we obtained service with you. Now you are going from us, and our misfortune is apparent to us. Be it so. Wherever you go, may God prosper you, and may our country be prosperous through you. So we entreat God. Our hearts are full, and we can say no more. So also, before you came here you were at Shorapur, and there, too, you made all happy, and made that district prosperous. Such praise have we heard from many persons who came from thence.

'Now our last request is this, that as you have bestowed on us so many obligations and so much love upon us, we, to show our gratitude to you, have signed this address, which all assembled have agreed on, and we pray you will be pleased to accept it. This is our unanimous representation, which you are to be pleased to accede to.

(Signed) 'JEWANJI RUSTOMJI,
SHANKAR RAO RUGGONATH,
Extra-Assistant Commissioners;

'And 1,123 *zemindars*, *patels*, and other respectable inhabitants.'

(Dated Naldrug, *Aug.* 27, 1857.)

I can never forget the scene in the public *kacheri* when this was read to me. My old friend, Shankar Rao Baba Sahib, read it with the tears running down his cheeks, and there were few dry eyes among the vast crowd that had collected. The old cry, 'Mahadeo Baba Ke Jey!' was raised outside and taken up by thousands. It was the first time I had heard it at Naldrug. I was much moved. Nothing, I thought, could exceed this simple but earnest expression of the feelings of the people towards me, and their manifestation of regard and affection was very grateful to my heart; and if I had stood between the people and wrong in the matter of land—if I had governed them justly to the best of my ability—if I had insured for them peace, and laid the foundation of prosperity, this was indeed a grateful reward—all I could have hoped or wished for on earth.[1]

That night as I left the fort and town, I found all the road and street lined with the people, cheering me with the old shout, 'Mahadeo Baba Ke Jey!' and many were weeping, and pressing round to bid farewell; and I was followed for more than two miles out of the town with the same cheer, by a crowd from which it seemed difficult to get away.

At every village I passed through that night, and till my frontier was reached, the village authorities, elders, and people came with their farewells and best wishes, in crowds, from all points within their reach, praying for my speedy and safe return. My departure from Shorapur had been affecting and painful to me, but the demeanour of the people here was, if possible, more touching and affectionate.

[1] In or near the Sholapur District there long flourished a native Christian called Mesoba Londhe of Watvad. He was noted for the circumstances of his conversion, and for an alleged connection with Meadows Taylor. In the course of 1917 a missionary organ published in Bombay had a long article about Mesoba.

It seems that in the Nizam's Territory, 'about fifty miles east of Barsi', between dates better not specified, but during Taylor's Naldrug period, Mesoba lived as a gang robber. This calling he doubled, as was quite possible in Hinduism, with that of a guru or spiritual leader. 'Physically he was a large man. He and his band robbed villages and carried off whatever they could secure. Col. Meadows Taylor, a noted writer on Indian customs, was the Magistrate of that district. He convicted Mesoba of theft and put him in jail for three years. Col. Taylor had schools in all the jails in his territory. In jail Mesoba learned to read.' And reading Christian books, though never having 'seen a missionary, nor a Christian, nor the Bible', he became a Christian.

CHAPTER XIV

1857–58

I ARRIVED at Jalna on the ninth day. I had intended to travel faster, but a feverish cold I caught on leaving Naldrug, when my palankeen doors were open and a chill night wind blowing through them, confined me to my bed for one whole day and night, and retarded my progress, so that I could not make double marches. The warm greetings and farewells did not cease till I reached the city of Bhir[1] in the Nizam's dominions,—everywhere the same reception, most hearty and affectionate.

The native district officer at Bhir, on behalf of the Nizam's Government, came out to meet me with a large retinue, a distance of six miles ; and I found my tents pitched in a very pleasant garden close to the city, and a most ample breakfast cooked at the officer's house, and ready to place upon my table. He pressed me very much to stay as long as I could, but I dared not linger ; and in the afternoon I pushed on again to a village on the Hyderabad road, where there was a good bungalow.

Next day I had to cross the Godavery at Shahgarh ; fortunately it was not in high flood, but it was not fordable. Here I found all my camels, baggage-ponies, and servants, clustered together on the bank of the river—the ferrymen would not permit them to pass ; and as soon as I came up

[1] This urgent journey from Naldrug to Buldana, due north through well over two degrees of latitude, may be clearly followed on the map. Bhir is the name of a district, a taluk and a town in the Aurungabad Division. The largest river is the Godavery, prominent below, which forms the northern boundary of the district. The town of Bhir had, in 1911, 16,000 inhabitants, a decrease from previous returns. Nothing more notable is recorded of it than that a tooth of Mohammed bin Tughlak is buried there.

there were some very ominous cries of *Deen! Deen!* [1] while the ferrymen, who had taken their boat to some distance, waved me off. I had no escort—only four men out of twenty-four who had been sent with me from Bhir; the other sixteen had already crossed the river. I had not brought my own cavalry escort from Naldrug; some of them still appeared very restless, and I thought it was safer to leave them where they were. As I and my servants were parleying with the boatmen, an old Byragi whom I had never seen before, raised the old cry loudly: 'Mahadeo Baba Ke Jey!' he shouted—and many joined, drowning the *Deen! Deen!* most completely; while on the opposite side of the river, near the town of Shahgarh, a large body of cavalry came in view, making it very doubtful to my mind what would be the next move. This, however, was soon decided by one of the horsemen, the officer in command of the party, tying a white scarf to his spear, and at the same time despatching two other boats with a few dismounted men to my assistance. On seeing this, the party who had set up the cry of *Deen! Deen!* bolted up the bank, looking sulky enough, and I saw them no more; while the three boats took me, my bearers, servants, baggage, and camels, across the river in safety.

The horsemen had been sent by an old friend of mine, the Talukdar of Ambarh,[2] with orders to see me safe over the river. He did not expect me so soon, or he would have sent them before. He had heard that the Musalmans of Shahgarh had betrayed a very fanatical spirit, and had said I was not to be allowed to proceed; and he feared for my safety.

This escort would not permit me to halt at Shahgarh, but carried me on to a village eight miles further, where they had

[1] 'For the Faith!' the Mohammedan call to arms. [M. T.]

'"Deen, Deen! cry to God for victory. Deen, Deen! the Prophet hears us, and Alí, and the holy martyrs, and so will ye be martyrs and enjoy Paradise if ye die." Again, again, his cry was raised, the fanatical cry of Islam, which no Moslem can hear without emotion.' (*Tara*, chapter xliv.)

[2] Ambarh is a village of between three and four thousand inhabitants, the headquarters of the south-eastern taluk of Aurungabad District. 'The river Godavari passes through the south of the *taluk*, which is composed of *regar* or black cotton soil.'

ordered a small tent to be pitched for me, and there I slept. Next morning we all went on to Ambarh. My old friend was ill and could not leave his house; but he sent his son with a large cavalcade to meet me, and entertained me most hospitably all day.

My friend, who was able to visit me in the evening, told me that he feared several mutineers of the Aurungabad cavalry were concealed at Shahgarh, and that a Musalman priest had been preaching rebellious addresses; but that he should send fifty men to the crossing place for the protection of travellers. I left the escort here that had accompanied me from Bhir. The men were sadly vexed at the scene at the river, and that they had not been with me; but as we could not all have crossed together, I, anticipating no difficulty, had desired them to precede me. I now dismissed them with a letter to the Talukdar of Bhir, thanking him for their services.

Next day I marched twenty miles, and arrived at Jalna.[1] I was rather amused at the 'cloud of cavalry' sent to attend me by my old friend, whose only regret was that he was not well enough to accompany me himself. Orders had been forwarded to a Parsi merchant at Jalna to see that a house was ready for me; and as the cantonment was nearly emptied of troops, there were plenty at my disposal, and I found myself located in a very comfortable well-furnished bungalow belonging to the Colonel of the 6th Cavalry. Here Major Gill,[2] who had been for some years employed by Government

[1] Jalna is the headquarters of the taluk of the same name in Aurungabad District. The town had a decreasing population, in 1911, of 19,000. It is locally believed to have been founded in the time of Rama. Jalna has some uncertain Moslem memories, and a ruined fort. It is little notable apart from the cantonments of which Taylor speaks, which were built in 1827, but which have been abandoned since 1903. There is a range of Jalna Hills, running eastward from Daulatabad (3,000 feet) into Berar.

[2] Robert Gill, one of the interesting Indian figures who can only be recovered in part. He is not in the *Dictionary of National Biography*. Mr. Buckland, who cannot give his birth, says of him: 'Major: antiquary, artist and sportsman: entered the Indian Army in 1842: his regimental service was apparently uneventful: he is remembered for his work.' From about 1845 he was employed, for some thirty years, making copies of the frescoes in the Buddhist excavations at Ajanta. 'With great labour, Gill, working in feverish jungle, and in

in copying the Buddhist frescoes in the caves of Ajanta, came to see me, and gave me a letter from Bullock, which had come in by express, begging me to wait for him at Jalna, which I was glad to do, especially as a heavy fall of rain set in, and marching would have been next to impracticable. Two days afterwards my friend joined me, and told me what had occurred. On the outbreak of the Mutiny several of his cavalry escort had broken away, very much as mine had done, and the whole district was reported to be unsound. He had asked for troops, which it was impossible to send him; and after a very sharp correspondence on both sides, our sudden exchange of districts was peremptorily ordered. I had been told nothing of this, but had simply acted according to the short urgent letter I had received; but the prospect of having to keep Berar quiet after what I now heard, was not encouraging by any means.

I was likewise told that I must be prepared to find the internal economy of the district very irregular. When Bullock had gone on furlough to England, his successor had not carried out the general instructions promptly, and I should find the progress made slow, but he hoped I would soon set things right; he had begun to work hard on his return, and thought he had put matters in training. I told him he would not have much trouble with my district, as it was in capital working order; and so we parted. This was no time to show vacillation or uneasiness, and I was determined to go through the country and among the people exactly as I should have done had I heard no unpleasant rumours. There were no troops to be had, so there was no use thinking about them. As much of the Contingent as could be spared, and several half-mutinous regiments of cavalry and infantry, were collected at Edlabad,[1] near Burhanpur, and prepared for service with

dark recesses (haunted by wild animals), copied in full size and in oil the principal frescoes, about thirty in number.' Gill was also an expert photographer, and published in conjunction with James Fergusson, whom Taylor afterwards knew (see note below). Major Gill killed above 150 tigers, mostly on foot. He died, apparently not an old man, in 1875, while being conveyed from Ajanta to Bhusawal, where he is buried.

[1] The Edlabad or Adilabad, in the north of the Nizam's Dominions, quite to the eastward, is some two hundred miles, right across Berar,

(then) Sir Hugh Rose's force ; and for the time, no bolder course could have been adopted. Nevertheless, the Resident was assailed fiercely by the press ; accused of shifting the responsibility of managing mutinous troops on others, and of ruining the chances of Sir Hugh Rose's success by placing in his rear a large brigade of the best troops in India, who could not possibly be depended on. But Colonel Davidson knew his men. He issued a spirited address to them, appealing to their loyalty, and encouraging them to go forward and win fame under Sir Hugh Rose. The men obeyed ; and after the brigade joined Sir Hugh, it shared in the whole of the Central India campaign with him, and behaved well to the very last. Colonel Davidson had in view a much higher aim than merely keeping the troops employed in the field. His object was to show that the Nizam had no sympathy with the re-establishment of the monarchy of Delhi ; and that his own troops were assisting the English to quell the Mutiny, and crush the authors of it ; and in this point the Resident's bold measure was successful beyond his hopes.

On the 19th July, the Residency at Hyderabad was attacked by a concourse of Rohillas and other city fanatics, who were easily repulsed ; but the Resident was at issue with the Commander of the Hyderabad Subsidiary Force, who not only differed from him on the question of retaining the Residency at all as a fortified post, but advised its total abandonment, and the location of all belonging to it within the cantonment. Happily the Resident took his own way, and he saw clearly that his desertion of the Residency would have the effect of weakening the Minister (now Sir Salar Jung, G.C.S.I.), and also the Nizam himself, both of whose lives had been threatened by fanatics. It was when it was determined that the Contingent Force should take the field, that my friend had applied for troops, and the utter impracticability of the request was resented. 'Berar,' wrote the Resident to me, 'which contains more than two millions of people, *must* be kept quiet by moral strength, for no physical force is at my disposal.'

Delhi, attacked first in June, and before which a position only was maintained till the siege began on the 1st September,

---

from Burhanpur, which is in the south-west corner of the Central Provinces, some fifty miles north of Taylor's headquarters at Buldana.

was taken by storm on the 14th, but resistance continued inside until the 20th. Every native in India who could think at all, had watched the progress of the siege from June to September with the greatest anxiety as to which would win the victory—England or the Mogul; and many doubted whether the small force of English in India could make any impression on the immense power of the native army of Bengal. And the long delay, to which they were so little accustomed in English operations generally, strengthened this feeling considerably.

As I approached the head station of Berar, Buldana,[1] I received deputations from the principal landholders, merchants, and bankers of the chief towns, who were all eager for authentic news; but I could discover no symptom whatever of disaffection. The great Musalman colony below the plateau of Buldana had been one of the chief points of anxiety to my predecessor; and, as soon as I could, I marched there, sending down a light tent before me. I gave no other warning, and was quite unexpected by the native officials and my English assistant, whom I found in charge. Though my sudden appearance at the head town of their county, when I had as yet visited no other, at first excited some surprise, and perhaps suspicion, we soon became excellent friends. At first I felt rather doubtful, as nobody came near me, and my servants heard very disagreeable rumours; but at length one leading man came forward, then another, and another, I suppose, to take my measure; and then all the people came, many hundreds, and raising the old cry, "Bolo Mahadeo Baba Ke

[1] A place of some 4,000 inhabitants, more than 2,000 feet above the sea. 'The town owes what little importance it possesses to its selection as the headquarters of a District.' The climate of much of the district is enervating, being both hot and moist. But Buldana, owing to its elevation, is 'the coolest and most pleasant station in Berar'.

Berar (or the Hyderabad Assigned Districts) is a province of 17,000 square miles, as Meadows Taylor says; while the two millions which he gives as the population are still under three millions. The Marathas, whose language is spoken by four-fifths of the people, call it Warhad. From the Assignment in 1853 Berar was administered by the Resident at Hyderabad until 1903, when it was transferred to the Chief Commissioner of the Central Provinces. Two years later the old six districts which Meadows Taylor governed for about half a year were rearranged into the four present districts: Amraoti, Akola, Buldana and Yeotmal.

Jey!' which some one set up, the whole assembly joined in heartily, and proffered service whenever and however I needed them. 'They would watch the frontier,' they said; 'they would not let in Sindia's disaffected people; they would follow me to Delhi if I would only take them there; they wanted no pay—only food, and ammunition for their matchlocks; they would be true and faithful to the English,'—and many more promises were made, and faithfully kept.

From that day they never gave me the least uneasiness; and, if I had had occasion to call them out, would, I firmly believe, have done their duty nobly.

I wrote what had occurred, privately, to the Resident, by express, and I believe my despatch was a very considerable relief to him, as he was under great anxiety about Berar.

I need say nothing upon the condition of the internal economy of Berar at this time. Cultivation and revenue alike seemed to have declined, and did not exhibit the elasticity of Naldrug. I had to set things to rights as much as I could, and the Commissioner wrote that he would come to me in January. Very hard work fell on me, as my assistants were new to the duties, and had not been trained to a regular system, which, had it been adopted from the first, would have rendered matters easy now to all. There was, too, a heavy arrear of appeals and civil suits; but every allowance was to be made, for the territory had undergone so many changes from one hand to another; and my friend Bullock's health having failed, and his being obliged to take furlough just after his appointment, had not given the district a fair chance. The climate was very enervating, and the district so extensive, that I felt very thankful my first appointment to it had been altered for Naldrug, as I am quite sure my health would never have held out under its relaxing influence. Indeed I felt anxious now as to whether I should be able to stand it; but this only experience would prove.

Buldana was a pleasant place on the south table-land, above the valley of Berar, and had been fixed upon as the head station on account of its fine climate; for there was the greatest possible difference in the air up there and that in the valley below. The views were beautiful down the wooded ravines, and my early morning rides were far more picturesque than any about Naldrug. But I had no time to stay there long, and, after a few days' rest, I took my establishment into the valley, and began work in earnest. It was not by any means pleasant, as I was obliged to find much fault with the managers of divisions, who, being provided with ample instructions, had neglected to carry them out, and had neither kept their own accounts in order, nor those of the villages under them. Neither were the village books nor the records properly kept. These were matters of detail, as to which I need not perplex my readers, for, except at great length, they could not be explained intelligibly; and if they were, it would not answer any purpose.

I confess I thought I had been badly paid at Naldrug, having received 300 rupees a-month less than had been granted to the Deputy-Commissioner in Berar, solely because the latter had a higher revenue and population: the area of both were nearly similar. However, it was no use grumbling now. I had done the work at Naldrug to the best of my ability, and now I was going to try to set things straight here, and I hoped to get the district rapidly into order. As yet I had received no additional pay. I, as second-class Deputy-Commissioner, was holding a first-class district; Bullock, as first-class Deputy-Commissioner, holding a second-class district. But we supposed some arrangement would be come to in time.

Although both Delhi and Lucknow had been taken, yet the pacification of the country was far from complete; and rebellion in the Central Provinces, close to my own northern frontier, had made, and was making, rapid progress.

There was now much more alarm and uneasiness than before the taking of Delhi, which was far too distant from us to excite more than passing interest.

I received many anonymous letters, apparently from friends, warning me of contemplated assassination, and stating that when I was disposed of, the native troops at Ellichpur were prepared to rise, and, aided by the military and predatory classes of the district, would plunder the chief towns, and join the rebel forces beyond the Satpura range which constituted my whole northern frontier. At Nemawar,[1] Captain Keatinge

[1] A district of Holkar, on the north bank of the Nurbudda.

had been obliged to conceal himself in the jungle, having his wife and children with him; and they escaped almost by a miracle.

At Jubbulpore and Saugor, rebellion was at its height, not only in the mutiny of native regiments, but by the risings of petty rajas and nawabs, and of the people of the district, always noted for their turbulent and predatory habits.

There was hardly one spot where loyalty prevailed; for as the regiments broke away from their several stations, with or without violence and murder, as it might be, all restraint was removed from the lawless classes of the people at large, and these were every day growing stronger under the evil spirit and licence which could not be checked.

On the eastern portion of Berar lay Nagpur, by no means to be trusted; and it was owing to the large force of faithful Madras troops who were stationed there that no serious outbreak occurred in favour of the deposed family, on whose behalf, it was reported, intrigue was busy throughout the whole country. On my western frontier lay Khandesh, not secure either. Nana Sahib had active agents there, as he aspired to be Peshwa; and all the northern frontier of that province was in contact with Sindia's and Holkar's territories, where rebellion was rife.

Berar was the centre of these three great provinces, which stretched across the whole of India, and formed, as it were, the barriers that were to prevent the rebellion from spreading southwards; and of the three, Berar was the most important perhaps, as, if the rebels had broken through the passes of the Satpura range—a very easy proceeding—and had been joined by the military classes and indigenous marauders of the province, it is impossible to say how far disaffection might have extended to the Nizam's dominions.

From October, therefore, as the circle of war and mutiny grew wider, reaching my northern frontier, the danger increased almost daily; and it was only the thorough attachment and loyalty of the people to the English rule which saved Berar, under God's blessing, from insurrection.

I have already mentioned the goodwill and proffered devotion of the Musalmans of the western portions of my district; and as I travelled up the valley slowly to Akola,[1] I was equally gratified by the conduct of the Rajputs, who resided there in large numbers. There had been fierce and bloody feuds between these two great classes from time to time, on occasions of religious festivals; and this seemed a good opportunity for them to break out again; for I had literally no troops on whom I could rely, and those at Ellichpur were more a source of uneasiness to me than anything else, as, although they were as yet orderly and quiet, it was felt that any excitement might cause them to break off and join their rebel brethren at Jubbulpore or in Central India. Their officers were very mistrustful of them, for many were from Oudh; and who could rely on them after the mutiny of Sindia's troops and their march to join the main body of the rebel forces?

I was grateful for the attachment evinced by the Rajputs of the Akola district, who also proffered service wherever and whenever it might be of use. All I could do was to ask their aid in watching the passes, and in apprehending parties from the north who might seek to sow rebellion among us. This they promised to do; and in two instances they actually did so, succeeding in arresting and bringing to justice a number of delegates from Sindia's mutinous troops at Burhanpur, whom I tried and sentenced to transportation and penal servitude. And these events prevented any further attempt of the like nature.

There were several petty rajas of the mountain tribes of Gonds who received hereditary allowances or stipends from the Berar administrators, and who were responsible for the several passes which led from the north. All these came to me and tendered their services, nor did any one case occur of disloyalty or neglect.

The northern frontier was thus made as secure as I could under these circumstances make it; but, in Colonel Davidson's expressive phrase, I was literally 'holding on by my eyelids'.

I will not deny that it was a period of fearful anxiety. No aid could be expected from without, and the anonymous

[1] A town of some 30,000 inhabitants, 'one of the principal centres of the cotton trade in Berar', headquarters of the former and the present district of Akola.

warnings were more frequent than ever, while evil reports flew daily through the country. My servants kept a hórse saddled for me every night in case of necessity for escape.

I had no guards except a few police, and I was carrying on my duties in my tents as usual: making the yearly settlement; examining village books, district books, and accounts; trying appeal and civil cases; holding criminal trials, and the like. One great benefit to me was my being able to speak the vernacular language, Marathi, fluently. The people felt that I understood them, and came to me freely with petitions as to any real or imaginary grievance.

There had been some corruption at work among my *chaprassis* or office attendants, which seemed to be of long standing; and I one night overheard a conversation between two of them who lay outside my tent walls, when they thought I was asleep, about division of the proceeds of their gains, upon the receipt of petitions, which would have been amusing enough but for the mischief that such extortion for presenting petitions to me occasioned. I at once adopted my Naldrug plan, which was to have a large box fitted with hinges and a padlock: a slit was cut in the lid, and notification made that all petitions henceforth were to be dropped into it, and that petitioners were to attend every afternoon, when the box would be opened before me, and the papers publicly read. The box was placed in an open space before my tent, and was presently filled with petitions; the two men, whose confidential talk I had overheard, were then called up. I took my usual seat outside my tent, and after addressing the crowd, I had the men's badges removed, and they were turned out of camp in disgrace.

I think, nay, I am positive, that if every Deputy-Commissioner, situated as I was, had such a box, they would find it an admirable plan.[1] It had an excellent effect in my district, and inspired great confidence among the people. Any frivolous complaint was at once dismissed; but many corrupt practices and grievances were brought to light; and as each petition was taken out of the box, the name of the petitioner

[1] This detail is given in *Seeta*, where Cyril Brandon, a young civilian in an indeterminate Non-Regulation Province, adumbrates many of Meadows Taylor's experiences in Berar, and earlier.

was called out, and every applicant knew that his paper was considered, and heard it read before me. A memorandum was then written on the back, referring it to the district native officer for report if necessary.

I was now fairly among the people; and though so often cautioned and advised of danger, I felt that reliance on them was the safest course. Once, in a Bombay paper, it was stated that I had been attacked and murdered; but I wrote to contradict the report before the departure of the mail for England, and the dear ones at home knew nothing of it; nor did I, as I see by my letters home, mention any current reports, and, indeed, I alluded very little to the condition of affairs at all, or my own cares. I lived, however, in a state of perpetual alarm, and every day added to the anxiety I endured. Every detail of deeds of violence in Central India—of which, almost daily, fresh rumours reached me, sometimes very much exaggerated—the arrival of every 'express', night or day, in camp—caused unavoidable excitement. Who could say what news it might not bring? At that time all Deputy-Commissioners of provinces and political officers used to send such expresses, when and how they could, to each other, giving local news, and with a request that the express might be forwarded to the next authority. Many a man in India was 'holding on', never flinching from his post, dying there bravely in many a terrible instance, or, when hope was gone, escaping with bare life, often through hosts of enemies, and thankful for that mercy. 'What if Berar should go?' I often thought; and how could I hope to escape? How thankful I was that I was alone—that I had only myself to think of! Had I had wife and children with me, as many had my anxiety would have been increased a thousandfold.

True, my people appeared steady and trustworthy, and business proceeded as usual, as I moved my camp from village to village; but Berar was 250 miles long, with an average breadth of 60 miles or more, and the population was two millions. Who could answer for all? And from day to day for some months, one felt as if in the morning one might be murdered before night, or at night be dead before the morning.

The Resident's anxiety on my account seemed to increase; but I assured him in my letters, which were rare, that so far

I could not trace any disaffection, and that a good spirit seemed to prevail among the people, even where I had felt most uneasiness myself. Still I often longed to be in the roughest scenes in Central India rather than bear the load of responsibility on my mind day and night: it was a terrible strain upon me.

I was at Ellichpur on the 9th December, and I stayed there till the 13th. It was very cold, the thermometer showing 36° and 40° in the mornings. It was the head civil station of a subdivision of my district, and I was greatly indebted to Captain Hamilton, who superintended it, for his watchful supervision of the frontier. The people were deeply attached to him, and gave him information freely. How welcome were the large baskets of delicious peaches grown in his garden at Chikalda, the sanitarium of Ellichpur! and I wished I could go up there again and revisit the old scenes.

The native officers of the cavalry and infantry both visited me, and I congratulated them on the honours which their regiments were winning in Central India. They appeared to be intensely gratified at the news which reached them from time to time, both in newspapers and private letters, and at the prospect which was opening for further good service under Sir Hugh Rose, whose forces were now advancing into the disturbed districts.

Many of the men also came to me 'for a talk', and raised the old cry of my regiment, which was known to all. So I hoped the disaffection of the cavalry at Ellichpur was a groundless rumour.

When the glorious news came from the Northern Provinces, the victory over the Gwalior troops at Cawnpore, and the second relief of Lucknow, with many other successful engagements in Central India, the year 1858 opened very brightly, and with good hope that the general campaign against the rebel forces would be brought to a brilliant conclusion in a few months. Already the various combinations of the rebel army and the various rebel chiefs had been much broken; now they were growing dispirited, and had nothing to fall back upon. When the constant arrival of troops from home made it manifest to all that England was fully roused, and was putting forth her strength and her enormous resources to save and help her sons, the hopes of the rebel leaders fell, and they felt their inability to war against her.

I am not, however, writing a history of the time,—that is in far abler hands than mine.[1] I can only relate what affected me personally.

My own position was decided by the Governor-General, who decreed, as I thought he would, that my friend was to be reinstated in Berar, and I to return to my old quarters —Naldrug. The Commissioner, Mr. Maltby, had been at Naldrug, had seen all my work, and approved of it, and had been much struck by the independent, though thoroughly respectful, demeanour of my Maratha farmers. They had visited him freely, and assured him of their prosperity and loyalty, and he wrote me a very flattering letter on the condition of the district generally. In Berar I had done my utmost to redeem irregularities and reconcile conflicting accounts; but three months had been too short a time to do all I wished, or to leave things as straight as I should have liked.

Bullock was to leave Naldrug at once, and wished me to meet him in the eastern portion of the district as soon as I could; and I too was anxious to get back to my old work before the very hot weather began. Berar was beginning to tell upon me; the old fever had returned in periodical attacks, and I was tormented with severe neuralgia, from which I could obtain no relief whatever. I had used the hot springs at Salbadli with some good effect, but it was not lasting, and I greatly dreaded the hot season. All the accounts had been sent in, and I found that one lakh out of two, set down for remission, was recoverable: the village books were now in order, and only careful supervision was needed.

While in the eastern portion of the district, I had been able to perform an essential service to Government, which had great effect on the war in Central India. One day I received an express from Colonel Hill, Assistant Quarter-master-General of the Madras army, attached to General Whitlock's force at Nagpur, which had not marched, and was

[1] Probably a compliment to Sir John Kaye, whose *Sepoy War* Taylor admired, and with whom he was somewhat associated. See note on Taylor's *People of India* in Chapter XVIII.

not able to do so, for want of draught and carriage bullocks. He requested I would, if possible, purchase and send to him 600 at once, leaving 400 more to follow; and added, if I could not manage this, there would be no hope of getting any except from Mysore. The Nagpur province either would not, or could not, supply them. I set to work directly. The province of Berar contains the finest draught cattle in India, and plenty were to be had at moderate prices. No sooner were my wants known than my camp was crowded with noble beasts. In two days I had got half the number, which were sent on under an escort of police, and day after day other herds were despatched; and this enabled the siege-train and heavy stores to be sent on without delay, so that eventually the whole force was set in motion, with an ample supply of trained cattle.

I received not only the thanks of the generals commanding for this assistance, but of the Governor of Madras in Council; and it was very clear that, if these cattle had not been sent up from the south, Whitlock's force could not have accomplished what it did in marching upon Jubbulpore, and, by a lucky stroke, capturing the Karwi treasures.[1] I thought myself fairly entitled to a share of the Karwi booty for the

[1] In Taylor's *History* appears the quiet claim: 'General Whitlock's column from Nagpoor, long delayed by want of draught cattle for his siege guns, was entering Bundelkhund.' Readers of Marbot may recall the sheer cleverness with which Davout, in 1812, marched into Russia with twelve thousand oxen, dragging supplies, but intended to be themselves eaten.

Sir George Cornish Whitlock, 1798–1868, is mentioned in all accounts of the intolerably fierce and small Central India fighting during the hot season of 1858, when the sun was the worst enemy. Rice Holmes speaks of his inactivity. Mr. Buckland writes that Whitlock captured 'Kirwi in June: gained a victory at Kirwi, Dec. 1858'. Allusions to the squabbles over the *Kirwee* booty, thus spelled, may be traced, if worth while, in several contemporary memoirs.

The *Imperial Gazetteer* tells what the more obvious history books, including Taylor's, fail in explaining. Karwi is a town of some 8,000 inhabitants, headquarters of the tahsil of the same name in Banda District, United Provinces. 'In 1829 it became the principal residence of a Maratha chieftain who lived in almost regal state, and built several beautiful temples and large wells. Numerous traders from the Deccan were thus attracted to Karwi. During the Mutiny, Narayan Rao, after the murder at Banda of the Joint-Magistrate of Karwi, assumed the government, and retained his independence for eight months amid the subsequent anarchy. The accumulations of his family constituted

service I had rendered ; but it was decreed afterwards by Sir J. Phillimore,[1] that as I did not belong to the force, 'my chance, *though just in equity*, was not admissible.'

In my letters home at this period I wrote very earnestly on the question of pressing the direct rule of the Crown in the future government of India, and that the time had arrived for a change to be made with advantage.

There was a very general impression that the great Company was only a farmer of the revenues ; and while royal houses would acknowledge and respect the Crown, they would have, especially after late events, no such feeling for the Company.

I suggested many other material changes as to high courts of justice and tenures of land, several of which have been carried out ; and I had the honour done me of some of my letters being read in the 'House'.

The letters written to my cousin Reeve,[2] and already given, embody most of my opinions and suggestions.

Strange indeed was the weird prophecy of Plassey in 1757–58 !

The Company's rule was to last for a hundred years. In 1857–58 it had virtually expired, and 1859 witnessed its total extinction !

It was my intention, after leaving my friend, to go direct *via* Aurungabad to Bhir. Mr. Maltby was now on his way to Berar, and Bullock and I moved on to meet him early in February, when he asked me to accompany him through the

---

the great treasure afterwards famous as "the Kirwee and Banda Prize Money."'

[1] Sir Robert Joseph Phillimore, 1810–1885, first baronet, was a civilian and judge. Of his quarrelsome brother, John George Phillimore, jurist, 1808–1865, who attacked Henry Reeve in 1863, Sir John Knox Laughton says that if he had known that Taylor's *Tara*, which had just received a laudatory article in the *Edinburgh Review*, was by a cousin, 'he would certainly have made it the subject of some more scurrilities'.

[2] Of 1857 Henry Reeve records this, and no more : 'It is singular that I have made no note with reference to the Indian Mutiny, which was the great and terrible event of the year. I remember Rawlinson saying to me as we rode in the Park that at this moment we held no land in India except that occupied by our armies. But this was an exaggeration. My cousin, Meadows Taylor, was in India during the Mutiny, and I corresponded with him regularly during the whole time of his service there' (Laughton's *Memoirs*).

district, and to visit with him the caves of Ajanta and Ellora. This would have been a very pleasant holiday for me; but again I was to be disappointed. We met the Commissioner near Amraoti,[1] on his way to Ellichpur, and the very next day came an 'express' from the Resident, directing me to lose not a moment in proceeding to Hyderabad on business relating to Shorapur.

I had seen by the papers a short time before, that the Raja had been suspected of treason, and that troops had been sent to watch the eastern and western frontiers of his district. Now I learned that he had attacked a small force[2] which had been ordered to Captain Campbell's assistance—this officer having been sent to Shorapur on a special mission; and the

[1] Amraoti is a cotton centre, a town, with the civil station, of some 40,000 inhabitants, headquarters of the taluk and district of the same name in Berar. Until the railway diverted the route to Bombay the Amraoti cotton was chiefly sent to the Ganges on pack bullocks. One merchant in one year is said to have sent off 100,000 bullock loads thus to Calcutta.

Did Taylor, fifty and fever-stricken, standing here in the sun to receive his official superior, have time to recall how, twenty years before, eager-hearted but even then stricken with fever, he had written chapter xxxiii. of the *Thug*?—'How Ameer Ali conducted himself in his debut as a Pindharee, and how the sahoukars of Oomraotee received their unwelcome visitors.'

'We entered the territories of the Nizam near the river Wurda, which we crossed, and in one march of nearly twenty-five coss reached Oomraotee. . . . I have once before described its riches and prosperity, and it was then far richer than it is now. As we rushed along, like the flood of a mighty river, every village on our route was instantly deserted by its inhabitants and left to our mercy.' There is comedy in the way in which Ameer Ali, entering Amraoti in advance of the host, patronises the frightened fat merchants in the market-place, lines his own pockets while making a good thing for his master Chitu, and genially arranges that the town shall be spared, and the Pindhari leaders entertained without any show of fear which might cause offence.

[2] 'This was treacherously attacked on February 7, 1858, by the Raja's tribe of Beydurs, with some Arabs and Rohillas; but after fighting all night they were repulsed, and early in the morning the movable column under Colonel Hughes, which had been watching the Beydur districts, came up by a forced march, and uniting with Captain Wyndham, drove the Beydurs back into the town of Shorapoor, a position of immense natural strength. The day after . . . preparations were being made to assault the place, when it was discovered to be entirely deserted' (*History*, p. 761).

Raja being defeated, had fled to Hyderabad, where he had been arrested.

Mr. Maltby spoke very kindly to me of all he had noted in the Naldrug district, and hoped I should soon be again at liberty to continue my work there, especially the survey operations. I ventured to ask whether I might be allowed anything for my labours in Berar ; but he could not say—and my travelling expenses had been a very serious pull upon my resources. I was to receive plenty of thanks ; but although these were very gratifying, they did not pay me for the very hard work and terrible anxiety I had gone through : but—there was one comfort—I had 'held on by my eyelids ! '

I pushed on now by double marches to Hingoli, and thence to Hyderabad, where I arrived on the 18th March, after having travelled 300 miles in sixteen days—not very fast perhaps ; but my continued travelling had blistered my people's feet, and I could not get on quicker.

I went of course to Mr. Palmer's house, and found him well and cheerful ; but the Resident would not hear of my being with any one but himself, and sent for me directly. I was very kindly received. He at once increased my pay, appointed me now Commissioner of Shorapur, on 1,800 rupees a-month, or, at the least, 1,500, and said his wish was to keep me altogether in the political department.

He told me all the high officials, and chiefly the Governor-General, were more than satisfied with what I had done in Berar.

CHAPTER XV

1858

THE Raja of Shorapur was a prisoner in the main-guard of the 'Royals' at Secunderabad, and I went three times to see him. He had deliberately rebelled against the British Government, and was to be tried for his life by a military commission, which would shortly assemble. As may be imagined, he was deeply affected on first seeing me, and he threw himself into my arms, quite unable to speak for some time. Even the honest fellows of the guard were moved, and much surprised that my appearance should have so sudden and extraordinary an effect upon their prisoner. In appearance he was much improved—he had grown stouter, fairer, and more manly; but though handsome, his features bore unmistakable signs of dissipation and excess, which I was sorry to see. Now, his face was so distorted with his emotions that it was difficult to judge what it would be in repose.

'O *appa, appa*!' was all he could cry, or rather moan, as he sat at my feet, his face buried in my lap, and his arms clasped tightly around me; 'O *appa*, I dare not look on your face! I have been so wicked—oh, so wicked! I have done every crime—I have even committed murder! Oh, if the earth had opened, and swallowed me up, it would only have been just. I cannot tell you all now, *appa*. My throat is parched, words will not come; but to-morrow, *appa*, you will come again—do come, and then I will tell you all.'

It was useless to remain then, and only painful to us both. So I promised to return on the morrow, and went away.

It was a sad case, and I feared there was no hope for him—none whatever. His unwarrantable disaffection began with that of the Southern Maratha country, where some of its chiefs had, as was proved afterwards, laid their plans for a general insurrection, in connection, no doubt, with Nana Sahib, and the general mutiny in the Bengal army; and the vigorous conduct of General Jacob alone prevented this rebellious movement.[1]

The Raja of Shorapur had been early inveigled into these intrigues, and was an active promoter of them. He was invited specially, as an ancient feudatory of the Peshwas, to join again the Maratha standard; and owing to his reputed wealth and the numbers of his clan, was not a chief to be overlooked by those disaffected.

If he could be induced to take the field with ten thousand men, the Beydurs of the Raichur Doab, of Bellary, Dharwar, and Belgaum, as well as those also of Mysore, would rise and follow him as their leader, and could plunder as they listed. His vanity and cupidity were excited, and he fell an easy prey to these representations.

Even after the Beydurs of the Southern Maratha country had received some very severe checks, the attitude of the Shorapur Raja was considered threatening and suspicious. He had collected Arabs and Rohilla mercenaries in addition to calling his own clan together, while he was more than

[1] The references in the text to Jacob, and to the Mutiny in Western India, were probably written after Taylor's attention had been drawn to the many errors in his *History*. Miss Penson writes:

'During my investigations the other day I came across something that I think might interest you. Taylor's *History* had been somewhat enthusiastically reviewed in the *Edinburgh Review* in 1877. Thereupon Major-General Sir G. Le Grand Jacob, who has written a book on Western India in the time of the Mutiny, wrote to the editor pointing out that the pages of Taylor's book dealing with the Mutiny and Western India were teeming with inaccuracies. And after some correspondence he sent letters written by Taylor to him acknowledging the errors. Taylor says that the book was written more hurriedly than he would have wished and that if he were able to bring out a new edition he would correct it. The comment on Taylor's inaccuracies to which I referred is found in the following article: "Taylor's Student's Manual of Indian History and the Edinburgh Review," by Major-General Sir G. Le Grand Jacob, K.C.S.I., C.B., Special Political Commissioner, Southern Mahratta Country, 1857–59 (London: C. Kegan Paul & Co., 1 Paternoster Sq., 1877). Published in *Political Tracts relating to India, China, etc.*, 1876–78. The pages of the *History* referred to are 759-761.'

suspected to hold communication with foreign mercenaries at Hyderabad. Those were anxious times, and it was impossible to allow any known conspiracy to exist, without watching it very narrowly. A strong force was sent, under Colonel Malcolm, and placed about equidistant between the Beydurs of Shorapur and those of the Southern Maratha country; Colonel Hughes, with a Madras force, watched the eastern frontier of Shorapur; and the Contingent troops at Lingsugur lay, as it were, between, ready to act in concert with either force, according to necessity.

The Resident, however, was very anxious to save the Raja, and to rescue him from his evil counsellors, feeling a peculiar interest in the boy who had for so long been a ward of the British Government; and early in January 1858 he despatched his assistant, Captain Rose Campbell, to Shorapur, to remonstrate with the Raja, and endeavour to bring him to a sense of his danger, and his promised allegiance to the British Government.

This considerate kindness was, unfortunately, thrown away.[1] The Raja was in the hands of the worst fanatics of the country, on all sides—even from Mysore and Arcot—and would listen to neither warning nor advice; and at length, when Captain Campbell received an intimation from the Raja's own servants and relatives that his life was in serious danger, the force from Lingsugur was ordered to support him, and arrived at Shorapur on the 7th February, encamping near the town. A narrow valley, surrounded on all sides by lofty hills and rocks, was pointed out as the camping-ground; but Captain Arthur Wyndham, who commanded the force, was too wary to be misled, and moved on to an open plain, where he was comparatively safe from any danger of surprise.

At night he was attacked by the Raja's whole force of Beydurs and foreign mercenaries; but he held his position bravely, and early in the morning Colonel Hughes, who was at Deodrug, twelve miles distant, and to whom a special messenger had been despatched, arrived with all his troops. It was very plain that had Captain Wyndham remained on the ground first pointed out to him, he would have endured

[1] 'Hast thou eaten my salt', asks the King of Bijapur in *Tara*, 'and found it so bitter that that of others seemed sweeter to thee?'

very heavy loss, if not total defeat. As it was, his force suffered but little, but he had inflicted serious damage on the Shorapur rebels.

Colonel Hughes arrived early on the morning of the 8th, and he and Captain Wyndham, with their united troops, drove the Beydurs and others from the hills into the town with severe loss. Unfortunately Captain Newberry, Madras cavalry, was killed in a charge against a body of Rohillas, and his subaltern, Lieut. Stewart, badly wounded. As the city of Shorapur was very strong, the approaches difficult of access, and the walls and bastions crowded with defenders, they did not attack it at once, but waited for Colonel Malcolm's force, which had moved close to the western frontier of Shorapur, and who had been requested to come on with all possible speed.

When this reached the ears of the Raja, and he heard also that Colonel Malcolm's force had with it a large proportion of English troops, who, together with two companies of the 74th Highlanders under Colonel Hughes, made a sufficiently imposing array—he saw that there was no chance of escape except by flight ; and, in the evening, accompanied by a few horsemen, he left Shorapur, and proceeded direct to Hyderabad.

He believed me to be at Naldrug, and intended to have given himself up to me there ; but hearing on his northern frontier that I had been removed to Berar, he changed his route, and made for Hyderabad, where he arrived with but two followers left. There, having made a fruitless attempt to gain the protection of the Arabs, he was found wandering about the bazaar, was apprehended, and taken to the Minister, Salar Jang, who at once sent him on to the Resident.

As soon as the Raja's flight became known, all the Beydurs and mercenaries left Shorapur during the night, and dispersed, whereupon the English forces marched into the city unopposed, and found it almost deserted.

Such is an outline of the occurrences that took place, and I hoped that when I next visited the Raja, he would disclose to me all the particulars of his rebellion and the causes that led to it. I found him much calmer during our second interview, but very reserved on many points.

'Do you remember, *appa*,' he said, 'that the day before

you left me, you warned me of the evil people who were about me; and you said, if I did not dismiss them, and lead a steady life, I should not hold Shorapur five years; and I promised you I would send them all away, and look after my own affairs?'

'I remember it well,' I replied, 'and how you wrote to me and told me that you were in trouble, and would come to me; and I sent you word to do so at once, for that I should now be near your border. But you never came, though I was there nearly a month, and I expected you.'

'No,' he said, 'they would not let me go to you, *appa*; and if I had gone it would have been no use; you could have done nothing. What was to be has come to pass, and I must bear my fate now, whatever it may be. When that evil wind blew, the people came and said it was the time to rise. The English had lost everything in the north, and were beaten everywhere; they could not keep the country, they said, and were flying to England as fast as they could get to their ships. This was told me, *appa*, by Brahmins and others from the south, from Poona, from everywhere.

'They promised, by their incantations, to raise me to be Raja of all the country—from Shorapur to Rameshwar[1]—and if I marched at the head of my twelve thousand, they said, all the country would rise, and we should be conquerors. Then Marathas from Poona, from Satara, from Kolhapur, from Mungoond,[2]

[1] '"Jey Sivaji Raja!" shall be cried from Delhi to Rameshwur' (*Tara*, chapter lxxvii.), with this note: 'The celebrated Hindu temple in the southern point of India.'

[2] If such a place exists, I have not been able to run it down. Considering the way in which many names are rendered in the first edition, this is probably a misprint for Nargund, a name prominent in the history of the period. Nargund is now a busy trading town of some 10,000 inhabitants, with many temples, in the Navalgund taluk of Dharwar District, Bombay, and near enough to the Hyderabad border. On the fall of the Peshwa it was confirmed by the British to the chief then in possession of the petty principality. This contained thirty-six towns and villages, with a population of about 25,000. At the time of the Mutiny the chief was one Bhaskar Rao, *alias* Baba Sahib.

On p. 761 of his *History* Taylor says: 'A very widespread conspiracy was attempted in the Southern Mahratta districts of the Bombay presidency, towards the close of 1857, which, however, only produced two outbreaks—one of the Rajah of Nurgoond, who treacherously murdered Mr. Manson, the political agent, who had gone to remonstrate with him.

from Bhim Rao,[1] who had secured all the disaffected people of Raichur, persuaded me to join them, and offered me what I pleased if I did so; but still I did not go. I was still true to the English and to you. I knew I was right. I did not move a man; nor did I allow one of my people even to go to the assistance of the Beydurs of Halgali, their brethren, many of whom were slain. And then my people rebelled against me, and called me a "coward and a fool", because I would not let them go. Arabs and Rohillas now came around me, and one man, worse than all the rest, swore to me on the Koran that the Arabs and Rohillas of Hyderabad, and all the Musalmans, had declared a crusade against the English; that the Madras troops would not fight, and they would all come and join me if I would rise. And these men and my own evil companions gave me brandy, and made me drunk, and they took my seal and used it, and led me into evil which I could not help, and did not know.

'When Captain Campbell came to me with the letter from the Resident, ask him whether I did not receive him with all honour and respect. But the people about me and the Hyderabad men said he was a Kafir and a Feringhi, and that he must die. Had not all true men put to death any English they could find? And they told me about Cawnpore, and Jhansi, and Delhi, and how all the English had been slain—even women and little children; and I thought of you—and of your children—girls too,—and I was grieved; but they made me drunk again, and they determined to murder Captain Campbell the next time he came; but I sent him private warnings, and this I could prove to you. Ask my uncles;

The fort of Nurgoond, which resisted, was afterwards captured and dismantled. The second, by a Brahmin named Bhim Rao, who gained temporary possession of the strong fortress of Kopul Droog, in the Raichore Dooab, and tried to raise the country, but failed. He was soon afterwards attacked by a Madras force from Bellary under Colonel Hughes, when he was killed in an attempt to retire to the upper works.'

Mr. Rice Holmes, in his *History of the Indian Mutiny*, calls Baba Sahib the ablest of the native chiefs. He does not mention Bhim Rao or Koppaldrug; but has a wordy account, covering a page, of the movements of Mr. Manson. See below, Mirgoona, another misprint for Nargund.

[1] See further accounts of this small rebel leader in the two chapters following.

ask ——, and ——, and others; they will tell you. Ask Captain Campbell if they did not warn him. I speak no lie, why should I? my life is not worth saving now. I have done too much crime to live; I dare not tell you all; you would not touch me or let me come near to you. O *appa*, *appa*! why did you leave me? If you had stayed with me, all would have been well! I tell you, if Captain Campbell had come to me again, no one, not I myself, could have saved his life; the men who were to cut him down were standing ready: but he attended to my warnings, and was saved.

'Then the troops came, and when I heard the first gun fired at night, I knew all was gone. I had no faith in my people's courage, although I had not been able to stop their madness, and I went up to a bastion and stood there all night. They told me—what a lie it was!—that the Lingsugur troops had lost their officers and fled! but when I saw, as day broke, the whole force and the English soldiers driving all my people before them into the city, and a shell burst close to the bastion where I was, killing some, and wounding more—ah! why did it not kill me?—when I saw this, I say, I knew there was no hope left, and I thought to myself, "I will go to *appa*, and give him up the *Samasthan* to do with as he pleases".

'I told Rangama (the eldest wife) to hide herself, and to tell the others all to hide for the night, and get on as well as they could to Naldrug to you. When I got to Narribol, I heard you had gone to Berar, and I turned through the hills and across the jungle to Hyderabad, riding the horse you bought for me. This is all my story, *appa*; it is true, all of it. If I can remember any more you ought to know, I will tell you. I wish you to know everything.'

Hours had passed while he poured out this tale; hours of intense suffering to him, and bitter self-reproach. Sometimes he would stop, and throw his arms round me passionately; sometimes kneel beside me, moaning piteously; again he would burst into loud hysterical sobs which shook his frame. I did my best to soothe him, and gradually he gave me the details narrated above. I have given only the heads, which I took down for the Resident's information. It would be impossible to remember his wild incoherent exclamations, his sudden recurrence to old scenes when he had played as a child about me, with his sisters; of the enjoyment they had had in the magic lantern I showed; of the little vessel on Bohnal lake, and the happy expeditions there: and all those recollections of his innocent early life, made the scenes through which he had lately passed the more grievous and full of reproach.

I asked him if he would like to see the Resident, who had promised to accompany me on my last visit to him if the Raja wished it. To my surprise, he drew himself up very proudly, and replied, haughtily—

'No, *appa*; he would expect me to ask my life of him, and I won't do that. Tell him, if you like, that if the great English people grant me my life, I and mine will be ever true to them; but I deserve to die for what I did, and I will not ask to live like a coward, nor will I betray my people.'

I think this speech, which I reported word for word, pleased the Resident better than anything he had heard of the Raja before.

'The poor lad has spirit in him,' he said; 'and I will not forget all you have told me of him.'

I went once more to see the Raja, the day before I left for Shorapur. I should soon see his wife and his other relations, and I wished to know whether he had any instructions or messages for them. He was calm, though he could not repress his old loving ways to me—but very quiet. I told him I was going by *dak* to Shorapur. 'What could I do for him there?'

'*Appa*,' he said, 'you remember once I said to you, that the British Government should have Shorapur if I left no heir; and I have none. I only wish now I had written this down; but at that time I had hope still: and I wish now to say, that I want you to have it yourself; the people love you, and you must never leave it. I will write this with my own hand, if they will give me pen and ink and some paper.'

'No,' I said, 'it could not be as you wish; and besides, the Government may pardon you when all is known.'

'And spare my life? No—I will never ask it.'

'That would not save it,' I answered. 'If Government is merciful, they will give you your life freely, without your asking it.'

'What do you think, *appa*? Shall I have to die?' he asked.

'I think so,' I said. 'It would be wrong in me to give you any false hope, or to raise the slightest shadow of one in your mind. Many have been false who should have remained true, and you were a child of the English.'

'Why do you reproach me?' he asked, sadly. 'You know all; it was not of my own will, when I was in my senses, *appa*.'

'I do not reproach you,' I said, 'for I do know all; but those who will try you do not. Speak the truth before them boldly, and exactly as you have done to me, and send for me if you think I can help you.'

'I will surely tell all,' he answered, calmly; 'but if they press me to disclose the names of those who excited me, I shall be silent. Government is powerful enough to crush them if they rise. But what can they do? Was I not the strongest among them? And yet, where am I now? Shall I, who have to face death, be faithless to those who trusted me months ago? Never, *appa*! I would rather die than be sent over the black water, or shut up in a fortress always. Suppose they sentence me to that, I could not bear it. No; the meanest Beydur could not live if he were imprisoned—and shall I, a Raja?'

'If you have to die,' said I, a good deal moved, for there was much nobility in his speech, 'die like a brave man.'

'I shall not tremble when they tie me up to a gun,' he answered, gravely. 'If you could be near me to the last, I should be happier. Only one thing, *appa*—do not let them hang me. I have done nothing to be hanged for, like a robber. Tell the Resident that is all the favour I ask. Promise me to tell him.' And I promised.

'I have nothing now to give you, *appa*,' he continued. 'They have taken away all I had, even my amulets; but take what you will at Shorapur, in remembrance of me. As to all my people in the palace, they are yours; and you will care for them, I know. I shall never see them again, now. I ask nothing more.'

Then, throwing himself into my arms, he clung to me for a long time, silently; then kissing me gently on the forehead, he said—

'Go, *appa*—go now. I shall never look upon your face or

hear your voice again; but I am thankful to have seen you. Tell them all that you have been with me, and that I was not a coward.'

And so I left him, among the men of the guard, who looked on with kindly, wondering eyes.

'He was very fond of you, sir,' said one of the sergeants, as I passed out, 'and before you came, was asking for you constantly. You must have been as a father to him.'

'He was like a child to me', I said, 'till evil people came between us, and temptation proved too strong for him. Now, I fear, it is too late to help him.'

I told the Resident all that had taken place, on my return, and all the Raja had said, especially about his not wishing to make any disclosures that would implicate his associates; and he respected the poor boy's reticence on these points.

'We will save him if we can, Taylor, when the time comes,' he said. 'Just now, things must take their course. But I am sure there is good stuff in the lad; and if we can save his life, he will be all the better for this experience.'

My bearers to Shorapur were laid; my servants and baggage had preceded me by some days—and they would, I hoped, have all ready on my arrival.

Mr. Palmer had no hope of the Raja's life being spared, but he took a great interest in him, and only feared that his death might be considered necessary as a warning to all the plotters in the South, of whom, no doubt, there were many, though there had been no actual rising except the unimportant one at Hyderabad, and the intrigues in the Southern Maratha country before mentioned.

I bade all Hyderabad friends farewell on the 30th March in the evening, and went on by stages to Shorapur, putting up in the villages during the day, for it was too hot to expose myself to the sun. The nights were, fortunately, cool and pleasant still, and I hoped to arrive at my long journey's end by the 3d April, when I should have travelled over 500 miles.

I reached the Bhima river on the morning of 3d April, long before it was light, indeed not long after midnight, hoping to get into Shorapur soon after daylight; but it was quite impossible. I found the river-bank crowded with people, from all the villages round, come to welcome me back again to my old scenes, and I had to wait to exchange greetings. Very warm and affectionate they were. 'Now', they said, 'they would have no more fears; all would take up their lands and go to work quietly, so long as I remained with them': and I assured them I should remain. All the head-men, *patels*, and *patwaris*, all the principal farmers and traders, assembled to give me the first greetings; and they told me the road was lined with crowds from all the country-side. Many had been waiting for days, as it was reported I should arrive sooner than I did. When I could get away from these, I passed on in the same manner from that village to the next, always with crowds running beside my palankeen, and a blaze of lights carried by the village torch-bearers. Now I had to stop while some old friend dismounted from his horse or pony to embrace me or kiss my feet; and again, when village authorities came out to meet me with their simple offerings and libations of water. I could, in truth, have dispensed with the crowds, for the dust rose heavily in the air, and there was no wind to scatter it, and the torches increased the heat perceptibly, while to sleep was out of the question. When day broke, the throng seemed greater and greater—men, women, and children pressing on my palankeen to touch my feet, or even my clothes—and, as I neared Shorapur, vast numbers, apparently thousands, came out to meet me, and my bearers could only advance at a slow walk, often being obliged to halt altogether. So, through the first suburb and up the steep road to the city, amidst shouts of the old cry of 'Mahadeo Baba', the scream of pipes and Beydurs' horns, and thumping of big and little drums, I was conducted into the first street, where further progress was clearly impossible.

I had never before seen even this excitable people so frantic; women weeping passionately, grasping my hands, kissing my clothes, or touching my feet—crying, 'Oh, you are come again; we see you; we shall suffer no more!' They raised their children above their heads and showed me to them, showering blessings on me the while.

The terraced house-tops were full likewise, and the shouts and cries quite indescribable. It was now eleven o'clock, and my slow progress through the town occupied almost an hour more. The sun was blazing hot, and I was faint and wearied out; still the showers of garlands, the handfuls of sweet powder and dyed rice, thrown on and over me, continued till I was close to the palace guard, when my bearers turned in, and I was free.

Captain Wyndham and all the officers had been most anxious, especially when the shouts were heard as I entered the streets; and my delay was so unaccountable that they feared I had met with opposition, till they were assured I was only 'being welcomed', and therefore abandoned their idea of sending a troop of cavalry, which they had ready, to my assistance.

I had never dreamed of such a welcome. It was intensely gratifying, and I was deeply affected by the feeling displayed by all, which could not be mistaken. Captain Wyndham and others had seen something of my reception from the roof of the palace, and had wondered not a little, as I had myself. It proved, at any rate, that I was not forgotten; and I thanked God for this from my heart very gratefully. The English officers congratulated me very warmly.

I was very glad of a refreshing bath and a substantial breakfast, which had been got ready for me; and then I lay down to have a sleep, which I needed much after the night's work. When I awoke, several old native friends were waiting for me. We were located in the new palace I had built for the Raja, which afforded good airy shelter for us all. The large upper room was the 'mess' and public room, and soon all the male members of the Raja's family and State officers assembled there—Pid Naik's sons, their uncles, and great-uncle.

All were as much concerned as I was at the unexpected events which had led to my second arrival at Shorapur; but they told me that for more than a year past they had lived in perpetual alarm at the conduct of the Raja, who seemed to have become quite deranged by constant intoxication.

In the evening I went to see the Ranis, who had assembled at the house of the father of the eldest Rani, close to the palace. As may be imagined, it was a sad and trying scene for us all. I could not either console them or hold out any hope that the Raja's life would be spared. They had, too, lost all they possessed, except the few ornaments they wore. When the Raja had desired them to escape the night he fled, they had gone out by the northern gate on foot, and made the best of their way to villages, where they were sheltered by the people. Some few women-servants followed them; but when they heard the Raja had gone to Hyderabad, and was a prisoner, they took advantage of a proclamation issued by Captain Campbell, and ventured back to Shorapur—not to the palace, as that was occupied by troops and soldiers, but to the house where I found them. Some of their clothes had been sent to them, but everything valuable was declared prize property, and was confiscated.

When the ladies grew more calm, I told them about my interviews with the Raja, and the various messages he had sent to them. They had almost expected to have heard before now of his public execution.

'I could not save him, *appa*,' cried Rangama, the chief Rani, whom I had petted as a child—'I could not save him; he was quite mad of late, drinking brandy those horrible men gave him constantly, which made him furious. Then, when he was quiet, he used to lay his head in my lap, and call for you, and tell me he knew he should lose the *Samasthan*, but that he would die like a soldier at the gates if the city were attacked. Again and again we all implored him to go to you, but we did not know you were so far away; and he always said if he left, the Rohillas and Arabs would plunder the city, because he owed them so much—and so he stayed.'

According to an arrangement made with the Resident, I issued a general amnesty to all except certain persons who had been leaders and exciters of this most miserable rebellion. The people of the city and of the suburbs were still in the villages to which they had fled; but now they returned. All the shops were opened; and in a few days the markets were full, and firewood, fruit, and vegetables were as plentiful as ever. Captain Wyndham's company occupied the palace, and were ordered to secure all valuables as 'prize'. My house was tenanted by a company of the 74th Highlanders. The troops of all arms had entered the city; but though property of every kind had been summarily looted, the people had remained unmolested.

In the treasury there remained nothing except a few State jewels; others had been hurriedly secreted, but were returned by those who had them in charge. I do not think a single article was missing, and any coin found had become prize-money.

I deeply regretted that all the old records had been either burnt or destroyed,—letters from former kings of Bijapur and Bidar, Rajas of Vijayanagar; of the Emperor Aurungzeb, with the impress of his large hand dipped in sandal-wood; of the Peshwas, and others. Great portions of these I had already translated, and had intended to continue when I should have leisure, hoping to complete a very interesting historical State paper; but all were gone now.[1]

The Resident allowed me to draw on the Residency treasury for as much as I required, and I got bills cashed as they were wanted for current expenditure. Many of the *patels* and heads of villages came in during the first week and assured me as to the cultivation of the country, and that such of the newly-cleared land as could be managed would be taken up at once; so altogether there seemed a fair prospect of revenue.

The investigation upon the occurrences which led to the rebellion was cut short as much as possible. There was no good in raking up old scores, especially as the Raja, as chief of all, had been the one responsible, and he was on his trial at Hyderabad. There was one man, a Musalman of Hyderabad, who had preached a holy war at Shorapur, and had been the instigator-in-chief of much trouble, and who, in concert with a wicked Brahmin whom I remembered, Krishna Shastri, pretended to miraculous power and divination. These two had, by their false prophecies and mischievous counsels, deluded the Raja more than any others; and, as dangerous characters, were worthy of death, or at least transportation for life.

The Brahmin eluded all pursuit, and disappeared. The Musalman, however, was apprehended after some time at Hyderabad, and sent to me for trial, when evidence was

[1] In a note to his *History*, p. 356, Taylor tells of these 'very valuable and interesting' records. 'They had been classed and arranged by me when in political charge of the State, with a view to complete translation; but on the capture of Shorapoor, after the rajah's rebellion in 1858, they were destroyed by the English troops in possession of the place.'

produced conclusive as to the projected murder of Captain Campbell, in which he was to have taken an active part; and his own treasonable conspiracies being distinctly proved, he was condemned to death. The sentence was confirmed by the Resident, and he was publicly hanged at Shorapur.

The great interest of the time was centred in the Raja's fate. There was no doubt, had he been taken in arms during the attack by Wyndham's force, that he would have been at once tried and summarily executed—and even now there seemed but small chance of his life; but the Resident wrote to me saying he thought, if I asked it, the Raja's life might be granted, especially if I explained with what ruffians he had been surrounded, and how misled.

I sent an 'express' at once with an earnest appeal for mercy.

A few hours after my arrival in Shorapur the old Brahmin priest came to me privately.

'Do you remember, Sahib,' he asked, 'what I once told you, and what the Rani said when we were with her at her bedside?'

'Perfectly,' I answered; 'you said the Raja would not live to complete his twenty-fourth year, and that he would lose his country.'

'Yes, Sahib,' he went on; 'part of the prediction is already fulfilled, and the rest will surely follow—it is quite inevitable.'

'Do you think the Raja knew of the prediction?' I inquired. 'If he did, it may have made him reckless.'

'I do not think he knew it,' replied the old priest; 'for the last time I saw the box it was in the treasury, with the seals unbroken, as you left it.'

(Captain Wyndham had secured the box, and kept the horoscope with the rolls of calculations as a curiosity, not knowing their purport.) [1]

'We cannot say', I continued, 'what may yet happen; the proceedings are not over, and the Resident and I are both determined to save the Raja's life if we can.'

[1] This horoscope, a very curious document, left to her by Mrs. Wyndham, is now in the possession of Miss Taylor. She has also a large picture of the Raja and his family painted by her father, as well as many water-colour sketches of Shorapur, Naldrug, and other places where he was in charge.

'It's no use, Sahib,' returned the Shastri, shaking his head mournfully; 'your intentions are merciful, but you are helpless before his fate. He will die—how, we may not see; but he must die—he cannot live. You, Sahib, and I, are the only two living that possess this secret, and you must be so good as to tell me directly you know his sentence. I cannot believe that the Government will spare him. I firmly expect that he will be blown away from a gun.'

When the Resident's letter came, I sent for the old Shastri and read it to him, and also my own strong appeal in reply. 'I hope the Raja's life is now safe,' I said. 'Listen to what I have written. The Governor-General, who is kind and merciful, will scarcely refuse this request, supported by the Resident.'

The old man shook his head sadly. 'Till the last day has passed to which the calculation extends, I have no hope,' he said; 'it cannot be wrong, and but little time remains. It grieves me, Sahib, to go over the figures again, but the present aspect of the planets is very calamitous to the Raja, and all through next month the combinations show extreme danger. We cannot help him, and you have done all you could; you can do no more—only wait.' So we did, anxiously.

From the time I had quitted Shorapur, no regular accounts appeared to have been made up; but I had been joined by my old head accountant, Sita Ram Rao, now Assistant Deputy-Commissioner, to whom I could offer better pay, and who was rejoiced to serve again under me. He knew all about the revenues of Shorapur, and could help materially. A schedule of the whole period of the Raja's administration was drawn out, and the result was that three and a half lakhs, or £35,000, of new debt had been contracted, while every rupee of the former surplus had altogether disappeared.

We had much to do in revising district accounts; but all was progressing well, and my life was a very pleasant one. I had charming companions in Wyndham and his wife, who became my very dear friends, and our love and friendship will continue while life lasts. They were interested in all my doings, and it used to be a great delight to me to show them all my roads and the improvements I had made during my residence at Shorapur. The roads were sadly out of repair, but we scrambled over them on horseback, and I soon had them put to rights again.

I could not get back my house while the 74th remained; but I held my *kacheri* in the hospital, and was constructing a large, airy, thatched barrack for the soldiers.

At last the news came.

The Raja of Shorapur had been sentenced to death; but the Resident had commuted his sentence to transportation for life, which was the most his power admitted of. This sentence had, however, been still further commuted by the Governor-General to four years' imprisonment in a fortress near Madras (I think Chingleput).[1] In addition, the Raja was to be allowed to have such of his wives as he pleased with him, and his own servants. If he showed evidence of reform and steadiness, his principality was to be restored to him.

I sent off at once for the Shastri.

'Listen', said I, 'to the gracious and merciful determination of the Governor-General. The Raja's life is safe; and if he is quiet and steady for four short years, he will regain his State! What could be more considerate or more lenient? What becomes now of the prophecy? This letter proves it is false.'

'I wish I could think so, Sahib,' he sighed, 'and that my poor young master were really safe; but, alas! he is in the greatest danger. Nay, it seems closer than ever now; but we shall see, Sahib. Sometimes a merciful God puts away the evil omens just as the fulfilment of them is imminent. I will go and tell the Rani this good news. I only wish the time were past, and that I could be happy in it too.'

The Rani would hardly believe the message I sent her. She and the other Ranis were to join the Raja almost directly, and were to make their preparations at once.

The head Rani, Rangama, asked me to come to her; and when I entered, quite regardless of etiquette, she threw herself into my arms, and danced about in the wildest glee. She had expected the news of her husband's death when she saw the old Shastri come into her rooms, and the revulsion of feeling was almost too much for her. She and one other Rani were to go. The third was no favourite with the Raja.

[1] Vellore, according to Taylor's *History*.

A few days after, the Resident's order finally came that the ladies were to be sent off on a certain day to meet the Raja at Karnul. Everything had been already prepared; there need be no delay; and I intended them to start that very afternoon. I took leave of them both in the morning, and had settled down to my work after breakfast was over. It chanced to be a day set apart for the arrangement of yearly allowances and gifts to Brahmins, and all the chief Brahmins were present, and the old Shastri among them. Several were seated at the table with me, assisting me, when suddenly I heard the clash of the express-runner's bells coming up the street. I thought it might be some message from Lingsugur, or some new arrangement for the Ranis' departure. The runner entered the palace court, and his packet was soon in my hands. It contained a few lines only, from the Resident:—

'The Raja of Shorapur shot himself this morning dead, as he arrived at his first encampment. I will write particulars when I know them.'

My countenance naturally changed; and the old Shastri, who was beside me, and had been reading over Sanskrit deeds and grants to me, caught hold of my arm, and, peering into my face, cried, almost with a shriek—

'He's dead! he's dead! I know it by your face—it tells me, Sahib, he's dead!'

'Yes,' I said, sorrowfully. 'Yes, he is dead; he shot himself at the first stage out of Secunderabad, and died instantly.'

Then ensued a sad scene of weeping and wailing; and one of my friends in the adjoining room, hearing the tumult, rushed in, crying, 'Thank God, you are safe! I feared something terrible had happened. Why are these people so agitated?'

'It is terrible enough,' I answered. 'The Raja has shot himself, and the news has just come by express.'

'Ah,' said the old priest, as soon as he could speak, 'he could not escape his fate, and the prophecy is fulfilled.'

It was, indeed, a strange accomplishment of the prediction. In a few more days the Raja would have completed his twenty-fourth year; and now he had died by his own hand! I sent for the Rani's father, and bade him break the news gently to his daughter. I could not bear to see the poor girl's misery, and I should have to visit her later ; so he and an old friend of his departed to perform their sad task.

The day after, I heard by another express the particulars. The Raja had been told of the Governor-General's commutation of his sentence, and was very deeply grateful for the mercy shown to him. He had promised earnestly to try and deserve the consideration which had been extended him, and was particularly pleased that he was to be allowed the society of his two Ranis, speaking joyously of the prospect of meeting them at Karnul.

He had travelled in a palankeen, with the officer commanding his escort near him, all the way to their camp.

When they arrived, the officer took off his belt, in which was a loaded revolver, hung it over a chair, and went outside the tent. While washing his face a moment afterwards, he heard a shot, and, running back, found the Raja lying on the ground quite dead. The ball had entered his stomach and passed through the spine.

Was the act intentional ? I think not. He had a trick always of taking up and examining everything lying near him, more especially if it were new to him ; and he had had this habit from childhood, and I had often checked him for it. I do not think he could ever have seen a revolver—and such a weapon would be too tempting to escape notice ; he would be sure to snap it, or meddle with the lock, and the pistol may have exploded without his intending it at all. No one was with him—no one saw him,—so that only conjectures could be raised about the event ; but I, who knew him well, do not believe it was suicide.

Whether accidental or intentional, the result was the same. The Raja was dead, and his kingdom was lost, ere he completed his twenty-fourth year ; and the grim old prophecy deduced from the horoscope was literally fulfilled !

CHAPTER XVI

1858–59

TOWARDS the end of May, Lord Elphinstone and the Resident had both been extremely anxious in regard to Shorapur and its Beydur population.

It had transpired at the Raja's trial, and had previously been suspected, that certain chiefs of the Southern Maratha country had formed a plan for insurrection ; but as the Raja had refused to give any names, or to implicate others in any way, no action could be taken : and the Raja simply pleaded in his defence that he had refused to join the rebellion when invited and pressed to do so. General Jacob had taken the precaution, very wisely, of disarming Miraj,[1] a very strong fort ; and his admirable check of formidable rebellion at Kolhapur, and the active measures he used, effectually crushed the hopes of the insurrectionists. I have little doubt that had the Raja gone to the assistance of the Beydurs of Halgali when they asked his aid, the whole of the Southern Maratha country and Raichur would have joined him in far greater force than they afterwards displayed when they rose at last on the 29th May 1858, under the chief of Mirgoona,[2]

[1] An old trading town, now of some 20,000 inhabitants, capital of Miraj State, senior branch, which is under the political agent of Kolhapur. Miraj is notable for the admirable missionary medical work carried on by the American Presbyterians.

[2] No such place, or chief, or victim can be traced, evidently because they are creations of the first printers of this autobiography. Mr. Thomson is Mr. Manson ; the chief is Baba Sahib, Raja of Nargund (see earlier note). Rice Holmes, following the narrative of General George Le Grand Jacob, giving the same dates, tells how on June 1st Colonel Malcolm defeated the Raja before Nargund, the fort of which

and openly murdered Mr. Thomson, a Bombay civilian, who had ventured to remonstrate with them.

The force was afterwards attacked by Colonel Malcolm and utterly routed on the 2d June : their chief was captured, tried, and executed.

Another rising was planned by one Bhim Rao, formerly a Government collector at Bellary, who with 250 men took up his position in the fort of Koppaldrug,[1] but was pursued and killed by Major Hughes and a detachment from Lingsugur. The remainder of the rebels were taken prisoners, and either hanged or shot.

There were many such parties in the Deccan ; and I confess that, when I heard of these troubles, I wondered what my Beydurs would do : but they had received sufficient warning in the fate of their Raja and in the prompt discomfiture of their rebellious neighbours, and not a man stirred or showed the slightest sign of insubordination. They even assisted me materially in guarding the frontier, and the ferries across the Bhima, against the insurgents who tried to pass through Shorapur. The Arabs of Hyderabad employed by the late Raja were satisfied that the Beydurs would soon join them if they could only enter the country, and were not a little discomfited to find these very people guarding their country against their entrance. So, finding they could get no sympathy, all disturbance ceased, and we were once more at peace ; and I could assure Lord Elphinstone, with whom I had been in private correspondence, that no apprehension of the Beydurs being induced to join the rebel party need be entertained.

---

was found empty the next morning. 'Baba Sahib had fled in the night. Frank Souter, the superintendent of police, rode with a few men in pursuit, and on the 2nd caught him, disguised as a pilgrim, in the jungle. Soon afterwards he was tried, condemned, and executed.'

The Malcolm of these chapters was not Taylor's earlier friend at the Hyderabad Residency, Captain D. Malcolm. This was the subsequent General Sir George Malcolm, 1818–1897. He was born in Bombay, a nephew of Sir John Malcolm ; and was in the old Bombay Army, from Kabul to Abyssinia. Buckland writes of him : 'Against Shorapur, 1858 : commanded in the operations against the Chief of Nargoond, 1858.' He had distinguished himself at Gujrat, 1849, leading a charge of 'the famous Sinde Horse', as mentioned in Taylor's *History*.

[1] See note, next chapter.

The victories won by Sir Hugh Rose, that of Gwalior, and the death of the Rani of Jhansi,[1] the capture of the Nawab of Banda and his treasure, Sir Hope Grant's proceedings in Oudh, and the seizure of Tantia Topi—all these went to prove that the power of the Mutiny was broken, and that India would soon be at peace in all its borders.

How earnestly I had looked forward to this year as the one in which I should again see all my dear ones in England! but now leave was impossible to obtain, and indeed no one would have asked it, except it were urgently needed for health's sake. Fortunately I was in too good condition to ask for a medical certificate, though at times I had much suffering. My father proposed to bring my children to me; but in my present position I felt it would hardly do. I had no home for them; my work was of a very unsettled nature, and the country was still very much disturbed. I consulted the Resident; but he earnestly begged me not to risk such a step, adding that he knew I sorely needed change, and it was better to wait another year, when leave could be obtained without difficulty. I felt he was right, and a very serious fit of illness in September warned me that I should soon need rest from work; but I recovered, and went on as usual again.

Authentic ghost-stories are comparatively rare; but a circumstance occurred at Shorapur which made a great impression on men's minds, and may be accepted as one.

There were two companies of the 74th Highlanders at Shorapur with Colonel Hughes's force. After the place was taken, one company was located, as I have before stated, in my house on the hill, the other remaining in camp below the town, till they should return to Bellary. One afternoon—I have forgotten the date—Capt. ——, the senior officer, was sitting in his tent writing letters for England, as the mail letters had to be forwarded by that evening's post, and had had the side wall of his tent opened for light and air, when a young man of his company appeared suddenly before him in his hospital dress, without his cap, and, without saluting him, said, 'I wish, sir, you would kindly have my arrears of pay

[1] A singularly poor chapter in *Seeta*, xlix., 'The Ranee of Jhansy', is devoted to this sovereign: Taylor felt sorry for her, and tried to idealise her.

sent to my mother, who lives at ——; please take down the address.' Capt. —— took down the address mechanically, and said, 'All right, my man, that will do'; and, again making no salute, the man went away. A moment after, Capt. —— remembered that the dress and appearance of the soldier, and his manner of coming in, were highly irregular, and desired his orderly to send the sergeant to him directly.

'Why did you allow —— to come to me in that irregular manner?' he asked, as soon as the sergeant came.

The man was thunderstruck. 'Sir,' he exclaimed, 'do you not remember he died yesterday in hospital, and was buried this morning? Are you sure, sir, you saw him?'

'Quite sure,' was the reply; 'and here is a memorandum I took down from him of his mother's address, to whom he wished his pay should be sent.'

'That is strange, sir,' said the sergeant; 'his things were sold by auction to-day, and I could not find where the money should be sent in the company's registry, but it may be in the general registry with the regiment.'

The books were searched; the address taken down was proved to be correct, and the circumstance made a profound impression upon all who knew the facts.

These Highlanders were capital fellows—very steady in a town where there were all sorts of temptations to excess. As the weather grew cooler, they got up a play—a melodrama—called, I think, 'The Maniac Lover', and acted it well in the *kacheri*. Many of the Shorapur 'gentry' and their wives being invited, the latter sat ensconced behind bamboo screens; and although no word could be understood, the natives applauded very vigorously. I wrote a ballad, entitled the 'Battle of Shorapur', with a very long string of verses, which became exceedingly popular, and detailed the march of the troops, the fight, with various incidents, and the final discomfiture of the rebels; and this was constantly sung with great spirit, all joining in the chorus. The men had also games of cricket, skittles, etc., to amuse them, and some were even fond of chess.

The officers were pleasant companions, and we generally dined together. They were succeeded by a company of H.M.'s 56th Regiment in June.

I laid out a new road into the town, which was about 24 feet wide and about a mile long, leading from the alley up to the north gate. Its deepest gradient was 1′ in 25′, and along it carts and pack-bullocks could travel easily. My plantations of mango and tamarind trees were generally thriving, and the oldest ones were now bearing fruit. Bohnal tank required no repairs, and was quite complete in all respects; but as to the others, nothing had been done, except a little at Kachaknur. No outlay upon public works had been permitted since I left.

By June all the arrangements of estates and pensions were reported as finished. There were objections to the Ranis receiving their estates back again, for the present at any rate; but an allowance of £1000 a-year was settled on Rangama, and pensions on the other ladies in proportion. Rangama was very grateful; she did not expect half so much. I often paid her a visit, and she was gradually growing more cheerful and resigned.[1]

The year closed pleasantly to me, though I could not get leave to England; but as soon as ever the prohibitions were

[1] A glimpse of this fallen family half a century later is given in the little volume of the Nawab Framurz Khan, called *Shorapur, an Ancient Beydur Raj*. It seems that, although the Rajas of Shorapur considered themselves Kshattriyas, yet in reality they were only Beydurs. Much of Indian social history is indicated in the statements: 'They were allowed by religion to eat everything', that is, they were so low that it did not matter what they ate. 'Later on they took it as a matter of dignity to abstain from certain things, and as they had bestowed Jagirs and Inams on Brahmins, the latter in return classed these Rajahs as Kshatriyas. . . . The daring deeds to which they accustomed themselves deprived them of their natural timidity and made them bold and fearless.'

As in many parts of India, personal names among the Beydurs are extremely few, and repeated to the point of confusion. The Kanarese word *appa* or father is added to the names of men, and *ama* or *avva*, mother, to the names of women. The wives of the last Raja would seem to have had but two names between them. Most of them were probably children in 1858. In 1906 the Nawab Framurz Khan wrote: 'The last Rajah Venkatappa Naik had nine wives, of whom Rani Bangarama III. and Rani Rangama VI. are still alive. After the State was ceded to His Highness the Nizam, allowances were granted to the nine Ranis.' There were three acknowledged cousins of the last Raja. The sons of two of these had been endowed by the Nizam, one of them upon a considerable scale, with grants including the historic Sagar.

withdrawn, I was prepared to ask for it. The survey in Naldrug was to be carried on according to my plan, as an experiment, although my present duties did not admit of my taking up the surveyorship.

The Governor-General was pleased to record of me that 'Captain Meadows Taylor has been deputed to Shorapur, where his past experience and local knowledge make his presence most invaluable.'

It was not yet decided who should take my place at Naldrug. Mr. Maltby had been obliged to go to England; and my friend Bullock was acting for him—without any hope, however, of obtaining the appointment permanently, as it was far too good for an 'uncovenanted servant' to aspire to! We had all hoped that the gracious proclamation issued on her Majesty's assumption of the Government of India, which I had the pleasure of reading in Urdu and Marathi to the people of Shorapur, would have extended to us, and done away with the invidious distinctions 'covenanted' and 'uncovenanted'; but it was not to be so.

At the close of the year I had a visit from the executive engineer in the Raichur district, who came to look at my contemplated works, and checked the levels and surveys of the great Kachaknur tank. There was a slight error of fourteen-hundredths of a foot detected in the outward bench-marks of the embankment; but in all other respects my work, even with the imperfect instruments I had used, was entirely correct. I proposed to go on and complete the tank; but until some decision was come to about the principality, no public work of magnitude could be attempted. The Resident had gone up to Calcutta to confer with Lord Canning, and perhaps the fate of Shorapur would be decided by them. However, in the end, it was left uncertain.

A very unpleasant affair had taken place at Hyderabad. At a reception which the Nizam had held, and at which the Minister and the Resident had both been present, a man had fired a loaded pistol either at the Resident or the Minister, who were coming out together. It could not be determined for whom the shot was intended. Fortunately the ball missed both, but wounded the Minister's foster-brother. The ruffian then drew his sword and made a cut at the Minister, which an attendant received upon his arm, and the villain was immediately cut down by Captain Hastings Fraser and others standing by. The scene had been exciting and disagreeable, and showed plainly that the germs of treason were not yet destroyed. There was, however, no further disturbance.

I could get no satisfactory answer to my application for furlough to England, being answered that, as soon as the question of the Shorapur State was decided, I should know my fate; and meanwhile, if it were at all possible, I was to hold on.

At the beginning of May 1859 I had finished my tour of the district, and made a settlement for the current year. The country was in a wretched condition. A great mass of the cultivation had been thrown up the year before. The farmers had been deprived of their best lands by the Raja, who had given them to his favourites. There were no proper accounts, and the whole was in worse confusion than when I had first taken over charge. Numbers of families had emigrated in disgust. I could give very little assurance to any, as to future settlements; and, indeed, I was forbidden to do so, for Government was still silent as to the destiny of the State.

I did what I could, but it amounted to very little. The people would not invest their capital unless the country were to remain under British rule, and I could not conscientiously counsel them to do so. 'Directly you went away the last time,' they said, 'the men about the Raja chose the best of our newly-cleared lands, and they were taken from us and given to them. True, you have now given them back to us; but can you assure us that the same won't happen again if your back is turned? Let us wait and see what will happen.'

No change occurred in my position until August, when, in addition to Shorapur, the whole of the Raichur Doab was put under my charge; and as Raichur had been deeply disaffected, I was desired to report upon its condition specially. I did not relish this employment; and I began to fear, too, that this accession to my duties would prevent my going to England, as I had hoped to do, the year following. I was now by no means strong, and I looked to the future with grave anxiety. With Raichur and Shorapur combined, I should have a country quite 20,000 square miles in area under my jurisdiction, and a population hardly under, perhaps exceeding, two millions. There was but one English assistant, with four native assistants, in Raichur; but my assistant in Shorapur, Sita Ram Rao, was a host in himself, and I could trust that province to him with every confidence.

It appeared, too, that I was to receive no additional pay for my extra work; but there was no help for it. The order came, and was obeyed with the best grace I could command.

I went to Lingsugur for a few days, and there performed the sad and painful task of reading the burial service over a dear friend's wife, who had died suddenly, and who expressed a wish that I should be the one to perform this last sad office for her. I could not stay long, but simply took charge of the province, returning again to Shorapur to investigate a trial for murder—a very difficult and complicated case, which no one but myself could dispose of. Captain and Mrs. Wyndham accompanied me, and remained till October, when we moved out to Bohnal, to begin my tour.

It was a delightful time, cool and pleasant. There had been a good monsoon, and the lake was full and running over. We had charming rides every morning over the roads, both old and new, and which were now as smooth as gravel-walks.

After a fortnight spent at Bohnal, where the schooner was in capital order and in constant use, we set out for the western frontier, so as to visit the great falls of the Krishna, which I wanted to show my friends. I took them also to the cairns and cromlechs I had discovered, and we all enjoyed our holiday at the falls most thoroughly.

Here the great river Krishna leaves the tableland of the Deccan, and falls, by a descent of 408 feet in about three miles, into the lower level of Shorapur. The fall itself is not perpendicular, but becomes a roaring cataract half a mile broad when the river is in flood. The scene then is indescribably grand, an enormous broken volume of water rushing down an incline of granite with a roar that can be easily heard at a distance of thirty miles, and a cloud of spray dashing up high into the air; while the irregularity of the incline, its huge rocks, and the deep holes which the waters have excavated, increase the wonderful effect of the cataract, and brilliant rainbows flash through the spray, changing with every breath of wind. Finally, the water falls into a deep pool, which becomes a whirling mass covered with billows that, rushing in every direction, clash and break against each other, sending up great piles of foam. As a Beydur standing beside me said, 'It is like all the white horses in the world fighting together, and tossing their manes into the air.' Nor was the simple fellow's illustration without point.

I had never seen such a sight during my life, and perhaps few cataracts in the world can surpass it, when in flood, for sublimity and beauty.

I believe few English people have visited this spot. I, at least, have never met any traveller who had heard of it. When we were there, the water was lower than on my first visit; but the effect of the fall, the rocky gorge below clothed with wood, and the grand old fort at the end, partly Hindu and partly Musalman, was very beautiful.[1]

Our route lay across the ford, which was a memorable spot in history, when the Musalman army crossed to engage that of Vijayanagar in the battle which was fought on the south bank of the Krishna in 1565. The ford had been carried by a bold stratagem. The Musalman leaders marched slowly up the left bank of the river for two days, watched by the Hindu troops, who left the ford almost unguarded. The Musalmans then doubled back, carried the defences of the ford by storm, and the whole army followed. By this utter defeat of their opponents, the Musalmans gained possession of the city of Vijayanagar and the whole of the northern portion of the kingdom.[2]

[1] A large part of such action as there is in *A Noble Queen* passes at this fort, Jaldrug (otherwise Shahdrug), a few miles above the junction of the Dhon, the river of the Bijapur plain, with the Krishna. 'If the crop on Dhon ripens, who can eat it? if it fails, who can eat?' There is much about these falls, not merely in the chapters called 'The Cataract of the Krishna' and 'The Storm and the Flood'. A Beydur chief, an ineffective repetition of the sympathetic hunchback cateran in *Tara*, uses the same comparison as above about wild horses. 'Although the water was yellow and muddy, yet the rosy light played among every giant stream, or tiny portion of the vast fall, causing rainbows to appear, to vanish, and to re-appear in every part of the spray on which the sun shone. . . . Beneath them the stupendous rushes of water from the great holes, rising in perpetual changes, seemed hung with these lovely garlands ever varying.'

[2] The story is told at more length in Taylor's *History*. 'By this great battle, which is usually called that of Talikote, though in reality

We found the remains of the defences still quite traceable at the ford, and corresponding in all respects with the description given by Ferishta. From hence to Lingsugur was only an easy march, and we returned into cantonments.

At the end of October I started on my first march to Mudgal.[1] I dared not loiter longer, and felt I must see with my own eyes, and hear with my own ears, before I could report specially upon the district.

I found a good road to Mudgal, and the canter in the fresh morning air was delicious. Mudgal is a fine old fort, built upon a group of granite rocks rising perhaps 100 feet above the plain. It had been a bone of contention from the earliest times of the Bahmani dynasty, and alternately fell into the possession of the Hindus or the Musalmans, whichever chanced to be, for the time, the strongest party. Now it was considerably ruined, but most picturesque, and I explored it thoroughly.

I could only stay two days, and these were mostly occupied in inquiring into a dispute relating to a Christian settlement there, which, as it involved religious jurisdiction between his Holiness the Pope and the Archbishop of Goa, I was incompetent to decide. The congregation were all weavers of blankets, and shepherds, originally converted by one of

---

fought nearly thirty miles to the south-west of that town, the Hindoo power of Southern India was destroyed.'

[1] Headquarters of the Lingsugur taluk, Raichur District, with a dwindling population of 7,000. 'The fort was the seat of the Yadava governors of Deogiri in 1250.' The 'small Roman Catholic colony in the town' of Mudgal is mentioned in the *Imperial Gazetteer* article.

Mudgal appears in Taylor's *History* in connection with the well-known story of the martyrs. And Seeta's grandfather thus tells another when giving her to Cyril Brandon: 'Many years ago—centuries—when the Hindoo princes of Beejanugger ruled over Southern India, and the Moslems held Goolburgah, there was a great war, on account of a daughter of our craft, who was very beautiful and learned, like Seeta. The Rajah of Beejanugger desired to carry her away from Moodgul, where she lived, and sent his horsemen to seize her; but the Moslems prevented this, and a bitter war followed, in which the Moslems were victorious. Then the Moslem king sent for the goldsmith's daughter, whom his son had seen and loved in secret, and married her to him; and she bore him children, who sat on the royal throne of Beedar.'

There is also much about Mudgal, and the Christians there, in *A Noble Queen*.

St. Francis Xavier's missionaries from Goa. It had been somewhat richly endowed by the several kings of the Adil Shahi dynasty of Bijapur, and it still retained these grants through all revolutions. There were two other congregations in the Doab, one being composed of potters at Raichur; the name of the place of the other I forget.[1] The church at Mudgal was a humble but respectable edifice, and service was performed by a deacon, the Mass in full being celebrated when a priest came from Goa on his rounds.

On my arrival some time after in England, I wrote to his Eminence Cardinal Wiseman about this congregation, furnishing him with all particulars respecting them, and received a courteous reply, to the effect that my communication was both valuable and extremely interesting, and would be duly forwarded to Rome.

I hoped next to visit the grand old city of Vijayanagar, and to add some sketches to my collection. At the town of Kanakgheri the Raja came out to welcome me, and entertained me most hospitably. Here I saw the finest Hindu temple I had yet visited. The interior was supported by huge pillars of granite, in the form of horses, on which female figures were mounted; the frieze and ceiling were richly ornamented in carving. I do not think it is much known, but it well repays a visit. After breakfast the Raja came to me, and Shorapur and its affairs were the subject of discussion. 'Could I give any hope', he asked, 'of its being restored to the family? would the British keep it? or would the Nizam have it?'

I could say nothing, for nothing had been determined upon. My friend, whom I had often before seen at Shorapur, deprecated the idea of the Nizam having Shorapur.

'Why should the people suffer more oppression?' he said. 'Of course I would wish to see it given back to the family—

[1] At the end of *Tara*, when (probably at Afzulpur near the Bhima) the dying Tara says, 'I come, O Mother,' she may have remembered her old goddess at Tuljapur. Or she may have been thinking of another Mother, 'since some Christian monks from Goa, who had established a mission at the town of Chittapoor, only a few miles distant, had come to beg alms of her'. There is this note: 'The mission still exists, and is visited periodically by priests from Goa. There are, or were, about seventy Christians in it who, with an affecting simplicity, preserve their faith in purity. They are shepherds, weavers, and distillers.'

my relatives; but if that may not be, why should the Nizam get it? The 12,000 Beydurs would far prefer the just rule of the English, and would not revert to their evil ways under you.'

Such was the old gentleman's opinion, and I agreed with him perfectly; but I had no hope of the restoration of the family being allowed. Pid Naik's eldest son, who was the next heir, was steady, sensible, and thoroughly loyal, having opposed his cousin, the late Raja, in all his insurrectionary movements; still, I thought the British Government would eventually annex the State, as an example and a warning to all others.

From Kanakgheri I went on to Anagundi, where the lineal descendant of the great Rajas of Vijayanagar resided.[1] He

[1] In his admirable *Brief History of the Indian Peoples*, Sir W. W. Hunter, telling of lesser powers founded by the nobles and the blood royal of Vijayanagar, says: 'Another scion, claiming the same high descent, lingers to the present day near the ruins of Vijayanagar, and is known as the Raja of Anagundi, a feudatory of the Nizam of Haidarabad.'

This romantic corner, so rich in historical interest, is well represented in the map of Hyderabad State. Anagundi, Hampi where Vijayanagar stood, and the large modern town of Hospet, feverish through irrigation, all appear.

To the end of Indian history the unregenerate student will be tempted to confuse the ruined Shiah city of Bijapur with the ruined Hindu capital a hundred miles to the south. This tendency is made irresistible by Meadows Taylor's way of spelling the latter, 'Beejanugger'. The only safety, as so often, lies in the standard of the *Imperial Indian Gazetteer*. Vijayanagar is so plainly the Town of Victory. The article upon it in the *Gazetteer*, evidently written by an enthusiast, is of extreme interest.

'The site of the old city is a strangely wild place to have been the birthplace and capital of an empire. The whole area is dotted with little rocky hills; and immediately to the north the wide and rapid Tungabhadra hurries along a boulder-strewn channel down rapids and through narrow gorges. The hills are of granite, weathered to every shade of colour from a bluish-grey to a rich golden brown, and have hardly a shrub or a blade of grass upon them.' For ten square miles there is nothing between heaven and earth but boulders. 'The city was founded in 1336; and its importance in South Indian history lies in the fact that it was a stronghold of the Hindus, and that for two and a half centuries it successfully opposed the southward movement of the Musalman arms.'

After the great defeat the puppet king of Vijayanagar is believed to have fled with 550 elephants laden with 100 millions sterling of treasure.

had sent me a very pressing invitation to comc and visit him, and volunteered to show all the marvels of Vijayanagar to me on my arrival. Anagundi, 'The Elephant's Corner', had once been a suburb of Vijayanagar, and proved to be one of the most curious places I had ever visited. To the north was a perfectly inaccessible range of bare granite hills, surmounted by piles of fantastic rocks, along the tops of which ran high walls, with bastions at intervals, in the Hindu style. The only entrance to this labyrinth of rocks was through a very narrow gorge on the eastern side, also strongly fortified by double walls and large bastions. Passing round the corners of these walls, the ground opened out to some degree, and was cultivated, affording a lovely view of the rugged hills on the south side of the Tungabhadra, a rough brawling river rushing through the valley.

The Raja had made a good road through his estate, and showed me many points which afforded exquisite views of wood, rock, and water, with the mountains in the background; and he always stopped the carriage at these places, to show me the prospect, with evident enjoyment. He was driving a handsome light phaeton, and met me at the barrier. He was a fine active young man, with a very pleasing and intelligent countenance, and we were soon good friends. He had

---

This may illustrate the meaninglessness of numbers in the East. The victorious Musalmans spent five months in deliberately destroying everything destructible within the city. 'The existing representative of the line is the Raja of Anegundi [*sic*] in the Nizam's Dominions, who possesses a small estate and draws a pension from the British Government.' The article upon Anegundi adds little. The word means 'elephant pit', where the elephants of the Vijayanagar Rajas were kept. The village has some 2,000 inhabitants. The region on both sides of the river is peculiarly sacred as the Kishkindha of the Ramayana, where Sita was seen by Hanuman, the minister of the king of the place, being borne through the air to Ceylon, and where the monkey host was gathered to deliver her.

Taylor has here given such a picture, intensely felt, of the place that there is the less need to sample what he has written of it in his *History*. He had no illusions about the material magnificence of Vijayanagar, however he may have exaggerated that of Bijapur. See the loving monograph upon this subject, Mr. Robert Sewell's *A Forgotten Empire*. For formal description, *Hampi Ruins*, described and illustrated by A. H. Longhurst, Superintendent of the Archaeol. Survey, Madras, 1917 may be consulted with advantage. The book is well illustrated.

prepared the porch of a temple on the bank of the river for me, and I found an ample breakfast provided, and his own servants in attendance.

The situation of the town among these most picturesque piles of rock was very curious. I went to return the Raja's visit in the afternoon, when he proposed to take me to his island in the evening. I willingly agreed. I found his reeeption-room nieely furnished in the English style; and we sat chatting pleasantly for a long time. He seemed pleased to find me aequainted with his family history—their wars with the Musalmans, and their final gallant struggle with the erusade against them in 1565.

'Ah!' he said, 'my ancestor, Ram Raj,[1] alone would have beaten them back; but the coalition of four kingdoms of the Deeean proved too strong for him. They are all gone now, and have left no trace exeept these cities—not a soul to pray for their manes, or light a lamp in their name; while I still am here, and represent my great ancestors as their lineal descendant. I have only the "Elephant Corner" of the great city to live in, it is true; but I am quite content, and the Nizam allows me this corner and its dependencies, while the English have granted me some lands on the south bank of the river, and a pension.'

[1] The Raja of Anagundi may be supposed to have known best who were his ancestors. A list furnished by him to another person is mentioned in Taylor's *History*, according to which the royal line must have had about one hundred descents even before the founding of Vijayanagar. Rama Raja, Maharaja, or Raya, whose name bears a halo as the champion of Hinduism fallen in battle, was plainly not of the old line, but the son of a minister. The opening of the next chapter mentions Achyuta Rao as an ancestor of the Raja of Anagundi.

The *Imperial Gazetteer* says: 'Achyuta (1530–1542) was a weak yet tyrannical ruler, and his conduct and mode of government ruined the Hindu cause in the South. His nobles rebelled against his authority, and all real power fell into the hands of three brothers. The chief of these was Rama Raja, who did much to repair the blunders of Achyuta and restore the prestige of the empire.' Yet by haughtiness he brought the confederacy upon Vijayanagar, and died at Talikot with one of his brothers.

Taylor in his *History*, leaning too heavily upon Ferishta, has made rather a tangle of the last generation of Vijayanagar history. A far clearer account, yet hardly recognisable as of the same events, is given in the *Short History of India* by J. Talboys Wheeler, who speaks of Vijayanagar by the alternative name of Narsinga.

In the evening he came quite alone, poling a small basket-boat.

'I always go down to the island by myself,' he said; 'it is such good fun shooting the rapid; but I have men there to paddle me up again in a bigger boat.'

I got into the little craft, and he pushed off into the stream, striking as directly across it as the current would allow. We were soon drawn into the rapid, and dashed on for a quarter of a mile at great speed—the Raja with his long bamboo pole fending the boat from rocks on either side very skilfully, and evidently intensely enjoying the excitement.

At the end of the shoot, we entered the still water, where the island was situated—a richly-wooded spot, laid out as a garden in the English style, well stocked with fruit-trees and a profusion of roses and gardenias, whose scent filled the evening air with perfume. In the centre was a pretty pavilion, also in the English style; and this was, the Raja told me, his favourite resort. There were numbers of tame pea-fowl; and at his peculiar call some cranes and flamingoes, with geese and ducks, all came flocking round us to be fed—a motley and curious collection. 'These are my pets,' said the Raja, 'and my children's too.'

When it was growing dark, his gardeners brought a large basket-boat to the landing-place, and six stout fellows paddled us up the rapid to my resting-place. I had spent a very interesting day, and my host pressed me much to remain some time; but this was impossible—my tents had already gone on to Hampi on the south bank of the river, where the old city commenced, and I had much to see there. 'If you really must go,' said the Raja, 'I will take you there myself in my large boat, and you will then see the views from the river, which are very striking, and more interesting than those on the road; but I wish you could stay—you are the only Englishman with whom I ever felt on easy terms of friendship; and none of your people seem to know or to remember who I am.'

The Raja was punctual to the time appointed next morning, and brought a stout crew with him, as we should have to paddle up several rapids; and before sunrise we were off.

It was a lovely voyage of several miles. At each bend of

the beautiful river new prospects opened, and new piles of granite rocks, some of them 500 feet in height, came in view, fringed with trees and brushwood, which softened their grim outlines, and rendered the effects of light and shade most charming. I took many sketches from the water, while the Raja looked on wonderingly, and longed to be able to do so likewise. At last the 'Gate of the River', as it is called, came in sight, where the stream lessens to a very narrow pass, bounded by piles of rock of the most fantastic forms imaginable; and leaving our boat at the landing-place, we walked up to the courtyard of the great temple, in the cloisters of which I found my servants had taken up a comfortable position, instead of pitching my tents.

'If I can, I will come to-morrow,' said the Raja; 'but in any case, you must not go till I return. I must be with you when you go over the great temple.'

I promised I would stay, and he took his leave.

After breakfast I ordered my palankeen, and wandered over the western portions of the city. I saw that the barriers of rocks extended to the south, forming a strong line of defence, the only aperture being a pass between them and the spurs of the Raman Mallay Mountain. This was the pass by which the Bahmani king, Mujahid Shah, entered the lines of defence in 1378, and endeavoured to take the city; but owing to the neglect of one of his generals, who had been directed to occupy an eminence to the west of the city, which was the real key to the place, and who failed in his duty, the king could only penetrate the first line of defence, where a huge image of Hanuman, the monkey-god, stands alone, carved out of a great granite boulder.

The king, on seeing it surrounded by Brahmins, charged and dispersed them; then dismounting, he struck the image with his steel mace, breaking off a portion of the right leg.[1]

'For this act', cried a dying Brahmin, 'thou shalt die before thou reach the city'—a prophecy strictly fulfilled; for

[1] 'Struck the image in the face, mutilating its features,' says Taylor in his *History*. A page is there given to the moving story of Mujahid Shah, who ascended the throne of Gulbarga at the age of nineteen in 1373, and was murdered four or five years later, according to the best authorities.

King Mujahid was assassinated on his march to Gulbarga. In Ferishta,[1] a vivid description is given of this battle; and the positions occupied by the contending parties are so exactly mentioned, that they are, to this day, easily traceable.

I spent all the day sketching. The Raja's sleeping-palace was a curious conception of Musalman-Gothic architecture,

[1] *C.* 1570–*c.* 1611, according to the *Encyclopædia Britannica.* The same dates are given in the article in *Cassell's Biographical Dictionary,* which may or may not be by Meadows Taylor. The actual dates are not known. 'This celebrated historian of the rise of the Mahometan power in India was born at Astrabad, on the shores of the Caspian.' There is a reference in *Tara*: 'Those were times when the service of Indian princes was eagerly sought for by Persians, Turks, Affghans, and even Abyssinians.' At the Deccan court, Bijapur, 'among others of his countrymen, the historian Mahomed Kasim Ferishta had been distinguished'. He had drifted thither from Ahmednagar. At an early age he gave up arms, and settled down, as king's librarian, to his too brief, studious life.

The article in *Cassell's Biographical Dictionary* says that Ferishta 'entered upon his great work of history with much diligence, and at the age of twenty-six [*sic*] he had completed the detail of the Beejapoor and other Deccan kings. The rest of the work he rendered most valuable and interesting. His style is nervous and elegant; and the wonderful labour bestowed upon his histories of the many Mahometan dynasties, even from the earliest times, is most remarkable.' But it was loose to write, anywhere near 1870, that Ferishta's 'history has been twice translated into English; the portion of it which related specially to the Deccan, by Colonel Dow, and the whole work by Colonel Briggs'. In *Tara* Taylor refers to Scott's 'Ferishta'. Among the works consulted for his own *History of India* were Briggs's *Translation of Ferishta's History,* Scott's *Deccan,* and Dow's *History of Hindostan.*

Ferishta is easily the outstanding Asiatic historian. In all Sanskrit there is no historian with the exception of Kalhana, invaluable both for the isolated story of Kashmir and for his genuine poetical quality. Yet history was outside orthodox Hindu mentality. The Moslem mind, less acute, did just admit an uncritical chronicle of names and haphazard events. But Ferishta compiles carefully, besides telling some good stories. He brings the chronicles of Hindustan within measurable distance of the coming of the English conquerors. The more scholarly of these therefore fastened upon him in the days when Persian, the court speech of half the East, was still eagerly studied.

Alexander Dow, whose translation of Ferishta appeared in 1768, worked his way as a sailor to Benculen, where he became secretary to the governor, later a colonel and a dramatist. Jonathan Scott, the next translator, was a brother of Major Scott, the mismanaging agent of Warren Hastings, to whom he had himself been Persian Secretary. His translations (1811) of several stories are still reprinted in the Oxford University Press *Arabian Nights.* There is yet no better translation

the upper rooms of which would make a delightful residence if purged from the bats, swallows, and wild-pigeons' nests. The fine tower, with a Gothic pavilion at the top, from whence there is a glorious view; the elephant stables and treasury, still perfect; and the ruins of the Raja's palaces, and their courtyards, which are very extensive—with a host of other picturesque scenes, and masses of ruins,—gave me more than enough to do with my pencil and my brush. Vijayanagar is well described by the Nawab Abdul Bazzak, a Persian merchant, who visited the city in 1443, and resided there. His account of the population and general aspect of the city, the religious ceremonials, and the splendour of the king's court, are very graphic and eminently truthful. The journal has been translated for the Hakluyt Society, and well repays perusal. I have described the temple in a volume published by Mr. Murray on the *Temples of Western India*, and I endeavoured to extract my information from the most authentic sources.

---

of Ferishta than that of General John Briggs, 1785–1875, sometime Resident at Satara and at Nagpur. It was reprinted at Calcutta in four volumes, 1908–10.

Elphinstone relied chiefly upon Ferishta, while Taylor's *History* would have been far more readable had he excluded whole sheets of uncouth names and indigestible details taken from the same source.

CHAPTER XVII

1859–60

AFTER breakfast, the Raja arrived in his chair, which he insisted upon my using, while he took my palankeen instead; and we set off for the temple which had been built by his ancestor, Achyuta Rao, in 1534–36. Anything more exquisitely beautiful, or so wondrously finished, could hardly be conceived —except, perhaps, the temple of Nandidrug,[1] which even excels this in some particulars; but that of Kanakgheri,

[1] 'The temple of Bhoga Nandishvara dates at least from the Chola period, the beginning of the eleventh century, but in the courtyard is a Pallava inscription 200 years older' (*Imperial Gazetteer*, article 'Nandi'). This is a village in the Kolar District of Mysore, on the road to Bangalore, through which Taylor had passed on his way to the Nilgiris a quarter of a century before. Here the only sentence in all these volumes of standardised information referring to one of Taylor's novels has two mistakes. 'East of the village is the mosque mentioned in Meadows Taylor's novel *Tippoo Sultaun*, the opening scenes of which are laid at Nandi.' The mosque must be the temple to Nandi, the bull of Siva (*sic transit gloria Nandi* as Dr. John Wilson of Bombay used to say on seeing one of them), already twice specified above. The travellers, on their undeniably slow progress towards 'the city', Seringapatam, arrive there in chapter xii.

'Shortly afterwards they rode into the outer court of the Temple of Nuudi, at the town under the fort of Nundidroog. . . . The court was a large square, contained in a sort of piazza formed by a colonnade of huge square blocks of granite placed in three rows, about twelve feet asunder, each piece probably sixteen feet in height; across these at the top, to form a roof, were transverse pieces of equal length.' As then profaned by the Musalmans, the temple made capital barracks. 'Before them, and above the piazzas, appeared the richly ornamented and curious high pyramidical roofs of the temples, and their massive and decorated gateway; and above all frowned the bare rock of the fort— a naked mass of about eight hundred feet perpendicular, arising from

which I had considered very marvellous, sinks into significance before this.

Lofty pillars of granite support the roof, carved out of solid blocks of stone ; some of these are fashioned like horses or lions ; on the horses' backs ride female figures : others have rows of slender figures round them, cut away from the main stem, giving a graceful airy effect, which is very charming. Every portion of the interior is covered with rich, minute carving, and some parts were polished like glass.

Outside, the basement consists of rows of elephants, above these run several courses of different ornaments of elegant patterns. The projecting eaves of the cornices are likewise elaborately carved ; and the whole presented an appearance of extreme lightness and grace, which I had not before noticed in any Hindu edifice. Tippoo Sultan, when encamped near Vijayanagar, had had a mine sprung in the roof, in the hope of destroying the building ; but it had only made a small hole, and Tippoo then said he had been warned in a dream not to attempt to destroy the holy temple. The deity to whom it was dedicated was Vithal or Krishna, and it had been the intention of one of the Raja's ancestors to have removed the holy image from Pandharpur to it, as being a more appropriate dwelling-place ; the god, however, refused to stir, and, in consequence, the building has never been fully consecrated.

Close to the exterior of the temple there is what appeared to me to be a richly-ornamented triumphal car, to be used on festivals ; but this proved to be also of granite—a great boulder having been wrought as it stood into the perfect

---

a rugged and woody slope of an equal height. The walls around the summit, which were built upon the very giddy verge, were bristling with cannon, and the numbers of men about showed that it possessed many defenders.'

This famous fortress overhead, Nandidrug, was taken by Lord Cornwallis in 1791. It stands close upon 5,000 feet above the sea, much higher than the Ramandrug described below. Points called Hyder's Drop and Tippoo's Drop are shown, whence British prisoners used to be hurled—sometimes purposely from heights not great enough to cause instant death. Taylor's hand, so unfailing where native life is concerned, fumbles with the English characters in this novel. The later chapters, about the officers confined at Nandidrug, are crude, and gruesome beyond anything in the *Thug*, because the artistic touch is lacking. Nandidrug was a favourite summer resort of Sir Mark Cubbon.

resemblance of a car, the wheels of which seemed only to require a push to make them turn, so well was the carving executed.

I had felt ill all day, and at last, in the middle of my drawing, such violent fever and ague came on as obliged me to give it up very unwillingly; and as the attack lasted some hours, my sketching came to an untimely end, and I was unable to see the remainder of the temple or the east side of the city.

However, before the fever began, I had managed to ascend the 'Matan Parwat', a stupendous pile of rocks, by the stone steps which had been cut in them; my bearers easily carried my chair—and from the top—an elevation probably of five hundred feet—I had enjoyed a magnificent view.[1] The whole area of the old city lay spread out before me—the noble temples, and their lines of building—the ranges of fantastic rocks piled on all sides—the course of the river, for miles above and below the 'Gate'—and the blue Raman Mallay Mountains, and their varied spurs, stretching away to the south.

The Raja pointed out to me all the objects of interest—the battle-fields of Mujahid Shah, and the Lake of Kamalapuram, glittering in the bright sunlight.[2] It was indeed a magnificent panorama, and one never to be forgotten.

I was very sorry to say farewell to the Raja, whose genuine and most courteous hospitality and agreeable manners had made a great impression upon me. I had been told I should find him haughty and repellent: on the contrary, he was entirely free from presumption, full of information and intelligence, active and manly in his habits, and of very prepossessing appearance—in every respect a 'gentleman',—and I was glad I had gone out of my way to visit him.

[1] 'To know Vijayanagar at its best, the visitor should climb the slippery steps leading to the little shrine on the top of the hill called Matanga Parvatam, and watch the evening light fade across the ruins; and if the fates are kind and grant him the added glory of a Deccan sunset, he will surely return content' (*Imperial Gazetteer*, article 'Vijayanagar').

[2] 'The best base from which to see what remains of the ruined city of Vijayanagar to-day . . . is Kamalapuram, 7 miles from Hospet railway station, where a deserted temple converted into a dwelling by a former Collector is now used as a travellers' bungalow' (*Imperial Gazetteer*, article 'Vijayanagar').

I stayed a day longer to recruit after my fit of fever, and went again to the great temple, and to the avenue of pilgrim's cloisters, and so round to the palace of the kings and its surroundings, all of the highest interest. The palaces could never have equalled those of Bijapur : there were no arches, and the roof had evidently been made of wood, covered with concrete, and supported on wooden pillars. These had either been destroyed on the spot or carried away, as no vestige of them remained. There was nothing to compare with the fort at Bijapur. The defences of Vijayanagar were mean and weak in comparison ; and the ancient Rajas, who had built the city, had evidently trusted more to the natural strength of the position than to the work raised by men's hands.

One Cesar Federicke, a Venetian merchant, gives a very interesting description of the city in 1565, after the residence there of the victorious Musalman kings for six months. He says :—

'The city was not altogether destroyed, but houses still stand empty, and there are dwelling in them nothing but tigers and other wild beasts. The *enceinte* of the city is about four-and-twenty miles, and within the walls are several mountains. The houses stand walled with earth, and no place, saving the palaces of the three tyrants and the pagodas, other than made with earth.'

Evidently, therefore, the city was exactly the same as the Hindu habitations of the present day,—the walls of houses being of mud, or clay and stone, and the roofs of clay beaten down—very substantial as long as the roof is good, but which crumbles away on the percolation of water.

In the large volume which illustrates the *Temples of Western India*, which I have before alluded to, many fine photographic illustrations of Vijayanagar will be found, and the views of the temple of Vithal or Vithoba are especially worthy of examination.

From Vijayanagar I ascended the pass through the Raman Mallay Mountain by a beautiful road constructed by the Madras engineers, at an easy gradient the whole way up. I was well enough now to ride, and enjoyed the lovely scenery to the full. At the top I found a nearly level plain, and a total change of climate from India to Europe. Ramandrug is,

I believe, about 4,000 feet above the sea-level,[1] and its climate is delicious throughout the year. Even during the hottest season the sea-breeze makes its way up, and there is no oppressive heat. Here there is a sanitarium, and I had sent word to the medical officer in charge that I was coming up for advice. I well remember we had to have a fire lighted that evening as it was so chilly, and that we sat over it till a late hour most thoroughly enjoying it. How I slept that night! All the evil demons that had been tormenting me—neuralgia, rheumatism, and all their doleful train, vanished as if by magic with the change of air. The doctor said I had been too long without a thorough change and rest from work, and that there was nothing for it but to take furlough and go home to England as soon as I could. He would not answer for my life, he said, if I remained at Shorapur through another hot season. I enjoyed some days at Ramandrug very much; my strength and appetite returned; I felt fresh vigour and renewed health, and could take a good long walk without fatigue. However, I might not stay; time was precious, and I set off again to my work.

I went to Kurga, where my tents were pitched, and where there was a fine ancient weir for irrigation, which required repair on my side, the authorities of Bellary having already restored their portion. The old Rajas of Vijayanagar had been great constructors of irrigation works from time to time, had thrown several dams across the Tungabhadra river, and had diverted the various streams so as to employ them extensively for the cultivation of rice, sugar-cane and cocoa-

[1] 3,256 feet, according to the *Imperial Gazetteer*. This is no more than the height of many a place, which says nothing about it, throughout the Deccan. Taylor's enjoyment here of 'The sleep that is among the lonely hills' was the measure of his need for a larger change. Ramandrug is as minute a sanitarium as Kipling ever laughed at. It is within Sandur State, but controlled from Bellary. There are 'some fifteen bungalows' belonging to people in Bellary, where the temperature averages twelve degrees higher. Chilly fogs during the monsoon make fires a necessity at Ramandrug.

Save for one monsoon on the Nilgiris in his youth Meadows Taylor never was at an Indian mountain station of good class. He relates below how narrowly he missed seeing Mahableshwar, in the neighbourhood of which he has laid perhaps his finest and most important historical scenes.

nut, ginger, turmeric, and other produce. At Kurga the constructor had been Achyuta Rao, and the inscription bore date 1537. This dam consisted for the most part of large loose blocks of granite, placed together on a broad base in a triangular form, and which had gradually become consolidated by silt. Many noble tanks, too, had been constructed by the Vijayanagar dynasty, the largest being nearly three square miles in area.

My district work now fairly began, and was fearfully heavy, while the petitions against one grievance or another became almost too numerous to attend or to settle at all as I could wish. Here the fever returned, and I could only do my work lying on my bed, for I was too weak to sit up much, and I began to fear I should soon fail utterly.

For change I went further north to Koppaldrug,[1] a marvellous fort indeed, being entirely impregnable. It consists of two fortifications, one, encircling the town, which had been remodelled by the French engineers in Tippoo's service, and all the bastions and cavaliers fitted with embrasures, and ramparts for heavy guns; the other fortification being of the great granite rock within the *enceinte*, the batteries of which command every portion of the land below on all sides to a great distance.

This hill-fort must be upwards of 500 feet high, and is inaccessible except by a flight of very rude rough steps which wind in and out among the rocks, and are in some places extremely narrow and unsafe. How many guns were ever carried up, it is impossible to say, but there were several old ones in the upper batteries. I went up this rock once, my bearers having contrived a light conveyance out of an arm-chair, and I travelled along easily. Had the insurgent Bhim Rao confined himself to operations against villages, he would have done much mischief, and roused the people, who seemed

[1] This is the Koppal of the map, *drug* meaning fort. The population has come down to some 7,000, from 9,000 a decade before. The *Imperial Gazetteer* gives it as an old hill fort and town in Raichur District, on the Southern Mahratta Railway. It figured in the wars of Tippoo. 'During the Mutiny of 1857, Bhim Rao, a rebel, obtained possession of it, but was slain with many others of his party, and the rest surrendered. . . . Sir John Malcolm described it as the strongest place he had seen in India. It is now the chief town in a jagir of Sir Salar Jang's family.'

ripe for insurrection ; but he got possession of Koppaldrug by a stratagem, and found himself there in a trap. He could not hold so large a place, and his party betook themselves to the steps of the fort, where many, including the Raja himself, were slain, and the rest were forced to surrender at discretion, for they had no food. I found the summit of this rock was composed of a large circular battery, and below it some deep cisterns in the naked rock contained beautiful clear water. About three miles south of Koppaldrug lay another rock-fort, if possible even stronger and more difficult of access, but not so high, and equally well provided with water in the same manner.

At Kukanur, near the border of the Dharwar Collectorate, I found a very beautiful Hindu temple dedicated to Siva. The pillars of the porch and hall were of polished greenstone, and seemed almost as if they had been turned in a lathe, the different circles of ornamentation were so exact ; and the designs were cut out as sharply in this tough, hard stone, as if they had been chased in metal. Near the town was a curious monolith of sandstone thirty-five feet in height, richly decorated, and having a figure of a cock on the top. There was a long inscription on the pillar, apparently in ancient Kanarese, and I regretted very much that no one was able to decipher it. A little further on I found another superb temple ; the ornamentation of its pillars was truly exquisite, and the designs so delicate that the various patterns were copied by the goldsmiths of the country for gold and silver ornaments.

This was the limit of my district, which contained, in addition to the foregoing, many illustrations of the Jain and Hindu architecture, dating from A.D. 76 to the 13th century. Many of their works are represented in the volumes before alluded to, but very many more certainly remain comparatively unknown. Had I been originally appointed to the Raichur district, I should have delighted in making myself acquainted with all these wonderful and very curious and beautiful buildings ; but as I have recorded, my lines fell in other places, and now I had not the time to devote to them as I wished. The archæological features of Raichur would have supplied a noble field for research. It had been the battle-ground of the ancient western Hindu and Jain dynasties, as well as the Musalman and Hindu, and each in succession had left their distinctive marks of occupation.

I pushed on to Gulbarga and Hamam Sagar, once a great city, as was apparent from its ruins, which spread over a large area. There was nothing, however, remarkable in them. Here my friend, the Rev. Mr. Keis, of whom I have before made mention, paid me a visit, as he happened to be in the neighbourhood on one of his tours, and we had a pleasant talk over old times. He had succeeded well in his work since our last meeting, and one whole village community had become Christians; they were weavers by trade. He was travelling about in his old fashion, a true missionary, going from village to village ministering to and teaching the people as he found occasion—everywhere welcome, and everywhere respected; for the people saw his earnestness, and his pure, humble, godly life, and loved him for his simplicity and his benevolence.

I visited the fort of Gajendragarh,[1] which belonged with its dependencies to a Southern Maratha chief, and also a remarkable place of pilgrimage near it on the side of the mountain, which proved exceedingly picturesque. Almost half-way up the hill, and at the foot of its precipitous sandstone top, is a cavern in which an image of Siva is placed. This is approached by steps, wide at foot and narrowing to the last gallery. The cavern is a natural aperture between two enormous blocks of granite; and on further examination of the hill, I found that the whole of the flat upper portion, which was upwards of 300 feet in height, with precipitous sides, rested upon granite, which had been raised from the plain around by some subterranean upheaval. The fort was built on a portion of this elevation, and as its chief had been implicated in the late insurrectionary movements, and his loyalty was still very doubtful, part of the walls and gates had recently been blown up, and the fort thereby rendered untenable.

I had now done what I could in the Raichur Doab, and I have not described my work minutely, as it was of the same character as that I had previously been employed upon, and there would be no use in multiplying details. The fever had

[1] A town in no other way notable, of some 9,000 inhabitants, in the Ron taluk of Dharwar District.

again returned, with neuralgia and other trying accompaniments, and I felt that something must soon be done. I could not hold on much longer. It was no use attempting anything more in Raichur, because it now transpired that the province was to be restored to the Nizam, and Naldrug also ; and that, as the revenues had largely increased, and were more than sufficient for the purpose for which the original cession had been made, the assignment would now be restricted to Berar, the whole of which, without any reservation, was to be retained, along with some portions to the south and east, which had not been included in the previous agreement.

Evidently the time had come when the Commission would be remodelled, but how it might affect me, it was impossible to tell. Had my health continued good, I should never have dreamed of leaving India, for I loved the country, and I loved the people ; but I felt I could no longer stay now. I had no wish to retire from active work, and hoped to return to live and die, if God willed it, among the people. And I thought in any case I could take leave and go as far as Malta, where my father would meet me, and I could bring back my children with me, and by that time the new arrangements would be completed, and I should know what position I would occupy when the new treaty with H.H. the Nizam was concluded.

I was obliged to admit now, that work was growing very difficult to me. Medicine seemed powerless to check the perpetual ague and fever, and a debility and want of energy came over me which I could not struggle against. The doctor at Lingsugur told me very plainly that I had no chance of recovery in India, and that if I stayed, my illness must go on from bad to worse. I sent up his report upon my case to the Resident, at the earnest entreaty of my friends, who thought me very ill, and made an application for two years' leave of absence, which was all I could hope to get under the rules.

I gave over charge of the Raichur Doab to Mr. Ricketts, my only Assistant, and, taking a sad farewell of my friends, whom I never then thought I should see again, I went to Shorapur to try and close my work there.

The Treasury was in a prosperous condition, and I was allowed to take from it the price of my house,[1] for which I

[1] This is now the 'New Durbar' at Shorapur.

fortunately held the late Raja's note of hand. I was very thankful for this piece of good fortune, although I had of course to put up with the loss of interest on my money.

At Shorapur the utmost anxiety prevailed as to the ultimate destiny of the State, but I could give no opinion whatever; and its fate remained yet uncertain. There was much dread that it would be made over to the Musalmans, their old hereditary enemies; and I found this fear was disturbing the people very much.

'We shall no longer be true Hindus,' was the general cry. 'Cows will be killed in our precincts, and the flesh will be sold in our streets. Hundreds of years have passed since this indignity has been offered us, and now we dare not resist it.'

What could I say? or what assurance could I give them that such would not be the case?

I grew better at Shorapur. I went out to Bohnal, and had a last sail on the beautiful lake. I left instructions for the completion of Kachaknur, in case it should ever be found practicable to go on with it. I looked round all the roads and plantations, and saw them in a satisfactory condition. I settled all estates belonging to individuals on a more permanent basis, and recommended that the Ranis should have theirs restored to them.

My last farewells to all the people were very trying. They saw I could not stay, and had little hope they should ever see me again. On the 25th February they asked me to preside at a last *durbar*, and presented me with the following address, which is literally translated :—

Translation of a Marathi Address, presented to Captain Meadows Taylor, Deputy-Commissioner of Shorapur, by the Inhabitants of Shorapur Territory, February 26, 1860.

(After compliments.)

'We, the undersigned Pundits, Alims, Raja's relatives, Government servants, merchants, Watandars or hereditary State servants, Jaghirdars, soldiers, ryots, and others, residents in and belonging to Shorapur principality, respectfully beg to subscribe the following Address to you, in the sanguine hope that you will accept it as a token of our respect and esteem towards you :—

'1. We unanimously beg to state that, on account of your being in readiness to return to England, we are plunged into much grief; but your health having declined, from your residence in this country for the long period of thirty-six years, engaged in the arduous service of Government, protecting and benefiting thousands of people with much care and benevolence, you are disabled by over-exertion from continuing any longer to perform your very laborious duties for the benefit of the country and its people, without some relaxation; therefore, you have necessarily determined to go home, and remain there, among your relatives and friends, and thus return with renewed vigour to support thousands of people in this country. But this, we hope, temporary, separation has overpowered our minds with sincere anxiety, and we have only one alternative to allay it—in the hope of expecting your happy and safe return amongst us soon, and humbly to pray to the ever-blessing Almighty to restore happiness upon you, your beloved father, and daughters, kindred and friends.

'2. Since your arrival in this country, you have done great things to secure happiness to the people; and though they are too numerous to be enumerated here, yet, by recapitulating some of them, as far as our abilities will allow us, we trust they will enable us to pass our time in joy, by frequently refreshing our hearts with their recitation until you return to this country. With this desire, we have ventured to intrude upon your precious time, in the hope that you will kindly pardon us, and permit us to say what we feel on this occasion.

'3. The cause of your first coming to this district was this: certain unsatisfactory circumstances having occurred, which threatened the welfare of the State and its Prince, in reference to their relations with the State of Hyderabad, the considerate British Government became a mediator between the two States, and appointed you Political Agent in this principality, in the year 1842. From that period until 1852, you administered the country very judiciously, and according to its requirements; and brought it into a very prosperous condition, both as regards the public revenue and the improvement of the morals of the people. All this is not only known to us who have this day assembled here, but it is patent to the world.

'4. In this district certain crime-thirsty wretches used, before your arrival, to commit atrocities to the injury and suffering of the people. But you, with the weapons of your judgment and discretion, extirpated their vices, and led them to pursue virtuous paths of life, thereby affording true security to life, honour, and property; and the country prospered day by day. In any country where courts of justice are established, and justice is properly administered, that country does not acquire a bad reputation. So the misrule which prevailed in this district before 1842 was speedily annihilated by the awe of your prompt and impartial justice, just as darkness vanishes on the appearance of the sun.

'5. By introducing wise measures into the revenue affairs of the State from 1842 to 1852 the people fearlessly cultivated waste lands, and thereby the revenue doubled in ten years. This advantage was not only secured to Government, but to the people; because during their former administration the people did not know the value of continuously holding any lands from which they could derive profit for their labour, whereas they now cultivated considerable quantities of land in excess of their former means, thus contributing to the public revenue, as well as adding to their profits. Hence in 1852 about one and a half lakhs of *bighas* [150,000 acres] of lease expired, and cleared fields were ready to yield full assessment in the following year, in addition to the ordinary cultivation of the State.

'6. From the increase thus obtained, works of public utility and remuneration—viz., roads, State buildings, tanks, wells, etc., were constructed, and avenues, gardens, groves, etc., were planted. This is one of the reasons by which your name and fame have become popular, and everlasting in this district.

'7. At this healthy state of affairs, the late Raja of Shorapur having attained majority, you considered it advisable that the management of the country should be intrusted to him, and Government having, on your recommendation, sanctioned the measure, you made over the principality to him, giving him your friendly and full advice in regard to his future conduct in his responsible and dignified position, and as to governing his people; and then you proceeded to join your new appointment of Deputy-Commissioner at Naldrug. There, too, by your amiable disposition, generosity, benevolence, ingenuity, and zeal, you created abundant security and happiness to the people of that country, and profit to Government. You built there new tanks, constructed roads, and other works of public utility, and thus became entitled to the respect and gratitude of the people. Convinced of your abilities, the Government sent you as Deputy-Commissioner to the district of Berar.

'8. Here, in this principality, for two or three years after the Raja's assumption of independent management of his country, he conducted his affairs tolerably well; but, at this period, he was unfortunately surrounded by a band of designing and capricious men, who took advantage of his youth, imbued him with bad notions, and, misusing his name, committed atrocities with impunity. This becoming known to the Resident at Hyderabad, he deputed his second Assistant to Shorapur for the purpose of ascertaining the true state of affairs, and dispersion of all ill-advisers.

'But while things were in this state, the Raja's intriguing band unauthorisedly fired at the Government troops who were encamped below the town; then the young Raja became alarmed for the consequences, and fled to Hyderabad, to seek refuge with the Government itself. The inhabitants of the town, beholding these things, fled for their lives, accompanied by their wives and children, abandoning their homes and property, lest worse things might happen to them. Immediately after the Raja's flight, the British troops took possession of the town, and plundered it for three days, thereby making it desolate and deserted. At this unhappy period we, of this place, were praying to God to send His messenger in your form for our relief; but as you were in a higher appointment, and in a distant country, we had not much hope of your coming at all. But lo! when God pleases and blesses, the very impossibilities become possibilities at once. So, according to the heartfelt desires of the people of this country, the Resident, by God's will and influence, suddenly thought of sending you here, and took the necessary measures accordingly. With what joy and thankfulness the population, old and young, great and small, received the intelligence of your nomination to this place (because we had our long-cherished hopes and confidence in your magnanimity and justice) is beyond all description. And our anticipations of good from you were greatly strengthened when we knew of your true feelings for the Raja when you saw him at Hyderabad. Your feelings were so affected and plunged into grief at the sight of that unfortunate Raja, that it was hardly possible, even for his own parents, to grieve at his misfortune more bitterly than you. Thus have you continuously manifested great interest and kindness towards this principality and its rulers; and this being universally known to the people, even before your arrival at Shorapur, those who had abandoned their homes in despair and anxiety, speedily returned without apprehension. All this, of course, depended upon your kind and humane disposition and goodwill towards the people.

'9. On your arrival here you caused all the anarchy and misrule that had taken place to disappear. You introduced new regulations, and secured a proper and correct system of management. From this much good and advantage have accrued to the people. By your constructing good roads around the town, much comfort and convenience have been enjoyed by the traders and people in general; and the praises which are merrily sung to your name by the travellers, old and young, on these roads, are indeed gratifying and pleasing to the hearers.

'10. The thousands of mango-trees, planted by you in and about the town during your former administration of this country, are now bearing abundant fruit; and, as you are now again planting thousands of trees, with great pains, for our benefit, we humbly pray to God that He will likewise ordain you shall be present here when these infant trees shall similarly bear fruit.

'11. You have used your full powers in securing and

continuing various rights, perquisites, *miras* or hereditary lands, and allowances, etc., which were enjoyed by the people; and if, in spite of your generous endeavours, any unfortunate person's expectations were not realised, it is no fault of yours, but his own misfortune. Consequently, we are all content with what you have done for us, and are under great obligations to you.

'12. When sedition and rebellion occurred here in 1858, certain senseless persons were concerned in them, and they were liable to heavy penalties; and if you had punished them, notwithstanding the proclamation of amnesty, you would not have exceeded the requirements of the law, nor their deserts; but, not considering their past violent and intriguing acts, you have saved their lives and honour from destruction. For this singular kindness, these people should be grateful and thankful to you for ever; and this assembly ardently believes they will be so.

'13. Another, the principal request and prayer of this assembly, is, that this principality should be restored to the family of the late Raja, in compassion for their misfortune, and the maintenance of charitable and other ancient institutions which have existed and have been enjoyed for centuries. To attain this end, we trust you will accord your support; but we are aware it depends mainly upon the future good conduct and loyalty, as also destiny, of the expectants of this dignity. It is the duty, nevertheless, of this assembly to pray constantly to the Almighty that Government will, in their exalted generosity, pardon all past misdemeanours, and indulgently protect the remnants of the late chief's family.

'14. That your projects for constructing a series of new roads and a market-place, and for lighting the town, as well as for erecting travellers' and strangers' homes, sinking wells, building tanks, etc., for the use and benefit of the people, as well as for improving the public revenue, should be carried out after your return, in renewed health, is the heartfelt prayer of this assembly.

'15. All your acts being of benevolence and for the good of the people, there is very little time to recount them all here; and it is likewise hardly possible to give preference to any one of them. We, therefore, most respectfully beg to entreat that you will kindly accept what we have briefly stated above, as a sincere expression of our feelings towards you, and we crave that you will pardon us for our rather long intrusion upon your time.

'16. It may only be known to the light of the world, the Sun, if there were any persons like you on the face of the earth; but, as far as our experience goes, we know not a more kind-hearted, equitable, painstaking, skilful, and benevolent gentleman than you; and we are constrained to think that your qualities have no parallel save in you.

'17. We are afraid that you may have tired of our loquacity; but, our hearts being full with heavy anxiety at the thought of our approaching temporary separation, and being unable to bear it without giving utterance to our feelings, we have ventured to occupy a good deal of your time, for doing which we have already craved your pardon.

'18. In conclusion, we most ardently hope that, by the blessing of the Almighty Protector, you will happily and safely reach your country, and meet your most beloved and endeared father, daughters, brothers and all who for a series of years have been intensely longing for your return, and cause them to rejoice. And we further heartily and sincerely pray to the Lord of the Universe to bestow upon you abundant longevity, renewed health, greater grandeur, and higher powers, and safely and happily bring you again to this country, in order that thousands of people may find a ready asylum in you for their protection, and so your fame and glory may be greatly aggrandised; and, by the grace of God, we confidently hope to realise these our desires and expectations.

'Again tendering our warmest, sincere, and affectionate but respectful thanks to you for the cordial support and courtesy you have usually evinced towards us, according to our respective positions in society, during your former and present career in this principality, we are proud that you carry with you our heartfelt gratitude and good wishes. May God bless you and yours for ever!

'We beg to remain, with the utmost respect, dear sir, your most obedient, faithful, obliged, and humble servants and well-wishers,

(Signed) 'Raja Venketappa Naik, sen.,
Raja Venketappa Naik Jellipalli,
Raja Krishnappa Naik,

and 987 others of the Raja's relations, Pundits, Jaghirdars, and other principal inhabitants of Shorapur.

(*True Translation.*)

'J. Sita Ram Rao,
Extra Assist. Commissr.'[1]

I cannot describe the scene; but its passionate character can be imagined from the purport of what is recorded above in the quaint, simple words of the people. None of them had been strangers to me; many had grown up from children

[1] This address, and that to Taylor upon his leaving Naldrug in August 1857, are truly admirable, showing what the Marathi language may be capable of. A much poorer address for similar circumstances, apparently made up from these two, is given in the depressing penultimate chapter of *Seeta.*

under my sight, and had now children of their own about their knees; others were old and greyheaded; and many whom I had known had gone to their rest. It was not an easy task to leave them all; but I had to go, and I do not think I am forgotten there even now. I intended to depart quietly in the night; but I found the chiefs of the Beydur clans assembled in the streets, and it was as difficult now to reach the north gate of the city as it had been to enter it two years before—only, instead of a clamour of joyous welcome, there was now sad wailing of women, while the men walked by me in utter silence. Now and then some one would exclaim, 'We have no one now to care for us; but our women will sing of you as they grind corn in the morning, and will light their lamps in your name at night. Come back to us; oh, come back!'

It was very sad and very solemn, and can never be forgotten. At every village the people came about me, the mothers holding up their children for me to put my hands upon their heads and bless them; and it was all so simple, so earnest, and so heartfelt, one could not but feel its sincerity. People ask me what I found in the natives to like so much. Could I help loving them when they loved me so? Why should I not love them? I had never courted popularity. I had but tried to be just to all, and to secure to the meanest applicant consideration of his complaint, by allowing unrestricted communication with myself.

Thousands wished to have signed the address had time permitted it; but there are quite enough signatures to show the attachment of the people to the only Englishman whom most of them had ever seen, and certainly the first who had exercised any authority over them. At Naldrug the sincere love of the people was shown in the address before given; in Berar I accepted the loyal and peaceful demeanour of the population as a marked proof of their attachment to me in the most trying crisis of the great rebellion.

In all I had ruled over 36,000 square miles of area, and a population of upwards of five millions of a most industrious and intelligent people, not only without a single complaint against my rule, but, as I think and hope, with a place in their affections and respect, gained by no other means than by exercising simple courtesy and justice to all. I was often told by various friends, 'You do too much for people who will never thank you.' I do not think so: I did not do half enough, and I could have done more had I had more help. God is my witness, I tried to do as much as I could, and heartily regretted being obliged, through physical inability, to leave undone many a measure of progress and advancement which I hoped to accomplish.

I travelled slowly to Hyderabad, for I could not bear long marches now, and stayed at the Residency, where there was still much to do before I could leave. Even now furlough to England was very difficult to obtain, and, but for the Resident's private intercession with the Governor-General, I should not have got it at all.

I was very glad to be able at this time to render my friend, Colonel Davidson, the Resident, an essential service in writing a series of letters to the *Friend of India* in justification of his conduct in remaining at the Residency after the officers commanding at Secunderabad had thought it desirable to leave it, and also in sending away the Contingent troops to act under Sir Hugh Rose. Both these acts of the Resident were severely censured, and deemed 'worse than rash'; but I considered that the complaints made were totally unfounded. Had the Resident gone into Secunderabad, the desertion of the Residency would have been looked upon as a sign of fear, and the loyal minister, Salar Jang, would have been left to his fate. What might have happened had he not been able to control the fanatical element of Hyderabad, or had the British all entrenched themselves at Secunderabad, who can say? By remaining firm, the Resident showed the minister that he had every confidence in him—a confidence which has been fully merited, and never abused by Sir Salar Jang.

I regarded the march of the Contingent, too, as a triumph of will over disaffection. No one denied that many of its members had trembled on the verge of mutiny, and no doubt, in their cantonment, they were sorely tempted and chafed by inaction. The effect, however, of the Nizam's troops having joined the English cause, while Sindia's soldiers coalesced with the rebels, soon became known and apparent to all, as the Hyderabad Contingent fought, as Lord Strathnairn himself has told me, more like Englishmen than natives. The honours they gained in the field kept them quiet, and as their loyalty was now beyond question, the whole of the Nizam's territory kept quiet also ; nor, with the one exception of the insurrection at Hyderabad, was there a single instance of treason to the English during the whole of that most trying period.

My letters were upheld and supported by the *Friend of India*, and I believe produced a good effect in England, although the opposition party was a very strong one. I pressed Colonel Davidson very earnestly to come home with me, for he was very ill ; but he would not leave his post, and died there the year following.[1]

I left Hyderabad at length,[2] and as the road *via* Homnabad and Naldrug was now finished, I went by it as far as Sholapur ; then there was the railway. At Naldrug I had left my plate and various articles in the treasury ; but, alas ! some one had, during these troublous times, broken open the plate-chest,

[1] Not until August 1862.

[2] This, despite Taylor's visit just before his death, was the end of an old song, of a long and affectionate connection with Hyderabad. Little memory of him now survives in the capital of the State which he served during well-nigh four decades. The alleged original of his Tara was long pointed out in Hyderabad.

In 1916 I was fortunate enough to get into communication with the one faithful local memory of him. William Palmer's daughter Lucy, Mrs. William Fallon, Taylor's sister-in-law, was alive a year later. For long survival she is worthy to be named with Miss Hogarth and with Miss Peabody, the sisters-in-law of Dickens and of Hawthorne, and their literary confidantes.

A niece wrote to Mrs. Fallon about Meadows Taylor, reminding her thus of an event eighty-four years earlier : 'He married your sister Mary, your father's eldest child.' But Mrs. Fallon was able herself to write : 'I was with Meadows Taylor in Shorapur and Naldrug. He was of a very loveable and amiable disposition. He was very much beloved by the people of Shorapur ; the women composed songs about him and sing to their children. . . I have just lately returned from Shorapur, where my husband's regiment was stationed for fourteen years. Meadows Taylor's memory is still fresh in the minds of the people there.'

It has not been possible to secure specimens of these songs or refrains on Taylor. To Mrs. Fallon I owe the knowledge of the book about Shorapur, by an Indian family friend, which makes the subject of a note. 'My youngest son,' she has written, 'is called Meadows after the old man.'

and several articles had been abstracted, most of which, however, I afterwards recovered; but I was much grieved at the loss of a small bag containing all the autograph letters I valued most, and a few little ornaments which my wife had always worn. They were of no value to any one intrinsically, and must have been taken for the sake of the bag, which was prettily embroidered in gold thread.

On the road I reached one of the stage bungalows for travellers, and, being very weak, was being lifted from my palankeen by one of my servants, when two gentlemen came forward to help me. 'Was I Captain Meadows Taylor,' they asked, 'who was anxiously expected at Malta?' 'Yes, I was'; and they told me they had been fellow passengers with my dear ones, who were awaiting me there, and gave me many particulars of them. Going home seemed at last to be growing a reality!

I passed a day and a night at Sholapur with my dear friend Abingdon Compton, and he urged me, if I missed the steamer, which seemed very probable, as I was too weak to travel very quickly, to go up to stay with his wife at Mahableshwar; and indeed, he said, I had better not go to England till the next steamer, as he knew Lord Elphinstone was at the Hills,[1] and wanted to see me, and, in any case, it was no use my waiting a fortnight in the heat at Bombay. I promised to go if I missed the steamer; but I was in time, having just two days to spare before it sailed.[2] How strangely

[1] Lord Elphinstone remained Governor only until May, and was dead by the July of this year—one of the true victims of the Mutiny.

[2] Miss Taylor writes: 'My father could not go to Mahableshwar because his passage to Malta was already taken, 1860—whether he was ever there in previous years I don't know.'

The likelihood is that he was not; and thus that he never saw the Mawuls or western valleys, 'the wild rugged country beyond Wye', where Maratha freedom rose, and of which he has made such vivid use in *Tara*. The proof of this would seem to be in Taylor's own descriptions of the scenes, near Mahableshwar, which framed the central episode in Hindu history. In his *History* the 'Mahabuleshwur mountains' are quite wrongly implied to be 6,000 feet above the sea.

The account of the Mahableshwar of sixty years ago may pass—even to the point where it is suggested that sails can be discerned on the sea thirty miles away. But not for a moment the description of the road to Pratapgarh. 'The forest, or jungle, had been partly cleared away

events happen! Had I missed that mail, I should have gone to Mahableshwar, and should, as I afterwards found, have been offered by Lord Elphinstone the 'Directorship of Jails', an appointment which I could have held, worth £2,500 a-year! He had kept it for me; but finding I had gone home on sick leave, was obliged to bestow it elsewhere. I should have stayed in India, and have taken up my appointment, telling my father to come on at once. I could have remained at the Hills, would have entered a new department of the service where there was no press of work, and where I could travel as I pleased. But luck was against me! Yet, why should I say

---

from its sides, but noble trees still hung over it, affording grateful shade as it wound round ravines and shoulders of the mountain in gradual but easy ascent; and the huge broad leaf of the teak tree, the graceful and feathery bamboo, and other masses of luxuriant foliage, rich with great creepers now covered with flowers, which hung from tree to tree in graceful festoons, or clung in dense masses about their tops,—presented endless and beautiful combinations with the bold upper precipices of the mountain itself, and the distant ranges behind it. Farther up, as the air grew fresher in the ascent, and you looked down into deep gloomy dells, or broad over the valley, or up to the rugged sides of the great mountain beyond,—a subtle blue atmosphere appeared to pervade everything; and this, the peculiar characteristic of those high tropical regions, seemed to increase in depth of colour,—and, without in reality obscuring the features of the scenery, to soften its rugged outlines, and blend its almost savage elements into harmony' (chapter lxx.).

Again, as Afzul Khan ascends to his doom: 'The wind had died away, and the sun shone with a blaze of heat unknown elsewhere, striking down among those moist narrow valleys with a power which would have been painful, but for the cool refreshing air by which it was tempered. The distant mountains glowed under the effect of the trembling exhalations, which, rising now unseen, tempered the colours of the distance to that tender blue and grey which melts into the tint of the sky. The rugged precipices above were softened in effect; and the heavy masses of foliage, festoons of creepers, and the dense woods, rich in colour, combined to enhance the wonderful beauty of the spot' (chapter lxxviii.).

These passages might come from the descriptions, in *Tippoo Sultaun*, of the Western Ghats hundreds of miles farther south, in Malabar—places which Taylor never saw, though such a negative is almost impossible to prove. He had much natural eloquence, a glowing imagination and style. Pratapgarh, according to the *Imperial Gazetteer*, is but 3,543 feet above the sea, a height greatly less than that of Nandidrug described above. Nor have its approaches—I have walked up there, and on to Mahableshwar—anything of the tropical character which Taylor gives to them. Those hillsides are bare, not to say bald.

this ? I might not have been able to stand the Indian climate longer, even at the Hills, and with lighter work. At all events, God willed it otherwise. I heard before I left, that Naldrug and Raichur were to be restored to the Nizam, and that Shorapur was to be given to him as a token of the appreciation of the British Government of his faithfulness and loyalty in the mutiny. So, what would have become of me without Lord Elphinstone's kind offer was not apparent, and I should have at once accepted it had I remained in India.

I had a pleasant party of fellow-passengers ; one poor fellow, who had been badly wounded by a bullet in the lungs, was specially consigned to my care, although, as his father said at parting, 'You do indeed look fearfully ill yourself.' And so I was ; the relaxing heat of Bombay, and all my final journey and preparations, had exhausted me terribly, and I had grown so fat and unwieldy that to move about was a trouble to me. I asked one lady on board, whose husband had been Political Agent in Miniawar [?],[1] why they had not come to me when obliged to fly ? 'We dared not,' she said, 'go to Berar. We were told you were a marked man, and dangerously popular. There would be no hope for us—nay, we heard you were already murdered ! '

Yes, we had almost all in that ship been through trying scenes and many dangers, and a merciful God had brought us out safely from the land.

We arrived at Malta in due course, very late, after midnight, and no passengers could land till morning. I was sitting with the poor fellow who had been my constant care, and who was so ill that night we thought him dying, when a gentleman came up to me. 'The P. and O. agent has come on board,' he said, 'and tells me he will take you and me ashore if we like, to-night. I know how anxious you are to go.' I put my night things in a small bag, and went. I could not stay behind. It was as much as I could do to get up the long flight of steps into Valetta, and I had to sit down often ; but at length the hotel was reached. All was quiet, every one in bed ; but this was no time for ceremony, and in a few minutes I held my darlings to my heart.

* * * * * *

[1] Probably for Kathiawar.

CHAPTER XVIII

1860–74

I NEED not dwell upon that time. Any one who has followed me through the latter years of my life in India, so lonely and so utterly cut off from all society of any kind, will appreciate what it was to me to find myself again with those dearest to me on earth, to learn to know them and be known by them. And the days flew by, I feeling stronger, and my face losing the deep-drawn lines of pain about my forehead and mouth, which my children said they 'ironed' out; and so they did, no doubt. I was, however, very far from well, although the excitement and delight of my first arrival had kept me up wonderfully. But Malta was growing hot, and we started for Naples, where we spent some delightful days, taking a fresh excursion every day—one to Pompeii and Herculaneum, the former presenting exactly the appearance of a Deccan town unroofed;[1] one to Baia, and another to Vesuvius, which we partly ascended, but my strength was not equal to much yet. My old Indian helmet, with a scarlet *pagari* tied round it, with gold ends, attracted much attention, and hats were raised as we drove along; and on passing the main guard, there rose a cry, 'Il Generale!' and the guard fell in and saluted, to our very great amusement. There was a sudden exodus from Naples, owing to a rumour of cholera, and an apprehended

[1] 'Furniture, such as we need, was unknown. A small cotton or woollen carpet laid down here and there, with a heavy cotton pillow covered with white calico, sufficed for sitting or reclining. . . The house, therefore, would have appeared bare in any of my readers' eyes; but it was neat and pleasant to look at: and one can imagine, though decorated in a higher style of art, the Roman houses at Pompeii to have been similar in most respects of plan and domestic arrangement' (*Tara*, chapter i.).

attack by Garibaldi, and we decamped with the rest. We landed at Civita Vecchia, a very motley crowd, and a general scramble began for luggage and places in the train. My red *pagari* stood me in good stead, however, and the officials came forward at once. Everything was at the service of 'Il Generale' or 'Eccellenza'.

'Air you a Ingine general, sir?' asked an American, as I was entering the carriage.

'No, sir, an Indian officer, but not a general,' I replied.

'Wal, sir, you air very fair for Ingy, you air. If you was to come to our country, they wouldn't know you for a Ingine; no, sir, they would not, I tell you, sir.'

We stayed a fortnight in Rome. We saw all the pictures and the statues and the palaces. We made excursions to Tivoli and to Hadrian's villa. We saw St. Peter's, too, under decoration for a great ceremony, and above all, I was introduced in the strangest manner to his Holiness the Pope. We had no tickets for the reserved seats for the occasion, not having secured them in time, and our old guide Stefano was sorely distressed at this. He, however, told us not to despair, 'he had a great friend, a priest, who was to take part in the ceremony,' and motioning me to follow, he marched straight to the door of the sacristy, and beckoned to his friend, explaining to him who I was, and how I had arrived too late to get tickets. I was bidden to enter, and was presented to a very benevolent-looking old gentleman as 'Il Generale Inglese'. I had hardly time to realise that it was the Pope himself, when he put out his hand to me, while I bent low and kissed it. He told me I was welcome, and desired the priest to see that we had good seats. We were conducted to a little door in one of the great pillars, where, ascending a spiral staircase, we found ourselves in a cosy little box, just large enough for four people, from which we saw and heard everything most perfectly.

'Did I not manage that well?' cried old Stefano, rubbing his hands.

What a world of new thought and beauty was opened to me! I revelled in the pictures and in the galleries at Rome; but even more, I believe, in those of Florence, where we literally lived in the Pitti Palace and the Uffizi. I think, however, I was most interested in the ancient remains—the statues and the busts—not only those of emperors, kings, and statesmen, but of the citizens and their wives, recalling the features of the age to which they belonged, the head-dresses and graceful draperies as worn at the period. Many of the women's faces struck me as being truly noble, and their figures too, and as more intellectual and handsomer in type than those of the men. We could have lingered in Florence, in Bologna, in Milan, in Venice so dreamy and so exquisite, for weeks, nay, months; but time was passing, and we left beautiful Italy—its pictures, statues, noble ancient remains, its churches, and its lakes behind us—and crossed over the Splügen Pass into Bavaria. Surely the world can contain no fairer spot than those lakes of Italy, and it is quite impossible to decide whether Maggiore, or Lugano, with its wild grand beauty, or fair Como, lying sparkling in the sun, carries off the palm, all are so lovely and all so different. I do not know and have not seen, the other Passes over the Alps, but I should think none can exceed the Splügen and the Via Mala in grandeur and in beauty; nor could I, an old road-maker, cease to marvel at the great science and daring displayed in the engineering work. From Chur—after a *détour* made to visit dear relations in Bavaria, and stay some days with them in their beautiful old *schloss*[1]—to Paris, by way of Basel and Strasbourg, a weary railway journey in very hot weather.

[1] It has always rather fascinated and puzzled me to know how Meadows Taylor came to have relatives in a Bavarian castle. The answer is in the *Life of Henry Reeve*, where, under the year 1873, recording an August journey in Switzerland and Germany, Reeve barely writes, '26th, to Syrgenstein.' But his wife annotates: 'Near the Lake of Constance, where some cousins of ours, the Whittles, bought an old schloss with some 300 acres, and settled about fifteen years ago.' Under 1877 Reeve refers to a cousin, Mrs. James Whittle, a great invalid, who wintered near Florence: 'But she is now returning to a Schloss (Syrgenstein) they have in Bavaria.'

Of these relatives Miss Taylor writes: 'They were a very quiet couple who, with her sister, found small incomes went further abroad; they were childless, and lived in several places in Germany and Italy at different times. It happened that just at the time mentioned they were renting an old Schloss near the Lake of Constance which was very picturesque, and the country around it very pretty.' The Whittles, like the Philip Taylors of Marseilles, 'were far off cousins with whom no subsequent intercourse was kept up'.

Paris was almost unbearable from the heat, and we only waited long enough to get a few clothes, and then on to London, and back to home-life once more. My health, which at first had seemed almost re-established, now again broke down, showing that the evil still existed; the fever returned perpetually; and the best physicians, both in London and Dublin, shook their heads. The news from India was not reassuring. The treaty of 1860 was now accomplished; the Raichur Doab and Naldrug were transferred to the Nizam, and the principality of Shorapur conferred upon him as a free gift in return for his loyal conduct during the mutiny. It was clear to me that except my Deputy-Commissionership, I had no hope of promotion, unless I should be made Settlement Officer.

My eighteen months' leave expired in November 1861, and I obtained an extension for six months more; and as I was in London on this business, I had the honour of being summoned by the then Secretary of State for India,[1] who was anxious for information in regard to Berar and its revenue settlement. He seemed to approve of the system I had introduced in Naldrug during 1856–57, and listened earnestly while I described its details; he requested me to write him an official letter on the subject, and hinted that, although the Head Commissionership might not be given to an 'uncovenanted servant', the appointment of Settlement Officer was one which I could hold.

Time passed. I confess I have no distinct memory of events. Constant illness, and, worse than all, a sort of debility of the brain, seemed to possess me, and were most distressing. I had not only lost my energy, but my memory also in great measure, and I was obliged to have every note looked over before it was posted, lest the sense should not be clear, or a strange jumble and repetition of words should be found. Indeed I grew worse and worse, and the thought that I should, if this continued, be obliged to give up India altogether, made me miserable. My doctors apprehended, I have since heard, paralysis of the brain, and entreated my family to oppose my return to active work. As the expiration of my leave drew near, I made desperate efforts to have it renewed still further,

[1] Sir Charles Wood, baronet, 1800–1885. He was Secretary of State for India from 1859 to 1866, when he was created Viscount Halifax.

offering to do without pay altogether if my place might be kept open for me. Sir Ranald Martin[1] told me six months more would, perhaps, recruit my health, and promised to back my petition: I had friends too at the India House to help me. But it was of no avail; the rules of the 'uncovenanted service' could not be broken, and my request was refused; so no alternative remained for me except to go out as I was, ill and weak, or to resign the service altogether. It was a hard battle. My heart was in my work, and I ardently longed to go back and try to carry on what I had been planning for the benefit of the people among whom I had lived my life, and whom I loved; but it seemed as if God, in His wisdom, had taken from me the power and strength I needed. 'If you go back', said Sir Ranald Martin, 'to the climate of Berar, you must die: you are totally unfit for duty, and the fever and ague are as bad as ever. Think of your life, and think of your children, and may God help you to a right decision. I never had a more painful case to deal with.'

I thought over all this earnestly, and asked for help and guidance, and I saw clearly that it would not be right to run into the jaws of death as it were; so I gave up the struggle, and sent in my resignation with a very heavy heart. No one knows, even now, what a bitter grief it was to me to do this; but I trust I did what was right. I returned to Dublin very much cast down. I was not able to do anything except paint, and I took refuge in this, and in music: any attempt at writing set my head throbbing; and neither words nor thoughts would come. I looked sadly at the commencement of a story I had begun years before in India, and wondered whether I should ever be able to complete it.

A friend, finding me one day sitting on a doorstep in Dublin, faint and sick, and shivering with ague, took me home and told me how his brother, who had suffered terribly from Australian bush-fever, had derived much benefit from homœopathy. I had tried everything else, and every physician

[1] Sir James Ranald Martin, 1793–1874, at this time President of the India Office Medical Board. He had written on the drainage of Calcutta, and *On the Influence of Tropical Climates on European Constitutions*.

of note without avail, and I promised my friend to consult the doctor he told me of, and to give the system a fair trial.

I told my story to the kind physician he recommended, and also honestly confessed my want of faith in the system.

'I don't mind that,' said the good man; 'but it is rather hard to ask me to cure a malady of thirty years' standing, when so many great men have failed. However, I will try to alleviate—I cannot cure it; and I trust, under God's blessing, to give you some help. But you were right not to return to India.'

I followed the prescriptions he gave me faithfully, and I amused myself by fishing, painting, and reading very light literature, and tried not to think about anything. The effect was really marvellous. I grew stronger and more energetic, and I felt some of my old power returning to me; and after a few months I went to my friend and asked his leave to begin to write.

'Do you feel able now?' he asked. 'If you do, begin; but you must be very cautious, and do not fatigue your brain. If you feel the least tired or confused, stop.'

I took his advice, and I began my novel of *Tara*. The incidents and actions of the story had been planned for nearly twenty years; and I knew all the scenes and localities described, as I had the story in my mind during my visit to Bijapur, and had noted the details accurately; while my long residence in an entirely native State, and my intimate acquaintance with the people, their manners, habits, and social organisation, gave me opportunities, which I think few Englishmen have ever enjoyed, of thoroughly understanding native life. One day, when talking of my projected book with my dear friend Mrs. Cashel Hoey,[1] whom I have known since she was a child,

[1] Miss Taylor writes of Mrs. Hoey: 'She was a very old friend of our family, and before she became a widow lived in Kensington and had very interesting guests on Friday afternoons. When I lived there I used to see a great deal of her. After Mr. Hoey's death she went to live at Bath, where she died. She seemed to lose touch with old friends; but I believe she gathered an interesting circle about her. She must have been an old woman. She was very clever and brilliant in conversation, with a great deal of Irish humour, and keen appreciation of a joke.'

Canon Taylor, of St. Just, has sent me this abstract of what is told of Frances Sarah Hoey in *Allibone's Dictionary of English Literature*: '"She was born in 1830 at Bushy Park, Co. Dublin, Ireland. She was the daughter of C. B. Johnston and she married (1) in 1846 A. M. Stewart

and whose career I have always watched with ever-increasing interest and affection, she said suddenly, 'Now you have the plot so clearly defined in your brain, come and write it out chapter by chapter; I will set it down exactly as you dictate to me.' We went together to my study, and locked the door, and there for six hours we worked at it, she writing in total silence, and a perfect sketch of the whole tale was made, the details of which were filled up afterwards. I never remember feeling so utterly exhausted in my life; but the relief when it was finished was intense, and we both were glad that we had resisted the entreaties to us to stop our work, and rest, which my children, fearing for me in my state of health, made more than once in vain. After this, I felt sure of my subject, and wrote confidently, but very slowly, for my brain had not regained its full strength yet; but the occupation interested me, and was a source of infinite delight. When my book was partly finished, I wrote to Messrs. Blackwood, offering it to them, and telling them how it had been promised twenty years before, for *Blackwood's Magazine*, when I had written the *Confessions of a Thug*.

My book was accepted, and, still writing very slowly, I finished and published it in 1863. It was most favourably received. All the leading papers—*The Times, Morning Post, Athenæum, Saturday Review*, and the Quarterlies—were loud in its praise;[1] and I only mention this at length, because I

---

and (2) in 1858 John Cashel Hoey. She is a constant contributor to periodical literature, writing criticism and fiction, and has translated a large number of works from the French and Italian." Then follows a list of twenty-seven novels and translations, and a further list of seven translations from the French in collaboration with John Lillie.'

[1] *Tara* was dedicated to the scholarly seventh Earl of Carlisle, K.G., 1802–1864, the friend of Prescott and of other literary men, then for the second time Viceroy of Ireland, who died in the following year. *The Times* said of *Tara*: 'For its rapid action, in fact, we have seldom read a better story, or one which is more full of incidents, sanguinary, trenchant, and robust.' *The Morning Post*: '*Tara* is a unique work. There is nothing like it in the English literature of fiction. No other writer has ever attempted the portrayal of Indian life, society, and interests, entirely free from any European admixture of character or incident. . . . *Tara* is all Indian.' *The Spectator*: 'This is a very remarkable book. It is a determined attempt to bring the interior Hindoo and Mussulman life of a great Mahratta province during the most exciting times home

had been very anxious as to my reception in the literary world, after a silence of so many years; and I was not a little gratified to find myself welcomed once more so warmly.

Tara was the first of the series of three historical romances which I had proposed to write on the three great modern periods of Indian history, which occurred at an interval of exactly a hundred years. *Tara* illustrated the rise of the Marathas, and their first blow against the Musalman power in 1657.[1]

---

to the hearts and understandings of Englishmen, to interest them in people with whom they have nothing except human nature in common.'

The shortest article in the October number of the *Edinburgh Review*, of hardly ten pages, was on *Tara*. As soon as the opportunity arose Reeve spoke up loyally, as again later, for Meadows Taylor. He welcomes the return, after a quarter of a century, of the author of the *Thug*. 'Few Englishmen have left behind them in India a more honourable reputation: for in addition to the not uncommon merit of successful administration in a large territory, it has been Captain Taylor's good fortune to endear himself to the population, to penetrate the native character in all its phases, and to live amongst the mingled races of Southern India as one of themselves. In this respect his career has widely differed from the dominant character of Indian civilians—a class to which he did not belong; and it is probably due to this cause that he writes of India, and the natives of India, with a degree of spirit, truth, and genuine sympathy hardly to be met with in any other English author.'

About one half of the article consists of the quotation of 'a remarkable episode, complete in itself, and admirably described'. This is the tragedy at Pratapgarh, Taylor's chapter lxxviii., as far as the words: 'Some escaped; but of the fifteen hundred men who had ridden there in their pride that morning, few lived to tell the tale.'

'India', the article ends, 'in which we have a far deeper interest than in any other part of Asia, is still but imperfectly known to England—perhaps, we might even add, to many of the English who have inhabited and governed it. To inspire his countrymen with a deeper interest in the past annals of the people of India is, we are informed by Captain Taylor, one of the objects he had in view in his work, and we think he has succeeded in it to a very remarkable degree.'

[1] This scheme, of which Taylor makes much in various places, was too symmetrical to be quite correct. It seems to have been a year or two later than 1657 that Shivaji slew Afzul Khan.

The date 1658 may be found, and I grew up in the same district, somehow identifying the death of Afzul Khan with the year, and practically the month, of Cromwell's death. But Hunter's *Brief History of the Indian Peoples*, the *Oxford Student's History of India*, and the *Imperial Gazetteer*, article 'Pratapgarh', all say 1659.

Ralph Darnell, my second work, was to illustrate the rise of the English political power in the victory of Plassey in June 1757.

Seeta, which was to be the third, was to illustrate the attempts of all classes alike to rid themselves of the English by the Mutiny of 1857.

Ralph Darnell, which appeared in 1865, was also well received, and I had every encouragement to persevere.[1]

I read a paper upon my discoveries of cairns, cromlechs, etc., in Shorapur, before the Royal Irish Academy, with illustrations and sketches of what I found, which, I believe, completely established the identity of those remains in India and in Europe, and, I have reason to think, was valuable archæologically. It was published in vol. xxiv. of the Society's *Transactions*, and illustrated with sixty-eight engravings. This had been a subject which, since I had made the first identification in relation to the cromlechs and cairns of Rajah Kolur, I had followed up with the greatest interest, until I obtained ample confirmation of my views in the cairns on Twizell Moor, Northumberland, in the autumn of 1864.[2]

I was placed in charge of the Indian Department of the Dublin Exhibition of 1865 by my friend Dr. Forbes Watson,[3]

[1] *Ralph Darnell* was dedicated, from Old Court, Harold's Cross, near Dublin, August 16, 1865, ' to my dear father, with the love of my life '. It offers not a hook by which any illustrative extract can be attached to the autobiography, save for the descriptions of two romantic Northumbrian houses inhabited by Taylor's kinsmen. The book deals with England of the eighteenth century, and with an Indian province of which he knew as little, Bengal. One is tempted to ask what had happened in the two years since the writing of *Tara*, so sketchy, so amazingly inferior, is its successor. Yet *Ralph Darnell* contained some elements of popularity, including a rather sickly sentiment. A second edition was issued in 1879.

[2] Other references are *J. Bs. Br. R.A.S.* iii. 179, iv. 380; *J. Ethnological Soc.* i. 157. Taylor's pioneer researches on the subject were of much interest.

[3] The second-hand copy of the first edition of *The Story of My Life*, two volumes, Blackwood, 1877, from which the present edition is being printed, bought at Oxford in 1915, has upon the top of the title-page of the first volume, in clear lead pencilling, the signature, Dr. Forbes Watson. Therefore this copy probably belonged once to Taylor's friend.

He appears (1827–1892) in Buckland and in the *Dictionary of National Biography*. Yet it is an indeterminate sort of fame that he has left,

and on the occasion of the visit of H.R.H. the Prince of Wales to the Exhibition, was called on to attend and explain various matters to him. He was especially struck by the large raised map of the eastern coast of India, constructed to scale by the late Mr. Montgomery Martin,[1] which I had painted afresh, and of which the Prince showed a very intimate knowledge. He had evidently studied Indian subjects deeply, and appeared gratified by the information I was able to give in regard both to the natural productions and the articles of manufacture displayed.

My next task was to write the historical and descriptive portions of two superb volumes of Photographs of the City of Bijapur and the Hindu Temples of the Southern Maratha country. These volumes were published by Mr. John Murray, the architectural portions being contributed by my friend Mr. James Fergusson.[2]

This led to my undertaking the descriptive letterpress of a work entitled *The People of India,* which consisted of a series of photographs of the different races, tribes, and orders of the people all over India, and involved much labour and research. The descriptions were necessarily very short, and

---

chiefly connected with just such exhibitions as the one here mentioned, then so much in vogue. He was for some years in the Bombay Medical service. The *Dictionary of National Biography* calls him a 'writer on India'; yet it was on such subjects as food grains, textile manufactures, and plant names, as official Reporter on the products of India. He published, with J. W. Kaye, *The People of India,* 8 vols., London, 1868–75.

[1] Another of the scholarly Indian surgeons, died 1868. Robert Montgomery Martin must have had an interesting life, for in youth he had roamed, as botanist and naturalist, all the shores of the Indian Ocean, getting later both to Hongkong and Jamaica in official capacities. His chief work was *The History, Antiquities, Topography, and Statistics of Eastern India* (1838), usually cited as *Eastern India,* a valuable work in three volumes, based on the survey by Buchanan Hamilton. This is still constantly consulted.

[2] 1808–1886. Fergusson was one of the few who have successfully entered Government service from business life. 'In ten years at his indigo factory made sufficient to retire upon. . . . He invested the historical study of architecture, particularly Indian architecture, with a new interest' (Buckland). The volumes are *Architecture at Beejapore,* London, 1866 (Taylor and Fergusson); *Architecture in Dharwar and Mysore* (Taylor), London, 1866. [In I.O. Library.]

as much information as possible had to be compressed into a few meagre lines. The work was brought out by the India Office, and no limit was affixed to it. Up to the present year (1874) six volumes have been completed. Eight were published.

I also began a series of Indian articles for Messrs. Cassell, Petter, and Galpin's Biographical Dictionary,[1] which, as far as I know, are the only contributions to Indian biography which exist. Of course the space here was also very circumscribed, and all I could do was to make the notices intelligible and useful for reference.

Thus I worked on, and employed myself as busily as I could, painting during my leisure hours. In 1868 we went abroad, and remained away for a year, wintering at that loveliest of places, Mentone—one of the sweetest spots, I think, the world contains.[2] How we all enjoyed it, and what glorious walks, donkey rides, and excursions we made! And the flowers—but they are too beautiful for description. We used to bring home basket-loads of crimson and scarlet anemones, violets, tulips, and a thousand more, less gay, perhaps, but none the less beautiful. I worked on at the biographies and descriptions all the winter, steadily refusing to be tempted out until the afternoon. A project for a *Child's History of India* was also growing in my brain, originated by a dear friend, a lady, coming to me one day with an armful of most stupendous-looking volumes, and

[1] The sub-title of this volume is: 'Original memoirs of the most eminent men and women of all ages and countries.' It is neither scholarly nor literary. There is no date, and the editor is nameless. There is a list of thirteen contributors, none better known than Colonel Meadows Taylor and Canon Payne Smith. All the Indian articles cannot be assigned to Taylor, for there is also a Captain W. W. Knollys, author of *Memoirs of Lord Combermere*.

Some of the major Indian articles, as that on Clive, afford internal evidence that they are by Taylor. He may have found these exercises useful for the *History of India* which was to follow. Messrs. Cassell have kindly looked up their books in the effort to identify for me Taylor's work. 'Whilst I find the record of numerous payments to Colonel Meadows Taylor for contributions to *Cassell's Biographical Dictionary*, there is nothing to indicate the articles for which payment was made.'

[2] This was the place where Taylor was to die. See the accounts of Mentone, with a dying man there, in the last chapter of *Seeta*, published 1872.

saying, as she threw them down wearily, 'Oh, Colonel Taylor, do tell me what I am to do. How can I teach the children the history of India out of those?' And indeed it seemed a truly formidable task. I was not able to set about a history of India just then, but later I confided the scheme to Messrs. Longman, who begged I would make mine a *Student's Manual of the History of India*; and this I eventually wrote some time later.[1] The work was very laborious, and involved much minute study, occupying me in all about two years.

I had not long returned from Mentone when I was solicited by the Institute of Civil Engineers of Ireland to deliver a lecture upon the method of constructing large earthen embankments and sluices for irrigation tanks in India; and as I was much interested in the subject, I made the lecture as comprehensive as I could, and described the system adopted so as to retain the rainfall as much as possible. I had all my own plans, elevations, surveys, and sections, and some details of ancient native work. My lecture was printed in the *Transactions* of the Society, and to my gratification, I was not only elected a member, but received a diploma as civil engineer, with liberty to practise as such within the United Kingdom.

My hard work over my *History* was delightfully interrupted during 1869 by an announcement from the Secretary of State for India that Her Most Gracious Majesty the Queen had been pleased, on the 2d of June, to appoint me a 'Companion of the Most Exalted Order of the Star of India'. The honour and gratification of the gift were enhanced by a communication from his Grace the Duke of Argyle, as he presented me with the order, that the selection of my name had been made by her Majesty herself.

I felt very grateful for this honour—which had been entirely unsolicited by me—not only as a recognition of any public service I had been able to perform during my Indian life, but as an assurance that I had not been forgotten though so long absent. Her Majesty had indeed recognised me at the first levee I attended after my return, and her words,

[1] 1st ed. 1870, 2nd ed. 1871 (I.O. library cat.), new edition, 1895, 1915.

'I am glad to see you back again,' will always be treasured by me, as a very gratifying proof of her kind interest in so humble a servant as myself.

In 1871 my *History* appeared, as complete as I could make it in the limited space necessarily at my disposal, and I trusted that, having now a compendium, as it were, at their command, Principals of colleges and schools would bring the History of India more into their educational course. I inquired in many directions, but I could not discover that Indian history was taught anywhere. Why, I know not, for surely there can scarcely be any subject of greater importance to Englishmen than the history of the noble dependencies won by their ancestors, which, one would think, would be both more useful, and perhaps more interesting, than many subjects which seem to form part of the essential education of our boys.

I had to take a long rest now. The labour of the *History* had very much exhausted me, and I spent the interval in travelling and painting, and was elected honorary member of the Royal Hibernian Academy. In 1872 I began *Seeta*, finishing it in June the same year;[1] and up to the time I write, I have not begun any more works of fiction.[2] After

[1] *Seeta* was dedicated 'to my dear daughters, Alice and Amy, for their devoted love and valuable patient assistance'.

The excellence with which this novel opens hardly holds beyond the first quarter part or so, when Seeta is united to her white husband. The remainder cannot be called good as a picture either of the English in India sixty years ago or of the Mutiny. Yet it was doubtless a relief to many readers to be among their countrymen at all after the generally native novels. This, together with the vein of sentiment, is enough to account for the popularity which *Seeta* long enjoyed. It gave the first detailed account of love across the gulf of race and religion. It had also topical interest, the Mutiny being then not fifteen years old.

[2] Several of Taylor's later friends are indicated in a somewhat involved sentence of Sir Bartle Frere's Introduction to the 1872 edition of *Pandurang Hari*: '*Pandurang Hari* has been so completely forgotten, that when Dr. George Birdwood recommended its republication, the publishers were indebted to the liberality of Lord Talbot de Malahide for one of the few copies of the book which could be traced by Captain Meadows Taylor in any library, with which he was acquainted, in the United Kingdom.'

Later are some grudging references to Taylor's novels. He appears to have been called 'captain' by many people to the end of his life.

this *Story of my Life* is finished, I hope, if I am spared, to revert to the romantic and medieval period of Deccan history, and write an illustration of it, the plot of which is growing in my brain.[1]

From time to time I contributed articles to the *Edinburgh Review*, on various subjects connected with India: every year one or more of these appeared. And I enjoyed this kind of literary labour very much, and am grateful it was given to me to do.[2]

Also, from time to time, I gave public lectures on subjects connected with India, both in Dublin, Birmingham, Whitehaven, and other places. I wanted to bring India nearer to England—to bring its people nearer our people; and if, by my simple descriptions of life among the natives, any have felt more interest in their Indian brothers and sisters, or have

---

He would seem to have retired as colonel, 'with the pension of his rank in the British service' which Henry Reeve mentions, only in 1862. His new grade was given currency by the advertisement of his novels as 'Colonel Taylor's Indian Tales'.

[1] It is to this period that the beautiful portrait belongs which Miss Taylor has presented as the frontispiece to this volume. It is dated, by the contemporary record of the photographer, Chancellor, Dublin, as of August 1873. To use this it has been necessary to sacrifice the one prefixed to the two-volume edition of the *Story of my Life*, Blackwood, 1877. It is a sacrifice, for the countenance there, too, is of rare charm and nobility, with such kind eyes.

Miss Taylor writes: 'I like the one in Court dress best of any he ever had: it is so exactly like him. The one in the first edition of the *Life* was taken by our cousin Colonel Mitford at Mitford when we were staying there; and after my father's death Colonel Mitford asked me as a favour to allow this photo to be used. I could not refuse, although I did not really think it as good as the other. When Mitford church was being restored various branches of the family had the offer of putting in windows if they wished. My father and uncles chose one of St. Peter in the chancel, to commemorate their mother. My father died before the window was ready; and Colonel Mitford suggested to me that *his* portrait (of course the head only) should be perpetuated as the Apostle. This was done; and his dear face looks down upon all the worshippers now and is really a memorial to him as well. There are six windows on the south side of the chancel in that beautiful church, the four Evangelists with St. Peter and St. Paul—St. Peter, I like to think, just beside the altar.'

[2] An acknowledgment to Henry Reeve, editor of the *Edinburgh Review* from 1855 to 1895. Messrs. Longmans have obliged me with this list of Taylor's articles:

been led to read and study more, my object has been attained. The following were the subjects of some of my lectures :—

'Ancient Literature of India.'

'Village Communities.'

'India Past and Present.'

'Some Great Men of India.'

'Some Great Women of India.'

And others, of which I have only notes.

I always found my audiences interested and amused; and I believe it only needs such illustrations to arouse an interest in, and bring India home to, the minds of English people.

I heard frequently from friends in India who did not forget to tell me about my old people and districts whenever they could hear of them. How Naldrug and the Raichur Doab are now administered I know not, or whether the revenue remains as it was under English management. Of Berar there is at least no question. I have already stated that a portion of the Bombay survey was introduced in 1860, and its benefit and progress have been wonderful. Not only do the people possess their holdings, instead of being merely 'tenants at will', liable to be dispossessed by any outbidder; but the cultivation has extended, as it was plain to see would be the case, with insured possession. All that is now wanting,

---

April 1862 . .	Cotton.
April 1864 . . .	Human Sacrifices in India.
Oct. 1865 . .	Rock Cut Temples.
July 1867 .	Indian Costumes.
Jan. 1869 .	Rural Bengal.
Oct. 1869 . . .	Fergusson, Tree Worship.
Jan. 1872 . . .	Central Provinces of India.
Jan. 1873 . .	Berar.
April 1875 . . .	Geology of India.

Of the intercourse with Henry Reeve which is known to have existed during Taylor's fifteen years at home, the only suggestion in Sir John Knox Laughton's *Memoirs of Henry Reeve* is a record in May 1873: 'Gladstone presided at the Literary Fund dinner. I took Meadows Taylor, who was staying with us.' The index to these volumes wrongly puts upon Taylor the authorship of 'our common friend's Memoirs', unnamed, mentioned in a letter from Lord Ebury to Reeve in 1886. These had something spiteful about Lady Blessington; but the *Story of my Life* certainly contains no spiteful word.

to my perception, to complete the land settlement—which is exactly in principle what I proposed for Naldrug in 1855—is the grant of title-deeds for estates and area of house occupation; and I hope these may be eventually issued. The increase of revenue has been enormous, and has accompanied the increase of cultivation. According to the Administrative Report of 1870–71, a final total of £905,467 was reached, which showed an increase of £504,985 in ten years; and as a large portion of the district is still unsurveyed, the revenue will, in the end, there is little doubt, exceed a million sterling. I trust this magnificent practical result may induce Government to undertake a perpetual settlement on the sound basis of proprietary right, instead of the many shifty measures which have hitherto been in operation.

I have little more to add. I went to India with only one friend there on whom I could rely, and upon him I had no claim except a slight relationship. I have had no education so to speak. What I know I have taught myself. I have gained my position, such as it is now, by steady hard work and perseverance; and that my humble services have been acknowledged by my Queen and my country in giving me the Star of India, is a recompense for which I am very grateful.

My literary work has been a great pleasure to me; but I can only write about the people among whom I lived, and whom I love and shall always love to the last. Had I known how to write about modern society, fast young ladies, *roué* young gentlemen, fair murderesses with golden hair, and all the 'sensation' tribe, I doubt not I should have filled my pockets better; but it was no use,—I was too old and stiff to change my ways. The old Tuljapur Brahmin spoke truly, 'Much, very much money, passed through my hands', and yet I continue poor. But I am thankful,—thankful for having sufficient to live on, though not riches; for loving and beloved children; for many, many dear friends, who make me welcome always in the North, and in Yorkshire, and in Norfolk (is not the hot corner kept for me at Didlington[1] when I am able to

[1] Didlington was the home, rich in books and in Egyptian and other antiquities, of Mr. and Mrs., afterwards Lord and Lady, Amherst.

Lady Amherst of Hackney was the daughter of Admiral Mitford of Hunmanby Hall, Yorkshire, Taylor's uncle. She was born in 1835,

shoot ?)—in London, where I sometimes go for a few weeks to have a glimpse of the great world and its doings—in Dublin, where, in my dear old home, I have a large circle of kind and loving friends. And is not this enough to make me happy and contented with my lot ?

One word, one last reflection in regard to India, may not be out of place. It is to advise all who go there in whatever capacity, or whatever position they may hold,—use true courtesy to natives of all degrees. My experience has taught me that large masses of men are more easily led than driven, and that courtesy and kindness and firmness will gain many a point which, under a hard and haughty bearing, would prove unattainable. By courtesy I do not mean undue familiarity—far from it; self-respect must always be preserved. But there is a middle course which, if rightly pursued in a gentlemanly fashion, not only exacts respect from natives of all classes, but gratitude and affection likewise.

Grateful to God for all the mercies of my life, for His sustaining power, and the ability to do what I have been able to accomplish through all my life, all that I hope for, in my humble sphere, is that my efforts may be accepted by Him, and that, in Sir Henry Lawrence's words, 'I may be thought of as one who strove to do his duty.'

MEADOWS TAYLOR.

OLD COURT, HAROLD'S CROSS, DUBLIN,
June 1874.

---

died November 1919. The following month died her daughter, Baroness Amherst (Lady William Cecil).

TAYLOR'S 'HISTORY OF INDIA'

After such an ending to such a *Life* it is hard to have to say certain things about the *History*; and I shall write less rather than more.

The *History*, which is still reprinted from the old plates, has a singularly pleasing *format* for so thick a volume. It was for long the only one of Taylor's works which brought in any income. It has eight hundred pages, amounting to something approaching half a million words, with a vast index.

My father, who bought the *History* after his voyage with Colonel Taylor, often took up the red-edged black volume. 'To think of calling that a *Student's Manual*!' I tried faithfully to learn Indian history from it; nor could any book be less adapted for the purpose.

Sir George Birdwood, a friend and admirer of the author, could not think well of the *History*, except for the views, impressions and opinions which it contains. These have more than a personal interest, being wonderfully mellow and reasonable. I have extracted about all the best of them in the notes preceding. Of similar excellence there remain only Taylor's descriptions of the Hindu and the Mohammedan character and modes of life, which he knew so thoroughly. They are delightful; but it would be out of proportion to give them here.

Though Sir George Birdwood tried also to except from his condemnation Taylor's accounts of Hyderabad State which he served, and of Indian history in his own generation, this is not possible. Nothing is better in the preceding autobiography than the reasoned discussion of the causes of the Mutiny in Chapter XIII. One would think that Taylor would excel in the account of the Mutiny through which he had valiantly passed, in the only part of India which he knew. Yet it is precisely his account of the Mutiny in Western India which has been riddled through and through with convicted errors by the chief military actor therein, Sir George Le Grand Jacob.

The effect of the repetition of dates, and of uncouth needless names, chiefly Moslem though at one period Maratha, is very bad. No principles of mnemonics or of literary art can justify the degree to which this is here carried. Surely if dates and names are to be retained they must be selected and adequately set forth. They defeat their own purpose, they cease to make clear, if scattered too mercilessly. Page 129 of Taylor's *History*, which is but two-thirds of a page, contains some two dozen dates or accumulations of figures, each quite certainly wrong, since all concern the early history of Kashmir. Page 151 is horrid with some thirty-three dates, text and margin, besides Moslem names more aggressive than most. This, with several others, is such a page for looks as no printers should ever have passed. Taylor was peculiarly ill served throughout his *History* by his printers, who probably had a trying handwriting to complain of. Many mistakes are due to them; but many are of the sort which cannot be put upon the printers.

At successive periods Taylor leans heavily upon at least three authorities, Ferishta, Grant Duff, and James Mill. It was an impossible task which he undertook to put through in two years. Sir George Forrest has told me at Oxford that as a young man he knew Meadows Taylor while the *History of India* was being written. 'You are attempting too much,' he used to say to Taylor. 'Choose some one period or subject which you can master, and upon that you may be able to do lasting work.' It was sound advice.

Of the *History* Miss Penson has noted: 'In the last part of the book dealing with British rule, of which alone I am at all competent to judge as to accuracy, there is a great deal of revision necessary. Even now it is difficult to be rid of the influence of Mill; and at the time when Taylor wrote Mill's apparently deliberate twisting of the truth had not been shown up. . . . Taylor's book is of a very convenient size; and it is interesting to see how his own experiences in India prevent him here and there from endorsing the traditional condemnation of the early Governors, while for the most part he retains the traditional version of the facts.'

So Reeve, to whom the *History* was dedicated as Taylor's cousin and 'faithful friend of many years,' was justified in calling it the most complete summary then in existence of the annals of India. The fact that there have been at least four editions shows that the book was wanted.

CHAPTER XIX

CONCLUSION

1874–76

DURING the autumn and winter of 1874–75, my dear father suffered much from bronchitis and general debility; but in the quiet of his own study, to which his health almost entirely confined him, he wrote his last novel, *A Noble Queen*, which appeared in chapters in *The Overland Mail*, and also in *The Week's News*, and was published by Messrs. H. King & Co. His friends earnestly hope that the story may be published shortly in volume form, and thus become known more widely than at present in England. In India it has been much appreciated, and eagerly looked for on the arrival of each mail; and, to quote *The Times of India*, 'apart from its historic and literary interest, it abounds with attractive and excellent descriptions of Indian scenery'. The story relates to the Musalman kingdoms of Bijapur and Ahmednagar; and its historic heroine is Chand Bibi, the dowager queen of Ali Adil Shah—its ideal heroine being Zora, the young granddaughter of an exiled dervish. My father also completed during these winter months the seventh and eighth volumes of the *People of India*. Whether this great work will be continued by the order of the Secretary of State for India is not yet apparent; but the materials are almost inexhaustible, and it deserves to be made as complete as possible.

In May 1875 my father's eyesight suddenly failed him, and he wrote the concluding pages of *A Noble Queen* with considerable difficulty.[1] It was hoped earnestly that this

[1] This did not appear in book form until 1878. It is surprising and creditable, considering the circumstances under which the novel was

dimness of vision was only temporary, and that, with renewed health, the precious sight might be regained. He visited London in order to obtain the best medical advice, and was told by the physicians that his best and only hope of recovery lay in passing the following winter in some warm, dry climate.

'I should like to go to India again, if you think the climate would suit me,' he said. And after a long and deliberate consultation, leave was given; and he was told he might revisit the old scenes, now made yet more attractive by the residence at Hyderabad of his married daughter.[1]

When the news of his determination to spend the winter in India reached Hyderabad, His Excellency, Sir Salar Jang, wrote in the kindest possible terms, expressing a hope that, if my father fulfilled his present intention, he would consider himself as his guest during his stay, and allow him to make all the arrangements he could for his comfort.

This invitation was gratefully accepted, and on the 12th

---

written, that it holds together as it does. The brief introduction is dated only a few weeks before Colonel Taylor sailed. His two novels published subsequently to the *History* suffered less than that work at the hands of the printers. Those who may yet read through *A Noble Queen* will keep from it a certain light upon the Western India of the end of the sixteenth century. As in his *History* at the same period, Taylor follows Ferishta meticulously, sometimes at the cost of the larger accuracy. The figure of the Queen is one of some sweetness.

Miss Taylor writes: 'I quite agree with you that *Tara* is my father's masterpiece; though I find, when I lend his books, that *Seeta* is the general favourite—I presume because it is more English. I love the *Noble Queen* too, but it does not come up to *Tara*.' 'Of all his books my father liked *Tara* best.'

[1] Colonel Taylor's younger daughter Amy had in 1873 married Mr. Krohn, tutor to the Nizam, Mir Mahbub Ali, who succeeded at the age of three in 1869 and died in 1911. Mrs. Krohn died in 1899, leaving three daughters.

Miss Taylor has written of her father: 'I know of no one now living except our dear cousin the Dowager Lady Amherst of Hackney who knew my father well. . . . She says beyond testifying to his marvellous versatility of talent and his great store of knowledge on very many subjects, including geology, antiquarian research, engineering, road and tank making, she can add nothing. Besides these, he was always busy with his hands; painting, doing needlework on canvas, making balls for children, never idle for a moment and always the same—gentle, loving, sweet-tempered and patient.'

of September 1875, he and I, with our faithful servant John,[1] sailed from Liverpool in the s.s. *Guy Mannering* for Bombay. The change of air and the sea voyage seemed to benefit my father's general health, though there was scarcely any improvement in his sight. His memory was so wonderfully clear, and his recollection of places and scenes so accurate, that our captain was astonished, and declared he was led to look for and find out many points of interest that he had, in previous voyages, overlooked. We arrived at Bombay on the 15th of October, and, after a rest of two days, started for Hyderabad. The long railway journey, of twenty-seven hours, was borne without much fatigue, and my father seemed to rally wonderfully under the delight and excitement of meeting those so dear to him once more. His loss of sight was a sad drawback, but his patience under this terrible affliction was very touching. He could see a little, but not enough to read or write himself, or employ himself in any way; and this to one of his indefatigably industrious habits was a trial which only those who knew him could appreciate. When not writing or reading he used to draw, or knit, or crotchet, and his delight was to surprise his friends with some specimen of his work. His interest in all that went on around him was as keen as ever; and the numerous visits he received from his native friends afforded him great pleasure. Some came from long distances, only to see him, to touch his feet, or bring their simple offerings of fruit, sugar-candy, and garlands of sweet jessamine; and it was very touching to see the love and reverence the people bore for him. One, a native of Shorapur, told him how the people yet bewailed his loss, and how the women sang ballads to his honour as they ground their corn, and related stories of him to their children. He seemed to be so essentially the *people's* friend; and that his memory and his deeds lived still in their hearts, was evident to all who saw the manner of their coming.

[1] This John was something of a character, who at least amused the children aboard. He was a clever and prized family servant. After Colonel Taylor's death he was for a short time in the service of Taylor's only nephew, the Rev. Robert Taylor, junior, then vicar of Muston near Filey. John, who was falling back into drink, returned to Ireland and was lost to sight.

Owing to the prolonged absence of H. E. Sir Salar Jang, both at Bombay and Calcutta, on the occasions of the visit of H.R.H. the Prince of Wales, my father did not see so much of the Minister as he otherwise would have done; and this was a source of much mutual regret. But everything that princely hospitality could suggest, in the providing of house, servants, horses and carriages, and every comfort, was done by Sir Salar Jang to render my father's stay as pleasant and as comfortable as possible. He was able to partake of the hospitalities of the palace, too, on several occasions, especially that of the grand *fête* given on the arrival of Sir Richard Meade as Resident at Hyderabad; and he was able also to accept and enjoy invitations to the Residency, and among other friends. One great regret to him was that his health did not admit of his taking the long journey to Calcutta, in order to be present at the great gathering of the members of the 'Order of the Star of India'. He wrote his apologies to Sir Bartle Frere, begging him, if he would, to make known to H.R.H. the reason of his non-attendance, and received in reply a note which gratified him exceedingly. Not only was Sir Bartle Frere desired by the Prince of Wales to assure Colonel Taylor how much he regretted being deprived of the opportunity of making his personal acquaintance, but he added that he wished Colonel Taylor especially to know what pleasure he had derived from the perusal of his works on the voyage out to India. This gracious message and recognition of his literary labours were very pleasant to him, and afforded another instance, among so many at that time, of the graceful thoughtfulness and kindly feeling of his Royal Highness. In January 1876 my father was once more attacked by his old enemy, the jungle fever, and for many days and nights it seemed doubtful whether he would be spared to us yet a while. On the advice of his medical attendants, we took him back to Bombay, the climate there being considered better for his complaint, as it was more relaxing, and had not the excessive irritating dryness of Hyderabad. He remained at Bombay for a month. During this time he received many visits from persons acquainted with his Indian career and literary works, and enjoyed, on several occasions, long and earnest conversations with them, especially on subjects connected with native education and literature.

On this latter point he was exceedingly anxious, and it was his purpose, had his life been spared, to have contributed a series of letters to *The Times of India* on the subject. In one letter, to a native gentleman friend, which has been largely quoted, after thanking him for his criticisms on *Seeta*, and admitting that it is impossible for a writer, not a Hindu, to describe Brahminical observances and caste customs with absolute correctness, he thus proceeds :—

'Now why do not you, or some one of your friends, take up the subject of novels or tales, and instruct *us* on the subject of your people ? If you wrote in Marathi, or Gujarati, you would have a vast audience. If in English, we—if the work were simply and truthfully written—would welcome the author warmly. Think of the still existing popularity of Goldsmith's *Vicar of Wakefield*, which is undying ; and how simple and pathetic the tale is. You have matter, too, for a hundred romances in Grant Duff's *History*, if you follow history ; but that is not needed for general interest so much as writing that will move the hearts of the people, and become the foundation of a national literature of fiction, healthy, pure, and instructive to future generations. Why should we know only the dark side of Hinduism, and see none of the bright and light side, from the pens of its sons, now so rapidly advancing and advanced in modern science and thought ? Any one of your people who might attempt this department of literature would, if he wrote simply, naturally, and without pedantry, secure for himself not only present reputation, but undying fame. I cannot believe the ability is wanting ; all that is required is to be stimulated to healthy exertion on a pure model to achieve a decided success.'

And on another occasion he writes :—

'I am glad to hear that my works have been read, if it be only to prove to those who read them that my interest in the people of India, of all classes, is as strong as ever, and increases with time. I would fain see the educated portion striving to strike out new lines of occupation for themselves ; and I do not despair of yet seeing illustrations of native life, native legends, and native history written by yourselves.[1] Such

[1] Taylor would have rejoiced to see the considerable output of historical fiction in Marathi and other vernaculars. What Seeta says no longer holds : 'While for us—no one writes now ; no one thinks ; we are as the dead, with those whose very language is dead too.'

as I am, though we strive never so much, cannot penetrate beyond the surface of that we see; and as for myself, in regard to *Tara*, *Seeta*, and my other books, where I have tried to work out phases of native character, male and female, I only hope I have produced pictures something like reality, and not caricatures. I think portions of *Tara* and *Seeta* would translate easily into Marathi; and I should like to hear that extracts of these books were done into Marathi to serve as reading-books for the new generation.[1] Until Marathi and other native languages have a homely literature of their own, I confess there is the want of a principle which would encourage many to better things.'

On the 15th March we embarked on board the s.s. *Australia*, belonging to the Rubattino Company, who had with great kindness reserved two cabins for my father's and my own use, without extra charge, in spite of an over-full complement of passengers. We were bound for Genoa, as we intended passing a little time in the south of France until the spring should be far enough advanced to permit of our return home. On the voyage my father became far more ill, and the loss of all power in his lower limbs was a great additional trial. He could no longer walk at all, and was carried up and down from his berth to his chair on deck. We reached Genoa, however, in safety on the 6th April, after a very calm voyage of twenty-one days, and travelled on next day to Mentone, where, becoming gradually worse and more and more helpless, he sank to rest peacefully and painlessly on the 13th of May 1876.

To the last my dear father retained all the brightness of his intellect, and his interest in all that passed. The night before his death he heard read with great pleasure the account of the arrival of H.R.H. the Prince of Wales in England, and spoke long and earnestly of the royal visit to India; of the good it was likely to produce there; of the courtesy which distinguished the Prince's behaviour to all natives of whatever degree, and his wish that such an example might be largely followed.

The papers both of England and India were filled with

[1] This reasonable wish has never been fulfilled. To this day the Government reading books in Marathi contain nothing from Taylor's writings. Yet his best cameos are from Maratha history, which he has idealised to the furthest permissible point.

notices, all speaking of the varied and great talents my dear father possessed as soldier, administrator, man of science and of letters ; but we, whose privilege it was to be with him in his home, knew him best as the tenderest and most loving of parents, the wise friend, the true-hearted, humble Christian gentleman, ever casting his cares upon Him who cared for him in his strange neglected boyhood and early manhood, and who helped him to become what he was in private life, and to attain the public distinctions which were awarded to him.[1]

He rests at Mentone, in that spot so sacred to many English families and homes, amid the lovely scenes he delighted in, and among the sweet flowers he loved so well.

A simple cross of white marble marks his grave, on which are inscribed the last words he uttered on earth :—

'The Eternal God is thy Refuge, and underneath are the everlasting Arms.'

ALICE M. TAYLOR.

HUNMANBY VICARAGE, *15th September* 1877.

---

[1] The *Edinburgh Review* for October 1877 contained an article of 33 pages on the *Story of my Life*, mellow and moderate. Extracts from it have already been given.

Towards the end the writer dwells upon what has been painfully evident in the text of the Autobiography, the way in which Taylor was hampered during his last years, and the circumstances of his retirement made difficult for him, by 'the invidious distinctions of covenanted and uncovenanted'. It is plain that his health might have been restored, or need never have been so injured, had he enjoyed the liberal privileges of furlough to England which his supposed betters enjoyed, instead of having to spend those cruel twenty years on end in India. 'That, if he had belonged to the regular Indian service, Taylor would have risen to the highest posts, is certain, for he exhibited almost every quality needed to deserve promotion ; that, being what he was, he should never have been allowed to rise higher than a district officer, or to receive even the salary of a humdrum collector, is hardly creditable to those concerned.' There is a reference which Taylor, with his peculiarly happy modesty, might not have endorsed, to the inadequacy of the only decorative reward conferred upon him in the Companionship of the Star of India.

MEADOWS TAYLOR OUTSIDE THE AUTOBIOGRAPHY

It is seldom that one biography is so neatly concluded by another as is *The Story of my Life* by Mr. Francis Henry Skrine's *Life of Sir William Wilson Hunter*. (Longmans, 1901.)

This thick volume is unique among Indian memoirs for its stimulating intellectual quality, besides poignant personal interest. Mr. Skrine has written up to his subject. As to Hunter, it is amazing, though but natural, how much better he wrote in his letters than in his books *ad hoc*. Napoleon used to say that he would go down to posterity with his Code in his hand. Hunter may take the same journey holding in his hand Skrine's *Life* of himself, with perhaps the exquisite *Brief History of the Indian Peoples*. The twenty-six volumes of the *Imperial Indian Gazetteer*, of which I have made lavish use in the notes preceding, are too many and too mutable to carry far. Already they contain hardly a paragraph as Hunter wrote it. Yet it was an achievement to initiate and to launch such a collection of indispensable information, with the principle within it of self-renewal.

Hunter was believed to make ruthless use of other people's work. In 1895 he told me at Oxford that, of the ten thousand articles which the *Gazetteer* then contained, he had written with his own hand—doubtless meaning written something in —not less than eight thousand and five hundred articles. This statement has been hotly contested, before and since. But there can be no hesitation about the value of Hunter's standardisation of Indian spelling. Of the two views on the transliteration of Indian names mentioned in the extracts below, Taylor's was no system at all. It was just the whim of the moment; so that, as already shown, Taylor's spelling varies not only from book to book, from decade to decade, as might be reasonable, but within the same book and actually upon the same page, becoming on the whole rather more uncouth towards the end. This flux, this eccentricity was tardily arrested by what used to be called the Hunterian system. All who resent having to give their minds to trivialities must feel grateful to have a standard of orthodoxy in Indian spelling completely established.

Hunter was born in 1840; dying before he was sixty in 1900, killed either by the Boer War or by his expanding labours upon the *History of British India*. When the extracts which show him to such advantage begin he was still a young man, known as Dr. Hunter, flushed with unusual success, engaged at Bombay in his happy life-work on the *Gazetteer*. There was a kindling quality about him, a touch of personal if not of literary genius.

Mr. Skrine thus annotates the first mention of Taylor's name: 'Colonel Philip Meadows Taylor, C.S.I., Author of the *Confessions of a Thug* (1839), *Tara* (1863), and other brilliant delineations of Indian society at critical stages of its history. . . . He was also an administrator of mark, and rendered splendid services to the Empire, which were poorly requited by the Government of the day'.

Hunter writes to his wife from Bombay, March 13, 1876: 'I am looking after Colonel Meadows Taylor, the Indian novelist. He was sent out for the cold weather to Haidarabad by Sir William Jenner, but has fairly broken down. Poor old man! it is fifty-two years since he entered the Haidarabad Contingent as a subaltern, and he has now become so blind and paralytic that he is carried about like a child by his daughter and a faithful Irish valet. To-day I am taking Miss Meadows Taylor to see our potters at work, and will see them safely shipped off for Europe on the morrow' (Skrine's *Life of Hunter*, p. 252).

Of a later date, the opening of 1878, Mr. Skrine writes of Hunter: 'His own toils and sufferings gave him a rare degree of sympathy for others. We have seen how he befriended Colonel Meadows Taylor during the last sad voyage of the great Indian novelist, who, like Sir Walter Scott, revealed the romance of a vanished past to British readers and, like him, vainly sought relief for an overtasked brain in foreign travel. His autobiography showed too late how poorly rewarded had been the veteran's services to the Empire, and its perusal impelled Hunter to press the claims of Colonel Meadows Taylor's daughter on the special consideration of the State.' And in a note: 'This transparently truthful autobiography was published in 1877,' etc.

Hunter writes to Sir Erskine Perry (see earlier note) of the India Council, February 12, 1878: 'I have learned quite accidentally that Miss Meadows Taylor is in straitened circumstances. As a Bengal civilian, I had been painfully impressed by her father's posthumous *Story of my Life*. I could not help contrasting the rewards which come as a matter of course in the covenanted service with the scanty promotion earned by his long and exceptional labours. Though technically an "uncovenanted officer", Colonel Meadows Taylor held what are now styled "covenanted" appointments, and yet he had no chance of reaching more lucrative posts, nor is there any pension for his daughter after his death. But it is rather as a man of letters than as an official that I venture to ask your Council as to whether it might be possible to do something in the matter. My personal acquaintance with Colonel Meadows Taylor was a slight one, and in public matters, as regards the revision of Indian proper names, he strongly took up the view opposed to that which it was my duty to carry out. But I have derived more knowledge of Indian life and native character from him than from any other Anglo-Indian writer. His works have given zest and reality to the daily routine of hundreds of young civilians and soldiers, teaching them to study the facts around them, and counteracting the besetting sin of Anglo-Indian life in our day—the tendency to regard India as a temporary place of business rather than as a career or a home. It has fallen to my lot to do something to systematise our knowledge of India, and so to render possible the present method of short periods of service and constant changes, or, at any rate, to strip that method of its most evident evils. The performance of this task has made me the more keenly alive to the administrative value of the influence which Colonel Meadows Taylor's works exercise. They form a most salutary reminder that Indian administration is not, and ought not to be, merely a matter of system, but one of individual knowledge. The stream of native life which Anglo-Indians see flowing past them with unconcerned or weary eyes, becomes to his readers a drama full of reality and pathos. I believe that I am only one among hundreds of Indian officials who owe their first awakening to this fact to Colonel Meadows Taylor's writings. Surely it must be possible to do something for the daughter of a common benefactor of this sort? I understand that Sir Salar Jang has given a small allowance of £60 a year, but out of his own purse and, therefore, dependent on his own life. The Indian Government spends little enough on literature, and has but few men of letters to pension or reward. The case is not one for relaxing the rules of the uncovenanted service or any other and thus creating an inconvenient precedent. It is the case of a man of rare literary excellence, who gave his whole life and leisure to Indian subjects (in themselves never more than barely remunerative), and has exercised an influence for good on two generations of Indian officials.'

Mr. Skrine adds this note: 'It is greatly to Hunter's credit that he, though one of the elect, should have felt the injustice of these galling class distinctions. Such breadth of view is rare, and still rarer is the generosity which extended a helping hand to the children of one who had opposed a reform very near his heart. The chivalrous intervention was entirely successful.'

Reeve, after consultations with Mr. William Blackwood and Sir Erskine Perry, wrote to the Viceroy, his old friend, enclosing Hunter's letter, and asking him to give Taylor's daughters '£100 a year each, with benefit to the survivor.' As Mr. Skrine says, 'Lord Lytton's sympathies as a man of letters were excited by this appeal.'

The big *Life of Henry Reeve* (Longmans, 1898), which has hitherto been so disappointing as regards Meadows Taylor, gives this letter which Lord Lytton wrote to Mr. Reeve from Government House, Simla, April 20th, 1878:

'I think you in nowise overestimate the value of Meadows Taylor's life and work in India, and I cordially recognise the exceptional claims of the two ladies, on whose behalf you have written to me, to the grant which I regret to hear they require. Their case is rather a difficult one to deal with, owing to the fact that nearly the whole work of Meadows Taylor's life was performed, not in the service of the Government of India, but in that of the Nizam's Government; and we are precluded, by rules as inflexible as the laws of the Medes and Persians, from granting public money to the distressed survivors of our own public servants on purely compassionate grounds. In my own opinion, however, the claim of these ladies may be fairly admitted on grounds furnished by their father's eminence, not only as a literary man, but also as an administrator, and the fact that his work, though not performed in the service of the Government of India, has been, and is, in various ways, unquestionably beneficial to India. I am glad to say that I have obtained the concurrence of my council in this view of the case, and we propose to grant 100*l.* a year to each of these ladies from the Indian revenues' (*Life of Reeve*, vol. ii. p. 258).

INDEX

THE END

HYDERABAD
DIVISIONS OF HYDERABAD
1 AURANGABAD DIVISION
2 GULBARGA DIVISION
3 GULSHANABAD (MEDAK) DIVISION
4 WARANGAL DIVISION
AURANGABAD
PARBHANI
NANDER
BHIR
OSMANABAD
ADILABAD
NIZAMABAD
KARIMNAGAR
WARANGAL
MEDAK
ATRAF I-BALDA
HYDERABAD
GULBARGA
NALGONDA
MAHBUBNAGAR
RAICHUR
BAY OF BENGAL
WESTERN GHATS OR SAHYADRI